Y0-BXI-093

BOOKMAN'S GUIDE TO AMERICANA

10th edition

by
LEE SHIFLETT

The Scarecrow Press, Inc.
Metuchen, N.J., & London
1991

British Library Cataloguing-in-Publication data available

Library of Congress Cataloging-in-Publication Data

Shiflett, Lee.
Bookman's guide to Americana / by Lee Shiflett. -- 10th ed.
p. cm.
Rev. ed. of: Bookman's guide to Americana / J. Norman Heard and Charles F. Hamsa. 9th ed. 1986.
ISBN 0-8108-2464-7 (alk. paper)
1. America--Bibliography--Catalogs. 2. Out-of-print books--Bibliography--Catalogs. I. Heard, J. Norman (Joseph Norman), 1922- Bookman's guide to Americana. II. Title.
Z1207.H43 1991
[E18]
016.97--dc20 91-25404

Manufactured in the United States of America

Printed on acid-free paper

ACKNOWLEDGMENTS

The booksellers who lent their time and expertise to this project by sending their catalogs are especially thanked. In particular, I wish to thank Steve Anderson of Ross & Haines and Jerry Johnson of J. A. Johnson in St. Paul, Minnesota, who were generous in their comments, criticisms, and cavils through various drafts. Their help has done much to enhance the usefulness of this compilation and, had I paid attention to all their kind efforts, it would have done even more.

Cinderella W. Hayes, General Librarian for Documents and Learning Center at Louisiana State University-Eunice, served as my Graduate Assistant through most of the project. Her bibliographic ability, diligence, and good sense have aided immeasurably in its completion.

Vivian A. Auld, Computer Resources Coordinator for the Louisiana State University School of Library and Information Science, has been instrumental in solving the many technical problems that were encountered. Her predecessor, John McLain, now Local Area Network Administrator at the Louisiana Cooperative Extension Service, and Wendy R Windham of the LSU/SLIS Research Annex and currently Technical Librarian at Exxon Chemical in Baton Rouge, were invaluable in escorting me through the maze created by my own ineptitude with word processing.

Finally, I wish to thank my wife, Mary Ellen, for the days she has spent proofreading, questioning the bibliographic anomalies, and generally making the work more difficult--and more accurate.

INTRODUCTION

The 10th edition of **The Bookman's Guide to Americana** includes items which have been offered for sale by North American booksellers since the appearance of the 9th edition in 1986. It is neither an attempt to systematically cover the broad field of Americana nor a bibliography. It is a priced checklist of books thought to be of interest to booksellers, librarians and collectors.

The term **Americana** has been used as broadly as possible to apply to books and pamphlets relating to the history, culture, literature, and life of North, Central, and South America. Though some items of extreme rarity are included, in the main, only those available in the North American book trade with some degree of regularity were considered for inclusion.

FORM

In each case, the author, title, place of publication, publisher, and date of publication are included. Each item listed has been verified in standard bibliographic tools. **The National Union Catalog Pre-1956 Imprints**, the **Dictionary Catalog of the Research Libraries of the New York Public Library, 1911-1971**, and **The Cumulative Book Index** have all been extensively used. In cases where the information available either from the booksellers or from other sources has been insufficient to identify a particular variant or a particular item of information, the information is followed by a question mark. Absence of a place of publication is noted by the abbreviation "s.l." (sine loco). Lack of the name of a publisher, printer, or some organization or person responsible for the production of the physical object is indicated by "s.n." (sine nomine).

Subsequent editions, printings, and other variations are either noted in the body of the citation (e.g. "signed limited ed.") or in brackets with the price of the copy (e.g. "1968 Oklahoma ed."). When the title of a subsequent edition or printing has changed significantly, and the relationship between or among the items is not clear, a separate entry has been established for the various forms. For example, Loring Moody's **History of the Mexican War** is the second edition of his 1847 book, **Facts for the People**. While the subtitle probably makes the relationship clear enough, both have been entered. A less clear relationship exists between John Bristed's **America and Her Resources** and his **Resources of the United States of America**, which represent the 1818 British and American editions of the same text. Both are entered as separate items.

The arrangement of entries and cross references is in accordance with the 1980 edition of the **ALA Filing Rules**. One pecularity of these rules important to this list is that prefixes not joined to the name (i.e. De Forest or La Cava) are treated as separate words. Thus, "De Forest" would come before "Defoe" and "La Cava" before Labarre." Similary, the various forms of "Mac" are filed according to their actual spellings rather than as if all forms such as "Mc," "M'," and "Mac" were spelled out. It is useful to consult possible variant spellings of the name when consulting the **Guide**. Another anomaly is the problem of different authors with the same name. Rather than rely on subtle or arbitrary means to distinguish among these, the entries are filed as though they were the same person. For example, books by Oliver Wendell Holmes are found in the midst of those of his son of the same name and Henry James, the historian of Harvard, is not distinguished from Henry James, the novelist.

CONDITION

For the past decade, **AB Bookman's Weekly** has published criteria attempting to standardize the terms used in the trade to describe the condition of items offered for sale by booksellers. The uses, abuses, and physical damages to which paper, bindings, and inks are subject are many and varied. Books do not easily fall into such precise categories of condition as items in other well established areas of collecting such as coins, in which the number of hairs on Lincoln's head can serve as an accurate indicator of wear. But there are certain consistencies in wear and damage that can be codified and the categories proposed by **AB** do represent an attempt to standardize the usage in the trade. A major problem with these categories is the middle ground. The gap between a book that would be described as "good" in this scheme--one that is "the average used and worn book that has all pages and leaves present"--and "very good," a "book that does show some small signs of wear--but no tears--on binding, paper or dust jacket," is a large one and one into which the preponderance of items listed in this compilation fall.

Unfortunately, most booksellers pay little attention to these guidelines, preferring a system that has the sanction of tradition and relies on the reputation of the individual bookseller for its validity. The condition of the item is one (if not the major) determinant of its value in the marketplace. One of the most difficult tasks of compiling the **Guide** has been that of determining the condition of individual items from the descriptions given by booksellers. It is assumed that the booksellers whose catalogs were consulted are all honest and honorable persons. But it is also clear that in some cases their enthusiasm for the book has the better of their objectivity. It is difficult to imagine a dealer who can consistently produce catalogs of several hundred mid-ninteenth century titles all of which are "fine." Many other booksellers seem to be over diligent in describing the copies they offer. "1/8 inch tear in inner margin of front fly" adds little to a description of a common item in otherwise "good" condition. But the real problem arises when enthusiasm for a title is combined with fastidiousness in describing a book's defects. Such descriptions as "bumped, rubbed, sunned, silverfished, mildewed--otherwise, mint" can be found in the catalogs of booksellers and can only lead to bemusement on the part of their readers.

In this compilation, it is assumed that a book without descriptive information bracketed in the price is in the range of condition that can be described as "good" to "very good" on the criteria used in **AB**. Major defects or conditions that would affect the value of the item are noted. Every attempt has been made where possible to preserve the language used by the bookseller who described the item.

One convention used in this compilation is of particular importance. "Signed" is used to designate a signature by the author. "Inscribed" is used to indicate a text in the author's hand and the author's signature in the book. "Presentation" is used to indicate an inscription presenting the copy to a specific individual. In cases where these addenda have been added to the copy by someone else of significance to the title, this is noted.

PRICES

The authority of a guide such as this rests on that of the booksellers from whose catalogs it has been compiled. The prices listed here are those placed by experienced booksellers on unique items in their stock which they have reason to expect will sell at that price. This does not, of course, mean that those items actually found a buyer at that price. Indeed, most booksellers who catalog feel the activity a success if a third of a particular catalog sells. While, in some cases, this may be attributable to an asking price that is too high for the market, other variables, such as the condition of the item, collecting tastes, the degree to which the mailing list used by the bookseller covered the potential market, the season of the fiscal year, and perhaps the weather all perplex the problem. Evaluating an individual item based on actual sale is somewhat meaningless. The prices listed in this **Guide** reflect the considered judgment of booksellers who survive the financial hardships of the trade and, as such, can be considered a fair and informed estimation of the value of an item.

In many cases, more than one price has been given. These prices do not represent in any way a range of values, but are the result of independent judgments based on unique physical items. In cases where only one price or two widely varying prices are given, it is advisable to consult earlier editions of the **Guide**, other price guides, and auction catalogs. The prices themselves, representing a point in a range of possible values for an item, may well be significantly higher or lower than that which another competent judge would place on a similar or even the same item. It is important to remember that in cross checking with other sources, historical works have, with some adjustment for inflation, tended to be stable while literature has been subject to a high degree of fluctuation based on collecting interests and fads. In the case of literary works especially, a quotation more than five years old may not be valid and one a decade old is probably useless.

Lee Shiflett
Turgid Manor
St. Gabriel, Louisiana

BOOKSELLER DIRECTORY

Catalogs from the booksellers listed below have been examined in the preparation of this guide. The compiler of this 10th edition of the **Bookman's Guide to Americana** is grateful to these dealers for their participation in the project and invites any bookseller interested in the compilation of the 11th edition of the guide to send catalogs listing Americana as well as their comments on and suggestions for the project to: Lee Shiflett, School of Library and Information Science, Louisiana State University, Baton Rouge, LA 70803.

Abraham Lincoln Bookshop, 18 East Chestnut Street, Chicago, IL 60611.
Richard H. Adelson, North Pomfret, VT 05053.
William H. Allen, 2031 Walnut Street, Philadelphia, PA 19103.
Andover Square Books, 805 Norgate Road, Knoxville, TN 37919.
Antique Books, 3651 Whitney Avenue, Hamden, CT 06518.
Argosy Book Store, Inc., 116 East 59th Street, New York, NY 10022.
Richard B. Arkway, Inc., 538 Madison Avenue, New York, NY 10022.
Authors of the West, 191 Dogwood Drive, Dundee, OR 97115.
Bauman Rare Books, 1215 Locust Street, Philadelphia, PA 19107.
Beebah Books, P. O. Box 37, Andover, KS 67002.
The Book Attic, 555 West Baseline, San Bernardino, CA 92410.
The Book Cellar, 124 Orangefair Mall, Fullerton, CA 92632.
The Book Shelf, 3675 Hillsdale Drive NE, Cleveland, TN 37312.
The Bookseller, Inc., 521 West Exchange Street, Akron, OH 44302.
The Bookshop, Inc., 400 West Franklin Street, Chapel Hill, NC 27516.
Bookworm and Silverfish, P. O. Box 639, Wytheville, VA 24382.
James Burmester, Manor House Farmhouse, North Stoke, Bath, BA1 9AT, England.
Art Carduner, 6228 Greene Street, Philadelphia, PA 19144.
Dawson's Books, 535 North Larchmont Boulevard, Los Angeles, CA 90004.
The Early West, Creative Publishing Company, Box 9292, College, TX 77840.
The Family Album, RD 1, Box 42, Glen Rock, PA 17327.
Bob Fein Books, 150 Fifth Avenue, New York, NY 10011.
Joseph J. Felcone, Inc., P. O. Box 366, Princeton, NJ 08540.
Ferndale Books, 405 Main Street, Ferndale, CA 95536.
Michael Ginsberg, Box 402, Sharon, MA 02067.
Paulette Greene, 140 Princeton Road, Rockville Center, NY 11570.
Heritage Book Shop, 8540 Melrose Avenue, Los Angeles, CA 90069.
Heritage Books, 866 Palmerston Avenue, Toronto, Ontario M6G 2S2.
Historical Newspapers and Journals, 9850 Kedvale, Skokie, IL 60076.
Holms Book Company, 274 Fourteenth Street, Oakland, CA 94612.
Hope Farm Bookshop, Strong Road, Cornwallville, NY 12418.
The Jenkins Company, P. O. Box 2085, Austin, TX 78768
J. A. Johnson, Box 16193, St. Paul, MN 55116.
Kenneth Karmoile, Inc., P. O. Box 464, Santa Monica, CA 90406.
John K. King Books, P. O. Box 33363, Detroit, MI 48232.
Leaves of Grass, 2433 Whitmore Lake Road, Ann Arbor, MI 48103.
T. N. Luther, P. O. Box 429, Taos, NM 87571 (succeeded by, T. A. Swinford, P. O.

Box 93, Paris, IL 91944).
M & S Rare Books, Inc., Weston, MA 02193.
George MacManus, 1317 Irving Street, Philadelphia, PA 19107.
Melvin Marcher, 6204 North Vermont, Oklahoma City, OK 73112.
Margolis and Moss, P. O. Box 2042 Santa Fé, NM 87504-2042.
Robert L. Merriam, Newell Road, Conway, MA 01341.
Mickler House, 154 Lake Drive, Chuluota, FL 32766.
Willis Monte, RD 1, Box 336, Cooperstown, NY 13326.
Kenneth Nebenzahl, 333 North Michigan Avenue, Chicago, IL 60601.
19th Century Shop, 1047 Hollins Street, Baltimore, MD 21223.
Oak Knoll Books, 414 Delaware Street, New Castle, DE 19720.
Old Erie Street Bookstore, 2128 East Ninth Street, Cleveland, OH 44115.
Palinurus, 2210 Delancy Place, Philadelphia, PA 19103.
A. Parker's Books, 1488 Main Street, Sarasota, FL 34236.
R. A. Petrilla, Box 306, Roosevelt, NJ 08555.
Poor Richard's Books, Ltd., 968 Balmoral Road, Victoria, British Columbia V8T 1A8.
Richard C. Ramer, 225 East 70th Street, New York, NY 10021.
William Reese, Co., 409 Temple Street, New Haven, CT 06511.
Frank E. Reynolds, P. O. Box 805, Newburyport, MA 01950.
J. E. Reynolds, 3801 Ridgewood Road, Willits, CA 95490.
Rose Tree Inn Book Shop, Tombstone, AZ 85638.
Leona Rostenberg & Madeleine B. Stern, 40 East 88th Street, New York, NY 10128.
Robert H. Rubin, P. O. Box 267, Brookline, MA 02146.
John Rybski, 2319 West 47th Place, Chicago, IL 60609.
Sadlon's, 109 North Broadway, DePere, WI 54115.
Schoyer's Books, 1404 S. Negley Avenue, Pittsburgh, PA 15217.
J. E. Taylor, 1451 McMichael Drive, Baton Rouge, LA 70815.
Tollivar's Books, 1634 Stearns Drive, Los Angeles, CA 90035.
Trails West Books, 1032 S. Boulder Road, Louisville, CO 80027.
George H. Tweney, 16660 Marine View Drive SW, Seattle, WA 98166.
Tyson's Old & Rare Books, 334 Westminister Street, Providence, RI 02903.
R. M. Weathérford, Inc., 10902 Woods Creek Road, Monroe, WA 98272.
West Side Book Shop, 113 W. Liberty, Ann Arbor, MI 48103.
Wheldon & Wesley's, Lytton Lodge, Codicote, Hitchin, Herts., SG4 8TE, England.
Whitlock Farm Booksellers, 20 Sperry Road, Bethany, CT 06525.
Wolf's Head Books, P. O. Box 1020, Morgantown, WV 26507-1020.
William P. Wreden, 206 Hamilton Avenue, Palo Alto, CA 94302-0056.
Clark Wright, 409 Royal Street, Waxahachie, TX 75165.
John Zwishon, 524 Salon Drive NE, Albuquerque, NM 87108.

Abbey, Charles Augustus. **Before the Mast in the Clippers.** NY: Derrydale; 1937. [$150.00]

Abbot, Willis John. **Battle Fields and Camp Fires.** NY: Dodd, Mead; 1890. [$35.00]

Abbot, Willis John. **Battle-Fields of '61.** NY: Dodd, Mead; 1889. [$35.00]

Abbot, Willis John. **Blue Jackets of '61.** NY: Dodd, Mead; 1886. [$22.00]

Abbott, Charles C. **A Naturalist's Rambles about Home.** NY: Appleton; 1885. [$20.00]

Abbott, Edward Charles. **We Pointed Them North.** lst ed. NY, Toronto: Farrar & Rinehart; 1939. [dj worn, $100.00] [1955 Oklahoma ed., $17.50]

Abbott, John Stevens Cabot. **Christopher Carson.** NY: Dodd & Mead; 1874. [$25.00]

Abbott, John Stevens Cabot. **Daniel Boone, the Pioneer of Kentucky.** NY: Dodd, Mead; 1872. [bumped, rubbed, frayed, $25.00]

Abbott, John Stevens Cabot. **History of Maine.** 2nd ed. Portland: Brown Thurston; 1892. [$75.00]

Abbott, Katharine Mixer. **Old Paths and Legends of the New England Border.** NY, London: Putnam; 1907. [$40.00]

Abbott, Lawrence Fraser. **Impressions of Theodore Roosevelt.** Garden City: Doubleday, Page; 1919. [$60.00]

Abbott, Lawrence Fraser. **Story of NYLIC.** NY: The Company; 1930. [$15.00]

Abbott, Newton Carl. **Montana in the Making.** 13th ed. Billings: Gazette; 1964. [$17.00]

Abbott, Wilbur Cortez. **New York in the American Revolution.** NY, London: Scribner; 1929. [$25.00]

Aberle, David Friend. **The Peyote Religion among the Navaho.** NY: Aldine; 1966. [$35.00]

Abernathy, John R. **In Camp with Theodore Roosevelt.** Oklahoma City: Times-Journal; 1933. [$60.00]

Abernathy, John R. **Son of the Frontier.** Croton-on-Hudson, NY: News Press; 1935. [inscribed, $65.00]

Abernethy, Arthur Talmage. **Moonshine.** Asheville, NC: Dixie; 1924. [inscribed, $12.50]

Abernethy, Thomas Perkins. **The Burr Conspiracy.** NY: Oxford UP; 1954. [$22.50] [$27.50]

Abernethy, Thomas Perkins. **The Burr Conspiracy.** NY: Oxford UP; 1954. [$22.50] [$27.50]

Abernethy, Thomas Perkins. **From Frontier to Plantation in Tennessee.** Chapel Hill: U. of North Carolina; 1932. [$50.00] [$35.00]

Abernethy, Thomas Perkins. **Three Virginia Frontiers.** University, LA: Louisiana State UP; 1940. [$15.00]

Abert, James William. **Western America in 1846-1847.** San Francisco: Howell; 1966. [$85.00]

Acheson, Sam Hanna. **35,000 Days in Texas.** NY: Macmillan; 1938. [$25.00]

Ackerman, Carl William. **George Eastman.** Boston, NY: Houghton Mifflin; 1930. [x-lib., $20.00]

Acrelius, Israel. **History of New Sweden.** Philadelphia: Hist. Soc. of PA; 1874. [$60.00]

Adair, James. **Adair's History of the American Indians.** Johnson City, TN: Watauga; 1930. [$135.00] [1953 Nashville reprint, $27.50]

Adair, James. **History of the American Indians.** 1st ed. London: Dilly; 1775. [$1650.00]

Adair, John. **The Navajo and Pueblo Silversmiths.** Norman: U. of Oklahoma; 1946. [$20.00]

Adam, Graeme Mercer. **The Canadian North West.** Toronto: Rose; 1885. [$85.00]

Adamic, Louis. **Dyamite.** 1st ed. NY: Viking; 1931. [$25.00]

Adams, Andy. **Log of a Cowboy.** Boston, NY: Houghton Mifflin; 1903. [$125.00]

Adams, Andy. **Reed Anthony, Cowman.** Boston, NY: Houghton Mifflin; 1907. [$65.00]

Adams, Andy. **A Texas Matchmaker.** Boston, NY: Houghton Mifflin; 1904. [$50.00] [$70.00]

Adams, Andy. **Wells Brothers.** Boston, NY: Houghton Mifflin; 1911. [$30.00]

Adams, Andy. **Why the Chisholm Trail Forks.** Austin: U. of Texas; 1956. [$25.00]

Adams, Ansel. **My Camera in Yosemite Valley.** Yosemite National Park; Boston: Adams; Houghton Mifflin; 1949. [fine, $500.00]

Adams, Charles Francis. **Charles Francis Adams, 1835-1915.** Boston, NY: Houghton Mifflin; 1916. [$17.50]

Adams, Charles Francis. **The Confederacy and the Transvaal.** Boston: Houghton Mifflin; 1901. [$20.00]

Adams, Charles Francis. **Constitutional Ethics of Secession, and, "War is Hell."** Boston: Houghton Mifflin; 1903. [$40.00]

Adams, Charles Francis. **Texas and the Massachusetts Resolutions.** Boston: Eastburn's; 1844. [$150.00]

Adams, Edward Clarkson Leverett. **Congaree Sketches.** Chapel Hill: U. of North Carolina; 1927. [silverfished, sunned, and stained, $50.00]

Adams, Emma Hildreth. **To and Fro in Southern California.** Cincinnati: W.M.B.C.; 1887. [$50.00]

Adams, Emma Hildreth. **To and Fro, Up and Down in Southern California, Oregon, and Washington Territory.** Cincinnati: Cranston & Stowe; 1888. [$75.00]

Adams, Francis Colburn. **Manuel Pereira; or, The Sovereign Rule of South Carolina.** Washington: Buell & Blanchard; 1853. [$225.00]

Adams, George Worthington. **Doctors in Blue.** NY: Schuman; 1952. [$22.50] [$32.50]

Adams, Hannah. **Summary History of New-England.** Dedham, MA: Mann & Adams; 1799. [rebacked, $500.00]

Adams, Henry. **Civil-Service Reform.** Boston: Fields, Osgood; 1869. [$195.00]

Adams, Henry. **The Degradation of the Democratic Dogma.** NY: Macmillan; 1919. [dj torn, $50.00]

Adams, Henry. **Democracy, an American Novel.** 1st ed. NY: Holt; 1880. [spine chipped, $100.00]

Adams, Henry. **Documents Relating to New-England Federalism 1800-1815.** Boston: Little, Brown; 1877. [$150.00]

Adams, Henry. **Historical Essays.** NY: Scribner; 1891. [$125.00]

Adams, Henry. **History of the United States of America: The Formative Years.** Boston: Houghton Mifflin; 1947. 2 v. [$25.00]

Adams, Henry. **Life of Albert Gallatin.** Philadelphia, London: Lippincott; 1879. [x-lib., $235.00]

Adams, Herbert Baxter. **Thomas Jefferson and the University of Virginia.** Washington: USGPO; 1888. [silverfished and stained, $17.50] [$30.00]

Adams, James Donald. **Copey of Harvard.** Boston: Houghton Mifflin; 1960. [silverfished and stained, $20.00]

Adams, James Truslow. **America's Tragedy.** NY, London: Scribner; 1934. [$16.50]

Adams, James Truslow. **Frontiers of American Culture.** NY: Scribner; 1944. [$17.50]

Adams, James Truslow. **History of New England.** Boston: Little, Brown; 1927. 3 v. [$35.00]

Adams, James Truslow. **Provincial Society, 1690-1763.** NY: Macmillan; 1927. [$10.00]

Adams, John. **Adams-Jefferson Letters.** Chapel Hill: U. of North Carolina; 1959. 2 v. [$40.00] [$45.00]

Adams, John. **Defence of the Constitutions of Government of the United States of America.** London: Dilly; 1787. 2 v. [$500.00] [rebacked, covers scuffed, $575.00]

Adams, John. **Diary and Autobiography.** Cambridge, MA: Harvard UP; 1961. 4 v. [$50.00]

Adams, John. **Familiar Letters of John Adams and His Wife Abigail Adams.** NY: Hurd and Houghton; 1876. [$35.00]

Adams, John. **Novanglus, and Massachusettensis.** Boston: Hews & Goss; 1819. [$150.00] [x-lib., $100.00]

Adams, John. **Statesman and Friend.** Boston: Little, Brown; 1927. [$40.00]

Adams, John Quincy. **Correspondence between John Quincy Adams, Esquire, President of the United States, and Several Citizens of Massachusetts Concerning the Charge of a Design to Dissolve the Union.** Boston: Daily Advertiser; 1829. [$75.00]

Adams, John Quincy. **Eulogy on the Life and Character of James Madison.** Boston: Eastburn; 1836. [$50.00]

Adams, John Quincy. **A Letter to the Hon. Harrison Gray Otis.** 3rd ed. Bristol, RI: Dearth and Sterry; 1808. [$40.00]

Adams, John Quincy. **Oration Addressed to the Citizens of the Town of Quincy on the Fourth of July, 1831.** Boston: Richardson, Lord & Holbrook; 1831. [$20.00]

Adams, John Quincy. **Oration Delivered before the Inhabitants of the Town of Newburyport.** Newburyport, MA: Morss and Brewster; 1837. [$25.00]

Adams, John Quincy. **Oration on the Life and Character of Gilbert Motier de Lafayette.** Washington: Gales and Seaton; 1835. [$75.00] [rear wrap torn, $60.00]

Adams, John Quincy. **Speech of . . . Relating to the Annexation of Texas.** Washington: Gales and Seaton; 1838. [$225.00]

Adams, Nathaniel. **Annals of Portsmouth.** Portsmouth, NH: The Author; 1825. [x-lib., $25.00]

Adams, Nehemiah. **A South-Side View of Slavery.** Boston: Marvin; 1854. [$85.00]

Adams, Oscar Fay. **Some Famous American Schools.** Boston: Estes; 1903. [$20.00]

Adams, Ramon F. **Charles M. Russell, the Cowboy Artist.** Pasadena, CA: Trail's End; 1948. [$75.00]

Adams, Ramon F. **Come an' Get It.** Norman: U. of Oklahoma; 1952. [1st printing, $75.00]

Adams, Ramon F. **Cowboy Lingo.** Boston: Houghton Mifflin; 1936. [$75.00]

Adams, Ramon F. **The Cowman & His Code of Ethics.** limited, signed ed. Austin: Encino; 1969. [$50.00]

Adams, Ramon F. **The Cowman & His Philosophy.** signed limited ed. Austin: Encino; 1967. [$40.00]

Adams, Ramon F. **The Cowman Says It Salty.** Tucson: U. of Arizona; 1971. [$35.00]

Adams, Ramon F. **A Fitting Death for Billy the Kid.** 1st ed. Norman: U. of Oklahoma; 1960. [dj frayed, $30.00] [$45.00]

Adams, Ramon F. **The Old-Time Cowhand.** NY: Macmillan; 1961. [dj rubbed, $45.00]

Adams, Ramon F. **Western Words.** Norman: U. of Oklahoma; 1945. [$50.00] [1968 issue, $25.00]

Adams, Romanzo Colfax. **Interracial Marriage in Hawaii.** NY: Macmillan; 1937. [$20.00]

Adamson, Hans Christian. **Rebellion in Missouri, 1861.** 1st ed. Philadelphia: Chilton; 1961. [$22.50]

Addams, Jane. **A New Conscience and an Ancient Evil.** NY: Macmillan; 1914. [3rd? printing, $23.50]

Addison, Albert Christopher. **The Romantic Story of the Puritan Fathers.** Boston: Page; 1912. [$25.00]

Ade, George. **Forty Modern Fables.** NY: Russell; 1901. [x-lib., $20.00]

Ade, George. **Hand-Made Fables.** London: Pearson; 1921. [x-lib., $12.50]

Ade, George. **Knocking the Neighbors.** Garden City: Doubleday, Page; 1912. [x-lib., foxed, $15.00]

Ade, George. **True Bills.** NY: Harper; 1904. [$15.00]

Adler, Selig. **The Isolationist Impulse.** NY: Free Press; 1957. [$17.50]

Admonishing Crime. see, Richmond, James Cook.

Adney, Edwin Tappan. **The Klondike Stampede.** NY, London: Harper; 1900. [$150.00]

Adventures of Theodore. Chicago: Smith & Devereaux; 1901. [$15.00]

Agassiz, Alexander. **A Visit to the Bermudas in March, 1894.** Cambridge: Harvard Museum of Comparative Zoology; 1895. [rebound, cover chipped, $22.00]

Agassiz, Louis. **Journey in Brazil.** Boston: Ticknor and Fields; 1868. [front hinge cracked, $75.00]

Agassiz, Louis. **Lake Superior.** Boston: Gould, Kendall and Lincoln; 1850. [lacking one plate of 16, rebound, $250.00]

Aiken, David Wyatt. **The Grange.** Philadelphia: Wagenseller; 1884. [$35.00]

Aiken, William Earl. **The Roots Grow Deep.** Cleveland: Lezius-Hiles; 1957. [$17.50]

Aikman, Duncan. **Calamity Jane and the Lady Wildcats.** 1st ed. NY: Holt; 1927. [$40.00] [Blue Ribbon reprint, $10.00]

Aiton, Arthur Scott. **Antonio de Mendoza.** Durham: Duke UP; 1927. [$75.00]

Aken, David. **Pioneers of the Black Hills.** [Milwaukee?: s.n.; 1920?]. [$75.00]

Akron, OH Historical Committee. **Centennial History of Akron, 1825-1925.** [Akron?]: Summit County Historical Society; 1925. [$40.00]

Alabama. Dept. of Agriculture. **Alabama's Resources and Future Prospects, 1897.** Birmingham: Roberts; 1897. [wraps clipped, creased, torn, $17.50]

Albaugh, William A. **Confederate Handguns.** Philadelphia: Riling and Lentz; 1963. [in mint dj and original shipping carton, $50.00]

Albaugh, William A. **The Original Confederate Colt.** NY: Greenberg; 1953. [$40.00]

Albaugh, William A. **Tyler, Texas, C.S.A.** Harrisburg, PA: Stackpole; 1958. [$40.00]

Albee, John. **New Castle.** Boston: Rand Avery Supply; 1884. [$40.00]

Albert, James W. see, United States. Army. Corps of Topographical Engineers.

Albion, Robert Greenhalgh. **The Rise of New York Port.** NY, London: Scribner; 1939. [$30.00]

Alcott, Amos Bronson. **Sonnets and Canzonets.** 1st ed. Boston: Roberts; 1882. [presentation from Sanborn, $65.00]

Alcott, Louisa May. **Hospital Sketches and Camp and Fireside Stories.** Boston: Roberts; 1890. [2nd printing?, $65.00]

Alcott, Louisa May. **Little Men.** Boston: Roberts; 1871. [front flyleaf missing, $125.00]

Alcott, Louisa May. **Little Women.** 1st ed. Boston: Roberts; 1868. 2 v. [1st printing, $2000.00] [1880 ed., $100.00]

Alcott, Louisa May. **Rose in Bloom.** Boston: Roberts; 1876. [$60.00]

Alcott, Louisa May. **Silver Pitchers and Independence.** Boston: Roberts; 1876. [lacks front endpaper, $60.00]

Alden, John Richard. **General Gage in America.** Baton Rouge: Louisiana State UP; 1948. [$40.00]

Aldrich, Bess Streeter. **A White Bird Flying.** NY: Appleton-Century-Crofts; 1931. [$35.00]

Aldrich, Lorenzo D. **Journal of the Overland Route to California & the Gold Mines.** Los Angeles: Dawson's; 1950. [with pocket map, $45.00]

Aldrich, Thomas Bailey. **XXXVI Lyrics and XII Sonnets.** Boston: Houghton Mifflin; 1881. [$15.00]

Aldridge, Alfred Owen. **Benjamin Franklin, Philosopher & Man.** 1st ed. Philadelphia: Lippincott; 1965. [$15.00]

Aldridge, Alfred Owen. **Franklin and His French Contemporaries.** NY: New York UP; 1957. [$20.00]

Alexander, Archibald. **Biographical Sketches of the Founder and Principal Alumni of the Log College.** Philadelphia: Presbyterian Board of Pub.; 1851. [$20.00]

Alexander, Charles. **Life and Times of Cyrus Alexander.** Los Angeles: Dawson's; 1967. [$30.00]

Alexander, Edward Porter. **Military Memoirs of a Confederate.** NY: Scribner; 1907. [inscribed, $145.00]

Alexander, Edwin P. **The Pennsylvania Railroad.** 1st ed. NY: Norton; 1947. [$30.00] [Bonanza reprint, $15.00]

Alexander, Hartley Burr. **The World's Rim.** Lincoln: U. of Nebraska; 1953. [$25.00]

Alexander, Holmes Moss. **The American Talleyrand.** 1st ed. NY: Harper; 1935. [$50.00]

Alexander, James Edward. **Transatlantic Sketches.** London: Bentley; 1833. 2 v. [rebound, $300.00]

Alexander, James McKinney. **The Islands of the Pacific.** NY: American Tract Soc.; 1895. [$25.00]

Alexander, James Waddell. **History of the University Club of New York.** NY: Scribner; 1915. [$20.00]

Alexander, Nancy. **Here Will I Dwell.** Salisbury, NC: Rowan; 1956. [bumped, mildewed, scattered ink notes, $45.00]

Alfriend, Frank H. **Life of Jefferson Davis.** Cincinnati; Philadelphia: Caxton; National; 1868. [$40.00]

Algren, Nelson. **Chicago.** 1st ed. Garden City: Doubleday; 1951. [$50.00]

Algren, Nelson. **A Walk on the Wild Side.** 1st ed. NY: Farrar, Straus and Cudahy; 1956. [presentation, near fine in dj, $130.00]

Alinsky, Saul David. **John L. Lewis.** NY: Putnam; 1949. [$15.00]

Allan, Herbert Sanford. **John Hancock, Patriot in Purple.** NY: Macmillan; 1948. [$15.00]

Allan, James T. **Central and Western Nebraska and the Experiences of Its Stock Growers.** Omaha: Republican; 1883. [$285.00]

Allardice, Robert Barclay. **Agricultural Tour in the United States and Upper Canada.** Edinburgh: Blackwood; 1842. [lacking rear endpaper, $200.00] [$175.00]

Alldredge, Eugene Perry. **Cowboys and Coyotes.** Nashville: Marshall & Bruce; 1945. [$20.00]

Allen & Ginter. **Game Birds of America.** 2nd ed. Richmond: Allen & Ginter; [18--?]. [$35.00]

Allen, Andrew J. **The American Pioneer.** 1st ed. Boston: Allen; 1854. [covers rubbed and soiled, $25.00]

Allen, Brasseya Johnson. **Pastorals, Elegies, Odes, Epistles and Other Poems.** Abingdon, MD: Ruff; 1806. [covers scuffed, $120.00]

Allen, Gardner Weld. **Our Navy and the West Indian Pirates.** Salem, MA: Essex Institute; 1929. [$50.00]

Allen, George. **An Appeal to the People of Massachusetts, on the Texas Question.** Boston: Little & Brown; 1844. [$135.00]

Allen, Hervey. **Action at Aquila.** 1st ed. NY: Farrar & Rinehart; 1938. [$35.00]

Allen, Hervey. **Israfel; the Life and Times of Edgar Allan Poe.** NY: Doran; 1926. 2 v. [inscribed, $165.00]

Allen, Hugh. **Rubber's Home Town.** 1st ed. NY: Stratford; 1949. [$20.00]

Allen, Ira. **Natural and Political History of the State of Vermont.** London: Myers; 1798. [with folding map, $1500.00]

Allen, James B. **The Company Town in the American West.** 1st ed. Norman: U. of Oklahoma; 1966. [$20.00]

Allen, James Lane. **Flute and Violin and Other Kentucky Tales and Romances.** NY: Harper; 1891. [$40.00]

Allen, James Lane. **Reign of Law.** NY, London: Macmillan; 1900. [$20.00]

Allen, James Stewart. **Reconstruction; the Battle for Democracy (1865-1876).** NY: International; 1937. [$25.00]

Allen, John Houghton. **Southwest.** 1st ed. Philadelphia: Lippincott; 1952. [$25.00]

Allen, Myron Oliver. **History of Wenham.** Boston: Bazin & Chandler; 1860. [spine torn and chipped, front hinge broken, $25.00]

Allen, T. D. **Navahos Have Five Fingers.** Norman: U. of Oklahoma; 1963. [$38.00]

Allen, William M. **Five Years in the West.** Nashville: Southern Methodist; 1884. [$750.00]

Allen, William Wallace. **California Gold Book.** San Francisco, Chicago: Donohue & Henneberry; 1893. [$150.00]

Alley, Felix Eugene. **Random Thoughts and the Musings of a Mountaineer.** 1st ed. Salisbury, NC: Rowan; 1941. [cover mildewed, dj stained, $25.00]

Allhands, James Lewellyn. **Gringo Builders.** Iowa City: Priv. Print.; 1931. [$85.00] [$75.00]

Allhands, James Lewellyn. **Railroads to the Rio.** Salado, TX: Jones; 1960. [$75.00]

Allhands, James Lewellyn. **Uriah Lott.** San Antonio: Naylor; 1949. [chipped dj, signed, $90.00]

Allison, John. **Notable Men of Tennessee.** Atlanta: Southern Hist. Assn.; 1905. 2 v. [binding worn and tattered, $35.00]

Allred, Berten Wendell. **Flat Top Ranch.** 1st ed. Norman: U. of Oklahoma; 1957. [$50.00]

Allsopp, Frederick William. **Folklore of Romantic Arkansas.** NY: Grolier; 1931. 2 v. [$125.00]

Allsopp, Frederick William. **History of the Arkansas Press.** Little Rock: Parke-Harper; 1922. [$25.00]

Almada, Bartolome Eligio. **Almada of Alamos.** Tucson: Arizona Silhouettes; 1962. [$27.00]

Almirall, Leon Vincent. **Canines and Coyotes.** Caldwell, ID: Caxton; 1941. [dj chipped, $45.00]

Alpert, Hollis. **The Barrymores.** NY: Dial; 1964. [$15.00]

Alsop, George. **A Character of the Province of Maryland.** NY: Gowans; 1869. [spine chipped and torn, worn, $45.00]

Alsop, Richard. **A Poem; Sacred to the Memory George Washington.** Hartford: Hudson and Goodwin; 1800. [$45.00]

Alter, J. Cecil. **James Bridger.** Salt Lake City: Shepard; 1925. [$150.00] [1962 Oklahoma ed., $30.00]

Altisonant, Lorenzo. see, Hoshour, Samuel K.

Altrocchi, Julia. **Snow Covered Wagons.** NY: Macmillan; 1936. [inscribed, $22.50]

Alvord, Clarence Walworth. **First Explorations of the Trans-Allegheny Region by the Virginians.** Cleveland: Clark; 1912. [bumped, rubbed, stained, $55.00]

Amaral, Anthony A. **Comanche.** Los Angeles: Westernlore; 1961. [$28.00] [$30.00]

Ambler, Charles Henry. **History of Transportation in the Ohio Valley.** Glendale, CA: Clark; 1932. [$75.00]

Ambler, Charles Henry. **History of West Virginia.** NY: Prentice-Hall; 1933. [$45.00]

American Battle Monuments Commission. **American Armies and Battlefields in Europe.** Washington: USGPO; 1938. [$20.00]

American Female Guardian Society and Home for the Friendless, New York. **Our Golden Jubilee.** NY: The Society; 1884. [$35.00]

American Heritage Book of the Revolution. NY: American Heritage; 1958. [$15.00]

American Jewish Historical Society. **Early History of Zionism in America.** NY: [s.n.]; 1958. [$20.00]

American Military Biography. Cincinnati: Chronicle; 1834. [rebound, $55.00]

American Tract Society. **The Color-Bearer: Francis A. Clary.** NY: American Tract Society; 1864. [cover worn and soiled, $40.00]

Americus. **Thoughts for the Times.** London: The Author; 1862. [disbound, $15.00]

Ames, Fisher. **Oration on the Sublime Virtues of General George Washington.** Boston: Young & Minns, etc.; 1800. [$45.00]

Ames, Mary. **Ten Years in Washington.** Hartford, CT: Worthington; 1876. [$25.00]

Amory, Cleveland. **Proper Bostonians.** NY: Dutton; 1947. [$10.00]

Amory, Robert. **Surf and Sand.** Andover, MA: Andover Press; 1947. [$65.00]

Amos, James E. **Theodore Roosevelt.** NY: Day; 1927. [$25.00]

Ampere, J. J. **Promenade en Amerique; Etats-Unis--Cuba--Mexique.** nouv. ed. Paris: Levy; 1856. 2 v. [$150.00] [$125.00] [$100.00]

Amsden, Charles Avery. **Navaho Weaving.** Albuquerque: U. of New Mexico; 1949. [$250.00] [1964 Rio Grande ed., $40.00]

Anburey, Thomas. **Travels through the Interior Parts of America in a Series of Letters.** London: Lane; 1789. 2 v. [$1000.00] [1923 Houghton ed., $150.00]

Anderson, Alexander D. **Silver Country.** NY: Putnam; 1877. [rebound, $65.00]

Anderson, Archer. **Robert Edward Lee.** Richmond: Jones; 1890. [presentation, silverfished, bumped, $30.00]

Anderson, Charles Carter. **Fighting by Southern Federals.** NY: Neale; 1912. [x-lib., $50.00] [$125.00]

Anderson, Edward Henry. **Brief History of the Church of Jesus Christ of Latter-Day Saints.** 4th rev. ed. Salt Lake City: Missions of the Church of Jesus Christ of Latter-Day Saints in America; 1926. [$45.00]

Anderson, Ephraim McDowell. **Memoirs: Historical and Personal.** Saint Louis: Times; 1868. [cover spotted, $325.00]

Anderson, Galusha. **Story of a Border City during the Civil War.** 1st ed. Boston: Allen; 1854. [$85.00]

Anderson, George A. **Bartlett Yancey.** Chapel Hill: U. of North Carolina; 1911. [$20.00]

Anderson, Jack. **McCarthy: the Man, the Senator, the "Ism."** Boston: Beacon; 1952. [$12.50]

Anderson, John Q. **A Texas Surgeon in the C. S. A.** Tuscaloosa, AL: Confederate Pub. Co.; 1957. [$40.00]

Anderson, Roger Charles. **Rigging of Ships in the Days of the Spritsail Topmast 1600-1720.** Salem, MA: Marine Res. Soc.; 1927. [$75.00]

Anderson, Rufus. **Hawaiian Islands.** Boston, NY: Gould and Sheldon; 1864. [$200.00]

Anderson, Sherwood. **Home Town.** 1st ed. NY: Alliance; 1940. [reinforced dj, $40.00]

Anderson, Sherwood. **Puzzled America.** NY, London: Scribner; 1935. [pencilled, worn dj, $15.00]

Anderson, Sherwood. **A Story Teller's Story.** 1st ed. NY: Huebsch; 1924. [fine in dj, $250.00]

Anderson, William Marshall. **The Rocky Mountain Journals of.** San Marino, CA: Huntington Library; 1967. [$85.00]

Anderson, William R. **First under the North Pole.** Cleveland: World; 1959. [$12.50]

Andre, Eugene. **A Naturalist in the Guianas.** London: Smith, Elder; 1904. [rebound, $60.00]

Andre, John. **Andre's Journal.** Boston: Bibliophile Soc.; 1903. 2 v. [$350.00]

Andre, John. **The Cow Chase.** London: Fielding; 1781. [$900.00]

Andreas, Alfred Theodore. **History of Chicago.** Chicago: Andreas; 1884-86. 3 v. [$350.00]

Andrews, Charles McLean. **Narratives of the Insurrections, 1675-1690.** NY: Scribner; 1915. [x-lib., $12.50] [$30.00]

Andrews, Christopher Columbus. **History of the Campaign of Mobile.** NY: Van Nostrand; 1867. [$95.00]

Andrews, Clarence Leroy. **The Story of Alaska.** Caldwell, ID: Caxton; 1944. [later printing, $12.50]

Andrews, Clarence Leroy. **Story of Sitka.** Seattle: Lowman and Henford; 1922. [$45.00]

Andrews, Edward Deming. **The People Called Shakers.** NY: Oxford UP; 1953. [$15.00]

Andrews, Elisha Benjamin. **History of the Last Quarter-Century in the United States.** NY: Scribner; 1896. 2 v. [$25.00]

Andrews, Eliza Frances. **War-Time Journal of a Georgia Girl, 1864-1865.** NY: Appleton; 1908. [$65.00]

Andrews, John. **History of the War with America, France, Spain, and Holland.** London: Fielding; 1785-86. 4 v. [$1000.00]

Andrews, Lorrin. **Grammar of the Hawaiian Language.** Honolulu: Mission Press; 1854. [$450.00]

Andrews, Mathew Page. **Founding of Maryland.** Baltimore; NY, London: Williams & Wilkins; Appleton-Century; 1933. [$40.00]

Andrews, Matthew Page. **Virginia, the Old Dominion.** limited, signed ed. Garden City: Doubleday; 1937. 2 v. [$110.00]

Andrews, Matthew Page. **The Women of the South in War Times.** Baltimore: Norman, Remington; 1920. [$28.00]

Andrews, Roger. **Old Fort Mackinac on the Hill of History.** Menominee, MI: Herald-Leader; 1938. [$37.50]

Andrews, William Loring. **James Lyne's Survey or, As It Is More Commonly Known, the Bradford Map.** NY: Dodd, Mead; 1900. [$125.00]

Andrews, William Loring. **New York As Washington Knew It after the Revolution.** NY: Scribner; 1905. [dj tape repaired, $175.00]

Andrist, Ralph K. **The Long Death.** NY: Macmillan; 1964. [$35.00]

Angle, Paul McClelland. **Here I Have Lived.** Springfield, IL: Abraham Lincoln Assn.; 1935. [$35.00]

Angle, Paul McClelland. **The Library of Congress.** Kingsport, TN: Kingsport Press; 1958. [$15.00]

Angoff, Charles. **H.L. Mencken.** NY: Yoseloff; 1956. [$17.50]

Angulo, Jaime de. **Indian Tales.** 1st ed. NY: Hill and Wang; 1953. [$25.00]

Angus, Henry Forbes. **British Columbia and the United States.** Toronto; New Haven: Ryerson; Yale UP; 1942. [$45.00]

Anson, Bert. **The Miami Indians.** 1st ed. Norman: U. of Oklahoma; 1970. [$35.00]

Anspach, Frederick Rinehart. **The Sons of the Sires.** Philadelphia: Lippincott, Grambo; 1855. [$20.00] [$40.00]

Anthony, Joseph R. **Life in New Bedford a Hundred Years Ago.** New Bedford: Reynolds; 1922. [$60.00]

Anthony, Katharine Susan. **Susan B. Anthony.** 1st ed. Garden City: Doubleday; 1954. [$27.50]

Apes, William. **Son of the Forest.** NY: The Author; 1829. [cover partly detached, $125.00] [$150.00]

Applegate, Frank Guy. **Native Tales of New Mexico.** Philadelphia, London: Lippincott; 1932. [dj repaired, $45.00]

Applegate, Jesse. **A Day with the Cow Column in 1843.** Chicago: Caxton Club; 1934. [very good, $135.00]

Appleman, Roy Edgar. **Charlie Siringo.** Washington: Potomac Corral, The Westerners; 1968. [signed, limited, $30.00]

Appler, Augustus C. **The Younger Brothers.** NY: Fell; 1955. [$15.00] [$30.00]

Appleton, LeRoy H. **Indian Art of the Americas.** NY: Scribner; 1950. [dj lacks spine, $65.00]

Appleton's Hand-Book of American Travel Northern and Eastern Tour. NY; London: Appleton; Low and Marston; 1870. [$50.00]

Arfwedson, Carl David. **Brief History of the Colony of New Sweden.** Lancaster, PA: Pennsylvania German Society; 1909. [$50.00]

Argyll, John Douglas Sutherland Campbell. **Canadian Pictures.** new ed. London: Religious Tract Society; 1885. [$125.00]

Argyll, John Douglas Sutherland Campbell. **A Trip to the Tropics and Home through America.** London: Hurst and Blackett; 1867. [$70.00]

Argyll, John Douglas Sutherland Campbell. **Yesterday & To-Day in Canada.** London: Allen; 1910. [$30.00, Canadian]

Ariel. see, Payne, Buckner H.

Arkansas. State Geologist. **Second Report of a Geological Reconnoissance of the Middle and Southern Counties of Arkansas.** Philadelphia: Sherman; 1860. [$350.00]

Armbruster, Eugene L. **The Eastern District of Brooklyn.** NY: [s.n.]; 1912. [$40.00]

Armes, George Augustus. **Ups and Downs of an Army Officer.** Washington: [s.n.]; 1900. [$150.00]

Armor, William C. **Lives of the Governors of Pennsylvania.** Norwich: Davis; 1874. [$85.00]

Armstrong, A. N. **Oregon.** Chicago: Scott; 1857. [rebound, $300.00] [inscribed, $300.00]

Armstrong, Benjamin G. **Early Life among the Indians.** Ashland, WI: Bowron; 1892. [paper darkened, $125.00]

Armstrong, Henry. **Gloves, Glory, and God.** Westwood, NJ: Revell; 1956. [$25.00]

Armstrong, Mary Frances Morgan. **Hampton and Its Students.** NY: Putnam; 1874. [$50.00]

Armstrong, Moses Kimball. **Early Empire Builders of the Great West.** St. Paul: Porter; 1901. [cover stains, $35.00] [$37.50]

Armstrong, Moses Kimball. **History and Resources of Dakota, Montana, and Idaho.** Pierre: Hipple; 1928. [reprint of 1866 ed?, $30.00]

Armstrong, Nelson. **Nuggets of Experience.** [San Bernardino?]: Times-Mirror; 1906. [$85.00]

Armstrong, William Ayres. **Miracle Hill.** Milwaukee, WI: Cramer, Aikens & Cramer; 1889. [$25.00]

Armstrong, Zella. **History of Hamilton County and Chattanooga, Tennessee.** Chattanooga: Lookout; 1931-40. 2 v. [bumped, mildewed, sunned, presentation, $125.00]

Arndt, Karl John Richard. **George Rapp's Harmony Society, 1785-1847.** Philadelphia: U. of Pennsylvania; 1965. [$37.50]

Arnold, Augustus C. L. **Philosophical History of Free-Masonry and Other Secret Societies.** NY: Clark, Austin & Smith; 1854. [$65.00]

Arnold, Benjamin F. **History of Whittier.** Whittier, CA: Western Print.; 1933, c1932. [covers soiled, $40.00]

Arnold, C. D. **The World's Columbian Exposition.** Chicago, St. Louis: National Chemigraph; 1893. [$60.00]

Arnold, Isaac Newton. **History of Abraham Lincoln, and the Overthrow of Slavery.** Chicago: Clarke; 1866. [$75.00]

Arnold, Isaac Newton. **Reminiscences of the Illinois Bar Forty Years Ago.** Chicago: Fergus; 1881. [$95.00]

Arnold, Oren. **Hot Irons; Heraldry of the Range.** NY: Macmillan; 1940. [1st printing, dj intact, $75.00]

Arnold, Oren. **Sun in Your Eyes.** Albuquerque: U. of New Mexico; 1947. [$10.00] [$15.00]

Arnold, Oren. **Thunder in the Southwest.** Norman: U. of Oklahoma; 1952. [$45.00]

Arnold, Oren. **Wild Life in the Southwest.** Dallas: Upshaw; 1935. [$35.00]

Arny, William Frederick Milton. **Centennial Celebration, Santa Fe, New Mexico, July 4, 1876.** Santa Fe: Williams & Shaw; 1876. [x-lib., $325.00]

Arrington, Alfred W. **Rangers and Regulators of the Tanaha.** NY: De Witt; 1856. [$125.00]

Arthur, John Preston. **Western North Carolina; a History.** Raleigh: Edwards & Broughton; 1914. [bumped, rubbed, $85.00] [$100.00]

Arthur, Stanley Clisby. **Audubon.** New Orleans: Harmanson; 1937. [inscribed, $125.00]

Arthur, Stanley Clisby. **Jean Laffite, Gentleman Rover.** New Orleans: Harmanson; 1952. [signed, limited, publisher's inscription, $165.00] [signed, bumped, sunned, rubbed, $45.00]

Arthur, T. S. **The Angel and the Demon.** Philadelphia: Evans; 1859. [$20.00]

Arthur, T. S. **Lovers and Husbands.** 1st ed. NY: Harper; 1845. [scuffed, $45.00]

Arthur, T. S. **Pride or Principle.** 2nd ed. Philadelphia: Lindsay & Blakiston; 1844. [rubbed, $50.00]

Arthur, T. S. **Sweethearts and Wives.** 1st ed. NY: Harper; 1843. [$50.00]

Artrip, Louise. **Memoirs of Daniel Fore (Jim) Chisholm and the Chisholm Trail.** Booneville, AR: Artrip; 1949. [$50.00]

Ashburn, Percy M. **Ranks of Death.** NY: Coward-McCann; 1947. [fine in dj, $35.00]

Ashby, Thomas Almond. **The Valley Campaigns.** NY: Neale; 1914. [$175.00]

Ashe, Thomas. **Memoirs and Confessions of Captain Ashe.** London: Colburn; 1815. 3 v. [$850.00]

Ashe, Thomas. **Travels in America Performed in 1806.** London: Sawyer; 1808. [x-lib., rebound, $600.00] [1808 Newburyport ed., $285.00]

Ashely, Willliam. see, Sunday, Billy.

Ashton, Dean Henderson. **Be It Ever So Humble.** Hopewell, NJ: [s.n.]; 1947. [$25.00]

Ashton, Wendell J. **Voice in the West.** NY: Duell, Sloan & Pearce; 1950. [$17.50]

Aswell, James. **God Bless the Devil!** see, Writer's Program. Tennessee.

Atascadero Estates, Inc. **Atascadero (Atas-ka-dero), California.** Atascadero, CA: Atascadero Press; 1923. [$45.00]

Athearn, Robert G. **Forts of the Upper Missouri.** Englewood Cliffs, NJ: Prentice-Hall; 1967. [$30.00]

Athearn, Robert G. **Rebel of the Rockies.** New Haven: Yale UP; 1962. [$50.00]

Athearn, Robert G. **William Tecumseh Sherman and the Settlement of the West.** 1st ed. Norman: U. of Oklahoma; 1956. [$25.00]

Atherton, Gertrude. **Ancestors.** NY: Harper; 1907. [$25.00]

Atherton, William. **Narrative of the Suffering & Defeat of the North-Western Army.** Frankfort, KY: Hodges; 1842. [$175.00]

Atkinson, Edward. **Cheap Cotton by Free Labor.** Boston: Williams; 1861. [$35.00]

Atkinson, G. H. **Address Delivered by . . . upon the Possession, Settlement, Climate and Resources of Oregon and the North-West Coast.** [s.l.: s.n.]; 1868. [$150.00]

Atkinson, George Wesley. **Bench and Bar of West Virginia.** Charleston: Virginia Law Book; 1919. [$50.00]

Atkinson, John Hampton. **Jesse and Martha Dean.** Boston: Meador; 1942. [$10.00]

Atkinson, Joseph. **The History of Newark, New Jersey.** Newark: Guild; 1878. [$60.00]

Atkinson, Mary Jourdan. **The Texas Indians.** San Antonio: Naylor; 1935. [signed, $85.00]

Atlee, Philip. **The Inheritors.** NY: Dial; 1940. [$125.00]

Atwater, Horace Cowles. **Incidents of a Southern Tour.** Boston: Magee; 1857. [$350.00]

Atwood, Albert William. **Gallaudet College: Its First One Hundred Years.** [Lancaster?, PA: s.n.]; 1964. [$15.00]

Atwood, Elmer Bagby. **Regional Vocabulary of Texas.** Austin: U. of Texas; 1962. [$85.00]

Auchampaugh, Philip Gerald. **James Buchanan and His Cabinet on the Eve of Secession.** Lancaster, PA: Priv. Print.; 1926. [$40.00]

Audubon, John James. **Audubon and His Journals.** NY: Scribner; 1897. 2 v. [$250.00]

Audubon, John James. **Audubon in the West.** Norman: U. of Oklahoma; 1965. [$25.00]

Audubon, John James. **Audubon's America.** Boston: Houghton Mifflin; 1940. [signed by editor, lacks slipcase, $75.00]

Audubon, John James. **Delineations of American Scenery and Character.** 1st trade ed. NY: Baker; 1926. [$65.00]

Audubon, John James. **Journal of John James Audubon: Made during His Trip to New Orleans.** Boston: Odd Volumes; 1929. [unopened, $250.00]

Audubon, John James. **Journal of John James Audubon: Made while Obtaining Subscriptions to His "Birds of America," 1840-1843.** Boston: Odd Volumes; 1929. [$250.00]

Audubon, John James. **Letters of . . . , 1826-1840.** Boston: Odd Volumes; 1930. 2 v. [$325.00]

Audubon, John James. **The Original Water-Color Paintings by John James Audubon for the Birds of America.** NY: American Heritage; 1966. [$150.00]

Auer, Harry Anton. **The North Country.** Cincinnati: Clarke; 1906. [$25.00]

Aughey, John H. **Tupelo.** Lincoln, NE: State Journal; 1888. [$30.00]

Augur, Helen. **American Jezabel.** NY: Brentano's; 1930. [$25.00]

Augur, Helen. **Secret War of Independence.** NY: Duell, Sloan and Pearce; 1955. [$12.50]

Aurand, Ammon Monroe. **The "Pow-Wow" Book.** Harrisburg, PA: Aurand; 1929. [in good dj, $75.00]

Austin, Emily M. **Mormonism.** Madison, WI: Cantwell; 1882. [$250.00]

Austin, Guy K. **Covered Wagon, 10 H.P.** London: Bles; 1936. [$25.00]

Austin, J. P. **Blue and the Gray.** Atlanta: Franklin; 1899. [x-lib., $25.00] [$65.00] [binding shabby, $27.50]

Austin, Mary Hunter. **Earth Horizon.** Boston, NY: Houghton Mifflin; 1932. [dj worn, $40.00]

Austin, Mary Hunter. **The Flock.** Boston, NY: Houghton Mifflin; 1906. [$45.00]

Austin, Mary Hunter. **Isidro.** Boston, NY: Houghton Mifflin; 1905. [$25.00] [$45.00]

Austin, Mary Hunter. **The Land of Journeys' Ending.** NY: Century; 1924. [dj chipped, $50.00] [$50.00]

Austin, Mary Hunter. **Land of Little Rain.** Boston, NY: Houghton Mifflin; 1903. [$150.00]

Austin, Mary Hunter. **Lands of the Sun.** Sierra ed. Boston, NY: Houghton Mifflin; 1927. [dj chipped, $40.00]

Austin, Mary Hunter. **Santa Lucia.** NY, London: Harper; 1908. [$40.00]

Austin, Mary Stanislas. **Philip Freneau: The Poet of the Revolution.** NY: Wessels; 1901. 2 v. [$40.00]

An Authentic Exposition of the "K.G.C.", "Knights of the Golden Circle." Indianapolis: Perrine; 1861. [$450.00]

Avary, Myrta Lockett. **Dixie after the War.** NY: Doubleday, Page; 1906. [$35.00]

Avary, Myrta Lockett. **A Virginia Girl in the Civil War.** NY: Appleton; 1903. [covers worn, $25.00]

Averill, Charles E. **Secret Service Ship.** Boston: Gleason; 1848, c1847. [spine crudely repaired, $75.00]

Avery, Elroy McKendree. **History of the United States and Its People.** Cleveland: Burrows; 1904-10. 7 v. [$300.00]

Avey, Elijah. **The Capture and Execution of John Brown.** Elgin, IL: Brethren; 1906. [$45.00]

Axelrad, Jacob. **Philip Freneau.** Austin: U. of Texas; 1967. [$20.00]

Axford, Joseph. **Around Western Campfires.** NY: Pageant; 1964. [$20.00]

Ayer, I. Winslow. **The Great Treason Plot in the North during the War.** Chicago: U.S. Publishing; 1895. [hinges cracked, $80.00]

Ayer, I. Winslow. **Life in the Wilds of America and Wonders of the West.** Grand Rapids, MI: Central; 1880. [$65.00]

Ayers, James J. **Gold and Sunshine.** Boston: Badger; 1922. [cover stained, $30.00]

Ayme, Jean Jacques. **Deportation et Naufrage de J.J. Ayme.** Paris: Maradan; 1800. [$175.00]

B., J. C. **Travels in New France.** Harrisburg: Pennsylvania Hist. Comm.; 1941. [$45.00]

Baber, Adin. **Nancy Hanks, the Destined Mother of a President.** Kansas, IL: dist. by Arthur Clark; 1963. [$35.00]

Babst, Earl D. **Michigan and the Cleveland Era.** Ann Arbor: U. of Michigan; 1948. [x-lib., $20.00] [$17.50]

Baca, Carlos C. de. **Vicente Silva.** [s.l.: s.n.]; 1938. [$50.00]

Bach, Marcus. **Of Faith and Learning.** Iowa City: School of Religion, State U. of Iowa; 1952. [$17.50]

Bache, Benjamin Franklin. **Truth Will Out!** Philadelphia: Aurora; 1798. [x-lib., $125.00]

Bachelder, John B. **Bachelder's Illustrated Tourists' Guide of the United States Popular Resorts, and How to Reach Them.** Boston: Bachelder; 1873. 2 v. in 1. [x-lib., $22.50]

Bachman, Calvin George. **Old Order Amish of Lancaster County.** Norristown, PA: Pennsylvania German Society; 1942. [x-lib., $70.00]

Back, George. **Narrative of the Arctic Land Expedition to the Mouth of the Great Fish River.** Philadelphia: Carey & Hart; 1836. [rebacked, $200.00]

Bacon, Edgar Mayhew. **The Hudson River from Ocean to Source.** NY, London: Putnam; 1902. [with five strip maps in pocket, $100.00]

Bacon, Edgar Mayhew. **Narragansett Bay.** NY, London: Putnam; 1904. [$60.00]

Bacon, Edwin M. **Walks and Rides in the Country round about Boston.** Boston, NY: Houghton Mifflin; 1898. [$45.00]

Bacon, Leonard. **Genesis of the New England Churches.** NY: Harper; 1874. [$30.00]

Bad Heart Bull, Amos. **Pictographic History of the Oglala Sioux.** Lincoln: U. of Nebraska; 1967. [$75.00]

Badeau, Adam. **Grant in Peace.** Hartford: Scranton; 1887. [$85.00]

Badeau, Adam. **Military History of Ulysses S. Grant.** NY: Appleton; 1881. 3 v. [$115.00]

Badlam, Alexander. **Wonders of Alaska.** San Francsico: Bancroft; 1890. [covers stained, $45.00]

Baerg, William J. **Birds of Arkansas.** Fayetteville: Agricultural Experiment Station, U. of Arkansas; 1931. [$35.00]

Baerlein, Henry. **Mexico, the Land of Unrest.** London: Herbert and Daniel; 1913. [$50.00]

Bagby, George William. **John Brown and Wm. Mahone.** Richmond: Johnston; 1880. [top wrap loose, $45.00]

Baggs, Mae Lacy. **Colorado, the Queen Jewel of the Rockies.** Boston: Page; 1920, c1918. [$17.50]

Bagley, Clarence. **Acquisition and Pioneering of Old Oregon.** Seattle: Argus; 1924. [$100.00]

Bail, Hamilton Vaughan. **Views of Harvard.** Cambridge: Harvard UP; 1949. [$25.00]

Bailey, Gamaliel. **American Progress.** Cincinnati: Shepard; 1846. [$75.00]

Bailey, Harold Harris. **Birds of Florida.** limited ed. Baltimore: William & Wilkins; 1925. [signed, covers soiled, $160.00]

Bailey, Harold Harris. **Birds of Virginia.** Lynchburg: Bell; 1913. [$125.00]

Bailey, James Henry. **Henrico Home Front, 1861-1865.** [Richmond?: s.n.]; 1963. [$12.50]

Bailey, Lynn Robison. **Indian Slave Trade in the Southwest.** Los Angeles: Westernlore; 1966. [$20.00] [$25.00]

Bailey, Paul Dayton. **Wovoka, the Indian Messiah.** Los Angeles: Westernlore; 1957. [$25.00]

Bailey, Rosalie Fellows. **Pre-Revolutionary Dutch Houses and Families in Northern New Jersey and Southern New York.** NY: Morrow; 1936. [$75.00]

Bain, John. **Tobacco in Song and Story.** NY: Caldwell; 1896. [bumped, rubbed, torn, deteriorating suede binding, $12.50]

Baird, Charles Washington. **History of the Huguenot Emigration to America.** NY: Dodd, Mead; 1885. 2 v. [$45.00]

Baird, Henry Carey. **The Eastern and the Western Questions; Turkey and the United States.** Philadelphia: Baird; 1877. [$25.00]

Baird, Robert. **Impressions and Experiences of the West Indies and North America in 1849.** Philadelphia: Lea & Blanchard; 1850. [$125.00] [binding frayed and rubbed, $40.00]

Baird, Robert. **Religion in the United States of America.** Glasgow and Edinburgh: Blackie; 1844. [$125.00]

Baird, Robert. **View of the Valley of the Mississippi, or, The Emigrant's and Traveller's Guide to the West.** 2nd ed. Philadelphia: Tanner; 1834. [$150.00]

Bakarich, Sarah Grace. **Gun-Smoke.** [s.l.: s.n.]; 1947. [$75.00] [signed, $60.00]

Bakeless, John Edwin. **Background to Glory.** Philadelphia: Lippincott; 1957. [$30.00]

Bakeless, John Edwin. **Daniel Boone.** NY: Morrow; 1939. [$37.50]

Bakeless, John Edwin. **Eyes of Discovery.** 1st ed. Philadelphia: Lippincott; 1950. [dj repaired, $15.00]

Baker, Carlos. **Ernest Hemingway.** NY: Scribner; 1969. [fine, $35.00]

Baker, Charlotte Alice. **True Stories of New England Captives Carried to Canada during the Old French and Indian Wars.** Cambridge: Hall; 1897. [$135.00]

Baker, De Witt Clinton. **Texas Scrap-Book.** 1st ed. NY: Barnes; 1875. [extremities worn, $250.00]

Baker, Edward Dickinson. **Masterpieces.** San Francisco: Shuck; 1899. [$25.00]

Baker, Henry H. **Reminiscent Story of the Great Civil War: Second Paper.** New Orleans: Ruskin; 1911. [$250.00]

Baker, La Fayette Charles. **History of the United States Secret Service.** Philadelphia: Baker; 1867. [worn, $22.50] [x-lib., $15.00]

Baker, La Fayette Charles. **The United States Secret Service in the Late War.** Philadelphia: Potter; 1874. [binding very worn, $14.50]

Baker, Nina Brown. **Cyclone in Calico.** 1st ed. Boston: Little, Brown; 1952. [$18.50]

Baker, Ray Palmer. **A Chapter in American Education; Rensselaer Polytechnic Institute, 1824-1924.** NY: Scribner; 1924. [$20.00]

Baker, Ray Stannard. **Following the Color Line.** NY: Doubleday, Page; 1908. [$45.00]

Baker-Crothers, Hayes. **Virginia and the French and Indian War.** Chicago: U. of Chicago; 1928. [$40.00]

Balch, Emily Greene. **Occupied Haiti.** NY: Writers Publishing; 1927. [$25.00]

Balch, Thomas Willing. **The Alabama Arbitration.** Philadelphia: Allen, Lane & Scott; 1900. [$30.00]

Balch, Thomas Willing. **The Alaska Frontier.** Philadelphia: Allen, Lane and Scott; 1903. [x-lib., $40.00]

Balch, William Ralton. **Life of James Abram Garfield.** Philadelphia: McCurdy; 1881. [$55.00]

Bald, Frederick Clever. **Detroit's First American Decade.** Ann Arbor: 1948. [fine in dj, $50.00]

Baldridge, Michael. **A Reminiscence.** Los Angeles: [s.n.]; 1959. [$15.00]

Baldwin, Ebenezer. **Annals of Yale College.** New Haven: Howe; 1831. [$25.00]

Baldwin, Joseph G. **Flush Times of Alabama and Mississippi.** NY: Appleton; 1853. [$325.00]

Baldwin, Leland Dewitt. **The Keelboat Age on Western Waters.** Pittsburgh: U. of Pittsburgh; 1941. [$40.00]

Baldwin, Leland Dewitt. **Pittsburgh.** Pittsburgh: U. of Pittsburgh; 1938. [$22.00]

Baldwin, Thomas. **Narrative of the Massacre by the Savages, of the Wife and Children of Thomas Baldwin.** NY: Martin and Wood; 1835. [$425.00]

Bale, Florence Gratiot. **Galena's Yesterdays.** Waukegan, IL: Bale; 1931. [covers soiled, $25.00]

Ball, Eve. **Ma'am Jones of the Pecos.** Tucson: U. of Arizona; 1969. [$35.00]

Ball, John. **Autobiography of.** Glendale, CA: Clark; 1925. [$75.00] [$50.00]

Ballads of the B.E.F. NY: Coventry; 1932. [$60.00]

Ballagh, James Curtis. **White Servitude in the Colony of Virginia.** Baltimore: Hopkins; 1895. [$45.00]

Ballantyne, R. M. **Hudson's Bay.** 3rd ed. London: Nelson; 1857. [$65.00]

Ballard, Colin Robert. **Military Genius of Abraham Lincoln.** 1st American ed. Cleveland: World; 1952. [$22.50]

Ballenger, Thomas Lee. **Around Tahlequah Council Fires.** Muskogee, OK: Motter; 1935. [signed, $45.00]

Ballou, Maturin Murray. **The New Eldorado.** Boston; NY: Houghton Mifflin; 1889. [$11.00]

Balme, Joshua Rhodes. **American States, Churches, and Slavery.** London: Hamilton, Adams; [1863?]. [$100.00]

Baltimore Citizens. **Proceedings of Sundry Citizens of Baltimore.** Baltimore: Wooddy; 1827. [$200.00]

Balzer, Robert Lawrence. **This Uncommon Heritage.** Los Angeles: Ritchie; 1970. [x-lib., $15.00]

Bancroft, Aaron. **Life of George Washington.** Boston: Phillips, Sampson; 1852. 2 v. in 1. [$35.00]

Bancroft, George. **History of the Formation of the Constitution of the United States of America.** 3rd ed. NY: Appleton; 1883, c1882. 2 v. [$45.00]

Bancroft, George. **History of the United States of America.** rev. ed. Boston: Little, Brown; 1879, c1878. 6 v. [$60.00]

Bancroft, Griffing. **Lower California.** NY, London: Putnam; 1932. [$80.00]

Bancroft, Hubert Howe. **History of Alaska. 1730-1885.** San Francisco: Bancroft; 1886. [$120.00]

Bancroft, Hubert Howe. **History of Arizona and New Mexico: 1530-1888.** San Francisco: History Co.; 1889. [$95.00]

Bancroft, Hubert Howe. **History of British Columbia: 1792-1887.** San Francisco: History Co.; 1887. [$60.00]

Bancroft, Hubert Howe. **History of California.** San Francisco: Bancroft; 1884-90. 7 v. [mixed printings, $175.00]

Bancroft, Hubert Howe. **History of Nevada, Colorado, and Wyoming, 1540-1888.** San Francisco: History Co.; 1890. [$70.00]

Bancroft, Hubert Howe. **History of North Mexican States and Texas.** San Francisco: Bancroft; 1884-1889. 2 v. [$200.00]

Bancroft, Hubert Howe. **History of Oregon.** San Francisco: History Co.; 1886-88. 2 v. [$85.00]

Bancroft, Hubert Howe. **History of the Life of Leland Stanford.** Oakland: Biobooks; 1952. [$20.00]

Bancroft, Hubert Howe. **History of Utah, 1540-1886.** San Francisco: History Co.; 1889. [$75.00]

Bancroft, Hubert Howe. **History of Washington, Idaho, and Montana: 1845-1889.** San Francisco: History Co.; 1890. [$75.00]

Bancroft, Hubert Howe. **The Native Races of the Pacific States of North America.** NY: Appleton; 1874-76. 5 v. [x-lib., $625.00]

Bandel, Eugene. **Frontier Life in the Army, 1854-1861.** Glendale, CA: Clark; 1932. [$150.00]

Bandelier, Adolf Francis Alphonse. **The Delight Makers.** NY: Dodd, Mead; 1890. [$125.00] [1916 2nd ed., $35.00]

Bandelier, Adolph Francis Alphonse. **A Scientist on the Trail.** Berkeley: Quivira; 1949. [x-lib., $75.00]

Bangor and Aroostook Railroad. **In the Maine Woods.** Bangor, ME: Bangor and Aroostook Railroad Co.; 1926. [$25.00]

Banks, Louis Albert. **White Slaves.** Boston: Lee and Shepard; 1892. [$20.00]

Banks, Robert Webb. **The Battle of Franklin.** NY, Washington: Neale; 1908. [some dampstain, $235.00]

Bankston, Marie Louise Benton. **Camp-Fire Stories of the Mississippi Valley Campaign.** New Orleans: Graham; 1914. [$25.00]

Banning, William. **Six Horses.** NY: Century; 1930. [hinges weak, $20.00]

Banta, Richard Elwell. **Indiana Authors and Their Books, 1816-1916.** Crawfordsville, IN: Wabash College; 1949. [$40.00]

Banta, William. **Twenty-Seven Years on the Texas Frontier.** Council Hill, OK: [s.n.]; 1933. [$35.00]

Baragwanath, John. **Pay Streak.** Garden City: Doubleday, Doran; 1936. [$15.00]

Baraka, Imamu Amiri. **Blues People.** 1st ed. NY: Morrow; 1965. [dj rubbed and chipped, $25.00]

Barbe-Marbois, Francois Marquis de. **Complot d'Arnold et de Sir Henry Clinton Contre les Etats-Unis d'Amerique et Contre le General Washington.** Paris: Didot; 1816. [$250.00]

Barbe-Marbois, Francois Marquis de. **Histoire de la Louisiane.** Paris: Didot; 1829. [$375.00] [$250.00]

Barbe-Marbois, Francois Marquis de. **History of Louisiana.** Philadelphia: Carey & Lea; 1830. [rebacked, foxed, $350.00] [$275.00]

Barbe-Marbois, Francois Marquis de. **Our Revolutionary Forefathers.** NY: Duffield; 1929. [$20.00]

Barber, Don. **Yale Songs.** New Haven: [s.n.]; 1893. [$12.50]

Barber, Edwin Atlee. **The Pottery and Porcelain of the United States.** 2nd ed. NY: Putnam; 1901. [$120.00]

Barber, John Warner. **Historical Collections of the State of New York.** NY: Tuttle; 1841. [one gathering loose, rubbed, browned, $180.00]

Barber, John Warner. **Historical, Poetical and Pictorial American Scenes.** New Haven: Bradley; 1850. [$40.00] [1851 printing, $45.00]

Barber, John Warner. **The History and Antiquities of New England, New York, New Jersey, and Pennsylvania.** 3rd ed. Hartford: Parsons; 1846, c1842. [$85.00]

Barber, John Warner. **History and Antiquities of New Haven.** New Haven, CT: Barber; 1831. [spine restored, $265.00] [1856 2nd ed., $145.00]

Barber, John Warner. **Views in New Haven and Its Vicinity: With a Particular Description to Each View.** New Haven: Barber; 1825. [foxed, $50.00]

Barber, Joseph. **Hawaii: Restless Rampart.** Indianapolis: Bobbs-Merrill; 1941. [$25.00] [$15.00] [$25.00]

Barbour, Harriot Buxton. **Sandwich, the Town That Glass Built.** Boston: Houghton Mifflin; 1948. [$15.00]

Barbour, Philip Norbourne. **Journals of the Late Brevet Major.** NY, London: Putnam; 1936. [$45.00]

Barbour, Thomas. **The Birds of Cuba.** 1st ed. Cambridge: Nuttal Ornithological Club; 1923. [x-lib., $60.00]

Barclay, James W. **Mormonism Exposed.** [s.l.: s.n.]; 1884. [$49.50]

Barclay, Robert. see, Allardice, Robert Barclay.

Bard, Floyd C. **Horse Wrangler.** 1st ed. Norman: U. of Oklahoma; 1960. [$25.00]

Bari, Valeska. see, Bary, Helen

Barker, Anselm Holcomb. **Anselm Holcomb Barker, 1822-1895.** limited ed. Denver: Golden Bell; 1959. [signed by editor, $100.00]

Barker, Benjamin. **Francisco or the Pirate of the Pacific.** Boston: Gleason's; 1845. [$125.00]

Barker, Burt Brown. **The McLoughlin Empire and Its Rulers.** Glendale, CA: Clark; 1959. [$50.00]

Barker, Charles Edwin. **With President Taft in the White House.** Chicago: Kroch; 1947. [$35.00]

Barker, Elliott Speer. **Beatty's Cabin.** Albuquerque: U. of New Mexico; 1953. [$25.00] [frayed dj, $12.00] [$25.00]

Barker, Eugene Campbell. **Life of Stephen F. Austin.** special limited ed. Nashville, Dallas: Cokesbury; 1925. [$300.00] [trade edition, $125.00]

Barker, Eugene Campbell. **Mexico and Texas, 1821-1835.** Dallas: Turner; 1928. [$100.00]

Barker, Jacob. **Conspiracy Trials of 1826 and 1827.** Philadelphia: Childs; 1864. [$45.00]

Barker, Joseph. **Recollections of the First Settlement of Ohio.** Marietta, OH: Marietta College; 1958. [$20.00]

Barkley, Alben William. **That Reminds Me--.** 1st ed. Garden City: Doubleday; 1954. [signed, $25.00]

Barler, Miles. **Early Days in Llano.** [Llano, TX?: s.n.; 1905?]. [$75.00]

Barlow, Joel. **The Vision of Columbus.** Hartford: Hudson and Goodwin; 1787. [$450.00] [1973 English Press, Paris ed., $250.00]

Barnard, Evan G. **A Rider of the Cherokee Strip.** Boston, NY: Houghton Mifflin; 1936. [$45.00] [$40.00] [$55.00]

Barnard, Harry. **Eagle Forgotten.** Indianapolis: Bobbs-Merrill; 1938. [$15.00]

Barnard, Harry. **Rutherford B. Hayes, and His America.** 1st ed. Indianapolis: Bobbs-Merrill; 1954. [$30.00]

Barnard, John Gross. **The Peninsular Campaign and Its Antecedents.** NY: Van Nostrand; 1864. [$45.00]

Barnard, Joseph Henry. **Journal.** Goliad bicentennial ed. [Refugio?, TX: Huson?]; 1949. [$135.00]

Barnes, Gilbert Hobbs. **The Antislavery Impulse 1830-1844.** NY, London: Appleton-Century; 1933. [$40.00]

Barnes, Will C. **Apaches & Longhorns.** Los Angeles: Ritchie; 1941. [$130.00]

Barnes, Will C. **Tales from the X-Bar Horse Camp.** Chicago: Breeders' Gazette; 1920. [inner hinge starting, $125.00]

Barnett, Joel. **A Long Trip in a Prairie Schooner.** [s.l.: s.n.]; 1928. [$100.00]

Barnhart, John Donald. **Henry Hamilton and George Rogers Clark in the American Revolution.** 1st ed. Crawfordsville, IN: Banta; 1951. [$60.00] [$45.00]

Barnhart, John Donald. **Indiana from Frontier to Industrial Commonwealth.** NY: Lewis Historical; 1954. 4 v. [$95.00]

Barnhart, John Donald. **Valley of Democracy.** Bloomington: Indiana UP; 1953. [$20.00] [$30.00]

Barns, George C. **Denver, the Man.** Wilmington, OH: [s.n.]; 1949, c1950. [$30.00]

Barnum, H. L. **The Spy Unmasked; or, Memoirs of Enoch Crosby.** NY; London: Harper; Newman; 1828. 2 v. in 1. [$50.00]

Barnum, P. T. **Life of P.T. Barnum.** NY: Redfield; 1855. [with Barnum's autograph laid in, $225.00]

Barnum, P. T. **Struggles and Triumphs.** Hartford: Burr; 1869. [$25.00] [1871 American News ed., $75.00] [1875 Buffalo Courier ed., in ratty binding, $15.00]

Barr, Alwyn. **Polignac's Texas Brigade.** 1st ed. Houston: Texas Gulf Coast Hist. Assn.; 1964. [$40.00]

Barratt, Raven. **Coronets and Buckskin.** Boston: Houghton Mifflin; 1957. [$10.00]

Barrett, Charles Simon. **The Mission, History and Times of the Farmers' Union.** Nashville: Marshall & Bruce; 1909. [$35.00]

Barrett, Harrison Delivan. **Life Work of Mrs. Cora L. V. Richmond.** Chicago: Hack & Anderson; 1895. [x-lib., $20.00]

Barrett, John Gilchrist. **Sherman's March through the Carolinas.** Chapel Hill: U. of North Carolina; 1956. [$25.00]

Barrett, Joseph Hartwell. **Abraham Lincoln and His Presidency.** Cincinnati: Clarke; 1903. 2 v. [$100.00]

Barrett, Joseph Hartwell. **Life of Abraham Lincoln.** Cincinnati: Moore, Wilstach, Keys; 1860. [$150.00]

Barrett, Joseph O. **History of "Old Abe."** Chicago: Sewell; 1865. [$300.00]

Barrett, Monte. **Tempered Blade.** Alamo ed. Indianapolis, NY: Bobbs-Merrill; 1946. [signed, $35.00]

Barrett, Samuel Alfred. **Material Aspects of Pomo Culture.** Milwaukee: Public Museum; 1952. 2 v. [$50.00]

Barrett, Samuel Alfred. **Pomo Myths.** Milwaukee: Public Museum; 1933. [$50.00]

Barringer, Paul B. **The Natural Bent.** Chapel Hill: U. of North Carolina; 1949. [$35.00]

Barron, Samuel Benton. **The Lone Star Defenders.** NY, Washington: Neale; 1908. [dj repaired, $850.00] [1964 Morrison ed., $35.00]

Barron, William. **History of the Colonization of the Free States of Antiquity Applied to the Present Contest between Great Britain and Her American Colonies.** London: Cadell; 1777. [rebound, $300.00]

Barrows, John. **Ubet.** Caldwell, ID: Caxton; 1934. [$100.00]

Barrows, William. **The General; or, Twelve Nights in the Hunters' Camp.** Boston: Lee and Shepard; 1869. [$45.00]

Barrows, William. **Oregon: The Struggle for Possession.** 3rd ed. Boston: Houghton Mifflin; 1885. [x-lib., $10.00]

Barrows, William. **The United States of Yesterday and of To-morrow.** Boston: Roberts; 1888. [$20.00] [$25.00]

Barrus, Clara. **Life and Letters of John Burroughs.** Boston, NY: Houghton Mifflin; 1925. 2 v. [$45.00]

Barry, Colman James. **The Catholic Church and German Americans.** Milwaukee: Bruce; 1953. [$20.00] [signed, $15.00]

Barry, Iris. **D. W. Griffith.** NY: Museum of Modern Art; 1940. [$25.00]

Barry, James Buckner. **A Texas Ranger and Frontiersman.** Dallas: Southwest; 1932. [$275.00]

Barry, John Stetson. **History of Massachusetts.** Boston: Phillips, Sampson; 1855-57. 3 v. [$100.00]

Barry, Joseph. **Annals of Harper's Ferry.** 2nd ed. Martinsburg, WV: Berkeley Union; 1872. [$75.00]

Barry, William E. **Chronicles of Kennebunk.** NY: Redfield-Kendrick-Odell; 1923. [$175.00]

Bartholomew, Ed Ellsworth. **Biographical Album of Western Gunfighters.** Houston: Frontier Press; 1958. [signed, $195.00] [hinges weak, $125.00]

Bartholomew, Ed Ellsworth. **Black Jack Ketchum.** Houston: Frontier Press; 1955. [$50.00]

Bartholomew, Ed Ellsworth. **Cullen Baker.** Houston: Frontier Press; 1954. [$45.00]

Bartholomew, Ed Ellsworth. **Jesse Evans.** 1st ed. Houston: Frontier Press; 1955. [signed limited ed., $35.00]

Bartholomew, Ed Ellsworth. **Wild Bill Longley.** Houston: Frontier Press; 1953. [$50.00]

Bartlett, John Russell. **Personal Narrative of Explorations and Incidents in Texas, New Mexico, California, Sonora, and Chihuahua.** NY, London: Appleton; 1854. 2 v. [$800.00] [$975.00] [$750.00] [1856 2 v. in 1 issue, $525.00]

Bartlett, Josiah. **Historical Sketch of Charlestown.** Boston: Eliot; 1814. [$35.00]

Bartlett, W. H. **Pilgrim Fathers.** London: Hall, Virtue; 1853. [$100.00]

Barton, Wilfred. **Road to Washington.** Boston: Badger; 1919. [$20.00]

Barton, William. **Memoirs of the Life of David Rittenhouse.** Philadelphia: Parker; 1813. [spine repaired, $150.00] [rebacked, $225.00]

Barton, William Eleazar. **The Lineage of Lincoln.** 1st ed. Indianapolis: Bobbs-Merrill; 1929. [$95.00]

Bartram, John. **Observations on the Inhabitants, Climate, Soil, Rivers, Productions, Animals, and Other Matters Worthy of Notice.** London: Whiston and White; 1751. [rebound, $4000.00]

Bartram, William. **Travels through North and South Carolina.** Philadelphia: James and Johnson; 1791. [restored, $2850.00]

Bary, Helen. **Course of Empire.** NY: Coward-McCann; 1931. [$12.50]

Bashford, Herbert. **A Man Unafraid.** San Francisco: Wagner; 1927. [$45.00]

Baskervill, William Malone. **Southern Writers.** Nashville: M. E. Church, South; 1897. [cover rubbed and spotted, $22.50]

Bass, Altha Leah (Bierbower). **Cherokee Messenger.** Norman: U. of Oklahoma; 1936. [inscribed, $125.00]

Bass, Charlotta A. **Forty Years.** Los Angeles: Bass; 1960. [$125.00]

Bass, Samuel. **Life and Adventures of.** Dallas: Commercial; 1878. [wraps chipped, $50.00]

Bassett, Edward H. **From Bull Run to Bristow Station.** St. Paul: North Central; 1962. [$17.50]

Bassett, John Spencer. **Anti-Slavery Leaders of North Carolina.** Baltimore: Hopkins; 1898. [$45.00]

Basso, Hamilton. **Beauregard, the Great Creole.** NY, London: Scribner; 1933. [x-lib., $30.00] [$45.00]

Batchelder, George Alexander. **Sketch of the History and Resources of Dakota Territory.** Yankton: Steam Power Printing; 1870. [$2000.00]

Batchelder, James. **Multum in Parvo.** San Francisco: Pacific Press; 1892. [$125.00]

Batchelder, Roger. **Camp Devens.** Boston: Small, Maynard; 1918. [$25.00]

Batchelder, Samuel Francis. **Bits of Harvard History.** Cambridge: Harvard; 1924. [$25.00]

Bate, Walter Nathaniel. **Frontier Legend; Texas Finale of Capt. William F. Drannan.** New Bern, NC: Dunn; 1954. [$20.00]

Bates, Charles Francis. **Custer's Indian Battles.** Bronxville, NY: [s.n.]; 1936. [signed, $40.00]

Bates, Edmond Franklin. **Authentic History of Sam Bass and His Gang.** Bandera, TX: Frontier Times; 1950. [$75.00]

Bates, Ernest Sutherland. **Story of the Supreme Court.** 1st ed. Indianapolis, NY: Bobbs-Merrill; 1936. [$17.50]

Bates, Finis Langdon. **Escape and Suicide of John Wilkes Booth.** Memphis: Pilcher; 1907. [hinges weak, $90.00]

Bates, Harry C. **Bricklayers' Century of Craftsmanship.** Washington: Bricklayers, Masons and Plasterers' International Union of America; 1955. [$25.00]

Bates, Henry Walter. **Naturalist on the River Amazons.** London: Murray; 1892. [hinges cracked, $50.00]

Bates, Samuel Penniman. **Our Country and Its People.** Boston: Fergusson; 1899. [joints broken, $100.00]

Bathe, Greville. **Oliver Evans.** Philadelphia: Historical Society of PA; 1935. [$150.00] [x-lib., $100.00]

Battey, Thomas C. **Life and Adventures of a Quaker among the Indians.** Boston: Lee and Shepard; 1875. [$75.00] [$35.00] [binding frayed, $150.00]

Battle, Kemp Plummer. **Memories of an Old-Time Tar Heel.** Chapel Hill: U. of North Carolina; 1945. [$12.50]

Batty, Beatrice. **Forty-Two Years amongst the Indians and Eskimo.** London: Religious Tract Soc.; 1893. [$50.00]

Baudry des Lozieres, Louis Narcisse. **Voyage a la Louisiane.** Paris: Dentu; 1802. [rebound in half calf, last leaf in facs., $750.00]

Baughman, Abraham J. **History of Richland County, Ohio, from 1808 to 1908.** Chicago: Clarke; 1908. 2 v. [$75.00]

Baughman, Theodore. **Oklahoma Scout.** Chicago: Conkey; [188-?]. [$30.00]

Baurmeister, Carl Leopold. **Revolution in America.** New Brunswick, NJ; Boston: Rutgers UP; Murray; 1957. [$25.00]

Baxley, Henry Willis. **What I Saw on the West Coast of South and North America, and at the Hawaiian Islands.** NY: Appleton; 1865. [$85.00]

Baxter, James Phinney. **Memoir of Jacques Cartier Sieur de Limoilou.** NY: Dodd, Mead; 1906. [$175.00]

Baxter, James Phinney. **Pioneers of New France in New England.** Albany, NY: Munsell; 1894. [$75.00]

Baxter, John Sydney. **America, Her Grandeur and Her Beauty.** Chicago: Union; [1904?]. [fine, $125.00]

Bay, Jens Christian. **Fortune of Books.** Chicago: Hill; 1941. [$60.00]

Bayard, Nicholas. **Narrative of an Attempt Made by the French of Canada upon the Mohaque's Country.** NY: Dodd, Mead; 1903. [$40.00]

Bayard, Samuel John. **A Sketch of the Life of Com. Robert F. Stockton.** NY: Derby & Jackson; 1856. [x-lib., $45.00]

Bayard, Samuel Preston. **Hill Country Tunes.** Philadelphia: American Folklore Soc.; 1944. [$24.00]

Bayer, Henry G. **The Belgians, First Settlers in New York and in the Middle States.** NY: Devin-Adair; 1925. [$40.00]

Bayles, William Harrison. **Old Taverns of New York.** NY: Allaben; 1915. [$40.00]

Baylies, Francis. **Historical Memoir of the Colony of New Plymouth.** Boston: Hilliard, Gray, Little, Wilkins; 1830. 2 v. [x-lib., $30.00]

Baylies, Francis. **Narrative of Major General Wool's Campaign in Mexico.** Albany: Little; 1851. [some wear and stains, $200.00][$300.00][worn, stained, browned, $200.00]

Baylor, George. **Bull Run to Bull Run.** Richmond: Johnson; 1900. [$100.00]

Baylor, Orval Walker. **John Pope.** Cynthiana, KY: Hobson; 1943. [bumped, mildewed, hinges weak, $35.00]

Bayne, Julia. **Tad Lincoln's Father.** Boston: Little, Brown; 1931. [$28.50]

Beach, Arthur Granville. **A Pioneer College; the Story of Marietta.** Chicago: Priv. Print.; 1935. [$25.00]

Beach, James Caleb. **Army vs. Notre Dame.** NY: Random; 1948. [$17.50]

Beach, Spencer Ambrose. **Apples of New York.** Albany: NY Dept. of Agriculture; 1905. 2 v. [$95.00]

Beadle, Erastus Flavel. **To Nebraska in '57.** NY: New York Public Library; 1923. [$45.00]

Beadle, John Hanson. **Life in Utah.** Philadelphia: National; 1870. [$75.00] [binding stained and loose, $60.00]

Beadle, John Hanson. **Western Wilds and the Men Who Redeem Them.** Cincinnati: Jones; 1878, c1877. [$75.00]

Beakes, Samuel W. **Past and Present of Washtenow County Michigan.** Chicago: Clarke; 1906. [spine chipped, hinges broken, covers scuffed, $100.00]

Beal, Merrill D. **History of Idaho.** NY: Lewis; 1959. 3 v. [$85.00]

Beal, Merrill D. **The Story of Man in Yellowstone.** Caldwell, ID: Caxton; 1949. [inscribed, dj chipped, $13.00]

Beale, David J. **Through the Johnstown Flood.** [Johnstown, Pa.?]: Edgewood; 1890. [x-lib., amateurishly rebacked, $15.00]

Beale, Howard K. **Theodore Roosevelt and the Rise of America to World Power.** Baltimore: Hopkins; 1956. [$30.00]

Beale, Richard Lee. **History of the Ninth Virginia Cavalry, in the War between the States.** Richmond: Johnson; 1899. [$850.00]

Beals, Carleton. **Brass-Knuckle Crusade.** NY: Hastings; 1960. [$25.00]

Beals, Carleton. **Fire on the Andes.** Philadelphia, London: Lippincott; 1934. [inscribed, $15.00]

Beals, Frank Lee. **Backwoods Baron.** Wheaton, IL: Morton; 1951. [$16.00]

Bean, Orestes U. **Corianton: an Aztec Romance.** [s.l.: s.n.; 1902?]. [$35.00]

Bean, William Gleason. **Stonewall's Man: Sandie Pendleton.** Chapel Hill: U. of North Carolina; 1959. [$25.00]

Bear, John W. **Life and Travels of.** Baltimore: Binswanger; 1873. [fine, $125.00]

Beard, Daniel Carter. **What to Do and How to Do It.** new ed. NY: Scribner; 1907. [$22.50]

Beard, John Relly. **Life of Toussaint L'Ouverture.** London: Ingram, Cooke; 1853. [$125.00]

Beardsley, Daniel Barna. **History of Hancock County [Ohio].** Springfield: Republic; 1881. [x-lib., $90.00]

Beardsley, Eben Edwards. **Life and Times of William Samuel Johnson.** 2nd ed. Boston: Houghton; 1886. [$35.00]

Beardsley, Levi. **Reminiscences.** NY: Vinten; 1852. [spine frayed, $145.00] [$75.00] [hinges weak, $60.00]

Beasley, Norman. **The Continuing Spirit.** NY: Duell, Sloan and Pearce; 1956. [$15.00]

Beasley, Norman. **Knudsen.** NY; London: Whittlesey; McGraw-Hill; 1947. [$15.00]

Beaton, Kendall. **Enterprise in Oil.** NY: Appleton Century Crofts; 1957. [$25.00]

Beattie, Kim. **Brother, Here's a Man! The Saga of Klondike Boyle.** NY: Macmillan; 1940. [2nd printing, $12.50]

Beatty, Charles. **Journal of a Two Months Tour.** Edinburgh: Maccliesh and Ogle; 1798. [disbound, $400.00]

Beaumont, William. **Experiments and Observations on the Gastric Juice, and the Physiology of Digestion.** Plattsburgh: Allen; 1833. [$1500.00] [1834 Boston imprint, rebacked, $1500.00] [2nd ed. 1847, $650.00]

Beauregard, G. T. **Commentary on the Campaign and Battle of Manassas, of July 1861.** NY, London: Putnam; 1891. [x-lib., $45.00]

Bechdolt, Frederick Ritchie. **Giants of the Old West.** NY, London: Century; 1930. [$35.00]

Bechdolt, Frederick Ritchie. **Tales of the Old-Timers.** NY, London: Century; 1924. [$22.00] [$25.00]

Bechdolt, Frederick Ritchie. **When the West Was Young.** NY: Century; 1922. [$25.00]

Beck, Earl Clifton. **Lore of the Lumber Camps.** rev. ed. Ann Arbor: U. of Michigan; 1948. [inscribed, worn dj, $40.00]

Beck, Henry Charlton. **Fare to Midlands.** 1st ed. NY: Dutton; 1939. [$40.00] [$35.00]

Beck, Henry Charlton. **More Forgotten Towns of Southern New Jersey.** NY: Dutton; 1937. [$22.50]

Beck, Warren A. **New Mexico; a History of Four Centuries.** 1st ed. Norman: U. of Oklahoma; 1962. [$27.50] [$25.00]

Becker, Stephen D. **Comic Art in America.** NY: Simon and Schuster; 1959. [$20.00]

Beckford, William. **Descriptive Account of the Island of Jamaica.** London: Egerton; 1790. 2 v. [2 vols. bound together, x-lib., front cover detached, title page defective, $200.00]

Beckman, Nellie Sims. **Unclean and Spotted from the World.** San Francisco: Whitaker & Ray; 1906. [$15.00]

Beckwith, Paul Edmond. **Creoles of St. Louis.** St. Louis: Nixon-Jones; 1893. [hinges reinforced, $150.00]

Beckwourth, James Pierson. **Life and Adventures of.** new ed. London; NY: Unwin; Macmillan; 1892. [$40.00]

Bedell, Mary Crehore. **Modern Gypsies.** NY: Brentano's; 1924. [$40.00]

Bedford-Jones, Henry. **The Mission and the Man.** Pasadena: San Pasqual; 1939. [presentation, $49.50]

Bedichek, Roy. **Karankaway Country.** 1st ed. Garden City: Doubleday; 1950. [$35.00]

Beebe, Lucius. **The American West.** 1st ed. NY: Dutton; 1955. [$45.00]

Beebe, Lucius. **Cable Car Carnival.** 1st ed. Oakland, CA: Hardy; 1951. [$15.00]

Beebe, Lucius. **Legends of the Comstock Lode.** 2nd ed. Carson City: Hardy; 1951. [$20.00]

Beebe, Lucius. **U.S. West.** NY: Dutton; 1949. [$17.50]

Beecher, Edward. **Narrative of Riots at Alton.** Alton, IL: Holton; 1838. [spine chipped, hinges cracked, foxed, $150.00] [foxed, $50.00]

Beecher, Henry Ward. **Eyes and Ears.** Boston: Ticknor and Fields; 1862. [$20.00]

Beecher, Henry Ward. **Star Papers.** NY: Derby; 1855. [$30.00] [$20.00]

Beechey, Frederick William. **Narrative of a Voyage to the Pacific and Beering's Strait.** London: Colburn and Bentley; 1831. 2 v. [$1000.00]

Beekman, George Crawford. **Early Dutch Settlers of Monmouth County, New Jersey.** 2nd ed. Freehold, NJ: Moreau; 1915. [$100.00]

Beer, Thomas. **Stephen Crane.** NY: Knopf; 1923. [$17.50] [$10.00]

Beers, Fannie A. **Memories.** Philadelphia: Lippincott; 1891, c1888. [bumped, frayed, rubbed, spotted, $15.00]

Beeson, John. **A Plea for the Indians.** 3rd ed. NY: Beeson; 1858. [corners worn, $225.00]

Beetle, David Harold. **West Canada Creek.** Utica, NY: Observer-Dispatch; 1946. [$20.00]

Behnke, Arno. **Sailing of a Refugee Ship.** NY: Schirmer; 1914. [$25.00]

Beidelman, William. **The Story of the Pennsylvania Germans.** Easton, PA: Express; 1898. [presentation, hinges cracked, $30.00]

Beirne, Francis F. **War of 1812.** 1st ed. NY: Dutton; 1949. [$25.00]

Belden, Albert Lord. **The Fur Trade of America and Some of the Men Who Made and Maintain It.** NY: Peltries; 1917. [$75.00]

Belden, George P. **Belden, the White Chief.** Cincinnati, NY: Vent; 1872. [$45.00] [$30.00]

Belden, Thomas Graham. **So Fell the Angels.** 1st ed. Boston: Little, Brown; 1956. [$25.00]

Belknap, Jeremy. **History of New-Hampshire.** Philadelphia: Aitken; 1784-92. 3 v. [rebound in 3/4 morocco, $1100.00]

Bell, Archie. **Sunset Canada.** Boston: Page; 1918. [$35.00, Canadian]

Bell, Frederick Jackson. **Room to Swing a Cat.** NY, Toronto: Longmans, Green; 1938. [1944 printing, $35.00]

Bell, Hiram Parks. **Men and Things.** Atlanta: Foote & Davies; 1907. [$60.00]

Bell, Horace. **Reminiscences of a Ranger.** Los Angeles: Yarnell, Caystile & Mathes; 1881. [$185.00] [1927 Hebberd ed., fine in dj, $45.00]

Bell, John Calhoun. **The Pilgrim and the Pioneer.** Lincoln, NE: International; 1906. [$25.00]

Bell, Landon Covington. **The Old Free State.** Richmond: Byrd; 1927. 2 v. [$85.00] [$125.00]

Bell, William Hemphill. **The Quiddities of an Alaskan Trip.** Portland, OR: Steel; 1873. [shaken, $525.00]

Belmont, Perry. **An American Democrat.** NY: Columbia UP; 1940. [x-lib., $15.00]

Belt, Thomas. **The Naturalist in Nicaragua.** 2nd ed. London: Bumpus; 1888. [$75.00]

Beltrami, Giacomo Costantino. **Pilgrimage in Europe and America Leading to the Discovery of the Sources of the Mississippi and Bloody River.** London: Hunt and Clarke; 1828. 2 v. [$625.00] [$400.00]

Bemis, Samuel Flagg. **The Diplomacy of the American Revolution.** NY, London: Appleton-Century; 1935. [$25.00]

Bemis, Samuel Flagg. **Jay's Treaty.** NY: Macmillan; 1924, c1922. [$35.00]

Bemis, Samuel Flagg. **John Quincy Adams and the Foundations of American Foreign Policy.** 1st ed. NY: Knopf; 1949. [$20.00]

Bemis, Samuel Flagg. **John Quincy Adams and the Union.** 1st ed. NY: Knopf; 1956. [$30.00]

Benchley, Robert. **20,000 Leagues under the Sea; or, David Copperfield.** Holt; 1928. [x-lib., $25.00] [Blue Ribbon reprint, $15.00]

Benchley, Robert. **Inside Benchley.** NY, London: Harper; 1942. [$25.00]

Bendbow, Hesper. **The Dismemberment of Maryland.** Baltimore: Murphy; 1890. [rebound, $35.00]

Bendire, Charles. **Life Histories of North American Birds.** Washington: USGPO; 1892. [$145.00]

Benedict, Harry Yandell. **Peregrinusings.** Austin: Ex-Students' Association of the U. of Texas; 1924. [$45.00]

Benet, Stephen Vincent. **John Brown's Body.** 1st trade ed. NY: Doubleday, Doran; 1928. [$30.00] [$17.50]

Benezet, Anthony. **Caution to Great Britain and Her Colonies.** London: Phillips; 1784. [$350.00]

Benjamin, Marcus. **John Bidwell.** Washington: [s.n.]; 1907. [$75.00]

Benjamin, Marcus. **Washington during War Time.** Washington: Adams; 1901. [$22.50]

Benjamin, Samuel Greene Wheeler. **Art in America.** NY: Harper; 1880. [$150.00]

Bennett, Estelline. **Old Deadwood Days.** NY: Sears; 1928. [lacks front endpaper, $25.00] [1935 London ed., $17.50]

Bennett, Frank Marion. **The Steam Navy of the United States.** Pittsburgh: Warren; 1896. [fine, $300.00]

Bennett, Fremont O. **The Chicago Anarchists and the Haymarket Massacre.** Chicago: Blakely; 1887. [rebacked, $150.00]

Bennett, George N. **William Dean Howells.** Norman: U. of Oklahoma; 1959. [$15.00]

Bennett, Ira Elbert. **History of the Panama Canal.** builders' ed. Washington: Historical Publishing Co.; 1915. [presentation, $75.00]

Bennett, John C. **History of the Saints.** Boston; NY: Leland & Whiting; Bradbury, Soden; 1842. [dampstained, spine worn, $59.50]

Bennett, Mildred R. **The World of Willa Cather.** NY: Dodd, Mead; 1951. [$17.50]

Bennett, Wendell Clark. **Ancient Arts of the Andes.** NY: Museum of Modern Art; 1954. [$20.00]

Bennett, Wendell Clark. **The Gallinazo Group, Viru Valley, Peru.** New Haven: Dept. of Anthropology, Yale; 1950. [$25.00]

Bennett, William P. **The First Baby in Camp.** Salt Lake City: Rancher Publishing Co.; 1893. [$90.00] [$50.00] [lacks folding plate, $20.00]

Bennett, William Wallace. **Memorials of Methodism in Virginia.** 2nd ed. Richmond: The Author; 1871. [bumped, silverfished, and sunned, $40.00]

Benschoter, George E. **Book of Facts Concerning the Early Settlement of Sherman County.** Loup City, NE: Northwestern; [1897?]. [$225.00]

Benson, Berry. **Berry Benson's Civil War Book.** Athens: U. of Georgia; 1962. [$37.50]

Benson, Egbert. **Vindication of the Captors of Major Andre.** NY: Priv. Print.; 1865. [quarto ed., x-lib., $150.00] [Sabin reprint, $100.00]

Benson, Henry Clark. **Life among the Choctaw Indians.** Cincinnati: Swormstedt & Poe; 1860. [$400.00]

Bent, George. **Life of.** 1st ed. Norman: U. of Oklahoma; 1968. [$35.00]

Bent, Newell. **American Polo.** NY: Macmillan; 1929. [$20.00]

Bent, Silas. **Justice Oliver Wendell Holmes.** reprint ed. Garden City: Garden City Pub. Co.; 1932. [$20.00]

Benton, Jesse James. **Cow by the Tail.** Boston: Houghton Mifflin; 1943. [$25.00] [dj intact, $40.00]

Benton, Joel. **Life of Hon. Phineas T. Barnum.** Philadelphia: Edgewood; 1891. [$30.00]

Benton, Joseph Augustine. **The California Pilgrim.** Sacramento; San Francisco: Alter; Marvin & Hitchcock; 1853. [$150.00]

Benton, Nathaniel Soley. **A History of Herkimer County.** Albany: Munsell; 1856. [map detached, $95.00]

Benton, Thomas Hart. **Historical and Legal Examination of That Part of the Decision of the Supreme Court of the United States in the Dred Scott Case Which Declares the Unconstitutionality of the Missouri Compromise Act.** NY: Appleton; 1857. [$75.00]

Benton, Thomas Hart. **Speech of . . . Delivered at Fayette, Howard County, Missouri, on Saturday, the First of September, 1849.** Jefferson City, MO: Lusk; 1849. [$250.00]

Benton, Thomas Hart. **Thirty Years' View.** NY; Providence: Appleton; Stickney; 1854. 2 v. [$65.00] [$100.00]

Benwell, Harry A. **History of the Yankee Division.** Boston: Cornhill; 1919. [cover stained, $27.50]

Berger, Thomas. **Little Big Man.** 1st ed. NY: Dial; 1964. [dj frayed, $50.00] [$60.00]

Berkeley, George Charles. **English Sportsman in the Western Prairies.** London: Hurt & Blackett; 1861. [inscribed, spine repaired, $425.00] [$150.00]

Berky, Andrew S. **Practitioner in Physick.** Pennsburg, PA: Schwenkfelder Library; 1954. [$20.00]

Bernard, John. **Retrospections of America, 1797-1811.** NY: Harper; 1887. [$45.00]

Bernard, Kenneth A. **Lincoln and the Music of the Civil War.** Caldwell, ID: Caxton; 1966. [$45.00]

Bernard, William Spencer. **American Immigration Policy, a Reappraisal.** 1st ed. NY: Harper; 1950. [$15.00]

Berney, Saffold. **Hand-Book of Alabama.** 2nd ed. Birmingham: Roberts; 1892. [bumped, silverfished, and worn, $25.00]

Bernhard, Karl Duke of Saxe-Weimar-Eisenach. **Reise Sr. Hoheit des Herzogs Bernhard zu Sachsen-Weimar-Eisenach durch Nord-Amerika in den Jahren 1825 und 1826.** Weimar: Hoffmann; 1828. 2 v. in 1. [$950.00]

Bernhardt, Christian. **Indian Raids in Lincoln County, Kansas, 1864 and 1869.** Lincoln: Sentinel; 1910. [wraps badly chipped, $20.00] [$35.00]

Bernhardt, Joshua. **The Railroad Labor Board.** Baltimore: Hopkins; 1923. [$30.00]

Bernheim, G. D. **History of the German Settlements and of the Lutheran Church in North and South Carolina.** Philadelphia: Lutheran Book Store; 1872. [x-lib., spine detached, $25.00]

Bernheimer, Charles Leopold. **Rainbow Bridge.** Garden City: Doubleday, Page; 1929, c1924. [$15.00]

Berquin-Duvallon. **Schilderung von Louisiana.** Weimar: Landes-Industrie-Comptoirs; 1804. [$475.00]

Berquin-Duvallon. **Vue de la Colonie Espagnole du Mississipi.** Paris: Expeditive; 1803. [$1250.00]

Berra, Yogi. **Yogi.** 1st ed. Garden City: Doubleday; 1961. [$15.00]

Berry, Don. **A Majority of Scoundrels.** 1st ed. NY: Harper; 1961. [dj rubbed, $60.00]

Berry, Don. **Moontrap.** NY: Viking; 1962. [$35.00]

Berthold, Eugenie. **Glimpses of Creole Life in Old St. Louis.** St. Louis: Missouri Historical Society; 1933. [$3.00]

Berthrong, Donald J. **The Southern Cheyennes.** 1st ed. Norman: U. of Oklahoma; 1963. [$30.00] [$40.00]

Berton, Pierre. **The Klondike Fever.** NY: Knopf; 1958. [$16.00] [$8.50]

Bethell, Arnold Talbot. **Early Settlers of the Bahamas and Colonists of North America.** 3rd ed. Holt, Eng.: Rounce & Wortley; 1937. [$40.00]

Bettersworth, John Knox. **Mississippi in the Confederacy.** Baton Rouge: Louisiana State UP; 1961. 2 v. [$85.00]

Bettersworth, John Knox. **People's College.** University: U. of Alabama; 1953. [$20.00]

Betts, Doris. **The Gentle Insurrection.** NY: Putnam; 1954. [dj sunned, signed, $75.00]

Bevan, Philip. **Songs of the War for the Union.** Cincinnati: Clarke; 1887. [$25.00]

Beveridge, Albert Jeremiah. **Abraham Lincoln, 1809-1858.** Boston: Houghton Mifflin; 1928. 2 v. [$40.00]

Beveridge, Albert Jeremiah. **Life of John Marshall.** Boston: Houghton Mifflin; 1916-1919. 4 v. [$50.00]

Beverley, Robert. **History of Virginia, in Four Parts.** 2nd ed. London: Tooke; 1722. [$1000.00]

Beyer, Walter Frederick. **Deeds of Valor.** Detroit: Perrien-Keydel; 1905. 2 v. [$75.00] [1907 issue, $47.50]

Biart, Lucien. **The Aztecs.** Chicago: McClurg; 1900, c1886. [$22.50]

Bickerstaff, Laura M. **Pioneer Artists of Taos.** Denver: Sage; 1955. [x-lib., $125.00] [soiled dj, $150.00]

Bickersteth, John Burgon. **Land of Open Doors.** London: Gardner, Darton; 1914. [$30.00, Canadian]

Biddle, Cordelia Drexel. **My Philadelphia Father.** 1st ed. Garden City: Doubleday; 1955. [$7.50]

Bidwell, John. **A Journey to California, 1841.** Berkley: Friends of the Bancroft Library; 1964. [$30.00]

Bidwell, John. **Life in California before the Gold Discovery.** Palo Alto: Osborne; 1966. [$35.00] [$20.00]

Bierce, Ambrose. **Black Beetles in Amber.** San Francisco: Western Authors; 1892. [2nd issue sold by Johnson & Emigh, wraps chipped, $225.00]

Bierce, Ambrose. **Dance of Death.** 2nd ed. San Francisco: Keller; 1877. [$85.00]

Bierce, Ambrose. **In the Midst of Life.** new ed. London: Chatto & Windus; 1898. [$40.00]

Bierce, Ambrose. **Write It Right.** 1st ed. NY, Washington: Neale; 1909. [$250.00]

Biesele, Rudolph Leopold. **History of the German Settlements in Texas.** Austin: Von Boeckmann-Jones; 1930. [$275.00] [$285.00]

Bigelow, Jacob. **Florula Bostoniensis.** 2nd ed. Boston: Cummings, Hilliard; 1824. [rebacked, $200.00]

Bigelow, John. **Memoir of the Life and Public Services of John Charles Fremont.** NY; Cincinnati: Derby & Jackson; Derby; 1856. [$40.00] [$60.00]

Bigelow, John. **Reminiscences of the Santiago Campaign.** NY, London: Harper; 1899. [$35.00]

Bigelow, John. **Retrospections of an Active Life.** NY: Baker & Taylor; 1909-1913. 5 v. [$125.00]

Bigg-Wither, Thomas Plantagenet. **Pioneering in South Brazil.** London: Murray; 1878. 2 v. [$500.00]

Biggers, Don Hampton. **German Pioneers in Texas.** 1st ed. Fredericksburg, TX: Fredericksburg Pub. Co.: 1925. [$135.00]

Biggs, James. **The History of Don Francisco de Miranda's Attempt to Effect a Revolution in South America.** Boston: Oliver and Munroe; 1808. [disbound, $85.00] [1809 ed., $75.00] [1811 ed., much of binding missing, $175.00]

Bigney, Mark Frederick. **The Forest Pilgrims, and Other Poems.** New Orleans: Gresham; 1867. [$45.00]

Bigney, T. O. **A Month with the Muses.** Pueblo, CO: Bigney; 1875. [$110.00]

Bi'kis, Dineh. **The Upward Trail.** Grand Rapids, MI: Eerdmans; 1935. [$15.00]

Biles, J. Hugh. **Early History of Ada.** 2nd ed. Ada, OK: Oklahoma State Bank; 1954. [$15.00]

Bill, Alfred Hoyt. **The Beleaguered City, Richmond, 1861-1865.** NY: Knopf; 1946. [$14.00] [$15.00]

Bill, Alfred Hoyt. **Rehearsal for Conflict.** 1st ed. NY: Knopf; 1947. [$27.50]

Bill, Ledyard. **Minnesota; Its Character and Climate.** NY: Wood & Holbrook; 1871. [$75.00]

Billberg, Eddy E. **War Cry of the Sioux.** Boston: Christopher; 1930. [$25.00]

Billias, George Athan. **General John Glover and His Marblehead Mariners.** 1st ed. NY: Holt; 1960. [dj soiled, chipped and torn, $15.00]

Billings, John David. **Hardtack and Coffee.** Minneapolis: Richards; 1888, c1887. [$200.00] [1888 Boston ed., $115.00] [1960 Lakeside reprint, $25.00]

Billingsley, Andrew. **Black Families in White America.** Englewood Cliffs: Prentice-Hall; 1968. [$18.50]

Billington, Ray Allen. **The Far Western Frontier, 1830-1860.** 1st ed. NY: Harper; 1956. [$25.00]

Bimba, Anthony. **The Molly Maguires.** NY: International; 1932. [worn, silverfished, dj badly chipped, $15.00]

Bingham, Caleb. **The Columbian Orator.** Boston: Bingham; 1817, c1810. [worn, $50.00]

Bingham, Hiram. **Bartimeus, of the Sandwich Islands.** NY: American Tract Soc.; 1851. [$25.00]

Bingham, Hiram. **Machu Picchu, a Citadel of the Incas.** New Haven; London: Yale UP; Oxford UP; 1930. [slipcase rubbed, $850.00]

Bingham, Hiram. **Residence of Twenty-One Years in the Sandwich Islands.** Hartford; NY: Huntington; Converse; 1847. [$150.00] [2nd ed., 1848, $125.00]

Bingham, John Armor. **Trial of the Conspirators, for the Assassination of President Lincoln.** Washington: USGPO; 1865. [$75.00]

Bingham, John H. **Short History of Brule County.** [s.l.: s.n.]; 1947. [$25.00]

Binkley, William Campbell. **The Expansionist Movement in Texas, 1836-1850.** Berkeley: U. of California; 1925. [$325.00]

Bird, Annie Laurie. **Boise.** Caldwell, ID: Caxton; 1934. [$135.00] [dj badly nicked, $100.00]

Bird, Arthur. **Looking Forward.** Utica, NY: Childs; 1899. [$75.00]

Bird, Harrison. **Navies in the Mountains.** NY: Oxford UP; 1962. [$40.00]

Bird, Isabella. see, Bishop, Isabella Lucy (Bird).

Bird, Yellow. see, Ridge, John Rollin.

Birge, Julius Charles. **The Awakening of the Desert.** Boston: Badger; 1912. [$45.00]

Birkbeck, Morris. **Letters from Illinois.** 1st ed. London: Taylor and Hessey; 1818. [$95.00] [Philadelphia, 1818, 154p. issue, $200.00; 112p. issue, $100.00]

Birkbeck, Morris. **Notes on a Journey in America.** Philadelphia: Richardson; 1817. [rebacked, $150.00] [1818 London ed., $225.00]

Birmingham, George A. **From Dublin to Chicago.** NY: Doran; 1914. [$25.00]

Birney, Hoffman. **Roads to Roam.** Philadelphia: Penn; 1930. [x-lib., $15.00]

Birney, Hoffman. **Vigilantes.** 1st ed. Philadelphia: Penn; 1929. [$40.00]

Bishop, Abraham. **Oration, in Honor of the Election of President Jefferson and the Peaceable Acquisition of Louisiana.** New Haven: Sidney's; 1804. [$65.00]

Bishop, Albert Webb. **Loyalty on the Frontier.** St. Louis: Studley; 1863. [spine chipped, some wear, $175.00]

Bishop, Harriet E. **Dakota War Whoop.** 1st ed. St. Paul: Merrill; 1863. [rear endpaper lacking, $175.00]

Bishop, Isabella Lucy (Bird). **The Hawaiian Archipelago.** 4th ed. NY: Putnam; 1881. [$50.00]

Bishop, Isabella Lucy (Bird). **A Lady's Life in the Rocky Mountains.** NY: Putnam; 1880, c1879. [$100.00]

Bishop, Isabella Lucy (Bird). **Six Months in the Sandwich Islands.** Honolulu: U. of Hawaii; 1964. [$22.00]

Bishop, Morris. **Champlaign.** NY: Knopf; 1948. [fine in dj, $25.00]

Bishop, Morris. **History of Cornell.** Ithaca, NY: Cornell UP; 1962. [$25.00]

Bishop, Morris. **Odyssey of Cabeza de Vaca.** 1st ed. NY, London: Century; 1933. [$40.00] [$45.00]

Bishop, Nathaniel Holmes. **Four Months in a Sneak-Box.** Boston; NY: Lee & Shepard; Dillingham; 1879. [$150.00] [later printing?, $65.00]

Bishop, Nathaniel Holmes. **The Pampas and Andes.** Boston: Lee & Shepard; 1869. [covers loose, $25.00]

Bishop, Nathaniel Holmes. **Voyage of the Paper Canoe.** Boston: Lee and Shepard; 1882. [$95.00]

Bishop, William Henry. **Mexico, California & Arizona.** NY: Harper; 1888, c1883. [$100.00]

Bixler, Julius Seelye. **Colby College (1813-1953).** NY: Newcomen Society; 1953. [$15.00]

Black, A. P. **End of the Long Horn Trail.** Selfridge, ND: Journal; [ca. 1936]. [$40.00]

Black, Eleanora. **Gold Rush Song Book.** San Francisco: Colt; 1940. [$35.00]

Black, Leonard. **Life and Sufferings of.** New Bedford: Lindsey; 1847. [$125.00]

Black, Norman Fergus. **History of Saskatchewan and the Old North West.** 2nd ed. Regina: North West Historical Co.; 1913. [corners bumped and worn, $295.00, Canadian]

Black, Robert Lounsbury. **Little Miami Railroad.** Cincinnati: [s.n.]; 1940. [$85.00]

Black Hawk. **Life of Ma-Ka-Tai-Me-She-Kia-Kiak or Black Hawk.** Boston; NY: Russell, Odiorne & Metcalf; Bancroft; 1834. [$125.00]

Blacker, Irwin R. **Old West in Fiction.** NY: Obolensky; 1961. [$17.50]

Blackford, Launcelot Minor. **Mine Eyes Have Seen the Glory.** Cambridge: Harvard UP; 1954. [$25.00]

Blackford, Susan Leigh. **Letters from Lee's Army.** NY: Scribner; 1947. [x-lib., $22.50] [$20.00]

Blackford, William Willis. **War Years with Jeb Stuart.** NY: Scribner; 1945. [$25.00]

Blackhills Views. Deadwood, SD: Peterson & Carwiler; 1903. [$125.00]

Blackmar, Frank Wilson. **Spanish Institutions of the Southwest.** Baltimore: Hopkins; 1891. [$225.00]

Blackmore, William. **Colorado: Its Resources, Parks, and Prospects.** London: Low and Marston; 1869. [$275.00]

Blackwelder, Bernice. **Great Westerner; the Story of Kit Carson.** Caldwell, ID: Caxton; 1962. [$22.00]

Blackwell, Robert. **Original Acrostics.** NY: The Author; 1871. [$22.50]

Blair, Emma Helen. **The Indian Tribes of the Upper Mississippi Valley and Region of the Great Lakes as Described by Nicolas Perrot.** Cleveland: Clark; 1911. 2 v. [$300.00] [$200.00] [$300.00]

Blair, Walter. **Half Horse, Half Alligator.** Chicago: U. of Chicago; 1956. [$20.00] [x-lib., $15.00]

Blair, Walter. **Mike Fink.** NY: Holt; 1933. [$30.00]

Blake, Clagette. **Charles Elliot.** London: Cleaver-Hume; 1960. [$12.50]

Blake, Forrester. **Johnny Christmas.** NY: Morrow; 1948. [$20.00]

Blake, John Lauris. **Farmer's Every-Day Book; or, Sketches of Social Life in the Country.** NY: Miller, Orton & Mulligan; 1856, c1850. [worn, $37.50]

Blake, William J. **History of Putnam County, N.Y.** NY: Baker & Scribner; 1849. [$125.00]

Blake, William O. **History of Slavery and the Slave Trade.** Columbus: Miller; 1858. [$65.00] [$40.00] [1860 printing, rebound, $50.00]

Blanchard, Jonathan. **A Debate on Slavery: Held on the First, Second, Third and Sixth Days of October, 1845.** 4th ed. Cincinnati; NY: Moore; Newman; 1846. [$25.00]

Blanchard, Rufus. **Discovery and Conquests of the Northwest.** Chicago: Cushing, Thomas; 1880. [$85.00]

Blanchard, Rufus. **History of Illinois, to Accompany an Historical Map of the State.** Chicago: National School Furnishing Co.; 1883. [with the map, $100.00]

Blanchard, William Oscar. **Geography of Southwestern Wisconsin.** Madison: Pub. by the State; 1924. [$15.00]

Blanchet, Francis Norbert. **Notices & Voyages of the Famed Quebec Mission to the Pacific Northwest.** Portland: Oregon Historical Society; 1956. [$50.00]

Bland, Richard. **Fragment on the Pistole Fee.** Brooklyn: Hist. Print. Club; 1891. [$35.00]

Blankenship, Russell. **And There Were Men.** 1st ed. NY: Knopf; 1942. [$15.00]

Blasingame, Ike. **Dakota Cowboy.** NY: Putnam; 1958. [$45.00]

Blatchley, Willis Stanley. **Indiana Weed Book.** 2nd ed. Indianapolis: Nature; 1920. [$12.50]

Bledsoe, Albert Taylor. **An Essay on Liberty and Slavery.** Philadelphia: Lippincott; 1856. [$25.00]

Bledsoe, Albert Taylor. **Is Davis a Traitor. . . ?** Baltimore: Innes; 1866. [$40.00]

Blegen, Theodore Christian. **Grass Roots History.** Minneapolis: U. of Minnesota; 1947. [$10.00]

Blennerhassett, Harman. **The Blennerhassett Papers.** Cincinnati: Moore, Wilstach, Keys; 1861. [$60.00]

Blessington, Joseph P. **Campaigns of Walker's Texas Division.** NY: Lange, Little; 1875. [$350.00]

Blews, Richard R. **Master Workmen.** Winona Lake, IN: Light and Life; 1960. [$17.50]

Blinn, Henry Clay. **Life and Gospel Experience of Mother Ann Lee.** East Canterbury, NH: Shakers; 1901. [$140.00]

Bliss, Richard W. **Our Lost Explorers: The Narrative of the Jeannette Arctic Expedition.** Hartford, CT; San Francisco: American Pub. Co.; Bancroft; 1882. [$50.00]

Bliss, Robert Woods. **Pre-Columbian Art.** 2nd ed. London: Phaidon; 1959. [$275.00]

Bliss, William Root. **September Days on Nantucket.** Boston; NY: Houghton Mifflin; 1902. [$20.00]

Block, Eugene B. **Great Train Robberies of the West.** NY: Coward-McCann; 1959. [$25.00]

Blodget, Lorin. **Climatology of the United States, and of the Temperate Latitudes of the North American Continent.** Philadelphia: Lippincott; 1857. [x-lib., spine mended, $175.00]

Blodget, William. see, Carnac, Turner.

Blumenschein, Helen G. **Sangre de Cristo.** Taos, NM: El Crepusculo; 1939. [$15.00]

Blumenthal, Walter Hart. **American Panorama.** Worcester, MA: St. Onge; 1962. [$35.00]

Boardman, Fon Wyman. **Columbia, an American University in Peace and War.** NY: Columbia UP; 1944. [$15.00]

Boardman, William H. **Lovers of the Woods.** NY: McClure, Phillips; 1901. [$30.00]

Boas, Franz. **Handbook of American Indian Languages.** Washington: USGPO; 1911-1922. 2 v. [$100.00]

Boatright, Mody Coggin. **And Horns on the Toads.** Dallas: Southern Methodist UP; 1959. [$35.00]

Boatright, Mody Coggin. **Backwoods to Border.** Austin: Texas Folklore Society; 1943. [$45.00]

Boatright, Mody Coggin. **From Hell to Breakfast.** Austin: Texas Folklore Society; 1944. [$55.00]

Boatright, Mody Coggin. **Gib Morgan, Minstrel of the Oil Fields.** Austin: Texas Folklore Society; 1945. [$75.00]

Boatright, Mody Coggin. **The Golden Log.** Dallas: Southern Methodist UP; 1962. [$30.00]

Boatright, Mody Coggin. **A Good Tale and a Bonnie Tune.** Dallas: Southern Methodist UP; 1964. [$40.00]

Boatright, Mody Coggin. **The Sky Is My Tipi.** 1st ed. Austin: Texas Folklore Society; 1949. [$65.00]

Boddam-Whetham, John Whetham. **Western Wanderings.** London: Bentley; 1874. [$175.00]

Boddy, E. Manchester. **Japanese in America.** Los Angeles: Boddy; 1921. [$40.00]

Bodenstedt, Friedrich Martin von. **Vom Atlantischen zum Stillen Ocean.** Leipzig: Brockhaus; 1882. [$250.00]

Bodge, George M. **Soldiers in King Philip's War.** Boston, MA: The Author; 1906. [$40.00] [$100.00]

Bodine, A. Aubrey. **My Maryland.** Baltimore: Bodine; 1952. [$15.00]

Boehm, John Philip. **Life and Letters of.** Philadelphia: Reformed Church; 1916. [$37.50] [$55.00]

Boewe, Charles E. **Prairie Albion.** 1st ed. Carbondale: Southern Illinois UP; 1962. [$40.00]

Bogen, Frederick W. **The German in America.** 2nd ed. Boston: Greene; 1851. [$36.00]

Boggs, Mae Helene Bacon. **My Playhouse Was a Concord Coach.** Oakland: Howell-North; 1942. [$325.00]

Bokum, Hermann. **Testimony of a Refugee from East Tennessee.** Philadelphia: [s.n.]; 1863. [$25.00]

Bolin, Major C. **Narrative of the Life and Adventures of.** Palo Alto: Osborne; 1966. [$55.00] [$40.00]

Bollaert, William. **William Bollaert's Texas.** 1st ed. Norman: U. of Oklahoma; 1956. [$35.00] [$45.00]

Boller, Henry A. **Among the Indians.** Philadelphia: Zell; 1868. [$1250.00] [1959 Lakeside ed., $35.00]

Bolles, Albert Sidney. **Industrial History of the United States.** Norwich, CT: Bill; 1879. [$50.00]

Bolles, Albert Sidney. **Pennsylvania, Province and State.** Philadelphia: Wanamaker; 1899. 2 v. [$50.00]

Bollinger, Edward Taylor. **The Moffat Road.** Denver: Sage; 1962. [$30.00]

Bolton, Charles Knowles. **The Founders.** Boston: Athenaeum; 1919-26. 3 v. [$175.00]

Bolton, Charles Knowles. **The Private Soldier under Washington.** NY: Scribner; 1902. [$27.50]

Bolton, Charles Knowles. **The Real Founders of New England.** Boston: Faxon; 1929. [$50.00]

Bolton, Charles Knowles. **Scotch Irish Pioneers in Ulster and America.** Boston: Bacon and Brown; 1910. [x-lib., $45.00]

Bolton, Herbert Eugene. **Anza's California Expeditions.** Berkeley: U. of California; 1930. 5 v. [$300.00]

Bolton, Herbert Eugene. **Athanase de Mezieres and the Louisiana-Texas Frontier.** Cleveland: Clark; 1914. 2 v. [$475.00] [$385.00]

Bolton, Herbert Eugene. **Coronado.** NY: Whittlesey; 1949. [chipped dj, $55.00]

Bolton, Herbert Eugene. **Drake's Plate of Brass.** see, California Historical Society.

Bolton, Herbert Eugene. **Pageant in the Wilderness.** see, Velez de Escalante, Silvestre.

Bolton, Herbert Eugene. **Spanish Exploration in the Southwest, 1542-1706.** NY: Scribner; 1916. [$150.00]

Bolton, Herbert Eugene. **Texas in the Middle Eighteenth Century.** Berkeley: U. of California; 1915. [$250.00]

Bolton, Horace Wilbert. **History of the Second Regiment Illinois Volunteer Infantry.** Chicago: Donnelley; 1899. [lacks front endpaper, $40.00]

Bolton, John. **An Account of the Loss of the American Clipper Ship Tontine.** Pittsburgh: Callow; 1861. [$40.00]

Bolton, Reginald Pelham. **A Woman Misunderstood.** NY: Schoen; 1931. [$30.00]

Bolton, Sarah Knowles. **The Present Problem.** NY: Putnam; 1874. [$35.00]

Bomberger, Christian Martin Hess. **The Battle of Bushy Run.** Jeannette, PA: Jeannette Pub. Co.; 1928. [$30.00]

Bon Homme Richard (Ship). **Log of the Bon Homme Richard.** Mystic, CT: Marine Hist. Assn.; 1936. [$75.00]

Bond, John Wesley. **Minnesota and Its Resources.** NY: Redfield; 1854. [$200.00] [1856 Keen & Lee ed., $115.00]

Bonner, Willard Hallam. **Pirate Laureate.** New Brunswick: Rutgers UP; 1947. [$10.00]

Bonney, Catharina Visscher. **A Legacy of Historical Gleanings.** Albany, NY: Munsell; 1875. 2 v. [$37.50]

Bonney, Edward. **The Banditti of the Prairies.** Norman: U. of Oklahoma; 1963. [$22.00]

Bonney, Orrin H. **Battle Drums and Geysers.** 1st ed. Chicago: Sage; 1970. [$40.00]

Bonnycastle, Richard Henry. **The Canadas in 1841.** London: Colburn; 1842. 2 v. [binding ugly and dirty, $125.00, Canadian]

Bonsal, Stephen. **When the French Were Here.** 1st ed. Garden City: Doubleday, Doran; 1945. [$15.00]

Bontekoe, Willem Ysbrandsz. **Memorable Description of the East Indian Voyage, 1618-25.** London: Routledge; 1929. [$38.50, Canadian]

Booth, Andrew B. **Records of Louisiana Confederate Soldiers.** see, Louisiana Commissioner of Military Records.

Booth, Charles G. **Los Angeles Murders.** see, Rice, Craig.

Booth, Edmund. **Edmund Booth (1810-1905), Forty-Niner.** Stockton, CA: San Joaquin Pioneer and Hist. Soc.; 1953. [$20.00]

Borcke, Heros von. **Memoirs of the Confederate War for Independence.** reprint ed. NY: Smith; 1938. 2 v. [$85.00] [$75.00]

Borden, Courtney Louise. **The Cruise of the Northern Light.** NY: Macmillan; 1928. [$24.00]

Borden, Lizzie. **Trial of Lizzie Borden.** 1st ed. Garden City: Doubleday, Doran; 1937. [$32.50]

The Border Ruffian Code in Kansas. NY: Tribune Office; 1856. [$60.00]

Borein, Edward. **Ed Borein's West.** Santa Barbara: Edward Borein Memorial; 1952. [fine in chipped dj, $100.00]

Borgmann, Carl Williams. **"UVM": the University of the State of Vermont, 1791.** NY: Newcomen Society; 1956. [$15.00]

Borland, Hal. **High, Wide and Lonesome.** Philadelphia: Lippincott; 1956. [$14.00]

Borup, George. **A Tenderfoot with Peary.** NY: Stokes; 1911. [$20.00]

Bossu Jean Bernard. **Travels in the Interior of North America, 1751-1762.** Norman: U. of Oklahoma; 1962. [$30.00]

Bossu, Jean Bernard. **Travels through That Part of North America Formerly Called Louisiana.** London: Davies; 1771. 2 v. [$1250.00]

Bostick, Daisy F. **Carmel.** Carmel, CA: Seven Arts; 1945. [$15.00]

Boston. **A Memorial of Charles Sumner.** Boston: City Council; 1874. [$45.00]

Boston. **A Memorial of the American Patriots Who Fell at the Battle of Bunker Hill, June 17, 1775.** Boston: City Council; 1889. [$65.00]

Boston. **A Short Narrative of the Horrid Massacre in Boston Perpetrated in the Evening of the Fifth Day of March, 1770.** NY: Doggett; 1849. [$100.00]

Boston. Convention of Delegates on Proposed Annexation of Texas, 1845. **Proceedings of a Convention.** Boston: Eastburn's; 1845. [$225.00]

Boston Slave Riot, and Trial of Anthony Burns. Boston: Fetridge; 1854. [$275.00]

Bosworth, Allan R. **New Country.** 1st ed. NY: Harper; 1962. [$25.00]

Botkin, B. A. **Lay My Burden Down.** see, Federal Writers' Project.

Botkin, Benjamin Albert. **Folk-Say.** Norman: U. of Oklahoma; 1930-1932. 2 v. [vol. 1 only, $40.00]

Botkin, Benjamin Albert. **Sidewalks of America.** 1st ed. Indianapolis: Bobbs-Merrill; 1954. [$15.00]

Botkin, Benjamin Albert. **Treasury of Railroad Folklore.** NY: Crown; 1953. [$30.00]

Botta, Carlo Giuseppe Guglielmo. **History of the War of Independence of the United States of America.** Philadelphia: Bailey; 1820-21. 3 v. [$375.00] [1848 2 vol. Phinney ed., some worming, $45.00]

Botts, John Minor. **The Great Rebellion.** NY: Harper; 1866. [$25.00]

Botts, John Minor. **Interesting and Important Correspondence between Opposition Members of the Legislature of Virginia and . . .** Washington: Towers; 1860. [$10.00]

Boucher, Jack E. **Absegami Yesteryear.** Egg Harbor City, NJ: Laureate; 1963. [$25.00]

Boucher, Jonathan. **Reminiscences of an American Loyalist, 1738-1789.** Boston, NY: Houghton Mifflin; 1925. [$65.00]

Bouchette, Joseph. **A Topographical Description of the Province of Lower Canada.** London: Faden; 1815. [$750.00]

Boudier de Villemert, Pierre Joseph. **The Friend of Women.** Philadelphia: Conrad; 1803. [$160.00]

Boudinot, Elias. **The Age of Revelation.** Philadelphia: Dickins; 1801. [$250.00]

Boudinot, Elias. **Journal or Historical Recollections of American Events during the Revolutionary War.** Philadelphia: Bourquin; 1894. [large paper ed., unbound, last page in facs., $175.00]

Boudinot, Elias. **Life, Public Services, Addresses, and Letters of.** Boston: Houghton Mifflin; 1896. 2 v. [$150.00]

Boudinot, Elias. **A Star in the West.** Trenton, NJ: Fenton, Hutchinson and Dunham; 1816. [binding worn and scuffed, $325.00]

Bougainville, Louis-Antoine de comte. **Adventure in the Wilderness.** 1st ed. Norman: U. of Oklahoma; 1964. [$35.00]

Boughton, Joseph S. **The Kansas Hand Book for 1878.** Lawrence: Daily Journal; 1878. [x-lib., lacks rear wrap, $125.00]

Bourke, John Gregory. **Apache Campaign in the Sierra Madre.** NY: Scribner; 1958. [$30.00]

Bourke, John Gregory. **On the Border with Crook.** NY: Scribner; 1891. [$225.00]

Bourne, Benjamin Franklin. **The Captive in Patagonia.** Boston: Lothrop; 1853. [$85.00]

Bourne, William Oland. **The House That Jeff Built.** NY: American News; 1868. [$125.00]

Bouton, Nathaniel. **The History of Concord.** Concord, NH: Sanborn; 1856. [$60.00]

Boutwell, George Sewall. **The Lawyer, the Statesman and the Soldier.** NY: Appleton; 1887. [$30.00]

Bowden, James. **History of the Society of Friends in America.** London: Gilpin; 1850. 2 v. [x-lib., rebound in 4 vols., $125.00]

Bowen, Benjamin Franklin. **America Discovered by the Welsh in 1170 A.** D. Philadelphia: Lippincott; 1876. [spine frayed, silverfished, very sunned, $35.00]

Bowen, Catherine Drinker. **John Adams and the American Revolution.** 1st ed. Boston: Little, Brown; 1950. [$20.00]

Bowen, Dana Thomas. **Lore of the Lakes Told in Story and Picture.** Daytona Beach, FL: Bowen; 1940. [$15.00]

Bowen, Dana Thomas. **Shipwrecks of the Lakes Told in Story and Picture.** Daytona Beach, FL: Bowen; 1952. [$17.50]

Bowen, Frank Charles. **America Sails the Seas.** NY: McBride; 1938. [$75.00]

Bowen, Henry L. **Memoir of Tristam Burges.** Providence; Philadelphia: Marshall, Brown; Marshall; 1835. [$40.00]

Bowen, James Lorenzo. **Scouting Dave.** NY: American News; [1865?]. [$85.00]

Bowen, John Joseph. **Strategy of Robert E. Lee.** NY: Crowell; 1914. [$25.00]

Bowen, Louise Hadduck. **Growing Up with a City.** NY: Macmillan; 1926. [$20.00]

Bowers, Claude Gernade. **Tragic Era.** Cambridge: Houghton Mifflin; 1929. [binding worn, $12.50]

Bowie, Effie Gwynn. **Across the Years in Prince George's County.** Richmond: Garrett and Massie; 1947. [$60.00]

Bowles, Samuel. **Across the Continent.** Springfield, MA; NY: Bowles; Hurd & Houghton; 1866. [$90.00] [$85.00]

Bowles, Samuel. **Our New West.** Hartford, CT; NY: Hartford Pub. Co.; Dennison; 1869. [$35.00]

Bowles, Samuel. **The Switzerland of America.** Springfield; NY: Bowles; American News; 1869. [$35.00] [$30.00]

Bowman, Heath. **Mexican Odyssey.** Chicago: Willett, Clark; 1936, c1935. [$10.00]

Bowman, Samuel Millard. **Sherman and His Campaigns.** NY; Cincinnati: Richardson; Vent; 1865. [bumped, frayed, sunned, spotted, $20.00] [$42.50]

Bownas, Samuel. **Account of the Life, Travels, and Christian Experiences in the Work of the Ministry of.** London: Phillips; 1795. [rebound, $50.00] [1805 Hull imprint, $50.00]

Boyd, David. **A History, Greeley and the Union Colony of Colorado.** Greeley, CO: Tribune; 1890. [covers stained, $65.00]

Boyd, E. **Saints & Saint Makers of New Mexico.** Santa Fe: Laboratory of Anthropology; 1946. [$150.00]

Boyd, James Penny. **Recent Indian Wars under the Lead of Sitting Bull, and Other Chiefs.** Philadelphia: Publishers Union; 1891. [$40.00]

Boyd, James Penny. **Vital Questions of the Day.** NY: Publishers' Union; 1894. [$35.00]

Boyd, Stephen Gill. **Indian Local Names with Their Interpretation.** York, PA: The Author; 1885. [$75.00]

Boyd, Thomas. **Mad Anthony Wayne.** NY, London: Scribner; 1929. [$28.50]

Boyd, Thomas. **Simon Girty.** 1st ed. NY: Minton, Balch; 1928. [$15.00]

Boyd, William Kenneth. **Some Eighteenth Century Tracts Concerning North Carolina.** Raleigh: Edwards & Broughton; 1927. [$65.00]

Boyden, Anna L. **Echoes from Hospital and White House.** Boston: Lothrop; 1884. [$40.00]

Boyer, Charles Shimer. **Early Forges & Furnaces in New Jersey.** 1st ed. Philadelphia; London: U. of Pennsylvania; Oxford UP; 1931. [$90.00]

Boyer, Mary G. **Arizona in Literature.** Glendale, CA: Clark; 1935. [$35.00]

Boykin, Edward. **Congress and the Civil War.** NY: McBride; 1955. [$15.00]

Boykin, Edward. **Ghost Ship of the Confederacy.** NY: Funk & Wagnalls; 1957. [$20.00] [signed, $37.50] [inscribed, $30.00]

Boykin, Edward. **Sea Devil of the Confederacy.** NY: Funk & Wagnalls; 1959. [$20.00]

Boynton, Charles Brandon. **History of the Navy during the Rebellion.** NY: Appleton; 1867-68. 2 v. [$125.00]

Boynton, Charles Brandon. **Journey through Kansas.** Cincinnati: Moore, Wilstach, Keys; 1855. [$225.00]

Boynton, Henry Van Ness. **Sherman's Historical Raid.** Cincinnati: Wilstach, Baldwin; 1875. [$50.00]

Boynton, Percy Holmes. **The Rediscovery of the Frontier.** Chicago: U. of Chicago; 1931. [$25.00]

Brace, Charles Loring. **The Dangerous Classes of New York.** 3rd ed. NY: Wynkoop & Hallenbeck; 1880. [x-lib., $50.00]

Brace, Charles Loring. **The New West.** NY: Putnam; 1869. [spine frayed, one hinge cracked, $50.00]

Bracht, Viktor. **Texas in 1848.** San Antonio: Naylor; 1931. [$125.00]

Brackenridge, Henry Marie. **History of the Western Insurrection in Western Pennsylvania.** Pittsburgh: Haven; 1859. [$125.00] [$75.00]

Brackenridge, Henry Marie. **Recollections of Persons and Places in the West.** 2nd ed. Philadelphia: Lippincott; 1868. [$35.00]

Brackenridge, Henry Marie. **Views of Louisiana; Together with a Journal of a Voyage up the Missouri River, in 1811.** Pittsburgh: Cramer, Spear, and Eichbaum; 1814. [$850.00] [$1000.00] [$850.00]

Brackenridge, Hugh Henry. **Indian Atrocities.** Cincinnati: James; 1867. [rebound, $100.00]

Bradbury, John. **Travels in the Interior of America, in the Years 1809, 1810, and 1811.** Liverpool: Smith and Galway; 1817. [$1500.00]

Braddy, Haldeen. **Cock of the Walk.** Albuquerque: U. of New Mexico; 1955. [$45.00]

Bradford, Alden. **History of Massachusetts, for Two Hundred Years.** Boston: Hilliard, Gray; 1835. [x-lib., $17.50] [$45.00]

Bradford, Alexander W. **American Antiquities, and Researches into the Origin and History of the Red Race.** NY; Boston: Dayton and Saxton; Saxton and Pierce; 1841. [foxed, covers rubbed, spine taped, $40.00]

Bradford, Gamaliel. **Lee the American.** Boston, NY: Houghton Mifflin; 1912. [spine faded, $22.50] [$15.00]

Bradford, Gamaliel. **Portraits of American Women.** Boston, NY: Houghton Mifflin; 1919. [$20.00] [$28.50]

Bradford, John. **John Bradford's Historical &c. Notes on Kentucky.** San Francisco: Grabhorn; 1932. [bumped, sunned, spine torn, $85.00]

Bradford, Ned. **Battles and Leaders of the Civil War.** NY: Hawthorn; 1956. [$15.00]

Bradford, Sarah H. **Scenes in the Life of Harriet Tubman.** 1st ed. Auburn, NY: Moses; 1869. [$55.00]

Bradford, William. **History of Plymouth Plantation 1620-1647.** Boston: Houghton Mifflin; 1912. 2 v. [$150.00] [rebound, $65.00]

Bradley, Alice Marie. **The World Looks at Texas.** Dallas: Tardy; 1936. [$40.00]

Bradley, Glenn Danford. **The Story of the Pony Express.** Chicago: McClurg; 1913. [$25.00]

Brady, Cyrus Townsend. **Britton of the Seventh.** Chicago: McClurg; 1914. [spine loose, $18.00]

Brady, Cyrus Townsend. **Northwestern Fights and Fighters.** patriot's ed. Garden City: Doubleday, Page; 1916, c1907. [$18.00]

Bragg, Jefferson Davis. **Louisiana in the Confederacy.** Baton Rouge: Louisiana State UP; 1941. [$40.00]

Brainerd, Chauncey Niles. **My Diary.** NY: Egbert, Bourne; 1868. [$20.00]

Brainerd, David. **Account of the Life of.** 1st ed. Boston: Henchman; 1749. [$325.00] [1765 Edinburgh ed., $175.00]

Brainerd, David. **Life and Diary of.** Chicago: Moody; 1949. [$17.50]

Brainerd, David. **Memoirs of.** New Haven: Converse; 1822. [$65.00]

Braman, D. E. E. **Braman's Information about Texas.** Philadelphia: Lippincott; 1858. [$450.00]

Branagan, Thomas. **Excellency of the Female Character Vindicated.** Philadelphia: Wyeth; 1828. [3rd printing?, $100.00]

Branagan, Thomas. **The Guardian Genius of the Federal Union.** NY: The Author; 1839. [$125.00]

Branch, Edward Douglas. **The Cowboy and His Interpreters.** NY: Appleton; 1926. [$70.00]

Branch, Edward Douglas. **Hunting of the Buffalo.** NY, London: Appleton; 1929. [$80.00]

Branch, Edward Douglas. **Westward.** NY: Appleton; 1930. [$75.00]

Branch, Mary Jones Polk. **Memoirs of a Southern Woman "Within the Lines."** Chicago: Branch; 1912. [silverfished, $35.00]

Brand, Max. **Alcatraz.** 1st ed. NY: Putnam; 1923. [$25.00]

Brand, Max. **The Gun Tamer.** 1st ed. NY: Dodd, Mead; 1929. [$20.00]

Brand, Max. **Max Brand's Best Stories.** NY: Dodd, Mead; 1967. [$20.00]

Brand, Max. **Notebooks and Poems of.** limited ed. NY: Dodd, Mead; 1957. [$50.00]

Brand, Max. **Trailin'!** 1st ed. NY, London: Putnam; 1920. [$20.00]

Brand, Max. **The White Wolf.** NY: Putnam; 1926. [$25.00]

Brandeis, Louis Dembitz. **Unpublished Opinions of.** Cambridge: Harvard UP; 1957. [$35.00]

Brandon, William. **Men and the Mountain.** NY: Morrow; 1955. [$20.00]

Brandt, Francis Burke. **The Majestic Delaware.** Philadelphia: Brandt and Gummere; 1929. [$20.00]

Brandt, Harry Alonzo. **Christopher Sower and Son.** Elgin, IL: Brethren Publishing; 1938. [$30.00]

Braunschweig, Johann Daniel von. **Ueber die Alt-Americanischen Denkmaler.** Berlin: Reimer; 1840. [rubbed, $225.00]

Brawley, Benjamin Griffith. **Your Negro Neighbor.** NY: Macmillan; 1918. [$15.00]

Braxton, Allen Caperton. **The Fifteenth Amendment, an Account of Its Enactment.** Lynchburg, VA: Bell; 1934. [$25.00]

Bray, Thomas. **Rev. Thomas Bray.** Baltimore: Murphy; 1901. [$45.00]

Brayer, Garnet M. **American Cattle Trails, 1540-1900.** 1st ed. Bayside, NY: Western Range Cattle Industry Study; 1952. [clothbound, $35.00]

Brayer, Herbert Oliver. **Pueblo Indian Land Grants of the "Rio Abajo," New Mexico.** Albuquerque: U. of New Mexico; 1939. [inscribed, $25.00]

Brayton, Matthew. **The Indian Captive.** Fostoria, OH: Gray; 1896. [$150.00]

Breakenridge, William M. **Helldorado.** Boston, NY: Houghton Mifflin; 1928. [$100.00] [$85.00]

Brearley, Harry Chase. **Fifty Years of a Civilizing Force.** NY: Stokes; 1916. [binding stained, $20.00]

Breazeale, J. W. M. **Life As It Is.** Knoxville: Williams; 1842. [rebacked, $1000.00]

Brebner, John Bartlet. **Explorers of North America, 1492-1806.** London: Black; 1933. [$55.00]

Brebner, John Bartlet. **New England's Outpost.** NY; London: Columbia UP; King; 1927. [$45.00, Canadian]

Breeling, Lutie Taylor. **When the Trail Was New in Mountraille.** [Ross?, ND: s.n.]; 1956. [$15.00]

Breen, Matthew Patrick. **Thirty Years of New York Politics Up-to-Date.** NY: The Author; 1899. [front hinge cracked, $25.00]

Breihan, Carl W. **Great Gunfighters of the West.** San Antonio: Naylor; 1962. [signed, dj worn, $25.00]

Breihan, Carl W. **Great Lawmen of the West.** London: Long; 1963. [$12.50]

Bremer, Frederika. **Homes of the New World.** NY: Harper; 1853. 2 v. [$95.00]

Brenckman, Frederick Charles. **History of the Pennsylvania State Grange.** Harrisburg: Pennsylvania State Grange; 1949. [$12.00]

Brenner, Anita. **Wind That Swept Mexico.** 1st ed. NY, London: Harper; 1943. [dj repaired, $97.50] [$85.00]

Brent, Rafer. **Great Western Heroes.** NY: Bartholomew; 1957. [$15.00]

Brereton, John. **A Briefe and True Relation of the Discoverie of the North Part of Virginia.** NY: Dodd, Mead; 1903. [shaken and stained, $25.00]

Brevoort, Elias. **New Mexico, Her Natural Resources and Attractions.** Santa Fe: Brevoort; 1874. [$285.00]

Brevoort, Henry. **Letters of Henry Brevoort to Washington Irving.** NY: Putnam; 1916. 2 v. [$45.00]

Brevoort, James Carson. **Verrazano the Navigator.** NY: Argus; 1874. [$200.00]

Brewer, Luther Albertus. **History of Linn County Iowa.** Chicago: Pioneer; 1911. 2 v. [x-lib., $100.00]

Brewer, William Henry. **Up and Down California in 1860-1864.** New Haven; London: Yale UP; Oxford UP; 1930. [$125.00]

Brewer, Willis. **Alabama, Her History, Resources, War Record, and Public Men.** Montgomery, AL: Barrett & Brown; 1872. [x-lib., $50.00]

Brewerton, George Douglas. **Overland with Kit Carson.** NY: Coward-McCann; 1930. [in good dj, $70.00]

Brewerton, George Douglas. **The War in Kansas.** NY: Derby & Jackson; 1856. [$90.00]

Brice, Wallace A. **History of Fort Wayne.** Fort Wayne, IN: Jones; 1868. [$225.00]

Brickell, John. **The Natural History of North-Carolona.** Dublin: Carson; 1737. [rebound, $1650.00]

Bridenbaugh, Carl. **Cities in the Wilderness.** NY: Ronald; 1938. [$30.00]

Bridenbaugh, Carl. **Colonial Craftsman.** NY: New York UP; 1950. [$25.00]

Bridge, James Howard. **Inside History of the Carnegie Steel Company.** NY: Aldine; 1903. [$50.00] [$40.00]

Bridges, George Wilson. **Annals of Jamaica.** London: Murray; 1828. 2 v. [v. 1 only, $75.00]

Bridges, Leonard Hal. **Lee's Maverick General.** 1st ed. NY: McGraw-Hill; 1961. [$35.00]

Bridgman, Howard Allen. **New England in the Life of the World.** Boston, Chicago: Pilgrim; 1920. [$15.00]

Briesen, Hans Von. **Why Not Know Florida.** Jacksonville: Drew; 1936. [$35.00]

Briggs, Emily Edson. **The Olivia Letters.** NY, Washington: Neale; 1906. [$95.00]

Briggs, Harold Edward. **Frontiers of the Northwest.** NY, London: Appleton-Century; 1940. [$40.00]

Briggs, Lloyd Vernon. **Arizona and New Mexico, 1882, California, 1886, Mexico, 1891.** Boston: Priv. Print.; 1932. [$150.00]

Briggs, Lloyd Vernon. **California and the West, 1881, and Later.** Boston: Priv. Print.; 1931. [$75.00] [presentation, $75.00]

Brill, Charles J. **Conquest of the Southern Plains.** 1st ed. Oklahoma City: Golden Saga; 1938. [$65.00]

Brimlow, George Francis. **Cavalryman out of the West.** Caldwell, ID: Caxton; 1944. [$70.00]

Brimlow, George Francis. **Harney County, Oregon, and Its Range Land.** Portland: Binfords & Mort; 1951. [$35.00]

Brininstool, Earl Alonzo. **Fighting Indian Warriors.** Harrisburg, PA: Stackpole; 1953. [$15.00]

Brininstool, Earl Alonzo. **Fighting Red Cloud's Warriors.** Columbus, OH: Hunter-Trader-Trapper; 1926. [$40.00]

Brininstool, Earl Alonzo. **Trail Dust of a Maverick.** NY: Dodd, Mead; 1914. [$40.00]

Brininstool, Earl Alonzo. **A Trooper with Custer.** Columbus, OH: Hunter-Trader-Trapper; 1925. [$55.00] [spine rubbed, $55.00] [1926 issue, $47.50] [1952 Stackpole revision, $45.00]

Brinton, Daniel Garrison. **Aboriginal American Authors and Their Productions.** Philadelphia: Brinton; 1883. [$125.00]

Brinton, Daniel Garrison. **The American Race.** Philadelphia: McKay; 1901. [$50.00]

Brinton, Daniel Garrison. **Notes on the Floridian Peninsula.** Philadelphia: Sabin; 1859. [$350.00]

Brisbin, James Sanks. **The Beef Bonanza.** Norman: U. of Oklahoma; 1959. [$12.00]

Brissot de Warville, Jacques Pierre. **The Commerce of America with Europe.** NY: Swords; 1795. [$150.00]

Brissot de Warville, Jacques Pierre. **Lettre de J.P. Brissot 'a M. Barnave.** Paris: Desenne; 1790. [$250.00]

Brissot de Warville, Jacques Pierre. **New Travels in the United States of America Performed in 1788.** NY: Swords; 1792. [$125.00] [1794 London ed., 2 vols., $575.00; $375.00]

Bristed, John. **America and Her Resources.** London: Colburn; 1818. [rebound, $150.00] [$100.00]

Bristed, John. **Resources of the United States of America.** NY: Eastburn; 1818. [front hinge cracked, minor worming, $300.00]

Bristol, Sherlock. **The Pioneer Preacher.** Chicago, NY: Revell; 1887. [$35.00]

Britt, Albert. **Great Indian Chiefs.** NY; London: Whittlesey; McGraw-Hill; 1938. [$25.00]

Britton, Wiley. **Union Indian Brigade in the Civil War.** Kansas City: Hudson; 1922. [$150.00] [$90.00]

Brockett, Linus Pierpont. **Handbook of the United States of America.** NY: Watson; 1884. [$50.00]

Brockett, Linus Pierpont. **Our Western Empire.** Philadelphia; Columbus, OH: Bradley, Garretson; Garretson; 1881. [$85.00]

Brockett, Linus Pierpont. **The Silk Industry in America.** NY: Silk Assn. of America; 1876. [$85.00]

Brodhead, John Romeyn. **History of the State of New York.** 1st ed. NY: Harper; 1853-71. 2 v. [v. 1 only, $75.00]

Brodie, Fawn. **No Man Knows My History.** NY: Knopf; 1946. [later printing, $12.50]

Brogan, Phil F. **East of the Cascades.** Portland, OR: Binfords & Mort; 1964. [$15.00]

Brokmeyer, Henry Conrad. **A Foggy Night at Newport.** St. Louis: Foote; 1860. [$65.00]

Brolaski, Harry. **Easy Money.** Cleveland: Searchlight; 1911. [backstrip partially missing, $45.00]

Bromley, Edward Augustus. **Minneapolis Album.** Minneapolis: Thresher; 1890. [worn, soiled, loose, $400.00]

Bronaugh, Warren Carter. **The Younger's Fight for Freedom.** Columbia, MO: Stephens; 1906. [$75.00] [$65.00]

Bronson, Sherlock A. **John Sherman.** Columbus: Derby; 1880. [$25.00]

Bronson, Walter Cochrane. **History of Brown University, 1764-1914.** Providence: The University; 1914. [$20.00]

Broocks, John H. **To Hell I Reckon.** 1st ed. Houston: Southwest; 1924. [$35.00]

Brooker, William H. **Texas: An Epitome of Texas History.** Columbus: Nitschke; 1897. [presentation, $225.00] [$250.00]

Brooks, Alfred Hulse. **Blazing Alaska's Trails.** Washington: Arctic Institute of North America; 1953. [$35.00]

Brooks, Bryant Butler. **Memoirs of.** Glendale, CA: Clark; 1939. [one of 150 copies, $125.00]

Brooks, Elbridge Streeter. **The Century Book of the American Revolution.** NY: Century; 1897. [$10.00]

Brooks, Geraldine. **Dames and Daughters of the Young Republic.** NY: Crowell; 1901. [$35.00]

Brooks, John Graham. **American Syndicalism.** 1st ed. NY: Macmillan; 1913. [x-lib., $15.00]

Brooks, John S. **First Administration of Oklahoma.** Oklahoma City: Brooks; 1908. [$85.00]

Brooks, Nathan Covington. **Complete History of the Mexican War.** Philadelphia; Baltimore: Grigg, Elliot; Hutchinson & Seebold; 1849. [hinges starting, $245.00]

Brooks, Noah. **First across the Continent.** NY: Scribner; 1901. [$25.00]

Brooks, Noah. **Washington in Lincoln's Time.** NY: Century; 1896. [$18.50]

Brooks, Robert Preston. **University of Georgia under Sixteen Administrations.** Athens: U. of Georgia; 1956. [$12.50]

Brooks, Robert Romano Ravi. **Williamstown: The First Two Hundred Years, 1753-1953.** Williamstown, MA: McClelland; 1953. [rubbed, stained, sunned, $20.00]

Brooks, Ulysses Robert. **Butler and His Cavalry in the War of Secession.** Columbia, SC: State; 1909. [lacks title page, worn and battered, $35.00] [$90.00]

Brooks, Van Wyck. **The Flowering of New England, 1815-1865.** 1st ed. NY: Dutton; 1936. [$20.00]

Brooks, Van Wyck. **New England: Indian Summer, 1865-1915.** 1st ed. NY: Dutton; 1940. [$15.00]

Brooks, Van Wyck. **Times of Melville and Whitman.** 1st ed. NY: Dutton; 1947. [$7.50] [$10.00]

Brooks, William Elizabeth. **Grant of Appomattox.** Indianapolis: Bobbs-Merrill; 1942. [x-lib., $15.00]

Brooks, William Elizabeth. **Lee of Virginia.** Indianapolis: Bobbs-Merrill; 1932. [$25.00]

Brosnan, Cornelius J. **Jason Lee.** NY: Macmillan; 1932. [$12.50]

Bross, William. **Legend of the Delaware.** Chicago: Knight and Leonard; 1887. [$85.00]

Brotherhead, William. **The Book of the Signers.** Philadelphia: Brotherhead; 1861. [soiled, $85.00]

Brough, James. **Princess Alice.** 1st ed. Boston: Little, Brown; 1975. [$12.50]

Brougham, John. **Lotos Leaves.** Boston: Gill; 1875. [$100.00]

Brown County. Territorial Pioneers Association. **Early History of Brown County, South Dakota.** [Aberdeen?, SD: s.n.]; 1965. [$25.00]

Brown, Alan Willard. **Hobart College.** NY: Newcomen Society; 1956. [$20.00]

Brown, Alexander. **The Genesis of the United States.** Boston, NY: Houghton Mifflin; 1890. 2 v. [$175.00]

Brown, Alexander Crosby. **The Dismal Swamp Canal.** Chesapeake, VA: Norfolk County Historical Society; 1967. [$12.50]

Brown, Dee Alexander. **Fort Phil Kearny.** NY: Putnam; 1962. [worn dj, $30.00]

Brown, Dee Alexander. **Trail Driving Days.** NY: Scribner; 1952. [torn dj, $30.00] [fine, $40.00]

Brown, Edmund G. **Reagan and Reality.** 1st ed. NY: Praeger; 1970. [$20.00]

Brown, Estelle. **Stubborn Fool.** Caldwell, ID: Caxton; 1952. [$15.00]

Brown, Everett Somerville. **Constitutional History of the Louisiana Purchase.** Berkeley: U. of California; 1920. [$90.00]

Brown, Floyd. **He Built a School with Two Dollars and Eighty-Five Cents.** Pine Bluff, AR: Brown; [1956?]. [$10.00]

Brown, Francis. **Edmund Niles Huyck.** NY: Dodd, Mead; 1935. [$15.00]

Brown, George Alfred. **Harold the Klansman.** Kansas City, MO: Western Baptist; 1923. [$45.00]

Brown, George Washington. **Old Times in Oildom.** Youngsville, PA: [s.n.]; 1909. [$45.00]

Brown, Henry. **History of Illinois.** NY: Winchester; 1844. [x-lib., rebound, $35.00]

Brown, Henry Collins. **Brownstone Fronts and Saratoga Trunks.** 1st ed. NY: Dutton; 1935. [$20.00]

Brown, Henry Collins. **The Lordly Hudson.** NY, London: Scribner; 1937. [signed, $250.00]

Brown, James. **History of Public Assistance in Chicago.** Chicago: U. of Chicago; 1941. [$20.00]

Brown, James Stuart. **Allaire's Lost Empire.** Freehold, NJ: Transcript Print. House; 1958. [$20.00]

Brown, Jennie Broughton. **Fort Hall on the Oregon Trail.** Caldwell, ID: Caxton; 1932. [$65.00]

Brown, Jesse. **The Black Hills Trails.** Rapid City, SD: Journal; 1924. [$150.00]

Brown, John Henry. **History of Texas; from 1685 to 1892.** St. Louis: Daniell; 1892. 2 v. [rebacked, $385.00]

Brown, John Henry. **Indian Wars and Pioneers of Texas.** Austin: Daniell; 1896. [first issue, $950.00] [$850.00]

Brown, John Henry. **Life and Times of Henry Smith.** Dallas: Aldridge; 1887. [$175.00] [$100.00]

Brown, John Mason. **The Political Beginnings of Kentucky.** Louisville: Morton; 1889. [$135.00]

Brown, John Mason. **To All Hands.** NY; London: Whittlesey; McGraw-Hill; 1943. [$15.00]

Brown, John P. **Old Frontiers.** Kingsport, TN: Southern; 1938. [$75.00]

Brown, Joseph Willard. **The Signal Corps, U.S.A. in the War of the Rebellion.** Boston: U. S. Veteran Signal Corps Assn.; 1896. [front hinge cracked, $150.00]

Brown, Louise Fargo. **Apostle of Democracy.** 1st ed. NY, London: Harper; 1943. [signed, $47.50]

Brown, Mark Herbert. **Before Barbed Wire.** 1st ed. NY: Holt; 1956. [dj worn, $55.00] [Bramhill reprint, dj frayed, $25.00]

Brown, Mark Herbert. **The Frontier Years.** NY: Holt; 1955. [dj chipped, $55.00]

Brown, Mark Herbert. **Plainsmen of the Yellowstone.** NY: Putnam; 1961. [dj chipped, $45.00]

Brown, Milton Wolf. **Story of the Armory Show.** [s.l.]: Hirshhorn Foundation; 1963. [$30.00]

Brown, Robert Leaman. **Colorado Ghost Towns.** Caldwell, ID: Caxton; 1972. [$25.00]

Brown, Robert Leaman. **An Empire of Silver.** Caldwell, ID: Caxton; 1968, c1965. [2nd printing, $15.00]

Brown, Robert Leaman. **Ghost Towns of the Colorado Rockies.** Caldwell, ID: Caxton; 1968. [1st printing, $20.00]

Brown, Robert Leaman. **Jeep Trails to Colorado Ghost Towns.** Caldwell, ID: Caxton; 1963. [1st printing, $20.00]

Brown, Rollo Walter. **Harvard Yard in the Golden Age.** NY: Current Books; 1948. [$20.00]

Brown, Samuel R. **The Western Gazetteer; or Emigrant's Directory.** Auburn, NY: Southwick; 1817. [$350.00]

Brown, William Griffee. **History of Nicholas County, West Virginia.** 1st ed. Richmond: Dietz; 1954. [signed, $47.50]

Brown, William H. **History of the First Locomotives in America.** NY: Appleton; 1871. [$150.00]

Brown, William Henry. **Portrait Gallery of Distinguished American Citizens.** NY: Baker; 1931. [$200.00]

Brown, William Samuel. **California Northeast.** Oakland: Biobooks; 1951. [$25.00]

Brown, William Wells. **The Black Man.** NY; Boston: Hamilton; Wallcut; 1863. [$175.00]

Brown, William Wells. **Narrative of.** Boston: Anti-Slavery Office; 1847. [rebound, $175.00]

Brown, William Wells. **Sketches of Places and People Abroad.** Boston: Jewett; 1855, c1854. [$175.00]

Brown-Reynolds Duel. St. Louis: Franklin Club; 1911. [$160.00]

Browne, Belmore. **The Conquest of Mt. McKinley.** Boston: Houghton Mifflin; 1956. [$25.00]

Browne, Francis Fisher. **Bugle-Echoes.** NY: White, Stokes, & Allen; 1886. [x-lib., $15.00]

Browne, J. Ross. **Adventures in the Apache Country.** NY: Harper; 1868. [$275.00] [1869 issue, $150.00]

Browne, J. Ross. **Crusoe's Island.** NY: Harper; 1864. [$75.00]

Browne, J. Ross. **Muleback to the Convention.** San Francisco: Book Club of California; 1950. [$55.00]

Brownell, Charles De Wolf. **Indian Races of North and South America.** Hartford; Chicago: Hurlbut, Scranton; Treat; 1864. [waterstained, handcolored plates, rebound, $40.00]

Browning, Charles Henry. **Welsh Settlement of Pennsylvania.** Philadelphia: Campbell; 1912. [$65.00]

Brownlee, Richard S. **Gray Ghosts of the Confederacy.** Baton Rouge: Louisiana State UP; 1958. [$25.00] [signed, $37.50]

Brownlow, William Gannaway. **Helps to the Study of Presbyterianism.** Knoxville: Heiskell; 1834. [$300.00]

Brownlow, William Gannaway. **Ought American Slavery to Be Perpetuated?** Philadelphia: Lippincott; 1858. [worn, $45.00]

Brownlow, William Gannaway. **Sketches of the Rise, Progress, and Decline of Secession.** Philadelphia; Cincinnati: Childs; Applegate; 1862. [$150.00] [badly worn, $45.00]

Brownson, Orestes Augustus. **American Republic.** NY: O'Shea; 1866. [x-lib., $20.00]

Broyles, J. Allen. **John Birch Society.** Boston: Beacon; 1964. [$12.50]

Bruce, Edward C. **The Century.** Philadelphia: Lippincott; 1877. [$45.00]

Bruce, John Roberts. **Gaudy Century.** NY: Random; 1948. [$12.50]

Bruce, Lenny. **How to Talk Dirty and Influence People.** 1st ed. Chicago: Playboy; 1965. [fine, $75.00]

Bruce, Miner Wait. **Alaska: Its History and Resources, Gold Fields, Routes and Scenery.** Seattle: Lowman & Hanford; 1895. [$75.00] [$100.00]

Bruce, Philip Alexander. **Social Life of Virginia in the Seventeenth Century.** Richmond: Whittet & Shepperson; 1907. [x-lib., $25.00] [2nd ed., Lynchburg, 1907, $12.50]

Bruce, Robert. **The Fighting Norths and Pawnee Scouts.** Lincoln, NE: [s.n.]; 1932. [$60.00]

Bruce, Robert V. **Lincoln and the Tools of War.** 1st ed. Indianapolis: Bobbs-Merrill; 1956. [$28.50] [$30.00]

Bruce, William Cabell. **Benjamin Franklin, Self-Revealed.** 2nd ed. NY, London: Putnam; 1923. 2 v. [$60.00]

Bruff, Joseph Goldsborough. **Gold Rush.** NY: Columbia UP; 1944. 2 v. [$200.00]

Brummelkamp, Anthony. **Landverhuizing.** Amsterdam: Hoogkamer; 1846. [$225.00]

Brush, Daniel Harmon. **Growing Up with Southern Illinois, 1820 to 1861.** Chicago: Donnelley; 1944. [$15.00]

Bryan, Daniel. **Lay of Gratitude.** Philadelphia: Carey & Lea; 1826. [some worming, foxed, $75.00]

Bryan, John Albury. **Missouri's Contribution to American Architecture.** St. Louis: Architectural Club; 1928. [x-lib., $35.00]

Bryan, William Jennings. **Memoirs of.** Philadelphia: United Publishers of America; 1925. [$12.50]

Bryant, Henry Edward Cowan. **Tar Heel Tales.** Charlotte: Stone & Barringer; 1910. [hinges weak, stained and worn, $35.00]

Bryant, William Cullen. **Discourse on the Life, Character and Genius of Washington Irving.** NY: Putnam; 1860. [rubbed, rebound, $65.00]

Bryant, William Cullen. **Letters of a Traveller, 2d series.** NY: Appleton; 1859. [1st state, $75.00]

Bryant, William Cullen. **Picturesque America; or, The Land We Live In.** NY: Appleton; 1872-74. 2 v. [$275.00] [$375.00]

Bryant, William Cullen. **Thirty Poems.** NY: Appleton; 1864. [$65.00]

Bryce, James Bryce viscount. **The American Commonwealth.** London, NY: Macmillan; 1888. [3 vol. issue, $250.00] [2 vol. issue, $75.00]

Bryner, Byron Cloyd. **Abraham Lincoln in Peoria.** 2nd ed. Peoria, IL: Lincoln Historical Publishing; 1926. [$25.00]

Bryson, James Gordon. **One Hundred Dollars & a Horse.** NY: Morrow; 1965, c1963. [$9.00]

Buchanan, James. **James Buchanan, His Doctrines and Policy.** NY: Greeley & McElrath; 1856. [$45.00]

Buck, Charles Nicholas. **Memoirs of.** Philadelphia: Walnut; 1941. [$25.00]

Buck, Daniel. **Indian Outbreaks.** Mankato, MN: [s.n.]; 1904. [$100.00]

Buck, Franklin Augustus. **Yankee Trader in the Gold Rush.** Boston, NY: Houghton Mifflin; 1930. [$25.00]

Buck, Irving Ashby. **Cleburne and His Command.** NY, Washington: Neale; 1908. [$350.00]

Buckeridge, Justin O. **Lincoln's Choice.** 1st ed. Harrisburg, PA: Stackpole; 1956. [$25.00]

Buckingham, Nash. **De Shootinest Gent'man.** NY: Putnam; 1943. [3rd printing, $20.00]

Bucklin, Sophronia E. **In Hospital and Camp.** Philadelphia: Potter; 1869. [$95.00]

Buckmaster, Henrietta. **Let My People Go.** 1st ed. NY: Harper; 1941. [$45.00]

Budd, Thomas. **Good Order Established in Pennsylvania and New-Jersey.** NY: Gowans; 1865. [$40.00] [$50.00] [Cleveland, 1902 ed., $25.00]

Buel, James William. **The Border Outlaws.** St. Louis: Historical Pub. Co.; 1881. [$85.00]

Buel, James William. **Life and Marvelous Adventures of Wild Bill.** Chicago: Belford, Clarke; 1880, c1879. [wrappers chipped, $1000.00]

Buettner, Johann Carl. **Narrative of Johann Carl Buettner in the American Revolution.** NY: Heartman; 1915. [320 numbered copies, $125.00]

Buffum, Edward Gould. **Six Months in the Gold Mines.** Philadelphia: Lea and Blanchard; 1850. [$450.00]

Buley, R. Carlyle. **The Old Northwest: Pioneer Period, 1815-1840.** Indianapolis: Indiana Historical Society; 1950. 2 v. [$35.00] [1951 printing, $25.00]

Bulfinch, Thomas. **Oregon and Eldorado.** Boston: Tilton; 1866. [rebound, $45.00]

Bulkeley, Alice Talcott. **Historic Litchfield.** Hartford, CT: Case, Lockwood & Brainard; 1907. [$25.00]

Bulkeley, John. **A Voyage to the South-Seas, in the Years 1740-1.** London: Robinson; 1743. [$775.00]

Bull, William Perkins. **From Strachan to Owen.** Toronto: Perkins Bull; 1938. [$15.00]

Bullard, Frederic Lauriston. **Tad and His Father.** Boston: Little, Brown; 1915. [$22.50]

Bullock, Helen Claire Duprey. **My Head and My Heart.** NY: Putnam; 1945. [$12.50]

Bullock, William. **Six Months' Residence and Travels in Mexico.** London: Murray; 1824. [$650.00]

Bullock, William. **Sketch of a Journey through the Western States.** London: Miller; 1827. [presentation, rebacked, x-lib., $1250.00]

Bumgardner, Edward. **Life of Edmund G. Ross.** Kansas City: Fielding-Turner; 1949. [$20.00]

Bungay, George W. **Off-Hand Takings.** NY: De Witt & Davenport; 1854. [$15.00]

Bunker Hill Songster. NY: Murphy; [185-?]. [$10.00]

Bunker, Robert Manson. **Other Men's Skies.** Bloomington: Indiana UP; 1956. [$12.50]

Bunkley, Josephine M. **Testimony of an Escaped Novice from the Sisterhood of St. Joseph, Emmettsburg, Maryland.** NY: Harper; 1855. [$67.50]

Bunnell, David C. **The Travels and Adventures of.** Palmyra, NY: Bortles; 1831. [lacking two plates, $450.00]

Bunnell, Fred G. **Captain Joshua Huddy.** Toms River, NJ: Ocean County Bureau of Publicity; 1941. [$15.00]

Bunnell, Lafayette Houghton. **Discovery of the Yosemite and the Indian War of 1851.** Chicago: Revell; 1880. [$275.00] [4th ed., 1911, $60.00]

Bunting, Bainbridge. **Taos Adobes.** 1st ed. Santa Fe: Museum of New Mexico; 1964. [$75.00]

Buntline, Ned. **Mysteries and Miseries of New York.** NY: Berford; 1848, c1847. [5 parts bound as one, text foxed, $175.00]

Bunton, Mary Taylor. **A Bride on the Old Chisholm Trail in 1886.** San Antonio: Naylor; 1939. [dj chipped, $75.00]

Burch, John P. see, Trow, Harrison.

Burden, Harold Nelson. **Manitoulin.** London: Simpkin, Marshall, Hamilton, Kent; 1895. [$45.00]

Burdett, Charles. **Life and Adventures of Christopher Carson.** Philadelphia: Evans; 1860. [backstrip chipped, $150.00]

Burdett, Charles. **Life of Kit Carson.** Philadelphia: Potter; 1866. [$30.00]

Burdett, Charles. **Margaret Moncrieffe: The First Love of Aaron Burr.** NY: Derby & Jackson; 1860. [$30.00]

Burdette, Robert Jones. **Greater Los Angeles & Southern California.** rev. ed. Chicago, Los Angeles: Lewis; 1910. [$75.00]

Burdick, Usher Lloyd. **History of the Farmers' Political Action in North Dakota.** Baltimore: Wirth; 1944. [bumped, sunned, $25.00]

Burdick, Usher Lloyd. **Last Days of Sitting Bull.** 1st ed. Baltimore: Wirth; 1941. [$65.00]

Burdick, Usher Lloyd. **Life and Exploits of John Goodall.** 1st ed. Watford City, ND: McKenzie County Farmer; 1931. [$45.00]

Burdick, Usher Lloyd. **Tales from Buffalo Land: The Story of Fort Buford.** Baltimore: Wirth; 1940. [$75.00]

Burdick, Usher Lloyd. **Tragedy in the Great Sioux Camp.** Baltimore: Proof Press; 1936. [$40.00]

Burge, Dolly Sumner. **A Woman's Wartime Journal.** 2nd ed. Macon, GA: Burke; 1927. [$55.00]

Burgess, John William. **Reminiscences of an American Scholar.** NY: Columbia UP; 1934. [$12.50] [$25.00]

Burgoyne, John. **A Letter from Lieut. Gen. Burgoyne to His Constituents.** London: Almon; 1779. [disbound, $150.00]

Burk, John. **History of Virginia.** Petersburg: Dickson & Pescud; 1804-1816. 4 v. [3/4 morocco, $850.00] [imprint varies, $850.00]

Burke, Edmund. **Account of the European Settlements in America in Six Parts.** 2nd ed. London: Dodsley; 1758. 2 v. [x-lib., spine repaired, $450.00] [3rd ed., 1760, rebound, $175.00] [4th ed., 1765, $375.00]

Burke, Edmund. **Letter from . . . to John Farr and John Harris.** 4th ed. London: Dodsley; 1777. [$125.00]

Burlend, Rebecca. **True Picture of Emigration.** London: Berger; 1848. [in original lavender wraps, $200.00] [1936 Lakeside reprint, $17.50]

Burleson, Georgiana Jenkins. **The Life and Writings of Rufus C. Burleson.** [Waco?,TX]: Burleson; 1901. [$125.00]

Burlin, Natalie Curtis. **The Indians' Book.** NY, London: Harper; 1923. [$85.00]

Burman, Ben Lucien. **Big River to Cross.** NY: Day; 1940. [$25.00]

Burnaby, Andrew. **Travels through the Middle Settlements in North-America.** London: Payne; 1775. [$600.00] [2nd ed., 1775, $350.00]

Burne, Alfred Higgins. **Lee, Grant and Sherman.** NY: Scribner; 1939. [$42.00]

Burnet, David Gouverneur. **David G. Burnet Letters.** La Grange, TX: La Grange Journal; [193-?]. [$250.00]

Burnet, Jacob. **Notes on the Early Settlement of the North-Western Territory.** Cincinnati: Derby, Bradley; 1847. [rebound, $100.00]

Burnett, Arthur C. **Yankees in the Republic of Texas.** Houston: Jones; 1952. [$45.00]

Burnett, James Jehu. **Sketches of Tennessee's Pioneer Baptist Preachers.** Nashville: Marshall & Bruce; 1919. [all published?, $60.00]

Burnett, Peter H. **Recollections and Opinions of an Old Pioneer.** NY: Appleton; 1880. [$300.00]

Burnham, Frederick Russell. **Scouting on Two Continents.** Los Angeles: Deach; 1934, c1926. [$15.00]

Burnham, Guy M. **Lake Superior Country in History and Story.** Ashland, WI: Daily Press; 1930. [$45.00]

Burns, George. **I Love Her, That's Why!** NY: Simon and Schuster; 1955. [$12.50]

Burns, James Aloysius. **History of Catholic Education in the United States.** NY: Benziger; 1937. [$17.50]

Burns, James Anderson. **The Crucible.** Oneida, KY: Oneida Institute; 1928. [$18.50]

Burns, Vincent Godfrey. **Female Convict.** NY: Macaulay; 1934. [spine frayed, $75.00]

Burns, Walter Noble. **Saga of Billy the Kid.** Garden City: Doubleday, Page; 1926. [hinge starting, $25.00] [Grosset & Dunlap reprint, $15.00]

Burns, Walter Noble. **Tombstone.** Garden City: Doubleday, Page; 1927. [$50.00] [Garden City Books reprint, $20.00]

Burns, William John. **Masked War.** NY: Doran; 1913. [$40.00]

Burpee, Lawrence Johnstone. **The Search for the Western Sea.** Toronto: Macmillan; 1935. 2 v. [$150.00] [1936 printing, $100.00]

Burr, Aaron. **Memoirs of.** NY: Harper; 1837-1838. 2 v. [lightly foxed, $40.00] [1855 reprint, spines chipped, $40.00]

Burr, Aaron. **Private Journal of.** NY: Harper; 1838. 2 v. [$150.00]

Burr, Aaron. **Reports of the Trials of Colonel Aaron Burr . . . for Treason.** Philadelphia: Hopkins and Earle; 1808. 2 v. [$450.00]

Burr, Anna Robeson. **Portrait of a Banker.** NY: Duffield; 1927. [worn, x-lib., $10.00]

Burr, Fearing. **The Town of Hingham in the Late Civil War.** Boston: The Town; 1876. [$30.00]

Burr, George Lincoln. **Narratives of the Witchcraft Cases, 1648-1706.** NY: Scribner; 1914. [$22.50]

Burr, Nelson Rollin. **The Anglican Church in New Jersey.** Philadelphia: Church Historical Society; 1954. [$35.00]

Burr, Timothy. **BISBA.** Trenton, NJ: Hercules; 1965. [dj over pict. covers, $75.00]

Burrage, Henry Sweetser. **Early English and French Voyages.** NY: Scribner; 1906. [$27.50]

Burrage, Henry Sweetser. **Thomas Hamlin Hubbard.** Portland, ME: [s.n.]; 1923. [$37.50]

Burrell, Abram Bogart. **Reminiscences of George La Bar.** Philadelphia: Claxton, Remsen & Haffelfinger; 1870. [$25.00] [$50.00]

Burritt, Elihu. **The Learned Blacksmith.** NY: Wilson-Erickson; 1937. [$15.00]

Burrough, Edward. **A Declaration of the Sad and Great Persecution and Martyrdom of the People of God, Called Quakers.** London: Wilson; 1660. [badly trimmed, some leaves torn, $850.00]

Burroughs, Burt Edward. **Legends and Tales of Homeland on the Kankakee.** Chicago: Regan; 1923. [presentation, $35.00]

Burroughs, Burt Edward. **Tales of an Old "Bordertown" and along the Kankakee.** Fowler, IN: Benton Review Shop; 1925. [$65.00]

Burroughs, Edgar Rice. **Escape on Venus.** 1st ed. Tarzana, CA: Burroughs; 1946. [tape repaired dj, $60.00]

Burroughs, Edgar Rice. **Llana of Gathol.** lst ed. Tarzana, CA: [s.n.]; 1948. [fine, $85.00]

Burroughs, Edgar Rice. **Tarzan and the Jewels of Opar.** 1st ed. Chicago: McClurg; 1918. [$115.00]

Burroughs, John. **Camping & Tramping with Roosevelt.** Boston, NY: Houghton Mifflin; 1907. [$45.00]

Burroughs, John. **In the Catskills.** Boston, NY: Houghton Mifflin; 1910. [$20.00]

Burroughs, John. **Notes on Walt Whitman.** 2nd ed. NY: Redfield; 1871. [$100.00]

Burroughs, Stephen. **Memoirs of the Notorious Stephen Burroughs of New Hampshire.** NY: Dial; 1924. [$15.00]

Burson, William. **Race for Liberty.** Wellsville, OH: Foster; 1867. [$225.00]

Burt, Maxwell Struthers. **Diary of a Dude-Wrangler.** NY, London: Scribner; 1924. [$35.00]

Burt, Olive Woolley. **American Murder Ballads and Their Stories.** NY: Oxford UP; 1958. [$20.00]

Burton, Harley True. **A History of the JA Ranch.** Austin: Von Boeckmann-Jones; 1928. [$650.00]

Burton, Jean. **Lydia Pinkham Is Her Name.** NY: Farrar, Straus; 1949. [scotch tape marks on cover, $10.00]

Burton, Jeff. **Black Jack Christian.** 1st ed. Santa Fe: Territorian; 1967. [x-lib., $20.00]

Burton, Maria Amparo. **The Squatter and the Don.** San Francisco: Carson; 1885. [worn, $40.00]

Burton, Richard Francis. **The City of the Saints and across the Rocky Mountains to California.** London: Longman, etc.; 1861. [rebound, $325.00]

Burton, Warren. **White Slavery: A New Emancipation Cause.** Worcester; Boston: Phillips; Little; 1839. [$40.00]

Busbey, Katherine Graves. **Home Life in America.** NY: Macmillan; 1910. [$20.00]

Busbey, L. White. **Uncle Joe Cannon.** NY: Holt; 1927. [bumped and rubbed, $7.50]

Busby, Levi E. **Life-Sketch of Rev. Charles A. Rose.** Salisbury, NC: Smith & Irvin; [190-?]. [$30.00]

Busch, George B. **Duty; The Story of the 21st Infantry Regiment.** Sendai, Japan: Hyappan; 1953. [signed, $30.00]

Busch, Moritz. **Wanderungen zwischen Hudson und Mississippi, 1851 und 1852.** Stuttgart, Tübingen: Cotta; 1854. 2 v. [$275.00]

Bush, George. **Future Builders.** NY: McGraw Hill; 1973. [$25.00]

Bush, George Gary. **Harvard.** Boston: Cupples, Upham; 1886. [$20.00]

Bush, Wesley A. **Paradise to Leeward.** NY: Van Nostrand; 1954. [$25.00]

Bushick, Frank H. **Glamorous Days.** 1st ed. San Antonio: Naylor; 1934. [$40.00]

Bushnell, David Ives. **The Choctaw of Bayou Lacomb, St. Tammany Parish, Louisiana.** Washington: USGPO; 1909. [$30.00]

Bushnell, Horace. **Reverses Needed.** Hartford: Hunt; 1861. [$15.00]

Bushong, Millard Kessler. **History of Jefferson County, West Virginia.** Charles Town, WV: Jefferson; 1941. [$45.00]

Busk, Henry William. **Sketch of the Origin and the Recent History of the New England Company.** London: Spottiswoode; 1884. [$75.00, Canadian]

Butcher, Harry Cecil. **My Three Years with Eisenhower.** NY: Simon and Schuster; 1946. [$10.00]

Butcher, Herbert Borton. **The Battle of Trenton.** Princeton: Princeton UP; 1934. [$15.00]

Butel-Dumont, Georges Marie. **Histoire et Commerce des Colonies Angloises, dans l'Amerique Septentrionale.** Londres, Paris: Breton; 1755. [rebacked, boards eroded, $450.00]

Butler, Anna B. **Centennial Records.** see, Woman's State Centennial Executive Committee, Wisconsin.

Butler, Benjamin Clapp. **Lake George and Lake Champlain from Their First Discovery to 1759.** Albany: Weed, Parsons; 1868. [$75.00]

Butler, Benjamin Franklin. **Autobiography and Personal Reminiscences of.** Boston: Thayer; 1892. [$35.00] [rebound, $15.00]

Butler, Benjamin Franklin. **Character and Results of the War.** Philadelphia: Printed for Gratuitous Distribution; 1863. [$30.00]

Butler, Benjamin Franklin. **Private and Official Correspondence of.** Norwood, MA: Plimpton; 1917. 5 v. [x-lib., $300.00]

Butler, Ellis Parker. **The Adventures of a Suburbanite.** Garden City: Doubleday, Page; 1911. [$15.00]

Butler, Frederick. **Memoirs of the Marquis de La Fayette.** Weathersfield, CT: Deming & Francis; 1825. [lacks portrait, $40.00]

Butler, James. **American Bravery Displayed.** Carlisle, PA: Phillips; 1816. [$200.00]

Butler, Margaret Manor. **Pictorial History of the Western Reserve 1796-1860.** Cleveland: Early Settlers Association of the Western Reserve; 1963. [$25.00]

Butler, Marvin Benjamin. **My Story of the Civil War and the Under-Ground Railroad.** Huntington, IN: United Brethren; 1914. [$100.00]

Butler, Ruth Lapham. **Doctor Franklin, Postmaster General.** 1st ed. Garden City: Doubleday, Doran; 1928. [$35.00]

Butler, William. **Mexico in Transition.** NY: Hunt & Eaton; 1892. [$35.00]

Butler, William Allen. **A Retrospect of Forty Years, 1825-1865.** NY: Scribner; 1911. [$30.00]

Butterfield, Consul Willshire. **An Historical Account of the Expedition against Sandusky under Col. William Crawford in 1782.** Cincinnati: Clarke; 1873. [$100.00]

Butterfield, Consul Willshire. **History of the Girtys.** Cincinnati: Clarke; 1890. [hinges cracked, $150.00] [1950 Long's College Book reprint, $70.00]

Butterfield, Consul Willshire. **Washington-Irvine Correspondence.** Madison, WI: Atwood; 1882. [$120.00]

Butterfield, L. H. **John Witherspoon Comes to America.** Princeton: Princeton UP; 1953. [$25.00]

Buttrick, Tilly. **Voyages, Travels and Discoveries of.** Boston: The Author; 1831. [$2750.00]

Butts, D. Gregory Claiborne. **From Saddle to City by Buggy, Boat and Railway.** Richmond: [s.n.]; 1922. [$35.00]

Bye, John O. **Back Trailing in the Heart of the Short-Grass Country.** [Everett?, WA: s.n.]; 1956. [signed, $75.00]

Byers, Chester. **Roping.** NY, London: Putnam; 1928. [$37.50]

Byington, Cyrus. **Dictionary of the Choctaw Language.** Washington: USGPO; 1915. [$45.00]

Bynum, Ernest Taylor. **Personal Recollections of Ex-Governor Watton.** Oklahoma City: [s.n.]; 1924. [$40.00]

Byrd, Richard Evelyn. **Alone.** NY: Putnam; 1938. [signed, $50.00]

Byrd, William. **William Byrd's Histories of the Dividing Line betwixt Virginia and North Carolina.** Raleigh: North Carolina Hist. Comm.; 1929. [silverfished, $35.00]

Byrn, Marcus Lafayette. **Life and Adventures of an Arkansaw [sic] Doctor.** NY: Byrn; [1879?]. [lacks rear wrap, $175.00]

Byrne, Patrick Edward. **Soldiers of the Plains.** NY: Minton, Balch; 1926. [foxed, $32.50]

Byrnes, Thomas F. **Professional Criminals of America.** NY: Cassell; 1886. [rebacked, $300.00]

Byron, George Anson. **Voyage of H. M. S. Blonde.** see, title.

Byron, John. **Narrative of.** London: Baker; 1768. [elegantly rebound, $200.00]

Cabell, James Branch. **Cream of the Jest.** NY: McBride; 1927. [2nd printing, $35.00]

Cabell, James Branch. **Domnei.** NY: McBride; 1930. [very good in dj, $95.00]

Cabell, James Branch. **Figures of Earth.** NY: McBride; 1925. [dj chipped, fine, $65.00] [4th printing, 1928, dj torn, $45.00]

Cabell, James Branch. **From the Hidden Way.** rev. ed. NY: McBride; 1924. [$40.00]

Cabell, James Branch. **Jurgen.** NY: McBride; 1927, c1919. [3rd printing, $20.00]

Cabell, James Branch. **The King Was in His Counting House.** 1st ed. NY, Toronto: Farrar & Rinehart; 1938. [sunned, dj torn, $65.00]

Cabell, James Branch. **The Music from Behind the Moon.** NY: Day; 1926. [$75.00]

Cabell, James Branch. **Preface to the Past.** NY: McBride; 1936. [$40.00]

Cabell, James Branch. **The Silver Stallion.** illustrated ed. NY: McBride; 1928. [$85.00]

Cabell, James Branch. **Smirt.** 1st ed. NY: McBride; 1934. [dj torn, $40.00]

Cabell, James Branch. **Something about Eve.** illustrated ed. NY: McBride; 1929. [dj torn, $60.00]

Cabell, James Branch. **There Were Two Pirates.** 1st ed. NY: Farrar, Straus; 1946. [very good in dj, $45.00]

Cabell, James Branch. **The White Robe.** NY: McBride; 1928. [$80.00]

Cabeza de Baca, Carlos. see, Baca, Carlos C. de.

Cabeza de Vaca, Alvar Nunez. see, Nunez Cabeza de Vaca, Alvar.

Cable, George Washington. **The Cavalier.** NY: Scribner; 1901. [1st state, inscribed, fine, $165.00]

Cable, George Washington. **The Grandissimes.** NY: Scribner; 1880. [$30.00]

Cable, George Washington. **Old Creole Days.** 1st ed. NY: Scribner; 1879. [$265.00] [1897 issue, inscribed, $175.00]

Cable, John Ray. **The Bank of the State of Missouri.** NY: Columbia UP; 1923. [$35.00]

Cabot, James Elliot. **Memoir of Ralph Waldo Emerson.** Boston, NY: Houghton Mifflin; 1887. 2 v. [$20.00]

Cackler, Christian. **Recollections of an Old Settler.** Kent, OH: Courier; 1904. [rebound, last leaf detached, $45.00]

Cadillac, Antoine de la Mothe. **The Western Country in the 17th Century.** Chicago: Lakeside; 1947. [$15.00]

Cadwallader, Sylvanus. **Three Years with Grant.** 1st ed. NY: Knopf; 1955. [$15.50]

Cadwell, Clara Gertrude. **De Barr's Friends, or, Number Seventeen.** Cleveland: Ohio Farmer; 1881. [$95.00]

Cady, Annie Cole. **The American Continent and Its Inhabitants before Its Discovery by Columbus.** Philadelphia: Gebbie; 1893, c1890. 2 v. [$365.00]

Caemmerer, Hans Paul. **Manual on the Origin and Development of Washington.** Washington: USGPO; 1939. [$30.00]

Caesar, Gene. **King of the Mountain Men.** 1st ed. NY: Dutton; 1961. [$35.00] [$20.00]

Cagle, Malcolm W. **The Sea War in Korea.** Annapolis: U.S. Naval Institute; 1957. [$45.00]

Cahoone, Sara S. **Sketches of Newport and Its Vicinity.** NY: Taylor; 1842. [binding crudely repaired, $35.00]

Caird, James. **Prairie Farming in America.** NY: Appleton; 1859. [dampstained, x-lib., $40.00]

Cairnes, John Elliott. **The Slave Power.** 2nd ed. NY: Carleton; 1862. [$35.00] [$50.00]

Cairns, Mary Lyons. **Grand Lake.** Denver: World; 1946. [worn dj, $30.00]

Calder, Isabel MacBeath. **Colonial Captivities, Marches and Journeys.** NY: Macmillan; 1935. [$20.00]

Calderon de la Barca, Madame. **Life in Mexico.** Boston: Little, Brown; 1843. 2 v. [$325.00]

Caldwell, James Fitz James. **History of a Brigade of South Carolinians.** Marietta, GA: Continental; 1951. [$30.00]

Caldwell, Martha Belle. **Annals of Shawnee Methodist Mission and Indian Manual Labor School.** Topeka, KS: Kansas State Hist. Soc.; 1939. [$15.00]

Caldwell, Robert Graham. **Red Hannah.** Philadelphia: U. of Pennsylvania; 1947. [$22.50]

Calhoun, Samuel H. **A Desperado in Arizona, 1858-1860.** Santa Fe: Stagecoach; 1964. [$55.00]

California Historical Society. **Drake's Plate of Brass.** San Francisco: California Hist. Soc.; 1937. [$15.00]

California: Its Past History: Its Present Position: Its Future Prospects. London: The Proprietors; 1850. [7 leaves in facs., 3 plates, $350.00]

Callahan, Charles Hilliard. **Washington, the Man and the Mason.** 2nd ed. Washington: National; 1913. [$17.50]

Callahan, James Morton. **American Relations in the Pacific and the Far East, 1784-1900.** Baltimore: Hopkins; 1901. [$35.00]

Callan, Louise. **Society of the Sacred Heart in North America.** 1st ed. London: Longmans, Green; 1937. [$35.00]

Callender, John. **An Historical Discourse on the Civil and Religious Affairs of the Colony of Rhode-Island and Providence Plantations.** Boston: Kneeland and Green; 1739. [marginal repairs, rebound, $550.00]

Callon, Milton W. **Las Vegas, New Mexico.** Las Vegas, NM: Daily Optic; 1962. [signed, $55.00]

Calver, William Louis. **History Written with Pick and Shovel.** NY: New York Hist. Soc.; 1950. [$30.00]

Calvin, Ross. **River of the Sun.** Albuquerque: U. of New Mexico; 1946. [$35.00]

Calvin, Ross. **Sky Determines.** rev. ed. Albuquerque: U. of New Mexico; 1948. [$25.00]

Cameron, Agnes Deans. **The New North.** NY: Appleton; 1912, c1909. [$65.00, Canadian]

Cameron, Rebecca. **Salted with Fire.** NY: Hale; 1872. [x-lib., frayed and stained, $25.00]

Cameron, William Evelyn. **Life and Character of Robert E. Lee.** [Petersburg?, VA: s.n.]; 1901. [$45.00]

Camp, William Martin. **San Francisco: Port of Gold.** Garden City: Doubleday; 1948. [$20.00]

Campa, Arthur Leon. **Treasure of the Sangre de Cristos.** 1st ed. Norman: U. of Oklahoma; 1963. [$35.00]

Campbell, Alexander. **The Destiny of Our Country.** Cannonsburg, PA: Philo Society; 1852. [$75.00]

Campbell, Archibald. **A Voyage round the World, from 1806 to 1812.** Edinburgh: Constable; 1816. [$850.00]

Campbell, Camilla. **Galleons Sail Westward.** Dallas: Mathis, Van Nort; 1939. [$45.00]

Campbell, Charles. **History of the Colony and Ancient Dominion of Virginia.** Philadelphia: Lippincott; 1860. [$60.00]

Campbell, Charles. **Introduction to the History of the Colony and Ancient Dominion of Virginia.** Richmond: Minor; 1847. [$80.00]

Campbell, Douglas. **The Puritan in Holland, England, and America.** NY: Harper; 1892. 2 v. [$35.00]

Campbell, Helen Jones. **Confederate Courier.** NY: St. Martin; 1964. [$22.50]

Campbell, James V. **Outlines of the Political History of Michigan.** Detroit: Schober; 1876. [inscribed, $65.00]

Campbell, John. **A Concise History of the Spanish America.** London: Stagg and Browne; 1741. [rebound, $500.00]

Campbell, John. **The Spanish Empire in America.** London: Cooper; 1747. [front cover detached, some water damage, $175.00]

Campbell, John Bayard Taylor. **Rose of Los Angeles.** Los Angeles: Tribune; 1929. [chipped dj, $20.00]

Campbell, Malcolm. **Malcolm Campbell, Sheriff.** Casper, WY: Wyomingana; 1932. [loose, worn, signed, $95.00]

Campbell, Maria Hull. **Revolutionary Services and Civil Life of General William Hull.** NY, Philadelphia: Appleton; 1848. [chipped, worn, $20.00]

Campbell, Marie. **Tales from the Cloud Walking Country.** Bloomington: Indiana UP; 1958. [some pencil notes, $15.00]

Campbell, Marjorie Wilkins. **The North West Company.** NY: St. Martin; 1957. [$25.00]

Campbell, Patrick. **Travels in the Interior Inhabited Parts of North America in the Years 1791 and 1792.** Toronto: Champlain Society; 1937. [$250.00]

Campbell, Thomas. **Gertrude of Wyoming.** London: Longman, etc.; 1809. [$110.00] [$250.00]

Campbell, Thomas Elliott. **Colonial Caroline.** Richmond: Dietz; 1954. [mildewed, $35.00]

Campbell, Thomas H. **History of the Cumberland Presbyterian Church in Texas.** Nashville: Cumberland Presbyterian; 1936. [$55.00]

Campbell, Thomas Jefferson. **The Upper Tennessee.** Chattanooga: Campbell; 1932. [$45.00] [signed, $50.00]

Campbell, Thomas Joseph. **The Jesuits, 1534-1921.** NY: Encyclopedia; 1921. 2 v. [$37.50]

Campbell, Tom W. **Two Fighters and Two Fines.** Little Rock: Pioneer; 1941. [$45.00]

Campbell, William Carey. **A Colorado Colonel and Other Sketches.** Topeka: Crane; 1901. [$20.00]

Campbell, William W. **Border Warfare of New York, during the Revolution.** NY: Baker & Scribner; 1849. [$85.00] [$75.00]

Campion, J. S. **On the Frontier.** 2nd ed. London: Chapman & Hall; 1878. [$100.00]

Canby, Henry Seidel. **Alma Mater.** NY: Farrar & Rinehart; 1936. [$17.50]

Canby, Henry Seidel. **The Brandywine.** NY, Toronto: Farrar & Rinehart; 1941. [$20.00]

Canfield, Chauncey L. **City of Six.** Chicago: McClurg; 1910. [$30.00]

Canfield, Chauncey L. **Diary of a Forty-Niner.** Stanford: Delkin; 1947. [$12.50]

Canfield, Mary Grace. **Lafayette in Vermont.** Rochester, NY: Canfield & Tack; 1934. [wraps torn, $15.00]

Cannon, Corodon S. **Cannon's Universal Proof of Money Making.** 2nd ed. Battle Creek, MI: Cannon; 1881. [$65.00]

Cannon, Frank Jenne. **Brigham Young and His Mormon Empire.** NY: Revell; 1913. [$50.00]

Cannon, George Q. **My First Mission.** Salt Lake City: Juvenile Instructor Office; 1879. [$125.00]

Canton, Frank M. **Frontier Trails.** 1st ed. Boston, NY: Houghton Mifflin; 1930. [$50.00] [$60.00]

Cantwell, Robert. **Laugh and Lie Down.** NY: Farrar & Rinehart; 1931. [$50.00]

Cantwell, Robert. **Nathaniel Hawthorne, the American Years.** NY: Rinehart; 1948. [$15.00]

Capen, Nahum. **The Republic of the United States of America.** NY, Philadelphia: Appleton; 1848. [slight wear and foxing, $150.00]

Capers, Walter Branham. **The Soldier-Bishop, Ellison Capers.** NY: Neale; 1912. [$115.00]

Capote, Truman. **In Cold Blood.** 1st ed. NY: Random; 1965. [$15.00]

Capron, Elisha Smith. **History of California from Its Discovery to the Present Time.** Boston; Cleveland: Jewett; Jewett, Proctor and Worthington; 1854. [$150.00]

Cardell, William S. **Story of Jack Halyard.** 5th ed. Philadelphia: Hunt; 1825. [$35.00]

Carey, Charles Henry. **History of Oregon.** Chicago, Portland: Pioneer Historical Publishing; 1922. [inscribed, $150.00]

Carey, Fred. **Mayor Jim.** Omaha, NE: Omaha Printing; 1930. [spine faded, $15.00]

Carey, Mathew. **Addresses of the Philadelphia Society for the Promotion of National Industry.** 4th ed. Philadelphia: Carey; 1819. [disbound, $75.00]

Carey, Mathew. **Essays on Political Economy.** 1st ed. Philadelphia: Carey & Lea; 1822. [some stains in text, $85.00]

Carey, Mathew. **Short Account of the Malignant Fever Lately Prevalent in Philadelphia.** 4th ed. Philadelphia: The Author; 1794. [x-lib., $150.00]

Carey, Thomas. **History of the Pirates.** Hartford: Benton; 1829. [$90.00]

Carleton, James Henry. **Battle of Buena Vista.** NY: Harper; 1848. [$185.00] [$200.00]

Carlisle, William L. **Bill Carlisle, Lone Bandit.** deluxe ed. Pasadena: Trail's End; 1946. [hinges loose, $80.00] [2nd ed., 1950, $30.00]

Carlton, Ambrose B. **The Wonderlands of the Wild West.** [s.l.: s.n.]; 1891. [x-lib., $175.00]

Carlton, Robert. **The New Purchase.** see, Hall, Baynard Rush.

Carmer, Carl Lamson. **Listen for a Lonesome Drum.** NY: Farrar & Rinehart; 1936. [$25.00]

Carmer, Carl Lamson. **Stars Fell on Alabama.** NY: Farrar & Rinehart; 1934. [$10.00]

Carmer, Carl Lamson. **The Susquehanna.** NY: Rinehart; 1955. [signed, $35.00]

Carmichael, A. C. (Mrs.). **Domestic Manners and Social Condition of the White, Coloured, and Negro Population of the West Indies.** 2nd ed. London: Whittaker; 1834. 2 v. [$285.00]

Carnac, Turner. **Facts and Arguments Respecting the Great Utility of an Extensive Plan of Inland Navigation in America.** Philadelphia: Duane; 1805. [rebound, $275.00]

Carnahan, James. **Dangers of a College Life.** Princeton, NJ: Robinson; 1843. [$40.00]

Carnegie, Andrew. **Autobiography of.** Boston, NY: Houghton Mifflin; 1920. [$17.50]

Carnegie Institute. **Memorial of the Celebration of the Carnegie Institute at Pittsburgh, Pa., April 11, 12, 13, 1907.** Pittsburgh: Trustees; 1907. [$17.50]

Carpenter, Edmund Janes. **America in Hawaii.** Boston: Small, Maynard; 1899. [x-lib., $20.00]

Carpenter, Edna Turley. **Tales from the Manchaca Hills.** New Orleans: Hauser; 1960. [presentation from editor, mildewed, dj chipped, $15.00]

Carpenter, Francis Bicknell. **Six Months at the White House with Abraham Lincoln.** NY: Hurd and Houghton; 1866. [$45.00] [2nd printing?, $75.00]

Carpenter, George N. **History of the Eighth Regiment Vermont Volunteers, 1861-1865.** Boston: Deland & Barta; 1886. [$100.00]

Carpenter, Hugh. **King's Mountain.** Knoxville: The Author; 1936. [$75.00]

Carpenter, Stephen Cullen. **Memoirs of the Hon. Thomas Jefferson.** NY: Printed for the Purchasers; 1809. 2 v. [$685.00]

Carr, Albert H. Z. **The World and William Walker.** 1st ed. NY: Harper & Row; 1963. [$10.00]

Carr, Ezra Slocum. **Patrons of Husbandry on the Pacific Coast.** San Francisco: Bancroft; 1875. [$125.00]

Carr, Harry. **The West Is Still Wild.** NY: Houghton; 1932. [$25.00]

Carr, John. **Pioneer Days in California.** Eureka, CA: Times; 1891. [x-lib., $100.00]

Carr, William Guy. **Checkmate in the North.** Toronto: Macmillan; 1944. [$20.00]

Carr, William H. A. **The Du Ponts of Delaware.** NY: Dodd, Mead; 1964. [$10.00]

Carraway, Gertrude Sprague. **Carolina Crusaders.** New Bern: Dunn; 1941. [slightly stained and sunned, $8.50]

Carrier, A. H. **Monument to the Memory of Henry Clay.** Philadelphia: Rulison; 1859. [$100.00]

Carriere, Joseph Medard. **Tales from the French Folk-Lore of Missouri.** Evanston: Northwestern UP; 1937. [$25.00]

Carrighar, Sally. **Moonlight at Midday.** NY: Knopf; 1958. [$8.00]

Carrighar, Sally. **One Day at Teton Marsh.** 1st ed. NY: Knopf; 1947. [$12.50]

Carrighar, Sally. **One Day on Beetle Rock.** NY: Knopf; 1945. [$20.00]

Carrington, Frances (Courtney). **My Army Life and the Fort Phil Kearney Massacre.** 2nd ed. Philadelphia: Lippincott; 1911. [x-lib., rear hinge cracked, $35.00]

Carrington, Henry Beebee. **Indian Question.** Boston: Whiting; 1884. [$300.00] [Boston, 1909, $125.00]

Carrington, Margaret Irvin. **Absaraka (Ab-Sa-Ra-Ka), Home of the Crows.** Chicago: Donnelley; 1950. [$27.00]

Carrington, Wirt Johnson. **History of Halifax County.** Richmond, VA: Appeals; 1924. [$40.00]

Carroll, Henry King. **Francis Asbury in the Making of American Methodism.** NY, Cincinnati: Methodist Book Concern; 1923. [$20.00]

Carroll, Wesley Philemon. **Moss Agates.** Cheyenne, WY: Daily Sun; 1890. [$150.00]

Carruthers, Olive. **Lincoln's Other Mary.** Chicago, NY: Ziff-Davis; 1946. [$16.50]

Carson, Ann Baker. **The Memoirs of the Celebrated and Beautiful Mrs. Ann Carson.** 2nd ed. Philadelphia, NY: [s.n.]; 1838. 2 v. in 1. [$75.00]

Carson, Hampton L. **The Supreme Court of the United States.** Philadelphia: Huber; 1891-92. 2 v. [vol. 1 only, $195.00]

Carson, Kit. **Kit Carson's Autobiography.** Chicago: Donnelley; 1935. [$25.00]

Carson, Kit. **Kit Carson's Own Story of His Life.** Taos, NM: [s.n.]; 1926. [$75.00] [1955 Memorial Foundation ed., signed by editor, $75.00]

Carson, Russell M. L. **Peaks and People of the Adirondacks.** Garden City: Doubleday, Page; 1927. [$37.50]

Carson, William Edward. **Historic Shrines of Virginia.** Richmond: Commission on Conservation and Development; 1934. [$15.00]

Carter, Everett. **Howells and the Age of Realism.** 1st ed. Philadelphia: Lippincott; 1954. [$15.00]

Carter, George Calvin. **Walter Kittredge, Minstrel of the Merrimack.** Manchester, NH: [s.n.]; 1953. [signed, $17.50]

Carter, Harvey Lewis. **Dear Old Kit.** 1st ed. Norman: U. of Oklahoma; 1968. [dj stained, $45.00]

Carter, Herbert Dyson. **Sea of Destiny.** NY: Greenberg; 1940. [$15.00, Canadian]

Carter, Hodding. **John Law Wasn't So Wrong.** Baton Rouge: Esso Standard Oil; 1952. [$20.00]

Carter, Robert G. see, Charlton, John B.

Carter, Robert Goldthwaite. **On the Border with Mackenzie.** NY: Antiquarian; 1961. [$100.00]

Carter, Susannah. **The Frugal Housewife.** Philadelphia: Carey; 1802. [$500.00]

Carter, William Harding. **Horses, Saddles and Bridles.** Leavenworth, KS: Ketcheson & Reeves; 1895. [$185.00]

Carteret, John Dunloe. **A Fortune Hunter.** Cincinnati: The Author; 1888. [$75.00]

Cartwright, W. C. **Gustave Bergenroth.** Edinburgh: Edmonston and Douglas; 1870. [$200.00]

Caruso, John Anthony. **The Appalachian Frontier.** 1st ed. Indianapolis: Bobbs-Merrill; 1959. [$17.50] [$23.00]

Caruso, John Anthony. **The Great Lakes Frontier.** 1st ed. Indianapolis: Bobbs-Merrill; 1961. [x-lib., $17.50]

Caruso, John Anthony. **The Mississippi Valley Frontier.** Indianapolis: Bobbs-Merrill; 1966. [$25.00]

Caruso, John Anthony. **Southern Frontier.** Indianapolis: Bobbs-Merrill; 1963. [x-lib., $15.00]

Caruthers, William. **Loafing along Death Valley Trails.** Palm Desert, CA: Desert Magazine; 1951. [$17.50]

Carvalho, Solomon Nunes. **Incidents of Travel and Adventure in the Far West.** NY: Derby & Jackson; 1857. [$100.00] [$110.00] [$175.00]

Carver, Hartwell. **Memorial for a Private Charter. . . to Build a Railroad from Some Point on the Mississippi or Missouri Rivers, or from Lake Michigan to the Pacific Ocean.** Washington: Gideon; 1849. [x-lib., $185.00]

Carver, Jonathan. **Three Years Travels throughout the Interior Parts of North-America.** Portsmouth, NH: Peirce; 1794. [rebacked, $250.00] [1797 Boston reprint, $150.00]

Casey, Charles. **Two Years on the Farm of Uncle Sam.** London: Bentley; 1852. [$125.00]

Casey, Robert Joseph. **The Black Hills and Their Incredible Characters.** 1st ed. Indianapolis: Bobbs-Merrill; 1949. [guide in pocket, dj chipped, $40.00] [lacks guide?, $25.00]

Casey, Robert Joseph. **Give the Man Room; The Story of Gutzon Borglum.** 1st ed. Indianapolis: Bobbs-Merrill; 1952. [$20.00]

Casey, Robert Joseph. **The Texas Border and Some Borderliners.** 1st ed. Indianapolis: Bobbs-Merrill; 1950. [$45.00]

Cash, W. T. **Florida Becomes a State.** see, Florida State Library.

Cash, Wilbur Joseph. **The Mind of the South.** NY: Knopf; 1941. [$20.00]

Caspipina, T. see, Duche, Jacob.

Casson, Henry. **"Uncle Jerry."** Madison, WI: Hill; 1895. [back cover nicked, $20.00] [$22.50]

Castaneda, Carlos Eduardo. **Mexican Side of the Texas Revolution, 1836.** Dallas: Turner; 1928. [$200.00]

Castel, Albert E. **A Frontier State at War: Kansas, 1861-1865.** Ithaca, NY: Cornell UP; 1958. [$30.00]

Castel, Albert E. **William Clarke Quantrill.** NY: Fell; 1962. [$25.00]

Castellane, Boni marquis de. **How I Discovered America.** NY: Knopf; 1924. [$20.00]

Castetter, Edward Franklin. **Yuman Indian Agriculture.** Albuquerque: U. of New Mexico; 1951. [$30.00]

Caswell, John Edwards. **Arctic Frontiers.** Norman: U. of Oklahoma; 1956. [$25.00]

Caswell, Mary S. Deering. **Address in Opposition to Woman Suffrage.** Boston: Massachusetts Association Opposed to the Further Extension of Suffrage to Women; [1913?]. [$20.00]

Cate, Wirt Armistead. **Lucius Q.C. Lamar.** Chapel Hill: U. of North Carolina; 1935. [$25.00]

Cate, Wirt Armistead. **Two Soldiers.** Chapel Hill: U. of North Carolina; 1938. [$45.00]

Cather, Willa. **December Night.** NY: Knopf; 1933. [dj chipped, $40.00] [$50.00]

Cather, Willa. **Early Stories.** NY: Dodd, Mead; 1957. [$20.00]

Cather, Willa. **O Pioneers!** Boston, NY: Houghton Mifflin; 1913. [$100.00]

Cather, Willa. **Shadows on the Rock.** 1st ed. NY: Knopf; 1931. [dj chipped and repaired, $25.00] [dj frayed, $50.00]

Catholic Church Pope (1492-1503: Alexander VI). **The Earliest Diplomatic Documents on America; the Papal Bulls of 1493 and the Treaty of Tordesillas.** Berlin: Gottschalk; 1927. [$150.00]

Catlin, George. **Catalogue of Catlin's Indian Gallery of Portraits, Landscapes, Manners and Customs, Costumes.** NY: Piercy & Reed; 1838. [$450.00]

Catlin, George. **Catlin's Notes of Eight Years' Travels and Residence in Europe with His North American Indian Collection.** 3rd ed. London: The Author; 1848. 2 v. [$350.00]

Catlin, George. **Illustrations of the Manners, Customs and Condition of the North American Indians.** 5th ed. London: Bohn; 1845. [$550.00] [9th ed., 1857, $350.00]

Catlin, George. **Letters and Notes on the Manners, Customs, and Conditions of the North American Indians.** NY: Wiley and Putnam; 1841. 2 v. [$1200.00] [London, 1841, $950.00] [4th ed., London, 1844, $850.00] [1892 reprint, x-lib., $200.00]

Catlin, George. **North American Indians.** Edinburgh: Grant; 1903. 2 v. [$275.00] [Philadelphia, 1913, color plates, $600.00]

Catlin, George. **O-Kee-Pa.** Philadelphia: Lippincott; 1867. [$4500.00]

Caton, John Dean. **Antelope and Deer of America.** NY; Boston: Hurd and Houghton; Houghton; 1877. [$150.00] [Forest and Stream reprint, 1877, $75.00]

Caton, John Dean. **Last of the Illinois: And a Sketch of the Pottawatomies.** Chicago: Rand, McNally; 1870. [$250.00]

Catton, Bruce. **Army of the Potomac.** Garden City: Doubleday; 1962. 3 v. [$25.00]

Catton, Bruce. **Centennial History of the Civil War.** 1st ed. Garden City: Doubleday; 1961-65. 3 v. [$30.00]

Catton, Bruce. **Stillness at Appomattox.** NY: Washington Square; 1953. [$14.50]

Caughey, John Walton. **California.** NY: Prentice-Hall; 1940. [$15.00]

Caughey, John Walton. **McGillivray of the Creeks.** 1st ed. Norman: U. of Oklahoma; 1938. [$75.00] [1959 printing, $25.00]

Caughey, John Walton. **Their Majesties the Mob.** Chicago: U. of Chicago; 1960. [$15.00]

Cauthorn, Henry Sullivan. **History of the City of Vincennes, Indiana from 1702 to 1901.** [s.l.]: Cauthorn; 1902. [$35.00]

Caverly, Robert Boodey. **Heroism of Hannah Duston.** Boston: Russell; 1874. [lacks frontis and endpapers, $35.00]

Cayley, Arthur. **Life of Sir Walter Ralegh, Knt.** 2nd ed. London: Cadell and Davies; 1806. 2 v. [x-lib., spines badly chipped, $65.00]

Cazenove, Theophile. **Cazenove Journal, 1794.** Haverford: Pennsylvania History Press; 1922. [$40.00]

Cazneau, Jane Maria. **Eagle Pass.** NY: Putnam; 1852. [$250.00]

Cendrars, Blaise. **Sutter's Gold.** NY, London: Harper; 1926. [$25.00]

Cerf, Bennett. **Shake Well before Using.** NY: Simon and Schuster; 1948. [$19.50]

Chadsey, Charles E. **The Struggle between President Johnson and Congress over Reconstruction.** NY: Columbia UP; 1896. [$35.00]

Chadwick, French Ensor. **Graves Papers and Other Documents.** NY: Naval History Society; 1916. [$40.00]

Chaffin, Lorah B. **Sons of the West.** Caldwell, ID: Caxton; 1941. [$85.00]

Chalfant, Willie Arthur. **Outposts of Civilization.** Boston: Christopher; 1928. [covers soiled, $60.00]

Chalkley, Thomas. **A Journal, or Historical Account, of the Life, Travels, and Christian Experiences, of That Faithful Servant of Jesus Christ.** Philadelphia: Chattin; 1754. [$140.00]

Chalmers, George. **Political Annals of the Present United Colonies from Their Settlement to the Peace of 1763.** London: The Author; 1780. [rebacked, $785.00]

Chalmers, Harvey. **Joseph Brant: Mohawk.** East Lansing: Michigan State UP; 1955. [$15.00]

Chamberlain, Mellen. **Documentary History of Chelsea.** Boston: Massachusetts Historical Society; 1908. 2 v. [$37.50]

Chamberlain, Mellen. **John Adams, the Statesman of the American Revolution.** Boston: Webster Society; 1884. [$35.00]

Chamberlain, Newell D. **The Call of Gold: True Tales on the Gold Road to Yosemite.** Mariposa, CA: Gazette Press; 1936. [$50.00]

Chamberlain, Samuel E. **My Confession.** NY: Harper; 1956. [$15.00]

Chambers, Frank Pentland. **The War behind the War, 1914-1918.** NY: Harcourt, Brace; 1939. [$15.00]

Chambers, John. **Autobiography of.** Iowa City: State Historical Society; 1908. [$20.00]

Chambers, John Whiteclay. **Draftees or Volunteers.** NY: Garland; 1975. [$25.00]

Chambers, Julius. **The Mississippi River and Its Wonderful Valley.** NY, London: Putnam; 1910. [$75.00]

Chambers, Lenoir. **Stonewall Jackson.** NY: Morrow; 1959. 2 v. [slipcase worn, $75.00]

Chambers, William. **Things As They Are in America.** London, Edinburgh: Chambers; 1854. [x-lib., $45.00]

Chambers, William Nisbet. **Old Bullion Benton.** 1st ed. Boston: Little, Brown; 1956. [worn dj, $20.00]

Chambrun, Charles Adolphe de Pineton marquis de. **Impressions of Lincoln and the Civil War.** NY: Random; 1952. [$16.00]

Champion, Salmon Fred. **From Southern California to Casco Bay.** San Bernardino: San Bernardino Pub. Co.; 1930. [$25.00]

Chandler, Alfred Dupont. **Pierre S. Du Pont and the Making of the Modern Corporation.** NY: Harper & Row; 1971. [$20.00]

Chandler, Elizabeth Margaret. **The Poetical Works of.** Philadelphia: Howell; 1836. [$85.00]

Chandler, Julian Alvin Carroll. **Colonial Virginia.** Richmond: Times-Dispatch; 1907. [$35.00]

Chandler, Julian Alvin Carroll. **The South in the Building of the Nation.** Richmond: Southern Historical Publication Society; 1909-1913. 13 v. [$300.00]

Chandless, William. **A Visit to Salt Lake.** London: Smith, Elder; 1857. [$400.00]

Chaney, George Leonard. **"Alo'ha!" A Hawaiian Salutation.** Boston: Roberts; 1880, c1879. [$25.00]

Channing, Edward. **The Story of the Great Lakes.** NY: Macmillan; 1909. [$10.00]

Channing, William Ellery. **A Letter to the Hon. Henry Clay, on the Annexation of Texas to the United States.** 3rd ed. Boston: Munroe; 1837. [lacks wraps, water stained, $50.00]

Channing, William Ellery. **Slavery.** 1st ed. Boston: Munroe; 1835. [$50.00]

Channing, William Ellery. **Thoughts on the Evils of a Spirit of Conquest, and on Slavery.** London: Green; 1837. [$125.00]

Chapelle, Georgette Louise Meyer. **What's a Woman Doing Here?** NY: Morrow; 1962, c1961. [$20.00]

Chapelle, Howard Irving. **American Sailing Craft.** NY: Kennedy; 1936. [spine faded, $27.50]

Chapelle, Howard Irving. **The History of American Sailing Ships.** NY: Norton; 1935. [$50.00] [Bonanza reprint, $15.00]

Chapin, Bela. **Poets of New Hampshire.** Claremont, NH: Adams; 1883. [$25.00]

Chapin, Frederick H. **Land of the Cliff-Dwellers.** Boston: Appalachian Mountain Club; 1892. [$85.00]

Chapin, Frederick H. **Mountaineering in Colorado.** Boston: Appalachian Mountain Club; 1889. [inscribed, $350.00]

Chapin, Lon F. **Thirty Years in Pasadena.** Los Angeles: Southwest; 1929. [$40.00]

Chapin, Louis N. **Brief History of the Thirty-Fourth Regiment, N. Y. S. V.** NY: [s.n.; 1903?]. [$100.00]

Chapman, Arthur. **Pony Express.** NY, London: Putnam; 1932. [$25.00] [$75.00]

Chapman, Charles. **The Ocean Waves.** London: Berridge; 1875. [presentation, $135.00]

Chapman, Charles Edward. **Colonial Hispanic America.** NY: Macmillan; 1933. [$10.00]

Chapman, Frederick Spencer. **Northern Lights.** London: Chatto and Windus; 1932. [2nd impression, $20.00, Canadian]

Chapman, Isaac A. **Sketch of the History of Wyoming.** Wilkesbarre, PA: Lewis; 1830. [$235.00] [binding chipped, covers detached, spine missing, $35.00]

Chapman, John Jay. **Treason & Death of Benedict Arnold.** 1st ed. NY: Moffat, Yard; 1910. [$25.00]

Chapman, John Jay. **William Lloyd Garrison.** 1st ed. NY: Moffat, Yard; 1913. [$20.00]

Chapman, Victor Emmanuel. **Victor Chapman's Letters from France.** 1st ed. NY: Macmillan; 1917. [$37.50]

Chapman Publishing Company. **Portrait and Biographical Record of Western Oregon.** Chicago: Chapman; 1904. [outer hinges partly cracked, $100.00]

Chappell, Fred. **The Inkling.** 1st ed. NY: Harcourt, Brace & World; 1965. [silverfished, dj scuffed, $25.00]

Chapple, Joe Mitchell. **Warren G. Harding.** Boston: Chapple; 1920. [$32.50]

Chard, Thomas S. **California Sketches.** Chicago: [s.n.]; 1888. [inscribed, $75.00]

Charles, Tom (Mrs.). **More Tales of the Tularosa.** Alamogordo, NM: Bennett; 1961. [$45.00]

Charles, Tom (Mrs.). **Tales of Tularosa.** rev. ed. Alamogordo, NM: [s.n.]; 1954. [inscribed, $65.00]

Charlevoix, Pierre Francois Xavier de. **The History of Paraguay.** Dublin: Wilson, Saunders; 1769. 2 v. [hinges partially split, $340.00] [one cover detached, $200.00] [1769 London imprint, $200.00]

Charlevoix, Pierre Francois Xavier de. **Journal of a Voyage to North America.** Chicago: Caxton Club; 1923. 2 v. [$400.00]

Charlot, Jean. **Charlot Murals in Georgia.** Athens: U. of Georgia; 1945. [$45.00]

Charlot, Jean. **Choris and Kamehameha.** Honolulu: Bishop Museum; 1958. [$50.00].

Charlton, John B. **The Old Sergeant's Story.** NY: Hitchcock; 1926. [$150.00]

Charnay, Desire. **Ancient Cities of the New World.** London: Chapman and Hall; 1887. [$150.00]

Charnwood, Godfrey Rathbone Benson. **Abraham Lincoln.** London: Constable; 1916. [$25.00]

Charnwood, Godfrey Rathbone Benson. **Theodore Roosevelt.** Boston: Atlantic Monthly; 1923. [$15.00]

Chase, Charles Monroe. **Editor's Run in New Mexico and Colorado.** Montpelier, VT: Argus and Patriot; 1882. [wraps chipped and soiled, $150.00]

Chase, Ezra B. **Teachings of Patriots and Statesmen.** Philadelphia: Bradley; 1860. [$65.00]

Chase, Francis. **Gathered Sketches from the Early History of New Hampshire and Vermont .** Claremont, NH: Tracy, Kenney; 1856. [$100.00]

Chase, Joseph Smeaton. **California Coast Trails.** Boston, NY: Houghton Mifflin; 1913. [$35.00]

Chase, Joseph Smeaton. **Yosemite Trails.** NY: Houghton Mifflin; 1911. [$40.00]

Chase, Mary Ellen. **Jonathan Fisher.** NY: Macmillan; 1948. [$12.50]

Chase, William Henry. **Pioneers of Alaska.** Kansas City, MO: Burton; 1951. [$19.00]

Chasles, Philarete. **Anglo-American Literature and Manners.** NY: Scribner; 1852. [$90.00]

Chastellux, Francois Jean. **Travels in North-America, in the Years 1780, 1781, and 1782.** 2nd ed. London: Robinson; 1787. 2 v. [$700.00] [$600.00] [1787 Dublin printing, $550.00]

Chateaubriand, Francois-Rene vicomte de. **The Interesting History of Atala, the Beautiful Indian of the Mississippi.** NY: Oram and Mott; 1818. [scuffed, front flyleaf missing, $50.00]

Chateaubriand, Francois-Rene vicomte de. **Recollections of Italy, England and America.** Philadelphia: Carey; 1816. [$150.00] [$100.00]

Chateaubriand, Francois-Rene vicomte de. **Travels in America and Italy.** London: Colburn; 1828. 2 v. [$275.00]

Chatterton, Fenimore. **Yesterday's Wyoming.** Aurora, CO: Powder River; 1957. [$35.00]

Chavez, Angelico. **From an Altar Screen; El Retablo.** NY: Farrar, Straus and Cudahy; 1957. [mended dj, $35.00]

Chavez, Angelico. **Origins of New Mexico Families in the Spanish Colonial Period.** Santa Fe: Historical Society of New Mexico; 1954. [$100.00]

Cheetham, James. **A Narrative of the Suppression by Col. Burr of the History of the Administration of John Adams.** NY: Denniston and Cheetham; 1802. [$65.00]

Cheetham, James. **View of the Political Conduct of Aaron Burr.** NY: Denniston & Cheetham; 1802. [$65.00]

Cheever, George Barrell. **The American Common-Place Book of Poetry.** Boston: Carter, Hendee; 1831. [$40.00]

Chenery, William Eastman. **Home Entertaining.** Boston: Lothrop, Lee & Shepard; 1912. [$16.50]

Chennault, Claire Lee. **Way of a Fighter.** NY: Putnam; 1949. [torn dj, $12.50]

Cherry, Peter Peterson. **The Western Reserve and Early Ohio.** Akron: Fouse; 1921. [$35.00]

Cherry, Thomas Crittenden. **Kentucky; the Pioneer State of the West.** Boston, NY: Heath; 1935. [$20.00]

Cheseldine, Raymond Minshall. **Ohio in the Rainbow.** Columbus: Heer; 1924. [$30.00]

Cheshire, Joseph Blount. **The Church in the Confederate States.** NY: Longmans, Green; 1912. [silverfished, presentation, $35.00]

Chesnut, Mary Boykin Miller. **Diary from Dixie.** NY: Appleton; 1905. [$85.00] [$50.00] [1949 Houghton ed., $35.00; $25.00]

Chesnutt, Charles Waddell. **The Conjure Woman.** Boston: Houghton Mifflin; 1900, c1899. [2nd printing, bumped, rubbed, sunned, $60.00]

Chester, Alden. **Courts and Lawyers of New York.** NY, Chicago: American Hist. Soc.; 1925. 3 v. [$125.00]

Chester, Samuel Hall. **Pioneer Days in Arkansas.** Richmond: Presbyterian Committee of Publication; 1927. [$65.00]

Chesterton, George Laval. **Narrative of Proceedings in Venezuela.** London: Arch; 1820. [spine replaced, lacks map, $85.00]

Chevalier, Michel. **Lettres sur l'Amerique du Nord.** 4th ed. Bruxelles: Wouters; 1844. 2 v. in 1. [worn, lacks map, $125.00]

Chevalier, Michel. **Mexico, Ancient and Modern.** London: Maxwell; 1864. [lacks map, $110.00]

Chevalier, Michel. **Society, Manners and Politics in the United States.** Boston: Weeks, Jordan; 1839. [$50.00] [$150.00]

Chevigny, Hector. **Lord of Alaska.** NY: Viking; 1942. [$10.00]

Chevigny, Hector. **Lost Empire.** NY: Macmillan; 1937. [inscribed, $12.50]

Cheyney, Edward Potts. **History of the University of Pennsylvania.** Philadelphia: U. of Pennsylvania; 1940. [$15.00]

Chicago and Its Environs: A Complete Guide to the City and the World's Fair. Columbian ed. Chicago: Kenkel; 1893. [$35.00]

Chicago Board of Local Improvements. **Sixteen-Year Record of Achievement. 1915-1931.** Chicago: Buckley, Dement; 1931. [$100.00]

Chicago Record's Book for Gold Seekers. Chicago: Chicago Record; 1897. [front cover rubbed, $45.00]

Chickering, Jesse. **Immigration into the United States.** Boston: Little and Brown; 1848. [$85.00]

Child, Lydia Maria. **Appeal in Favor of That Class of Americans Called Africans.** Boston: Allen and Ticknor; 1833. [some wear to spine, $200.00] [$150.00]

Child, Lydia Maria. **The Family Nurse.** Boston: Hendee; 1837. [hinge cracked, covers rubbed, $75.00]

Child, Lydia Maria. **Letters from New York.** London: Bentley; 1843. [$45.00]

Child, Theodore. **Spanish-American Republics.** NY: Harper; 1891. [$45.00]

Childs, Herbert. **El Jimmy, Outlaw of Patagonia.** London: Hutchinson; 1936. [$25.00]

Chinard, Gilbert. **Thomas Jefferson, the Apostle of Americanism.** Boston: Little, Brown; 1929. [$30.00]

Chinard, Gilbert. **Treaties of 1778.** see, France.

Chipman, Daniel. **Memoir of Thomas Chittenden.** Middlebury, VT: The Author; 1849. [$40.00]

Chipman, Norton Parker. **The Tragedy of Andersonville.** 2nd ed. [Sacramento?, CA: s.n.; 191-?]. [$35.00]

Chisholm, Adam Stuart Muir. **The Independence of Chile.** Boston: Sherman, French; 1911. [$20.00]

Chittenden, Hiram Martin. **The American Fur Trade of the Far West.** NY: Harper; 1902. 3 v. [near mint, $750.00] [$675.00] [1935 2 vol. Press of the Pioneers ed., $100.00]

Chittenden, Hiram Martin. **History of Early Steamboat Navigation on the Missouri River.** NY: Harper; 1903. 2 v. [$300.00]

Chittenden, Hiram Martin. **The Yellowstone National Park.** Cincinnati: Stewart & Kidd; 1920. [$10.00] [1924 rev. Haynes ed., $35.00]

Chittenden, L. E. **Capture of Ticonderoga.** Rutland: Tuttle; 1872. [$30.00] [$30.00] [$20.00]

Chittenden, L. E. **Personal Reminiscences.** NY: Richmond, Croscup; 1893. [x-lib., $20.00] [$35.00] [x-lib., $12.50] [$27.50]

Chittick, Victor Lovitt Oakes. **Ringed-Tailed Roarers.** Caldwell, ID: Caxton; 1943, c1941. [$15.00]

Chivers, T. H. **Nacoochee.** NY: Dean; 1837. [$425.00]

Choate, Joseph Hodges. **Life of.** London: Constable; 1920. 2 v. [$60.00]

Chreitzberg, Abel McKee. **Early Methodism in the Carolinas.** Nashville: Methodist Episcopal Church, South; 1897. [silverfished and sunned, $85.00]

Christian, Edgar Vernon. **Unflinching.** NY, London: Funk & Wagnalls; 1938. [$14.00]

Christie, Robert A. **Empire in Wood.** Ithaca: Cornell; 1956. [$27.50]

Christman, Henry. **Tin Horns and Calico.** NY: Holt; 1945. [$15.00]

Church, Benjamin. **History of King Philip's War.** Boston: Wiggin; 1865. 2 v. [$225.00]

Church, Benjamin. **History of Philip's War.** 2nd ed. Boston: Frost; 1827. [hinges weak, $45.00]

Church, Benjamin. **History of the Great Indian War of 1675 and 1676.** rev. ed. NY: Dayton; 1860. [$40.00]

Church, George Earl. **Aborigines of South America.** London: Chapman and Hall; 1912. [$50.00]

Church, Herbert E. **Making a Start in Canada.** London: Seeley; 1889. [$110.00, Canadian]

Church, Samuel Harden. **A Short History of Pittsburgh: 1758-1908.** NY: De Vinne; 1908. [$15.00] [$12.50]

Church, Thomas. see, Church, Benjamin.

Church, William Conant. **Life of John Ericsson.** NY: Scribner; 1906-07. 2 v. [$45.00]

Church, William Conant. **Ulysses S. Grant and the Period of National Preservation and Reconstruction.** Garden City, NY: Garden City Pub. Co.; 1926, c1897. [$12.50]

Cieza de Leon, Pedro de. **The Incas.** 1st ed. Norman: U. of Oklahoma; 1959. [$15.00]

Cisco, Jay Guy. **Historic Sumner County, Tennessee.** Nashville: Folk-Keelin; 1909. [$65.00]

Cist, Charles. **Cincinnati in 1841.** Cincinnati: The Author; 1841. [$90.00]

Cist, Henry Martyn. **Army of the Cumberland.** NY: Scribner; 1882. [$30.00]

Clap, Thomas. **Annals or History of Yale-College.** New Haven: Hotchkiss; 1766. [$600.00]

Clapp, Theodore. **Autobiographical Sketches and Recollections.** Boston: Phillips, Sampson; 1857. [$200.00]

Clapper, Olive Ewing. **Washington Tapestry.** 1st ed. NY; London: Whittlesey; McGraw-Hill; 1946. [dj chipped, $20.00]

Clark, Allen Culling. **Abraham Lincoln in the National Capital.** Washington: Roberts; 1925. [$30.00]

Clark, Champ. **My Quarter Century of American Politics.** NY, London: Harper; 1920. 2 v. [$20.00]

Clark, Charles L. **Lockstep and Corridor.** Cincinnati: U. of Cincinnati; 1927. [x-lib., $12.50]

Clark, Charles M. **A Trip to Pike's Peak and Notes by the Way.** Chicago: Rounds; 1861. [$800.00] [$925.00]

Clark, Daniel. **Proofs of the Corruption of Gen. James Wilkinson and of His Connexion with Aaron Burr.** Philadelphia: Hall, Pierie; 1809. [$750.00]

Clark, Edna Maria. **Ohio Art and Artists.** Richmond: Garrett and Massie; 1932. [$125.00]

Clark, Emmons. **History of the Second Company of the Seventh Regiment (National Guard) N. Y. S. Militia.** NY: Gregory; 1864. [vol. 1 all published, $40.00]

Clark, George Ramsey. **Short History of the United States Navy.** Philadelphia: Lippincott; 1927. [$12.50]

Clark, George Rogers. **Capture of Old Vincennes.** Indianapolis: Bobbs-Merrill; 1927. [$25.00]

Clark, George Rogers. **Col. George Rogers Clark's Sketch of His Campaign in the Illinois in 1778-9.** Cincinnati: Clarke; 1869. [$225.00] [$150.00]

Clark, George Rogers. **The Conquest of the Illinois.** Chicago: Donnelly; 1920. [$17.50]

Clark, George Thomas. **Leland Stanford.** Stanford; London: Stanford UP; Oxford UP; 1931. [$30.00]

Clark, Henry W. **History of Alaska.** NY: Macmillan; 1930. [$25.00]

Clark, Hollis. **Taught by Mail.** Bozeman, MT: The Author; 1917. [$25.00]

Clark, James Albert. **The Wyoming Valley, Upper Waters of the Susquehanna, and the Lackawanna Coal-Region.** Scranton, PA: Clark; 1875. [x-lib., $375.00]

Clark, James Anthony. **Spindletop.** NY: Random House; 1952. [chipped dj, $25.00] [signed, $45.00] [lacks dj, $25.00]

Clark, John Alonzo. **Gleanings by the Way.** Philadelphia; NY: Simon; Carter; 1842. [$60.00]

Clark, John Hawkins. **Overland to the Gold Fields of California in 1852.** Topeka: Kansas Historical Quarterly; 1942. [$40.00]

Clark, Joseph Lynn. **History of Texas.** Boston; NY: Heath; 1940. [$10.00]

Clark, O. S. **Clay Allison of the Washita.** [Attica, IN: Williams]; 1922. [$350.00]

Clark, Robert Lorenzo. **History of the Presbytery of Westminster and Its Antecedents.** Chicago: Regan; 1924. [$50.00]

Clark, Samuel A. **History of St. John's Church, Elizabeth Town, New Jersey.** Philadelphia: Lippincott; 1857. [$25.00]

Clark, Sterling B. F. **How Many Miles from St. Jo?** San Francisco: Priv. Print.; 1929. [$35.00]

Clark, Susie Champney. **The Round Trip from the Hub to the Golden Gate.** Boston; NY: Lee and Shepard; Dillingham; 1890. [$25.00]

Clark, Thomas Dionysius. **The Rural Press and the New South.** Baton Rouge: Louisiana State UP; 1948. [$15.00] [$35.00]

Clark, Thomas Dionysius. **The Southern Country Editor.** Indianapolis: Bobbs-Merrill; 1948. [$20.00]

Clark, Walter Halsey. **History of Platte Presbytery.** Kansas City, MO: Tiernan-Dart; 1910. [$45.00]

Clark, Walter Van Tilburg. **The City of Trembling Leaves.** NY: Random; 1945. [$20.00]

Clark, Walter Van Tilburg. **The Track of the Cat.** NY: Random; 1949. [dj chipped, $20.00] [$25.00]

Clark, Walter Van Tilburg. **The Watchful Gods.** NY: Random; 1950. [$40.00]

Clark, William. **Westward with Dragoons.** Fulton, MO: Bell; 1937. [inscribed by editor, $125.00]

Clark, William Bell. **Gallant John Barry.** NY: Macmillan; 1938. [$20.00]

Clark, William Horace. **Ships and Sailors: The Story of Our Merchant Marine.** Boston: Page; 1938. [$50.00]

Clarke, A. B. **Travels in Mexico and California.** Boston: Wright & Hasty; 1852. [$1000.00] [$1250.00]

Clarke, Asia Booth. **The Unlocked Book.** 1st ed. London: Faber & Faber; 1938. [$27.50]

Clarke, Dwight Lancelot. **Stephen Watts Kearny.** 1st ed. Norman: U. of Oklahoma; 1961. [$40.00] [$55.00]

Clarke, James Freeman. **Anti-Slavery Days.** NY: Worthington; 1884. [$40.00]

Clarke, John. **Letters to a Student in the University of Cambridge, Massachusetts.** Boston: Hall; 1796. [$150.00]

Clarke, John B. **Sketches of Successful New Hampshire Men.** Manchester: Clarke; 1882. [$50.00]

Clarke, M. St. Clair. **Legislative and Documentary History of the Bank of the United States.** Washington: Gales and Seaton; 1832. [x-lib., $200.00]

Clarke, O. P. **Colonel of the 10th Cavalry.** Utica, NY: Childs; 1891. [$37.50]

Clarke, Olive Rand. **Vacation Excursion from Massachusetts Bay to Puget Sound.** Manchester, NH: Clarke; 1884. [$25.00]

Clarke, Ollie E. **Fort Griffin.** Albany, TX: Chamber of Commerce; 1935. [$65.00]

Clarke, Samuel A. **Pioneer Days of Oregon History.** Portland: Gill; 1905. 2 v. [x-lib., $35.00]

Clarke, T. Wood. **Emigres in the Wilderness.** NY: Macmillan; 1941. [$25.00] [$28.50]

Clarkson, Thomas. **Essay on the Slavery and Commerce of the Human Species.** 3rd ed. Philadelphia: Crukshank; 1787. [$150.00]

Clavigero, Francesco Saverio. **Historia de la Antigua o Baja California.** Mejico: Navarro; 1852. [rebound, $500.00]

Clavigero, Francesco Saverio. **The History of Mexico Collected from Spanish and Mexican Historians.** London: Robinson; 1787. 2 v. [$225.00]

Clay, Henry. **The Life and Speeches of Henry Clay.** NY: Greeley & McElrath; 1843. 2 v. [covers worn, $45.00]

Clay, Jehu Curtis. **Annals of the Swedes on the Delaware.** Philadelphia: Pechin; 1835. [$150.00] [2nd ed., 1858, $42.00]

Clay, John. **My Life on the Range.** Chicago: Priv. Print.; 1924. [$275.00] [1962 Oklahoma ed., $45.00]

Clay-Clopton, Virginia. **A Belle of the Fifties.** NY: Doubleday, Page; 1905, c1904. [$55.00] [$35.00]

Clayton, Augustin S. **Life of Martin Van Buren.** see, Crockett, Davy.

Clayton, Powell. **The Aftermath of the Civil War, in Arkansas.** NY: Neale; 1915. [$150.00] [$145.00] [$125.00]

Clayton, W. Woodford. **History of Davidson County, Tennessee.** Philadelphia: Lewis; 1880. [$250.00]

Cleaveland, Agnes Morley. **No Life for a Lady.** Boston: Houghton Mifflin; 1941. [$50.00]

Cleaveland, Agnes Morley. **Satan's Paradise.** Boston: Houghton Mifflin; 1952. [$20.00]

Cleaves, Freeman. **Rock of Chickamauga.** 1st ed. Norman: U. of Oklahoma; 1948. [$47.50]

Clegern, Wayne M. **British Honduras.** Baton Rouge: Louisiana State UP; 1967. [$20.00]

Cleland, Robert Glass. **Cattle on a Thousand Hills.** 2nd ed. San Marino, CA: Huntington; 1951. [spine sunned, $25.00] [1969 reprint, $30.00]

Cleland, Robert Glass. **From Wilderness to Empire.** NY: Knopf; 1944. [$25.00]

Cleland, Robert Glass. **The Irvine Ranch of Orange County, 1810-1950.** San Marino, CA: Huntington; 1952. [$80.00]

Cleland, Robert Glass. **Place Called Sespe.** Alhambra, CA: Priv. Print.; 1940. [1953 printing, $35.00]

Cleland, Robert Glass. **This Reckless Breed of Men.** 1st ed. NY: Knopf; 1950. [$45.00] [1963 printing, $20.00]

Clem, Gladys Bauserman. **Stories of the Shenandoah.** [Staunton?, VA: s.n.]; 1948. [$15.00]

Clemenceau, Georges. **American Reconstruction, 1865-1870 and the Impeachment of President Johnson.** NY; Toronto: Dial; Longmans, Green; 1928. [$15.00]

Clement, John. **Sketches of the First Emigrant Settlers in Newton Township.** Camden, NJ: Chew; 1877. [$85.00]

Clement, Maud Carter. **History of Pittsylvania County, Virginia.** Lynchburg: Bell; 1929. [$60.00]

Clendenin, Henry Wilson. **Autobiography of.** Springfield, IL: State Register; 1926. [$17.50]

Cleveland, Grover. **Government in the Chicago Strike of 1894.** Princeton: Princeton UP; 1913. [$25.00]

Cleveland, Grover. **Letters of Grover Cleveland, 1850-1908.** Boston, NY: Houghton Mifflin; 1933. [$17.50] [$45.00]

Cleveland, Grover. **Writings and Speeches of.** NY: Cassell; 1892. [$45.00]

Cleveland, Henry. **Alexander H. Stephens in Public and Private.** Philadelphia, Chicago: National; 1866. [$25.00]

Clinch, Bryan James. **California and Its Missions.** San Francisco: Whitaker & Ray; 1904. 2 v. [x-lib., $100.00]

Cline, Gloria Griffen. **Exploring the Great Basin.** Norman: U. of Oklahoma; 1963. [$35.00]

Cline, Howard Francis. **Latin American History.** Austin: U. of Texas; 1967. 2 v. [x-lib., $27.50]

Cline, Isaac Monroe. **Storms, Floods and Sunshine.** New Orleans: Pelican; 1945. [$45.00]

Clinton, Henry. **The American Rebellion.** New Haven: Yale UP; 1954. [$25.00]

Clopper, Edward Nicholas. **An American Family.** Cincinnati: [s.n.]; 1950. [$45.00]

Clopton, A. G. **An Eulogy on the Life and Character of Dr. Ashbel Smith.** Jefferson, TX: Iron News; 1886. [$150.00]

Cloquet, Jules. **Recollections of the Private Life of General Lafayette.** London: Baldwin and Cradock; 1835. [x-lib., $30.00] [$50.00] [$125.00]

Cloquet, Jules. **Souveniers sur la Vie Privee du General Lafayette.** Paris: Galignani; 1836. [$75.00]

Clos, Jean Henri. **Glory of Yorktown.** Yorktown, VA: Historical Society; 1924. [$20.00]

Cloud, William F. **Church and State or, Mexican Politics from Cortez to Diaz.** Kansas City, MO: Peck & Clark; 1896. [$50.00]

Clover, Samuel Travers. **On Special Assignment.** NY: Argossy-Argonaut; 1965. [$35.00]

Clugston, William George. **Rascals in Democracy.** NY: Smith; 1940. [$15.00]

Clum, Woodworth. **Apache Agent.** Boston, NY: Houghton Mifflin; 1936. [$65.00]

Clyde, John Cunningham. **Rosbrugh, a Tale of the Revolution.** Easton, PA: [s.n.]; 1880. [worn, $50.00]

Clyman, James. **James Clyman, Frontiersman, 1792-1881.** definitive ed. Portland, OR: Champoeg; 1960. [unopened, $125.00]

Clymer, Joseph Floyd. **Treasury of Early American Automobiles.** NY: McGraw-Hill; 1950. [$15.00]

Coan, Lydia Bingham. **Titus Coan.** Chicago: Revell; 1884. [$25.00]

Coates, Robert M. **The Outlaw Years.** NY: Macaulay; 1930. [$25.00] [$30.00]

Cobb, Eben. **The Star of Endor.** Hyde Park, MA: Cobb; 1891. [$30.00]

Cobb, Irvin Shrewsbury. **Old Judge Priest.** NY: Doran; 1916. [first state, $35.00]

Cobb, John Storer. **Quartercentury of Cremation in North America.** Boston: Knight and Millet; 1901. [spine soiled and torn, $25.00] [x-lib., $45.00]

Cobb, Oliver W. **Rose Cottage.** Easthampton, MA: Easthampton News; 1940. [$25.00]

Cobb, Sanford Hoadley. **Story of the Palatines.** NY, London: Putnam; 1897. [$75.00]

Cobbett, William. **The Guillotina.** see, Hopkins, Lemuel.

Cobbett, William. **A Kick for a Bite.** 2nd ed. Philadelphia: Bradford; 1796. [$75.00]

Cobbett, William. **Letters on the Late War between the United States and Great Britain.** NY: Belden; 1815. [$300.00]

Cobbett, William. **Life and Adventures of Peter Porcupine.** London: Nonesuch; 1927. [$40.00]

Cobbett, William. **Porcupine's Works.** London: Cobbett and Morgan; 1801. 12 v. [$725.00]

Cobbett, William. **The Pride of Britannia Humbled.** NY; Philadelphia; Baltimore: Boyle; Reynolds; Campbell; 1815. [x-lib., $150.00]

Cobbett, William. **A Year's Residence in the United States of America.** 2nd ed. London: Sherwood, Neely, and Jones; 1819. [$375.00]

Coblentz, Stanton Arthur. **The Swallowing Wilderness.** NY: Yoseloff; 1961. [$20.00]

Coblentz, Stanton Arthur. **Villains and Vigilantes.** NY: Wilson-Erickson; 1936. [$20.00] [$45.00]

Coburn, Frank Warren. **Battle of April 19, 1775.** 2nd ed. Lexington, MA: Lexington Historical Society; 1922. [$35.00]

Coburn, Walt. **Pioneer Cattleman in Montana.** 1st ed. Norman: U. of Oklahoma; 1968. [$25.00] [$35.00]

Cochrane, Charles Stuart. **Journal of a Residence and Travels in Colombia during the Years 1823 and 1824.** London: Colburn; 1825. 2 v. [$425.00]

Cocke, Preston. **Battle of New Market and the Cadets of the Virginia Military Institute May 15, 1864.** [Richmond?: s.n.]; 1914. [$45.00]

Codman, John. **Arnold's Expedition to Quebec.** special ed. NY, London: Macmillan; 1903. [$90.00]

Codman, John. **The Round Trip by Way of Panama through California, Oregon, Nevada, Utah, Idaho, and Colorado.** NY: Putnam; 1879. [spine rubbed and broken, $75.00]

Cody, Willliam Frederick. **Life and Adventures of "Buffalo Bill."** Chicago: Stanton; 1917. [$45.00]

Coe, George Washington. **Frontier Fighter.** Boston, NY: Houghton Mifflin; 1934. [plates loose, $45.00]

Coe, Wilbur. **Ranch on the Ruidoso.** 1st ed. NY: Knopf; 1968. [$50.00]

Coffin, Addison. **Life and Travels of.** Cleveland: Hubbard; 1897. [$75.00]

Coffin, Charles Carleton. **Drum-Beat of the Nation.** NY: Harper; 1888. [$10.00]

Coffin, Joshua. **Sketch of the History of Newbury, Newburyport, and West Newbury.** Boston: Drake; 1845. [$65.00]

Coffin, Levi. **Reminiscences of.** 2nd ed. Cincinnati: Clarke; 1880. [x-lib., shaken, $17.50]

Coffin, Robert Peter Tristram. **Kennebec, Cradle of Americans.** NY, Toronto: Farrar & Rinehart; 1937. [$9.00]

Coffinberry, Andrew. **The Forest Rangers.** Columbus, OH: Wright & Legg; 1842. [$125.00]

Coggins, Jack. **Arms and Equipment of the Civil War.** Garden City: Doubleday; 1962. [$20.00]

Cohen, George. **Jews in the Making of America.** Boston: Stratford; 1924. [$15.00]

Cohen, I. Bernard. **Benjamin Franklin: His Contribution to the American Tradition.** 1st ed. Indianapolis: Bobbs-Merrill; 1953. [$20.00]

Cohen, Isidor. **Historical Sketches and Sidelights of Miami, Florida.** Miami: Priv. Print.; 1925. [$50.00]

Cohn, Joseph Hoffman. **I Have Fought a Good Fight.** NY: American Board of Missions to the Jews; 1953. [$20.00]

Coit, Charles Guernsey. **Federal Reserve Bank of Richmond.** NY: Columbia UP; 1941. [$22.50]

Coke, Henry John. **A Ride over the Rocky Mountains to Oregon and California.** London: Bentley; 1852. [spine repaired, $400.00]

Colbert, Elias. **Chicago and the Great Conflagration.** Cincinnati, NY: Vent; 1871. [dampstained, $24.00] [$45.00]

Colburn, Frona. **In Old Vintage Days.** San Francisco: Nash; 1937. [cover faded, $70.00]

Colburn, Harvey C. **The Story of Ypsilanti.** [s.l.: s.n.; 1923?]. [$25.00]

Colburn, Zerah. **Memoir of.** Springfield: Merriam; 1833. [$300.00]

Colby, Merle. **Guide to Alaska.** see, Federal Writers' Project.

Colden, Cadwallader David. **History of the Five Indian Nations of Canada.** London: Osborne; 1747. [rebound, $1000.00] [1755, 3rd ed. in 2 vols., $400.00] [1902 New Amsterdam ed. in 2 vols., $40.00]

Colden, Cadwallader David. **Memoir Prepared at the Request of a Committee of the Common Council of the City of New York.** NY: Corporation of New York; 1825. [$1250.00]

Cole, Cornelius. **California Three Hundred and Fifty Years Ago.** San Francisco; NY: Carson; Dillingham; 1888. [$45.00]

Cole, Cornelius. **Memoirs of.** NY: McLoughlin; 1908. [x-lib., $30.00]

Cole, Cyrenus. **I Remember, I Remember.** Iowa City: State Hist. Soc.; 1936. [$10.00]

Cole, Fay-Cooper. **Kincaid.** Chicago: U. of Chicago; 1951. [$25.00]

Cole, George E. **Early Oregon.** Spokane: Shaw & Borden; 1905. [dj nicked, $75.00] [spine flaking, $15.00]

Cole, Gilbert L. **In the Early Days along the Overland Trail in Nebraska Territory, in 1852.** Kansas City: Hudson; 1905. [$75.00] [$100.00]

Cole, Harry Ellsworth. **Stagecoach and Tavern Tales of the Old Northwest.** Cleveland: Clark; 1930. [$60.00]

Coleman, Emma Lewis. **New England Captives Carried to Canada between 1677 and 1760.** Portland, ME: Southworth; 1925. 2 v. [$150.00]

Coleman, Mary Haldane (Begg). **Virginia Silhouettes.** Richmond: Dietz; 1934. [some underlining, $25.00]

Coleman, R. V. **The First Frontier.** NY: Scribner; 1948. [$12.00]

Coleman, William. **A Collection of the Facts and Documents, Relative to the Death of Major-General Alexander Hamilton.** Boston, NY: Houghton Mifflin; 1904. [$35.00]

Coleman, William Macon. **History of the Primitive Yankees.** Washington: Columbia; 1881. [$40.00]

Coleridge, Henry Nelson. **Six Months in the West Indies, in 1825.** London: Murray; 1826. [title page repaired, $100.00]

Colfax, Schuyler. **The "Laws" of Kansas.** NY: Greeley & McElrath; 1856. [$40.00]

Colles, Christopher. **Survey of the Roads of the United States of America, 1789.** Cambridge: Harvard UP; 1961. [$50.00]

Collier, Calvin L. **War Child's Children.** Little Rock: Pioneer; 1965. [$27.50]

Collier, John. **Indians of the Americas.** 1st ed. NY: Norton; 1947. [$45.00]

Collier, John. **Shadows Which Haunt the Sun-Rain.** Johnsville, PA: Stone House; 1917. [$125.00]

Collier, Sargent F. **Down East.** Boston: Houghton Mifflin; 1953. [$20.00]

Collier, William Ross. **Dave Cook of the Rockies.** NY: Wilson; 1936. [$40.00]

Collier, William Ross. **Reign of Soapy Smith.** 1st ed. Garden City: Doubleday, Doran; 1935. [$50.00]

Collin, Nicholas. **Journal and Biography of.** Philadelphia: New Jersey Society of Pennsylvania; 1936. [$30.00] [$25.00]

Collings, Ellsworth. **Adventures on a Dude Ranch.** Indianapolis: Bobbs-Merrill; 1940. [$30.00]

Collins, Anna C. **History of the Methodist Episcopal Church on Port Republic and Smithville Charge.** Camden, NJ: Gazette Printing; 1892. [$50.00]

Collins, Dennis. **The Indian's Last Fight.** 1st ed. Girard, KS: Press of the Appeal to Reason; 1915. [$150.00]

Collins, Hubert Edwin. **Warpath & Cattle Trail.** NY: Morrow; 1928. [$65.00] [spine loose, $30.00]

Collins, Varnum Lansing. **Princeton, Past and Present.** Princeton: Princeton UP; 1945. [$20.00]

Collis, Septima Maria. **A Woman's Trip to Alaska.** NY: Cassell; 1890. [2nd issue, $75.00]

Coloney, Myron. **Manomin.** St. Louis: The Author; 1866. [lacks front endpaper, spine faded, $75.00] [rebound, $125.00]

Colt, Miriam Davis. **Went to Kansas.** Watertown, NY: Ingalls; 1862. [$285.00] [$450.00]

Colt, Samuel. **Samuel Colt's Own Record of Transactions with Captain Walker and Eli Whitney, Jr.** Hartford: CT Hist. Soc.; 1949. [$135.00]

Colton, Calvin. **Annexation of Texas.** NY: Greeley & McElrath; 1844. [$185.00]

Colton, Calvin. **The Last Seven Years of the Life of Henry Clay.** NY: Barnes; 1856. [$45.00]

Colton, George Hooker. **Tecumseh.** NY: Wiley & Putnam; 1842. [$15.00]

Colton, Henry E. **Mountain Scenery.** Raleigh, NC; Philadelphia: Pomeroy; Hayes & Zell; 1859. [lacks map, covers worn, $100.00]

Colton, Joseph Hutchins. **Colton's Traveler and Tourist's Guide-Book.** NY: Colton; 1850. [lacks map, $45.00, Canadian]

Colton, Joseph Hutchins. **The State of Indiana Delineated.** NY: Colton; 1838. [with folding map, $950.00]

Colton, Joseph Hutchins. **The Western Tourist; or, Emigrant's Guide.** NY: Colton; 1846. [$165.00]

Colton, Julia Maria. **Annals of Old Manhattan, 1609-1664.** NY: Brentano's; 1901. [$12.50]

Colton, Matthias Baldwin. **Civil War Journal & Correspondence.** limited ed. Philadelphia: Macrae; 1931. [$225.00]

Colton, Ray Charles. **The Civil War in the Western Territories.** 1st ed. Norman: U. of Oklahoma; 1959. [$30.00]

Colton, Walter. **California Diary.** Oakland: Biobooks; 1948. [$50.00] [$45.00]

Colton, Walter. **Deck and Port.** NY: Barnes; 1850. [some foxing, $65.00]

Colton, Walter. **Three Years in California.** NY: Barnes; 1850. [lacks map, $100.00]

Columbus, Christophe. **Letter of Christopher Columbus.** Albany, NY: McDonough; 1900. [$15.00]

Colyar, Arthur St. Clair. **Life and Times of Andrew Jackson.** Nashville: Marshall & Bruce; 1904. 2 v. [$75.00]

Combe, George. **Notes on the United States of North America during a Phrenological Visit in 1838-9-40.** Edinburgh: Maclachlan, Stewart; 1841. 3 v. [$300.00]

Combs, Joseph F. **Gunsmoke in the Redlands.** San Antonio: Naylor; 1968. [$30.00]

Comeau, Napoleon Alexander. **Life and Sport on the North Shore of the Lower St. Lawrence and Gulf.** 2nd ed. Quebec: Telegraph; 1923. [spine worn, $40.00] [spine taped, $19.50] [$45.00]

Commager, Henry Steele. **The Blue and the Gray.** 1st ed. Indianapolis: Bobbs-Merrill; 1950. 2 v. [$22.50]

Commager, Henry Steele. **The Spirit of 'Seventy-Six.** Indianapolis: Bobbs-Merrill; 1958. 2 v. [$35.00]

Commonwealth of Pennsylvania, ex relatione Paul Daniel Gonzalve Grand d'Hauteville. **Report of the d'Hauteville Case.** Philadelphia: Martien; 1840. [$50.00]

Compendium of History and Biography of North Dakota. Chicago: Ogle; 1900. [$135.00]

Comstock, Sarah. **Old Roads from the Heart of New York.** NY, London: Putnam; 1915. [inscribed, $27.50]

Conant, Alban Jasper. **Foot-Prints of Vanished Races in the Mississippi Valley.** St. Louis: Barns; 1879. [inscribed, $55.00]

Conard, Howard Louis. **"Uncle Dick" Wootton.** Columbus, OH: Long's; 1950. [$50.00]

Condie, Thomas. **History of the Pestilence Commonly Called Yellow Fever, Which Almost Desolated Philadelphia.** Philadelphia: Folwell; 1799. [$225.00]

Cone, Mary. **Two Years in California.** Chicago: Griggs; 1876. [bright, $80.00]

Confederate States of America. President. **Compilation of the Messages and Papers of the Confederacy Including the Diplomatic Correspondence, 1861-1865.** Nashville: United States Pub. Co.; 1906. 2 v. [x-lib., $30.00]

Conference on the History of Western America. **Probing the American West.** Santa Fe: Museum of New Mexico; 1962. [$20.00]

Conger, Arthur Latham. **Rise of U.S. Grant.** NY: Century; 1931. [$20.00]

Connell, Evan S. **Son of the Morning Star.** San Francisco: North Point; 1984. [1st printing, $35.00]

Connelley, William Elsey. **Ingalls of Kansas.** Topeka: The Author; 1909. [$45.00]

Connelley, William Elsey. **John Brown.** Topeka, KS: Crane; 1900. [$65.00]

Connelley, William Elsey. **Quantrill and the Border Wars.** Cedar Rapids, IA: Torch; 1910. [$140.00] [$165.00]

Connelley, William Elsey. **Wild Bill and His Era.** NY: Press of the Pioneers; 1933. [$85.00]

Conner, Howard M. **The Spearhead.** 1st ed. Washington: Infantry Journal; 1950. [$55.00]

Connett, Eugene Virginius. **Duck Shooting along the Atlantic Tidewater.** NY: Morrow; 1947. [$75.00] [Bonanza reprint, $35.00]

Connett, Eugene Virginius. **Yachting in North America.** NY: Van Nostrand; 1948. [$65.00]

Connor, Henry Groves. **John Archibald Campbell.** Boston, NY: Houghton Mifflin; 1920. [bumped, rubbed, frayed, $22.00]

Connor, Robert Digges Wimberly. **North Carolina, Rebuilding an Ancient Commonwealth, 1584-1925.** Chicago: American Historical Society; 1929. 4 v. [bumped, rubbed, $50.00]

Connor, Seymour V. **The Peters Colony of Texas.** Austin: Texas State Historical Association; 1959. [$200.00]

Conover, George W. **Sixty Years in Southwest Oklahoma.** Andarko, OK: Plummer; 1927. [$75.00]

Conrad, David Holmes. **Memoir of Rev. James Chisholm.** NY: Protestant Episcopal Society for the Promotion of Evangelical Knowledge; 1856. [$20.00]

Conrad, Earl. **Harriet Tubman.** Washington: Associated Publishers; 1943. [$45.00]

Conrad, Earl. **Jim Crow America.** NY: Duell, Sloan and Pearce; 1947. [$10.00]

Conrad, Earl. **Mr. Seward for the Defense.** NY: Rinehart; 1956. [$20.00]

Conrad, Thomas Nelson. **The Rebel Scout.** Washington: National; 1904. [$110.00]

Conway, Moncure Daniel. **Barons of the Potomack and the Rappahannock.** NY: Grolier; 1892. [$125.00]

Conway, William Martin Conway. **The Bolivian Andes.** NY, London: Harper; 1901. [lacks front fly-leaf, $50.00]

Conwell, Russell Herman. **History of the Great Fire in Boston, November 9 and 10, 1872.** Boston: Russell; 1873. [$50.00]

Conwell, Russell Herman. **Life, Speeches, and Public Services of James A. Garfield.** Boston: Russell; 1881. [$35.00]

Conwell, Russell Herman. **Why and How: Why the Chinese Emigrate.** Boston; NY: Lee and Shepard; Lee, Shepard and Dillingham; 1871. [hinges cracked, one plate detached, $60.00]

Conyngham, Kate. see, Ingraham, Joseph Holt.

Cook, David J. **Hands Up.** Denver: Robinson; 1897. [$125.00]

Cook, Harry T. **The Borough of the Bronx, 1639-1913.** NY: The Author; 1913. [$45.00]

Cook, James. **A Voyage to the Pacific Ocean.** London: Nicol & Cadell; 1784. 3 v. [$4600.00]

Cook, James H. **Fifty Years on the Old Frontier.** New Haven: Yale UP; 1923. [$75.00]

Cook, James M. **Lane of the Llano.** Boston: Little, Brown; 1936. [$75.00]

Cook, John R. **The Border and the Buffalo.** Topeka, KS: Crane; 1907. [$100.00]

Cook, Joseph. **Extracts from Sketches of Ticonderoga.** Ticonderoga, NY: Sentinel; [1899?]. [$37.50]

Cook, Joseph Witherspoon. **Diary and Letters of.** Laramie, WY: Republican; 1919. [silverfished, $75.00] [$150.00]

Cook, Marc. **Wilderness Cure.** NY: Wood; 1881. [$85.00]

Cook, Roy Bird. **Annals of Fort Lee.** Charleston, WV: West Virginia Review; 1935. [signed, $15.00]

Cook, Roy Bird. **Family and Early Life of Stonewall Jackson.** 2nd ed. Richmond: Old Dominion; 1925. [$38.50]

Cook, Roy Bird. **Lewis County in the Civil War, 1861-1865.** Charleston, WV: Jarrett; 1924. [$125.00]

Cook, William Henry. **Letters of a Ticonderoga Farmer.** Ithaca: Cornell UP; 1946. [$25.00]

Cooke, Alistair. **Douglas Fairbanks.** NY: Museum of Modern Art; 1940. [$20.00]

Cooke, John Esten. **Essay on the Invalidity of Presbyterian Ordination.** Lexington, KY: Reporter; 1829. [$125.00]

Cooke, John Esten. **Life of Stonewall Jackson.** NY: Richardson; 1863. [$50.00]

Cooke, John Esten. **Mohun.** NY: Dillingham; 1896. [$22.50]

Cooke, John Esten. **Outlines from the Outpost.** Chicago: Lakeside; 1961. [$35.00]

Cooke, John Esten. **Stonewall Jackson: A Military Biography.** NY: Appleton; 1866. [$200.00]

Cooke, John Esten. **Stonewall Jackson and the Old Stonewall Brigade.** Charlottesville: U. of Virginia; 1954. [$35.00]

Cooke, John Esten. **Stories of the Old Dominion.** NY: Harper; 1879. [$45.00]

Cooke, John Esten. **Surry of Eagle's-Nest.** NY: Bunce and Huntington; 1866. [$75.00] [$100.00]

Cooke, John Esten. **Wearing of the Gray.** NY; Baltimore: Treat; Morrow; 1867. [$125.00]

Cooke, Philip St. George. **Conquest of New Mexico and California.** Oakland: Biobooks; 1942 [i.e. 1952]. [$25.00]

Cooke, Philip St. George. **Exploring Southwestern Trails, 1846-1854.** Glendale, CA: Clark; 1938. [$125.00]

Cookridge, E. H. see, Spiro, Edward.

Coolbrith, Ina D. **Songs from the Golden Gate.** Boston, NY: Houghton Mifflin; 1885. [presentation, $75.00]

Coolidge, Dane. **Arizona Cowboys.** 1st ed. NY: Dutton; 1938. [$50.00]

Coolidge, Dane. **Death Valley Prospectors.** 1st ed. NY: Dutton; 1937. [inscribed, $40.00] [$25.00]

Coolidge, Dane. **The Fighting Danites.** NY: Dutton; 1934. [$25.00]

Coolidge, Susan. **Short History of the City of Philadelphia.** Boston: Roberts; 1887. [x-lib., $20.00]

Coombe, Thomas. **Peasant of Auburn.** London: Elmsly; 1783. [signed, $100.00]

Cooper, Courtney Ryley. **High Country.** Boston: Little, Brown; 1926. [$25.00]

Cooper, Courtney Ryley. **Last Frontier.** Boston: Little, Brown; 1923. [presentation, $25.00]

Cooper, Jacob Calvin. **Military History of Yamhill County.** [McMinnville?, OR: s.n.]; 1899. [$225.00]

Cooper, James Fenimore. **Last of the Mohicans.** 1st ed. Philadelphia: Carey & Lea; 1826. 2 v. [x-lib., worn, several gatherings loose, $750.00]

Cooper, James Fenimore. **Letter to His Countrymen.** NY: Wiley; 1834. [lacks front endpaper, $150.00]

Cooper, James Fenimore. **Notions of the Americans.** Philadelphia: Carey, Lea & Carey; 1828. 2 v. [$100.00] [1828 London ed., $300.00]

Cooper, James Fenimore. **The Wept of Wish Ton-Wish.** Philadelphia: Carey, Lea & Carey; 1829. 2 v. [2 vols. bound together-vol. 2 first, $375.00] [$125.00]

Cooper, Samuel. **The Crisis; or, A Full Defence of the Colonies.** London: Griffin; 1766. [waterstained and trimmed, $850.00]

Cooper, Susan Fenimore. **Mount Vernon.** NY: Appleton; 1859. [bumped, soiled, spine frayed, $25.00]

Cooper, Susan Fenimore. **Rural Hours.** NY, London: Putnam; 1850. [$65.00]

Cooper, Thomas. **Some Information Respecting America.** London: Johnson; 1794. [rebound, $300.00] [$175.00]

Cooper, Waller Raymond. **Southwestern at Memphis, 1848-1948.** Richmond: Knox; 1949. [$20.00]

Cooper, William Arthur. **Portrayal of Negro Life.** Durham, NC: Seeman; 1936. [signed, bumped, rubbed, $75.00]

Copley, Frank Barkley. **Frederick W. Taylor.** NY: Harper; 1923. 2 v. [$75.00]

Copway, George. **Life, History, & Travels of Kah-Ge-Ga-Gah-Bowh.** 2nd ed. Philadelphia: Harmstead; 1847. [x-lib., $60.00] [1850 NY ed., $100.00]

Corcoran, Michael. **Captivity of General Corcoran.** Philadelphia: Barclay; 1864. [$125.00]

Cordley, Richard. **History of Lawrence, Kansas.** Lawrence: Journal; 1895. [$59.50]

Corkran, David H. **The Creek Frontier, 1540-1783.** 1st ed. Norman: U. of Oklahoma; 1967. [$48.00]

Corle, Edwin. **Burro Alley.** limited, signed ed. NY: Duell, Sloan & Pearce; 1938. [$40.00]

Corle, Edwin. **Coarse Gold.** signed, limited ed. NY; Boston: Duell, Sloan & Pearce; Little, Brown; 1952. [$30.00]

Corle, Edwin. **Desert Country.** NY: Duell, Sloan and Pearce; 1941. [presentation, $35.00]

Corle, Edwin. **Fig Tree John.** NY: Liveright; 1935. [dj chipped, $35.00]

Corle, Edwin. **The Gila.** NY: Rinehart; 1951. [worn dj, $25.00]

Corle, Edwin. **The Royal Highway.** Misson Bell ed. Indianapolis: Bobbs-Merrill; 1949. [$25.00]

Cornelius, Elias. **The Little Osage Captive.** Boston; NY: Armstrong and Crocker & Brewster; Haven; 1822. [$75.00]

Cornell, Julien D. **Trial of Ezra Pound.** NY: Day; 1966. [$22.50]

Corner, William. **San Antonio de Bexar.** San Antonio: Bainbridge & Corner; 1890. [$125.00]

Corney, Peter. **Voyages in the Northern Pacific.** Honolulu: Thrum; 1896. [boards warped, $325.00] [$425.00]

Cornplanter, Jesse J. **Iroquis Indian Games and Dances.** [s.l.: s.n.; 1903?]. [$80.00]

Cornwall, Bruce. **Life Sketch of Pierre Barlow Cornwall.** San Francisco: Robertson; 1906. [presentation, $250.00]

Corpus Christi Caller-Times. **100 Years of Ranching.** Corpus Christi: Caller-Times; 1953. [$25.00]

Corrigan, Douglas. **That's My Story.** NY: Dutton; 1938. [signed, $22.50]

Corse, Carita Doggett. **Dr. Andrew Turnbull and the New Smyrna Colony of Florida.** Jacksonville, FL: Drew; 1919. [$35.00]

Corse, Carita Doggett. **Florida; Empire of the Sun.** Tallahassee: Florida State Hotel Commission; 1930. [$22.50]

Corser, Harry Prosper. **Legendary Lore of the Alaska Totems.** Juneau: Purity Pharmacy; 1910. [$70.00]

Cort, Cyrus. **Enoch Brown Sesqui-Centennial Memorial Services, August 4, 1914; and Fort McCord Dedicatory Services, October 29, 1914.** Reading, PA: Beaver; 1915. [$15.00]

Cortes, Hernando. **Letters of Cortes.** NY: Putnam; 1908. 2 v. [$60.00]

Cossley-Batt, Jill Lillie Emma. **Last of the California Rangers.** NY, London: Funk & Wagnalls; 1928. [$45.00] [$50.00]

Costello, Augustine E. **Our Firemen.** NY: Costello; 1887. [rebound, $125.00]

Costello, John Benjamin. **Swindling Exposed from the Diary of William B. Moreau.** Syracuse: Costello; 1907. [$95.00]

Cosulich, Bernice. **Tucson.** 1st ed. Tucson: Arizona Silhouettes; 1953. [$25.00]

Cotner, Thomas Ewing. **The Military and Political Career of Jose Joaquin de Herrera, 1792-1854.** Austin: U. of Texas; 1949. [$45.00]

Cotter, John L. **Archeological Excavations at Jamestown Colonial National Historical Park and Jamestown National Historic Site, Virginia.** Washington: National Park Service; 1958. [$17.50]

Cotterill, Robert Spencer. **The Southern Indians.** 1st ed. Norman: U. of Oklahoma; 1954. [$48.00]

Couch, William T. **Culture in the South.** Chapel Hill: U. of North Carolina; 1935, c1934. [$25.00]

Coughlin, Richard. **Adirondack Region.** Watertown, NY: Santway Photo-Craft; 1921. [$27.50]

Coulter, E. Merton. **Auraria.** Athens: U. of Georgia; 1956. [x-lib., $15.00]

Coulter, E. Merton. **College Life in the Old South.** NY: Macmillan; 1928. [$25.00]

Coulter, E. Merton. **William G. Brownlow.** Chapel Hill: U. of North Carolina; 1937. [$35.00] [1971 U. of Tennessee ed., $15.00]

Coulter, John. **Adventures on the Western Coast of South America, and the Interior of California.** London: Longman, etc.; 1847. 2 v. [light foxing, $300.00]

Couper, William. **One Hundred Years at V. M. I.** Richmond: Garrett and Massie; 1939. 4 v. [$75.00]

Coursey, Oscar William. **Beautiful Black Hills.** Mitchell, SD: Educator Supply; 1926. [$38.00]

Court of Neptune and the Curse of Liberty. 1st ed. NY: Vanwinkle, Wiley; 1817. [loose binding, $75.00]

Coutant, Charles Griffin. **History of Wyoming.** Laramie: Chaplin, Spafford & Mathison; 1899. [vol. 1 all published, spine repaired, $125.00]

Couts, Cave Johnson. **From San Diego to the Colorado in 1849.** Los Angeles: Ellis; 1932. [$75.00]

Couts, Cave Johnson. **Hepah, California!** Tucson: Arizona Pioneers' Historical Society; 1961. [$45.00]

Covarrubias, Miguel. **Indian Art of Mexico and Central America.** 1st ed. NY: Knopf; 1957. [$75.00]

Covarrubias, Miguel. **Mexico South; the Isthmus of Tehuantepec.** NY: Knopf; 1946. [$35.00] [x-lib., $15.00]

Cowan, Bud. **Range Rider.** 1st ed. Garden City: Doubleday, Doran; 1930. [$30.00]

Cowan, John F. **A New Invasion of the South.** NY: Board of Officers, Seventy-First Infantry; 1881. [bumped, rubbed, silverfished, scribbled on front endpaper, $35.00] [$45.00] [$125.00]

Cowen, Philip. **Memories of an American Jew.** signed, limited ed. NY: International; 1932. [$35.00]

Cowles, Florence Call. **Early Algona.** Des Moines: Register and Tribune; 1929. [$35.00]

Cowley, Charles. **Leaves from a Lawyer's Life.** Lowell; Boston: Penshallow; Lee & Shepard; 1879. [weak hinges, bumped, $85.00]

Cox, Isaac. **Annals of Trinity County.** Eugene, OR: Holmes; 1940. [book fine, slipcase worn, $190.00]

Cox, Jacob Dolson. **Atlanta.** NY: Scribner; 1882. [$30.00]

Cox, John. **Quakerism in the City of New York, 1657-1930.** NY: Priv. Print.; 1930. [$35.00]

Cox, John Harrington. **Folk-Songs of the South.** Cambridge: Harvard UP; 1925. [$30.00] [2nd printing, $35.00]

Cox, Palmer. **Frontier Humor.** Chicago: Donohue, Henneberry; [189-?]. [$40.00]

Cox, Ross. **Adventures on the Columbia River.** London: Colburn and Bentley; 1831. 2 v. [bound in one vol., $600.00] [x-lib., $850.00] [1832 NY ed., $125.00]

Cox, Ross. **The Columbia River.** 2nd ed. London: Colburn and Bentley; 1832. 2 v. [presentation, rebound, x-lib., $350.00]

Cox, Samuel Sullivan. **Eight Years in Congress.** NY: Appleton; 1865. [$35.00]

Cox, Sandford C. **Recollections of the Early Settlement of the Wabash Valley.** Lafayette, IN: Courier; 1860. [front hinge loose, $225.00] [dampstained, $75.00]

Cox, William Edward. **Southern Sidelights.** Raleigh: Edwards & Broughton; 1942. [$30.00]

Cox, William Robert. **Luke Short and His Era.** 1st ed. Garden City: Doubleday; 1961. [$35.00]

Coxe, Daniel. **A Description of the English Province of Carolana.** London: Symon; 1727. [full morocco, with map, $3500.00]

Coxe, John Redman. **The American Dispensatory.** 3rd ed. Philadelphia: Dobson; 1814. [$175.00]

Coxe, Tench. **A View of the United States of America.** Philadelphia: Hall, Wrigley & Berriman; 1794. [rebound, $200.00] [rebacked, $485.00] [$275.00]

Cozzens, Issachar. **Geological History of Manhattan or New York Island.** NY: Dean; 1843. [$185.00]

Crabb, Alexander Richard. **Empire on the Platte.** 1st ed. Cleveland: World; 1967. [$45.00]

Crabb, Alfred Leland. **Breakfast at the Hermitage.** 1st ed. Indianapolis, NY: Bobbs-Merrill; 1945. [$20.00]

Crabb, Alfred Leland. **Dinner at Belmont.** 1st ed. Indianapolis, NY: Bobbs-Merrill; 1942. [$12.50]

Crabb, Alfred Leland. **Home to Tennessee.** 1st ed. Indianapolis: Bobbs-Merrill; 1952. [$20.00]

Crabb, Alfred Leland. **Lodging at the Saint Cloud.** 1st ed. Dublin: National Press; 1946. [signed, $35.00]

Crabb, Alfred Leland. **A Mockingbird Sang at Chickamauga.** 1st ed. Indianapolis: Bobbs-Merrill; 1949. [$20.00]

Crabb, Alfred Leland. **Nashville: Personality of a City.** 1st ed. Indianapolis: Bobbs-Merrill; 1960. [$20.00]

Crabb, Alfred Leland. **Peace at Bowling Green.** 1st ed. Indianapolis: Bobbs-Merrill; 1955. [worn dj, $17.50]

Craig, Hardin. **Woodrow Wilson at Princeton.** 1st ed. Norman: U. of Oklahoma; 1960. [$15.00]

Craig, Hugh. **Nicaragua Canal.** San Francisco: Chamber of Commerce; 1898. [$25.00]

Craig, Neville B. **The History of Pittsburgh.** Pittsburgh: Weldin; 1917. [$15.00]

Crakes, Sylvester. **Five Years a Captive among the Black-Feet Indians.** Columbus: Osgood & Pearce; 1858. [lacking front fly-leaf, $850.00]

Cram, Mildred. **Old Seaport Towns of the South.** NY: Dodd, Mead; 1917. [$25.00]

Cramer, John Henry. **Lincoln under Enemy Fire.** Baton Rouge: Louisiana State UP; 1948. [signed, $28.50]

Cramer, Zadok. **The Navigator: Containing Directions for Navigating the Monongahela, Allegheny, Ohio and Mississippi Rivers.** 8th ed. Pittsburgh: Cramer, Spear and Eichbaum; 1814. [$850.00]

Cranch, William. **Memoir of the Life, Character, and Writings of John Adams.** Washington: Elliot; 1827. [$45.00]

Crandall, Marjorie Lyle. **Confederate Imprints.** Boston: Boston Atheneum; 1955. 2 v. [$150.00]

Crane, Leo. **Desert Drums.** Boston: Little, Brown; 1928. [$50.00] [$35.00]

Crane, Leo. **Indians of the Enchanted Desert.** Boston: Little, Brown; 1925. [$40.00]

Crane, Mary Powell. **Life of James R. Powell and Early History of Alabama and Birmingham.** Brooklyn: Braunworth; 1930. [$60.00]

Crane, Stephen. **Active Service.** 2nd ed. NY: Stokes; 1899. [$35.00]

Crane, Stephen. **George's Mother.** London: Arnold; 1896. [$100.00]

Crane, Stephen. **The Little Regiment.** NY: Appleton; 1896. [$100.00] [2nd printing, $90.00]

Crane, Stephen. **Maggie, a Girl of the Streets.** NY: Appleton; 1896. [covers worn, $75.00]

Crane, Stephen. **The Open Boat and Other Tales of Adventure.** NY: Doubleday & McClure; 1898. [fly leaf lacking, $225.00] [$180.00]

Crane, Stephen. **The O'Ruddy.** NY: Stokes; 1903. [near fine, $100.00]

Crane, Stephen. **Red Badge of Courage.** NY: Appleton; 1896, c1895. [2nd issue, $100.00]

Crane, Stephen. **Third Violet.** 1st ed. NY: Appleton; 1897. [fine, $175.00]

Crane, Verner Winslow. **Benjamin Franklin and a Rising People.** 1st ed. Boston: Little, Brown; 1954. [$25.00]

Cranston, Paul F. **Camden County, 1681-1931.** Camden, NJ: Camden County Chamber of Commerce; 1931. [$20.00]

Cranwell, John Philips. **Men of Marque.** NY: Norton; 1940. [$40.00]

Cranwell, John Philips. **Notes on Figures of Earth.** NY: McBride; 1929. [$30.00]

Craven, Avery Odelle. **Edmund Ruffin, Southerner.** NY, London: Appleton; 1932. [$30.00]

Craven, John Joseph. **Prison Life of Jefferson Davis.** NY: Carleton; 1866. [$35.00] [$40.00]

Craven, Margaret. **I Heard the Owl Call My Name.** 1st ed. Toronto: Clarke, Irwin; 1967. [$25.00]

Craven, Wesley Frank. **Legend of the Founding Fathers.** NY: New York UP; 1956. [$10.00]

Craven, Wesley Frank. **Southern Colonies in the Seventeenth Century.** Baton Rouge: Louisiana State UP; 1949. [$20.00]

Cravens, John Nathan. **James Harper Starr.** Austin: Daughters of the Republic of Texas; 1950. [$35.00]

Crawford, Charles Howard. **Scenes of Earlier Days in Crossing the Plains to Oregon.** Petaluma, CA: Studdert; 1898. [$300.00] [$135.00]

Crawford, Lewis Ferandus. **Badlands and Broncho Trails.** Bismarck, ND: Capital; 1922. [$20.00]

Crawford, Lewis Ferandus. **Rekindling Camp Fires.** Bismarck, ND: Capital; 1926. [$55.00]

Crawford, Morris De Camp. **Heritage of Cotton.** 1st ed. NY: Putnam; 1924. [$15.00]

Crawford, Mary Caroline. **Famous Families of Massachusetts.** Boston: Little, Brown; 1930. 2 v. [$22.50]

Crawford, Thomas Edgar. **The West of the Texas Kid, 1881-1910.** 1st ed. Norman: U. of Oklahoma; 1962. [$35.00]

Crawford, William L. **Crawford on Baileyism.** Dallas: Eclectic News; 1897 [i.e. 1907]. [$35.00]

Creekmore, Betsey Beeler. **Dark and Bloody Ground.** NY: Fell; 1967. [$15.00]

Creel, George. **Sam Houston.** NY: Cosmopolitan; 1928. [$45.00]

Cremin, Lawrence Arthur. **History of Teachers College, Columbia University.** NY: Columbia UP; 1954. [$27.50]

Cremony, John C. **Life among the Apaches.** San Francisco, NY: Roman; 1868. [$225.00] [$350.00] [1954 Arizona Silhouettes ed., $25.00]

Cresson, William Penn. **Francis Dana, a Puritan Diplomat at the Court of Catherine the Great.** NY; Toronto: Dial; Longmans, Green; 1930. [$20.00]

Cresson, William Penn. **The Holy Alliance.** NY: Oxford UP; 1922. [$35.00]

Crevecoeur, Michel-Guilluame Saint Jean de. see, St. John de Crevecoeur, J. Hector.

Crews, Harry. **The Hawk Is Dying.** 1st ed. NY: Knopf; 1973. [fine in dj, $20.00]

Crichfield, George Washington. **American Supremacy.** NY: Brentano's; 1908. 2 v. [$55.00]

Crichton, Kyle Samuel. **Law and Order, Ltd.** Santa Fe: New Mexican Publishing; 1928. [worn dj, $100.00]

Crissey, Forrest. **Where Opportunity Knocks Twice.** Chicago: Reilly & Britton; 1914. [$20.00]

Crissey, Theron Wilmot. **History of Norfolk, Litchfield County, Connecticut.** Everett, MA: Massachusetts Pub. Co.; 1900. [rebound, $75.00]

Crite, Allan Rohan. **Three Spirituals from Earth to Heaven.** Cambridge: Harvard UP; 1948. [$25.00]

Crittenden, Henry Huston. **Battle of Westport and National Memorial Park.** Kansas City: Lowell; 1938. [$65.00]

Croasdaile, Henry E. **Scenes on Pacific Shores.** London: Town and Country; 1873. [cover soiled and worn, $50.00]

Crocchiola, Stanley Francis Louis. see, Stanley, F.

Crockett, Davy. **An Account of Col. Crockett's Tour to the North and down the East.** Philadelphia; Boston: Carey and Hart; Ticknor; 1835. [$250.00] [$175.00]

Crockett, Davy. **Life of Martin Van Buren.** Philadelphia: Wright; 1835. [$125.00]

Crockett, Davy. **Sketches and Eccentricities of.** 11th ed. NY: Harper; 1833. [$225.00]

Crofutt, George A. **Crofutt's Grip-Sack Guide of Colorado.** 1st ed. Omaha; Denver: Overland; Alvord; 1881. [rebacked, $200.00]

Crofutt, George A. **Crofutt's New Overland Tourist, and Pacific Coast Guide.** Omaha: Overland; 1884. [$75.00]

Croix, Teodoro de. **Teodoro de Croix and the Northern Frontier of New Spain.** Norman: U. of Oklahoma; 1941. [$25.00]

Crompton, F. C. B. **Glimpse of Early Canadians: Lahontan.** Toronto: Nelson; 1925. [$45.00]

Cromwell, Otelia. **Lucretia Mott.** Cambridge: Harvard UP; 1958. [$28.50]

Cronau, Rudolf. **Army of the American Revolution and Its Organizer.** NY: Cronau; 1923. [signed, $22.00]

Cronau, Rudolf. **Drei Jahrhunderte Deutschen Lebens in Amerika.** Berlin: Reimer; 1909. [$85.00]

Crook, George. **General George Crook.** 1st ed. Norman: U. of Oklahoma; 1946. [$38.00]

Crooks, Esther Josephine. **The Ring Tournament in the United States.** Richmond: Garrett and Massie; 1936. [$17.50]

Crooks, George Richard. **Life of Bishop Matthew Simpson.** NY: Harper; 1890. [$35.00]

Crosby, Sylvester Sage. **The Early Coins of America.** Chicago: Green; 1945. [x-lib., $50.00]

Cross, Dorothy. **Archaeology of New Jersey.** Trenton: Archaeological Society of New Jersey; 1941-1956. 2 v. [$300.00]

Cross, Robert D. **Emergence of Liberal Catholicism in America.** Cambridge: Harvard UP; 1958. [$17.50]

Croswell, Mary E. **Story of Hollywood.** Hollywood, CA: Hollywood Board of Trade; 1905. [$25.00]

Crotty, Daniel G. **Four Years Campaigning in the Army of the Potomac.** Grand Rapids, MI: Dygert; 1874. [hinges weak, $135.00]

Crouse, Nellis Maynard. **French Pioneers in the West Indies, 1624-1664.** NY: Columbia UP; 1940. [x-lib., $15.00] [$35.00]

Crouse, Nellis Maynard. **The Search for the North Pole.** NY: Smith; 1947. [$18.00]

Crowe, Earle. **Men of El Tejon.** Los Angeles: Ritchie; 1957. [$30.00]

Crowninshield, Francis Welch. **The Unofficial Palace of New York.** NY: [s.n.]; 1939. [$17.50]

Croy, Homer. **He Hanged Them High.** 1st ed. NY: Duell, Sloan and Pearce; 1952. [$35.00]

Croy, Homer. **Jesse James Was My Neighbor.** NY: Duell, Sloan and Pearce; 1949. [$30.00] [$60.00]

Croy, Homer. **Last of the Great Outlaws: The Story of Cole Younger.** 1st ed. NY: Duell, Sloan and Pearce; 1956. [$30.00] [$40.00]

Croy, Homer. **Wheels West.** NY: Hastings; 1955. [$20.00]

Crozier, Emmet. **Yankee Reporters.** NY: Oxford UP; 1956. [$24.00]

Cruickshank, Helen Gere. **Flight into Sunshine.** NY: Macmillan; 1948. [$15.00]

Crumb, Frederick W. **Tom Quick.** Narrowsburg, NY: Delaware Valley; 1936. [x-lib., $25.00]

Cruse, Mary Anne. **Cameron Hall.** Philadelphia: Lippincott; 1867. [covers worn, $45.00]

Cruse, Thomas. **Apache Days and After.** Caldwell, ID: Caxton; 1941. [x-lib., $18.50]

Cruz, Martin de la. **Badianus Manuscript.** Baltimore: Hopkins; 1940. [$135.00]

Culbertson, Thaddeus A. **Journal of an Expedition to the Mauvaises Terres and the Upper Missouri in 1850.** Washington: USGPO; 1952. [$35.00]

Culbreth, David Marvel Reynolds. **The University of Virginia.** NY: Neale; 1908. [$27.50]

Culin, Stewart. **Games of the North American Indians.** Washington: USGPO; 1907. [$65.00]

Cull, John Augustine. **Bride of Mission San Jose.** NY: Abingdon; 1920. [$12.50]

Cullen, Countee. **The Black Christ & Other Poems.** NY, London: Harper; 1929. [$30.00]

Cullen, Countee. **Caroling Dusk.** 1st ed. NY, London: Harper; 1927. [$15.00]

Cullen, Countee. **Color.** NY: Harper; 1925. [$12.50]

Cullen, Countee. **One Way to Heaven.** NY, London: Harper; 1932. [$45.00]

Culley, John Henry. **Cattle, Horses, & Men of the Western Range.** Los Angeles Ritchie; 1940. [signed, $125.00]

Culver, I. F. **Alabama Resources.** see, Alabama. Department of Agriculture.

Cuming, Fortescue. **Sketches of a Tour to the Western Country through the States of Ohio and Kentucky.** Pittsburgh: Cramer, Spear & Eichbaum; 1810. [$950.00] [$850.00]

Cumming, Hiram. **Secret History of the Perfidies, Intrigues, and Corruptions of the Tyler Dynasty.** Washington, NY: The Author; 1845. [$135.00]

Cummings, E. E. **&.** NY: Priv. Print.; 1925. [shabby, $75.00]

Cummings, E. E. **The Enormous Room.** 1st ed. NY: Boni & Liveright; 1922. [covers very soiled, $25.00]

Cummings, E. E. **XLI Poems.** NY: Dial; 1925. [dj chipped, $250.00]

Cummins, Ella Sterling. see, Mighels, Ella Sterling.

Cummins, Sarah J. **Autobiography and Reminiscences.** Freewater, OR: Allen; 1914. [$100.00]

Cuneo, John R. **Robert Rogers of the Rangers.** NY: Oxford UP; 1959. [$27.50]

Cunningham, Eugene. **Triggernometry.** Caldwell, ID: Caxton; 1941. [$35.00]

Cunningham, Robert Oliver. **Notes on the Natural History of the Strait of Magellan and West Coast of Patagonia.** Edinburgh: Edmonston and Douglas; 1871. [rebound, $150.00]

Cunz, Dieter. **The Maryland Germans.** Princeton: Princeton UP; 1948. [$40.00] [x-lib., $22.50]

Curley, Walter J. P. **Letters from the Pacific: 1943-1946.** [s.l.]: Curley; 1959. [$32.50]

Curran, Michael Philip. **Life of Patrick A. Collins.** Norwood, MA: Norwood; 1906. [$25.00]

Currier, John J. **History of Newbury, Mass., 1635-1902.** Boston: Damrell & Upham; 1902. [$65.00]

Curti, Merle Eugene. **Growth of American Thought.** 2nd ed. NY: Harper; 1951. [$15.00]

Curtis, Charles P. **The Oppenheimer Case.** NY: Simon and Schuster; 1955. [$35.00]

Curtis, Edith Roelker. **A Season in Utopia.** NY: Nelson; 1961. [$12.50]

Curtis, Francis. **The Republican Party.** NY: Putnam; 1904. 2 v. [chipped dj, $75.00]

Curtis, George Ticknor. **Life of Daniel Webster.** NY: Appleton; 1870. 2 v. [$60.00]

Curtis, George Ticknor. **Life of James Buchanan.** NY: Harper; 1883. 2 v. [$85.00]

Curtis, George William. **Lotus-Eating.** NY: Harper; 1852. [$125.00]

Curtis, Natalie. see, Burlin, Natalie Curtis.

Curtis, Newton Martin. **From Bull Run to Chancellorsville.** NY, London: Putnam; 1906. [$55.00]

Curtiss, Arthur Lester Byron. **Life and Adventures of Nat Foster.** 2nd ed. Utica, NY: Griffiths; 1912. [$30.00]

Curtiss, Arthur Lester Byron. **Story of a Pass in the Adirondacks.** Boston: Gorham; 1917. [$50.00]

Curtiss, Daniel S. **Western Portraiture, and Emigrants' Guide.** NY: Colton; 1852. [inscribed, $200.00]

Curwood, James Oliver. **The Alaskan.** NY: Cosmopolitan; 1923. [$10.00]

Cushing, Caleb. **Outlines of the Life and Public Services, Civil and Military, of William Henry Harrison.** Boston: Eastburn's; 1840. [$45.00]

Cushing, Caleb. **The Treaty of Washington.** NY: Harper; 1873. [$50.00] [$35.00]

Cushing, Thomas. **History of the Counties of Gloucester, Salem, and Cumberland New Jersey .** Philadelphia: Everts & Peck; 1883. [rebound, $185.00]

Cushman, Dan. **The Great North Trail.** 1st ed. NY: McGraw-Hill; 1966. [dj torn, $20.00] [$18.00]

Cushman, Horatio Bardwell. **History of the Choctaw, Chickasaw and Natchez Indians.** Greenville, TX: Headlight; 1899. [$250.00]

Cushman, Rebecca. **Swing Your Mountain Gal.** Boston, NY: Houghton Mifflin; 1934. [light mildew, dj soiled and torn, $30.00]

Custer, Elizabeth Bacon. **Boots and Saddles.** NY: Harper; 1885. [1st state, $45.00] [$50.00]

Custer, Elizabeth Bacon. **Following the Guidon.** NY: Harper; 1890. [covers scuffed, $27.50] [$50.00]

Custer, Elizabeth Bacon. **Tenting on the Plains.** NY: Webster; 1887. [$100.00] [1889 reissue, $75.00] [1893 issue, $20.00]

Custer, George Armstrong. **The Custer Story.** NY: Devin-Adair; 1950. [$24.00]

Custer, George Armstrong. **My Life on the Plains.** London: Folio Society; 1963. [$35.00]

Cutbush, James. **American Artist's Manual.** Philadelphia: Johnson & Warner; 1814. 2 v. [$375.00]

Cutchins, John Abram. **History of the Twenty-Ninth Division, "Blue and Gray," 1917-1919.** Philadelphia: MacCalla; 1921. [$35.00]

Cutler, Carl C. **Greyhounds of the Sea.** 1st ed. NY, London: Putnam; 1930. [$75.00]

Cutler, Jervis. **A Topographical Description of the State of Ohio, Indiana Territory, and Louisiana.** Boston: Williams; 1812. [rebacked, some foxing, $1500.00] [$2000.00]

Dabney, Owen P. **True Story of the Lost Shackle.** Salem, OR: Capital; 1897. [spine chipped, $150.00]

Dabney, Robert Lewis. **Life and Campaigns of Lieut.-Gen. Thomas J. Jackson.** NY; Richmond: Blelock; National; 1866. [$65.00]

Dabney, Wendell Phillips. **Cincinnati's Colored Citizens.** Cincinnati: Dabney; 1926. [$90.00]

Daddow, Samuel Harries. **Coal, Iron, and Oil.** Pottsville, PA; Philadelphia: Bannan; Lippincott; 1866. [$125.00]

Daggett, John. **Sketch of the History of Attleborough.** Boston: Usher; 1894. [$95.00]

Dahlinger, Charles William. **Pittsburgh.** NY: Putnam; 1916. [$29.00]

Dairy World. **Hand-Book of Ford County, Kansas.** Chicago: Burch; 1887. [$250.00]

Dakin, Susanna. **A Scotch Paisano.** Berkeley: U. of California; 1939. [x-lib., $17.50] [tear in spine of dj, $49.50]

Dale, Edward Everett. **Cherokee Cavaliers.** 1st ed. Norman: U. of Oklahoma; 1939. [$90.00]

Dale, Edward Everett. **Cow Country.** Norman: U. of Oklahoma; 1943. [$20.00]

Dale, Edward Everett. **Indians of the Southwest.** 1st ed. Norman: U. of Oklahoma; 1949. [$40.00]

Dallas, Francis Gregory. **Papers of.** NY: Naval Hist. Soc.; 1917. [binding soiled, $25.00]

Dallas, Robert Charles. **History of the Maroons.** London: Longman and Rees; 1803. 2 v. [rebound, vol. 2 lacks frontis, $150.00]

Dally, Joseph W. **Woodbridge and Vicinity.** New Brunswick, NJ: Gordon; 1873. [$95.00]

Dalrymple, John. **Address of the People of Great Britain to the Inhabitants of America.** London: Cadell; 1775. [lacks rear wrapper, $185.00]

Dalton, Emmett. **When the Daltons Rode.** 1st ed. Garden City: Doubleday, Doran; 1931. [$90.00] [1937 Sun Dial ed., $50.00]

Dalton, John Edward. **Forged in Strong Fires.** Caldwell, ID: Caxton; 1948. [$40.00]

Daly, Dominick. **Adventures of Roger L'Estrange.** London: Sonnenschein; 1896. [$45.00]

Daly, James. **For Love & Bears.** Chicago: Gray; 1886. [$225.00] [corners worn, $175.00]

Dalzell, George W. **The Flight from the Flag.** Chapel Hill: U. of North Carolina; 1940. [$25.00]

Dame, Lawrence. **Yucatan.** 1st ed. NY: Random; 1941. [$12.50]

Damon, Ethel Moseley. **Sanford Ballard Dole and His Hawaii.** Alto, CA: Pacific Books; 1957. [$10.00]

Damon, Samuel Chenery. **Puritan Missions in the Pacific.** New Haven: Hunnewell; 1868 [cover 1869]. [$45.00]

Dana, Charles Anderson. **The United States Illustrated.** NY: Meyer; [1855?]. 2 v. [$2500.00]

Dana, Charles W. **The Garden of the World; or, The Great West.** Boston: Wentworth; 1856. [extremities chipped, $85.00]

Dana, David D. **The Fireman.** 2nd ed. Boston: French; 1858. [$150.00]

Dana, Edmund. **Geographical Sketches on the Western Country.** Cincinnati: Looker, Reynolds; 1819. [$850.00] [$1000.00]

Dana, James Dwight. **Corals and Coral Islands.** NY: Dodd, Mead; 1879. [rebound, $175.00]

Dana, Julian. **Sutter of California.** NY: Halcyon; 1938, c1934. [frayed dj, $9.00]

Dana, Richard Henry. **The Journal.** Cambridge: Harvard UP; 1968. 3 v. [$50.00]

Dana, Richard Henry. **Poems.** Boston: Bowles and Dearborn; 1827. [shaken, $88.00]

Dana, Richard Henry. **To Cuba and Back.** Boston: Ticknor and Fields; 1859. [$75.00] [$100.00]

Dana, Richard Henry. **Two Years before the Mast.** Chicago: Lakeside; 1930. [$65.00]

Danckaerts, Jasper. **Journal of a Voyage to New York, and a Tour in Several of the American Colonies in 1679-80.** Brooklyn: Long Island Hist. Soc.; 1867. [$75.00]

Dane, George Ezra. **Ghost Town.** NY: Tudor; 1948, c1941. [$20.00].

Danford, Harry Edmund. **Trail of the Gray Dragoon.** NY: Vinal; 1928. [$17.50]

Dangerfield, George. **Chancellor Robert R. Livingston.** 1st ed. NY: Harcourt, Brace; 1960. [$23.50]

Dangerfield, George. **Era of Good Feelings.** 1st ed. NY: Harcourt, Brace; 1952. [$20.00]

Daniel, Ferdinand Eugene. **Recollections of a Rebel Surgeon and Other Sketches.** Chicago: Clinic; 1901, c1899. [silverfished, crayon marks, $17.50]

Daniel, Frederick S. **Richmond Howitzers in the War.** Richmond: [s.n.]; 1891. [x-lib., $125.00] [$300.00]

Daniel, John Warrick. **Life and Reminiscences of Jefferson Davis.** see, title

Daniel, Lizzie. **Confederate Scrap-Book.** Richmond: Hill; 1893. [$30.00]

Daniels, George Fisher. **Huguenots in the Nipmuck Country or Oxford prior to 1713.** Boston: Estes & Lauriat; 1880. [$35.00]

Daniels, Jonathan. **Clash of Angels.** NY: Brewer and Warren, Payson and Clarke; 1930. [bumped, soiled, sunned, $20.00]

Daniels, Jonathan. **The Devil's Backbone.** 1st ed. NY: McGraw-Hill; 1962. [worn dj, $30.00] [$18.00]

Daniels, Jonathan. **Prince of Carpetbaggers.** 1st ed. Philadelphia: Lippincott; 1958. [$16.00]

Daniels, Josephus. **Editor in Politics.** Chapel Hill: U. of North Carolina; 1941. [$30.00]

Dannett, Sylvia G. L. **She Rode with the Generals.** Edinburgh, NY: Nelson; 1960. [$16.00]

Danskin, Washington A. **How and Why I Became a Spiritualist.** Boston; NY: Marsh; Munson; 1858. [$30.00]

Darby, William. **Geographical Description of the State of Louisiana.** Philadelphia: Bioren; 1816. [$600.00]

Darby, William. **Tour from the City of New York, to Detroit.** NY: Kirk & Mercein; 1819. [$400.00]

Dargan, Olive Tilford. **From My Highest Hill.** Philadelphia, NY: Lippincott; 1941. [bumped, sunned, hinges cracked, $40.00]

Darley, George Marshall. **Pioneering in the San Juan.** Chicago, NY: Revell; 1899. [inscribed, $90.00]

Darlington, Mary C. **History of Colonel Henry Bouquet and the Western Frontiers of Pennsylvania, 1747-1764.** [s.n.: s.l.]; 1920. [$50.00]

Darlington, William. **Flora Cestrica.** 3rd ed. Philadelphia: Lindsay & Blakiston; 1853. [x-lib., $100.00]

Darnell, Elias. **A Journal.** Philadelphia: Lippincott, Grambo; 1854. [$225.00]

Darrah, William Culp. **Powell of the Colorado.** Princeton: Princeton UP; 1951. [$20.00]

Darrow, Clarence. **Attorney for the Damned.** NY: Simon and Schuster; 1957. [$15.00]

Darrow, Clarence. **Story of My Life.** NY, London: Scribner; 1932. [$25.00]

Dartmouth College. **Report of the Case of the Trustees of Dartmouth College against William H. Woodward.** Portsmouth, NH: Foster; 1819. [$500.00]

Daugherty, Harry Micajah. **Inside Story of the Harding Tragedy.** NY: Churchill; 1932. [$12.50]

Davenport, Bishop. **A History and New Gazetteer or Geographical Dictionary of North America and the West Indies.** NY: Benedict; 1842. [$75.00]

Davenport, Montague. **Under the Gridiron.** London: Tinsley; 1876. [$75.00]

David, Ebenezer. **A Rhode Island Chaplain in the Revolution.** Providence: Society of the Cincinnati; 1949. [$40.00]

David, Henry. **History of the Haymarket Affair.** NY: Farrar & Rinehart; [$30.00]

David, Robert Beebe. **Finn Burnett, Frontiersman.** 1st ed. Glendale, CA: Clark; 1937, c1936. [$90.00]

Davidson, Charles Theodore. **America's Unusual Spot.** Cleveland, TN: White Wing; 1954. [dj torn & taped, $20.00]

Davidson, Edward H. **Hawthorne's Last Phase.** New Haven: Yale UP; 1949. [$15.00]

Davidson, Grace Gillam. **Early Records of Georgia.** Macon, GA: Burke; 1932. 2 v. [bumped and mildew stained, $100.00]

Davidson, James Wood. **The Florida of To-Day.** NY: Appleton; 1889, c1888. [$25.00]

Davidson, Lucretia Maria. **Amir Khan.** NY: Carvill; 1829. [$85.00]

Davidson, Philip Grant. **Propaganda and the American Revolution.** Chapel Hill: U. of North Carolina; 1941. [$20.00]

Davie, John Constanse. **Letters from Buenos Ayres and Chile.** London: Ackermann; 1819. [lacks half-title, x-lib., $200.00]

Davies, David. **Oshkosh, Wisconsin, Welsh Settlement Centennial, 1847-1947.** Amarillo, TX: Russell; 1947. [x-lib., $25.00]

Davies, Richard. **Account of the Convincement, Exercises, Services, and Travels, of That Ancient Servant of the Lord.** 2nd ed. London, Philadelphia: Chattin; 1752. [$100.00]

Davis, Andrew McFarland. **Confiscation of John Chandler's Estate.** Boston, NY: Houghton Mifflin; 1903. [$50.00]

Davis, Arthur Kyle. **More Traditional Ballads of Virginia.** Chapel Hill: U. of North Carolina; 1960. [mildewed, $20.00]

Davis, Arthur Kyle. **Virginia Communities in War Time.** Richmond: Virginia War History Commission; 1926-27. 2 v. [$35.00]

Davis, Britton. **The Truth about Geronimo.** New Haven; London: Yale UP; Oxford UP; 1929. [$40.00] [$45.00]

Davis, Burke. **The Cowpens-Guilford Courthouse Campaign.** 1st ed. Philadelphia: Lippincott; 1962. [$20.00]

Davis, Burke. **Gray Fox: Robert E. Lee and the Civil War.** NY: Rinehart; 1956. [$15.00]

Davis, Burke. **Jeb Stuart.** 1st ed. NY: Rinehart; 1957. [$30.00] [worn dj, $17.50]

Davis, Clyde Brion. **The Arkansas.** NY, Toronto: Farrar & Rinehart; 1940. [$30.00]

Davis, Deering. **The American Cow Pony.** Princeton: Van Nostrand; 1962. [$16.00] [$35.00]

Davis, Duke. **Flashlights from Mountain and Plain.** Bound Brook, NJ: Pentecostal Union; 1911. [$60.00]

Davis, Edward J. P. **Historical San Diego.** San Diego: Davis; 1953. [$15.00]

Davis, Edwin Adams. **Of the Night Wind's Telling.** Norman: U. of Oklahoma; 1946. [$14.00]

Davis, Ellis A. **Historical Encyclopedia of Texas.** rev. ed. Dallas: Texas Historical Society; [1937?]. 2 v. [$125.00]

Davis, Elmer Orville. **The First Five Years of the Railroad Era in Colorado.** Golden: Sage Books; 1948. [$45.00]

Davis, Forrest. **Huey Long.** 1st ed. NY: Dodge; 1935. [$15.00]

Davis, George Lynn-Lachlan. **The Day-Star of American Freedom.** NY: Scribner; 1855. [worn, $40.00]

Davis, George Thompson Brown. **Metlakahtla.** Chicago: Ram's Horn; 1904. [$25.00]

Davis, Gherardi. **The United States Navy and Merchant Marine from 1840-1880.** NY: Gilliss; 1923. [inscribed limited ed., $150.00]

Davis, Harold Lenoir. **Honey in the Horn.** 1st ed. NY: Harper; 1935. [$20.00]

Davis, Harold Lenoir. **Proud Riders and Other Poems.** 1st ed. NY, London: Harper; 1942. [$35.00]

Davis, Harold Lenoir. **Team Bells Woke Me.** NY: Morrow; 1953. [$40.00] [$50.00]

Davis, Harold Lenoir. **Winds of Morning.** NY: Morrow; 1952. [dj frayed, $20.00] [$25.00]

Davis, Harold Palmer. **Black Democracy; the Story of Haiti.** NY: Dial; 1928. [$20.00]

Davis, Henry Turner. **Solitary Places Made Glad.** Cincinnati: Cranston & Stowe; 1890. [$125.00]

Davis, J. H. **The Possum Creek Poultry Club.** Chatham, NY: Fanciers' Review; 1895. [$90.00]

Davis, Jefferson. **Rise and Fall of the Confederate Government.** NY: Appleton; 1881. 2 v. [$100.00] [1958 Yoseloff ed., $35.00]

Davis, Jerome. **The Russian Immigrant.** NY: Macmillan; 1922. [x-lib., $10.00]

Davis, John. **Travels of Four Years and a Half in the United States of America.** London: Ostell; 1803. [spine chipped, $600.00] [1910 Bibliophile Soc. ed. in two vols., $125.00]

Davis, Julia. **The Shenandoah.** NY, Toronto: Farrar & Rinehart; 1945. [$15.00]

Davis, Kenneth Sydney. **The Hero: Charles A. Lindbergh and the American Dream.** 1st ed. Garden City: Doubleday; 1959. [$15.00]

Davis, Mary Lee. **Alaska, the Great Bear's Cub.** Boston: Wilde; 1930. [$27.50]

Davis, Mary Lee. **Uncle Sam's Attic.** Boston: Wilde; 1930. [$25.00] [$10.00]

Davis, Mary Lee. **We Are Alaskans.** Boston: Wilde; 1931. [$15.00]

Davis, Matthew L. **Memoirs of Aaron Burr.** see, Burr, Aaron.

Davis, Nicholas A. **The Campaign from Texas to Maryland.** Austin: Steck; 1961. [$45.00] [$50.00]

Davis, Nicholas A. **Chaplain Davis and Hood's Texas Brigade.** San Antonio: Principia; 1962. [$35.00]

Davis, Richard Harding. **Soldiers of Fortune.** NY: Scribner; 1897. [$40.00]

Davis, Richard Harding. **Three Gringos in Venezuela and Central America.** NY: Harper; 1896. [$25.00]

Davis, Richard Harding. **The West from a Car Window.** NY: Harper; 1892. [first state, $85.00]

Davis, Susan Lawrence. **Authentic History, Ku Klux Klan, 1865-1877.** NY: The Author; 1924. [$25.00]

Davis, T. E. **From New Jersey to California '97.** Somerville, NJ: Bateman; 1897. [$35.00]

Davis, Thomas. **Rhode Island Politics, and Journalism.** Providence: Greene; 1866. [$20.00]

Davis, Varina Howell. **Jefferson Davis.** NY: Belford; 1890. 2 v. [$175.00] [$150.00]

Davis, Walter Bickford. **Illustrated History of Missouri.** St. Louis; Cincinnati: Hall; Clarke; 1876. [$135.00]

Davis, William Morris. **Nimrod of the Sea.** NY: Harper; 1874. [$150.00]

Davis, William Watts Hart. **The Fries Rebellion, 1798-99.** Doylestown, PA: Doylestown Pub. Co.; 1899. [$135.00] [$100.00]

Davis, William Watts Hart. **El Gringo.** NY: Harper; 1857. [$350.00]

Davis, William Watts Hart. **The Spanish Conquest of New Mexico.** Doylestown, PA: [s.n.]; 1869. [presentation, $225.00]

Davis, Winfield J. **History of Political Conventions in California, 1849-1892.** Sacramento: California State Library; 1893. [$125.00]

Dawes, Rufus R. **Service with the Sixth Wisconsin Volunteers.** Marietta, OH: Alderman; 1890. [$125.00] [x-lib., $85.00]

Dawley, T. R. **Incidents of American Camp Life.** NY: Hurst; 1866. [second issue, $35.00]

Dawson, Carl Addington. **Group Settlement; Ethnic Communities in Western Canada.** Toronto: Macmillan; 1936. [x-lib., $25.00]

Dawson, Carl Addington. **Pioneering in the Prairie Provinces.** Toronto: Macmillan; 1940. [x-lib., $25.00]

Dawson, Carl Addington. **Settlement of the Peace River Country.** Toronto: Macmillan; 1934. [x-lib., $27.50]

Dawson, Francis W. **Our Women in the War.** Charleston, SC: Walker, Evans & Cogswell; 1887. [$75.00]

Dawson, Henry Barton. **Battles of the United States by Sea and Land.** NY: Johnson, Fry; 1858. 2 v. [$165.00]

Dawson, Moses. **A Historical Narrative of the Civil and Military Services of Major-General William H. Harrison.** Cincinnati: Dawson; 1824. [lacks errata slip, $100.00]

Dawson, Sarah Morgan. **Confederate Girl's Diary.** Boston, NY: Houghton Mifflin; 1913. [front endpaper missing, $48.50] [$65.00]

Day, A. Grove. **Coronado's Quest.** Berkeley, Los Angeles: U. of California; 1940. [$50.00]

Day, Donald. **Big Country: Texas.** NY: Duell, Sloan & Pearce; 1947. [$30.00] [$35.00]

Day, Jack Hays. **The Sutton-Taylor Feud.** [s.l.]: The Author; 1937. [$35.00]

Day, James M. **Jacob De Cordova, Land Merchant of Texas.** Waco: Texian; 1962. [$45.00] [$55.00]

Dayton, Eldorous Lyons. **Give 'Em Hell Harry.** NY: Devin-Adair; 1956. [$25.00]

De Barthe, Joseph. **Life and Adventures of Frank Grouard.** St. Joseph, MO: Combe; 1894. [rebacked, new endpapers, $325.00] [1958 Oklahoma ed., $25.00]

De Benneville, George. **Some Remarkable Passages in the Life of.** rev. ed. Germantown, PA: Cleaves; 1890. [$40.00]

De Cordova, Jacob. **Texas, Her Resources and Her Public Men.** 1st ed. Philadelphia: Lippincott; 1858. [binding repaired, $750.00]

De Costa, Benjamin Franklin. **Lake George.** NY: Randolph; 1868. [$75.00]

De Cou, George. **Burlington.** Philadelphia: Harris and Partridge; 1945. [$45.00] [$40.00]

De Cou, George. **Moorestown and Her Neighbors.** Philadelphia: Harris & Partridge; 1929. [$30.00]

De Forest, John William. **History of the Indians of Connecticut.** Hartford: Hamersley; 1852. [$50.00]

De Forest, John William. **A Volunteer's Adventures.** 1st ed. New Haven: Yale UP; 1946. [worn dj, $25.00] [$30.00] [$25.00]

De Hass, Wills. **History of the Early Settlement and Indian Wars of Western Virginia.** Wheeling, Philadelphia: Hoblitzell; 1851. [$100.00]

De Koven, Anna Farwell. **Life and Letters of John Paul Jones.** London: Laurie; [1913?]. 2 v. [$125.00] [1913 Scribner ed., $125.00]

De La Fontaine, Oliver Roberts. **The Great Understander.** Aurora, IL: Walter; 1931. [$45.00] [$80.00]

De Leon, Thomas Cooper. **Four Years in Rebel Capitals.** Mobile, AL: Gossip Printing; 1890. [lacks front endpaper, $100.00] [x-lib., $35.00]

De Mare, Marie. **G. P. A. Healy, American Artist.** NY: McKay; 1954. [$15.00]

De Massey, Ernest. see, Massey, Ernest de.

De Mille, George E. **Catholic Movement in the American Episcopal Church.** Philadelphia: Church Historical Society; 1941. [$25.00]

De Quille, Dan. see, Wright, William.

De Ros, John Frederick Fitzgerald. **Personal Narrative of Travels in the United States and Canada in 1826.** London: Ainsworth; 1827. [$400.00] [rebound, $300.00] [$350.00]

De Rupert, A. E. D. **Californians and Mormons.** NY: Lovell; 1881. [backstrip worn, $95.00]

De Shields, James T. **Border Wars of Texas.** Tioga, TX: Herald; 1912. [inscribed, $375.00] [$135.00]

De Veaux, Samuel. **The Falls of Niagara.** Buffalo: Hayden; 1839. [x-lib., $75.00]

De Veaux, Samuel. **The Traveller's Own Book to Saratoga Springs, Niagara Falls and Canada.** Buffalo: Faxon & Read; 1841. [one map torn, $75.00]

De Voto, Bernard. **Across the Wide Missouri.** Boston: Houghton Mifflin; 1947. [$45.00]

De Voto, Bernard. **The Chariot of Fire.** NY: Macmillan; 1926. [$25.00]

De Voto, Bernard. **The Crooked Mile.** NY: Minton, Balch; 1924. [$30.00]

De Voto, Bernard. **The Easy Chair.** Boston: Houghton Mifflin; 1955. [$15.00]

De Voto, Bernard. **Forays and Rebuttals.** Boston: Little, Brown; 1936. [$12.50]

De Voto, Bernard. **The House of Sun-Goes-Down.** NY: Macmillan; 1928. [$20.00]

De Voto, Bernard. **The Literary Fallacy.** Boston: Little, Brown; 1944. [$12.50]

De Voto, Bernard. **We Accept with Pleasure.** Boston: Little, Brown; 1934. [signed, $30.00]

De Voto, Bernard. **Women and Children First.** Boston: Houghton Mifflin; 1956, c1955. [$15.00]

De Voto, Bernard. **Year of Decision, 1846.** 1st ed. Boston: Little, Brown; 1943. [worn dj, $35.00]

De Windt, Harry. **Through the Gold-Fields of Alaska to Bering Straits.** NY, London: Harper; 1898. [$75.00, Canadian]

De Witt, David Miller. **The Judicial Murder of Mary E. Surratt.** Baltimore: Murphy; 1895. [$125.00]

De Wolff, J. H. **Pawnee Bill.** [s.l.]: Pawnee Bill's Historic Wild West Company; 1902. [$100.00] [spine restored, $75.00]

Deaderick, John Barron. **Strategy in the Civil War.** Harrisburg, PA: Military Service; 1946. [$15.00]

Dean, Henry Clay. **Crimes of the Civil War, and Curse of the Funding System.** Baltimore: Innes; 1868. [rebacked, $45.00]

Dean, Winnie Mims. **Jefferson, Texas, Queen of the Cypress.** Dallas: Mathis, Van Nort; 1953. [$45.00] [$40.00]

Deane, Samuel. **History of Scituate, Massachusetts.** Boston: Loring; 1831. [$60.00]

Deane, Samuel. **The New England Farmer; or, Georgical Dictionary.** 2nd ed. Worchester: Thomas; 1797. [some worming, $200.00]

Dearborn, Henry. **Revolutionary War Journals of.** Chicago: Caxton Club; 1939. [$95.00]

Dearborn, Henry Alexander Scammell. **Letters on the Internal Improvements and Commerce of the West.** Boston: Lewis; 1839. [$125.00]

Dearborn Independent. **The International Jew.** Dearborn, MI: Dearborn Pub.; 1920-1922. 4 v. [$50.00]

Dearing, Mary Rulkotter. **Veterans in Politics.** Baton Rouge: Louisiana State UP; 1952. [$45.00]

Deason, Beecher. **Seven Years in Texas Prisons.** [s.l.: s.n.; 192-?]. [$85.00]

Deatherage, C. P. **The Early History of the Lumber Trade of Kansas City.** Kansas City, MO: Retail Lumberman; 1924. [covers soiled, $8.00]

Debo, Angie. **Prairie City.** NY: Knopf; 1944. [$15.00]

Debo, Angie. **Rise and Fall of the Choctaw Republic.** 1st ed. Norman: U. of Oklahoma; 1934. [$120.00]

Debo, Angie. **The Road to Disappearance.** Norman: U. of Oklahoma; 1941. [$114.00]

Debs, Eugene V. **Walls and Bars.** Chicago: Socialist Party; 1927. [$50.00]

Debs, Eugene V. **Writings and Speeches.** NY: Hermitage; 1948. [$15.00]

Decker, Amelia Stickney. **That Ancient Trail.** Trenton: Petty; 1942. [signed, $40.00]

Defoe, Daniel. **The History and Remarkable Life of the Truly Honourable Colonel Jacque.** NY: Christy; 1844. [$40.00]

Delabarre, Edmund Burke. **Dighton Rock.** NY: Neale; 1928. [$45.00]

Delafield, John. **Inquiry into the Origin of the Antiquities of America.** NY: Colt, Burgess; 1839. [x-lib., with frontis, $350.00] [1839 Cincinnati issue, rebound, lacks frontis, $100.00]

Deland, Margaret Wade. **Florida Days.** Boston: Little, Brown; 1889. [$85.00] [$100.00]

Delano, Alonzo. **Across the Plains and among the Diggings.** NY: Wilson-Erickson; 1936. [$65.00]

Delano, Alonzo. **Alonzo Delano's California Correspondence.** Sacramento: Sacramento Book Collectors Club; 1952. [$75.00]

Delano, Alonzo. **Life on the Plains and among the Diggings.** NY: Saxton; 1859. [4th printing, shaken, $95.00]

Delano, Alonzo. **Old Block's Sketch Book.** Santa Ana, CA: Fine Arts; 1947. [$35.00]

Delano, Amasa. **Narrative of Voyages and Travels in the Northern and Southern Hemispheres.** 2nd ed. Boston: House; 1818. [front joint repaired, $500.00]

Delaplaine, Edward S. **Francis Scott Key.** 1st ed. Brooklyn: Biography Press; 1937. [signed and numbered, $135.00]

Delaplaine, Edward S. **Life of Thomas Johnson.** limited ed. NY: Hitchcock; 1927. [$65.00]

Delke, James Almerius. **History of the North Carolina Chowan Baptist Association, 1806-1881.** Raleigh: Edwards, Broughton; 1882. [very silverfished, $150.00]

Dellenbaugh, Frederick Samuel. **A Canyon Voyage.** NY: Putnam; 1908. [$65.00]

Dellenbaugh, Frederick Samuel. **North-Americans of Yesterday.** NY, London: Putnam; 1900. [4th printing, rebound, $175.00]

Dellenbaugh, Frederick Samuel. **The Romance of the Colorado River.** NY, London: Putnam; 1902. [hinges cracked, $150.00]

Delteil, Joseph. **Lafayette.** NY: Minton, Balch; 1928. [$20.00]

Deming, Henry Champion. **Life of Ulysses S. Grant.** Hartford, Cincinnati, Scranton: National; 1868. [endpapers stained, $25.00] [binding worn, $14.50]

Deming, William Chapin. **Roosevelt in the Bunk House.** 2nd ed. Laramie: Laramie Printing; 1927. [$20.00]

Demoss, Estyl Lee. **Flyin' T Ranch.** Dallas: Royal; 1964. [$25.00]

Denig, Edwin Thompson. **Five Indian Tribes of the Upper Missouri.** 1st ed. Norman: U. of Oklahoma; 1961. [$40.00]

Denison, Frederic. **Westerly and Its Witnesses.** Providence: Reid; 1878. [$40.00]

Denison, Merrill. **Harvest Triumphant.** NY: Dodd, Mead; 1949. [$20.00]

Denslow, Ray Vaughn. **Civil War and Masonry in Missouri.** [St. Louis?]: Grand Lodge, Ancient Free and Accepted Masons of the State of Missouri; 1930. [$25.00]

Densmore, Frances. **The American Indians and Their Music.** NY: Womans; 1926. [presentation, $22.50]

Densmore, Frances. **Chippewa Music.** Washington: USGPO; 1910. [vol. 1 only, $22.50]

Denver Post. **Rocky Mountain Empire.** see, Howe, Elvon L.

Depew, Chauncey M. **My Memories of Eighty Years.** NY: Scribner; 1922. [$15.00]

Depew, Chauncey M. **One Hundred Years of American Commerce.** NY: Haynes; 1895. [$100.00]

Derbec, Etienne. **A French Journalist in the California Gold Rush.** Georgetown, CA: Talisman; 1964. [fine, $95.00]

Derleth, August William. **Countryman's Journal.** NY: Duell, Sloan and Pearce; 1963. [$12.00]

Derleth, August William. **Village Daybook: A Sac Prairie Journal.** Chicago: Pellegrini & Cudahy; 1947. [inscribed, $25.00]

Derleth, August William. **The Wisconsin.** 1st ed. NY: Farrar & Rinehart; 1942. [chipped dj, $25.00]

Derrick, Samuel Melanchthon. **Centennial History of South Carolina Railroad.** Columbia, SC: State Company; 1930. [x-lib., $45.00]

Desmet, Pierre Jean. see, Smet, Pierre-Jean de.

Detroit Post and Tribune. **Zachariah Chandler.** Detroit: Post and Tribune; 1880. [$50.00]

Dett, R. Nathaniel. **Religious Folk-Songs of the Negro as Sung at Hampton Institute.** Hampton, VA: Hampton Institute; 1927. [$40.00]

Deutsch, Albert. **The Mentally Ill in America.** 1st ed. Garden City: Doubleday, Doran; 1937. [$10.00]

Devens, Richard Miller. **Reminiscences of the Blue and Gray, '61-'65.** Chicago: Preston; 1895. [browning, $39.50]

Devinny, V. **Story of a Pioneer.** Denver: Reed; 1904. [presentation, lacks front endpaper, $60.00] [ink stains, $65.00]

Dewees, Francis Percival. **The Molly Maguires.** Philadelphia: Lippincott; 1877. [$40.00]

Dewees, Jacob. **The Great Future of America and Africa.** Philadelphia: Orr; 1854. [front cover badly damaged, $85.00]

Dewees, William B. **Letters from an Early Settler of Texas.** 2nd ed. Louisville: New Albany Tribune; 1858. [second printing, $425.00]

Dewey, Adelbert Milton. **Life and Letters of Admiral Dewey.** NY: Eaton & Mains; 1899. [$35.00]

Dexter, Henry Martyn. **England and Holland of the Pilgrims.** Boston, NY: Houghton Mifflin; 1905. [rebound, lacks frontis, $25.00]

Di Maggio, Joe. **Lucky to Be a Yankee.** NY: Field; 1946. [$15.00]

Diaz del Castillo, Bernal. **The True History of the Conquest of Mexico.** NY: McBride; 1938. [$10.00]

Dicey, Edward. **Six Months in the Federal States.** London, Cambridge: Macmillan; 1863. 2 v. [$175.00]

Dick, Everett Newfon. **The Sod-House Frontier, 1854-1890.** 1st ed. NY: Appleton-Century; 1937. [$45.00]

Dick, Everett Newfon. **Vanguards of the Frontier.** 1st ed. NY, London: Appleton-Century; 1941. [$40.00]

Dickerson, Edward Nicoll. **Joseph Henry and the Magnetic Telegraph.** NY: Scribner; 1885. [$20.00]

Dickerson, Oliver Morton. **The Navigation Acts and the American Revolution.** Philadelphia: U. of Pennsylvania; 1951. [$30.00]

Dickerson, Philip Jackson. **History of the Osage Nation.** [Pawhuska, OK?: s.n.]; 1906. [$85.00] [$125.00]

Dickey, Luther Samuel. **History of the Eighty-Fifty Regiment Pennsylvania Volunteer Infantry, 1861-1865.** NY: Powers; 1915. [$50.00] [$65.00]

Dickey, Roland F. **New Mexico Village Arts.** Albuquerque: U. of New Mexico; 1949. [$45.00]

Dickinson, Emily. **Complete Poems of.** Boston: Little, Brown; 1924. [$20.00]

Dickinson, Emily. **Poems 1st-3d Series.** Boston: Little, Brown; 1896-1898, c1890-1896. 3 v. [crisp, $125.00]

Dickinson, Emily. **The Single Hound.** Boston: Little, Brown; 1914. [$150.00]

Dickinson, John. **Letters from a Farmer in Pennsylvania to the Inhabitants of the British Colonies.** NY: Outlook; 1903. [Imperial Japan ed., $150.00]

Dickinson, John. **Political Writings.** Wilmington: Bonsal and Niles; 1801. 2 v. [$250.00]

Dickinson, Jonathan. **God's Protecting Providence.** 3rd ed. London: Sowle; 1720. [$750.00]

Dickson, Harris. **The Story of King Cotton.** NY, London: Funk and Wagnalls; 1937. [$17.50]

Dickson, Samuel. **San Francisco Is Your Home.** Stanford: Stanford UP; 1947. [$5.00]

Diffenderffer, Frank Ried. **German Immigration into Pennsylvania through the Port of Philadelphia, 1700 to 1775 Part II. The Redemptioners.** Lancaster, PA: The Author; 1900. [x-lib., $40.00]

Digby, William. **The British Invasion from the North.** Albany, NY: Munsell; 1887. [x-lib., rebound, $175.00]

Diggins, John V. **Pioneer on the Delaware.** Chester, PA: Downham; 1964. [$17.50]

Dill, James Renwick. **The Saloon a Nuisance and License Unconstitutional.** 2nd ed. [s.l.: s.n.]; 1900. [$29.50]

Dillaway, Charles Knapp. **A History of the Grammar School; or, "The Free Schoole of 1645 in Roxburie."** Boston: Crosby, Nichols, Lee; 1860. [x-lib., $17.50]

Dillin, John Grace Wolfe. **The Kentucky Rifle.** 3rd ed. NY: Ludlum and Beebe; 1946. [$75.00]

Dillon, John Forrest. **John Marshall.** Chicago: Callaghan; 1903. 3 v. [$135.00]

Dillon, Richard H. **J. Ross Browne, Confidential Agent in Old California.** Norman: U. of Oklahoma; 1965. [$20.00]

Dillon, Richard H. **The Legend of Grizzly Adams.** NY: Coward-McCann; 1966. [dj soiled, $35.00]

Dillon, Richard H. **Meriwether Lewis.** NY: Coward-McCann; 1965. [2nd impression, $20.00]

Dillon, Richard H. **Wells, Fargo Detective.** NY: Coward-McCann; 1969. [$17.50]

Dimock, Marshall Edward. **Developing America's Waterways.** Chicago: U. of Chicago; 1935. [$15.00]

Dimsdale, Thomas Josiah. **The Vigilantes of Montana.** 3rd ed. Helena: State; 1915. [$200.00]

Dinsmoor, Robert. **Incidental Poems.** Haverhill, MA: Thayer; 1828. [$150.00]

Dinsmore, John Walker. **The Scotch-Irish in America.** Chicago: Winona; 1906. [front flyleaf missing, $24.00]

Disbrow, Edward Delavan. **The Man without a Gun.** Boston: Chapman & Grimes; 1936. [$20.00]

Disturnell, John. **Northern Traveller.** NY: Disturnell; 1844. [$75.00] [$65.00]

Ditzion, Sidney Herbert. **Marriage, Morals, and Sex in America.** NY: Bookman Associates; 1953. [$17.50]

Dix, Edwin Asa. **Champlain, the Founder of New France.** NY: Appleton; 1903. [$12.50]

Dixie, Florence Lady. **Across Patagonia.** NY: Worthington; 1881. [shabby, $25.00]

Dixon, Billy. **Life and Adventures of.** Guthrie, OK: Co-Operative Pub. Co.; 1914. [$300.00]

Dixon, Billy. **Life of "Billy" Dixon.** rev. ed. Dallas: Turner; 1927. [$125.00]

Dixon, Edward Henry. **Scenes in the Practice of a New York Surgeon.** NY: DeWitt & Davenport; 1855. [$85.00]

Dixon, George. **Voyage round the World.** see, Portlock, Nathaniel.

Dixon, J. M. **The Valley and the Shadow.** NY: Russell; 1868. [$35.00]

Dixon, Joseph Kossuth. **The Vanishing Race.** Garden City: Doubleday, Page; 1913. [$200.00]

Dixon, Keith A. **Hidden House.** Flagstaff: Northern Arizona Society of Science and Art; 1956. [$20.00]

Dixon, Thomas. **The Clansman.** 1st ed. NY: Doubleday, Page; 1905. [$30.00]

Dixon, Thomas. **The Life Worth Living.** NY: Doubleday, Page; 1905. [hinges weak, rubbed, $20.00]

Dixon, William Hepworth. **New America.** Philadelphia: Lippincott; 1867. [sunned, $45.00]

Dixon, Winifred Hawkridge. **Westward Hoboes.** NY: Scribner; 1921. [$35.00]

Dobie, Charles Caldwell. **San Francisco: A Pageant.** NY, London: Appleton-Century; 1939. [$16.50]

Dobie, J. Frank. **Apache Gold & Yaqui Silver.** Boston: Little, Brown; 1939. [$40.00] [$55.00]

Dobie, J. Frank. **The Ben Lilly Legend.** Boston: Little, Brown; 1950. [binding faded, $45.00] [near fine dj, $100.00] [1952 London ed., $30.00]

Dobie, J. Frank. **Bob More, Man and Bird Man.** Austin, TX: Southwest Review; 1941. [$175.00]

Dobie, J. Frank. **Coffee in the Gourd.** Austin: Texas Folklore Society; 1935. [$45.00]

Dobie, J. Frank. **Coronado's Children.** 1st ed. Dallas: Southwest Press; 1930. [$125.00]

Dobie, J. Frank. **Cow People.** 1st ed. London: Hammond; 1964. [$60.00] [x-lib., 12.50]

Dobie, J. Frank. **Follow de Drinkin' Gou'd.** Austin: Texas Folklore Society; 1928. [$55.00]

Dobie, J. Frank. **Guide to Life and Literature of the Southwest with a Few Observations.** Austin: U. of Texas; 1943. [$50.00] [1952 Southern Methodist ed., $50.00]

Dobie, J. Frank. **I'll Tell You a Tale.** 1st ed. Boston: Little, Brown; 1960. [$55.00]

Dobie, J. Frank. **John C. Duval.** 2nd ed. Dallas: Southern Methodist UP; 1965, c1939. [$25.00]

Dobie, J. Frank. **Man, Bird, and Beast.** Austin: Texas Folklore Society; 1930. [$75.00]

Dobie, J. Frank. **The Mustangs.** Boston: Little, Brown; 1952. [with fine dj, $100.00] [worn dj, $35.00] [$65.00] [later printing, $25.00]

Dobie, J. Frank. **On the Open Range.** 1st ed. Dallas: Southwest; 1931. [$150.00]

Dobie, J. Frank. **Rattlesnakes.** Boston: Little, Brown; 1965. [dj faded, $24.00]

Dobie, J. Frank. **Roadrunner in Fact and Folk-Lore.** Austin, TX: Texas Game, Fish and Oyster Commission; 1939. [$75.00]

Dobie, J. Frank. **Some Part of Myself.** 1st ed. Boston: Little, Brown; 1967. [$35.00

Dobie, J. Frank. **Southwestern Lore.** 1st ed. Dallas: Texas Folklore Soc.; 1931 [$50.00]

Dobie, J. Frank. **Spur-of-the-Cock.** Austin: Texas Folklore Society; 1933. [$50.00]

Dobie, J. Frank. **Tales of Old-Time Texas.** 1st ed. Boston: Little, Brown; 1955. [$35.00]

Dobie, J. Frank. **Texian Stomping Grounds.** Austin: Texas Folklore Society; 1941. [$45.00]

Dobie, J. Frank. **Tone the Bell Easy.** Austin: Texas Folklore Society; 1932. [dj faded, $50.00] [$45.00]

Dobie, J. Frank. **Tongues of the Monte.** 1st ed. Garden City: Doubleday, Doran; 1935. [first issue, $185.00]

Dobie, J. Frank. **Vaquero of the Brush Country.** 1st ed. Dallas: Southwest; 1929. [first state bound in rattlesnake, $225.00] [$275.00]

Dobie, J. Frank. **The Voice of the Coyote.** 1st ed. Boston: Little, Brown; 1949. [near fine dj, $100.00] [$45.00] [with dj, $60.00] [$50.00]

Dockery, A. V. **Black Bass and Other Fishing in North Carolina.** Raleigh: Commercial; 1909. [bumped, silverfished, spine frayed, $30.00]

Documentary History of the State of New York. Albany: Weed, Parsons; 1849-51. 4 v. [one vol wormed, $100.00]

Dodd, E. Merrick. **American Business Corporations until 1860.** Cambridge: Harvard UP; 1954. [$20.00]

Dodd, Ephraim Shelby. **Diary of.** Austin: Steck; 1914. [$75.00]

Dodd, William Edward. **Jefferson Davis.** Philadelphia: Jacobs; 1907. [$25.00]

Dodd, William Edward. **Life of Nathaniel Macon.** Raleigh, NC: Edwards & Broughton; 1903. [bumped, rubbed, lacks front endpaper, $50.00]

Doddridge, Joseph. **Notes, on the Settlement and Indian Wars, of the Western Parts of Virginia & Pennsylvania.** Wellsburgh, VA: Gazette; 1824. [rebound half morocco, $375.00] [1876 2nd ed., $65.00]

Dodge, Fred. **Under Cover for Wells Fargo.** Boston: Houghton Mifflin; 1969. [$25.00]

Dodge, Grenville Mellen. **The Battle of Atlanta and Other Campaigns.** Council Bluffs, IA: Monarch; 1911. [$45.00]

Dodge, Grenville Mellen. **Personal Recollections of President Abraham Lincoln, General Ulysses S. Grant and General William T. Sherman.** Council Bluffs, IA: Monarch; 1914. [$42.50]

Dodge, Jacob Richards. **West Virginia: Its Farms and Forests, Mines and Oilwells.** Philadelphia: Lippincott; 1865. [$115.00] [x-lib., $200.00]

Dodge, Richard Irving. **The Black Hills.** NY: Miller; 1876. [$95.00] [$125.00] [1965 Ross & Haines reprint, $25.00]

Dodge, Richard Irving. **Our Wild Indians.** Hartford; Chicago: Worthington; Nettleton; 1883. [$100.00] [$85.00] [$80.00]

Dodge, Richard Irving. **The Plains of the Great West and Their Inhabitants.** NY: Putnam; 1877. [$45.00]

Doig, Ivan. **This House of Sky.** 1st ed. NY: Harcourt Brace Jovanovich; 1978. [$25.00]

Domenech, Emmanuel Henri Dieudonne. **Missionary Adventures in Texas and Mexico.** London: Longman; 1858. [inner hinges stained, $350.00]

Domenech, Emmanuel Henri Dieudonne. **Seven Years' Residence in the Great Deserts of North America.** London: Longman; 1860. 2 v. [with map, $500.00]

Donald, David Herbert. **Lincoln's Herndon.** NY: Knopf; 1948. [$12.50]

Donald, Henderson Hamilton. **The Negro Freedman.** NY: Schuman; 1952. [$35.00]

Donaldson, Alfred Lee. **History of the Adirondacks.** NY: Century; 1921. 2 v. [$125.00]

Donaldson, Thomas C. **Indians Taxed and Not Taxed.** see, United States. Census Office. 11th Census, 1890.

Donan, Patrick. **Utah.** Buffalo: Matthews-Northrup; 1891. [$45.00]

Donehoo, George Patterson. **Harrisburg.** Harrisburg, PA: Telegraph; 1927. [$45.00]

Donkin, Robert. **Military Collections and Remarks.** NY: Gaine; 1777. [$1500.00]

Donoho, Milford Hill. **Circle-Dot.** Topeka: Crane; 1907. [$75.00]

Donovan, Frank Pierce. **The First through a Century.** St. Paul: Itasca; 1954. [$15.00]

Donovan, Frank Pierce. **Mileposts on the Prairie.** 1st ed. NY: Simmons-Boardman; 1950. [$25.00]

Donovan, Robert J. **PT109.** 1st ed. NY: McGraw-Hill; 1961. [$10.00]

Dooley, John Edward. **John Dooley, Confederate Soldier.** Washington: Georgetown UP; 1945. [$25.00] [$40.00]

Dorman, Rushton M. **Origin of Primitive Superstitions and Their Development into the Worship of Spirits and Doctrine of Spiritual Agency among the Aborigines of America.** Philadelphia: Lippincott; 1881. [recased, spine repaired, $35.00]

Dornburgh, Henry. **Why the Wilderness Is Called Adirondack.** Glens Falls, NY: Daily Times; 1885. [$75.00]

Dorr, Rheta Louise Childe. **Susan B. Anthony.** NY: Stokes; 1928. [$30.00]

Dorsey, George Amos. **The Arapaho Sun Dance.** Chicago: Field Museum; 1903. [$80.00]

Dorsey, George Amos. **Indians of the Southwest.** Chicago: Atchison, Topeka & Santa Fe; 1903. [$20.00]

Dorsey, George Amos. **The Ponca Sun Dance.** Chicago: Field Museum; 1905. [$25.00]

Dorsey, James Owen. **Dictionary of the Biloxi and Ofo Languages.** Washington: USGPO; 1912. [$45.00]

Dorsey, James Owen. **Omaha and Ponka Letters.** Washington: USGPO; 1891. [lacks wrappers, $10.00]

Dorsey, Stephen Palmer. **Early English Churches in America, 1607-1807.** NY: Oxford UP; 1952. [$40.00]

Dorson, Richard Mercer. **Davy Crockett, American Comic Legend.** NY: Rockland Editions; 1939. [$85.00]

Dos Passos, John. **The Head and Heart of Thomas Jefferson.** 1st ed. Garden City: Doubleday; 1954. [$25.00]

Dos Passos, John. **Three Soldiers.** NY: Doran; 1921. [$20.00]

Doten, Dana. **The Art of Bundling.** Weston, VT; NY: Countryman; Farrar & Rinehart; 1938. [$30.00]

Doten, Lizzie. **Poems from the Inner Life.** 7th ed. Boston: White; 1869. [$40.00]

Doty, Silas. **Life of.** Detroit: Alved; 1948. [$15.00]

Doubleday, Abner. **Chancellorsville and Gettysburg.** NY: Scribner; 1882. [$35.00]

Doubleday, Russell. **Cattle-Ranch to College.** NY: Doubleday & McClure; 1899. [lacks front endpaper, $25.00]

Dougal, William H. **Off for California.** 1st ed. Oakland: Biobooks; 1949 [i.e. 1950]. [$25.00] [$35.00]

Doughty, Arthur G. **The Cradle of New France.** London: Longmans, Green; 1909. [$20.00, Canadian]

Douglas, C. L. **Cattle Kings of Texas.** Dallas: Baugh; 1939. [2nd printing, $110.00]

Douglas, C. L. **Gentlemen in the White Hats.** Dallas: South-West; 1934. [$150.00]

Douglas, George Mellis. **Lands Forlorn.** NY: Putnam; 1914. [$150.00]

Douglas, George William. **The Many-Sided Roosevelt.** NY: Dodd, Mead; 1907. [$30.00]

Douglas, Henry Kyd. **I Rode with Stonewall.** Chapel Hill: U. of North Carolina; 1940. [$25.00]

Douglas, Marjory Stoneman. **The Everglades.** NY: Rinehart; 1947. [signed, $25.00]

Douglas, Stephen Arnold. **Letters.** Urbana: U. of Illinois; 1961. [$22.50]

Douglas, William O. **Beyond the High Himalayas.** 1st ed. Garden City: Doubleday; 1952. [signed, chipped dj, $45.00]

Douglas, William O. **My Wilderness.** Garden City: Doubleday; 1961. [$10.00]

Douglas, William O. **Of Men and Mountains.** NY: Harper; 1950. [$10.00]

Douglass, Frederick. **Life and Times of.** Hartford, CT: Park; 1882, c1881. [$85.00]

Douglass, Frederick. **My Bondage and My Freedom.** NY: Miller, Orton & Mulligan; 1855. [$150.00] [1856 issue, $75.00]

Douglass, Frederick. **Narrative of the Life of Frederick Douglass.** Boston: Anti-Slavery Office; 1845. [spine repaired, $250.00] [$175.00]

Douglass, William. **A Summary, Historical and Political, of the First Planting, Progressive Improvements, and Present State of the British Settlements in North-America.** London: Baldwin; 1755. 2 v. [with Jeffery's map facing title of vol. 1, $1000.00]

Douthit, Mary Osborn. **The Souvenir of Western Women.** Portland, OR: Anderson & Duniway; 1905. [$100.00]

Dow, Charles Mason. **Anthology and Bibliography of Niagara Falls.** Albany: State of New York; 1921. 2 v. [$60.00, Canadian]

Dow, George Francis. **The Arts & Crafts in New England, 1704-1775.** Topsfield, MA: Wayside; 1927. [$100.00]

Dow, George Francis. **Every Day Life in the Massachusetts Bay Colony.** Boston: Society for the Preservation of New England Antiquities; 1935. [rebound, $35.00]

Dow, George Francis. **Fort Western on the Kennebec.** Augusta, ME: Gannett; 1922. [$15.00]

Dow, George Francis. **The Pirates of the New England Coast, 1630-1730.** Salem, MA: Marine Research Soc.; 1923. [$75.00] [$100.00]

Dow, George Francis. **Slave Ships and Slaving.** Salem, MA: Marine Research Soc.; 1927. [$65.00] [$100.00]

Dow, George Francis. **Whale Ships and Whaling.** Salem, MA: Marine Research Soc.; 1925. [$125.00]

Dow, Peggy. **Vicissitudes.** Philadelphia: Rakestraw; 1815. [rebound, portrait torn, $150.00] [5th ed., 1833, $50.00]

Dowd, Jerome. **Life of Braxton Craven.** Raleigh: Edwards & Broughton; 1896. [hinges weak, bumped, $35.00]

Dowd, Jerome. **Negro in American Life.** NY, London: Century; 1926. [$21.95]

Dowd, Jerome. **Sketches of Prominent Living North Carolinians.** Raleigh: Edwards & Broughton; 1888. [hinges weak, silverfished, $35.00]

Dowdey, Clifford. **Experiment in Rebellion.** Garden City: Doubleday; 1947, c1946. [$20.00]

Dowdey, Clifford. **The Great Plantation.** NY: Rinehart; 1957. [$15.00]

Dowdey, Clifford. **Lee's Last Campaign.** 1st ed. Boston: Little, Brown; 1960. [$25.00]

Dowie, John Alexander. **Zion's Holy War against the Hosts of Hell in Chicago.** Chicago: Zion; 1900. [$50.00]

Downes, Randolph Chandler. **Council Fires on the Upper Ohio.** Pittsburgh: U. of Pittsburgh; 1940. [$45.00]

Downey, Fairfax Davis. **Famous Horses of the Civil War.** NY: Nelson; 1959. [2nd printing, $35.00]

Downey, Fairfax Davis. **Guns at Gettysburg.** NY: McKay; 1958. [$40.00] [$32.50]

Downey, Fairfax Davis. **Indian-Fighting Army.** NY: Scribner; 1941. [$50.00]

Downey, Fairfax Davis. **Our Lusty Forefathers.** NY: Scribner; 1947. [$10.00]

Downey, Fairfax Davis. **Sound of the Guns.** NY: McKay; 1956. [$20.00]

Downey, Sheridan. **They Would Rule the Valley.** San Francisco: [s.n.]; 1947. [$7.50]

Downie, William. **Hunting for Gold.** San Francisco: California Pub. Co.; 1893. [$175.00]

Downing, Antoinette Forrester. **The Architectural Heritage of Newport, Rhode Island.** Cambridge: Harvard UP; 1952. [$250.00]

Downing, Elliot Rowland. **A Naturalist in the Great Lakes Region.** Chicago: U. of Chicago; 1922. [$18.00]

Doyle, Helen MacKnight. **Mary Austin, Woman of Genius.** 1st ed. NY: Gotham; 1939. [$25.00]

Drago, Harry Sinclair. **Great American Cattle Trails.** NY: Dodd, Mead; 1965. [$20.00]

Drago, Harry Sinclair. **River of Gold.** NY: Dodd, Mead; 1945. [$20.00]

Drago, Harry Sinclair. **Suzanna.** NY: Macaulay; 1922. [dj repaired, $35.00]

Drago, Harry Sinclair. **Wild, Woolly & Wicked.** 1st ed. NY: Potter; 1960. [limited, $60.00] [trade ed., $25.00]

Dragoon Campaigns to the Rocky Mountains. see, Hildreth, James.

Drake, Benjamin. **The Life and Adventures of Black Hawk.** 7th ed. Cincinnati: Conclin; 1847. [$125.00]

Drake, Benjamin. **Life of Tecumseh, and His Brother the Prophet.** Cincinnati; Philadelphia: Rulison; Quaker City; 1855. [corners bumped, sunned, $150.00]

Drake, Daniel. **Pioneer Life in Kentucky, 1785-1800.** NY: Schuman; 1948. [$35.00]

Drake, Francis Samuel. **Tea Leaves.** Boston: Crane; 1884. [$85.00] [$75.00]

Drake, James Madison. **Historical Sketches of the Revolutionary and Civil Wars.** NY: Webster; 1908. [$45.00]

Drake, James Madison. **The History of the Ninth New Jersey Veteran Vols.** Elizabeth: Journal Printing House; 1889. [$150.00]

Drake, Samuel Adams. **Bunker Hill: The Story Told in Letters.** Boston: Nichols and Hall; 1875. [$37.50]

Drake, Samuel Adams. **Burgoyne's Invasion of 1777.** Boston: Lothrop, Lee & Shepard; 1889. [$25.00]

Drake, Samuel Adams. **Heart of the White Mountains.** NY: Harper; 1882, c1881. [hinges cracked, $65.00]

Drake, Samuel Adams. **Our Colonial Homes.** Boston: Lee and Shepard; 1894. [$45.00]

Drake, Samuel Gardner. **Aboriginal Races of North America.** 15th ed. NY: Hurst; 1880. [rebound, $40.00]

Drake, Samuel Gardner. **Biography and History of the Indians of North America.** 3rd ed. Boston; NY: Perkins; Carvill; 1834. [$75.00] [11th ed., 1851, $45.00]

Drake, Samuel Gardner. **The Book of the Indians of North America.** Boston: Drake; 1833. [$100.00]

Drake, Samuel Gardner. **Indian Captivities.** Auburn, NY: Derby and Miller; 1851. [$35.00]

Drake, Samuel Gardner. **Result of Some Researches among the British Archives for Information Relative to the Founders of New England.** Boston: New Eng. Hist. and Gen. Register; 1860. [$125.00]

Drannan, William F. **Thirty-One Years on the Plains and in the Mountains.** Chicago: Rhodes & McClure; 1904. [$30.00]

Draper, Andrew Sloan. **Rescue of Cuba.** Boston, NY: Silver, Burdett; 1899. [spine stained, $35.00]

Draper, Lyman Copeland. **King's Mountain and Its Heroes.** Cincinnati: Thomson; 1881. [recased, $375.00]

Draper, William R. **Old Grubstake Days in Joplin.** Girard, KS: Haldeman-Julius; 1946. [$5.00]

Drayton, Daniel. **Personal Memoir of.** Boston: Marsh; 1855. [rebound, $50.00]

Dreiser, Theodore. **An American Tragedy.** NY: Boni and Liveright; 1925. 2 v. [$20.00] [$12.50] [limited signed, $200.00]

Dreiser, Theodore. **Epitaph.** NY: Heron; 1929. [signed, worn slipcase, $85.00]

Dreiser, Theodore. **Hoosier Holiday.** NY, London: Lane; 1916. [$50.00]

Dreiser, Theodore. **Moods, Cadenced and Declaimed.** limited ed. NY: Boni and Liveright; [spine faded, frayed slipcase, signed, $95.00]

Dreiser, Theodore. **A Traveler at Forty.** NY: Century; 1913. [x-lib., $17.50]

Dresel, Gustav. **Houston Journal.** Austin: U. of Texas; 1954. [$85.00]

Dressler, Albert. **California's Pioneer Circus.** San Francisco: Crocker; 1926. [$12.50]

Drew, Benjamin. **A North-Side View of Slavery.** Boston: Jewett; 1856. [$100.00]

Drewry, Patrick H. **The Story of a Church.** Petersburg, VA: Plummer; 1923. [bumped, silverfished, stained, $15.00]

Drucker, Philip. **Indians of the Northwest Coast.** NY: McGraw-Hill; 1955. [$15.00]

Drumheller, Dan. **"Uncle Dan" Drumheller Tells Thrills of Western Trails in 1854.** Spokane, WA: Inland-American; 1925. [inscribed, $125.00]

Drury, Clifford Merrill. see also, Spalding, Henry Harmon.

Drury, Clifford Merrill. **Henry Harmon Spalding.** Caldwell, ID: Caxton; 1936 [inscribed, $25.00]

Drury, Wells. **An Editor on the Comstock Lode.** NY, Toronto: Farrar & Rinehart; 1936. [$35.00]

Du Bois, W. E. B. **Dusk of Dawn.** NY: Harcourt, Brace; 1940. [$35.00]

Du Bois, W. E. B. **Some Notes on Negro Crime, Particularly in Georgia.** Atlanta: Atlanta UP; 1904. [spine missing, $50.00]

Du Bose, John Witherspoon. **Life and Times of William Lowndes Yancey.** Birmingham, AL: Roberts; 1892. 2 v. [$85.00]

Duane, William. **Politics for American Farmers.** Washington: Weightman; 1807. [x-lib., dampstained, $125.00]

Duane, William. **Truth Will Out!** see, Bache, Benjamin Franklin.

Duane, William. **Visit to Colombia in the Years 1822 & 1823.** Philadelphia: Palmer; 1826. [$300.00]

Dubbs, Joseph Henry. **Historic Manual of the Reformed Church in the United States.** Lancaster, PA: [s.n.]; 1885. [$50.00]

Dubbs, Joseph Henry. **History of Franklin and Marshall College.** Lancaster, PA: Franklin and Marshall College Alumni Association; 1903. [$25.00]

Dubofsky, Melvyn. **We Shall Be All; A History of the Industrial Workers of the World.** Chicago: Quadrangle; 1969. [$30.00]

Duchaussois, Pierre Jean Baptiste. **Mid Snow and Ice.** London: Burns, Oates & Washbourne; 1923. [$45.00]

Duche, Jacob. **Observations on a Variety of Subjects.** Philadelphia: Dunlap; 1774. [$275.00]

Ducoudray-Holstein, Henri La Fayette Villaume. **Memoirs of Simon Bolivar.** Boston: Goodrich; 1829. [$50.00]

Dudley, G. W. **Lost Account of the Battle of Corinth and Courtmartial of Gen. Van Dorn.** Jackson, TN: McCowat-Mercer; 1955. [$38.50]

Duer, William Alexander. **Life of William Alexander.** NY: Wiley & Putnam; 1847. [$17.50] [rebound, $50.00]

Duff, John J. **A. Lincoln, Prairie Lawyer.** 1st ed. NY: Rinehart; 1960. [$40.00]

Duffus, Robert Luther. **The Santa Fe Trail.** London, NY: Longmans, Green; 1931. [$75.00]

Dufresne, Frank. **Alaska's Animals & Fishes.** NY: Barnes; 1946. [$35.00]

Duganne, A. J. H. **Camps and Prisons.** 2nd ed. NY: Robens; 1865. [$750.00]

Duganne, A. J. H. **The Mission of Intellect.** NY: Larkin; 1853. [$60.00]

Dugdale, Richard Louis. **The Jukes.** 6th ed. NY: Putnam; 1900. [$29.50]

Dugmore, Arthur Radclyffe. **In the Heart of the Northern Forests.** London: Chatto and Windus; 1930. [$50.00, Canadian]

Dugmore, Arthur Radclyffe. **The Romance of the Newfoundland Caribou.** Philadelphia; London: Lippincott; Heinemann; 1913. [$75.00, Canadian]

Duhring, Henry. **Remarks on the United States of America with Regard to the Actual State of Europe.** London; NY: Simpkin and Marshall; Jackson; 1833. [$150.00]

Duke, Cordia Sloan. **6,000 Miles of Fence.** Austin: U. of Texas; 1961. [$25.00]

Dulany, Daniel. **Considerations on the Propriety of Imposing Taxes in the British Colonies.** London: Almon; 1766. [$250.00]

Dulieu, Marie Henri Joseph. **Mississippi et Indiana; Souvenirs d'Amerique.** Bruxelles: Ve Parent; 1862. [$225.00]

Dulles, Foster Rhea. **American Red Cross: A History.** 1st ed. NY: Harper; 1950. [fine in dj, $25.00]

Dumond, Annie Hamilton Nelles. **Hard Times.** St. Louis: The Author; 1895. [$20.00]

Dumond, Dwight Lowell. **The Secession Movement, 1860-1861.** NY: Macmillan; 1931. [$45.00]

Dunbar, Edward Ely. **Romance of the Age.** NY: Appleton; 1867. [x-lib., $15.00]

Dunbar, Mary Conway. **My Mother Used to Say.** Boston: Christopher; 1959. [$25.00]

Dunbar, Paul Laurence. **Complete Poems.** NY: Dodd, Mead; 1922. [$15.00]

Dunbar, Paul Laurence. **Poems of Cabin and Field.** NY: Dodd, Mead; 1899. [$60.00]

Dunbar, Seymour. **History of Travel in America.** Indianapolis: Bobbs-Merrill; 1915. 4 v. [large paper issue, $250.00] [trade issue, $125.00] [1937 Tudor ed., $35.00; $50.00]

Dunbar, Willis Frederick. **Michigan through the Centuries.** NY: Lewis; 1955. 4 v. [$95.00]

Duncan, John M. **Travels through Part of the United States and Canada in 1818 and 1819.** Glasgow; London: University Press; Hurst, Robinson; 1823. 2 v. [$350.00]

Duncan, Louis Caspar. **Medical Men in the American Revolution.** Carlisle Barracks, PA: Medical Field Service School; 1931. [x-lib., $30.00]

Duncan, Robert Lipscomb. **Buffalo Country.** NY: Dutton; 1959. [$18.00]

Duncan, Robert Lipscomb. **Reluctant General; the Life and Times of Albert Pike.** 1st ed. NY: Dutton; 1961. [$40.00]

Dunham, Allison. **Mr. Justice.** Chicago: U. of Chicago; 1956. [$30.00]

Dunkle, John J. **Prison Life during the Rebellion.** Singer's Glen, VA: Funk's; 1869. [$75.00]

Dunlap, William. **History of the Rise and Progress of the Arts of Design in the United States.** NY: Scott; 1834. 2 v. [$175.00] [Boston 1918, 3 vol. ed., $225.00]

Dunlop, William S. **Lee's Sharpshooters.** Little Rock: Tunnah & Pittard; 1899. [$200.00]

Dunn, Edward D. **Double-Crossing America by Motor.** NY, London: Putnam; 1933. [torn dj, $30.00] [$55.00]

Dunn, J. E. **Indian Territory.** Indianapolis: American Printing; 1904. [$75.00]

Dunn, Jacob Piatt. **Greater Indianapolis.** Chicago: Lewis; 1910-1939. 3 v. [$150.00]

Dunn, Jacob Piatt. **Massacres of the Mountains.** NY: Archer; 1958. [$40.00]

Dunn, Samuel Orace. **American Transportation Question.** NY, London: Appleton; 1912. [$15.00]

Dunn, Samuel Orace. **Government Ownership of Railways.** NY, London: Appleton; 1918. [$15.00]

Dunne, Peter Masten. **Juan Antonio Balthasar.** Tucson: Arizona Pioneers' Historical Society; 1957. [$75.00]

Dunovant, William. **In Memory of R. E. Lee.** Houston: [s.n.]; 1898. [$65.00]

Dupuy, Richard Ernest. **Soldier's Album.** Boston: Houghton Mifflin; 1946. [$8.00]

Dupuy, Richard Ernest. **Where They Have Trod: The West Point Tradition in American Life.** NY: Stokes; 1940. [$25.00]

Durand, George Harrison. **Joseph Ward of Dakota.** Boston, NY: Pilgrim; 1913. [$25.00]

Durand, James R. **James Durand, an Able Seaman of 1812.** New Haven; London: Yale UP; Oxford UP; 1926. [$12.50]

Durand, William Frederick. **Robert Henry Thurston.** NY: American Society of Mechanical Engineers; 1929. [$30.00]

Durand of Dauphiné. **A Huguenot Exile in Virginia.** NY: Press of the Pioneers; 1934. [$40.00]

Durante, Jimmy. **Night Clubs.** NY: Knopf; 1931. [$12.50]

Durham, George. **Taming the Nueces Strip.** Austin: U. of Texas; 1962. [$55.00]

Durham, Nelson W. **History of Spokane and Spokane County, Washington.** Spokane: Clarke; 1912. 3 v. [$185.00]

Durkin, Joseph T. **Stephen R. Mallory.** Chapel Hill: U. of North Carolina; 1954. [x-lib., $17.50]

Durocher, Leo Ernest. **The Dodgers and Me.** Chicago: Ziff-Davis; 1948. [$17.50]

Dusenberry, William Howard. **The Mexican Mesta.** Urbana: U. of Ilinois; 1963. [$35.00]

Duss, John Samuel. **The Harmonists.** Harrisburg, PA: Pennsylvania Book Service; 1943. [$40.00] [$17.50]

Duval, John C. **Adventures of Big-Foot Wallace.** 1st ed. Philadelphia: Claxton, Remsen & Haffelfinger; 1871. [first issue, $550.00]

Duval, John C. **Early Times in Texas.** Austin: Gammel; 1892. [$250.00] [1935 Steck ed., $37.50]

Duyckinck, Evert A. **National Portrait Gallery of Eminent Americans.** NY: Johnson, Fry; 1861-1864. 2 v. [half morocco, $85.00]

Duyckinck, Evert A. **Nationale Geschichte des Krieges fur die Union.** NY: Johnson, Fry; [1863?]. 2 v. [$125.00]

Dwight, Margaret Van Horn. **Journey to Ohio in 1810.** New Haven: Yale UP; 1913, c1912. [$22.50] [$15.00]

Dwight, Theodore. **The Character of Thomas Jefferson.** Boston: Weeks, Jordan; 1839. [spine worn, $70.00] [$150.00]

Dwight, Theodore. **History of the Hartford Convention.** NY; Boston: White; Russell, Odiorne; 1833. [$185.00]

Dwight, Timothy. **Greenfield Hill.** NY: Childs and Swaine; 1794. [title page damaged, rear wrap torn, $75.00]

Dwight, Timothy. **Memories of Yale Life and Men, 1854-1899.** NY: Dodd, Mead; 1903. [$27.50]

Dwight, Timothy. **Travels in New-England and New-York.** New-Haven: Dwight; 1821-22. 4 v. [$350.00] [$250.00] [1823 London ed. in 4 vols. rebound, $235.00]

Dwight, Wilder. **Life and Letters.** Boston: Ticknor and Fields; 1868. [stained, $45.00]

Dyckman, J. G. **The American Militia Officer's Manual.** 2nd ed. NY: Holmes; 1825. [$200.00]

Dyer, D. B. (Mrs.). **"Fort Reno"; or, Picturesque "Cheyenne and Arrapahoe Army Life."** NY: Dillingham; 1896. [$200.00]

Dyer, Edward Oscar. **Gnadensee, the Lake of Grace.** Boston, Chicago: Pilgrim; 1903. [worn, $12.50]

Dyer, Frank Lewis. **Edison, His Life and Inventions.** NY, London: Harper; 1929. 2 v. [$45.00]

Dyer, John Percy. **Tulane.** NY: Harper & Row; 1966. [$25.00]

Dykstra, Robert R. **The Cattle Towns.** 1st ed. NY: Knopf; 1968. [$20.00] [$38.00]

Eames, Wilberforce. **The First Year of Printing in New York.** NY: New York Public Library; 1928. [$12.00]

Earle, Alice. **Two Centuries of Costume in America, MDCXX-MDCCCXX.** NY, London: Macmillan; 1903. 2 v. [$75.00] [$40.00]

Earle, Pliny. **Marathon.** 1st ed. Philadelphia: Perkins; 1841. [inscribed, $50.00]

Earle, Swepson. **The Chesapeake Bay Country.** 3rd ed. Baltimore: Thomsen-Ellis; 1929. [signed, $37.50]

Earle, Swepson. **Maryland's Colonial Eastern Shore.** Baltimore: Munder-Thomsen; 1916. [$100.00]

Early, Eleanor. **New Orleans Holiday.** NY: Rinehart; 1947. [$7.50]

Early, Jubal Anderson. **Lieutenant General Jubal Anderson Early.** Philadelphia: Lippincott; 1912. [$200.00]

Early, Jubal Anderson. **Memoir of the Last Year of the War for Independence.** Toronto: Lovell & Gibson; 1866. [$200.00] [1866 Lynchburg ed., $100.00]

East Tennessee Historical Society, Knoxville. Knox County History Committee. **The French Broad-Holston Country.** Knoxville: Tennessee Historical Society; 1946. [x-lib., $20.00]

East Tennessee Land Company. **Two Years of Harriman, Tennessee.** NY: South; [1892?]. [$75.00]

Eastburn, Robert. **The Dangers and Sufferings of.** Cleveland: Burrows; 1904. [$40.00]

Easterby, James Harold. **History of the College of Charleston.** Charleston, SC: [s.n.]; 1935. [$25.00]

Eastman, Charles Alexander. **Indian Heroes and Great Chieftans.** Boston: Little, Brown; 1918. [inscribed, $50.00]

Eastman, Edwin. **Seven and Nine Years among the Camanches and Apaches.** Jersey City, NJ: Johnson; 1873. [$75.00]

Eastman, Mary Henderson. **Chicora and Other Regions of the Conquerors and the Conquered.** Philadelphia: Lippincott, Grambo; 1854. [$500.00]

Eastman, Mary Henderson. **Romance of Indian Life.** Philadelphia: Lippincott, Grambo; 1853. [second issue, $550.00]

Eastman, Samuel Coffin. **White Mountain Guide Book.** 6th ed. Concord, NH: Eastman; 1866. [$35.00]

Easton, Emily. **Roger Williams, Prophet and Pioneer.** Boston, NY: Houghton Mifflin; 1930. [$47.50]

Easton, John. **Narrative of the Causes Which Led to Philip's Indian War.** Albany: Munsell; 1858. [$350.00]

Easton, Robert Olney. **The Happy Man.** NY: Viking; 1943. [$17.50]

Easton, Robert Olney. **Lord of Beasts.** Tucson: U. of Arizona; 1961. [$22.00]

Eaton, Allen Hendershott. **Handicrafts of the Southern Highlands.** NY: Sage; 1937. [$35.00]

Eaton, Anna Ruth. **Origin of Mormonism.** NY: Woman's Executive Committee of Home Missions; 1881. [$125.00]

Eaton, Elon Howard. **Birds of New York.** Albany: SUNY; 1910-1914. 2 v. [$150.00]

Eaton, Frank. **Pistol Pete.** 1st ed. Boston: Little, Brown; 1952. [presentation, $25.00]

Eaton, John. **Grant, Lincoln and the Freedman.** NY: Longman and Green; 1907. [x-lib., $35.00]

Eaton, John Henry. **Leben des Generals-Majors Andreas Jackson.** Reading: Ritter; 1831. [rubbed, $115.00]

Eaton, John Henry. **The Life of Major General Andrew Jackson.** 3rd ed. Philadelphia: McCarty & Davis; 1828. [rebound, $55.00]

Eaton, John Henry. **Memoirs of Andrew Jackson.** Boston: Ewer; 1828. [front hinge starting, $165.00]

Eavenson, Howard Nicholas. **Map Maker & Indian Traders.** Pittsburgh: U. of Pittsburgh; 1949. [$125.00]

Eaves, Charles Dudley. **Post City, Texas.** Austin: Texas State Hist. Assn.; 1952. [$35.00]

Eberlein, Harold Donaldson. **American Georgian Architecture.** Bloomington: Indiana UP; 1952. [$37.50]

Eberlein, Harold Donaldson. **Colonial Interiors.** NY: Helburn; 1938. [$35.00]

Eberlein, Harold Donaldson. **Practical Book of Early American Arts and Crafts.** Philadelphia, London: Lippincott; 1916. [$85.00]

Eckenrode, Hamilton James. **James Longstreet: Lee's War Horse.** Chapel Hill: U. of North Carolina; 1936. [$40.00]

Eckenrode, Hamilton James. **Jefferson Davis.** NY: Macmillan; 1923. [$45.00]

Eckenrode, Hamilton James. **Political History of Virginia during the Reconstruction.** Baltimore: Hopkins; 1904. [x-lib., $20.00]

Ecker, Grace Dunlop. see, Peter, Grace Dunlop.

Eckert, Allan W. **The Frontiersmen.** Boston: Little, Brown; 1967. [$30.00]

Eckhardt, George H. **Pennsylvania Clocks and Clockmakers.** NY: Devin-Adair; 1955. [$23.00] [$25.00]

Eddis, William. **Letters from America.** London: The Author; 1792. [$375.00]

Eddy, Mary Baker. **Mind-Healing.** 3rd ed. Boston: The Author; 1888. [$75.00]

Eddy, Mary Baker. **The Personal and the Impersonal Saviour.** Boston: Christian Science Publishing Society; 1888. [$50.00]

Eddy, Mary Olive. **Ballads and Songs from Ohio.** NY: Augustin; 1939. [$30.00]

Eddy, Thomas Mears. **The Patriotism of Illinois.** Chicago: Clarke; 1865-66. 2 v. [binding worn, some internal staining, $125.00]

Edgar, William C. **Judson Moss Bemis.** Minneapolis: Bellman; 1926. [$10.00]

Edmonds, George. see, Meriwether, Elizabeth Avery.

Edmonds, S. Emma E. **Nurse and Spy in the Union Army.** Hartford: Jones; 1865. [$40.00]

Edmonds, Walter Dumaux. **They Fought with What They Had.** 1st ed. Boston: Little, Brown; 1951. [torn dj, $25.00]

Edmondston, Catherine Deveroux. **Journal 1860-1866.** Mebane, NC: Priv. Print.; [1954?]. [$65.00]

Edmunds, A. C. **Pen Sketches of Nebraskans.** Lincoln, Omaha: Wilbur; 1871. [hinges cracking, $200.00]

Edmundson, William. **Journal of the Life, Travels, Sufferings and Labour of Love.** 2nd ed. London: Hinde; 1774. [$85.00]

Edward, David B. **The History of Texas; or, The Emigrant's, Farmer's, and Politician's Guide.** Cincinnati: James; 1836. [lacks map, $450.00]

Edwards, Bryan. **Historical Survey of the French Colony in the Island of St. Domingo.** London: Stockdale; 1797. [$250.00]

Edwards, Bryan. **History, Civil and Commercial, of the British Colonies in the West Indies.** 4th ed. London: Stockdale; 1807. 3 v. [rebound, $200.00]

Edwards, Frank S. **Campaign in New Mexico with Colonel Doniphan.** London: Hodson; 1848. [$750.00]

Edwards, John A. **In the Western Tongue.** Wichita, KS: McCormick-Armstrong; 1920. [$25.00]

Edwards, John Newman. **Biography, Memoirs, Reminiscences and Recollections.** Kansas City: Edwards; 1889. ["gnawed at bottom," $47.50]

Edwards, John Newman. **Shelby's Expedition to Mexico.** Austin: Steck; 1964. [$37.50]

Edwards, Jonathan. **The Justice of God in the Damnation of Sinners.** Northampton, MA: Wright; [1800?]. [$100.00]

Edwards, Jonathan. **Sermons on the Following Subjects . . .** Hartford: Hudson and Goodwin; 1780. [$350.00]

Edwards, Philip Leget. **California in 1837.** Sacramento: Johnson; 1890. [$225.00]

Edwards, Richard. **Edwards's Great West and Her Commercial Metropolis.** St. Louis: Edwards's Monthly; 1860. [$85.00]

Edwards, Samuel E. **The Ohio Hunter.** Battle Creek, MI: Review and Herald; 1866. [$600.00]

Edwards, Thomas Augustus. **Daring Donald McKay.** Erie, PA: Herald; 1886. [$125.00]

Edwards, William B. **The Story of Colt's Revolver.** Harrisburg, PA: Stackpole; 1953. [$50.00]

Edwards, William Seymour. **Into the Yukon.** Cincinnati: Clarke; 1905, c1904. [$32.50] [$35.00] [$70.00, Canadian]

Edwards, William Seymour. **On the Mexican Highlands with a Passing Glimpse of Cuba.** Cincinnati: Jennings and Graham; 1906. [x-lib., $85.00]

Egan, Howard. **Pioneering the West, 1846 to 1878.** Richmond, UT: Egan Estate; 1917. [$65.00] [$75.00]

Egan, Michael. **The Flying, Gray-Haired Yank.** [s.l.]: Edgewood; 1888. [$85.00]

Egerton, Hugh Edward. **Causes and Character of the American Revolution.** Oxford: Clarendon; 1923. [$35.00]

Eggenhofer, Nick. **Wagons, Mules, and Men.** NY: Hastings; 1961. [$45.00]

Eggleston, Edward. **The Transit of Civilization from England to America in the Seventeenth Century.** NY: Appleton; 1901. [$20.00]

Egle, William Henry. **Illustrated History of the Commonwealth of Pennsylvania.** Harrisburg: Goodrich; 1876. [$50.00]

Egmont, John Perceval. **Journal of.** Athens: U. of Georgia; 1962. [$25.00]

Ehle, John. **The Free Men.** 1st ed. NY: Harper & Row; 1965. [$30.00]

Ehrenberg, Hermann. **With Milam and Fannin.** Dallas: Tardy; 1935. [worn, $95.00]

Eickmann, Walter Theodore. **History of West New York, New Jersey.** West New York: [s.n.]; 1948. [$25.00]

Eide, Arthur Hansin. **Drums of Diomede: The Transformation of the Alaska Eskimo.** Hollywood, CA: House-Warven; 1952. [$12.50]

Einstein, Lewis. **Divided Loyalties.** London: Cobden-Sanderson; 1933. [$30.00]

Eisele, Wilbert Edwin. **The Real Wild Bill Hickok.** Denver: Andre; 1931. [$45.00]

Eisenschiml, Otto. **American Iliad.** Indianapolis: Bobbs-Merrill; 1947. [$15.00]

Eisenschiml, Otto. **As Luck Would Have It.** 1st ed. Indianapolis: Bobbs-Merrill; 1948. [$20.00] [$30.00]

Eisenschiml, Otto. **Celebrated Case of Fitz John Porter.** 1st ed. Indianapolis: Bobbs-Merrill; 1950. [$22.50]

Eisenschiml, Otto. **Story of Shiloh.** Chicago: Civil War Round Table; 1946. [signed in slipcase, $25.00]

Eisenschiml, Otto. **Why the Civil War?** 1st ed. Indianapolis: Bobbs-Merrill; 1958. [$15.00]

Eisenschiml, Otto. **Why Was Lincoln Murdered?** 1st ed. Boston: Little, Brown; 1937. [inscribed, $38.50] [$20.00]

Elder, David Paul. **California the Beautiful.** San Francisco: Elder; 1911. [$65.00]

Elder, David Paul. **The Old Spanish Missions of California.** San Francisco: Elder; 1913. [dj rubbed and chipped, $60.00] [$45.00]

Eldredge, Zoeth Skinner. **Beginnings of San Francisco.** San Francisco: Eldredge; 1912. 2 v. [binding faded, $65.00]

Elias, Solomon Philip. **Stories of Stanislaus.** Los Angeles: [s.n.]; 1924. [$55.00]

Eliel, Paul. **The Waterfront and General Strikes, San Francisco, 1934.** San Francisco: Hooper; 1934. [$20.00]

Eliot, Charles William. **Harvard Memories.** Cambridge: Harvard UP; 1923. [$25.00]

Eliot, Charles William. **A Late Harvest.** Boston: Atlantic Monthly; 1924. [$17.50]

Eliot, Ellsworth. **Yale in the Civil War.** New Haven: Yale UP; 1932. [mildewed, $15.00]

Eliot, John. **A Biographical Dictionary.** Boston: Cushing and Appleton; 1809. [$40.00]

Eliot, John. **Brief Narrative of the Progress of the Gospel among the Indians of New England.** Boston: Wiggin & Lunt; 1868. [scuffed, small paper ed., $100.00]

Eliot, Samuel Atkins. **A Sketch of the History of Harvard College.** Boston: Little, Brown; 1848. [$15.00] [boards broken, $20.00]

Eliot, T. S. **Ash-Wednesday.** 1st American trade ed. NY, London: Putnam; 1930. [dj torn, $30.00]

Eliot, T. S. **The Confidential Clerk.** 1st American ed. NY: Harcourt, Brace; 1954. [$12.50]

Eliot, T. S. **On Poetry and Poets.** NY: Farrar, Straus and Cudahy; 1957. [1st printing, $12.50]

Elkins, John M. **Indian Fighting on the Texas Frontier.** Amarillo: Russell & Cockrell; 1929. [$50.00]

Elkinton, Joseph Scotton. **Selections from the Diary and Correspondence of.** Philadelphia: Leeds & Biddle; 1913. [$20.00]

Ellet, Elizabeth Fries. **The Court Circles of the Republic.** Hartford: Hartford Pub. Co.; 1869. [$85.00]

Ellet, Elizabeth Fries. **Pioneer Women of the West.** Philadelphia: Porter & Coates; 1873. [$85.00]

Ellet, Elizabeth Fries. **Women of the American Revolution.** 5th ed. NY: Baker and Scribner; 1850-53. 3 v. [$100.00]

Ellicott, Andrew. **Journal of.** Philadelphia: Dobson; 1803. [some tears mended, $2250.00]

Elliot, Daniel Giraud. **The Wild Fowl of the United States and British Possessions.** NY: Harper; 1898. [signed, x-lib., $50.00]

Elliot, William. **The Washington Guide.** Washington: Taylor; 1837. [rebound, $200.00]

Elliot, William Joseph Alexander. **The Spurs.** Spur, TX: Texas Spur; 1939. [$325.00]

Elliott, Claude. **Leathercoat.** San Antonio: Standard; 1938. [presentation, $95.00]

Elliott, E. N. **Cotton Is King, and Pro-Slavery Arguments.** Augusta, GA: Pritchard, Abbott & Loomis; 1860. [recased, $125.00]

Elliott, Henry Wood. **Our Arctic Province.** NY: Scribner; 1887. [corners worn, $100.00]

Elliott, Howard. **Truth about the Railroads.** Boston, NY: Houghton Mifflin; 1913. [$15.00]

Elliott, Robert Greene. **Agent of Death.** NY: Dutton; 1940. [$15.00]

Ellis, Agnes L. **Lights and Shadows of Sewickley Life.** Pittsburg: Foster; 1891. [$20.00]

Ellis, Amanda Mae. **Bonanza Towns.** 1st ed. Colorado Springs: Denton; 1954. [$30.00]

Ellis, Amanda Mae. **Pioneers.** 1st ed. [Colorado Springs?: s.n.]; 1955. [$30.00]

Ellis, Charles M. **History of Roxbury Town.** Boston: Drake; 1848, c1847. [$65.00]

Ellis, Edward Sylvester. **Camp-Fires of General Lee, from the Peninsula to the Appomattox Court-House.** Philadelphia: Harrison; 1886. [$30.00]

Ellis, Edward Sylvester. **The Indian Wars of the United States.** Chicago: Kenyon; 1902. [2nd printing, $110.00]

Ellis, Edward Sylvester. **The Life of Pontiac, the Conspirator.** NY: Hurst; 1910. [$5.00]

Ellis, Elmer. **Henry Moore Teller.** Caldwell, ID: Caxton; 1941. [$25.00]

Ellis, George Edward. **History of the Battle of Bunker's (Breed's) Hill.** Boston: Lockwood, Brooks; 1875. [$27.50]

Ellis, Henry. **Voyage to Hudson's-Bay by the Dobbs Galley and California.** London: Whitridge; 1748. [$1100.00]

Ellis, John B. **Free Love and Its Votaries.** NY: United States Pub. Co.; 1870. [$145.00]

Ellis, John Tracy. **Life of James Cardinal Gibbons.** Milwaukee: Bruce; 1952. 2 v. [x-lib., $25.00]

Ellis, William. **A Journal of a Tour around Hawaii.** Boston; NY: Crocker & Brewster; Haven; 1825. [rebound, $425.00]

Ellis, William. **Narrative of a Tour through Hawaii or Owhyhee.** 2nd ed. London: Fisher and Jackson; 1827. [$275.00] [x-lib., $250.00]

Ellis, William. see also, Rickman, John.

Ellis, William Turner. **Memories.** Eugene: U. of Oregon; 1939. [soiled and loose, $65.00]

Ellison, William Henry. **A Self-Governing Dominion: California, 1849-1860.** Berkeley: U. of California; 1950. [$20.00]

Ellsworth, Henry William. **Valley of the Upper Wabash, Indiana.** NY: Pratt, Robinson; 1838. [$350.00]

Elmer, Lucius Q. C. **History of the Early Settlement and Progress of Cumberland County, New Jersey.** Bridgeton, NJ: Nixon; 1869. [$45.00]

Elovitz, Mark H. **A Century of Jewish Life in Dixie.** University: U. of Alabama; 1974. [$20.00]

Elsbree, Oliver Wendell. **Rise of the Missionary Spirit in America.** Williamsport, PA: Williamsport Printing and Binding; 1928. [x-lib., pencil notes, $15.00]

Ely, Salem. **Centennial History of the Villages of Iroquois and Montgomery and the Township of Concord.** Chicago: Regan; 1918. [$27.50]

Emerson, Bettie Alder Calhoun. **Historic Southern Monuments.** NY and Washington: Neale; 1911. [$275.00]

Emerson, Ellen Russell. **Indian Myths.** Boston: Osgood; 1884. [map badly torn, rear hinge cracked, $47.50]

Emerson, Ralph Waldo. **The Conduct of Life.** Boston: Ticknor and Fields; 1860. [$75.00]

Emerson, Ralph Waldo. **English Traits.** Boston: Phillips, Sampson; 1856. [$135.00]

Emerson, Ralph Waldo. **Letters and Social Aims.** Boston: Osgood; 1876. [first printing, $80.00] [later printing, $55.00]

Emerson, Ralph Waldo. **Letters of.** NY: Columbia UP; 1939. 6 v. [$125.00]

Emerson, Ralph Waldo. **Oration Delivered before the Phi Beta Kappa Society, at Cambridge, August 31, 1837.** Boston: Munroe; 1837. [$250.00] [1838 edition, $75.00]

Emerson, Ralph Waldo. **Records of a Lifelong Friendship.** Boston, NY: Houghton Mifflin; 1910. [$40.00]

Emerson, Ralph Waldo. **Representative Men.** 1st ed. Boston: Phillips, Sampson; 1850. [1st issue, $175.00]

Emmart, Emily Walcott. **The Badianus Manuscript.** see, Cruz, Martin de la.

Emmert, David. **Reminiscences of Juniata College.** Huntingdon, PA: The Author; 1901. [$14.00]

Emmett, Chris. **Fort Union and the Winning of the Southwest.** 1st ed. Norman: U. of Oklahoma; 1965. [$22.50]

Emmett, Chris. **Shanghai Pierce.** 1st ed. Norman: U. of Oklahoma; 1953. [$35.00]

Emmett, Chris. **Texas Camel Tales.** 1st ed. San Antonio: Naylor; 1932. [first issue, $350.00]

Emmitt, Robert. **The Last War Trail.** 1st ed. Norman: U. of Oklahoma; 1954. [1st printing, $42.00] [later printing, $20.00]

Emmons, Della Florence. **Sacajawea of the Shoshones.** Portland, OR: Binfords & Mort; 1943. [$25.00]

Emmons, Richard. **The Battle of Bunker Hill or the Temple of Liberty.** 2nd ed. Boston: [s.n.]; 1841. [$12.50] [10th ed., 1939, $30.00]

Emmons, Richard. **The Fredoniad.** Boston: Munroe & Francis; 1827. 4 v. [$225.00]

Emory, William H. **Notes of a Military Reconnaissance.** see, United States. Army. Corps of Topographical Engineers.

Encyclopedia of the New West. Marshall TX: Biographical Publishing; 1881. [$850.00]

Endicott, H. Wendell. **Adventures in Alaska.** NY: Stokes; 1928. [$25.00]

Engel, Samuel. **Essai sur Cette Question.** Amsterdam: Rey; 1767. [$1500.00]

Engel, Samuel. **Memoires et Observations Geographique et Critiques sur la Situation des Pays Septentrionaux de l'Asie et l'Amerique.** Lausanne: Chapius; 1765. [lacks maps, $185.00]

Engelhardt, Zephyrin. **Mission San Juan Bautista.** Santa Barbara: Mission Santa Barbara; 1931. [$12.50]

Engelhardt, Zephyrin. **San Juan Capistrano Mission.** Los Angeles: Standard; 1922. [cover waterstained, $27.50]

Englebert, Omer. **Last of the Conquistadors, Junipero Serra, 1713-1784.** 1st ed. NY: Harcourt, Brace; 1956. [$38.50]

Entick, John. **General History of the Late War.** London: Dilly; 1763-1764. 5 v. [10 maps, some spine wear, $1100.00]

Erdman, Loula Grace. **A Time to Write.** NY: Dodd, Mead; 1969. [$17.50]

Erdman, Loula Grace. **The Wide Horizon.** NY: Dodd, Mead; 1956. [$17.50]

Ernst, Morris Leopold. **A Love Affair with the Law.** NY: Macmillan; 1968. [$18.50]

Erskine, Gladys Shaw. **Broncho Charlie.** NY: Crowell; 1934. [$45.00]

Ervin, Spencer. **Henry Ford vs. Truman H. Newberry.** NY: Smith; 1935. [binding faded, $20.00]

Erwin, Allan A. **The Southwest of John Horton Slaughter.** 1st ed. Glendale, CA: Clark; 1965. [$65.00]

Escobosa, Hector A. **Seattle Story.** Seattle: McCaffrey; 1948. [$10.00]

Essary, John Thurman. **Tennessee Mountaineers in Type.** NY: Cochrane; 1910. [$45.00]

Estabrooks, Henry L. **Adrift in Dixie.** NY: Carleton; 1866. [x-lib., spine torn, $45.00]

Estep, E. Ralph. **El Toro.** Detroit: Packard; 1909. [$50.00]

Estergreen, M. Morgan. **Kit Carson.** 1st ed. Norman: U. of Oklahoma; 1962. [$30.00]

Estvan, Bela. **War Pictures from the South.** NY: Appleton; 1863. [$75.00]

Etzenhouser, Rudolph. **The Book of Mormon and Its Translator.** Independence, MO: Ensign; 1899. [$35.00]

Evans, Albert S. **Our Sister Republic.** Hartford; Toledo: Columbian; Bliss; 1870. [$60.00]

Evans, Arthur L. **Fifty Years of Football at Syracuse University, 1889-1939.** Syracuse: Syracuse U. Football History Comm.; 1939. [$27.50]

Evans, Elwood. **The State of Washington.** [s.l.]: World's Fair Commission; [1893?]. [$85.00]

Evans, Estwick. **A Pedestrious Tour of Four Thousand Miles, through the Western States and Territories, during the Winter and Spring of 1818.** Concord, NH: Spear; 1819. [$300.00]

Evans, John Henry. **Charles Coulson Rich.** NY: Macmillan; 1936. [$40.00]

Evans, William Bacon. **Jonathan Evans and His Time, 1759-1839.** Boston: Christopher; 1959. [$15.00]

Evans, William Franklin. **Border Skylines.** Dallas: Baugh; 1940. [presentation, $65.00]

Everest, Charles William. **Poets of Connecticut.** Hartford: Case, Tiffany and Burnham; 1843. [$25.00]

Everett, Edward. **Address of Hon. Edward Everett at the Consecration of the National Cemetery at Gettysburg.** Boston: Little, Brown; 1864. [$125.00]

Everett, Edward. **Life of George Washington.** NY; Boston: Sheldon; Gould and Lincoln; 1860. [$45.00]

Everett, Edward. **An Oration Delivered on the Battlefield of Gettysburg (November 19, 1863).** NY: Baker & Godwin; 1863. [$1500.00]

Everett, Edward. **Orations and Speeches on Various Occasions.** Boston: American Stationer's Company; 1836. [$70.00]

Everett, George G. **Cattle Cavalcade in Central Colorado.** 1st ed. Denver: Golden Bell; 1966. [$40.00]

Everett, Marshall. **Great Chicago Theater Disaster.** [s.l.]: Publishers Union of America; 1904. [$20.00]

Evjen, John Oluf. **Scandinavian Immigrants in New York.** Minneapolis: Holter; 1916. [$35.00]

Ewan, N. R. **Early Brickmaking in the Colonies.** Camden, NJ: Camden County Hist. Soc.; 1938. [$10.00]

Ewell, James. **The Planter's and Mariner's Medical Companion.** Philadelphia: Bioren; 1807. [worn, foxed, pencil & ink notes, $350.00]

Ewell, John Louis. **Story of Byfield.** Boston: Littlefield; 1904. [$40.00]

Ewell, Richard Stoddert. **Making of a Soldier.** Richmond: Whittet & Shepperson; 1935. [$35.00]

Ewers, John Canfield. **The Blackfeet.** 1st ed. Norman: U. of Oklahoma; 1958. [$50.00]

Ewers, John Canfield. **Indian Life on the Upper Missouri.** 1st ed. Norman: U. of Oklahoma; 1968. [$48.00]

Ewing, Hugh. **The Black List.** NY: Collier; 1893. [x-lib., reading copy, $25.00]

Eye Witness. **The Dalton Brothers.** see, Valcourt-Vermont, Edgar de.

Eyre, Alice. **The Famous Fremonts and Their America.** Santa Ana, CA: Fine Arts; 1948. [$50.00]

Fagan, James Octavius. **Labor and the Railroads.** Boston: Houghton Mifflin; 1909. [$25.00]

Fages, Pedro. **The Colorado River Campaign, 1781-1782.** Berkeley: U. of California; 1913. [$45.00]

Fahey, John. **The Flathead Indians.** 1st ed. Norman: U. of Oklahoma; 1974. [$30.00]

Fairbanks, Douglas. **Laugh and Live.** NY: Britton; 1917. [$35.00]

Fairbanks, George Rainsford. **The Spaniards in Florida.** Jacksonville: Drew; 1868. [$125.00]

Fairchild, David. **The World Grows round My Door.** NY, London: Scribner; 1947. [$20.00]

Fairchild, James Harris. **The Underground Railroad.** [Cleveland?]: Western Reserve Historical Soc.; 1895. [$115.00]

Fairfield, Ula Marguerite. **Pioneer Lawyer.** Denver: Kistler; 1946. [inscribed, $45.00]

Faithfull, Emily. **Three Visits to America.** Edinburgh: Douglas; 1884. [$100.00]

Falckner, Daniel. **Daniel Falckner's Curieuse Nachricht from Pennsylvania.** Lancaster: New Era; 1905. [$40.00]

Falconer, Thomas. **Letters and Notes on the Texan Santa Fe Expedition, 1841-1842.** NY: Dauber & Pine; 1930. [$165.00]

Fales, Edward Lippitt. **Songs and Song-Legends of Dahkotah Land.** St. Paul, MN: Highland Pub. Co.; 1882. [$30.00]

Fane, Julian Henry Charles. **Tannhauser.** Mobile: Goetzel; 1863. [$125.00]

Fanning, Peter. **Great Crimes of the West.** San Francisco: Barry; 1929. [$40.00]

Farber, James. **Texas, C.S.A.** NY: Jackson; 1947. [signed, $45.00] [worn dj, $35.00]

Fargo, Clarence B. **History of Frenchtown.** NY: Fargo; 1933. [$25.00]

Faris, John Thomson. **Roaming the Eastern Mountains.** NY: Farrar & Rinehart; 1932. [$14.00]

Faris, John Thomson. **Romance of Forgotten Towns.** NY, London: Harper; 1924. [x-lib., $12.50]

Faris, John Thomson. **Romance of the Rivers.** 1st ed. NY, London: Harper; 1927. [$25.00]

Faris, John Thomson. **Seeing Canada.** Philadelphia: Lippincott; 1924. [$20.00]

Faris, John Thomson. **Seeing the Eastern States.** Philadelphia, London: Lippincott; 1922. [$10.00]

Faris, John Thomson. **Seeing the Far West.** Philadelphia & London: Lippincott; 1920. [$15.00]

Faris, John Thomson. **Seeing the Middle West.** Philadelphia, London: Lippincott; 1923. [$10.00]

Faris, John Thomson. **Seeing the Sunny South.** Philadelphia, London: Lippincott; 1921. [$12.50]

Farley, James Aloysius. **Behind the Ballots.** 1st ed. NY: Harcourt, Brace; 1938. [inscribed, $20.00]

Farmer, H. H. **Virginia before and during the War.** Henderson, KY: The Author; 1892. [$22.50]

Farnham, Thomas Jefferson. **Life, Adventures and Travels in California.** pictorial ed. NY; St. Louis: Nafis & Cornish; Van Dien & Macdonald; 1849. [rebacked, $150.00]

Farnham, Thomas Jefferson. **Travels in the Great Western Prairies, the Anahuac and Rocky Mountains, and in the Oregon Territory.** Poughkeepsie: Killey and Lossing; 1841. [foxed, $750.00] [1843 Greeley & McElrath ed., $125.00]

Farquhar, Arthur B. **The First Million the Hardest.** Garden City: Doubleday, Page; 1922. [$50.00]

Farr, Finis. **Margaret Mitchell of Atlanta.** NY: Morrow; 1965. [$15.00]

Farrar, C. C. S. **The War, Its Causes and Consequences.** Cairo, Memphis: Blelock & Co; 1864. [$30.00]

Farrar, Charles A. J. **From Lake to Lake.** Jamaica Plains, MA: Jamaica; 1887. [$17.50]

Farrar, Emmie Ferguson. **Old Virginia Houses.** NY: Hastings; 1955-1957. 2 v. [$40.00]

Farrell, James T. **This Man and This Woman.** NY: Vanguard; 1951. [$15.00]

Farrow, Marion Humphreys. **Troublesome Times in Texas.** 2nd ed. San Antonio: Naylor; 1960, c1959. [dj torn, $25.00]

Fast, Howard. **The Last Frontier.** NY: Blue Heron; 1953, c1941. [$25.00]

Fatout, Paul. **Ambrose Bierce.** 1st ed. Norman: U. of Oklahoma; 1951. [$20.00]

Faulk, Odie B. **Land of Many Frontiers.** NY: Oxford UP; 1968. [$35.00]

Faulk, Odie B. **Last Years of Spanish Texas, 1778-1821.** The Hague: Mouton; 1964. [$20.00]

Faulkner, William. **Absalom, Absalom!** 1st ed. NY: Random; 1936. [severe insect damage, $75.00]

Faulkner, William. **Doctor Martino.** 1st ed. NY: Smith and Haas; 1934. [dj chipped, $300.00]

Faulkner, William. **Go Down, Moses.** 1st ed. NY: Random; 1942. [1st state, dj chipped, $200.00]

Faulkner, William. **A Green Bough.** 1st ed. NY: Smith and Haas; 1933. [$250.00] [$150.00]

Faulkner, William. **The Hamlet.** 1st ed. NY: Random; 1940. [fine in dj, $350.00]

Faulkner, William. **Intruder in the Dust.** NY: Random; 1948. [spine rubbed, $35.00]

Faulkner, William. **Light in August.** 1st ed. NY: Smith and Haas; 1932. [1st printing, $395.00]

Faulkner, William. **The Mansion.** 1st ed. NY: Random; 1959. [lacks dj, $125.00]

Faulkner, William. **Requiem for a Nun.** NY: Random; 1951. [$55.00] [1st issue, $50.00]

Faulkner, William. **Sound and the Fury.** NY: Cape & Smith; 1929. [one hinge open, dj pasted on endpaper, $50.00]

Faulkner, William. **These 13.** limited signed ed. NY: Cape & Smith; 1931. [$800.00]

Faulkner, William. **The Town.** 1st trade ed. NY: Random; 1957. [fine, $200.00]

Faulkner, William. **The Wild Palms.** 1st ed. NY: Random; 1939. [dj soiled and chipped, x-lib., $65.00]

Faunce, Hilda. **Desert Wife.** Boston: Little, Brown; 1934. [x-lib., rebound, $20.00] [$22.50]

Fauset, Arthur Huff. **Sojourner Truth.** Chapel Hill: U. of North Carolina; 1938. [$20.00]

Faux, William. **Memorable Days in America.** London: Simpkin and Marshall; 1823. [rebound, $150.00]

Faversham, Julie Opp. **The Squaw Man.** NY, London: Harper; 1906. [$15.00]

Favour, Alpheus H. **Old Bill Williams.** Chapel Hill: U. of North Carolina; 1936. [$45.00]

Fay, Bernard. **Franklin the Apostle of Modern Times.** Boston: Little, Brown; 1929. [$10.00]

Fay, Bernard. **Notes on the American Press at the End of the Eighteenth Century.** NY: Grolier; 1927. [$225.00]

Fay, Bernard. **The Two Franklins.** Boston: Little, Brown; 1933. [$25.00]

Fay, Sidney Bradshaw. **Origins of the World War.** 2nd ed. NY: Macmillan; 1950. 2 vols. in 1. [$20.00]

Fay, Stephen. **Beyond Greed.** NY: Viking; 1982. [$12.50]

Fearon, Henry Bradshaw. **Sketches of America.** London: Longman, etc.; 1818. [outer hinge cracking, $250.00] [$175.00]

Featherstonhaugh, George William. **Canoe Voyage up the Minnay Sotor.** London: Bentley; 1847. 2 v. [$300.00]

Featherstonhaugh, George William. **Excursion through the Slave States.** NY: Harper; 1844. [disbound, $75.00]

Federal Writer's Project. see also, Writers' Program

Federal Writers' Project. **Guide to Alaska.** NY: Macmillan; 1943. [signed by editor, $25.00]

Federal Writers' Project. **Lay My Burden Down.** Chicago: U. of Chicago; 1945. [$15.00]

Federal Writers' Project. **Washington, City and Capital.** Washington: USGPO; 1937. [$30.00]

Federal Writers' Project. Illinois. **Illinois.** Chicago: McClurg; 1939. [$30.00]

Federal Writers' Project. New Jersey. **Story of Dunellen.** Dunellen, NJ: Art Color; 1937. [$30.00]

Federal Writers' Project. New Orleans. **New Orleans City Guide.** Boston: Houghton Mifflin; 1938. [$15.00]

Federal Writers' Project. New York (City). **The Italians of New York.** NY: Random; 1938. [$20.00] [worn dj, $40.00]

Federal Writers' Project. Pennsylvania. **Philadelphia.** 1st ed. Philadelphia: William Penn Assn.; 1937. [$40.00]

Feidelson, Charles. **Symbolism and American Literature.** Chicago: U. of Chicago; 1953. [$15.00]

Fell, Sarah M. **Genealogy of the Fell Family.** Philadelphia: Sickler; 1891. [x-lib., $45.00]

Fenley, Florence. **Oldtimers of Southwest Texas.** Uvalde: Hornby; 1957. [$100.00]

Fenley, Florence. **Oldtimers; Their Own Stories.** Uvalde: Hornby; 1939. [inscribed, $275.00]

Fennell, James. **Apology for the Life of.** Philadelphia: Maxwell; 1814. [$250.00]

Ferber, Edna. **Peculiar Treasure.** NY: Garden City Pub. Co.; 1940. [clean copy in very good dj, $22.50]

Ferguson, Charles D. **California Gold Fields.** Oakland: Biobooks; 1948. [$35.00]

Ferguson, Charles D. **The Experiences of a Forty-Niner during Thirty-Four Years' Residence in California and Australia.** Cleveland: Williams; 1888. [$100.00]

Ferguson, Jesse Babcock. **Spirit Communion.** Nashville: Union and American; 1854. [outer hinges cracked, $125.00]

Ferguson, Melville F. **Motor Camping on Western Trails.** NY & London: Century; 1925. [$32.50]

Fergusson, Erna. **Murder & Mystery in New Mexico.** 1st ed. Albuquerque: Armitage; 1948. [worn dj, $50.00] [x-lib., $25.00]

Fergusson, Erna. **Our Southwest.** NY, London: Knopf; 1940. [dj worn, $20.00]

Fergusson, Harvey. **Blood of the Conquerors.** NY: Knopf; 1921. [$35.00]

Fergusson, Harvey. **Home in the West.** 1st ed. NY: Duell, Sloan and Pearce; 1944. [$25.00]

Fergusson, Harvey. **Rio Grande.** 1st ed. NY: Knopf; 1933. [$25.00]

Fern, Fanny. **Fresh Leaves.** NY: Mason; 1857. [$22.00]

Fernald, Charles. **County Judge in Arcady.** Glendale, CA: Clark; 1954. [$45.00]

Fernald, Chester Bailey. **Gentleman in the Barrel.** San Francisco: Book Club of California; 1939. [$30.00]

Fernald, Merritt Caldwell. **History of the Maine State College and the University of Maine.** Orono, ME: U. of Maine; 1916. [covers stained, $20.00]

Fernandez, Nicholas. **Dying Declaration of.** [NY?: s.n.]; 1830. [$100.00]

Fernow, Berthold. **Ohio Valley in Colonial Days.** Albany: Munsell; 1890. [$85.00] [$100.00]

Ferris, Benjamin. **History of the Original Settlements on the Delaware.** Wilmington: Wilson & Heald; 1846. [$150.00] [$100.00]

Ferris, Benjamin G. **Utah and the Mormons.** NY: Harper; 1854. [$150.00] [1856 issue, rebound, $35.00]

Ferris, Benjamin G. (Mrs.). **The Mormons at Home.** NY: Dix & Edwards; 1856. [$125.00] [$65.00]

Ferris, Jacob. **The States and Territories of the Great West.** NY: Miller, Orton, and Mulligan; 1856. [$300.00]

Ferris, Warren Angus. **Life in the Rocky Mountains 1830-1835.** Salt Lake City: Rocky Mountain Book Shop; 1940. [$75.00]

Fertig, James Walter. **The Secession and Reconstruction of Tennessee.** Chicago: U. of Chicago; 1898. [$25.00]

Fessenden, Thomas Green. **Modern Philosopher.** 2nd ed. Philadelphia: Lorenzo; 1806. [front cover detached, $95.00]

Fetherstonhaugh, R. C. **The Royal Canadian Mounted Police.** NY: Carrick & Evans; 1938. [$15.00]

Fidfaddy, Frederick Augustus. **Adventures of Uncle Sam in Search after His Lost Honor.** Middletown, CT: Richards; 1816. [front cover detached, $200.00]

Fidler, Isaac. **Observations on Professions, Literature, Manners, and Emigration in the United States and Canada.** London: Whittaker, Treacher; 1833. [$150.00]

Fiedler, George. **Mineral Point.** Mineral Point, WI: Hist. Soc.; 1962. [$17.50]

Fiedler, Leslie A. **Love and Death in the American Novel.** NY: Criterion; 1960. [$15.00]

Field, Edward. **Colonial Tavern.** Providence: Preston and Rounds; 1897. [$45.00]

Field, Edward. **Esek Hopkins.** Providence: Preston & Rounds; 1898. [$85.00]

Field, Edward. **Revolutionary Defences in Rhode Island.** Providence: Preston and Rounds; 1896. [$30.00]

Field, Eugene. **Poems of Childhood.** NY: Scribner; 1904. [$60.00]

Field, Henry Martyn. **Blood Is Thicker Than Water.** NY: Munro; 1886. [front map torn, rear wrap missing, $65.00] [inscribed, $225.00]

Field, Henry Martyn. **Bright Skies and Dark Shadows.** NY: Scribner; 1890. [$65.00]

Field, Henry Martyn. **Our Western Archipelago.** NY: Scribner; 1895. [$100.00]

Field, Joseph E. **Three Years in Texas.** Austin: Steck; 1935. [$45.00]

Field, Matthew C. **Prairie and Mountain Sketches.** 1st ed. Norman: U. of Oklahoma; 1957. [$35.00]

Field, Maunsell Bradhurst. **Memories of Many Men and of Some Women.** NY: Harper; 1874. [$65.00]

Field, Stephen Johnson. **California Alcalde.** Oakland: Biobooks; 1950. [$25.00]

Field, Stephen Johnson. **Personal Reminiscences of Early Days in California.** [San Francisco?]: The Author; 1880. [$200.00]

Fielder, Herbert. **Sketch of the Life and Times and Speeches of Joseph E. Brown.** Springfield, MA: Springfield Print.; 1883. [$85.00]

Fielding, Loraine Hornaday. **French Heels to Spurs.** NY, London: Century; 1930. [$35.00]

Fields, William Claude. **Fields for President.** NY: Dodd, Mead; 1940. [$17.50]

Finch, Edith. **Carey Thomas of Bryn Mawr.** NY: Harper; 1947. [$15.00]

Finck, Henry Theophilus. **Pacific Coast Scenic Tour from Southern California to Alaska.** NY: Scribner; 1890. [$55.00] [$35.00]

Finck, William J. **Lutheran Landmarks and Pioneers in America.** Philadelphia: General Council; 1913. [$15.00] [$12.50]

Findley, William. **Observations on "The Two Sons of Oil."** Pittsburgh: Patterson & Hopkins; 1812. [$175.00]

Finerty, John Frederick. **War-Path and Bivouac.** 2nd ed. Chicago: [s.n.; 1890?]. [$85.00]

Finger, Charles Joseph. **The Distant Prize.** NY, London: Appleton-Century; 1935. [$35.00]

Fink, Colin Garfield. **Drake's Plate of Brass Authenticated.** San Francisco: California Historical Society; 1938. [$15.00]

Finley, James Bradley. **Autobiography of.** Cincinnati: Methodist Book; 1857. [$13.00]

Finley, John Huston. **The French in the Heart of America.** NY: Scribner; 1915. [$30.00]

Finley, Ruth Ebright. **The Lady of Godey's.** Philadelphia, London: Lippincott; 1931. [$45.00]

Finley, Ruth Ebright. **Old Patchwork Quilts and the Women Who Made Them.** Philadelphia, London: Lippincott; 1929. [$50.00]

Finney, Thomas McKean. **Pioneer Days with the Osage Indians.** Bartlesville, OK: [s.n.]; 1925. [$65.00]

Finnie, Richard. **Lure of the North.** Philadelphia: McKay; 1940. [$25.00]

First Reformed Church (Easton, PA). **Some of the First Settlers of "The Forks of the Delaware" and Their Descendants.** Easton: Kieffer; 1902. [$65.00]

Fisher, Frederick V. **Transformation of Job.** 1st ed. Elgin, IL: Cook; 1900. [$35.00]

Fisher, George Adams. **Yankee Conscript.** Philadelphia: Daughaday; 1864. [$175.00]

Fisher, Henry Lee. **Olden Times.** York, PA: Fisher; 1888. [$26.00]

Fisher, Hugh Dunn. **The Gun and the Gospel.** 2nd ed. Chicago, NY: Medical Century; 1899. [$45.00]

Fisher, John R. **Camping in the Rocky Mountains.** NY: Holt; 1880. [$45.00]

Fisher, Orceneth. **Sketches: Texas in 1840.** Waco: Texian; 1964. [$45.00]

Fisher, Ovie Clark. **King Fisher.** 1st ed. Norman: U. of Oklahoma; 1966. [$25.00]

Fisher, Ovie Clark. **Texas Heritage of the Fishers and the Clarks.** Salado, TX: Jones; 1963. [$50.00]

Fisher, Sydney George. **The Struggle for American Independence.** Philadelphia, London: Lippincott; 1908. 2 v. [$50.00]

Fisher, Sydney George. **The True Benjamin Franklin.** Philadelphia: Lippincott; 1899. [$10.00]

Fisher, Vardis. **Children of God.** 1st ed. NY, London: Harper; 1939. [$45.00]

Fisher, Vardis. **Sonnets to an Imaginary Madonna.** NY: Vinal; 1927. [$150.00]

Fisher, Vardis. **Tale of Valor.** 1st ed. Garden City: Doubleday; 1958. [$17.50]

Fisher, Vardis. **Toilers of the Hills.** 1st ed. Boston: Houghton Mifflin; 1928. [$50.00]

Fisher, William Arms. **One Hundred and Fifty Years of Music Publishing in the United States.** Boston: Ditson; 1933, c1934. [$25.00]

Fisk, James Liberty. **Expedition of Captain Fisk to the Rocky Mountains.** Washington: [USGPO?]; 1864. [$100.00] [$85.00]

Fisk, Theophilus. **The Nation's Bulwark.** New Haven: Examiner and Watch Tower of Freedom; 1832. [$125.00]

Fiske, Frank Bennett. **The Taming of the Sioux.** Bismarck, ND: Tribune; 1917. [$75.00]

Fiske, John. **The American Revolution.** Boston, NY: Houghton Mifflin; 1897. 2 v. [$50.00]

Fiske, John. **The Dutch and Quaker Colonies in America.** Boston, NY: Houghton Mifflin; 1899. 2 v. [clean & bright, $40.00] [$20.00]

Fiske, John. **The Mississippi Valley in the Civil War.** Boston, NY: Houghton Mifflin; 1900. [$17.50] [$20.00] [$25.00]

Fiske, John. **Old Virginia and Her Neighbours.** Boston, NY: Houghton Mifflin; 1897. 2 v. [$40.00]

Fitch, Abigail Hetzel. **Junipero Serra.** Chicago: McClurg; 1914. [$30.00]

Fitch, James Marston. **American Building.** London: Batsford; 1948. [$15.00]

Fitch, John. **Annals of the Army of the Cumberland.** 1st ed. Philadelphia: Lippincott; 1863. [$100.00]

Fitch, Michael Hendrick. **The Chattanooga Campaign.** Madison: Wisconsin History Commission; 1911. [x-lib., $15.00]

Fite, Emerson David. **The Presidential Campaign of 1860.** NY: Macmillan; 1911. [$55.00]

Fithian, Philip Vickers. **Journal & Letters of.** Williamsburg, VA: Colonial Williamsburg; 1943. [$25.00] [$35.00]

Fitz, Grancel. **North American Head Hunting.** NY: Oxford UP; 1957. [$15.00]

Fitzgerald, F. Scott. **All the Sad Young Men.** 1st ed. NY: Scribner; 1926. [1st issue, $250.00] [dj slightly wrinkled, $800.00]

Fitzgerald, F. Scott. **The Beautiful and Damned.** 1st ed. NY: Scribner; 1922. [1st printing, hinge split, no dj, $35.00] [1st issue, $250.00] [1st issue, lacks dj, $75.00]

Fitzgerald, F. Scott. **Great Gatsby.** NY: Scribner; 1925. [1st issue, $325.00]

Fitzgerald, F. Scott. **Tales of the Jazz Age.** NY: Scribner; 1922. [1st issue, without dj, $200.00] [1st issue, $200.00]

Fitzgerald, F. Scott. **Taps at Reveille.** NY: Scribner; 1935. [1st printing 2nd state, chipped dj, $300.00] [later state, $200.00]

Fitzgerald, F. Scott. **The Vegetable.** 1st ed. Scribner; 1923. [$265.00]

Fitzhugh, George. **Cannibals All!** Richmond, VA: Morris; 1857. [rebound, $50.00]

Fitzhugh, Lester Newton. **Terry's Texas Rangers.** Houston: Civil War Round Table; 1958. [$25.00]

Fitzpatrick, John Clement. **George Washington, Colonial Traveller, 1732-1775.** Indianapolis: Bobbs-Merrill; 1927. [$45.00]

Five Fur Traders of the Northwest. St. Paul: Minnesota Hist. Soc.; 1965. [$18.00]

Five Years in the West. see, Allen, William M.

Fladeland, Betty. **James Gillespie Birney.** Ithaca: Cornell UP; 1955. [$30.00]

Flagg, Edmund. **The Far West.** NY: Harper; 1838. 2 v. [worn, $175.00]

Flanders, G. M. (Mrs.). **The Ebony Idol.** NY: Appleton; 1860. [$50.00]

Flanders, Henry. **Life of John Marshall.** Philadelphia: Johnson; 1905. [front hinge weak, $25.00]

Flavel, John. **Husbandry Spiritualized.** Elizabethtown, NJ: Kollock; 1794. [$85.00]

Fleharty, J. J. **Social Impurity.** Cincinnati: The Author; 1875. [$50.00]

Fleming, George Thornton. **History of Pittsburgh and Environs.** NY, Chicago: American Historical Soc.; 1922. 5 v. [$115.00]

Fleming, Vivian Minor. **Campaigns of the Army of Northern Virginia.** Richmond: Byrd; 1928. [$90.00]

Fleming, Walter Lynwood. **Documentary History of Reconstruction.** Cleveland: Clark; 1906-07. 2 v. [$250.00] [x-lib., $225.00]

Fletcher, Daniel Cooledge. **Reminiscences of California and the Civil War.** Ayer, MA: Turner; 1894. [$125.00] [$85.00]

Fletcher, Ernest More. **The Wayward Horseman.** Denver: Sage; 1958. [$30.00]

Fletcher, F. N. **Early Nevada; the Period of Exploration, 1776-1848.** Reno: Carlisle; 1929. [$110.00]

Fletcher, Inglis. **Roanoke Hundred.** 1st ed. Indianapolis: Bobbs-Merrill; 1948. [signed, $15.00]

Fletcher, John Gould. **Arkansas.** Chapel Hill: U. of North Carolina; 1947. [$40.00]

Fletcher, Robert Henry. **Free Grass to Fences.** NY: University Publishers; 1960. [$55.00] [$45.00]

Fletcher, Robert Samuel. **History of Oberlin College.** Oberlin: Oberlin College; 1943. 2 v. [$25.00]

Flexner, James Thomas. **The Traitor and the Spy.** 1st ed. NY: Harcourt, Brace; 1953. [$10.00] [$15.00]

Flickinger, Robert Elliott. **The Choctaw Freedmen and the Story of Oak Hill Industrial Academy.** Pittsburgh, PA: Presbyterian Board of Missions for Freedmen; 1914. [$27.50]

Flickinger, Robert Elliott. **Pioneer History of Pocahontas County, Iowa.** Fonda, IA: Sanborn; 1904. [x-lib., rebound, $75.00]

Flint, Grover. **Marching with Gomez.** Boston, NY: Lamson, Wolffe; 1898. [x-lib., $15.00]

Flint, Timothy. **The History and Geography of the Mississippi Valley.** 2nd ed. Cincinnati: Flint and Lincoln; 1832. 2 v. in 1. [$185.00] [rebound, $75.00] [3rd ed., 1833, newly rebound, $45.00]

Florida State Library. **Florida Becomes a State.** Tallahassee: Florida Centennial Commission; 1945. [presentation from W. T. Cash, $25.00]

Flower, George. **History of the English Settlement in Edwards County, Illinois.** Chicago: Fergus; 1882. [$40.00]

Flower, Milton Embick. **James Parton.** Durham: Duke UP; 1951. [$40.00]

Floyd, N. J. **Thorns in the Flesh.** Lynchburg, VA: Bell; 1884. [$45.00]

Flynn, Errol Leslie. **Showdown.** NY: Sheridan; 1946. [$17.50]

Flynn, Paul V. **History of St. John's Church, Newark.** Newark, NJ: New Jersey Trade Review; 1908. [$35.00]

Foerster, Norman. **The American Scholar.** Chapel Hill: U. of North Carolina; 1929. [$12.50]

Foerster, Robert Franz. **Italian Emigration of Our Times.** Cambridge: Harvard UP; 1919. [x-lib., $15.00; $25.00]

Folk, Edgar Estes. **The Mormon Monster.** Chicago, NY: Revell; 1900. [hinges glued, $50.00] [$40.00]

Folmsbee, Stanley John. **Tennessee Establishes a State University.** Knoxville: U. of Tennessee; 1961. [$10.00]

Folsom, George. **History of Saco and Biddeford.** Saco, ME: Putnam; 1830. [one signature loose, $125.00]

Folsom, George. **Mexico in 1842.** NY: Folsom; 1842. [rebacked, x-lib., $1350.00]

Foltz, Charles Steinman. **Surgeon of the Seas.** 1st ed. Indianapolis: Bobbs-Merrill; 1931. [$22.50]

Fonda, Johnstown &. Gloversville Railroad Co. **Camera Sketches of Sacandaga Park.** Gloversville, NY: Passenger Department; [189-?]. [$35.00]

Foner, Philip Sheldon. **Frederick Douglass.** NY: Citadel; 1964. [2nd printing, $22.50]

Font, Pedro. **Font's Complete Diary.** Berkeley: U. of California; 1933. [$85.00]

Fontaine, James. **Memoirs of a Huguenot Family.** NY: Putnam; [1900?]. [$75.00]

Fontana, Bernard L. **Papago Indian Pottery.** Seattle: U. of Washington; 1962. [$20.00]

Foote, Andrew H. **Africa and the American Flag.** NY: Appleton; 1854. [bumped, cocked, sunned, worn, torn, $45.00]

Foote, Corydon Edward. **With Sherman to the Sea.** NY: Day; 1960. [$12.50]

Foote, Henry Stuart. **Texas and the Texans.** 1st ed. Philadelphia: Thomas, Cowperthwait; 1841. 2 v. [$950.00]

Foote, Henry Stuart. **War of the Rebellion.** NY: Harper; 1866. [$85.00]

Foote, Henry Wilder. **Robert Feke.** Cambridge: Harvard UP; 1930. [$85.00]

Foote, Henry Wilder. **Three Centuries of American Hymnody.** Cambridge: Harvard UP; 1940. [$35.00]

Footner, Hulbert. **New Rivers of the North.** NY: Outing; 1912. [$20.00]

Forbes, Alexander. **California; a History of Upper and Lower California.** San Francisco: Nash; 1937. [$125.00] [$150.00]

Forbes, Allan. **France and New England.** Boston: State Street Trust; 1925-1929. 3 v. [$35.00]

Forbes, Allan. **Towns of New England and Old England, Ireland and Scotland.** NY: Tudor; 1936, c1920-1921. 2 v. in 1. [$25.00]

Forbes, Edwin. **A Civil War Artist at the Front.** NY: Oxford UP; 1957. [$17.50]

Forbes, Jack D. **Apache, Navaho, and Spaniard.** 1st ed. Norman: U. of Oklahoma; 1960. [$27.50]

Forbes, John. **Writings of General John Forbes Relating to His Service in North America.** Menasha, WI: Collegiate; 1938. [$35.00]

Forbes, John Murray. **Letters and Recollections of.** Boston, NY: Houghton Mifflin; 1899. 2 v. [$30.00]

Forbush, Bliss. **Elias Hicks, Quaker Liberal.** NY: Columbia UP; 1956. [$20.00]

Forbush, Edward Howe. **History of the Game Birds, Wild-Fowl and Shore Birds of Massachusetts and Adjacent States.** Boston: Wright & Potter; 1912. [$25.00]

Forbush, Edward Howe. **Natural History of the Birds of Eastern and Central North America.** Boston: Houghton Mifflin; 1939. [$40.00]

Force, Peter. **Tracts and Other Papers.** Washington: Force; 1836-46. 4 v. [$500.00] [rebound, $400.00]

Ford, Arthur Peronneau. **Life in the Confederate Army.** NY, Washington: Neale; 1905. [$150.00]

Ford, Corey. **Donovan of OSS.** 1st ed. Boston: Little, Brown; 1970. [$15.00]

Ford, Henry. **The International Jew.** see, Dearborn Independent.

Ford, James. **Genealogy of the Ford Family.** Wabash, IN: Plain Dealer; 1890. [presentation, $75.00]

Ford, Lemuel. **March of the First Dragoons to the Rocky Mountains in 1835.** Denver: Eames; 1957. [limited ed. signed by editor, $100.00]

Ford, Paul Leicester. **The Many-Sided Franklin.** NY: Century; 1899. [$25.00]

Ford, Paul Leicester. **The New England Primer.** NY: Dodd, Mead; 1899. [$45.00]

Ford, Ruth. **Requiem for a Nun, a Play.** NY: Random; 1959. [fine in soiled dj, $65.00]

Ford, Thomas. **A History of Illinois.** Chicago; NY: Griggs; Ivison & Phinney; 1854. [shaken, $450.00]

Ford, Tirey Lafayette. **California State Prisons.** San Francisco: Star; 1910. [$45.00]

Ford, Worthington Chauncey. **The Controversy between Lieutenant-Governor Spotswood, and His Council and the House of Burgesses.** Brooklyn: Historical Print. Club; 1891. [$45.00]

Ford, Worthington Chauncey. **Washington as an Employer and Importer of Labor.** Brooklyn: Priv. Print.; 1889. [$25.00]

Ford Motor Company. **Ford at Fifty.** NY: Simon and Schuster; 1953. [$22.50]

Fordham, Elias Pym. **Personal Narrative of Travels.** Cleveland: Clark; 1906. [$100.00] [x-lib., $50.00]

Fore-Top-Man. see, Mercier, Henry James.

Foreman, Grant. **Advancing the Frontier, 1830-1860.** Norman: U. of Oklahoma; 1933. [$85.00] [dj chipped, $125.00]

Foreman, Grant. **Adventure on Red River.** see, United States. War Department.

Foreman, Grant. **Down the Texas Road.** 1st ed. Norman: U. of Oklahoma; 1936. [wraps spotted, $25.00]

Foreman, Grant. **Five Civilized Tribes.** Norman: U. of Oklahoma; 1934. [$125.00] [dj repaired, $110.00]

Foreman, Grant. **Fort Gibson.** 2nd ed. Norman: U. of Oklahoma; 1943. [$15.00]

Foreman, Grant. **History of Oklahoma.** 1st ed. Norman: U. of Oklahoma; 1942. [$25.00]

Foreman, Grant. **Indians & Pioneers.** New Haven; London: Yale UP; Oxford UP; 1930. [$95.00] [1936 Oklahoma ed., $30.00]

Foreman, Grant. **Marcy & the Gold Seekers.** Norman: U. of Oklahoma; 1968, c1939. [$20.00]

Foreman, Grant. **Pioneer Days in the Early Southwest.** 1st ed. Cleveland: Clark; 1926. [$125.00]

Foreman, Grant. **Sequoyah.** Norman: U. of Oklahoma; 1938. [$80.00] [1959 issue, $14.00]

Foreman, John. **The Philippine Islands.** 2nd ed. NY: Scribner; 1899. [$75.00]

Forester, C. S. **The Age of Fighting Sail.** 1st ed. Garden City: Doubleday; 1956. [later printing, $12.50]

Forgan, James Berwick. **Recollections of a Busy Life.** NY: Bankers; 1924. [$17.50]

"The Forks of the Delaware" Illustrated. Easton, PA: Eschenbach; 1900. [$175.00]

Forman, Samuel S. **Narrative of a Journey down the Ohio and Mississippi in 1789-90.** Cincinnati: Clarke; 1888. [$150.00]

Formby, John. **The American Civil War.** NY: Scribner; 1910. [$10.00]

Fornell, Earl Wesley. **The Galveston Era.** Austin: U. of Texas; 1961. [$45.00]

Forrest, Earle Robert. **Arizona's Dark and Bloody Ground.** Caldwell, ID: Caxton; 1936. [$60.00] [$85.00]

Forrest, Earle Robert. **Lone War Trail of Apache Kid.** limited signed ed. Pasadena, CA: Trail's End; 1947. [$90.00]

Forrest, Earle Robert. **Missions and Pueblos of the Old Southwest.** Chicago: Rio Grande; 1965. [$35.00]

Forrestal, Peter P. **The Venerable Padre Fray Antonio Margil de Jesus.** Austin: Texas Catholic Historical Society; [1932?]. [$30.00]

Forrester, Glenn C. **Falls of Niagara.** NY: Van Nostrand; 1928. [$20.00, Canadian]

Forrester, Izola Louise. **This One Mad Act.** Boston: Hale, Cushman & Flint; 1937. [$35.00]

Forster, Walter Otto. **Zion on the Mississippi.** Saint Louis: Concordia; 1953. [$35.00] [$45.00]

Forsythe, George Alexander. **Story of the Soldier.** NY: Appleton; 1900. [$100.00]

Fortier, Alcee. **Louisiana Studies.** New Orleans: Hansell; 1894. [$45.00]

Fortson, John Lake. **Pott Country and What Has Come of It.** Shawnee, OK: Pottawatomie County Historical Society; 1936. [$40.00]

Foss, Sam Walter. **Back Country Poems.** Boston: Lee and Shepard; 1894. [$15.00]

Fossett, Frank. **Colorado: Its Gold and Silver Mines Farms and Stock Ranges, and Health and Pleasure Resorts.** NY: Crawford; 1879. [x-lib., $85.00] [hinges cracked, $35.00] [$65.00]

Foster, Hannah Webster. **The Coquette.** 2nd ed. Charlestown, MA: Larkin; 1802. [disbound, $150.00]

Foster, John Wells. **The Mississippi Valley.** Chicago: Griggs; 1869. [$125.00]

Foster, John Wells. **Pre-Historic Races of the United States of America.** 3rd ed. Chicago: Griggs; 1874. [$20.00]

Foster, John Young. **New Jersey and the Rebellion.** Newark, NJ: Dennis; 1868. [$75.00]

Foster, Robert Frederick. **Practical Poker.** NY: Brentano's; 1905. [$45.00]

Foster, Stephen S. **The Brotherhood of Thieves.** Boston: Anti-Slavery Office; 1844. [$65.00]

Foster, William Z. **The Great Steel Strike and Its Lessons.** NY: Huebsch; 1920. [$50.00]

Fothergill, John. **Account of the Life and Travels in the Work of the Ministry, of.** Philadelphia: Chattin; 1754. [$150.00]

Fougera, Katherine Gibson. **With Custer's Cavalry.** Caldwell, ID: Caxton; 1940. [$100.00]

Fountain, Paul. **The Eleven Eaglets of the West.** London: Murray; 1905. [$25.00]

Fountain, Paul. **The Great Deserts and Forests of North America.** London, NY: Longmans, Green; 1901. [$60.00]

Fountain, Paul. **The Great Mountains and Forests of South America.** London: Longmans, Green; 1904. [$40.00]

Fowke, Gerard. **Antiquities of Central and Southeastern Missouri.** Washington: USGPO; 1910. [$35.00]

Fowler, A. Richard. **From the Pulpit to the Penitentiary.** Greenville, SC: Greenville News; 1901. [$28.50]

Fowler, Gene. **Illusion in Java.** NY: Random; 1939. [presentation, chipped dj, $35.00]

Fowler, Gene. **Timber Line.** Garden City: Garden City Books; 1951, c1933. [in dj, $15.00]

Fowler, Harlan Davey. **Camels to California.** Stanford: Stanford UP; 1950. [$50.00]

Fowler, Jacob. **Journal of.** NY: Harper; 1898. [x-lib., $100.00]

Fowler, O. S. **A Home for All.** NY: Fowler and Wells; 1854. [spine rubbed, $125.00]

Fowler, O. S. **Illustrated Self-Instructor in Phrenology and Physiology.** NY: Fowler and Wells; 1853. [$50.00]

Fowler, O. S. **The Practical Phrenologist.** Sharon Station, NY: Fowler; 1869. [signed, $17.50]

Fowler, Orin. **History of Fall River.** Fall River, MA: Almy & Milne; 1862. [$45.00]

Fowler, William Worthington. **Woman on the American Frontier.** Hartford: Scranton; 1878, c1876. [$75.00]

Fox, Ebenezer. **Adventures of.** Boston: Fox; 1848. [$45.00] [$50.00]

Fox, George. **The Short Journal and Itinerary Journals of.** Cambridge, Eng.: University Press; 1925. [$35.00]

Fox, James D. **True History of the Reign of Terror in Southern Illinois.** Aurora, IL: Fox; 1884. [$37.50]

Fox, John. **Crittenden.** NY: Scribner; 1900. [$20.00]

Fox, John. **Trail of the Lonesome Pine.** NY: Scribner; 1908. [$17.50]

Fox, William F. **Regimental Losses in the American Civil War, 1861-1865.** Albany, NY: Albany Pub. Co.; 1893, c1889. [$85.00]

Foxborough, MA Centennial Executive Committee. **Foxborough's Official Centennial Record, Saturday, June 29, 1878.** Boston: Town Centennial Committee; 1879. [$15.00]

Foy, Eddie. **Clowning through Life.** NY: Dutton; 1928. [$55.00]

Frackelton, Will. **Sagebrush Dentist.** Chicago: McClurg; 1941. [$45.00]

France. **Treaties of 1778, and Allied Documents.** Baltimore: Hopkins; 1928. [$25.00]

France, Lewis B. **Mountain Trails and Parks in Colorado.** 1st ed. Denver: Chain, Hardy; 1888. [$35.00]

France, Lewis B. **Pine Valley.** Denver: Chain and Hardy; 1891. [$45.00]

Franchere, Gabriel. **Adventure at Astoria, 1810-1814.** 1st ed. Norman: U. of Oklahoma; 1967. [$20.00]

Franchere, Gabriel. **A Voyage to the Northwest Coast of America.** Chicago: Lakeside; 1954. [$20.00]

Francis, John W. **New York during the Last Half Century.** NY: Trow; 1857. [$45.00] [$50.00]

Franck, Harry Alverson. **Roaming in Hawaii.** NY: Stokes; 1937. [$20.00]

Frank, Herman Washington. **Scrapbook of a Western Pioneer.** Los Angeles: Times-Mirror; 1934. [signed, $40.00]

Frank, John Paul. **Mr. Justice Black.** 1st ed. NY: Knopf; 1949, c1948. [$20.00]

Frank, Waldo David. **Birth of a World.** Boston: Houghton Mifflin; 1951. [$15.00]

Frankfurter, Felix. **The Case of Sacco and Vanzetti.** Boston: Little, Brown; 1927. [4th printing?, $35.00]

Frankfurter, Felix. **The Commerce Clause under Marshall, Taney and Waite.** Chapel Hill: U. of North Carolina; 1937. [$25.00]

Frankfurter, Felix. **Felix Frankfurter Reminisces.** NY: Reynal; 1960. [$35.00]

Frankfurter, Felix. **Mr. Justice Holmes and the Supreme Court.** Cambridge: Harvard UP; 1938. [$45.00]

Franklin, Benjamin. **A Collection of the Familiar Letters and Miscellaneous Papers.** Boston: Bowen; 1833. [front cover detached, $85.00]

Franklin, Benjamin. **The Complete Works in Philosophy, Politics, and Morals.** London: Johnson; 1806. 3 v. [$850.00]

Franklin, Benjamin. **Letters and Papers of Benjamin Franklin and Richard Jackson, 1753-1785.** Philadelphia: American Philosophical Society; 1947. [$30.00]

Franklin, Benjamin. **Letters of Benjamin Franklin & Jane Mecom.** Princeton: Princeton UP; 1950. [$20.00]

Franklin, Benjamin. **Mr. Franklin.** New Haven: Yale UP; 1956. [$20.00]

Franklin, Benjamin. **The Old Mistresses' Apologue (1745).** Philadelphia: Rosenbach Foundation; 1956. [$10.00]

Franklin, Benjamin. **Political, Miscellaneous, and Philosophical Pieces.** London: Johnson; 1779. [lacks portrait, inner hinge reinforced, $350.00] [$550.00]

Franklin, Benjamin. **The Private Life of the Late Benjamin Franklin.** London: Parsons; 1793. [rebound, $450.00]

Franklin, Benjamin. **Satires and Hoaxes of.** Mount Vernon: Peter Pauper; 1935. [$25.00]

Franklin, Benjamin. **Weg zum Gluck.** Ephrata, PA: Mayer; 1796. [$200.00]

Franklin, Benjamin. **The Works of.** Boston; New Orleans: Tappan, Whittemore, and Mason; Mygatt; 1840. 10 v. [$250.00]

Franklin, Benjamin. **Writings of.** NY, London: Macmillan; 1907. 10 v. [x-lib., $150.00]

Franklin, Samuel Rhoades. **Memories of a Rear-Admiral.** NY, London: Harper; 1898. [$15.00]

Franks, J. M. **Seventy Years in Texas.** Gatesville, TX: [s.n.]; 1924. [$100.00]

Frantz, Joe Bertram. **The American Cowboy.** 1st ed. Norman: U. of Oklahoma; 1955. [$35.00]

Frantz, Joe Bertram. **Gail Borden, Dairyman to a Nation.** 1st ed. Norman: U. of Oklahoma; 1951. [$45.00] [$25.00]

Frary, Ihna Thayer. **Early American Doorways.** Richmond: Garrett and Massie; 1937. [$40.00]

Frary, Ihna Thayer. **Early Homes in Ohio.** Richmond: Garrett and Massie; 1936. [$35.00]

Frary, Ihna Thayer. **Ohio in Homespun and Calico.** Richmond: Garrett and Massie; 1942. [$35.00]

Frary, Ihna Thayer. **Thomas Jefferson, Architect and Builder.** Richmond: Garrett and Massie; 1931. [$75.00]

Fraser, Georgia. **The Stone House of Gowanus.** NY: Witter and Kintner; 1909. [$30.00]

Frazer, Joseph Jack. **Iron Face.** Chicago: Caxton Club; 1950. [$85.00]

Frederick, James Vincent. **Ben Holladay, the Stagecoach King.** Glendale: Clark; 1940. [$75.00]

Fredman, Joseph George. **Jews in American Wars.** 5th ed. Washington: Jewish War Veterans of the USA; 1954. [$38.50]

Freed, Clyde H. **Story of Railroad Passenger Fares.** Washington: [s.n.]; 1942. [$25.00]

Freel, Margaret Walker. **Our Heritage.** Asheville, NC: Miller; 1956, c1957. [$35.00]

Freeman, Douglas Southall. **Lee of Virginia.** NY: Scribner; 1958. [$16.00]

Freeman, Douglas Southall. **The South to Posterity.** NY: Scribner; 1939. [$100.00]

Freeman, George D. **Midnight and Noonday.** Caldwell, KS: Freeman; 1892. [$200.00]

Freeman, Lewis Ransome. **Down the Columbia.** NY: Dodd, Mead; 1921. [$30.00]

Freeman, Lewis Ransome. **Waterways of Westward Wandering.** NY: Dodd, Mead; 1927. [$22.00] [$30.00]

Freeman, Samuel. **The Massachusetts Justice.** 2nd ed. Boston: Thomas; 1802. [$85.00]

Fregault, Guy. **Le Grand Marquis.** Montreal: Fides; 1952. [$20.00, Canadian]

Fremantle, Arthur James Lyon. **The Fremantle Diary.** Boston: Little, Brown; 1954. [$22.50]

Fremantle, Arthur James Lyon. **Three Months in the Southern States.** NY: Bradburn; 1864. [$125.00]

Fremont, Elizabeth Benton. **Recollections of.** NY: Hitchcock; 1912. [$85.00]

Fremont, Jessie Benton. **Mother Lode Narratives.** Ashland, OR: Osborne; 1970. [$30.00]

Fremont, Jessie Benton. **Story of the Guard.** Boston: Ticknor and Fields; 1863. [$95.00]

Fremont, John Charles. **Memoirs of My Life.** Chicago, NY: Belford, Clarke; 1887. [vol. 1 all published, $275.00]

Fremont, John Charles. **Report of the Exploring Expedition to the Rocky Mountains in the Year 1842 and to Oregon and North California in the Years 1843-44.** Senate ed. Washington: Gales and Seaton; 1845. [$1000.00] [$900.00] [1846 London ed., $650.00]

French, Allen. **The Day of Concord and Lexington.** Boston: Little, Brown; 1925. [$45.00]

French, Allen. **The Siege of Boston.** NY: Macmillan; 1911. [$17.50]

French, Francis Ormond. **Exeter and Harvard Eighty Years Ago.** Chester, NH: Priv. Print.; 1932. [$35.00]

French, Harry W. **Art and Artists in Connecticut.** Boston; NY: Lee and Shepard; Dillingham; 1879. [$75.00]

French, Joseph Lewis. **A Gallery of Old Rogues.** NY: King; 1931. [$12.50]

French, Joseph Lewis. **The Pioneer West.** Garden City: Garden City Pub. Co.; 1937. [$9.00]

French, Wilde James. **Wild Jim: The Texas Cowboy and Saddle King.** Antioch, IL: French; 1890. [$900.00]

French, William. **Some Recollections of a Western Ranchman.** London: Methuen; 1927. [$300.00]

Freneau, Philip Morin. **Poems Written and Published during the American Revolutionary War.** 3rd ed. Philadelphia: Bailey; 1809. 2 v. [rebacked, $275.00]

Freneau, Philip Morin. **Poems, Written between the Years 1768 & 1794.** new ed. Monmouth, NJ: The Author; 1795. [rebound, $325.00]

Freneau, Philip Morin. **Some Account of the Capture of the Ship "Aurora."** NY: Mansfield & Wessels; 1899. [spine faded, corners bumped, $35.00]

Frey, Carroll. **The First Air Voyage in America.** Philadelphia: Penn Mutual Life Insurance; 1943. [$15.00]

Fribourg, Marjorie G. **Supreme Court in American History.** Philadelphia: Macrae-Smith; 1965. [$15.00]

Fridge, Ike. **History of the Chisum War; or Life of Ike Fridge.** Electra, TX: Smith; 1927. [some spine wear, $250.00]

Friedheim, Eric. **Fighters Up.** Philadelphia: Macrae-Smith; 1945. [$45.00]

Friend, Llerena. **Sam Houston, the Great Designer.** Austin: U. of Texas; 1954. [$55.00] [$35.00]

Friends, Society of. **Some Account of the Conduct of the Religious Society of Friends towards the Indian Tribes in the Settlement of the Colonies of East and West Jersey and Pennsylvania.** London: Marsh; 1844. [$325.00]

Fries, John. **Das Erste und Zweite Verhor von.** Allentown, PA: [s.n.]; 1839. [$100.00]

Frink, Margaret Ann Alsip. **Journal of the Adventures of a Party of California Gold-Seekers.** [Oakland?, CA: s.n. 1897?]. [$1500.00]

Frink, Maurice. **Cow Country Cavalcade.** Denver: Old West; 1954. [dj chipped and sunned, $40.00]

Frink, Maurice. **When Grass Was King.** Boulder: U. of Colorado; 1956. [dj worn, $75.00]

Frisbie, Levi. **Discourse, before the Society for Propagating the Gospel among the Indians and Others in North America.** Charlestown, MA: Etheridge; 1804. [$85.00]

Fritz, Florence. **Unknown Florida.** Coral Gables: U. of Miami; 1963. [$15.00]

Fritz, Samuel. **Journal of the Travels and Labours of.** London: Hakluyt; 1922. [$40.00]

Frizzell, Lodisa. **Across the Plains to California in 1852.** NY: New York Public Library; 1915. [$65.00]

Frobel, Julius. **Seven Years' Travel in Central America, Northern Mexico, and the Far West of the United States.** London: Bentley; 1859. [x-lib., $200.00]

Froiseth, Jennie Anderson. **The Women of Mormonism.** Detroit, MI: Paine; 1882. [$40.00] [later printing, $35.00]

From New Jersey to California '97. Somerville, NJ: Bateman; 1897. [$20.00]

Frost, A. B. **Book of Drawings.** NY: Collier; 1904. [extremities rubbed, $60.00]

Frost, Donald McKay. **Notes on General Ashley, the Overland Trail, and South Pass.** Worcester, MA: American Antiquarian Soc.; 1945. [$75.00]

Frost, H. Gordon. **I'm Frank Hamer.** Austin: Pemberton; 1968. [$60.00]

Frost, John. **Book of the Army.** NY, Philadelphia: Appleton; 1846, c1845. [$100.00]

Frost, John. **The Mexican War and Its Warriors.** New Haven: Mansfield; 1848. [$70.00] [$125.00] [1850 printing, $50.00]

Frost, Robert. **Complete Poems of.** signed limited ed. NY: Holt; 1949. [$465.00]

Frost, Robert. **A Further Range.** signed limited ed. NY: Holt; 1936. [$150.00]

Frost, Robert. **New Hampshire.** NY: Holt; 1923. [$95.00]

Frost, Robert. **A Way Out.** signed limited ed. NY: Harbor; 1929. [$175.00]

Frothingham, Richard. **The Centennial: Battle of Bunker Hill.** Boston: Little, Brown; 1875. [$35.00]

Frothingham, Richard. **History of the Siege of Boston, and of the Battles of Lexington, Concord, and Bunker Hill.** 3rd ed. Boston: Little, Brown; 1872. [$85.00]

Frothingham, Richard. **Rise of the Republic of the United States.** Boston: Little, Brown; 1872. [$50.00]

Froude, James Anthony. **The English in the West Indies.** NY: Scribner; 1888. [$35.00]

Fry, Frederich. **Fry's Traveler's Guide and Descriptive Journal of the Great North-Western Territories.** Cincinnati: Applegate; 1865. [$750.00]

Fry, Henry Peck. **The Modern Ku Klux Klan.** Boston: Small, Maynard; 1922. [$85.00]

Fry, James Barnet. **Army Sacrifices.** NY: Van Nostrand; 1879. [$300.00] [loose, $50.00]

Fry, James Barnet. **Operations of the Army under Buell.** NY: Van Nostrand; 1884. [$90.00]

Fuentes, Manuel Atanasio. **Lima; or, Sketches of the Capital of Peru.** Paris: Didot; 1866. [$300.00]

Fuess, Claude Moore. **Rufus Choate.** NY: Minton, Balch; 1928. [$15.00]

Fuller, Anna. **Peak and Prairie.** NY: Putnam; 1894. [$35.00]

Fuller, Claud E. **The Rifled Musket.** Harrisburg, PA: Stackpole; 1958. [$30.00]

Fuller, Emeline L. **Left by the Indians.** NY: Eberstadt; 1936. [$35.00]

Fuller, George Washington. **A History of the Pacific Northwest.** NY: Knopf; 1931. [$50.00] [2nd ed., 1947, $15.00]

Fuller, Henry Clay. **Adventures of Bill Longley.** Nacogdoches, TX: Baker; [n.d.] [$110.00]

Fuller, John Frederick Charles. **Grant & Lee.** London: Eyre and Spottiswoode; 1933. [$20.00]

Fuller, Margaret. see, Ossoli, Sarah Margaret

Fulton, Ambrose Cowperthwaite. **A Life's Voyage.** NY: The Author; 1898. [$175.00]

Fulton, John Farquhar. **Benjamin Silliman.** NY: Schuman; 1947. [dj torn, $22.00]

Fulton, Maurice G. **History of the Lincoln County War.** Tucson: U. of Arizona; 1968. [signed by editor, $75.00]

Funk, Charles Earle. **A Hog on Ice.** 1st ed. NY: Harper; 1948. [$25.00]

Funk, John Fretz. **Mennonite Church and Her Accusers.** Elkhart, IN: Mennonite Pub. Co.; 1878. [$50.00]

Funk, Nellis Rebok. **Pictorial History of the Great Dayton Flood.** Dayton, OH: Otterbein; 1913. [$30.00]

Furlong, Charles Wellington. **Let 'er Buck.** 3rd ed. NY: Putnam; 1923. [$25.00] [$30.00]

Furman, Bess. **White House Profile.** Indianapolis: Bobbs-Merrill; 1951. [$15.00]

Furman, Moore. **The Letters of Moore Furman.** NY: Hitchcock; 1912. [$85.00]

Furnas, J. C. **Goodbye to Uncle Tom.** NY: Sloane; 1956. [$12.50]

Furnas, J. C. **The Road to Harpers Ferry.** London: Faber; 1961. [$15.00]

Futrell, Robert Frank. **The United States Air Force in Korea 1950-1953.** NY: Duell, Sloan and Pearce; 1961. [$42.50]

Gabriel, Ralph Henry. **The Course of American Democratic Thought.** 2nd ed. NY: Wiley; 1956. [$15.00]

Gage, Jack R. **Tensleep and No Rest.** 2nd ed. Casper, WY: Prairie; 1959. [$25.00]

Gaillardet, Frederic. **Sketches of Early Texas and Louisiana.** Austin: U. of Texas; 1966. [$85.00]

Gaither & Addison. **The Washington Directory, and National Register, for 1846.** Washington: Gaither & Addison; 1846. [$275.00]

Galdames, Luis. **A History of Chile.** Chapel Hill: U. of North Carolina; 1941. [$25.00]

Gale, Albert Liscomb. **Bryan the Man.** Boston: Earle; 1908. [$12.50]

Gale, George. **Historic Tales of Old Quebec.** Quebec: Telegraph Printing; 1923, c1920. [$10.00]

Gale, George. **Upper Mississippi.** Chicago, NY: Clarke Oakley and Mason; 1867. [$250.00]

Gallagher, Bertrand E. **Utah's Greatest Manhunt.** Salt Lake City: Gallagher; 1913. [$55.00]

Gallagher, Buell G. **American Caste and the Negro College.** NY: Columbia UP; 1938. [$20.00]

Gallagher, Helen Mar Pierce. **Robert Mills, Architect of the Washington Monument, 1781-1855.** NY: Columbia UP; 1935. [$40.00]

Gallagher, William Davis. **Facts and Conditions of Progress in the North-West.** Cincinnati: Derby; 1850. [rebound, $75.00]

Gallatin, Albert. **The Oregon Question.** NY: Bartlett & Welford; 1846. [$35.00]

Gallatin, Albert. **A Sketch of the Finances of the United States.** NY: Davis; 1796. [x-lib., $425.00]

Gallatin, Albert. **Speech of Albert Gallatin . . . on the Important Question Touching the Validity of the Elections Held in the Four Western Counties of the State.** Philadelphia: Woodward; 1795. [disbound, $150.00]

Gallatin, Albert. **Writings of.** Philadelphia: Lippincott; 1879. 3 v. [x-lib., covers soiled, $75.00]

Galloway, Charles Betts. **Jefferson Davis, a Judicial Estimate.** [s.l.: s.n.]; 1908. [$45.00]

Gambrell, Herbert Pickens. **Anson Jones.** Garden City: Doubleday; 1948. [signed, $65.00] [worn dj, $25.00]

Ganilh, Anthony. **Ambrosio de Letinez.** NY: Francis; 1842. 2 v. [$850.00]

Ganzhorn, John W. **I've Killed Men.** 1st American ed. NY: Devin-Adair; 1959. [$30.00]

Garber, John Palmer. **Valley of the Delaware.** Philadelphia, Chicago: Winston; 1934. [$30.00]

Garceau, Jean. **"Dear Mr. G--."** 1st ed. Boston: Little, Brown; 1961. [$12.50]

Gard, Robert Edward. **Johnny Chinook.** London, NY: Longmans, Green; 1945. [$15.00, Canadian]

Gard, Wayne. **The Chisholm Trail.** Norman: U. of Oklahoma; 1954. [x-lib., inscribed & signed, 1st printing, $125.00] [$125.00] [2nd printing, $25.00]

Gard, Wayne. **Frontier Justice.** 1st ed. Norman: U. of Oklahoma; 1949. [$25.00]

Gard, Wayne. **Great Buffalo Hunt.** NY: Knopf; 1960, c1959. [$14.00]

Gard, Wayne. **Rawhide Texas.** Norman: U. of Oklahoma; 1965. [$35.00]

Gard, Wayne. **Sam Bass.** Boston, NY: Houghton Mifflin; 1936. [$75.00]

Gardiner, Abraham Sylvester. **Tom Quick; or, The Era of Frontier Settlement.** Chicago: Knight & Leonard; 1888. [$40.00]

Gardiner, Mabel Henshaw. **Chronicles of Old Berkeley.** Durham, NC: Seeman; 1938. [$35.00]

Gardner, Erle Stanley. **Neighborhood Frontiers.** NY: Morrow; 1954. [inscribed, $20.00]

Gardner-Sharp, Abbie. see, Sharp, Abigale Gardner.

Garfield, Viola Edmundson. **The Wolf and the Raven.** 1st ed. Seattle: U. of Washington; 1948. [$30.00]

Garland, Claude Mallory. **Washington and His Portraits.** Chicago: Guilford; 1931. [$25.00]

Garland, Hamlin. **Back-Trailers from the Middle Border.** NY: Macmillan; 1928. [inscribed, $100.00]

Garland, Hamlin. **Book of the American Indian.** 1st ed. NY: Harper; 1923. [$250.00]

Garland, Hamlin. **Captain of the Gray-Horse Troop.** NY, London: Harper; 1902. [$25.00]

Garland, Hamlin. **Cavanagh, Forest Ranger.** 1st ed. NY: Harper; 1910. [$25.00] [$30.00]

Garland, Hamlin. **Crumbling Idols.** Cambridge: Harvard UP; 1960. [$17.50]

Garland, Hamlin. **A Daughter of the Middle Border.** NY: Macmillan; 1921. [$17.50

Garland, Hamlin. **Forty Years of Psychic Research.** NY: Macmillan; 1936. [$17.50]

Garland, Hamlin. **Her Mountain Lover.** NY: Century; 1901. [$25.00] [$20.00]

Garland, Hamlin. **Hesper.** 1st ed. NY, London: Harper; 1903. [$25.00]

Garland, Hamlin. **Main-Travelled Roads.** Boston: Arena; 1892, c1891. [$75.00]

Garland, Hamlin. **Moccasin Ranch.** NY, London: Harper; 1909. [$17.50]

Garland, Hamlin. **Roadside Meetings.** 1st ed. NY: Macmillan; 1930. [$25.00] [repaired, $25.00]

Garland, Hamlin. **Son of the Middle Border.** NY: Macmillan; 1917. [$25.00] [$20.0

Garland, Hamlin. **The Spirit of Sweetwater.** 1st ed. Philadelphia; NY: Curti Doubleday & McClure; 1898. [$35.00]

Garland, Hamlin. **Victor Ollnee's Discipline.** NY, London: Harper; 1911. [$30.00]

Garneau, Francois Xavier. **History of Canada.** Montreal: Lovell; 1860. 3 v. [$125.00]

Garneau, Joseph Jr. **Nebraska.** Omaha: Rees; 1893. [$85.00]

Garner, Bess Adams. **Windows in an Old Adobe.** Pomona, CA: Progress-Bulletin; 1939. [$12.50]

Garnett, Algernon S. **Treatise on the Hot Springs of Arkansas.** St. Louis: Van Beck, Barnard & Tinsley; 1874. [$100.00]

Garnett, William Care. **Tidewater Tales.** Dunnsville, VA: Tidewater; 1927. [$25.00]

Garrard, Lewis Hector. **Wah-To-Yah & the Taos Trail.** San Francisco: Grabhorn; 1936. [$175.00] [U. of Oklahoma, 1955, $20.00]

Garretson, James Edmund. **Brushland.** Philadelphia: Lippincott; 1882. [$50.00]

Garrett, Julia Kathryn. **Green Flag over Texas.** NY, Dallas: Cordova; 1939. [$135.00]

Garrett, Pat F. **Authentic Life of Billy, the Kid.** Houston: Frontier Press; 1953. [$22.50]

Garrett, Pat F. **Authentic Story of Billy the Kid.** NY: Atomic Books; 1946. [$18.00] [$10.00]

Garrison, George Pierce. **Texas: A Contest of Civilizations.** Boston, NY: Houghton Mifflin; 1903. [$65.00]

Garwood, Darrell. **Crossroads of America.** 1st ed. NY: Norton; 1948. [$12.50]

Gasparin, Agenor comte de. **America before Europe.** NY: Scribner; 1862. [$25.00]

Gass, Patrick. **Journal of the Voyages and Travels of a Corps of Discovery under the Command of Captain Lewis and Captain Clarke.** London: Budd; 1808. [rebound, $1000.00] [1904 McClurg ed., $100.00]

Gates, Susa Young. **Women of the "Mormon" Church.** Independence, MO: Zion's; 1928. [$35.00]

Gay, Frederick A. **Sketches of California.** NY: [s.n.]; 1848. [$950.00]

Gayarre, Charles. **School for Politics.** 3rd ed. NY; New Orleans: Appleton; Ellis; 1877. [x-lib., $100.00]

Geer, Andrew Clare. **Reckless.** 1st ed. NY: Dutton; 1955. [$15.00]

Geer, John James. **Beyond the Lines; or, A Yankee Prisoner Loose in Dixie.** Philadelphia: Daughaday; 1863. [$65.00]

Geer, Theodore Thurston. **Fifty Years in Oregon.** NY: Neale; 1912. [front hinge repaired, $25.00]

Geer, Walter. **Campaigns of the Civil War.** NY: Brentano's; 1926. [$50.00]

Geiger, Louis George. **University of the Northern Plains.** Grand Forks: U. of North Dakota; 1958. [$15.00]

Geiger, Vincent Eply. **Trail to California.** New Haven; London: Yale UP; Oxford UP; 1945. [$40.00]

Geiser, Samuel Wood. **Naturalists of the Frontier.** Dallas: Southern Methodist University; 1937. [$125.00] [2nd ed., 1948, $18.00]

Gemmill, William Nelson. **The Salem Witch Trials.** Chicago: McClurg; 1924. [$30.00]

General Scott and His Staff. Philadelphia: Grigg, Elliot; 1848. [$75.00] [$50.00]

Genin, Thomas Hedges. **The Napolead.** St. Clairsville, OH: Howard; 1833. [$150.00]

Gentry, Claude. **Private John Allen.** Decatur, GA: Bowen; 1951. [$25.00]

Georgetown University, Washington D. C. Alumni Association. **Blue and Gray: Georgetown University and the Civil War.** Washington: [s.n.]; 1961. [$15.00]

Gerhard, Frederick. **Illinois as It Is.** Chicago; Philadelphia: Keen and Lee; Desilver; 1857. [$175.00]

Gerould, Katharine Fullerton. **The Aristocratic West.** NY, London: Harper; 1925. [$25.00]

Gerould, Katharine Fullerton. **Hawaii; Scenes and Impressions.** NY: Scribner; 1916. [$25.00]

Gerry, Elbridge. **Diary of.** NY: Brentano's; 1927. [$22.50]

Gerson, Noel Bertram. **The Yankee from Tennessee.** 1st ed. Garden City: Doubleday; 1960. [$12.50]

Gerstacker, Friedrich. **Wild Sports in the Far West.** London, NY: Routledge; 1854. [covers worn, $55.00] [1968 Duke UP ed., fine, $40.00]

Gessler, Clifford. **Tropic Landfall: The Port of Honolulu.** Garden City: Doubleday, Doran; 1942. [$14.00]

Getty, J. Paul. **My Life and Fortunes.** 1st ed. NY: Duell, Sloan & Pearce; 1963. [$15.00]

Ghadiali, Dinshah Pestanji Framji. **Spectro-Chrome Metry Encyclopaedia.** 2nd ed. Malaga, NJ: Spectro-Chrome Institute; 1939-40. 3 v. [$90.00]

Ghent, William James. **The Early Far West.** 1st ed. NY, Toronto: Longmans, Green; 1931. [spine loose, $35.00]

Ghent, William James. **The Road to Oregon.** 1st ed. London, NY: Longmans, Green; 1929. [$50.00] [1934 Tudor ed., $25.00]

Gibbes, James Guiguard. **Who Burnt Columbia?** Newberry, SC: Aull; 1902. [frontis lacking, $100.00]

Gibbon, John Murray. **Steel of Empire.** 1st ed. Indianapolis: Bobbs-Merrill; 1935. [$35.00]

Gibbon, Thomas Edward. **Mexico under Carranza.** Garden City: Doubleday, Page; 1919. [$35.00]

Gibbons, James Sloan. **Banks of New York.** NY: Appleton; 1858. [$40.00]

Gibbons, Phebe H. **"Pennsylvania Dutch" and Other Essays.** 3rd ed. Philadelphia: Lippincott; 1882. [$30.00]

Gibbs, George. **Memoirs of the Administrations of Washington and John Adams.** NY: Van Norden; 1846. 2 v. [$110.00] [mildewed, waterstained, covers warped, $35.00]

Gibbs, James M. **History of the First Battalion Pennsylvania Six Months Volunteers and the 187th Regiment Pennsylvania Volunteer Infantry.** Harrisburg: Central; 1905. [$100.00]

Gibbs, Jim. **Pacific Graveyard.** Portland: Oregon Historical Society; 1950. [$45.00]

Gibbs, Josiah Francis. **Lights and Shadows of Mormonism.** Salt Lake City: Tribune; 1909. [$60.00]

Gibson, Albert M. **A Political Crime.** NY: Gottsberger; 1885. [$45.00]

Gibson, Arrell Morgan. **Life and Death of Colonel Albert Jennings Fountain.** Norman: U. of Oklahoma; 1965. [$30.00]

Gibson, Charles. **The Aztecs under Spanish Rule.** Stanford: Stanford UP; 1964. [$35.00]

Gibson, Florence Elizabeth. **Attitudes of the New York Irish toward State and National Affairs.** NY: Columbia UP; 1951. [$35.00]

Gibson, George Rutledge. **Journal of a Soldier under Kearny and Doniphan, 1846-1847.** Glendale, CA: Clark; 1935. [$75.00]

Gibson, Jesse. **Thomas Bone.** Toronto: Upper Canada Tract Society; [19-?]. [$15.00, Canadian]

Gibson, John Mendinghall. **Those 163 Days.** NY: Coward-McCann; 1961. [$12.50] [$22.50]

Gibson, Joseph Thompson. **History of the Seventy-Eighth Pennsylvania Volunteer Infantry.** Pittsburgh: Pittsburgh Printing; 1905. [$110.00]

Gibson, Otis. **The Chinese in America.** Cincinnati: Hitchcock & Walden; 1877. [worn, $60.00]

Gibson, W. Hamilton. **Highways and Byways.** NY: Harper; 1883. [$40.00]

Giddings, Joshua Reed. **Exiles of Florida.** Columbus, OH: Follett, Foster; 1858. [$30.00]

Giffen, Fannie Reed. **Oo-Mah-Ha Ta-Wa-Tha (Omaha City).** Lincoln: The Authors; 1898. [$45.00]

Giffen, Guy James. **California Expedition.** Oakland, CA: Biobooks; 1951. [$15.00]

Giffen, Helen S. **Casas & Courtyards.** Oakland, CA: Biobooks; 1955. [$50.00]

Gifford, John Clayton. **Billy Bowlegs and the Seminole War.** Coconut Grove, FL: Triangle; 1925. [$35.00]

Gihon, John H. **Geary and Kansas.** Philadelphia: Rhodes; 1857. [$80.00] [$65.00]

Gilbert, Fabiola (Cebeza De Baca). **We Fed Them Cactus.** Albuquerque: U. of New Mexico; 1954. [fine in dj, $35.00]

Gilbert, J. Warren. **Blue and Gray.** Harrisburg, PA: Evangelical; 1922. [$12.00]

Gilbert, Olive. **Narrative of Sojourner Truth.** Boston: The Author; 1875. [$200.00]

Gilder, Rodman. **The Battery.** Boston: Houghton Mifflin; 1936. [$30.00]

Gilder, William Henry. **Schwatka's Search.** NY: Abercrombie & Fitch; 1966. [$17.50]

Giles, Harry F. **Beauties of the State of Washington.** Olympia: Lamborn; 1916. [$8.50]

Giles, Leonidas B. **Terry's Texas Rangers.** Austin: Von Boeckman-Jones; 1911. [in morocco slipcase, $1250.00]

Giles, Rosena A. **Shasta County, California.** Oakland: Biobooks; 1949. [inscribed, $45.00] [$25.00] [presentation, $30.00]

Giles, Valerius Cincinnatus. **Rags and Hope.** NY: Coward-McCann; 1961. [$25.00]

Gill, William Davis. **Texas Yarns and Jokes.** San Antonio: Naylor; 1952. [x-lib., $15.00]

Gillett, Ezera Hall. **History of the Presbyterian Church in the United States of America.** rev. ed. Philadelphia: Presbyterian Board of Publications and Sabbath-School Work; 1873. 2 v. [$75.00]

Gillett, James B. **Six Years with the Texas Rangers, 1875 to 1881.** Austin: Von Boeckmann-Jones; 1921. [$200.00] [$150.00] [$265.00] [$125.00] [1925 Yale ed., $45.00] [1943 Lakeside ed., $25.00]

Gilliam, Albert M. **Travels over the Table Lands and Cordilleras of Mexico during the Years 1843 and 44.** Philadelphia: Moore; 1846. [shaken, $600.00]

Gillingham, Robert Cameron. **Rancho San Pedro.** Los Angeles: Dominguez Estate; 1961. [inscribed, $100.00]

Gillis, William Robert. **Gold Rush Days with Mark Twain.** NY: Boni; 1930. [$30.00]

Gillmor, Frances. **Traders to the Navajos.** Boston, NY: Houghton Mifflin; 1934. [signed, chipped dj, $40.00]

Gillmore, Parker. **Prairie and Forest.** NY: Harper; 1874. [$65.00]

Gilman, Daniel Coit. **Building of the University.** San Francisco: Carmany; 1872. [$20.00]

Gilmore, James Roberts. **Down in Tennessee, and Back by Way of Richmond.** NY: Carleton; 1864. [$28.50] [spine chipped, $35.00]

Gilmore, James Roberts. **John Sevier as a Commonwealth-Builder.** NY: Appleton; 1887. [$35.00]

Gilmore, James Roberts. **Personal Recollections of Abraham Lincoln and the Civil War.** Boston: Page; 1898. [$28.50]

Gilpin, Alec Richard. **The War of 1812 in the Old Northwest.** East Lansing: Michigan State UP; 1958. [$20.00, Canadian] [$22.50]

Gilpin, William. **The Central Gold Region.** Philadelphia; St. Louis: Sower, Barnes; Woodward; 1860. [$120.00]

Giovannoli, Harry. **Kentucky Female Orphan School, a History.** Midway, KY: [s.n.]; 1930. [$15.00]

Gipson, Frederick. **The Cow Killers.** Austin: U. of Texas; 1956. [inscribed by illustrator, $25.00]

Gipson, Frederick. **Fabulous Empire.** Boston: Houghton Mifflin; 1946. [$35.00]

Gipson, Frederick. **Hound-Dog Man.** 1st ed. NY: Harper; 1949. [$25.00]

Gipson, Lawrence Henry. **Lewis Evans.** Philadelphia: Historical Society of Pennsylvania; 1939. [$85.00]

Girdler, Tom Mercer. **Boot Straps.** NY: Scribner; 1944, c1943. [$15.00]

Gish, Anthony. **American Bandits.** Girard, KS: Haldeman Julius; 1938. [$10.00]

Gittinger, Roy. **The Formation of the State of Oklahoma (1803-1906).** Berkeley: U. of California; 1917. [$45.00] [1939 Oklahoma ed., dj faded, $25.00]

Glace, William H. **Early History and Reminiscences of Catasauqua in Pennsylvania.** Allentown: Searle & Dressler; 1914. [inscribed, $50.00]

Gladstone, Thomas H. **Kansas; or, Squatter Life and Border Warfare in the Far West.** London, NY: Routledge; 1857. [$225.00]

Glass, Robert Camillus. **Virginia Democracy.** Springfield, IL: Democratic Historical Association; 1937. 3 v. [$85.00]

Glasscock, Carl Burgess. **Bandits and the Southern Pacific.** NY: Stokes; 1929. [$45.00]

Glasscock, Carl Burgess. **Gold in Them Hills.** 1st ed. Indianapolis: Bobbs-Merrill; 1932. [$25.00]

Glasscock, Carl Burgess. **Here's Death Valley.** 1st ed. Indianapolis, NY: Bobbs-Merrill; 1940. [$25.00] [$17.50]

Glasscock, Sallie. **Dreams of an Empire.** San Antonio: Naylor; 1951. [$45.00]

Glazier, Willard. **Down the Great River.** Philadelphia: Hubbard; 1893. [$25.00]

Glazier, Willard. **Headwaters of the Mississippi.** Chicago: Rand McNally; 1894, c1892. [$20.00]

Glazier, Willard. **Ocean to Ocean on Horseback.** Philadelphia: Edgewood; 1900. [corners bent, back cover badly chipped, $20.00]

Glazier, Willard. **Peculiarities of American Cities.** Philadelphia: Hubbard; 1885. [$25.00] [$40.00]

Glazier, Willard. **Three Years in the Federal Cavalry.** NY: Ferguson; 1874. [$25.00]

Gleason, J. Duncan. **Islands and Ports of California.** NY: Devin-Adair; 1958. [$25.00]

Glenn, Thomas Allen. **Some Colonial Mansions and Those Who Lived in Them (1st & 2nd Series).** Philadelphia: Coates; 1899-1900. 2 v. [$150.00] [2nd series only, $45.00]

Glover, Edwin A. **Bucktailed Wildcats.** NY: Yoseloff; 1960. [$30.00]

Gobel, Gert. **Langer als ein Menschenleben in Missouri.** St. Louis: Witter's; 1877. [rebound, $175.00] [$185.00]

Godcharles, Frederic Antes. **Chronicles of Central Pennsylvania.** NY: Lewis; 1944. 4 v. [$110.00]

Goddard, Frederick Bartlett. **Where to Emigrate and Why.** Philadelphia, Cincinnati: Peoples; 1869. [$175.00] [restored, $100.00] [1869 NY imprint, $135.00]

Goddard, Pliny Earle. **Beaver Indians.** NY: American Museum of Natural History; 1916. [$15.00]

Goddard, Pliny Earle. **Indians of the Southwest.** 4th ed. NY: American Museum of Natural History; 1931. [$15.00]

Goddard, Pliny Earle. **Jicarilla Apache Texts.** NY: American Museum of Natural History; 1911. [$20.00]

Godfrey, Carlos Emmor. **The Commander-in-Chief's Guard, Revolutionary War.** Washington: Stevenson-Smith; 1904. [rebound, $75.00]

Goerner, Fred G. **Search for Amelia Earhart.** Garden City: Doubleday; 1966. [signed, $15.00]

Goldberg, Isaac. **President Harding's Illegitimate Daughter.** Girard, KS: Haldeman-Julius; 1929. [$20.00]

Goldbloom, Maurice. **Strikes under the New Deal.** NY: League for Industrial Democracy; 1935. [$25.00]

The Golden Book of California. Berkeley: California Alumni Assn.; 1937. [$20.00]

Golden, Gertrude. **The American Indian Then and Now.** San Antonio: Naylor; 1957. [$15.00]

Golder, Frank Alfred. **March of the Mormon Batallion from Council Bluffs to California.** NY, London: Century; 1928. [dampstained, $25.00] [$45.00]

Golder, John. **Life of the Honourable William Tilghman.** Philadelphia: The Author; 1829. [rebacked, $65.00]

Goldman, Emma. **Anarchism and Other Essays.** 3rd ed. NY: Mother Earth; 1917. [$50.00]

Goldman, Eric Frederick. **John Bach McMaster, American Historian.** Philadelphia; London: U. of Pennsylvania; Oxford UP; 1943. [$12.50]

Goldsborough, Charles Washington. **The United States' Naval Chronicle, Vol. 1.** Washington: Wilson; 1824. [all published, x-lib., $150.00]

Gollomb, Joseph. **Master Highwaymen.** NY: Macaulay; 1927. [$20.00]

Gongaware, George Jonas. **History of the German Friendly Society of Charleston, South Carolina.** Richmond: Garrett & Massie; 1935. [$15.00]

Gooch, Fanny Chambers. see, Inglehart, Fanny Chambers Gooch.

Gooch, T. C. **Texans and Their State.** Fort Worth: Texas Biographical Association; [1918?]. [$135.00]

Goode, John. **Recollections of a Lifetime.** NY: Neale; 1906. [$65.00]

Goodenough, Caroline Louisa. **Legends, Loves and Loyalties of Old New England.** Rochester, MA: The Author; 1930. [$25.00]

Goodhew, Edna F. **Echoes from Half a Century.** Los Angeles: Los Angeles Pacific College; 1960. [$15.00]

Goodlander, Charles W. **Memoirs and Recollections of.** Fort Scott, KS: Monitor; 1900. [spine sunned, $75.00] [$125.00] [2nd printing in 1900?, $30.00]

Goodloe, Albert Theodore. **Some Rebel Relics from the Seat of War.** Nashville: The Author; 1893. [$250.00] [x-lib., $100.00]

Goodman, Thomas M. **Sergeant Thomas M. Goodman's "Thrilling Record."** Maryville, MO: Rush; 1960. [$20.00]

Goodrich, Charles A. **The Family Tourist.** Philadelphia: Bradley; 1848. [x-lib., $25.00]

Goodrich, Charles A. **Lives of the Signers to the Declaration of Independence.** NY: Leavitt; 1829. [$40.00]

Goodrich, Frederick Elizur. **Life and Public Services of Winfield Scott Hancock.** Boston: Lee & Shepard; 1880. [$25.00]

Goodrich, Lloyd. **Winslow Homer.** NY: Macmillan; 1944. [$75.00]

Goodspeed, Edgar Johnson. **As I Remember.** NY: Harper; 1953. [$15.00]

Goodspeed, Edgar Johnson. **History of the Great Fires in Chicago and the West.** NY, Chicago: Goodspeed; 1871. [$40.00]

Goodspeed, Thomas Wakefield. **History of the University of Chicago.** Chicago: U. of Chicago; 1916. [x-lib., $25.00]

Goodspeed, Weston Arthur. **Counties of Porter and Lake, Indiana.** 1st ed. Chicago: Battey; 1882. [$90.00]

Goodwin, Cardinal Leonidas. **The Trans-Mississippi West.** NY: Appleton; 1922. [x-lib., $125.00] [$135.00]

Goodwin, Charles Carroll. **As I Remember Them.** Salt Lake City: Commercial Club; 1913. [$165.00]

Goodwin, Grenville. **Social Organization of the Western Apache.** Chicago: U. of Chicago; 1942. [$70.00]

Goodwin, Hermon Camp. **Pioneer History.** NY: Burdick; 1859. [$65.00]

Goodwyn, Frank. **Life on the King Ranch.** NY: Crowell; 1951. [$25.00]

Goodwyn, Frank. **Lone-Star Land.** 1st ed. NY: Knopf; 1955. [$12.50]

Goolrick, John Taquette. **Fredericksburg and the Cavalier Country.** Richmond: Garrett & Massie; 1935. [$20.00]

Gordon, Armistead Churchill. **In the Picturesque Shenandoah Valley.** Richmond: Garrett & Massie; 1930. [$15.00]

Gordon, Armistead Churchill. **Memories and Memorials of William Gordon McCabe.** Richmond: Old Dominion; 1925. 2 v. [$67.50]

Gordon, Armistead Churchill. **Men and Events: Chapters of Virginia History.** Staunton, VA: McClure; 1923. [silverfished, $15.00]

Gordon, Armistead Churchill. **William Fitzhugh Gordon.** NY: Neale; 1909. [$50.00]

Gordon, Elizabeth Putnam. **Women Torch-Bearers.** 2nd ed. Evanston, IL: Woman's Christian Temperance Union; 1924. [$17.50]

Gordon, Jan. **On Wandering Wheels through Roadside Camps from Maine to Georgia.** NY: Dodd, Mead; 1928. [$15.00]

Gordon, John Brown. **Reminiscences of the Civil War.** NY: Scribner; 1903. [$100.00] [1904 printing, $50.00]

Gordon, Welche. **Jesse James and His Band of Notorious Outlaws.** special ed. Chicago: Laird & Lee; 1892. [$150.00]

Gordon, William. **History of the Rise, Progress, and Establishment, of the Independence of the United States of America.** NY: Hodge, Allen, and Campbell; 1789. 3 v. [$1250.00]

Gorgas, Marie Cook. **William Crawford Gorgas.** Garden City: Doubleday, Page; 1924. [loose, $35.00]

Gorham, George Congdon. **Life and Public Services of Edwin M. Stanton.** Boston, NY: Houghton Mifflin; 1899. 2 v. [$65.00]

Gorostiza, Manuel Eduardo de. **Gorostiza Pamphlet.** Washington: [s.n.]; 1838. [$500.00]

Gosling, William Gilbert. **Labrador.** London: Rivers; 1910. [$100.00]

Gosnell, Harpur Allen. **Guns on the Western Waters.** Baton Rouge: Louisiana State UP; 1949. [$35.00] [$20.00]

Goss, Warren Lee. **The Soldier's Story of His Captivity at Andersonville, Belle Isle, and Other Rebel Prisons.** Boston: Lee and Shepard; 1867. [$65.00]

Gosselman, Carl August. **Resa i Norra Amerika.** Nykoping: [s.n.]; 1835. [$300.00]

Gossler, Jacob L. **An Old Turnpike-Road.** NY: Baker & Taylor; 1888. [$15.00]

Gottesman, Rita Susswein. **Arts and Crafts in New York.** NY: NY Hist. Soc.; 1938. [$50.00]

Gottschalk, Paul. **Earliest Diplomatic Documents on America.** see, Catholic Church. Pope (1491-1503: Alexander VI).

Gouge, William M. **Fiscal History of Texas.** Philadelphia: Lippincott, Grambo; 1852. [$585.00]

Gould, Charles Newton. **Travels through Oklahoma.** Oklahoma City: Harlow; 1928. [$50.00]

Gould, Emerson W. **Fifty Years on the Mississippi.** Saint Louis: Nixon-Jones; 1889. [$250.00] [1951 Long's reprint, $40.00]

Goulder, William Armistead. **Reminiscences.** Boise, ID: Regan; 1909. [$175.00]

Govan, Gilbert Eaton. **A Different Valor.** Indianapolis: Bobbs-Merrill; 1956. [signed, $30.00] [$30.00] [$35.00]

Graber, Henry William. **Life Record of.** Dallas: Graber; 1916. [$1250.00]

Grace, Albert L. **Heart of the Sugar Bowl: The Story of Iberville.** Plaquemine, LA: Franklin; 1946. [signed, $45.00]

Gracy, David B. **Littlefield Lands.** 1st ed. Austin: U. of Texas; 1968. [$15.00]

Grady, Benjamin Franklin. **The Case of the South against the North.** Raleigh, NC: Edwards & Broughton; 1899. [$55.00]

Grady, Joseph F. **Adirondacks; Fulton Chain-Big Moose Region.** Little Falls, NY: Journal & Courier; 1933. [$75.00]

Graff, John Franklin. **"Graybeard's" Colorado.** Philadelphia: Lippincott; 1882. [x-lib., worn, $30.00]

Graham, George Washington. **Mecklenburg Declaration of Independence, May 20, 1775.** NY, Washington: Neale; 1905. [$115.00]

Graham, Gerald Sandford. **The Walker Expedition to Quebec, 1711.** London: Navy Records Society; 1953. [$35.00]

Graham, James Augustus. **The James A. Graham Papers, 1861-1884.** Chapel Hill: U. of North Carolina; 1928. [$50.00]

Graham, James Robert. **The Planting of the Presbyterian Church in Northern Virginia.** Winchester, VA: Norton; 1904. [bumped, rubbed, silverfished, and sunned, $45.00]

Graham, James Stevenson. **A Scotch-Irish Canadian Yankee.** NY: Putnam; 1939. [$30.00, Canadian]

Graham, Jared Benedict. **Handset Reminiscences.** Salt Lake City: Century; 1915. [$150.00]

Graham, John A. **Descriptive Sketch of the Present State of Vermont.** London: Fry; 1797. [rebound, $500.00]

Graham, Matthew John. **Ninth Regiment, New York Volunteers (Hawkins' Zouaves).** NY: Cody; 1900. [$100.00]

Graham, Philip. **Early Texas Verse.** Austin: Steck; 1936. [$30.00]

Graham, Robert Bontine Cunningham. **The Horses of the Conquest.** Norman: U. of Oklahoma; 1949. [$35.00]

Graham, Stephen. **In Quest of El Dorado.** NY: Appleton; 1923. [$17.50] [$20.00]

Graham, William Alexander. **The Custer Myth.** limited ed. Harrisburg, PA: Stackpole; 1953. [$45.00] [Bonanza reprint, fine, $25.00]

Grahame, James. **History of the United States of North America.** 2nd ed. Philadelphia: Blanchard and Lea; 1856. 2 v. [$65.00]

Gramm, Carl H. **The Germans in New Brunswick, New Jersey.** Cleveland: Central Publishing; 1938. [$25.00]

Grammont, Justin. **League of the Merrimack.** Manchester, NH: Fisk & Moore; 1848. [wraps stained, $150.00]

Grand, Gordon. **Redmond C. Stewart.** NY, London: Scribner; 1938. [$35.00]

Grand, W. Joseph. **Illustrated History of the Union Stockyards.** Chicago: Knapp; 1901, c1896. [$55.00]

Grandy, Moses. **Narrative of the Life of.** 2nd American ed. Boston: Johnson; 1844. [$85.00]

Grange, Herbert. **An English Farmer in Canada and a Visit to the States.** London: Blackie; 1904. [$25.00, Canadian]

Granick, Harry. **Underneath New York.** NY, Toronto: Rhinehart; 1947. [$15.00]

Grant, Anne MacVicar. **Memoirs of an American Lady.** London: Longman, Hurst, Rees and Orme; 1808. 2 v. [$385.00] [1901 Dodd, Mead ed., $70.00; $125.00] [1846 Appleton ed., $95.00] [1809 Wells ed. in one vol., rebacked, $85.00]

Grant, Blanche Chloe. **Taos Indians.** 1st ed. Taos, NM: [s. n.]; 1925. [$90.00]

Grant, Blanche Chloe. **Taos Today.** 1st ed. Taos, NM: Grant; 1925. [signed, $35.00]

Grant, Blanche Chloe. **When Old Trails Were New.** NY: Press of the Pioneers; 1934. [covers and spine faded. $50.00] [$100.00]

Grant, Bruce. **Isaac Hull.** Chicago: Pellegrini and Cudahy; 1947. [$10.00]

Grant, George Monro. **Ocean to Ocean: Sandford Fleming's Expedition through Canada in 1872.** London: Campbell; 1873. [$225.00]

Grant, Ulysses S. **Personal Memoirs of.** NY: Webster; 1885-86. 2 v. [loose, $40.00] [$65.00] [$60.00]

Gras, Norman Scott Brien. **The Massachusetts First National Bank of Boston, 1784-1934.** Cambridge: Harvard UP; 1937. [$25.00]

Grattan, Clinton Hartley. **Bitter Bierce.** Garden City: Doubleday, Doran; 1929. [$20.00] [$35.00]

Grattan, Clinton Hartley. **The Three Jameses.** NY: New York UP; 1962, c1932. [$15.00]

Grattan, Thomas Colley. **Civilized America.** 2nd ed. London: Bradbury and Evans; 1859. 2 v. [spines worn, $85.00]

Gratz, Rebecca. **Letters of.** Philadelphia: Jewish Pub. Soc. of America; 1929. [$25.00]

Graves, H. A. **Reminiscences and Events in the Ministerial Life of Rev. John Wesley DeVilbiss.** Galveston, TX: Shaw; 1886. [$385.00]

Graves, Jackson Alpheus. **California Memories, 1857-1930.** 1st ed. Los Angeles: Times-Mirror; 1930. [signed, $55.00]

Graves, John. **Goodbye to a River.** 1st ed. NY: Knopf; 1960. [$65.00]

Graves, Lawrence L. **History of Lubbock.** Lubbock: West Texas Museum Assn.; 1959. [$20.00]

Graves, William Whites. **Life and Letters of Rev. Father John Schoenmakers, S.J.** Parsons, KS: Commercial; 1928. [$35.00]

Gray, Arthur Amos. **Men Who Built the West.** Caldwell, ID: Caxton; 1945. [$15.00]

Gray, Frank S. **For Love & Bears.** see, Daly, James.

Gray, Frank S. **Pioneering in Southwest Texas.** [Copperas Cove?, TX: s.n.]; 1949. [$45.00]

Gray, Harold Studley. **Character "Bad."** 1st ed. NY, London: Harper; 1934. [$15.00]

Gray, Horace. **A Legal Review of the Case of Dred Scott.** Boston: Crosby, Nichols; 1857. [presentation, lacks back wrapper, $150.00]

Gray, Hugh. **Letters from Canada.** London: Longman, etc.; 1809. [rebacked, $300.00]

Gray, William F. **From Virginia to Texas.** Houston: Young; 1965. [$65.00]

Gray, Wood. **The Hidden Civil War.** NY: Viking; 1942. [$30.00]

Graydon, Alexander. **Memoirs of a Life.** Harrisburgh: Wyeth; 1811. [$100.00] [$65.00]

Graydon, Alexander. **Memoirs of His Own Time.** Philadelphia: Lindsay & Blakiston; 1846. [$35.00]

Great Industries of the United States. Hartford, Chicago: Burr & Hyde; 1872, c1871. [rebound, $50.00]

Greatorex, Eliza Pratt. **Summer Etchings in Colorado.** NY: Putnam; 1873. [$120.00]

Greeley, Horace. **Life of Col. Fremont.** NY: Greeley & M'Elrath; 1856. [$35.00]

Greeley, Horace. **Political Text Book for 1860.** NY: Tribune Assn.; 1860. [$60.00]

Greely, Adolphus Washington. **Handbook of Alaska.** NY: Scribner; 1909. [map in pocket, $45.00]

Greely, Adolphus Washington. **Reminiscences of Adventure and Service.** NY, London: Scribner; 1927. [$50.00]

Greely, Adolphus Washington. **Three Years of Arctic Service.** NY: Scribner; 1886. 2 v. [$175.00]

Green, Ashbel. **Memoirs of the Rev. Joseph Eastburn.** Philadelphia: Mentz; 1828. [$35.00]

Green, Calvin. **Summary View of the Millennial Church.** see, Shakers.

Green, Charles R. **Early Days in Kansas.** Olathe, KS: Green; 1913. [$35.00]

Green, Doron. **History of Bristol Borough in the County of Bucks, State of Pennsylvania.** Camden, NJ: Magrath; 1911. [$75.00]

Green, Fletcher Melvin. **Constitutional Development in the South Atlantic States, 1776-1860.** Chapel Hill: U. of North Carolina; 1930. [$25.00]

Green, Fletcher Melvin. **The Lides Go South . . . and West.** Columbia: U. of South Carolina; 1952. [creased, old, worn, presentation, $25.00]

Green, Harry Clinton. **The Pioneer Mothers of America.** NY: Putnam; 1912. 3 v. [$100.00]

Green, John Riley. **Fun and Philosophy.** Dallas: Johnston; 1930. [$75.00]

Green, John Williams. **Johnny Green of the Orphan Brigade.** Lexington: U. of Kentucky; 1956. [signed by editor, $35.00]

Green, Paul. **The Common Glory.** Chapel Hill: U. of North Carolina; 1948. [dj chipped and worn, $25.00]

Green, Paul. **The Lord's Will, and Other Carolina Plays.** NY: Holt; 1925. [mildewed, hinges weak, $20.00]

Green, Thomas Jefferson. **Journal of the Texian Expedition against Mier.** NY: Harper; 1845. [spine repaired, $650.00] [rebacked, $925.00] [$785.00]

Green, Thomas Marshall. **The Spanish Conspiracy.** Cincinnati: Clarke; 1891. [$250.00]

Green, Wharton Jackson. **Recollections and Reflections.** Raleigh, NC: Edwards and Broughton; 1906. [inscribed, $385.00]

Greene, Francis Vinton. **The Mississippi.** NY: Scribner; 1882. [x-lib., $35.00]

Greene, Francis Vinton. **The Revolutionary War and the Military Policy of the United States.** NY: Scribner; 1911. [$40.00]

Greene, George Washington. **German Element in the War of American Independence.** NY; Cambridge: Hurd & Houghton; Riverside; 1876. [$45.00] [$40.00]

Greene, Katherine Glass. **Winchester, Virginia, and Its Beginnings.** Strasburg, VA: Shenandoah; 1926. [$40.00]

Greene, Laurence. **The Filibuster; the Career of William Walker.** 1st ed. Indianapolis, NY: Bobbs-Merrill; 1937. [$25.00] [$20.00]

Greene, Le Roy. **Shelter for His Excellency.** Harrisburg: Stackpole; 1951. [$15.00]

Greene, Lorenzo Johnston. **The Negro in Colonial New England, 1620-1776.** NY: Columbia UP; 1942. [$75.00]

Greenhow, Robert. **The History of Oregon and California.** 2nd ed. Boston: Little and Brown; 1845. [lacks map, $75.00] [1874 Freeman & Bolles ed., x-lib., $150.00]

Greenleaf, Moses. **Statistical View of the District of Maine.** Boston: Cummings and Hilliard; 1816. [lacking separately issued map, $250.00]

Greenslet, Ferris. **The Lowells and Their Seven Worlds.** Boston: Houghton Mifflin; 1946. [$10.00]

Greenwood, Annie Pike. **We Sagebrush Folks.** NY, London: Appleton-Century; 1934. [$22.50]

Greenwood, John. **The Revolutionary Services of.** NY: De Vinne; 1922. [$125.00]

Greer, James Kimmins. **Bois d'Arc to Barb'd Wire.** Dallas: Dealey and Low; 1936. [signed, $150.00]

Greer, James Kimmins. **Colonel Jack Hays.** 1st ed. NY: Dutton; 1952. [signed, $150.00] [$100.00] [$85.00]

Greever, William S. **Arid Domain.** Stanford: Stanford UP; 1954. [$35.00]

Greever, William S. **The Bonanza West.** 1st ed. Norman: U. of Oklahoma; 1963. [worn dj, $17.50]

Gregg, Alexander. **History of the Old Cheraws.** Columbia, SC: State Company; 1925. [covers scuffed, $125.00]

Gregg, Jacob Ray. **Pioneer Days in Malheur County.** Los Angeles: Morrison; 1950. [signed, $35.00]

Gregg, Josiah. **Commerce of the Prairies.** NY; London: Langley; Wiley and Putnam; 1844. 2 v. [$2000.00] [missing one map, $800.00] [1968 Citadel ed., $14.00] [1845 2nd ed., $750.00]

Gregg, Josiah. **Diary & Letters of.** Norman: U. of Oklahoma; 1941-44. 2 v. [$85.00]

Gregory, Dick. **Nigger.** 1st ed. NY: Dutton; 1964. [$12.50]

Gregory, John G. **History of Milwaukee, Wisconsin.** Chicago, Milwaukee: Clarke; 1931. 4 v. [$175.00]

Gregory, Thomas B. **Our Mexican Conflicts.** NY: Hearst's; 1914. [$25.00]

Grellet, Stephen. **Memoirs of the Life and Gospel Labors of.** Philadelphia: Longstreth; 1860. 2 v. [$45.00]

Grenfell, Wilfred Thomason. **Down North on the Labrador.** NY, Chicago: Revell; 1911. [$15.00]

Grenfell, Wilfred Thomason. **Labrador: The Country and the People.** NY: Macmillan; 1909. [$25.00] [$20.00, Canadian]

Grey, William. see, White, William Francis.

Grey, Zane. **Call of the Canyon.** 1st ed. NY and London: Harper; 1924. [chipped dj, $30.00] [$20.00]

Grey, Zane. **Forlorn River.** 1st ed. NY: Harper; 1927. [$20.00]

Grey, Zane. **Great Game Fishing at Catalina.** Chicago: Santa Catalina Island Co.; 1919. [$200.00]

Grey, Zane. **Horse Heaven Hill.** 1st ed. NY: Harper; 1959. [$20.00]

Grey, Zane. **Lone Star Ranger.** NY, London: Harper; 1915, c1914. [$25.00]

Grey, Zane. **Man of the Forest.** 1st ed. NY: Harper; 1920. [$20.00]

Grey, Zane. **Nevada.** 1st ed. NY and London: Harper; 1928. [$20.00]

Grey, Zane. **The Rainbow Trail.** 1st ed. NY: Harper; 1915. [$50.00]

Grey, Zane. **Shepherd of Guadaloupe.** 1st ed. NY: Harper; 1930. [$20.00]

Grey, Zane. **Trail Driver.** 1st ed. NY, London: Harper; 1936. [$20.00]

Grey, Zane. **Vanishing American.** 1st ed. NY: Harper; 1925. [$20.00]

Grey, Zane. **Wild Horse Mesa.** 1st ed. NY: Harper; 1928. [$20.00]

Grey Owl. **The Men of the Last Frontier.** London: Country Life; 1937. [$25.00]

Griffin, Clarence W. **Western North Carolina Sketches.** Forest City, NC: Courier; 1941. [water stained, warped, $60.00]

Griffin, Edward Dorr. **A Plea for Africa.** NY: Gould; 1817. [$65.00]

Griffin, John Howard. **Land of the High Sky.** Midland, TX: First National Bank; 1959. [$40.00]

Griffin, John S. **A Doctor Comes to California.** San Francisco: California Historical Society; 1943. [$75.00] [$35.00]

Griffin, Martin Ignatius Joseph. **Commodore John Barry "The Father of the American Navy."** centennial ed. Philadelphia: The Author; 1903. [$50.00] [$85.00]

Griffin, Martin Ignatius Joseph. **Stephen Moylan, Muster-Master General.** Philadelphia: The Author; 1909. [$50.00]

Griffin, Solomon Bulkley. **Mexico of To-Day.** NY: Harper; 1886. [$30.00]

Griffis, William Elliot. **Millard Fillmore.** Ithaca, NY: Andrus & Church; 1915. [$40.00]

Griffith, George Washington Ewing. **My 96 Years in the Great West.** Los Angeles: [s.n.]; 1929. [cover worn, $15.00] [$40.00] [$20.00] [$40.00]

Griggs, Robert Fiske. **The Valley of Ten Thousand Smokes.** Washington: National Geographic Society; 1922. [$95.00] [$65.00]

Grigsby, Hugh Blair. **The Virginia Convention of 1776.** Richmond: Randolph; 1855. [binding stained, torn, worn, interior foxed, $20.00]

Grigsby, Melvin. **Smoked Yank.** Sioux Falls: Dakota Bell; 1888. [$40.00] [$45.00]

Grimshaw, William. **History of South America.** NY: Collins & Hannay; 1830. [joints cracked and worn, $40.00]

Grinnell, George Bird. **American Big Game in Its Haunts.** NY: Forest and Stream; 1904. [spine faded, $200.00]

Grinnell, George Bird. **The Cheyenne Indians.** New Haven: Yale UP; 1923. 2 v. [presentation, $200.00] [1962 Cooper Square reprint, $45.00]

Grinnell, George Bird. **The Fighting Cheyennes.** Norman: U. of Oklahoma; 1956, c1915. [$40.00]

Grinnell, George Bird. **Hunting and Conservation.** New Haven: Yale UP; 1925. [spine faded, $175.00]

Grinnell, George Bird. **Trails of the Pathfinders.** Toronto: Briggs; 1911. [$50.00]

Grinnell, George Bird. **When Buffalo Ran.** New Haven: Yale UP; 1920. [$75.00]

Grinnell, Joseph. **Gold Hunting in Alaska.** Elgin, IL, Chicago: Cook; 1901. [$65.00]

Grinnell, Josiah Bushnell. **Men and Events of Forty Years.** Boston: Lothrop; 1891. [$85.00]

Grinnell, Josiah Bushnell. **Sketches of the West.** 2nd ed. Milwaukie; NY: Hopkins; Burgess, Stringer; 1847. [spine repaired, with folding map, $750.00]

Grinnell, Lawrence I. **Canoeable Waterways of New York State and Vicinity.** 1st ed. NY: Pageant; 1956. [$60.00]

Grisham, Noel. **Tame the Restless Wind.** Austin: San Felipe; 1968. [$25.00]

Griswold, Don L. **Colorado's Century of "Cities."** [s.l.: s.n.]; 1958. [$30.00]

Griswold, Rufus Wilmot. **The Poets and Poetry of America.** 11th ed. Philadelphia: Hart; 1852. [$95.00]

Griswold, Rufus Wilmot. **The Republican Court.** new ed. NY: Appleton; 1855. [$60.00] [$55.00] [1856 issue, $40.00]

Griswold, Wayne. **Kansas, Her Resources and Developments.** Cincinnati: Clarke; 1871. [$225.00]

Grivas, Theodore. **Military Governments in California, 1846-1850.** Glendale, CA: Clark; 1963. [$50.00]

Groce, George Cuthbert. **William Samuel Johnson.** NY: Columbia UP; 1937. [$20.00]

Grone, Carl von. **Briefe uber Nord-Amerika und Mexiko.** Braunschweig, NY: Westermann; 1850. [$125.00]

Grose, Parlee Clyde. **Case of Private Smith and the Remaining Mysteries of the Andrews Raid.** McComb, OH: General; 1963. [$7.50]

Grossman, Joel B. **Lawyers and Judges.** NY: Wiley; 1965. [$17.50]

Grove, Frederick Philip. **Consider Her Ways.** Toronto: Macmillan; 1947. [publisher's presentation slip, $30.00]

Grove, Frederick Philip. **Our Daily Bread.** Toronto: Macmillan; 1928. [$20.00]

Grove, Frederick Philip. **Over Prairie Trails.** Toronto: McClelland and Stewart; 1922. [$30.00]

Grove, Frederick Philip. **The Turn of the Year.** Toronto: McClelland & Stewart; 1923. [$25.00]

Grover, David H. **Diamondfield Jack.** Reno: U. of Nevada; 1968. [$20.00]

Grubar, Francis S. **William Ranney.** Washington: Corcoran Gallery; 1962. [$25.00]

Grue, Joseph. **Out of the Rockies.** Ogden, UT: Grue; 1953. [signed, $10.00]

Gruening, Ernest. **The State of Alaska.** NY: Random; 1954. [$17.50]

Grund, Francis J. **Aristocracy in America.** London: Bentley; 1839. 2 v. [with the four portraits, $250.00] [lacks portraits, $75.00]

Gue, Benjamin T. **History of Iowa.** NY: Century History; 1903. 4 v. [$125.00]

Guerin, Elsa Jane. **Mountain Charley.** Norman: U. of Oklahoma; 1968. [$18.00]

Guernsey, Charles Arthur. **Wyoming Cowboy Days.** NY: Putnam; 1936. [chipped dj, $55.00] [$55.00] [$85.00]

Guild, George B. **Brief Narrative of the Fourth Tennessee Cavalry Regiment, Wheeler's Corps, Army of Tennessee.** Nashville: [s.n.]; 1913. [$265.00]

Guild, Jo C. **Old Times in Tennessee.** Nashville: Tavel, Eastman & Howell; 1878. [$200.00]

Guillou, Charles F. B. **Oregon and California Drawings, 1841 and 1847.** San Francisco: Book Club of California; 1961. [$85.00]

Guinness, Geraldine. see, Taylor, Mary Geraldine Guinness.

Guizot, Francois Pierre Guillaume. **Essays on the Character and Influence of Washington in the Revolution of the United States of America.** 2nd ed. Boston: Munroe; 1851. [$85.00]

Gulick, Sidney Lewis. **The American Japanese Problem.** NY: Scribner; 1914. [$50.00]

Gummere, Amelia Mott. **Friends in Burlington.** Philadelphia: Collins; 1884. [$40.00]

Gummere, Amelia Mott. **The Quaker; a Study in Costume.** Philadelphia: Ferris & Leach; 1901. [$60.00]

Gunderson, Robert Gray. **Log-Cabin Campaign.** Lexington: U. of Kentucky; 1957. [$20.00]

Gunn, Donald. **History of Manitoba.** Ottawa: Maclean, Roger; 1880. [slight wear, $75.00]

Gunnison, Almon. **Rambles Overland.** Boston: Universalist; 1884. [$17.50]

Gunnison, John Williams. **The Mormons, or, Latter-Day Saints, in the Valley of the Great Salt Lake.** Philadelphia: Lippincott, Grambo; 1852. [$250.00] [x-lib., $325.00] [1856 issue, $60.00; $100.00]

Gunther, John. **Eisenhower, the Man and the Symbol.** 1st ed. NY: Harper; 1952. [$20.00]

Gurney, Joseph John. **A Winter in the West Indies.** London: Murray; 1840. [rebacked, $125.00]

Gurowski, Adam. **Diary.** Boston: Lee and Shepard; 1862. [$25.00]

Gurowski, Adam. **Slavery in History.** NY: Burdick; 1860. [$50.00]

Guthrie, Alfred Bertram. **The Big Sky.** NY: Sloane; 1947. [chipped dj, $20.00]

Haas, Oscar. **Chronological History of the Singers of German Songs in Texas.** 1st ed. New Braunfels, TX: Zeitung; 1948. [signed, rubbed, foxed, $20.00]

Haberly, Loyd. **Pursuit of the Horizon.** NY: Macmillan; 1948. [$30.00] [$25.00]

Hackett, Charles Wilson. **Revolt of the Pueblo Indians of New Mexico and Otermin's Attempted Reconquest.** Albuquerque: U. of New Mexico; 1942. 2 v. [$150.00]

Hackett, James. **Narrative of the Expedition Which Sailed from England in 1817, to Join the South American Patriots.** London: Murray; 1818. [lighty soiled, $375.00]

Hadden, James. **History of Uniontown.** Akron, OH: New Werner; 1913. [$125.00]

Hadfield, William. **Brazil, the River Plate, and the Falkland Islands.** London: Longman, Brown, Green, and Longmans; 1854. [$275.00]

Hafen, Ann Woodbury. **The Lost Crow.** Denver: Aiken & Bagshaw; 1935. [$50.00]

Hafen, LeRoy Reuben. **Broken Hand.** trade ed. Denver: Old West; 1931. [$275.00]

Hafen, LeRoy Reuben. **Fort Laramie and the Pageant of the West, 1834-1890.** Glendale, CA: Clark; 1938. [$125.00]

Hafen, LeRoy Reuben. **Handcarts to Zion.** Glendale, CA: Clark; 1960. [$45.00]

Hafen, LeRoy Reuben. **The Overland Mail, 1849-1869.** Cleveland: Clark; 1926. [$175.00]

Hafen, LeRoy Reuben. **Overland Routes to the Gold Fields.** Glendale, CA: Clark; 1942. [$90.00]

Hafen, LeRoy Reuben. **Western America.** NY: Prentice-Hall; 1941. [$40.00]

Hagan, William Thomas. **The Sac and Fox Indians.** 1st ed. Norman: U. of Oklahoma; 1958. [$45.00] [$20.00]

Hagedorn, Hermann. **The Bugle That Woke America.** NY: Day; 1940. [$12.50]

Hagedorn, Hermann. **Roosevelt in the Bad Lands.** Boston; NY: Houghton Mifflin; 1921. [$24.00]

Hageman, John Frelinghuysen. **History of Princeton and Its Institutions.** 2nd ed. Philadelphia: Lippincott; 1879. 2 v. [$150.00]

Hagen, Norris C. **Vikings of the Prairie.** 1st ed. NY: Exposition; 1958. [$20.00]

Hagner, Lillie May. **Alluring San Antonio through the Eyes of an Artist.** San Antonio: Naylor; 1940. [$10.00]

Haig-Brown, Roderick Langmere. **Fisherman's Spring.** Toronto: Collins; 1951. [$35.00]

Haig-Brown, Roderick Langmere. **Return to the River.** NY: Morrow; 1941. [$60.00] [1946 Toronto ed., presentation, $95.00, Canadian]

Haig-Brown, Roderick Langmere. **A River Never Sleeps.** NY: Morrow; 1946. [dj frayed, $40.00] [inscribed, $95.00, Canadian]

Haig-Brown, Roderick Langmere. **The Whale People.** London: Collins; 1962. [$25.00]

Haight, Anne Lyon. **Portrait of Latin America as Seen by Her Print Makers.** NY: Hastings House; 1946. [$12.50]

Hain, Harry Harrison. **History of Perry County, Pennsylvania.** Harrisburg: Hain-Moore; 1922. [$90.00]

Haines, Francis. **The Nez Perces.** 1st ed. Norman: U. of Oklahoma; 1955. [$50.00]

Halbak, Carl D. **With Faith in Their Hearts.** Buffalo: National Gypsum; 1950. [$20.00]

Hale, Albert. **Old Newburyport Houses.** Boston: Clarke; 1912. [$100.00]

Hale, Annie Riley. **Rooseveltian Fact and Fable.** NY: Broadway; 1908. [$45.00]

Hale, Edward Everett. **Kanzas and Nebraska.** Boston: Phillips, Sampson; 1854. [soiled and chipped, lacks front endpaper, $125.00]

Hale, Edward Everett. **The Man without a Country.** NY: Limited Editions Club; 1936. [signed by artist, $45.00] [1940 Haddon Craftsmen ed., $45.00]

Hale, Edward Everett. **One Hundred Years Ago.** Boston: Lockwood, Brooks; 1875. [$35.00]

Hale, John Peter. **Trans-Allegheny Pioneers.** Cincinnati: Graphic; 1886. [$250.00] [$150.00]

Hale, Nathaniel Claiborne. **Virginia Venturer.** Richmond: Dietz; 1951. [$15.00]

Hale, Richard Lunt. **The Log of a Forty-Niner.** Boston: Brimmer; 1923. [$35.00]

Hale, Salma. **History of the United States.** London: Miller; 1826. [$85.00]

Hale, Will T. **History of De Kalb County, Tennessee.** Nashville: Hunter; 1915. [$60.00]

Hale, William Harlan. **Horace Greeley.** 1st ed. NY: Harper; 1950. [$15.00]

Haley, J. Evetts. **Charles Goodnight.** Boston, NY: Houghton Mifflin; 1936. [$150.00]

Haley, J. Evetts. **Fort Concho and the Texas Frontier.** San Angelo, TX: Standard-Times; 1952. [$100.00]

Haley, J. Evetts. **George W. Littlefield, Texan.** 1st ed. Norman: U. of Oklahoma; 1943. [dj badly worn, $75.00]

Haley, J. Evetts. **The Heraldry of the Range.** Canyon, TX: Panhandle Plains Hist. Soc.; 1949. [fine in dj, $350.00]

Haley, J. Evetts. **Jeff Milton.** 1st ed. Norman: U. of Oklahoma; 1948. [$85.00] [$100.00] [dj worn, $50.00] [later printing, $16.50]

Haley, J. Evetts. **A Texan Looks at Lyndon.** Canyon, TX: Palo Duro; 1964. [first issue with sub-title in black print, $20.00]

Haley, J. Evetts. **The XIT Ranch of Texas, and the Early Days of the Llano Estacado.** Chicago: Lakeside; 1929. [$350.00] [1953 Oklahoma ed., signed, $85.00]

Haliburton, Thomas Chandler. **The Bubbles of Canada.** London: Bentley; 1839. [covers faded and stained, spine splitting, $110.00, Canadian]

Haliburton, Thomas Chandler. **The Clockmaker.** Philadelphia: Carey, Lea, and Blanchard; 1838. [$40.00]

Haliburton, Thomas Chandler. **Historical and Statistical Account of Nova-Scotia.** Halifax: Howe; 1829. 2 v. [rebound, $300.00]

Hall, Abraham Oakey. **The Congressman's Christmas Dream and the Lobby Member's Happy New Year.** NY: Scribner; 1870. [$35.00]

Hall, Abraham Oakey. **Old Whitey's Christmas Trot.** NY: Harper; 1857. [$35.00]

Hall, Ansel Franklin. **Guide to Yosemite.** San Francisco: Sunset; 1920. [$15.00]

Hall, Basil. **Extracts from a Journal Written on the Coasts of Chili, Peru, and Mexico, in the Years 1820, 1821, 1822.** 3rd ed. Edinburgh: Constable; 1824. 2 v. [hinges crudely repaired with tape, $125.00]

Hall, Basil. **Forty Etchings from Sketches Made with the Camera Lucida, in North America, in 1827 and 1828.** Edinburgh: Cadell & Co.; 1829. [fine, $850.00]

Hall, Basil. **Travels in North America in the Years 1827 and 1828.** Edinburgh; London: Cadell; Simpkin and Marshall; 1829. 3 v. [$225.00]

Hall, Baynard Rush. **The New Purchase.** NY, Philadelphia: Appleton; 1843. 2 v. [$225.00]

Hall, Benjamin Homer. **History of Eastern Vermont.** NY: Appleton; 1858. [x-lib., $35.00]

Hall, Bert L. **Roundup Years.** rev. ed. [s.l.: s.n.]; 1956. [signed, $75.00]

Hall, Carrie A. **Romance of the Patchwork Quilt in America.** Caldwell, ID: Caxton; 1935. [x-lib., $12.50]

Hall, Carroll Douglas. **Terry-Broderick Duel.** San Francisco: Colt; 1939. [$100.00]

Hall, Charles Swain. **Benjamin Tallmadge.** NY: Columbia UP; 1943. [$12.00]

Hall, Clayton Colman. **Baltimore.** NY: Lewis; 1912. 3 v. [$75.00]

Hall, Clayton Colman. **The Lords Baltimore and the Maryland Palatinate.** Baltimore: Murphy; 1902. [$35.00]

Hall, Clayton Colman. **Narratives of Early Maryland.** NY: Scribner; 1910. [$20.00]

Hall, Clifford J. **York County and the World War.** York, PA: [s.n.]; 1920. [$30.00]

Hall, Donald John. **Enchanted Sand.** NY: Morrow; 1933. [$12.50]

Hall, Edward T. **The Spanish Main.** Buffalo: Courier; 1888. [badly chipped covers; $20.00]

Hall, Fayrer. **Importance of the British Plantations in America to This Kingdom.** London: Peele; 1731. [new boards, $1200.00]

Hall, George Lyman. **Sometime Again.** Seattle: Superior; 1945. [$10.00]

Hall, H. P. **Observations.** 3rd ed. St. Paul: [s.n.]; 1904. [$35.00]

Hall, Harrison. **Hall's Distiller.** Philadelphia: Bioren; 1813. [$425.00]

Hall, James. **Legends of the West.** 2nd ed. Philadelphia: Key & Biddle; 1833. [dampstained, $150.00]

Hall, James. **Narrative of a Most Extraordinary Work of Religion in North Carolina.** Philadelphia: Woodward; 1802. [disbound, some ink stains, $50.00]

Hall, James. **Notes on the Western States.** Philadelphia: Hall; 1838. [rebound, $125.00]

Hall, James. **Sketches of History, Life, and Manners, in the West.** Philadelphia: Hall; 1835. 2 v. [rebacked, $135.00]

Hall, James. **The West; Its Commerce and Navigation.** Cincinnati: Derby; 1848. [$175.00]

Hall, John. **History of the Presbyterian Church in Trenton, New Jersey.** NY: Randolph; 1859. [$35.00]

Hall, Tom. **Fun and Fighting of the Rough Riders.** NY: Stokes; 1899. [$150.00]

Hallenbeck, Cleve. **Land of the Conquistadores.** Caldwell, ID: Caxton; 1950. [$50.00]

Hallenbeck, Cleve. **Legends of the Spanish Southwest.** Glendale, CA: Clark; 1938. [$60.00] [$45.00]

Haller, Mabel. **Early Moravian Education in Pennsylvania.** Nazareth, PA: Moravian Historical Society; 1953. [$20.00]

Hallock, Charles. **Camp Life in Florida.** NY: Forest and Stream; 1876. [$85.00]

Hallowell, Howard Thomas. **How a Farm Boy Built a Successful Corporation.** Jenkintown, PA: Standard Pressed Steel; 1951. [$15.00]

Hallum, John. **Biographical and Pictorial History of Arkansas.** Albany: Weed, Parsons; 1887. [lacks title page, reading copy, $45.00]

Halsell, H. H. **Cowboys and Cattleland.** Nashville: Parthenon; 1937. [$100.00]

Halsey, Edmund Drake. **History of Morris County, New Jersey.** NY: Munsell; 1882. [rebound, $125.00]

Halsey, Francis Whiting. **Pioneers of Unadilla Village, 1784-1840.** Unadilla, NY: St. Matthew's Church; 1902. [$125.00]

Halsey, Frank Davis. **Goal Lines.** Princeton: Princeton UP; 1922. [$15.00]

Halstead, Murat. **Galveston: The Horrors of a Stricken City.** Chicago: American Publishers' Assn.; 1900. [$40.00]

Halstead, Murat. **Life and Distinguished Services of William McKinley.** Chicago: Donohue; 1901. [$25.00]

Hamill, John. **Strange Career of Mr. Hoover under Two Flags.** NY: Faro; 1931. [$20.00]

Hamilton, Alexander. **The Federalist on the New Constitution, Written in 1788.** new ed. Hallowell, ME: Glazier, Masters & Smith; 1842. [$250.00]

Hamilton, Alexander. **Gentleman's Progress.** Chapel Hill: U. of North Carolina; 1948. [$22.50]

Hamilton, Alexander. **Letter from Alexander Hamilton, Concerning the Public Conduct and Character of John Adams.** 3rd ed. NY: Furman & Loudon; 1800. [$35.00]

Hamilton, Alexander. **Observations on Certain Documents Contained in No. V & VI of "The History of the United States for the Year 1796".** Philadelphia: Printed pro Bono Publico; 1800. [$125.00]

Hamilton, Alice. **Exploring the Dangerous Trades.** Boston: Little, Brown; 1943. [$25.00]

Hamilton, Charles. **Braddock's Defeat.** 1st ed. Norman: U. of Oklahoma; 1959. [$25.00] [$13.00]

Hamilton, Charles. **Cry of the Thunderbird.** NY: Macmillan; 1950. [$12.50]

Hamilton, Edward Pierce. **Fort Ticonderoga.** 1st ed. Boston: Little, Brown; 1964. [$25.00]

Hamilton, Holman. **Zachary Taylor.** 1st ed. Indianapolis: Bobbs-Merrill; 1941-51. 2 v. [$75.00]

Hamilton, James McLellan. **From Wilderness to Statehood.** Portland, OR: Binfords & Mort; 1957. [$25.00]

Hamilton, John C. **Life of Alexander Hamilton.** NY: Appleton; 1840. 2 v. [$75.00]

Hamilton, John Taylor. **History of the Church Known as the Moravian Church.** Bethlehem, PA: Times; 1900. [$65.00]

Hamilton, Joseph Gregoire de Roulhac. **Henry Ford.** NY: Holt; 1927. [foxed, $25.00]

Hamilton, Patrick. **The Resources of Arizona.** 2nd ed. San Francisco: Bancroft; 1883. [$200.00]

Hamilton, Peter Joseph. **Colonial Mobile.** Boston, NY: Houghton Mifflin; 1897. [$60.00]

Hamilton, Schuyler. **History of the National Flag of the United States of America.** Philadelphia: Lippincott, Grambo; 1852. [$75.00]

Hamilton, Thomas. **Men and Manners in America.** 2nd American ed. Philadelphia: Carey, Lea & Blanchard; 1833. 2 v. [$135.00] [rebound in one vol., $50.00]

Hamilton, Walter. **Legions of Purgatory and Hell.** Kansas City, MO: Burd & Fletcher; 1911. [spine worn, $25.00]

Hamilton, William Thomas. **My Sixty Years on the Plains.** NY: Forest and Stream; 1905. [$250.00] [1951 Long's reprint, $40.00]

Hamilton, Wilson. **The New Empire and Her Representative Men.** Oakland, CA: Pacific; 1886. [$35.00]

Hamley & Company. **Hamley's Cowboy Catalog.** Pendleton, OR: Hamley; 1929. [$45.00]

Hamlin, Charles Eugene. **Life and Times of Hannibal Hamlin.** Cambridge: Riverside; 1899. [$85.00]

Hamlin, Griffith A. **In Faith and History.** St. Louis: Bethany; 1965. [$15.00]

Hamlin, Talbot. **Benjamin Henry Latrobe.** NY: Oxford UP; 1955. [$30.00]

Hamlin, William Lee. **The True Story of Billy the Kid.** Caldwell, ID: Caxton; 1959. [$65.00]

Hammell, George M. **Passing of the Saloon.** Cincinnati: Rowe; 1908. [$50.00]

Hammerton, John Alexander. **The Real Argentine.** NY: Dodd, Mead; 1915. [$15.00]

Hammett, Samuel A. **Stray Yankee in Texas.** NY: Redfield; 1853. [$150.00]

Hammond, George Peter. **Narratives of the Coronado Expedition, 1540-1542.** Albuquerque: U. of New Mexico; 1940. [$110.00]

Hammond, John. **John Hammond on Record.** NY: Summit; 1977. [$20.00]

Hammond, John Hays. **Autobiography of.** NY: Farrar & Rinehart; 1935. 2 v. [rebound, lacks case, $55.00]

Hammond, L. M. see, Whitney, Luna M.

Hammond, Samuel H. **Hills, Lakes, and Forest Streams.** NY; Boston: Derby; Phillips, Sampson; 1854. [$75.00]

Hammond, William G. **Remembrance of Amherst.** NY: Columbia UP; 1946. [$27.50]

Hamner, Laura Vernon. **Light 'n Hitch.** 1st ed. Dallas: American Guild; 1958. [$45.00] [limited ed., $85.00]

Hamner, Laura Vernon. **Short Grass and Longhorns.** Norman: U. of Oklahoma; 1943. [$45.00]

Hampton Institute. **Twenty-Two Years' Work of the Hampton.** Hampton, VA: Normal School Press; 1893. [bumped, silverfished, sunned, x-lib., $20.00]

Hanbury, David T. **Sport and Travel in the Northland of Canada.** NY; London: Macmillan; Arnold; 1904. [$125.00]

Hanchett, Lafayette. **The Old Sheriff and Other True Tales.** NY: Margent; 1937. [$37.50]

Hancock, Cornelia. **South after Gettysburg.** Philadelphia: U. of Pennsylvania; 1937. [$25.00]

Hancock, Samuel. **The Narrative of.** NY: McBride; 1927. [1 of 65 copies large paper, $175.00] [trade ed., $30.00]

Hand-Book of Colorado. Denver: Blake & Willett; 1874. [4th ed.?, $250.00]

Handleman, Howard. **Bridge to Victory.** NY: Random; 1943. [$10.00]

Handlin, William Wallace. **American Politics.** New Orleans: Hinton; 1864. [presentation, $150.00]

Handsome Lake. **Code of Handsome Lake, the Seneca Prophet.** Albany: SUNY; 1913. [$30.00]

Handy, W. C. **Father of the Blues.** London: Sidgwick and Jackson; 1957. [x-lib., $15.00]

Hanes, Bailey C. **Bill Doolin, Outlaw O.T.** Norman: U. of Oklahoma; 1968. [$25.00]

Hanighen, Frank Cleary. **Santa Anna, the Napoleon of the West.** NY: Coward-McCann; 1934. [$50.00]

Hanke, Lewis. **Aristotle and the American Indians.** Chicago: Regnery; 1959. [worn dj, $15.00]

Hanks, Sidney Alvarus. **Scouting for the Mormons on the Great Frontier.** Salt Lake City: Deseret News; 1948. [inscribed by Ephriam Hanks, $40.00]

Hanna, Alfred Jackson. **Flight into Oblivion.** Richmond: Johnson; 1938. [presentation, $35.00]

Hanna, Alfred Jackson. **A Prince in Their Midst: The Adventurous Life of Achille Murat on the American Frontier.** Norman: U. of Oklahoma; 1946. [$15.00]

Hanna, Charles A. **The Wilderness Trail.** NY, London: Putnam; 1911. 2 v. [$250.00]

Hanna, John Smith. **History of the Life and Services of Captain Samuel Dewees.** Baltimore: Neilson; 1844. [hinges weak, $150.00]

Hannibal, P. M. **Thrice a Pioneer.** Dannebrog, NE: Hannibal; 1901. [$125.00]

Hans, Frederic Malon. **The Great Sioux Nation.** 1st ed. Chicago: Donohue; 1907. [$75.00] [$85.00]

Hanson, Alexander Contee. **Remarks on the Proposed Plan of a Federal Government.** Annapolis: Green; 1788. [$55.00]

Hanson, Charles E. **The Plains Rifle.** Harrisburg, PA: Stackpole; 1960. [$65.00]

Hanson, John Wesley. **Historical Sketch of the Old Sixth Regiment of Massachusetts Volunteers.** Boston: Lee and Shepard; 1866. [$50.00]

Haraszti, Zoltan. **John Adams & the Prophets of Progress.** Cambridge: Harvard UP; 1952. [$20.00]

Harbaugh, Henry. **Life of Rev. Michael Schlatter.** Philadelphia: Lindsay and Blakiston; 1857. [$125.00]

Harben, Will. **Northern Georgia Sketches.** Chicago: McClurg; 1900. [$50.00]

Harbison, Massy. **Narrative of the Sufferings of.** 4th ed. Beaver, PA: Henry; 1836. [$250.00]

Harcourt, Robert. **A Relation of a Voyage to Guiana.** London: Hakluyt; 1928. [$40.00]

Harden, John William. **The Devil's Tramping Ground.** Chapel Hill: U. of North Carolina; 1949. [$12.50]

Hardie, James. **Account of the Yellow Fever, Which Occurred in the City of New York.** NY: Marks; 1822. [$275.00]

Hardin, John Wesley. **Life of.** Seguin, TX: Smith & Moore; 1896. [title page torn, $185.00] [1961 Oklahoma ed., $35.00]

Hardin, Philomelia. **Every Body's Cook and Receipt Book.** 1st ed. Cleveland: Sanford; 1842. [chipped spine, $1600.00]

Harding, Earl. **Untold Story of Panama.** NY: Athene; 1959. [front hinge open, $12.50]

Hardman, Francis. **Frontier Life.** see, Sealsfield, Charles.

Hardy, Allison. **Wild Bill Hickok.** Girard, KS: Haldeman-Julius; 1943. [$30.00]

Hardy, Campbell. **Forest Life in Acadie.** London: Chapman & Hall; 1869. [$200.00]

Hardy, Mary McDowell Duffus. **Through Cities and Prairie Lands.** NY: Worthington; 1881. [$95.00]

Hardy, William Harris. **No Compromise with Principle.** NY: American Book-Stratford Press; 1946. [$65.00]

Hare, Lloyd Custer Mayhew. **Thomas Mayhew.** NY, London: Appleton; 1932. [$50.00]

Hargrave, Joseph James. **Red River.** Montreal: Lovell; 1871. [$300.00]

Haring, Clarence Henry. **The Spanish Empire in America.** NY: Oxford UP; 1947. [$45.00]

Hariot, Thomas. **A Briefe and True Report of the New Found Land of Virginia.** NY: Dodd, Mead; 1903. [bumped, rubbed, frayed, and spotted $37.50] [$30.00]

Harkey, Daniel R. **Mean as Hell.** Albuquerque: U. of New Mexico; 1948. [2nd printing, $50.00]

Harlow, Alvin Fay. **Old Waybills.** NY, London: Appleton-Century; 1934. [$75.00]

Harlow, Dana D. **Prairie Echoes.** [Aberdeen?, SD: s.n.]; 1961. [$45.00]

Harlow, Frederick Pease. **The Making of a Sailor.** Salem, MA: Marine Research Society; 1928. [$85.00]

Harlow, Rex Francis. **Oklahoma Leaders.** Oklahoma City: Harlow; 1928. [$85.00]

Harman, Samuel W. **Hell on the Border.** Fort Smith, AR: Hell on the Border; 1953. [$25.00] [$30.00]

Harmon, Appleton Milo. **Journals of.** Glendale, CA: Clark; 1946. [$25.00]

Harmon, Daniel Williams. **Journal of Voyages and Travels in the Interiour of North America.** Andover: Flagg and Gould; 1820. [$1000.00] [rebacked, $525.00]

Harney, Richard J. **History of Winnebago County, Wisconsin.** [s.l.: s.n.]; 1880. [$110.00]

Harpending, Asbury. **The Great Diamond Hoax.** San Francisco: Barry; 1913. [$50.00] [$30.00] [$35.00]

Harper, Frances Ellen Watkins. **Iola Leroy.** Philadelphia: Garrigues; 1892. [$150.00]

Harper, Ida Husted. **Life and Work of Susan B. Anthony.** Indianapolis: Bowen-Merrill; 1898-1908. 3 v. [$100.00]

Harper, Minnie Timms. **Old Ranches.** Dallas: Dealey and Lowe; 1936. [$35.00]

Harper, Robert S. **Lincoln and the Press.** NY: McGraw-Hill; 1951. [$16.50] [$30.00]

Harrell, John Mortimer. **The Brooks and Baxter War.** St. Louis: Slawson; 1893. [$175.00]

Harrington, Bates. **How 'Tis Done.** Syracuse: Pattison; 1890. [$125.00]

Harrington, Charles. **Summering in Colorado.** Denver: Richards; 1874. [$125.00] [front hinge cracked, $70.00]

Harrington, Fred Harvey. **Fighting Politician, Major General N. P. Banks.** Philadelphia: U. of Pennsylvania; 1948. [$35.00]

Harris, A. C. **Alaska and the Klondike Gold Fields.** [s.l.: s.n.]; 1897. [$35.00]

Harris, Albert Wadsworth. **Cruise of a Schooner.** Chicago: Priv. Print.; 1911. [presentation, $225.00] [$65.00]

Harris, Alexander. **Review of the Political Conflict in America.** NY: Pollock; 1876. [$100.00]

Harris, Charles Townsend. **Memories of Manhattan in the Sixties and Seventies.** NY: Derrydale; 1928. [$50.00]

Harris, Evelyn L. K. **From Humble Beginnings.** 1st ed. Charleston: West Virginia Labor History Pub. Fund; 1960. [$25.00]

Harris, Frank. **My Reminiscences as a Cowboy.** NY: Boni; 1930. [$10.00]

Harris, Franklin Stewart. **The Fruits of Mormonism.** NY: Macmillan; 1925. [$25.00]

Harris, Joel Chandler. **Aaron in the Wildwoods.** Boston, NY: Houghton Mifflin; 1897. [$50.00]

Harris, Joel Chandler. **Free Joe and Other Georgian Sketches.** 1st ed. NY: Scribner; 1887. [$125.00]

Harris, Joel Chandler. **Life of Henry W. Grady.** NY: Cassell; 1890. [$45.00]

Harris, Joel Chandler. **On the Plantation.** NY: Appleton; 1892. [$22.50]

Harris, Joel Chandler. **On the Wing of Occasions.** NY: Doubleday, Page; 1900. [$25.00]

Harris, Joel Chandler. **The Shadow between His Shoulder-Blades.** Boston: Small, Maynard; 1909. [$200.00]

Harris, Joel Chandler. **The Tar-Baby and Other Rhymes of Uncle Remus.** NY: Appleton; 1904. [$145.00]

Harris, Nathaniel Edwin. **Autobiogrpahy.** Macon, GA: Burke; 1925. [$37.50]

Harris, Thaddeus Mason. **Journal of a Tour into the Territory Northwest of the Alleghany Mountains.** Boston: Manning & Loring; 1805. [rubbed and some foxing, $500.00]

Harris, Thomas Le Grand. **The Trent Affair.** Indianapolis: Bobbs-Merrill; 1896. [bumped, sunned, $17.50]

Harris, Thomas Mealey. **Assassination of Lincoln.** Boston: American Citizen; 1892. [$75.00] [$60.00]

Harris, William C. **Prison-Life in the Tobacco Warehouse at Richmond.** Philadelphia: Childs; 1862. [$50.00]

Harris, William Richard. **The Catholic Church in Utah.** Salt Lake City: Intermountain Catholic; 1909. [$150.00]

Harrison, Benjamin. **Views of an Ex-President.** Indianapolis: Bowen-Merrill; 1901. [$60.00]

Harrison, Benjamin Samuel. **Fortune Favors the Brave.** 1st. Los Angeles: Ritchie; 1953. [$15.00]

Harrison, Burton (Mrs.). **Recollections Grave and Gay.** NY: Scribner; 1911. [$30.00]

Harrison, Edith Ogden. **"Strange to Say-."** Chicago: Kroch; 1949. [$25.00]

Harrison, Jonathan Baxter. **The Latest Studies on Indian Reservations.** Philadelphia: Indian Rights Association; 1887. [$65.00]

Harrison, Joseph Tecumseh. **Story of the Dining Fork.** limited ed. Cincinnati: Krehbiel; 1927. [$45.00]

Harrison, Peleg Dennis. **The Stars and Stripes and Other American Flags.** Boston: Little, Brown; 1906. [$20.00]

Harrison, Walter. **Pickett's Men.** NY: Van Nostrand; 1870. [$100.00]

Hart, Albert Bushnell. **The Monroe Doctrine.** Boston: Little, Brown; 1916. [$30.00]

Hart, Albert Bushnell. **Varick Court of Inquiry.** see, Varick, Richard.

Hart, Ann Clark. **Lone Mountain.** San Francisco: Pioneer; 1937. [$25.00]

Hart, Charles Henry. **Browere's Life Masks of Great Americans.** limited ed. NY: De Vinne; 1899. [$85.00]

Hart, Fred H. **Sazerac Lying Club.** 1st ed. San Francisco: Keller; 1878. [$125.00]

Hart, Gerald E. **The Fall of New France, 1755-1760.** Montreal; NY: Putnam; Drysdale; 1888. [$50.00] [$85.00]

Hart, Herbert M. **Old Forts of the Southwest.** 1st ed. Seattle: Superior; 1964. [$25.00]

Hart, Jerome Alfred. **In Our Second Century.** San Francisco: Pioneer; 1931. [$25.00]

Hart, Joseph C. **Miriam Coffin.** 2nd ed. NY: Harper; 1835. 2 v. [$200.00]

Harte, Bret. **"Excelsior."** 1st ed. NY: Morgan's; 1877. [1st printing, $150.00]

Harte, Bret. **In a Hollow of the Hills.** Boston, NY: Houghton Mifflin; 1895. [$17.50]

Harte, Bret. **Letters of.** Boston, NY: Houghton Mifflin; 1926. [$35.00] [$25.00]

Harte, Bret. **Sally Dows and Other Stories.** 1st ed. Boston, NY: Houghton Mifflin; 1893. [$17.50]

Harte, Bret. **Susy.** 1st ed. Boston, NY: Houghton Mifflin; 1893. [$17.50]

Harte, Bret. **Tales of the Gold Rush.** NY: Limited Editions Club; 1944. [$50.00]

Harte, Bret. **Thankful Blossom.** Boston: Osgood; 1877. [$75.00]

Harte, Bret. **Three Partners.** Boston; NY: Houghton Mifflin; 1897. [bumped, $80.00]

Hartmann, Sadakichi. **Tanka and Haikai.** San Francisco: [s.n.]; 1916. [covers scuffed, $55.00]

Hartsough, Mildred Lucille. **From Canoe to Steel Barge on the Upper Mississippi.** Minneapolis: U. of Minnesota; 1934. [$30.00]

Hartt, Charles Frederick. **Ehayer Expedition.** Boston: Fields, Osgood; 1870. [$55.00]

Hartwig, Georg Ludwig. **The Polar World.** NY: Harper; 1869. [$35.00]

Harvey, George Brinton McClellan. **Henry Clay Frick.** NY, London: Scribner; 1928. [$20.00]

Harvey, Oscar Jewell. **History of Wilkes-Barre, Luzerne County, Pennsylvania.** Wilkes-Barre: Raeder; 1909-1930. 6 v. [$350.00]

Haskell, Franklin Aretas. **The Battle of Gettysburg.** Madison: Wisconsin History Commission; 1908. [$35.00]

Haskell, Henry C. **City of the Future.** Kansas City, MO: Glenn; 1950. [signed, $10.00] [$12.50]

Haskell, John Cheves. **Haskell Memoirs.** NY: Putnam; 1960. [$22.50]

Haskell, William B. **Two Years in the Klondike and Alaskan Gold-Fields.** Hartford, CT: Hartford Pub. Co.; 1898. [binding soiled, $75.00]

Haskins, George Lee. **Law and Authority in Early Massachusetts.** NY: Macmillan; 1960. [$25.00]

Hassell, Cushing Biggs. **History of the Church of God from the Creation to A. D. 1885.** Middletown, NY: Beebe; 1886. [$60.00]

Hassett, William D. **Off the Record with F.D.R., 1942-1945.** New Brunswick: Rutgers UP; 1958. [$15.00]

Hassler, Edgar Wakefield. **Old Westmoreland.** Pittsburgh: Weldin; 1900. [$95.00]

Hassler, Warren W. **General George B. McClellan.** 1st ed. Baton Rouge: Louisiana State UP; 1957. [$25.00]

Hassrick, Royal B. **The Sioux.** 1st ed. Norman: U. of Oklahoma; 1964. [$27.50]

Hastings, Frank Stewart. **Ranchman's Recollections.** Chicago: Breeder's Gazette; 1921. [$125.00]

Hatch, Alden. **Remington Arms in American History.** NY: Rinehart; 1956. [$25.00]

Hatch, Vernelle A. **Illustrated History of Bradford, McKean County, PA.** Bradford, PA: Burk; 1901. [$45.00]

Hatcher, Edmund Neuson. **The Last Four Weeks of the War.** Columbus, OH: Hatcher; 1891. [$65.00] [1892 Co-Operative reprint, $45.00]

Hatcher, O. Latham. **A Mountain School.** Richmond: Garrett & Massie; 1930. [$25.00]

Hatcher, William B. **Edward Livingston.** University: Louisiana State UP; 1940. [$35.00]

Hatcher, William Eldridge. **John Jasper.** NY, Chicago: Revell; 1908. [lightly silverfished, $17.50]

Hatfield, Edwin Francis. **History of Elizabeth, New Jersey.** NY: Carlton & Lanahan; 1868. [$75.00]

Hathaway, Benjamin. **The League of the Iroquois and Other Legends.** Chicago: Griggs; 1882, c1880. [$35.00]

Haven, Alice B. **All's Not Gold That Glitters.** NY: Appleton; 1863, c1853. [front hinge cracked, contents soiled, $25.00]

Haven, Charles Chauncy. **Thirty Days in New Jersey Ninety Years Ago.** Trenton: State Gazette; 1867. [presentation, x-lib., $40.00]

Haven, Charles T. **History of the Colt Revolver.** NY: Morrow; 1940. [$135.00]

Havighurst, Walter. **Annie Oakley of the Wild West.** NY: Macmillan; 1954. [dj chipped, $25.00] [$15.00]

Havighurst, Walter. **Land of Promise.** NY: Macmillan; 1946. [$10.00]

Havighurst, Walter. **River to the West.** NY: Putnam; 1970. [$17.50]

Haviland, Laura Smith. **A Woman's Life Work.** 5th ed. Grand Rapids, MI: Shaw; 1881. [$50.00]

Hawaiian Islands Dept. of Foreign Affairs. **The Hawaiian Islands, Their Resources, Agricultural, Commercial and Financial.** Honolulu: Hawaiian Gazette; 1896. [$125.00]

Hawes, Joel. **Tribute to the Memory of the Pilgrims, and a Vindication of the Congregational Churches of New England.** 2nd ed. Hartford: Burgess; 1836. [$25.00]

Hawkes, Wells. **Moonshine Strategy and Other Stories.** Baltimore: Ottenheimer; 1906. [x-lib., $45.00]

Hawkeye, Harry. see, Love, Paul Emilius.

Hawkins, Alfred. **Hawkins's Picture of Quebec.** Quebec: Neilson and Cowan; 1834. [$975.00]

Hawkins, Benjamin. **Letters of Benjamin Hawkins, 1796-1806.** Savannah, GA: Georgia Historical Society; 1916. [wraps creased, sunned, torn, $65.00]

Hawkins, Walace. **Case of John C. Watrous.** Dallas: University Press; 1950. [$40.00]

Hawks, Francis L. **History of North Carolina.** 3rd ed. Fayetteville: Hale; 1859, c1856. 2 v. [x-lib., shaken, torn and worn, $60.00]

Hawks, Francis L. **Relation of Maryland.** NY: Sabin; 1865. [$125.00]

Hawks, John. **Orderly Book and Journal of.** NY: Brewer; 1911. [$65.00]

Hawley, Zerah. **Journal of a Tour through Connecticut, Massachusetts, New-York, the North Part of Pennsylvania and Ohio.** New Haven: Converse; 1822. [some worming, rebound, $650.00]

Hawn, William. **All around the Civil War.** NY: Wynkoop, Hallenbeck, Crawford; 1908. [$35.00]

Haworth, Paul Leland. **George Washington, Country Gentleman.** Indianapolis: Bobbs-Merrill; 1925. [signed, browning, lacks map, $17.50]

Hawthorne, Hildegarde. **California's Missions.** NY; London: Appleton-Century; 1942. [$20.00] [$10.00]

Hawthorne, Nathaniel. **Complete Writings of.** Old Manse ed. Boston, NY: Houghton Mifflin; 1900. 22 v. [$200.00]

Hawthorne, Nathaniel. **The House of Seven Gables.** Boston: Ticknor, Reed and Fields; 1851. [$350.00] [October ads., $250.00]

Hawthorne, Nathaniel. **Life of Franklin Pierce.** Boston: Ticknor, Reed and Fields; 1852. [cover dampstained, $285.00] [$200.00]

Hawthorne, Nathaniel. **The Marble Faun.** Boston: Ticknor and Fields; 1860. 2 v. [$225.00]

Hawthorne, Nathaniel. **Passages from the American Note-Books.** Boston: Ticknor and Fields; 1868. 2 v. [1st printing, $175.00]

Hawthorne, Nathaniel. **The Scarlet Letter.** 1st ed. Boston: Ticknor, Reed and Fields; 1850. [fine, $750.00] [1851 London ed., $450.00]

Hawthorne, Nathaniel. **Septimius Felton.** Boston: Osgood; 1872. [$85.00]

Hawthorne, Nathaniel. **The Snow-Image and Other Twice-Told Tales.** Boston: Ticknor, Reed, and Fields; 1852. [$180.00] [$250.00]

Hawthorne, Nathaniel. **Tanglewood Tales.** Boston: Ticknor, Reed and Fields; 1853. [1st printing, very worn and shaken, $125.00]

Hawthorne, Nathaniel. **Transformation.** 1st ed. London: Smith, Elder; 1860. 3 v. [1st printing, rebacked, $1200.00]

Hawthorne, Nathaniel. **True Stories from History and Biography.** Boston: Ticknor, Reed and Fields; 1851. [2nd issue, one gathering loose, $65.00]

Hawthorne, Nathaniel. **Twice-Told Tales.** new ed. Boston: Ticknor, Reed, and Fields; 1853. 2 v. [$90.00]

Hay, John. **Jim Bludso of the Prairie Belle and Little Breeches.** Boston: Osgood; 1871. [$60.00]

Hay, Thomas Robson. **The Admirable Trumpeter.** Garden City: Doubleday, Doran; 1941. [$38.50]

Hay, Thomas Robson. **Hood's Tennessee Campaign.** NY: Neale; 1929. [$145.00]

Hay, Walter G. **Thru Maine by Camera.** [s.l.: s.n.; 19--?]. [$40.00]

Haycox, Ernest. **Alder Gulch.** Boston: Little, Brown; 1942. [$20.00]

Hayden, Horace Edwin. **Genealogical and Family History of the Wyoming and Lackawanna Valleys, Pennsylvania.** NY, Chicago: Lewis; 1906. 2 v. [$125.00]

Hayden, Horace H. **Geological Essays.** Baltimore: Robinson; 1820. [insect damaged, foxed, $35.00]

Haydon, Arthur Lincoln. **The Riders of the Plains.** London; Toronto: Melrose; Clark; 1910. [front hinge weak, $50.00]

Haydon, Frederick Stansbury. **Aeronautics in the Union and Confererate Armies.** Baltimore: Hopkins; 1941. [vol. 1 all published, $150.00]

Hayes, Augustus Allen. **New Colorado and the Santa Fe Trail.** NY: Harper; 1880. [$60.00] [$85.00]

Hayes, Ernest Henry. **Forty Years on the Labrador.** NY, Chicago: Revell; 1930. [$8.00]

Hayes, I. I. **The Open Polar Sea.** NY: Hurd and Houghton; 1867. [$50.00] [inscribed, $185.00] [1885 Routledge ed., x-lib., $20.00]

Hayes, Jess G. **Boots and Bullets.** Tucson: U. of Arizona; 1968, c1967. [2nd printing, $20.00]

Hayes, Jess G. **Sheriff Thompson's Day.** Tucson: U. of Arizona; 1968. [$30.00]

Hayes, John. **Rural Poems.** Carlisle, PA: Loudon; 1807. [$40.00]

Hayes, Johnson J. **Land of Wilkes.** Wilkesboro, NC: Wilkes County Historical Society; 1962. [mildew, dj chipped, $60.00]

Hayward, John. **The New England Gazetteer.** Boston: Hayward; 1839. [foxed, $45.00]

Hayward, Walter Brownell. **Bermuda Past and Present.** NY: Dodd, Mead; 1912. [$12.50]

Haywood, John. **Civil and Political History of the State of Tennessee.** Nashville: M. E. Church, South; 1891. [spine split and chipped, boards hanging by threads, binding scorched, $35.00]

Hazard, Lucy Lockwood. **The Frontier in American Literature.** Oakland: The Author; 1927. [$25.00]

Hazel, Harry. **The Nun of St. Ursula.** see, Jones, Justin.

Head, Thomas A. **Campaigns and Battles of the Sixteenth Regiment, Tennessee Volunteers.** McMinnville, TN: Womack; 1961. [$50.00]

Headley, Joel Tyler. **The Adirondack.** new ed. NY: Scribner; 1864. [$100.00]

Headley, Joel Tyler. **Farragut, and Our Naval Commanders.** NY; Chicago: Treat; Lilley; 1867. [$35.00]

Headley, Joel Tyler. **Life and Travels of General Grant.** Philadelphia; Boston: Hubbard; Thompson; 1879. 2 v. in 1. [$25.00]

Headley, Joel Tyler. **Washington and His Generals.** NY: Baker and Scribner; 1847. 2 v. [$20.00]

Headley, Phineas Camp. **Life of General Lafayette.** Auburn, NY: Miller, Orton, & Mulligan; 1854. [$35.00]

Heap, Gwinn Harris. **Central Route to the Pacific from the Valley of the Mississippi to California.** Philadelphia: Lippincott, Grambo; 1854. [x-lib., $500.00] [$250.00]

Heaps, Willard Allison. **The Singing Sixties.** Norman: U. of Oklahoma; 1960. [$10.00]

Heard, Isaac V. D. **History of the Sioux War and Massacres of 1862 and 1863.** NY: Harper; 1863. [$150.00]

Hearn, Lafcadio. **Chita.** NY: Harper; 1889. [front hinge cracked, $100.00]

Hearn, Lafcadio. **La Cuisine Creole.** 2nd ed. New Orleans: Hansell; 1922. [$225.00]

Hearn, Lafcadio. **Interpretations of Literature.** NY: Dodd, Mead; 1920. 2 v. [spines torn, $20.00]

Hearn, Lafcadio. **Japan.** NY, London: Macmillan; 1904. [$225.00]

Hearn, Lafcadio. **Kokoro.** Boston: Houghton Mifflin; 1896. [worn dj, $45.00]

Hearn, Lafcadio. **Kotto.** 1st ed. NY: Macmillan; 1902. [1st state, $165.00]

Hearn, Lafcadio. **Shadowings.** Boston: Little, Brown; 1900. [$160.00]

Heartman, Charles Fred. **An Immigrant of a Hundred Years Ago.** Hattiesburg, MS: Book Farm; 1941. [$45.00]

Heath, William. **Memoirs of Major-General Heath.** Boston: Thomas; 1798. [$325.00]

Hebard, Grace Raymond. **The Bozeman Trail.** Cleveland: Clark; 1922. 2 v. [ink marginal notes, $175.00] [$275.00]

Hebard, Grace Raymond. **The Pathbreakers from River to Ocean.** 2nd ed. Chicago: Lakeside; 1912, c1911. [$25.00]

Hebard, Grace Raymond. **Sacajawea.** Glendale, CA: Clark; 1933. [$150.00]

Hebard, Grace Raymond. **Washakie.** Cleveland: Clark; 1930. [$175.00] [$200.00]

Hebert, Frank. **40 Years Prospecting and Mining in the Black Hills of South Dakota.** Rapid City: Daily Journal; 1921. [$200.00]

Hebert, Walter H. **Fighting Joe Hooker.** 1st ed. Indianapolis: Bobbs-Merrill; 1944. [x-lib., $20.00] [$40.00] [$47.50]

Hebrew Union College. Jewish Institute of Religion. American Jewish Archives. **Essays in American Jewish History.** Cincinnati: [s.n.]; 1958. [$20.00]

Hecht, Ben. **Cutie.** Chicago: Hechtshaw; 1924. [front endpaper slit, soiled, $48.50]

Hecht, Ben. **To Quito and Back.** 1st ed. NY: Covici, Friede; 1937. [soiled, chipped dj, $50.00]

Heck, Earl Leon Werley. **Augustine Herrman.** Richmond: Byrd; 1941. [$37.50]

Hecker, Isaac Thomas. **Questions of the Soul.** NY: Appleton; 1855. [title page stained, $100.00]

Heckewelder, John Gottlieb Ernestus. **History, Manners, and Customs of the Indian Nations.** new ed. Philadelphia: Hist. Soc. of PA; 1876. [$60.00]

Heckewelder, John Gottlieb Ernestus. **Narrative of the Mission of the United Brethren among the Delaware and Mohegan Indians.** Philadelphia: McCarty & Davis; 1820. [$250.00] [1907 Cleveland ed., $185.00]

Hedges, William Hawkins. **Pike's Peak . . . or Busted!** Evanston, IL: Branding Iron; 1954. [$40.00]

Hedrick, Ulysses Prentiss. **The Grapes of New York.** Albany: Lyon; 1908. [hinges cracked, $30.00]

Heg, Hans Christian. **The Civil War Letters of.** Northfield, MN: Norwegian-American Historical Assn.; 1936. [$40.00] [$25.00]

Hegemann, Elizabeth Compton. **Navaho Trading Days.** Albuquerque: U. of New Mexico; 1963. [$55.00]

Heilprin, Angelo. **Mont Pelee and the Tragedy of Martinique.** Philadelphia, London: Lippincott; 1903. [hinges weak, $25.00]

Heimann, Robert K. **Tobacco and Americans.** 1st ed. NY: McGraw-Hill; 1960. [$20.00]

Heizer, Robert Fleming. **The California Indians.** Berkeley: U. of California; 1960, c1951. [$12.50]

Held, John. **Works of.** NY: Washburn; 1931. [$17.50]

Heller, William Jacob. **Historic Easton from the Window of a Trolley-Car.** Easton, PA: Express; 1911. [$45.00]

Helm, Mary S. **Scraps of Early Texas History.** Austin: The Author; 1884. [$675.00]

Helm, William Pickett. **Harry Truman.** 1st ed. NY: Duell, Sloan and Pearce; 1947. [$12.50]

Helmer, William J. **The Gun That Made the Twenties Roar.** Highland Park, NJ: Gun Room; 1969. [$30.00]

Helms, Anton Zacharias. **Travels from Buenos Ayres, by Potosi, to Lima with an Appendix.** 2nd ed. London: Phillips; 1807. [map foxed, $150.00] [$60.00]

Helper, Hinton Rowan. **Dreadful California.** Indianapolis: Bobbs-Merrill; 1948. [$25.00]

Helper, Hinton Rowan. **The Impending Crisis of the South.** NY: Burdick; 1857. [$40.00] [13th printing?, $85.00] [1860 issue, badly worn spine, $15.00]

Helps, Arthur. **Life of Las Casas.** London: Bell and Daldy; 1868. [front hinge cracked, $45.00]

Helps, Arthur. **The Spanish Conquest in America.** London: Parker; 1855-61. 4 v. [$350.00] [1856-61 Harper ed. in 4 vols., $90.00]

Hemenway, Abby Maria. **Poets and Poetry of Vermont.** Rutland: Tuttle; 1858. [$150.00]

Hemenway, Frederick Vinton. **History of the Third Division United States Army in the World War.** Andernach-on-the-Rhine: Dumont; 1919. [$65.00]

Hemingway, Ernest. **Across the River and into the Trees.** NY: Scribner; 1950. [$10.00]

Hemingway, Ernest. **A Farewell to Arms.** 1st ed. NY: Scribner; 1929. [1st state in dj, $450.00]

Hemingway, Ernest. **For Whom the Bell Tolls.** 1st ed. NY: Scribner; 1940. [torn dj, $200.00]

Hemingway, Ernest. **Green Hills of Africa.** 1st ed. NY: Scribner; 1935. [first printing, sunned in dj, $220.00]

Hemingway, Ernest. **Men at War.** NY: Crown; 1942. [$45.00] [$15.00]

Hemingway, Ernest. **Men without Women.** 1st ed. NY: Scribner; 1927. [lacks dj, $125.00]

Hemingway, Ernest. **The Torrents of Spring.** 1st ed. NY: Scribner; 1926. [lacks dj, $225.00]

Hemingway, Ernest. **The Wild Years.** NY: Dell; 1962. [browned, paperback, $25.00]

Hemingway, Ernest. **Winner Take Nothing.** 1st ed. NY: Scribner; 1933. [dj reinforced, $350.00] [lacks dj, $55.00]

Henderson, Alice. **Brothers of Light.** 1st ed. NY: Harcourt, Brace; 1937. [$60.00]

Henderson, Archibald. **Conquest of the Old Southwest.** NY: Century; 1920. [bumped and soiled, $20.00] [$35.00]

Henderson, Archibald. **Cradle of Liberty.** Charlotte, NC: Mecklenburg Historical Assn.; 1955. [signed, $25.00]

Henderson, Archibald. **Washington's Southern Tour, 1791.** Boston, NY: Houghton Mifflin; 1923. [$85.00]

Henderson, George Francis Robert. **The Civil War: A Soldier's View.** Chicago: U. of Chicago; 1958. [$35.00]

Henderson, George Francis Robert. **Stonewall Jackson and the American Civil War.** 1st ed. London, NY: Longmans, Green; 1898. 2 v. [$100.00] [1900 reprint, $35.00] [1949 reprint, $35.00]

Hendrick, Burton Jesse. **The Lees of Virginia.** Boston: Little, Brown; 1935. [dj nicked, $30.00]

Hendrick, Burton Jesse. **Lincoln's War Cabinet.** 1st ed. Boston: Little, Brown; 1946. [$15.00]

Hendrick, Burton Jesse. **Statesmen of the Lost Cause.** NY: Literary Guild; 1939. [$15.00]

Hendricks, George David. **Bad Man of the West.** San Antonio: Naylor; 1941. [dj worn and chipped, $35.00]

Hendrickson, James E. **Joe Lane of Oregon.** New Haven: Yale UP; 1967. [$10.00]

Hendrickson, Walter Brookfield. **David Dale Owen.** Indianapolis: Indiana Historical Bureau; 1943. [$25.00]

Hening, William Waller. **The New Virginia Justice Comprising the Office and Authority of a Justice of the Peace.** 3rd ed. Richmond: The Author; 1820. [foxed, $175.00]

Henkel, David. **David Henkel against the Unitarians.** New Market, VA: Henkel; 1830. [$60.00]

Henle, Fritz. **Mexico: 64 Photographs.** Chicago; NY: Ziff-Davis; 1945. [$17.50]

Henley, Constance Matilda. **Grandmother Drives South.** NY: Putnam; 1943. [$15.00]

Hennepin, Louis. **Description de la Louisiane.** Paris: Hure; 1683. [folding map in facsimile, heavy worming in margins, $400.00]

Hennepin, Louis. **A New Discovery of a Vast Country in America.** Chicago: McClurg; 1903. 2 v. [$100.00]

Hennighausen, Louis Paul. **History of the German Society of Maryland.** Baltimore: Harrison; 1909. [$30.00]

Henry, Alexander. **New Light on the Early History of the Greater Northwest.** NY: Harper; 1897. 3 v. [$450.00]

Henry, Alexander. **Travels and Adventures in Canada and the Indian Territories.** NY: Riley; 1809. [with portrait, $1000.00]

Henry, J. T. **The Early and Later History of Petroleum.** Philadelphia: Rodgers; 1873. [worn, $250.00]

Henry, James. **Sketches of Moravian Life and Character.** Philadelphia: Lippincott; 1859. [$50.00]

Henry, John Joseph. **Account of Arnold's Campaign against Quebec.** Albany, NY; 1877. [$185.00]

Henry, John Joseph. **An Accurate and Interesting Account of the Hardships and Sufferings of That Band of Heroes, Who Traversed the Wilderness.** Lancaster PA: Greer; 1812. [3/4 morocco, $350.00] [disbound, $150.00] [$300.00]

Henry, O. **Cabbages and Kings.** 1st ed. NY: McClure, Phillips; 1904. [x-lib., $100.00]

Henry, O. **The Gentle Grafter.** 1st ed. NY: McClure; 1908. [1st state, $50.00]

Henry, O. **Heart of the West.** 1st ed. NY: McClure; 1907. [$35.00] [$40.00] [spine faded, $50.00]

Henry, O. **The Hiding of Black Bill.** NY: Ridgway; 1908. [$125.00]

Henry, O. **The Trimmed Lamp.** 1st ed. NY: McClure, Philips; 1907. [$10.00]

Henry, Robert Selph. **Story of the Confederacy.** new ed. NY: Grosset & Dunlap; 1936. [taped dj, $10.00]

Henry, Robert Selph. **The Story of the Mexican War.** 1st ed. Indianapolis: Bobbs-Merrill; 1950. [$40.00]

Henry, Stuart Oliver. **Conquering Our Great American Plains.** NY: Dutton; 1930. [$40.00]

Henry, Will. **San Juan Hill.** NY: Random; 1962. [dj sunned and chipped, $30.00] [$17.50]

Henry, William Seaton. **Campaign Sketches of the War with Mexico.** NY: Harper; 1847. [wraps detached, $240.00]

Hensel, William Uhler. **The Christiana Riot and the Treason Trials of 1851.** Lancaster, PA: New Era; 1911. [$40.00]

Henshall, James A. **Camping and Cruising in Florida.** Cincinnati: Clarke; 1884. [spotted, $25.00] [1888 printing, $125.00]

Henshall, James A. **More about the Black Bass.** Cincinnati: Clarke; 1889. [$75.00]

Henson, Josiah. **Autobiography of.** Boston: Russell; 1879. [$50.00]

Henson, Josiah. **Father Henson's Story of His Own Life.** Boston, Cleveland: Jewett; 1858. [spine chipped, $60.00] [$75.00]

Hepburn, William Murray. **Purdue University: Fifty Years of Progress.** Indianapolis: Hollenbeck; 1925. [$25.00]

Hepworth, George H. **The Whip, Hoe, and Sword.** Boston: Walker, Wise; 1864. [$27.00]

Herbert, Charles. **A Relic of the Revolution.** Boston: Pierce; 1847. [$100.00]

Heriot, George. **Travels through the Canadas.** London: Phillips; 1807. [rebound in buckram, lacks 5 maps of 22, $1000.00] [x-lib., $1800.00]

Herman, William. **Dance of Death.** see, Bierce, Ambrose.

Herndon, Dallas T. **Centennial History of Arkansas.** Chicago, Little Rock: Clarke; 1922. 3 v. [$165.00]

Herndon, Sarah Raymond. **Days on the Road.** NY: Burr; 1902. [$125.00]

Herndon, William Henry. **Herndon's Lincoln.** Chicago, NY: Belford, Clarke; 1889. 3 v. [$275.00] [$375.00] [2nd ed., 1890, $85.00]

Heroes and Hunters of the West. Philadelphia: Bliss; 1858. [smudged, foxed, worn, $25.00]

Herold, David E. **The Assassination of President Lincoln and the Trial of the Conspirators.** Cincinnati, NY: Moore, Wilstach & Boldwin; 1865. [rebound, $325.00] [$425.00] [1865 Philadelphia imprint, $350.00]

Herr, John Knowles. **Story of the U.S. Cavalry, 1775-1942.** 1st ed. Boston: Little, Brown; 1953. [worn dj, $45.00] [$35.00] [$40.00]

Herrick, Cheesman Abiah. **History of Girard College.** Philadelphia: Girard College; 1927. [shaken, $20.00]

Herskovits, Melville J. **Rebel Destiny.** London; NY: Whittlesey; McGraw-Hill; 1934. [$25.00]

Hess, Lizzie. **As Clay in the Potter's Hands.** Lancaster, PA: Hess; 1955. [$10.00]

Heston, Alfred M. **Absegami: Annals of Eyren Haven and Atlantic City, 1609 to 1904.** Camden, NJ: [s.n.]; 1904. 2 v. [$250.00]

Heston, Alfred M. **Jersey Waggon Jaunts.** Pleasantville, NJ: Atlantic County Historical Society; 1926. 2 v. [$90.00]

Heusinger, Edward Werner. **Early Explorations and Mission Establishments in Texas.** San Antonio: Naylor; 1936. [$125.00]

Heusser, Albert H. **The Forgotten General.** Paterson, NJ: Franklin; 1928. [$65.00]

Heverly, Clement Ferdinand. **History of Albany Township, 1800-1885.** Towanda, PA: Bradford; 1885. [$65.00]

Hewatt, Alexander. **Historical Account of the Rise and Progress of the Colonies of South Carolina and Georgia.** London: Donaldson; 1779. 2 v. [$1750.00]

Hewett, Edgar L. **Chaco Canyon and Its Monuments.** Albuquerque: U. of New Mexico; 1936. [$45.00]

Hewett, Edgar L. **Landmarks of New Mexico.** 3rd ed. Albuquerque: U. of New Mexico; 1953. [$25.00]

Hewett, Edgar L. **Pueblo Indian World.** Albuquerque: U. of New Mexico and the School of American Research; 1945. [$45.00]

Hewett, Waterman Thomas. **Cornell University, a History.** NY: University Publishing Society; 1905. 4 v. [$125.00]

Hewins, Amasa. **Hewins's Journal.** Boston: Athenaeum; 1931. [$65.00]

Heyman, Max L. **Prudent Soldier.** Glendale, CA: Clark; 1959. [$125.00]

Heyward, Du Bose. **Carolina Chansons.** NY: Macmillan; 1922. [inscribed, $75.00]

Heywood, Ezra H. **Uncivil Liberty.** Princeton, MA: Co-Operative; 1870. [wraps stained, $125.00]

Hiatt, Noble W. **The Silversmiths of Kentucky.** 1st ed. Louisville: Standard; 1954. [$125.00]

Hibben, Frank C. **Treasure in the Dust.** Philadelphia: Lippincott; 1951. [$16.00]

Hickman, William Adams. **Brigham's Destroying Angel.** NY: Crofutt; 1872. [dampstained, lacks rear endpaper, title page taped, $75.00] [$90.00] [1904 SLC reprint, $65.00]

Hickok, Laurens P. **A System of Moral Science.** Schenectady: Van Debogert; 1853. [x-lib., $35.00]

Hicks, Edwin P. **Belle Starr and Her Pearl.** Little Rock: Harper; 1963. [signed, $75.00]

Hicks, Granville. **The Great Tradition.** rev. ed. NY: Macmillan; 1935. [$15.00]

Higdon, Hal. **The Union vs. Dr. Mudd.** Chicago: Follett; 1964. [$15.00]

Higginbotham, Sanford W. **The Keystone in the Democratic Arch.** Harrisburg: Pennsylvania Historical and Museum Commission; 1952. [$45.00]

Higginson, Alexander Henry. **Hunting in the United States and Canada.** Garden City: Doubleday, Doran; 1928. [$60.00]

Higginson, Ella. **Alaska, the Great Country.** new ed. NY: Macmillan; 1919. [$18.00] [1926 issue, $20.00]

Higginson, Thomas Wentworth. **Army Life in a Black Regiment.** Boston: Fields, Osgood; 1870. [$100.00]

Higinbotham, John David. **When the West Was Young.** Toronto: Ryerson; 1933. [$65.00, Canadian]

Hildreth, James. **Dragoon Campaigns to the Rocky Mountains.** NY: Wiley & Long; 1836. [$225.00] [$175.00]

Hildreth, Richard. **Despotism in America.** 2nd ed. Boston, NY: Anti-Slavery Society; 1840. [$65.00] [1854 Jewett ed., $75.00; $85.00; $50.00]

Hildreth, Richard. **The White Slave.** Boston; Milwaukie: Tappan and Whittemore; Rood and Whittemore; 1852. [binding very faded, $150.00]

Hildreth, Samuel Prescott. **Memoirs of Early Pioneer Settlers of Ohio.** Cincinnati: Derby; 1854. [rebound, $100.00]

Hildreth, Samuel Prescott. **Pioneer History.** Cincinnati; NY: Derby; Barnes; 1848. [x-lib., $150.00]

Hildrup, Jesse Stephen. **Missions of California and the Old Southwest.** Chicago: McClurg; 1907. [$40.00]

Hill, Alfred James. **History of Company E, of the Sixth Minnesota Regiment of Volunteer Infantry.** [St. Paul?]: Lewis; 1899. [rebound, $125.00]

Hill, Alice Polk. **Tales of the Colorado Pioneers.** 1st ed. Denver: Pierson & Gardner; 1884. [$225.00]

Hill, Daniel Harvey. **Bethel to Sharpsburg.** Raleigh: Edwards & Broughton; 1926. 2 v. [$175.00]

Hill, Frederick Trevor. **Lincoln, the Lawyer.** NY: Century; 1906. [$15.00]

Hill, George Canning. **Benedict Arnold.** Boston: Libby; 1858. [$30.00]

Hill, George William. **History of Ashland County, Ohio.** Cleveland: Williams; 1880. [$125.00]

Hill, J. L. **The End of the Cattle Trail.** Long Beach, CA: Moyle; [192-?]. [$85.00] [$50.00]

Hill, Joseph John. **History of Warner's Ranch and Its Environs.** presentation ed. Los Angeles: Priv. Print.; 1927. [$75.00]

Hill, Laurance Landreth. **La Reina.** Los Angeles: Security Trust & Savings Bank; 1929. [$9.00]

Hill, Norman Newell. **History of Coshocton County, Ohio.** Newark, OH: Graham; 1881. [$45.00]

Hill, Ralph Nading. **Sidewheeler Saga.** NY: Rinehart; 1953. [$20.00]

Hillard, Elias Brewster. **The Last Men of the Revolution.** Hartford: Moore; 1864. [5 of the 6 lithographs of homes, $400.00] [1968 Barre ed., $25.00]

Hillard, George Stillman. **Life and Campaigns of George B. McClellan.** Philadelphia: Lippincott; 1864. [$35.00]

Hilliard d'Auberteuil, Michel Rene. **Essais Historiques et Politiques sur les Anglo-Americains.** Bruxelles:[s.n.]; 1781-82. 4 pts. in 2 v. [worn joints, $850.00]

Hillman, Charles F. **"Old Timers": British and American in Chile.** Santiago: Moderna; [1901?]. [$125.00]

Himes, Joshua. see, Miller, William.

Hind, Henry Youle. **Narrative of the Canadian Red River Exploring Expedition of 1857: and of the Assinniboine and Saskatchewan Exploring Expedition of 1858.** London: Longman, etc.; 1860. 2 v. [$750.00] [$875.00]

Hind, Henry Youle. **North-West Territory.** Toronto: Lovell; 1859. [$250.00]

Hinds, William Alfred. **American Communities.** Oneida, NY: American Socialist; 1878. [$100.00]

Hines, Harvey K. **Illustrated History of the State of Washington.** Chicago: Lewis; 1894. [spine repaired, $150.00]

Hines, Walker Downer. **War History of American Railroads.** New Haven; London: Yale UP; Oxford UP; 1928. [$45.00]

Hingham, MA. **History of the Town.** Hingham: The Town; 1893. 3 v. in 4. [$185.00]

Hinkley, Julian Wisner. **Narrative of Service with the Third Wisconsin Infantry.** Madison: Wisconsin History Commission; 1912. [$45.00]

Hinman, Wilbur F. **Corporal Si Klegg and His "Pard."** 12th ed. Cleveland: Hamilton; 1900, c1887. [$25.00]

Hinton, John Howard. **History and Topography of the United States of North America.** new ed. Boston: Walker; 1834. 2 v. [one signature loose, $150.00] [$350.00] [3rd ed., bound in one vol., $125.00].

Hinton, Richard Josiah. **The Handbook to Arizona.** San Francisco; NY: Payot, Upham; American News; 1878. [$250.00]

Hippisley, Gustavus. **Narrative of the Expedition to the Rivers Orinoco and Apure, in South America.** London: Murray; 1819. [$600.00]

Hirshson, Stanley P. **Grenville M. Dodge.** Bloomington: Indiana UP; 1967. [$25.00]

Historic Spots in California. Stanford: Stanford UP; 1948. [$25.00]

Historical and Pictorial Record of Camp Dix, New Jersey. [s.l.: s.n.; ca. 1918?]. [$35.00]

Historical Society of Geauga County, Ohio. **Pioneer and General History of Geauga County.** see, title.

History of Cedar County, Iowa. Chicago: Western Historical; 1878. [loose worn binding, $25.00]

History of Cedar County with a History of Iowa. Chicago and Cedar Rapids: Historical Publishing Co.; 1901. 2 v. [$55.00]

History of Columbia College on Morningside. NY: Columbia UP; 1954. [$27.50] [$25.00]

History of Columbia University, 1754-1904. NY; London: Columbia UP; Macmillan; 1904. [$27.50]

History of Napa and Lake Counties, California. San Francisco: Slocum, Bowen; 1881. [front hinge weak, $150.00]

History of Rock County, Wisconsin. Chicago: Western Historical; 1879. [rebound, $85.00]

History of the State of Rhode Island with Illustrations from Original Sketches. Philadelphia: Hoag, Wade; 1878. [$250.00]

History of Winnebago County, Ill. Chicago: Kett; 1877. [with biographical dictionary, $150.00]

Hitchcock, Edward. **Religious Lectures on Peculiar Phenomena in the Four Seasons.** 2nd ed. Amherst: Adams; 1851. [$85.00]

Hitchcock, Enos. **A Discourse, on the Dignity and Excellence of the Human Character; Illustrated in the Life of General George Washington.** Providence: Carter; 1800. [$50.00]

Hitchcock, Ethan Allen. **Fifty Years in Camp and Field.** NY, London: Putnam; 1909. [$200.00]

Hitchcock, Ethan Allen. **A Traveler in Indian Territory.** Cedar Rapids: Torch; 1930. [$150.00]

Hitchcock, Frank. **A True Account of the Capture of Frank Rande.** Peoria: Franks; 1897. [very good, $650.00]

Hitchcock, Frederick Lyman. **History of Scranton and Its People.** NY: Lewis; 1914. 2 v. [$100.00]

Hitchcock, Frederick Lyman. **War from the Inside.** Philadelphia: Lippincott; 1904, c1903. [$85.00]

Hitchcock, Ripley. **Etching in America.** NY: White, Stokes, & Allen; 1886. [$125.00]

Hitchcock, Ripley. **The Louisiana Purchase, and the Exploration.** Boston: Ginn; 1903. [$45.00]

Hittell, John Shertzer. **Guide Book to San Francisco.** San Francisco: Bancroft; 1888. [worn, $60.00]

Hittell, John Shertzer. **Hittell's Hand-Book of Pacific Coast Travel.** San Francisco: Bancroft; 1887. [worn, $75.00]

Hittell, Theodore Henry. **Adventures of James Capen Adams.** Boston: Crosby, Nichols, Lee; 1860. [$175.00] [1911 Scribner ed., $35.00]

Hoad, Louise Green. **Kickapoo Indian Trails.** 1st ed. Caldwell, ID: Caxton; 1944. [$20.00]

Hoadley, John Chipman. **Memorial of Henry Sanford Gansevoort.** Boston: Rand, Avery; 1875. [rebound, $50.00]

Hoar, George Frisbie. **Autobiography of Seventy Years.** NY: Scribner; 1903. 2 v. [$30.00]

Hobart, Aaron. **Historical Sketch of Abington, Plymouth County, Massachusetts.** Boston: Dickinson; 1839. [$50.00]

Hobbs, James. **Wild Life in the Far West.** Hartford: Wiley, Waterman & Eaton; 1872. [$450.00] [$300.00] [2nd issue, 1873, $80.00]

Hobbs, Jean. **Hawaii: a Pageant of the Soil.** Stanford; London: Stanford UP; Oxford UP; 1935. [$15.00]

Hobby, Laura Aline. **Washington the Lover.** Dallas: Southwest; 1932. [$20.00]

Hobson, Richmond Pearson. **Grass beyond the Mountains.** Philadelphia: Lippincott; 1951. [$15.00]

Hochbaum, H. Albert. **The Canvasback on a Prairie Marsh.** Washington: American Wildlife Institute; 1944. [$45.00] [covers warped, spotted, $25.00]

Hochderffer, George. **Flagstaff Whoa!** Flagstaff: Museum of Northern Arizona; 1965. [$45.00]

Hodge, Frederick Webb. **Handbook of American Indians North of Mexico.** Washington: USGPO; 1907-10. 2 v. [shaken, corners worn, $65.00] [$150.00] [$125.00]

Hodge, Hiram C. **Arizona as It Is.** NY: Hurd and Houghton; 1877. [$150.00] [$75.00]

Hodges, William Romaine. **Carl Wimar.** Galveston, TX: Reymershoffer; 1908. [x-lib., $30.00]

Hodgman, Stephen Alexander. **The Nation's Sin and Punishment.** NY: American News; 1864. [$40.00]

Hodgson, Adam. **Letters from North America.** London: Hurst, Robinson; 1824. 2 v. [$450.00]

Hodgson, Adam. **Remarks during a Journey through North America in the Years 1819, 1820, and 1821.** NY: 1823. [$150.00]

Hodgson, William. **Society of Friends in the Nineteenth Century.** Philadelphia: Smith, English; 1875-76. 2 v. [$50.00]

Hoehling, Adolph A. **Last Train from Atlanta.** NY: Yoseloff; 1958. [$17.00]

Hoff, J. Wallace. **Two Hundred Miles on the Delaware River.** Trenton, NJ: Brandt; 1893. [$75.00]

Hoffman, Benneville Ottomar. **Snarl of a Cynic.** Ephrata, PA: Heitler; 1868. [$32.00]

Hoffman, Robert V. **The Revolutionary Scene in New Jersey.** NY: American Historical; 1942. [$45.00] [$35.00]

Hoffmann, Hemmann. **Californien, Nevada und Mexico.** Basel: Schweighauser; 1871. [$125.00]

Hofstadter, Richard. **The Development of Academic Freedom in the United States.** NY: Columbia UP; 1955. [$20.00]

Hogan, John Joseph. **On the Mission in Missouri, 1857-1868.** Kansas City, MO: Heilmann; 1892. [$50.00] [$65.00] [$75.00]

Hogan, William Ransom. **The Texas Republic: A Social and Economic History.** Norman: U. of Oklahoma; 1946. [$85.00] [$65.00]

Hoge, Peyton Harrison. **Moses Drury Hoge.** Richmond: Presbyterian Committee of Publication; 1899. [x-lib., $50.00]

Hogg, James Stephen. **Speeches and State Papers of.** Austin: State; 1905. [$150.00]

Hogner, Dorothy Childs. **Westward, High, Low, and Dry.** NY: Dutton; 1938. [worn dj, $30.00]

Hogue, Wayman. **Back Yonder.** NY: Minton, Balch; 1932. [$26.00]

Hohman, Elmo Paul. **The American Whaleman.** NY: Longmans, Green; 1928. [$35.00]

Hohman, Johann Georg. **Der Lang Verborgene Freund.** Neu Berlin, PA: [s.n.]; 1843. [$35.00]

Hoig, Stan. **The Sand Creek Massacre.** 1st ed. Norman: U. of Oklahoma; 1961. [$40.00]

Hokanson, Nels Magnus. **Swedish Immigrants in Lincoln's Time.** NY, London: Harper; 1942. [3rd printing, $17.50]

Hoke, Jacob. **The Great Invasion of 1863.** Dayton, OH: Shuey; 1887. [$75.00]

Holand, Hjalmar Rued. **Old Peninsula Days.** Ephraim, WI: Pioneer; 1925. [signed, $25.00]

Holbrook, Stewart Hall. **The Columbia.** NY: Rinehart; 1956. [$15.00]

Holbrook, Stewart Hall. **Little Annie Oakley & Other Rugged People.** NY: Macmillan; 1948. [$25.00]

Holbrook, Stewart Hall. **Machines of Plenty.** NY: Macmillan; 1955. [poor dj, $12.50]

Holbrook, Stewart Hall. **The Rocky Mountain Revolution.** 1st ed. NY: Holt; 1956. [$20.00]

Holbrook, Stewart Hall. **Wyatt Earp, U. S. Marshal.** NY: Random; 1956. [$15.00]

Holbrook, Stewart Hall. **The Yankee Exodus.** NY: Macmillan; 1950. [$20.00]

Holden, Edward Singleton. **Catalogue of Earthquakes on the Pacific Coast, 1769-1897.** Washington: Smithsonian; 1898. [lacks wraps, $39.50]

Holden, William Curry. **Alkali Trails.** Dallas: Southwest; 1930. [$150.00]

Holden, William Curry. **Studies of the Yaqui Indians of Sonora, Mexico.** Lubbock: Texas Tech; 1936. [$45.00]

Holder, Charles Frederick. **Adventures of Torqua.** Boston: Little, Brown; 1902. [worn, $100.00]

Holder, Charles Frederick. **Channel Islands of California.** Chicago: McClurg; 1910. [$100.00]

Holder, Charles Frederick. **Life in the Open.** NY, London: Putnam; 1906. [$70.00] [$60.00]

Holdredge, Helen O'Donnell. **Mammy Pleasant.** NY: Putnam; 1953. [$15.00]

Holdredge, Helen O'Donnell. **Mammy Pleasant's Partner.** NY: Putnam; 1954. [$15.00]

Holland, Annie Jefferson. **The Refugees.** Austin: The Author; 1892. [$45.00]

Holland, Josiah Gilbert. **Life of Abraham Lincoln.** Springfield, MA: Bill; 1866. [$45.00]

Holland, Mary A. Gardner. **Our Army Nurses.** Boston: Lounsbery, Nichols & Worth; 1897. [$50.00]

Hollander, Jacob Harry. **Financial History of Baltimore.** Baltimore: Hopkins; 1899. [$50.00]

Holley, Frances Chamberlain. **Once Their Home.** Chicago: Donohue & Henneberry; 1890. [slightly rubbed, $125.00] [$150.00]

Holley, George Washington. **The Falls of Niagara.** NY: Armstrong; 1883. [$45.00]

Holley, Marietta. **Samantha at Saratoga.** Philadelphia: Hubbard; 1887. [$12.50]

Holley, Marietta. **Samantha at the World's Fair.** NY: Funk & Wagnalls; 1893. [$15.00]

Holley, Marietta. **Samantha in Europe.** NY: Funk & Wagnalls; 1896. [$15.00]

Holley, Mary Austin. **Texas.** Lexington: Clarke; 1836. [$1950.00]

Holliday, Charles William. **The Valley of Youth.** Caldwell, ID: Caxton; 1948. [$25.00]

Holliday, Walter Harry. **Mining-Camp Melodies.** 1st ed. Butte, MO: Oates & Roberts; 1924. [$125.00]

Hollis, John Porter. **Early Period of Reconstruction in South Carolina.** Baltimore: Hopkins; 1905. [x-lib., $25.00]

Hollister, Gideon Hiram. **The History of Connecticut.** 2nd ed. Hartford: Case, Tiffany; 1857. 2 v. [x-lib., rebound, $35.00]

Hollister, Horace. **Contributions to the History of the Lackawanna Valley.** NY: Tinson; 1857. [$46.00] [$85.00]

Hollister, Ovando James. **Boldly They Rode.** Lakewood, CO: Golden; 1949. [$32.50]

Hollon, W. Eugene. **Beyond the Cross Timbers.** 1st ed. Norman: U. of Oklahoma; 1955. [$27.50] [signed, $40.00] [$30.00]

Hollon, W. Eugene. **The Lost Pathfinder, Zebulon Montgomery Pike.** 1st ed. Norman: U. of Oklahoma; 1949. [$40.00]

Hollon, W. Eugene. **The Southwest.** NY: Knopf; 1961. [$25.00]

Holloway, John N. **History of Kansas.** Lafayette, IN: James, Emmons; 1868. [rebound, x-lib., $25.00]

Holloway, Laura C. **Ladies of the White House.** Philadelphia: Bradley; 1880. [$15.00]

Holman, Albert M. **Pioneering in the Northwest.** Sioux City: Deitch & Lamar; 1924. [$45.00] [$35.00]

Holman, Frederick Van Voorhies. **Dr. John McLoughlin.** Cleveland: Clark; 1907. [$65.00]

Holmes, Abiel. **American Annals.** Cambridge, MA: Hilliard; 1805. 2 v. [$150.00] [1829 ed., $32.00]

Holmes, Alice A. **Lost Vision.** NY: De Vinne; 1888. [$15.00]

Holmes, John Beck. **Historical Sketches of the Missions of the United Brethren for Propagating the Gospel among the Heathen.** 2nd ed. London: The Author; 1827. [$100.00]

Holmes, Mead. **A Soldier of the Cumberland.** Boston: American Tract Society; 1864. [$50.00]

Holmes, Oliver Wendell. **Autocrat of the Breakfast-Table.** 1st ed. Boston: Phillips, Sampson; 1858. [1st issue, $260.00] [2nd issue, $75.00] [2nd printing, $100.00]

Holmes, Oliver Wendell. **Elsie Venner.** 1st ed. Boston: Ticknor and Fields; 1861. 2 v. [1st printing, $175.00] [1891 Houghton ed., $20.00]

Holmes, Oliver Wendell. **The Guardian Angel.** Boston: Ticknor and Fields; 1867. [spine frayed, one hinge cracked, $60.00]

Holmes, Oliver Wendell. **Holmes-Laski Letters.** Cambridge: Harvard UP; 1953. 2 v. [$35.00]

Holmes, Oliver Wendell. **Holmes-Pollock Letters.** Cambridge: Harvard UP; 1941. 2 v. [spines faded, $35.00] [2nd ed., 1961, $25.00]

Holmes, Oliver Wendell. **The Iron Gate and Other Poems.** Boston: Houghton Mifflin; 1880. [$125.00]

Holmes, Oliver Wendell. **The Mind and Faith of Justice Holmes.** NY: Little, Brown; 1943. [$20.00]

Holmes, Oliver Wendell. **Our Hundred Days in Europe.** Boston, NY: Houghton Mifflin; 1887. [$75.00]

Holmes, Oliver Wendell. **Poems.** London: Rich; 1846. [$150.00]

Holmes, Oliver Wendell. **Songs in Many Keys.** Boston: Ticknor and Fields; 1862. [$30.00]

Holmes, Oliver Wendell. **Songs of Many Seasons.** Boston: Osgood; 1875. [$95.00]

Holmes, Oliver Wendell. **Speeches.** Boston: Little, Brown; 1913. [$38.50]

Holmes, Oliver Wendell. **Works.** Boston: Houghton Mifflin; 1892. 13 v. [$220.00]

Holmes, Oliver Wendell. **The Writings of.** Cambridge: Riverside Press; 1891-96. 16 v. [spines faded, $100.00]

Holmes, Sarah Katherine. **Brokenburn.** Baton Rouge: Louisiana State UP; 1956, c1955. [2nd printing, $25.00]

Holsinger, Henry Ritz. **Holsinger's History of the Tunkers and the Brethren Church.** Lathrop, CA: Pacific Press; 1901. [rebacked, $165.00]

Holt, Joseph. **The Evil, and the Remedy for the Privy System of New Orleans.** New Orleans: Hansell; 1879. [$35.00]

Holt, Roy David. **Schleicher County.** Eldorado, TX: Success; 1930. [$45.00]

Holthusen, Henry Frank. **James W. Wadsworth, Jr.** NY, London: Putnam; 1926. [$85.00]

Holzworth, John Michael. **The Wild Grizzlies of Alaska.** NY, London: Putnam; 1930. [$65.00]

Honeyman, Abraham Van Doren. **History of Union County, New Jersey 1664-1923.** NY: Lewis; 1923. 3 v. [$90.00]

Honeywell, Roy John. **Chaplains of the United States Army.** Washington: Chief of Chaplains; 1958. [x-lib., $40.00]

Hood, John Bell. **Advance and Retreat.** New Orleans: Beauregard; 1880. [rebound, $35.00] [$75.00] [1959 Indiana UP ed., $45.00]

Hoofs, Claws and Antlers of the Rocky Mountains. see, Wallihan, Allen Grant.

Hook, Sidney. **Education for Modern Man.** NY: Dial; 1946. [$17.50]

Hooker, Richard. **Aetna Life Insurance Company: Its First Hundred Years.** Hartford: Aetna; 1956. [$20.00]

Hooker, Richard. **Story of an Independent Newspaper.** NY: Macmillian; 1924. [$45.00]

Hooker, William Francis. **The Bullwhacker.** Yonkers-on-Hudson, Chicago: World; 1924. [$20.00]

Hooker, William Francis. **The Prairie Schooner.** Chicago: Saul; 1918. [$50.00]

Hoole, William Stanley. **Four Years in the Confederate Navy.** Athens: U. of Georgia; 1964. [$25.00]

Hooper, Osman Castle. **History of Ohio Journalism.** Columbus: Spahr & Glenn; 1933. [$17.50]

Hoover, Herbert. **The Basis of Lasting Peace.** NY: Van Nostrand; 1945. [inscribed, $75.00]

Hoover, Herbert. **The Challenge to Liberty.** NY, London: Scribner; 1934. [$12.50] [$15.00]

Hoover, Margaret Hocker. **Concerning Collegeville.** [Philadelphia?: s.n.]; 1966. [$25.00]

Hope, Ascott R. see, Moncrieff, Asott Robert Hope.

Hopkins, John Abel. **Economic History of the Production of Beef Cattle in Iowa.** Iowa City: State Historical Society; 1928. [$25.00]

Hopkins, Lemuel. **The Guillotina.** Philadelphia: Bradford; 1796. [$85.00]

Hopkins, Manley. **Hawaii: The Past, Present, and Future of Its Island-Kingdom.** London: Longmans, Green; 1866. [$185.00]

Hopkins, Sarah Winnemucca. **Life among the Piutes.** Boston: Cupples, Upham; 1883. [$150.00] [inscribed, binding very worn, $100.00]

Horan, James David. **Confederate Agent.** NY: Crown; 1954. [$25.00] [$14.50] [$17.50] [1960 printing, $15.00]

Horan, James David. **Desperate Men.** NY: Putnam; 1949. [$18.00]

Horan, James David. **Desperate Women.** NY: Putnam; 1952. [$30.00]

Horan, James David. **The Great American West.** NY: Crown; 1959. [$30.00] [Bonanza reprint, $15.00]

Horan, James David. **Pictorial History of the Wild West.** NY: Crown; 1954. [$30.00]

Horan, James David. **The Pinkerton Story.** NY: Putnam; 1951. [2nd printing, $20.00]

Horgan, Paul. **The Centuries of Santa Fe.** 1st ed. NY: Dutton; 1956. [$12.50] [$16.00] [$28.00] [signed, $25.00]

Horgan, Paul. **The Devil in the Desert.** 1st ed. NY: Longmans, Green; 1952, c1950. [chipped dj, $35.00]

Horgan, Paul. **Great River: The Rio Grande in North American History.** NY: Rinehart; 1954. 2 v. [$45.00] [slip case worn, $25.00]

Horgan, Paul. **Lamy of Santa Fe.** NY: Farrar, Straus and Giroux; 1975. [$30.00]

Horka-Follick, Lorayne. **Los Hermanos Penitentes.** Los Angeles: Westernlore; 1969. [$25.00]

Horn, Calvin. **New Mexico's Troubled Years.** 1st ed. Albuquerque: Horn & Wallace; 1963. [$35.00]

Horn, Robert Cannon. **Annals of Elder Horn.** NY: Smith; 1930. [$35.00] [$25.00]

Horn, Sarah Ann. **Narrative of the Captivity of Mrs. Horn.** St. Louis: Keemle; 1839. [front board missing, small tears in some leaves, $4700.00]

Horn, Stanley Fitzgerald. **The Army of Tennessee.** 1st ed. Indianapolis: Bobbs Merrill; 1941. [$75.00] [1952 Oklahoma ed., $30.00]

Horn, Stanley Fitzgerald. **The Hermitage.** Richmond: Garrett & Massie; 1938. [presentation, dj chipped, $45.00]

Horn, Stanley Fitzgerald. **Invisible Empire.** Boston: Houghton Mifflin; 1939. [chipped dj, $40.00]

Hornaday, William Temple. **Camp-Fires on Desert and Lava.** NY: Scribner; 1908. [binding weak, $35.00]

Hornaday, William Temple. **Hornaday's American Natural History.** 12th ed. NY, London: Scribner; 1927. [aged, $25.00]

Hornaday, William Temple. **Our Vanishing Wild Life.** NY: Scribner; 1913. [bumped, $20.00]

Hornby, Harry Paulson. **Going Around.** Uvalde, TX: Hornby; 1945. [$45.00]

Horner, Harlan Hoyt. **Lincoln and Greeley.** Urbana: U. of Illinois; 1953. [$20.00]

Hornor, William Stockton. **This Old Monmouth of Ours.** Freehold, NJ: Moreau; 1932. [$110.00]

Hornot, Antoine. **Anecdotes Americaines.** Paris: Vincent; 1776. [$175.00]

Horry, Peter. **Life of General Francis Marion.** see, Weems, Mason Locke.

Horsford, Eben Norton. **The Defences of Norumbega.** Boston, NY: Houghton Mifflin; 1891. [foxed, $35.00]

Horsford, Eben Norton. **Discovery of the Ancient City of Norumbega.** Cambridge: Priv. Print.; [1890?]. [$75.00]

Horsford, Eben Norton. **The Landfall of Leif Erickson.** 1st ed. Boston: Damrell and Upham; 1892. [soiled covers, $75.00]

Horton, Rushmore G. **Youth's History of the Great Civil War in the United States.** NY: Van Evrie, Horton; 1866. [$25.00]

Hoshour, Samuel Klinefetter. **Letters to Squire Pedant in the East.** 4th ed. Indianapolis: Print. and Pub. House; 1870. [$125.00]

Hosier, Helen Kooiman. **Walter Knott.** Fullerton, CA: Plycon; 1973. [$12.50]

Hosmer, George Lawrence. **An Historical Sketch of the Town of Deer Isle, Maine.** Boston: Fort Hill; 1905. [$40.00]

Hosmer, James Kendall. **The Color-Guard.** Boston: Walker, Wise; 1864. [$55.00] [$50.00]

Hosmer, James Kendall. **Short History of the Mississippi Valley.** Boston, NY: Houghton Mifflin; 1901. [$30.00]

Hotchkin, James Harvey. **History of the Purchase and Settlement of Western New York.** NY: Dodd; 1848. [rehinged, $85.00]

Hotchkin, Samuel Fitch. **Ancient and Modern Germantown, Mount Airy and Chestnut Hill.** Philadelphia: Ziegler; 1889. [$125.00]

Hotchkin, Samuel Fitch. **Rural Pennsylvania in the Vicinity of Philadelphia.** Philadelphia: Jacobs; 1897. [$125.00]

Hotchkin, Samuel Fitch. **The York Road.** Philadelphia: Binder & Kelly; 1892. [$75.00]

Hotchkiss, Charles F. **On the Ebb.** New Haven: Tuttle; 1878. [$100.00]

Hotten, John Camden. **Our Early Emigrant Ancestors.** 2nd ed. NY: Bouton; 1880. [worn, $25.00]

Hotz, Gottfried. **Indian Skin Paintings from the American Southwest.** 1st ed. Norman: U. of Oklahoma; 1970. [$30.00]

Hough, Alfred Lacey. **Soldier in the West.** Philadelphia: U. of Pennsylvania; 1957. [$17.50]

Hough, Emerson. **The Covered Wagon.** 1st ed. NY: Appleton; 1922. [$30.00] [dj chipped, $90.00]

Hough, Emerson. **Law of the Land.** 1st ed. Indianapolis: Bobbs-Merrill; 1904. [$35.00] [$40.00]

Hough, Emerson. **Out of Doors.** NY and London: Appleton; 1915. [$40.00] [$50.00]

Hough, Emerson. **Way to the West.** Indianapolis: Bobbs-Merrill; 1903. [$65.00]

Hough, Frank Olney. **Campaign on New Britain.** Washington: Historical Division, U.S. Marine Corps; 1952. [$45.00]

Houghteling, Leila. **Income and Standard of Living of Unskilled Laborers in Chicago.** Chicago: U. of Chicago; 1927. [$25.00]

Houghton, Louise. **Our Debt to the Red Man.** Boston: Stratford; 1918. [$20.00]

House That Jeff Built. see, Bourne, William Oland.

House, Boyce. **City of Flaming Adventure.** San Antonio: Naylor; 1949. [$15.00]

House, Boyce. **Cowtown Columnist.** San Antonio: Naylor; 1946. [dj repaired, $10.00]

Houston, David Franklin. **Eight Years with Wilson's Cabinet.** Garden City: Doubleday, Page; 1926. 2 v. [$30.00]

Houston, Sam. **Autobiography of.** Norman: U. of Oklahoma; 1954. [$20.00]

Houstoun, Matilda Charlotte Jesse Fraser. **Texas and the Gulf of Mexico; or, Yachting in the New World.** London: Murray; 1844. 2 v. [$875.00]

Hover, John Calvin. **Memoirs of the Miami Valley.** Chicago: Law; 1919-20. 3 v. [$110.00]

Hovey, Sylvester. **Letters from the West Indies.** NY: Gould and Newman; 1838. [some dampstaining, $100.00]

Howard, Benjamin C. see, United States. Supreme Court.

Howard, H. R. **History of Virgil A. Stewart.** NY: Harper; 1836. [lacks backstrip, dampstained, $150.00] [rebound, marginal waterstains, $250.00]

Howard, James Henri. **The Ponca Tribe.** Washington: USGPO; 1965. [$27.50]

Howard, John Tasker. **Stephen Foster.** NY: Tudor; 1939. [$45.00]

Howard, Joseph Kinsey. **Strange Empire.** NY: Morrow; 1952. [$17.50]

Howard, O. O. **My Life and Experiences among Our Hostile Indians.** Hartford, CT: Worthington; 1907. [$150.00]

Howard, Samuel Meek. **Illustrated Comprehensive History of the Great Battle of Shiloh.** Gettysburg, SD: Howard; 1921. [$200.00]

Howard of Glossop, Winifred Mary (DeLisle) Howard baroness. **Journal of a Tour in the United States, Canada and Mexico.** London: Low, Marston; 1897. [$45.00]

Howay, Frederic William. **British Columbia and the U. S.** see, Angus, Henry Forbes.

Howbert, Irving. **Memories of a Lifetime in the Pike's Peak Region.** NY, London: Putnam; 1925. [$50.00]

Howe, Charles Willis. **Timberleg of the Diamond Tail.** San Antonio: Naylor; 1949. [$25.00]

Howe, Edgar Watson. **Plain People.** NY: Dodd, Mead; 1929. [2nd printing, $15.00]

Howe, Edgar Watson. **Story of a Country Town.** Atchison, KS: Howe; 1883. [$90.00]

Howe, Elias. **American Dancing Master, and Ball-Room Prompter.** Boston: Howe; 1862. [$65.00]

Howe, Elvon L. **Rocky Mountain Empire.** 1st ed. Garden City: Doubleday; 1950. [inscribed, $35.00] [$15.00]

Howe, Henry. **Diary of a Circuit Rider.** Minneapolis: Voyageur; 1933. [$25.00]

Howe, Henry. **The Great West.** enlarged ed. NY; Cincinnati: Tuttle; Howe; 1859. 2 v. in 1. [spine worn, $50.00] [$30.00]

Howe, Henry. **Historical Collections of Ohio.** Cincinnati: Howe; 1852. [rebound, $65.00]

Howe, Henry. **Life and Death on the Ocean.** Cincinnati: Howe; 1870. [$45.00]

Howe, Julia Ward. **Words for the Hour.** Boston: Ticknor and Fields; 1857. [$75.00]

Howe, Julia Ward. **The World's Own.** Boston: Ticknor and Fields; 1857. [$75.00]

Howe, Mark De Wolfe. **Justice Oliver Wendell Holmes.** Cambridge: Harvard UP; 1957-1963. 2 v. [$50.00]

Howe, Mark De Wolfe. **Life and Letters of George Bancroft.** NY: Scribner; 1908. 2 v. [$50.00] [$20.00]

Howe, Octavius T. **Argonauts of '49.** Cambridge: Harvard UP; 1923. [$40.00] [$45.00]

Howe, Paul Sturtevant. **Mayflower Pilgrim Descendants in Cape May County, New Jersey.** Cape May: Hand; 1921. [$65.00]

Howe, S. Ferdinand. **The Commerce of Kansas City in 1886.** Kansas City, MO: Howe; 1886. [title page reinforced, $175.00]

Howells, John Mead. **Architectural Heritage of the Merrimack.** NY: Architectural Book; 1941. [$150.00]

Howells, John Mead. **Architectural Heritage of the Piscataqua.** NY: Architectural Book; 1937. [$75.00]

Howells, John Mead. **Lost Examples of Colonial Architecture.** NY: Helburn; 1931. [$150.00]

Howells, William Dean. **Between the Dark and the Daylight.** NY, London: Harper; 1907. [$12.50]

Howells, William Dean. **The Elevator.** Boston: Osgood; 1885. [$10.00]

Howells, William Dean. **A Hazard of New Fortunes.** NY: Harper; 1911. [$12.50]

Howells, William Dean. **Literature and Life.** NY, London: Harper; 1902. [$25.00]

Howells, William Dean. **Lives and Speeches of Abraham Lincoln and Hannibal Hamlin.** Columbus, OH: Follett, Foster; 1860. [$125.00]

Howells, William Dean. **My Mark Twain.** NY, London: Harper; 1910. [$65.00]

Howells, William Dean. **Questionable Shapes.** NY, London: Harper; 1903. [$15.00]

Hower, Ralph Merle. **History of an Advertising Agency.** rev. ed. Cambridge: Harvard UP; 1949. [$25.00]

Howison, John. **Sketches of Upper Canada.** Edinburgh; London: Oliver & Boyd; Whitaker; 1821. [$275.00]

Howitt, Emanuel. **Selections from Letters Written during a Tour through the United States in the Summer and Autumn of 1819.** Nottingham: Dunn; 1820. [$685.00]

Howitt, Mary Botham. **Poems of.** Philadelphia: Hunt; 1846. [$50.00]

Howitt, William. **Colonization and Christianity.** London: Longman, etc.; 1838. [$45.00]

Howlett, William Joseph. **Life of the Right Reverend Joseph P. Machebeuf.** Pueblo, CO: Franklin; 1908. [rebound, $100.00]

Hoyt, Edward Jonathan. **Buckskin Joe.** Lincoln: U. of Nebraska; 1966. [$25.00]

Hoyt, Epaphras. **Antiquarian Researches.** Greenfield, MA: Phelps; 1824. [folding plate repaired, $175.00]

Hoyt, George Henry. **Kansas and the Osage Swindle.** Washington: Gibson; 1868. [$175.00]

Hoyt, Henry Franklin. **A Frontier Doctor.** Boston, NY: Houghton Mifflin; 1929. [signed, $65.00; $75.00]

Hoyt, J. K. **Pen and Pencil Pictures on the Delaware, Lackawanna, and Western Railroad.** NY: Cadwell; 1874. [$75.00]

Hoyt, Ray. **"We Can Take It."** NY: American Book Co.; 1935. [soiled and frayed, $65.00]

Hrdlicka, Ales. **Physical Anthropology of the Lenape or Delawares and of the Eastern Indians in General.** Washington: USGPO; 1916. [$25.00]

Hrdlicka, Ales. **Recent Discoveries Attributed to Early Man in America.** Washington: USGPO; 1918. [$35.00]

Hubbard, Bernard Rosecrans. **Mush, You Malemutes!** NY: America; 1932. [cover stains, $18.00]

Hubbard, Elbert. **The Doctors.** East Aurora: Roycrofters; 1909. [$12.50] [$35.00]

Hubbard, Elbert. **In the Spotlight.** East Aurora: Roycrofters; 1917. [$12.50]

Hubbard, Jeremiah. **A Teacher's Ups and Downs from 1858 to 1879.** Richmond, IN: Palladium; 1879. [$75.00]

Hubbard, William. **A General History of New England from the Discovery to MDCLXXX.** Cambridge: Hillard & Metcalf; 1815. [$100.00]

Hubbard, William. **History of the Indian Wars in New England from the First Settlement to the Termination of the War with King Philip in 1677.** Roxbury, MA: Woodward; 1865. 2 v. [$200.00]

Hubbell, Jay Broadus. **The South in American Literature, 1607-1900.** Durham: Duke UP; 1954. [$25.00]

Hubley, Bernard. **History of the American Revolution.** Northumberland, PA: Kennedy; 1805. [original boards, $550.00]

Hudleston, Francis Josiah. **Gentleman Johnny Burgoyne.** Indianapolis: Bobbs-Merrill; 1927. [$15.00] [1928 London ed., $12.50]

Hudson, Arthur Palmer. **Folksongs of Mississippi.** Chapel Hill: U. of North Carolina; 1936. [$35.00]

Hudson, David. **History of Jemima Wilkinson.** Geneva, NY: Hull; 1821. [2 leaves supplied, rubbed, $375.00] [1844 2nd ed., $100.00]

Hudson, Mary Worrell Smith. **Esther the Gentile.** Topeka, KS: Crane; 1888. [$50.00]

Hudson, Sue F. **Background of Ho-Ho-Kus History.** [Hohokus?]: Woman's Club of Ho-Ho-Kus, NJ; 1953. [$35.00]

Hudson, Tom. **Three Paths along a River.** Palm Desert, CA: Desert-Southwest; 1964. [$17.50]

Hudson, Will E. **Icy Hell.** NY: Stokes; 1937. [$25.00]

Hudson, William Henry. **Idle Days in Patagonia.** London: Chapman & Hall; 1893. [x-lib., $100.00]

Hudson, Wilson Mathis. **The Sunny Slopes of Long Ago.** Dallas: Southern Methodist UP; 1966. [$35.00]

Hudson's Bay Company. **Saskatchewan Journals and Correspondence.** London: Hudson's Bay Record Society; 1967. [$75.00]

Hughes, Charles Evans. **The Supreme Court of the United States.** NY: Columbia UP; 1928. [2nd printing?, $17.50]

Hughes, Elizabeth. **The California of the Padres.** San Francisco: Choynski; 1875. [morocco slipcase, $125.00]

Hughes, John Taylor. **Doniphan's Expedition.** Cincinnati: James; 1847. [144 pp. 2nd? ed., $250.00] [1907 Topeka ed., $125.00]

Hughes, Langston. **Simple Speaks His Mind.** 1st ed. NY: Simon and Schuster; 1950. [minor wear, badly chipped dj, $35.00]

Hughes, Richard B. **Pioneer Years in the Black Hills.** Glendale, CA: Clark; 1957. [$100.00]

Hughes, Robert William. **Popular Treatise on the Currency Question Written from a Southern Point of View.** NY: Putnam; 1879. [presentation, $20.00]

Hughes, Thomas. **G. T. T.: Gone to Texas.** NY: Macmillan; 1884. [$285.00]

Hughes, William J. **Rebellious Ranger.** 1st ed. Norman: U. of Oklahoma; 1964. [chipped dj, $37.50] [$85.00] [$60.00]

Huhner, Leon. **Jews in America in Colonial and Revolutionary Times.** NY: Gertz; 1959. [$20.00]

Huie, William Bradford. **Ruby McCollum.** NY: Dutton; 1956. [$12.50]

Hulbert, Archer Butler. **Forty-Niners.** Boston: Little, Brown; 1931. [cover stained, $15.00]

Hulbert, Archer Butler. **The Niagara River.** NY: Putnam; 1908. [$50.00]

Hulbert, Archer Butler. **The Old National Road.** Columbus: Heer; 1901. [very x-lib., $22.00] [$60.00]

Hull, Clifton E. **Shortline Railroads of Arkansas.** 1st ed. Norman: U. of Oklahoma; 1969. [$35.00]

Hull, Cordell. **Memoirs of.** NY: Macmillan; 1948. 2 v. [$25.00]

Hull, William Isaac. **William Penn and the Dutch Quaker Migration to Pennsylvania.** Swarthmore: Swarthmore College; 1935. [$50.00]

Humboldt, Alexander von. **Personal Narrative of Travels to the Equinoctial Regions of the New Continent, during the Years 1799-1804.** Philadelphia: Carey; 1815. [$375.00]

Hume, John F. **The Abolitionists.** NY, London: Putnam; 1905. [$50.00]

Humphrey, Zephine. **Green Mountains to Sierras.** NY: Dutton; 1936. [corners bumped, spine faded, $20.00]

Humphreys, Andrew Atkinson. **From Gettysburg to the Rapidan.** NY: Scribner; 1883. [$40.00]

Humphreys, Andrew Atkinson. **Virginia Campaign of '64 and '65.** NY: Scribner; 1883. [2 maps badly torn, $35.00]

Humphreys, David. **Historical Account of the Incorporated Society for the Propagation of the Gospel in Foreign Parts.** London: Downing; 1730. [lacks the two maps, $200.00] [rebacked, $1000.00]

Hundley, Will M. **Squawtown.** Caldwell, ID: Caxton; 1939. [x-lib., $10.00]

Hungerford, Edward. **Men and Iron.** NY: Crowell; 1938. [$30.00]

Hungerford, Edward. **Men of Erie.** NY: Random; 1946. [$17.50]

Hungerford, Edward. **Wells Fargo.** NY: Random; 1949. [$17.50] [$20.00]

Hunt, Aurora. **The Army of the Pacific.** Glendale, CA: Clark; 1951. [$150.00]

Hunt, Aurora. **Kirby Benedict, Frontier Federal Judge.** Glendale, CA: Clark; 1961. [$25.00] [$32.00] [$30.00]

Hunt, Charles Havens. **Life of Edward Livingston.** NY: Appleton; 1864. [$65.00]

Hunt, Elvid. **History of Fort Leavenworth 1827-1927.** Fort Leavenworth, KS: General Service Schools Press; 1926. [rebound, $60.00]

Hunt, Frazier. **Cap Mossman.** NY: Hastings; 1951. [x-lib., $15.00] [$35.00]

Hunt, Frazier. **Custer.** NY: Cosmopolitan; 1928. [fine, $35.00]

Hunt, Frazier. **MacArthur and the War against Japan.** NY: Scribner; 1944. [$10.00]

Hunt, Frazier. **Tragic Days of Billy the Kid.** NY: Hastings; 1956. [$25.00] [$38.00]

Hunt, Gaillard. **Fragments of Revolutionary History.** Brooklyn: Historical Printing Club; 1892. [$45.00]

Hunt, George T. **The Wars of the Iroquois.** Madison: U. of Wisconsin; 1940. [$85.00]

Hunt, Henry M. **Crime of the Century; or, The Assassination of Dr. Patrick Henry Cronin.** [s.l.: s.n.]; 1889. [$30.00]

Hunt, James Halsey. **Three Runs in the Adirondacks and One in Canada.** NY: Putnam; 1892. [$100.00]

Hunt, Lenoir. **Bluebonnets and Blood.** founders' ed. Houston: Texas Books; 1938. [numbered and signed, $125.00]

Hunt, Robert Lee. **A History of Farmer Movements in the Southwest, 1873-1925.** College Station: A. and M. College of Texas; 1935. [$100.00]

Hunt, Rockwell Dennis. **A Short History of California.** NY: Crowell; 1929. [$15.00]

Hunter, C. L. **Sketches of Western North Carolina.** Raleigh: News; 1877. [spine torn, bumped, silverfished, $60.00]

Hunter, George. **Reminiscences of an Old Timer.** San Francisco: Crocker; 1887. [sunned, $150.00]

Hunter, John Dunn. **Manners and Customs of Several Indian Tribes Located West of the Mississippi.** Philadelphia: Maxwell; 1823. [disbound, foxed, $175.00]

Hunter, John Dunn. **Memoirs of a Captivity among the Indians of North America.** London: Longman; 1823. [$200.00] [3rd ed., 1824, $175.00]

Hunter, John Marvin. **Old Camp Verde, the Home of the Camels.** Bandera, TX: Frontier Times; 1936. [$40.00]

Hunter, John Marvin. **Peregrinations of a Pioneer Printer.** Grand Prairie, TX: Frontier Times; 1954. [$55.00]

Hunter, John Marvin. **Pioneer History of Bandera County.** Bandera, TX: Hunter's; 1922. [$185.00] [1936 reprint as "Brief History . . .," $65.00]

Hunter, John Marvin. **Trail Drivers of Texas.** 2nd ed. Nashville: Cokesbury; 1925. [$200.00] [1963 Argosy-Antiquarian ed., $250.00]

Hunter, Martin. **Canadian Wilds.** Columbus, OH: Harding; 1935. [$12.00]

Hunter, Milton R. **Utah, the Story of Her People, 1540-1947.** Salt Lake City: Deseret News; 1946. [$15.00]

Hunter, Robert Hancock. **Narrative of.** Austin, TX: Cook; 1936. [$125.00]

Hunter, Thomas Lomax. **Columns from the Cavalier.** Richmond: Dietz; 1935. [$8.50]

Hunter, William S. Jr. **Hunter's Panoramic Guide from Niagara Falls to Quebec.** Montreal; Boston: Dawson; Jewett; 1857. [$100.00]

Huntington, Bill. **Both Feet in the Stirrups.** [Billings?, MT: s.n.]; 1959. [$45.00]

Huntington, Elijah Baldwin. **History of Stamford, Connecticut.** Stamford: The Author; 1868. [$85.00]

Huntington, George. **Robber and Hero.** Northfield, MN: Christian Way; 1895. [$65.00]

Huntley, Elizabeth Valentine. **Peninsula Pilgrimage.** Richmond: Whittet & Shepperson; 1941. [$45.00]

Huntley, George William. **Story of the Sinnamahone.** Williamsport, PA: Williamsport Printing & Binding; 1936. [$50.00]

Hurd, Duane Hamilton. **History of Merrimack and Belknap Counties, New Hampshire.** Philadelphia: Lewis; 1885. [$120.00]

Hurd, Duane Hamilton. **History of Worcester County, Massachusetts.** Philadelphia: Lewis; 1889. 2 v. [$150.00]

Hurlbut, Henry Higgins. **Chicago Antiquities.** Chicago: The Author; 1881. [$50.00]

Hurn, Ethel Alice. **Wisconsin Women in the War between the States.** Madison: Wisconsin History Commission; 1911. [$27.00]

Husband, Joseph. **Year in a Coal-Mine.** Boston, NY: Houghton Mifflin; 1911. [$15.00]

Hutcheson, Harold. **Tench Coxe.** Baltimore: Hopkins; 1938. [some pencilled notes, $17.50]

Hutcheson, Joseph Chappell. **We March but We Remember.** Houston: Jones; 1941. [$55.00]

Hutchings, J. M. **In the Heart of the Sierras.** Oakland, CA: Pacific; 1886. [$350.00]

Hutchings, J. M. **Scenes of Wonder and Curiosity in California.** San Francisco: Hutchings & Rosenfield; 1860. [$375.00]

Hutchins, Robert Maynard. **The Higher Learning in America.** New Haven; London: Yale UP; Oxford UP; 1936. [$15.00]

Hutchins, Thomas. **An Historical Narrative and Topographical Description of Louisiana and West Florida.** Philadelphia: The Author; 1784. [rebound, $2500.00]

Hutchinson, Cecil Alan. **Frontier Settlement in Mexican California.** New Haven: Yale UP; 1969. [$50.00]

Hutchinson, Clinton Carter. **Resources of Kansas.** Topeka: The Author; 1871. [with folding map, $225.00]

Hutchinson, William. **The Spirit of Masonry.** NY: Collins; 1800. [hinges mended, $85.00]

Hutchinson, William Henry. **California.** Palo Alto: American West; 1969. [1st issue, dj repaired, $20.00]

Hutchinson, William Henry. **Whiskey Jim and a Kid Named Billie.** Clarendon, TX: Clarendon; 1967. [$25.00]

Hutchison, Bruce. **The Fraser.** NY: Rinehart; 1950. [$13.00]

Hutchison, Isobel Wylie. **North to the Rime-Ringed Sun.** NY: Hillman-Curl; 1937. [$17.50]

Hutchison, John Russell. **Reminiscences, Sketches and Addresses.** Houston: Cushing; 1874. [$175.00]

Hutt, Frank Walcott. **History of Bristol County, Massachusetts.** NY, Chicago: Lewis; 1924. 3 v. [$100.00]

Hyatt, Harry Middleton. **Folk-Lore from Adams County, Illinois.** NY: Hyatt Foundation; 1935. [$35.00]

Hyde, Edmund Morris. **The Lehigh University.** South Bethlehem, PA: [s.n.]; 1896. [$20.00]

Hyde, George E. **Indians of the High Plains.** 1st ed. Norman: U. of Oklahoma; 1959. [$40.00]

Hyde, George E. **Indians of the Woodlands.** 1st ed. Norman: U. of Oklahoma; 1962. [$25.00]

Hyde, George E. **Pawnee Indians.** Denver: U. of Denver; 1951. [$45.00]

Hyde, George E. **A Sioux Chronicle.** 1st ed. Norman: U. of Oklahoma; 1956. [$25.00] [$30.00]

Hyde, George E. **Spotted Tail's Folk.** Norman: U. of Oklahoma; 1961. [fine in dj, $45.00]

Hyer, Julien Capers. **Land of Beginning Again.** Atlanta: Tupper & Love; 1952. [fine, $25.00]

Hyman, Mac. **No Time for Sergeants.** NY: Random; 1954. [$8.50] [$15.00]

Ichihashi, Yamato. **Japanese Immigration.** San Francisco: Marshall; 1915. [spine faded, $30.00]

Ichihashi, Yamato. **Japanese in the United States.** Stanford; London: Stanford UP; Oxford UP; 1932. [$30.00]

Ickes, Anna. **Mesa Land.** Boston, NY: Houghton Mifflin; 1933. [$20.00]

Ickes, Harold L. **Autobiography of a Curmudgeon.** NY: Reynal & Hitchcock; 1943. [signed, $17.50]

Ickis, Alonzo Ferdinand. **Bloody Trails along the Rio Grande.** limited ed. Denver: Old West; 1958. [signed by editor, $125.00]

Illinois in 1837. Philadelphia: Mitchell; 1837. [$275.00]

Imhoff, Alexander Jesse. **Life of Rev. Morris Officer, A.M.** Dayton, OH: United Brethren; 1876. [$85.00]

Imlay, Gilbert. **A Description of the Western Territory of North America.** Dublin: Jones; 1793. [$500.00]

Imlay, Gilbert. **Topographical Description of the Western Territory of North America.** 3rd ed. London: Debrett; 1797. [$2000.00]

Immigrants' Guide to Minnesota in 1856. St. Anthony, [MN?]; NY: Wales; Ivison & Phinney; 1856. [$450.00] [lacks map, $125.00]

Importance of the British Plantations in America. see, Hall, Fayrer.

Imray, James. **Sailing Directions for the West Coast of North America.** London: Imray; 1853. [$250.00]

Indiana Historical Society. **Walam Olum or Red Score.** Indianapolis: Indiana Historical Society; 1954. [$75.00]

Ingersoll, Charles Jared. **Discourse Concerning the Influence of America on the Mind.** Philadelphia: Small; 1823. [$15.00]

Ingersoll, Charles Jared. **Historical Sketch of the Second War between the United States of America and Great Britain.** Philadelphia: Lea and Blanchard; 1849. [$55.00]

Ingersoll, Ernest. **The Crest of the Continent.** Chicago: Donnelley; 1885. [$45.00] [$45.00]

Ingersoll, Lurton Dunham. **History of the War Department of the United States.** Washington: Mohun; 1879. [$35.00]

Ingham, George Thomas. **Digging Gold among the Rockies.** Philadelphia: Edgewood; 1882. [x-lib., paper brittle, $35.00]

Ingham, Harvey. **Northern Border Brigade.** [Des Moines?: s.n.; 1926?]. [presentation, $100.00]

Ingham, Mary Bigelow James. **Women of Cleveland and Their Work.** Cleveland: Ingham; 1893. [$45.00] [$30.00]

Inglehart, Fanny Chambers Gooch. **The Boy Captive of the Texas Mier Expedition.** San Antonio: Wood; 1909. [presentation, $85.00]

Inglehart, Fanny Chambers Gooch. **Face to Face with the Mexicans.** NY: Fords, Howard, & Hulbert; 1887. [$150.00]

Ingraham, Joseph Holt. **Marie, or, The Fugitive!** Boston: Yankee Office; 1845. [waterstained, $125.00]

Ingraham, Joseph Holt. **Neal Nelson.** Boston: Williams; 1845. [front wrap missing. $60.00]

Ingraham, Joseph Holt. **The South-West.** NY: Harper; 1835. 2 v. [x-lib., $200.00]

Ingraham, Joseph Holt. **The Sunny South.** Philadelphia: Evans; 1860. [$85.00]

Ingraham. Prentiss. **Land of Legendary Lore.** Easton, MD: Gazette; 1898. [$65.00]

Ingram, J. S. **The Centennial Exposition, Described and Illustrated.** Philadelphia: Hubbard; 1876. [$20.00] [$50.00]

Ingram, John H. **Edgar Allan Poe.** London: Hogg; 1880. 2 v. [$300.00]

Inman, Henry. **The Great Salt Lake Trail.** NY: Macmillan; 1898. [very x-lib., spine taped, $12.50] [$100.00]

Inman, Henry. **The Old Santa Fe Trail.** NY: Macmillan; 1897. [x-lib., $125.00] [$150.00]

Innis, Harold Adams. **Peter Pond.** Toronto: Irwin and Gordon; 1930. [$95.00, Canadian]

International Polar Expedition, 1882-1883. **Report of the International Polar Expedition to Point Barrow, Alaska.** Washington: USGPO; 1885. [$150.00]

Ireland, James. **Life of.** Winchester, VA: Foster; 1819. [some dampstains, $75.00]

Irving, John Treat. **Indian Sketches Taken during an Expedition to the Pawnee Tribes, 1833.** Norman: U. of Oklahoma; 1955. [$25.00]

Irving, Theodore. **The Conquest of Florida by Hernando de Soto.** Philadelphia: Carey, Lea & Blanchard; 1835. 2 v. [$150.00]

Irving, Washington. **Adventures of Captain Bonneville, U.S.A.** Norman: U. of Oklahoma; 1961. [$25.00]

Irving, Washington. **The Alhambra.** London: Colburn and Bentley; 1832. 2 v. [$175.00]

Irving, Washington. **Astoria.** 1st ed. Philadelphia: Carey, Lea, & Blanchard; 1836. 2 v. [$250.00] [1st state, $450.00] [map in vol. 1 missing, $250.00] [$200.00] [rebound, $150.00] [$500.00]

Irving, Washington. **Chronicle of the Conquest of Granada.** Philadelphia: Carey, Lea & Carey; 1829. 2 v. [$200.00]

Irving, Washington. **History of New York.** NY: Inskeep & Bradford; 1809. 2 v. [map in facs., $650.00]

Irving, Washington. **History of the Life and Voyages of Christopher Columbus.** London: Murray; 1828. 4 v. [spine very worn, $150.00] [1838 NY ed., lacks map, in 3 vols., $100.00]

Irving, Washington. **Life of George Washington.** 1st ed. NY: Putnam; 1859. 5 v. [$225.00]

Irving, Washington. **The Rocky Mountains.** 1st American ed. Philadelphia: Carey, Lea, & Blanchard; 1837. 2 v. [lacks maps, rebound, $75.00]

Irving, Washington. **Salmagundi.** NY: Longworth; 1807-08. 2 v. [$280.00] [1824 London ed. in one vol., $35.00]

Irving, Washington. **Sketch Book of Geoffrey Crayon.** NY: Van Winkle; 1819-1820. 7 pts. in 1 v. [$150.00]

Irving, Washington. **A Tour on the Prairies.** Philadelphia: Carey, Lea & Blanchard; 1835. [rear hinge split, $125.00] [1835 London ed., $125.00; $150.00]

Irving, Washington. **Voyages and Discoveries of the Companions of Columbus.** London: Murray; 1831. [$40.00]

Irving, Washington. **Washington Irving and the House of Murray.** 1st ed. Knoxville: U. of Tennessee; 1969. [$17.50]

Irving, Washington. **Western Journals of.** 1st ed. Norman: U. of Oklahoma; 1944. [$15.00]

Irwin, Marjorie Felice. **The Negro in Charlottesville and Albemarle County.** Charlottesville: U. of Virginia; 1929. [$35.00]

Irwin, Ray Watkins. **Diplomatic Relations of the United States with the Barbary Powers.** Chapel Hill: U. of North Carolina; 1931. [bumped, sunned, $20.00]

Irwin, Richard Bache. **History of the Nineteenth Army Corps.** NY: Putnam; 1892. [$100.00]

Ise, John. **Sod and Stubble.** NY: Wilson-Erickson; 1936. [$40.00]

Iselin, Columbus O'Donnell. **Log of the Schooner Chance.** NY: Gilliss; 1927. [$85.00]

Isely, Bliss. **Early Days in Kansas.** Wichita, KS: Eagle; 1927. [$8.00]

Ives, Joseph C. **Report upon the Colorado River.** see, United States. Army. Corps of Engineers.

Ives, Martin V. B. **Through the Adirondacks in Eighteen Days.** NY: Wynkoop Hallenbeck Crawford; 1899. [$75.00]

Ivey, Joseph Benjamin. **My Memoirs.** Greensboro, NC: Piedmont; 1940. [signed, bumped, rubbed, boards warped, $35.00]

Jack, Ellen Elliott. **Fate of a Fairy.** Chicago: Donohue; 1910. [$45.00]

Jackson, Alice Fanny. **Three Hundred Years American.** Madison: State Historical Society of Wisconsin; 1951. [$12.50] [$20.00]

Jackson, Alonzo C. **Conquest of California.** [s.l.]: Priv. Print.; 1953. [$25.00]

Jackson, Andrew. **Messages.** Concord, NH: Brown; 1837. [$135.00]

Jackson, Andrew. **The Statesmanship of Andrew Jackson.** NY: Tandy-Thomas; 1909. [$45.00]

Jackson, Donald Dean. **Custer's Gold.** New Haven: Yale UP; 1966. [$17.50]

Jackson, Francis. **A History of the Early Settlement of Newton County of Middlesex, Massachusetts.** Boston: Stacy and Richardson; 1854. [spine chipped and repaired, $45.00]

Jackson, Frederick George. **A Thousand Days in the Arctic.** NY, London: Harper; 1899. [$125.00]

Jackson, George. **Sixty Years in Texas.** 2nd ed. Dallas: Wilkinson; 1908. [inscribed, $285.00]

Jackson, Halliday. **Civilization of the Indian Natives.** Philadelphia; NY: Gould; Hopper; 1830. [publisher's presentation, $125.00]

Jackson, Helen Hunt. **A Century of Dishonor.** new enl. ed. Boston: Roberts; 1887, c1885. [$35.00]

Jackson, Helen Hunt. **Glimpses of California and the Missions.** Boston: Little, Brown; 1914. [cover rubbed, $25.00]

Jackson, Helen Hunt. **Hetty's Strange History.** Boston: Roberts; 1877. [$125.00]

Jackson, Helen Hunt. **Ramona.** Boston: Roberts; 1884. [1st printing, $175.00]

Jackson, Isaac Rand. **Life of William Henry Harrison.** Philadelphia: Sherman; 1840. [$75.00] [1840 Marshall issue, 3rd?, hinges weak, spotted, $90.00]

Jackson, Isaac Rand. **Sketch of the Life and Public Services of William Henry Harrison.** NY: Harper; 1836. [first printing, $85.00]

Jackson, John. **Brief Memoir of.** Philadelphia: [s.n.]; 1856. [$65.00]

Jackson, Joseph. **Development of American Architecture, 1783-1830.** Philadelphia: McKay; 1926. [$22.50]

Jackson, Joseph Henry. **Anybody's Gold.** NY, London: Appleton-Century; 1941. [$30.00]

Jackson, Joseph Henry. **Bad Company.** 1st ed. NY: Harcourt, Brace; 1949. [$40.00]

Jackson, Joseph Henry. **Gold Rush Album.** NY: Scribner; 1949. [$40.00] [$25.00]

Jackson, Joseph Henry. **Tintypes in Gold.** 1st ed. NY: Macmillan; 1939. [$40.00]

Jackson, Mary E. **Topeka Pen and Camera Sketches.** Topeka, KS: Crane; 1890. [$25.00]

Jackson, Percival E. **The Wisdom of the Supreme Court.** 1st ed. Norman: U. of Oklahoma; 1962. [$30.00]

Jackson, Ralph Semmes. **Home on the Double Bayou.** Austin: U. of Texas; 1961. [$35.00]

Jackson, Robert. **Treatise on the Fever of Jamaica.** Philadelphia: Campbell; 1795. [$375.00]

Jackson, Thomas W. **From Rhode Island to Texas.** Chicago: Jackson; 1912. [$35.00]

Jackson, W. Turrentine. **Treasure Hill.** Tucson: U. of Arizona; 1963. [1st printing, $20.00]

Jackson, William Henry. **Picture Maker of the Old West.** NY: Scribner; 1947. [$75.00]

Jackson, William Henry. **Time Exposure.** NY: Putnam; 1940. [$40.00]

Jacobs, Bela. **Memoir of.** Boston: Gould, Kendall & Lincoln; 1837. [spine ends frayed, lacks front endpaper, $125.00]

Jacobs, Bruce. **Heroes of the Army.** 1st ed. NY: Norton; 1956. [spine faded, $15.00]

Jacobs, Henry Eyster. **The German Emigration to America, 1709-1740.** Lancaster, PA: Pennsylvania-German Society; 1898. [$60.00]

Jacobs, Michael. **Notes on the Rebel Invasion of Maryland and Pennsylvania and the Battle of Gettysburg.** Philadelphia: Lippincott; 1864. [map loose, $65.00] [$40.00]

Jacobs, Orange. **Memoirs of.** Seattle: Lowman & Hanford; 1908. [inscribed, $100.00]

Jacobson, Pauline. **City of the Golden 'Fifties.** Berkeley, Los Angeles: U. of California; 1941. [$20.00]

Jahns, Patricia. **Frontier World of Doc Holliday.** NY: Hastings; 1957. [$27.50]

Jahns, Patricia. **Violent Years.** NY: Hastings; 1962. [$25.00]

James, Ahlee. **Tewa Firelight Tales.** NY: Longmans, Green; 1927. [$45.00]

James, Arthur Edwin. **Chester County Clocks and Their Makers.** 1st ed. West Chester, PA: Chester County Hist. Soc.; 1947. [$125.00]

James, Arthur Wilson. **Virginia's Social Awakening.** Richmond: Garrett and Massie; 1939. [$15.00]

James, Bushrod Washington. **Alaskana; or, Alaska in Descriptive and Legendary Poems.** Philadelphia: Porter & Coates; 1892. [$20.00]

James, Edgar. **The Allen Outlaws.** Baltimore: Phoenix; 1912. [$50.00]

James, Edwin. **Account of an Expedition from Pittsburgh to the Rocky Mountains.** London: Longman, etc.; 1823. 3 v. [rebacked, $2000.00] [1823 Philadelphia ed. in 2 vols., elegantly rebound, $4000.00]

James, Frank Cyril. **Growth of Chicago Banks.** NY, London: Harper; 1938. 2 v. [$35.00]

James, George Wharton. **California, Romantic and Beautiful.** Boston: Page; 1914. [$30.00]

James, George Wharton. **In & around the Grand Canyon.** rev. ed. Boston: Little, Brown; 1911. [$35.00]

James, George Wharton. **In and out of the Old Missions of California.** Boston: Little, Brown; 1905. [$20.00]

James, George Wharton. **Indian Blankets and Their Makers.** 1st ed. Chicago: McClurg; 1914. [$200.00]

James, George Wharton. **Lake of the Sky.** Pasadena, CA: James; 1915. [$50.00]

James, George Wharton. **Travelers' Handbook to Southern California.** Pasadena, CA: James; 1904. [$12.50]

James, George Wharton. **Utah, the Land of Blossoming Valleys.** Boston: Page; 1922. [1st printing, $65.00]

James, George Wharton. **Wonders of the Colorado Desert.** Boston: Little, Brown; 1907. 2 v. [$200.00]

James, Henry. **Charles W. Eliot.** Boston, NY: Houghton Mifflin; 1930. 2 v. [$30.00]

James, Henry. **Daisy Miller.** Leipzig: Tauchnitz; 1879. [$25.00]

James, Henry. **English Hours.** Cambridge: Riverside; 1905. [front hinge cracked, $30.00]

James, Henry. **The Finer Grain.** Leipzig: Tauchnitz; 1910. [front hinge cracked, $30.00]

James, Henry. **Italian Hours.** Boston, NY: Houghton Mifflin; 1909. [$50.00]

James, Henry. **The Portrait of a Lady.** 1st American ed. Boston, NY: Houghton Mifflin; 1882. [x-lib., badly worn, $25.00]

James, Henry. **The Sacred Fount.** 1st ed. NY: Scribner; 1901. [$17.50]

James, Henry. **Transatlantic Sketches.** 1st ed. Boston: Osgood; 1875. [first binding, $225.00]

James, James Alton. **Life of George Rogers Clark.** Chicago: U. of Chicago; 1928. [$25.00]

James, Jesse. **Jesse James, My Father.** Cleveland: Buckeye; 1906. [$37.50]

James, John. **My Experience with Indians.** Austin: Gammel's; 1925. [$27.50]

James, Marquis. **Andrew Jackson, the Border Captain.** Indianapolis: Bobbs-Merrill; 1933. [$15.00]

James, Marquis. **The Cherokee Strip.** NY: Viking; 1945. [signed, $14.00]

James, Marquis. **Mr. Garner of Texas.** Indianapolis: Bobbs-Merrill; 1939. [$50.00]

James, Marquis. **The Raven: A Biography of Sam Houston.** 1st ed. Indianapolis: Bobbs-Merrill; 1929. [1st printing, $50.00] [later printing, $20.00]

James, Reese Davis. **Old Drury of Philadelphia.** Philadelphia; London: U. of Pennsylvania; Oxford UP; 1932. [$50.00]

James, Will. **All in the Day's Riding.** NY, London: Scribner; 1933. [$25.00] [1945 Cleveland ed., $10.00]

James, Will. **The American Cowboy.** NY: Scribner; 1942. [$35.00]

James, Will. **Big-Enough.** NY, London: Scribner; 1931. [$37.50]

James, Will. **Cow Country.** NY, London: Scribner; 1927. [$45.00]

James, Will. **Cowboy in the Making.** NY, London: Scribner; 1937. [$45.00]

James, Will. **The Dark Horse.** NY, London: Scribner; 1939. [$32.50]

James, Will. **The Drifting Cowboy.** NY, London: Scribner; 1925. [$65.00]

James, Will. **Flint Spears.** NY: Scribner; 1938. [$35.00]

James, Will. **Home Ranch.** NY, London: Scribner; 1935. [$45.00] [1948 Cleveland ed., $10.00]

James, Will. **In the Saddle with Uncle Bill.** NY, London: Scribner; 1935. [$45.00]

James, Will. **Lone Cowboy: My Life Story.** NY: Scribner; 1930. [$50.00]

James, Will. **Look-See with Uncle Bill.** NY: Scribner; 1938. [$32.50]

James, Will. **Scorpion.** NY: Scribner; 1936. [spine loose, $32.50]

James, Will. **Sun Up.** NY, London: Scribner; 1931. [$45.00]

James, Will. **The Three Mustangeers.** NY, London: Scribner; 1933. [$50.00]

James, Will. **Will James' Book of Cowboy Stories.** NY: Scribner; 1951. [$45.00]

James, Will. **The Will James Cowboy Book.** NY: Scribner; 1938. [$20.00]

James, Will. **Young Cowboy.** NY: Scribner; 1935. [$20.00]

James, Will S. **Cow-Boy Life in Texas.** Chicago: Donohue, Henneberry; 1893. [fine, $275.00] [$225.00]

James, William. **A Full and Correct Account of the Chief Naval Occurrences of the Late War between Great Britain and the United States of America.** London: Egerton; 1817. [$485.00] [1818 London ed. in two vols., spines worn, $350.00]

Jameson, Anna Brownell. **Winter Studies and Summer Rambles in Canada.** Toronto: Nelson; 1944, c1943. [$10.00]

Jameson, Henry B. **Heroes by the Dozen.** 1st, Kansas centennial ed. Abilene: Shadinger-Wilson; 1961. [$25.00]

Jameson, J. Franklin. **Narratives of New Netherland, 1609-1664.** NY: Scribner; 1909. [$25.00]

Jamison, James Carson. **With Walker in Nicaragua.** Columbia, MO: Stephens; 1909. [$250.00] [$225.00]

Janes, Edward C. **A Boy and His Gun.** NY: Barnes; 1951. [$25.00]

Janney, Samuel Macpherson. **The Last of the Lenape' and Other Poems.** Boston: Perkins & Mavin; 1839. [$100.00]

Janson, Charles William. **The Stranger in America.** London: Cundee; 1807. [$700.00] [elegantly rebound, $850.00] [1935 Press of the Pioneers ed., $37.50]

Janson, Florence Edith. **The Background of Swedish Immigration, 1840-1930.** Chicago: U. of Chicago; 1931. [$30.00]

Janvier, Thomas Allibone. **The Aztec Treasure-House.** NY: Harper; 1890. [$50.00]

Jaques, Florence Page. **As Far as the Yukon.** NY: Harper; 1951. [$25.00]

Jaques, Florence Page. **Canadian Spring.** NY: Harper; 1947. [$25.00]

Jaques, Florence Page. **Snowshoe Country.** Minneapolis: U. of Minnesota; 1944. [$15.00]

Jarchow, Merrill E. **Earth Brought Forth.** St. Paul: Minnesota Hist. Soc.; 1949. [$12.50]

Jardine, L. J. **Letter from Pennsylvania to a Friend in England.** Bath: Cruttwell; 1795. [unbound, $750.00]

Jarman, Rufus. **A Bed for the Night.** 1st ed. NY: Harper; 1952. [$17.50]

Jarrell, Randall. **A Sad Heart at the Supermarket.** 1st ed. NY: Atheneum; 1962. [$25.00]

Jarvis, Lucy Cushing. **Sketches of Church Life in Colonial Connecticut.** New Haven: Tuttle, Morehouse & Taylor; 1902. [rebound, $30.00]

Jay, Charles W. **My New Home in Northern Michigan.** Trenton, NJ: Sharp; 1874. [$35.00]

Jay, John. **Correspondence and Public Papers of.** NY, London: Putnam; 1890-1893. 4 v. [$200.00]

Jay, William. **Life of John Jay.** NY: Harper; 1833. 2 v. [$35.00]

Jay, William. **Review of the Causes and Consequences of the Mexican War.** 3rd ed. Boston; Philadelphia; NY: Mussey; Hunt; Dodd; 1849. [$85.00]

Jay, William. **A View of the Action of the Federal Government, in Behalf of Slavery.** NY: Taylor; 1839. [$135.00]

Jeffers, Robinson. **Be Angry at the Sun.** NY: Random; 1941. [dj chipped, $45.00]

Jeffers, Robinson. **Cawdor.** 1st trade ed. NY: Liveright; 1928. [dj chipped and rubbed, $50.00]

Jeffers, Robinson. **Descent to the Dead.** limited, signed ed. NY: Random; 1931. [$350.00]

Jeffers, Robinson. **The Double Axe.** 1st ed. NY: Random; 1948. [dj torn, $50.00]

Jeffers, Robinson. **Give Your Heart to the Hawks.** 1st ed. NY: Random; 1933. [spine sunned and frayed, $25.00]

Jeffers, Robinson. **Selected Poetry of.** NY: Random; 1959. [$16.00]

Jeffers, Robinson. **Themes in My Poems.** San Francisco: Book Club of California; 1956. [$200.00]

Jefferson, Joseph. **Autobiography of.** London; NY: Unwin; Century; 1890. [$75.00]

Jefferson, Thomas. **Complete Anas of Thomas Jefferson.** NY: Round Table; 1903. [$45.00]

Jefferson, Thomas. **Correspondence between Thomas Jefferson and Pierre Samuel du Pont de Nemours, 1798-1817.** Boston, NY: Houghton Mifflin; 1930. [$35.00]

Jefferson, Thomas. **Documents Relating to the Purchase & Exploration of Louisiana.** Boston: Houghton Mifflin; 1904. [$175.00]

Jefferson, Thomas. **A Jefferson Profile.** NY: Day; 1956. [$12.50]

Jefferson, Thomas. **Jefferson's Notes, on the State of Virginia; with the Appendixes--Complete.** Baltimore: Pechin; 1800. [$500.00]

Jefferson, Thomas. **Observations sur la Virginie.** Paris: Barrois; 1786. [$3200.00]

Jefferson, Thomas. **Thomas Jefferson's Garden Book, 1766-1824.** Philadelphia: American Philosophical Society; 1944. [$30.00]

Jefferson, Thomas. **Writings of.** Washington: Taylor & Maury; 1853-54. 9 v. [$350.00]

Jefferys, Thomas. **Natural and Civil History of the French Dominions in North and South America.** London: Jefferys; 1760. 2 pt. in 1 v. [$7500.00]

Jeffrey, William Hartley. **Richmond Prisons 1861-1862.** St. Johnsbury, VT: Republican; 1893. [$40.00] [$60.00]

Jeffreys, Raymond John. **Fabulous "Dutch" Zellers.** Columbus, OH: Capitol College; 1948. [$12.50]

Jencks, E. N. **A Plea for Polygamy.** NY: Panurge; 1929. [$45.00]

Jenkins, Charles Francis. **Button Gwinnett.** 1st ed. Garden City: Doubleday, Page; 1926. [$85.00]

Jenkins, James Gilbert. **Life and Confessions of.** Napa City, CA: Allen and Wood; 1864. [$285.00]

Jenkins, John Stilwell. **James Knox Polk, and a History of His Administration.** Auburn, Buffalo: Beardsley; 1850. [$85.00] [1854 New Orleans ed., $85.00]

Jenkins, John Stilwell. **Life of Silas Wright.** Auburn, NY: Alden & Markham; 1847. [$45.00]

Jenkins, Minnie. **Girl from Williamsburg.** Richmond: Dietz; 1951. [dj worn, $25.00]

Jenkins, Stephen. **Greatest Street in the World.** NY: Putnam; 1911. [$27.50]

Jenkins, William Sumner. **Pro-Slavery Thought in the Old South.** Chapel Hill: U. of North Carolina; 1935. [$40.00]

Jenkinson, Isaac. **Aaron Burr; His Personal and Political Relations with Thomas Jefferson and Alexander Hamilton.** Cleveland: Clark; 1902. [$45.00]

Jenkinson, Michael. **Ghost Towns of New Mexico.** 1st ed. Albuquerque: U. of New Mexico; 1967. [$20.00]

Jenness, Diamond. **Indians of Canada.** 3rd ed. Ottawa: Cloutier; 1955. [$20.00] [1963 Duhamel ed, $27.00]

Jennewein, John Leonard. **Calamity Jane of the Western Trails.** Huron, SD: Dakota Books; 1953. [$50.00] [$45.00]

Jenney, Walter Proctor. **The Mineral Wealth, Climate and Rain-Fall, and Natural Resources of the Black Hills of Dakota.** Washington: USGPO; 1876. [wrappers detached, $150.00]

Jennings, Alphonso J. **Through the Shadows with O. Henry.** NY: Fly; 1921. [lacks front endpaper, spine cocked, $15.00] [$25.00]

Jennings, Louis John. **Eighty Years of Republican Government in the United States.** London: Murray; 1868. [$50.00]

Jennings, Napoleon Augustus. **A Texas Ranger.** NY: Scribner; 1899. [spine darkened, $425.00] [1930 Southwest ed., $85.00]

Jennings, Walter Wilson. **Transylvania, Pioneer University of the West.** NY: Pageant; 1955. [bumped, rubbed, mildewed, $25.00]

Jensen, Jens Marinus. **History of Provo, Utah.** Provo: The Author; 1924. [$75.00]

Jensen, Merrill. **The New Nation.** 1st ed. NY: Vintage; 1950. [$15.00]

Jernegan, Marcus Wilson. **Laboring and Dependent Classes in Colonial America.** Chicago: U. of Chicago; 1931. [$30.00]

Jerome, Chauncey. **History of the American Clock Business for the Past Sixty Years.** New Haven: Dayton; 1860. [$150.00]

Jessye, Eva A. **My Spirituals.** NY: Robbins-Engel; 1927. [chipped dj, $30.00]

Jesuits. Letters from Missions (North America). **Jesuit Relations and Allied Documents.** NY: Boni; 1925. [dj worn, $37.50]

Jewett, Charles. **Speeches, Poems, and Miscellaneous Writings.** Boston: Jewett; 1849. [$50.00]

Jewett, Sarah Orne. **The Tory Lover.** Boston, NY: Houghton Mifflin; 1901. [1st printing, $95.00]

Jewitt, John Rodgers. **Narrative of the Adventures and Sufferings of.** Ithaca, NY: Andrus, Gauntlett; 1851. [$125.00]

Joel, Joseph A. **Rifle Shots and Bugle Notes.** NY: Grand Army Gazette; 1884, c1883. [shaken, stained, $25.00]

Johannsen, Albert. **The House of Beadle and Adams and Its Dime and Nickle Novels.** 1st. Norman: U. of Oklahoma; 1950. 3 v. [lacks supplement vol. 3, $125.00]

Johns, Henry T. **Life with the Forty-Ninth Massachusetts Volunteers.** Pittsfield: The Author; 1864. [x-lib., $75.00] [$85.00] [2nd ed., 1890, $50.00]

Johns, John. **Memoir of the Life of the Right Rev. William Meade.** Baltimore: Innes; 1867. [$45.00]

Johnson, Adam Rankin. **The Partisan Rangers of the Confederate States Army.** Louisville, KY: Fetter; 1904. [$300.00]

Johnson, Amandus. **The Instruction for Johan Printz, Governor of New Sweden.** Philadelphia: Swedish Colonial Society; 1930. [$30.00]

Johnson, Amandus. **Swedish Contributions to American Freedom.** Philadelphia: Swedish Colonial Foundation; 1953-57. 2 v. [$65.00]

Johnson, Amandus. **The Swedish Settlements on the Delaware.** Philadelphia; NY: U. of Pennsylvania; Appleton; 1911. 2 v. [$150.00]

Johnson, Andrew. **The Great Impeachment and Trial of Andrew Johnson.** Philadelphia: Peterson; 1868. [$65.00]

Johnson, Andrew. **Speeches of.** Boston: Little, Brown; 1865. [$30.00]

Johnson, Andrew. **Trial of Andrew Johnson.** Washington: USGPO; 1868. 3 v. [spine ends and corners chipped, $100.00]

Johnson, Brita Elizabeth. **Maher-Shalal-Hash-Baz; or, Rural Life in Old Virginia.** Claremont, VA: Olson; 1923. [covers spotted, $12.50]

Johnson, Charles Britten. **Letters from the British Settlement in Pennsylvania.** Philadelphia; London: Hall; Miller; 1819. [$500.00] [lacks map, $200.00]

Johnson, Clifton. **Highways and Byways of the Rocky Mountains.** NY, London: Macmillan; 1910. [$25.00]

Johnson, E. S. **American Military Biography.** see, title.

Johnson, Edward. **Wonder-Working Providence of Sions Saviour in New England.** limited ed. Andover, MA: Draper; 1867. [$150.00]

Johnson, Emory Richard. **American Railway Transportation.** 2nd ed. NY, London: Appleton; 1910. [$15.00]

Johnson, Francis White. **History of Texas and Texans.** Chicago, NY: American Hist. Soc.; 1914. 5 v. [$485.00] [x-lib., rebound, $325.00]

Johnson, Frederick H. **Guide to Niagara Falls and Its Scenery.** Philadelphia: Childs; 1864. [$75.00]

Johnson, George. **All Red Line.** Ottawa: Hope; 1903. [$50.00, Canadian]

Johnson, Gerald White. **Roosevelt: Dictator or Democrat?** NY, London: Harper; 1941. [$12.50]

Johnson, Guion Griffis. **Ante-Bellum North Carolina.** Chapel Hill: U. of North Carolina; 1937. [in dj, $100.00]

Johnson, Homer Uri. **From Dixie to Canada.** 2nd ed. Orwell, OH: Johnson; 1896. [vol. 1 all published, $50.00]

Johnson, Hugh S. **The Blue Eagle, from Egg to Earth.** 1st ed. Garden City: Doubleday, Doran; 1935. [x-lib., $10.00]

Johnson, Jack. **Jack Johnson in the Ring and Out.** Chicago: National Sports; 1927. [$45.00]

Johnson, James Weldon. **Book of American Negro Spirituals.** NY: Viking; 1925. [$40.00]

Johnson, James Weldon. **Negro Americans, What Now?** NY: Viking; 1934. [$25.00]

Johnson, Jane Snodgrass. **History of Lake County with Biographies.** [Waukegan?, IL: s.n.]; 1939. [$20.00]

Johnson, John. **Orderly Book of Sir John Johnson during the Oriskany Campaign.** Albany, NY: Munsell; 1882. [$275.00] [$200.00]

Johnson, John Lipscomb. **The University Memorial.** Baltimore: Turnbull; 1871. [rebound, $65.00]

Johnson, Joseph. **Traditions and Reminiscences Chiefly of the American Revolution in the South.** Charleston, SC: Walker & James; 1851. [$250.00]

Johnson, Laurence Ayres. **Over the Counter and on the Shelf.** NY: Bonanza; 1961. [$12.50]

Johnson, Lewis Franklin. **Famous Kentucky Tragedies and Trials.** Cleveland: Banks-Baldwin; 1943. [$75.00]

Johnson, Lorenzo Dow. **The Spirit of Roger Williams.** Boston: Cassady and March; 1839. [$50.00]

Johnson, Malcolm Malone. **Crime on the Labor Front.** NY: McGraw-Hill; 1950. [$20.00]

Johnson, Oliver. **William Lloyd Garrison and His Times.** Boston; NY: Russell; Drew; 1880. [$30.00]

Johnson, Overton. **Route across the Rocky Mountains.** Princeton: Princeton UP; 1932. [$25.00]

Johnson, Reverdy. **Remarks on Popular Sovereignty.** Baltimore: Murphy; 1859. [$50.00]

Johnson, Richard W. **Memoir of Maj. Gen. George H. Thomas.** Philadelphia: Lippincott; 1881. [$75.00]

Johnson, Robert G. **Historical Account of the First Settlement of Salem, in West Jersey.** Philadelphia: Rogers; 1839. [$75.00]

Johnson, Robert Underwood. **Battles and Leaders of the Civil War.** NY: Century; 1884-1887. 4 v. in 8. [worn, torn, hinges weak, $125.00] [1956 Yoseloff ed., $75.00] [1956 Castle reprint, box split, $47.50]

Johnson, Rossiter. **Campfire and Battlefield.** NY: Bryan, Taylor; 1894. [$50.00] [binding worn $45.00]

Johnson, Sam Houston. **My Brother, Lyndon.** 1st ed. NY: Cowles; 1970. [dj scuffed, $20.00]

Johnson, Stanley Currie. **History of Emigration from the United Kingdom to North America.** London: Routledge; 1913. [$40.00]

Johnson, Theodore Taylor. **Sights in the Gold Region, and Scenes by the Way.** 1st ed. NY: Baker and Scribner; 1849. [spine worn, $175.00] [$325.00]

Johnson, Virginia Weisel. **The Unregimented General.** Boston: Houghton Mifflin; 1962. [$25.00]

Johnson, Walter C. **The South and Its Newspapers, 1903-1953.** Chattanooga: Southern Newspaper Publishers Assn.; 1954. [$17.50]

Johnson, Warren Barlow. **From the Pacific to the Atlantic.** Webster, MA: Cort; 1887. [$75.00] [$50.00]

Johnson, William Cost. **Speech of William Cost Johnson on Resolutions Which He Had Offered Proposing to Appropriate Public Land for Educational Purposes.** Washington: Gales and Seaton; 1838. [$45.00]

Johnson, William Henry. **French Pathfinders in North America.** Boston: Little, Brown; 1919. [$17.50]

Johnson, Willis Ernest. **South Dakota; a Republic of Friends.** Pierre: Capital; 1911. [worn, $35.00]

Johnson, Willis Fletcher. **History of the Johnstown Flood.** [s.l.]: Edgewood; 1889. [spine chipped, $10.00]

Johnson, Willis Fletcher. **Life of Sitting Bull and History of the Indian War of 1890-91.** Philadelphia: Edgewood; 1891. [$45.00] [$50.00]

Johnson, Willis Fletcher. **Life of Wm. Techumseh Sherman.** Philadelphia: Hubbard; 1891. [browned, $17.50] [1891 Edgewood imprint, $25.00]

Johnston, Abraham Robinson. **Marching with the Army of the West, 1846-1848.** Glendale, CA: Clark; 1936. [$125.00]

Johnston, Bernice Eastman. **California's Gabrielino Indians.** Los Angeles: Southwest Museum; 1962. [$30.00]

Johnston, Charles. **Narrative of the Incidents Attending the Capture, Detention, and Ransom of.** NY: Harper; 1827. [binding worn, endpapers missing, $275.00] [$180.00] [rebound, stained, $150.00] [hinges cracking, $385.00]

Johnston, Charles Haven Ladd. **Famous Scouts.** Boston: Page; 1910. [$25.00]

Johnston, David E. **History of Middle New River Settlements and Contiguous Territory.** Huntington, WV: Standard; 1906. [$90.00] [$100.00]

Johnston, George. **History of Cecil County, Maryland.** Elkton, MD: The Author; 1881. [map detached, $100.00]

Johnston, Hank. **Railroads of the Yosemite Valley.** 1st ed. Long Beach, CA: Johnston-Howe; 1963. [$25.00]

Johnston, Harry V. **My Home on the Range.** Saint Paul: Webb; 1942. [$30.00]

Johnston, Henry Phelps. **Nathan Hale, 1776.** NY: De Vinne; 1901. [$50.00]

Johnston, Henry Phelps. **The Storming of Stony Point on the Hudson, Midnight, July 15, 1779.** NY: White; 1900. [$35.00]

Johnston, Henry Phelps. **The Yorktown Campaign and the Surrender of Cornwallis, 1781.** NY: Harper; 1881. [$30.00] [$45.00]

Johnston, Joseph Eggleston. **Narrative of Military Operations.** NY: Appleton; 1874. [x-lib., $55.00] [$90.00]

Johnston, Josiah Stoddard. **Speech of Mr. Johnston, of Louisiana: The Resolution of Mr. Foot, of Connecticut, Relative to the Public Lands, Being under Consideration.** Washington: Gales & Seaton; 1830. [$15.00]

Johnston, Margaret H. **In Acadia.** New Orleans: Hansell; 1893. [$12.50]

Johnston, William Graham. **Experiences of a Forty-Niner.** Pittsburgh: [s.n.]; 1892. [with folding map, $850.00]

Johnston, William Graham. **Life and Reminiscences from Birth to Manhood.** Pittsburgh: Knickerbocker; 1901. [$65.00]

Johnston, William Graham. **Overland to California.** Oakland: Biobooks; 1948. [$55.00]

Johnston, William Preston. **Johnstons of Salisbury.** New Orleans: Graham; 1897. [$45.00]

Johnston, William Preston. **Life of Gen. Albert Sidney Johnston.** NY: Appleton; 1878. [$125.00]

Jolly, Ellen Ryan. **Nuns of the Battlefield.** Providence, RI: Visitor; 1927. [lacks front endpaper, $15.00]

Jones, Abner Dumont. **Illinois and the West.** Boston; Philadelphia: Weeks, Jordan; Marshall; 1838. [$200.00]

Jones, Alexander. **Cymry of '76.** NY: Sheldon, Lamport; 1855. [rebound, $50.00]

Jones, Alice Johnson. **In Dover on the Charles.** Newport, RI: Milne; 1906. [$25.00]

Jones, Anson. **Memoranda and Official Correspondence Relating to the Republic of Texas.** NY: Appleton; 1859. [$485.00] [$590.00]

Jones, Archer. **Confederate Strategy from Shiloh to Vicksburg.** Baton Rouge: Louisiana State UP; 1961. [x-lib., $20.00]

Jones, Arthur Edward. **Old Huronia.** [Toronto?: s.n.]; 1908. [wraps worn, $35.00]

Jones, Buehring H. **Sunny Land.** Baltimore: Innes; 1868. [half morocco, $225.00]

Jones, Charles Colcock. **Antiquities of the Southern Indians Particularly of the Georgia Tribes.** NY: Appleton; 1873. [$225.00]

Jones, Charles Colcock. **Dead Towns of Georgia.** Savannah: Morning News; 1878. [$250.00]

Jones, Charles Colcock. **Georgians during the War between the States.** Augusta: Chronicle; 1889. [$25.00]

Jones, Charles Colcock. **Indian Remains in Southern Georgia.** Savannah: Cooper; 1859. [presentation, $150.00]

Jones, Charles Henry. **History of the Campaign for the Conquest of Canada in 1776.** Philadelphia: Porter & Coates; 1882, c1881. [$34.00]

Jones, Charles Jesse. **Buffalo Jones' Forty Years of Adventure.** Topeka, KS: Crane; 1899. [$125.00]

Jones, Charles Sheridan. **Truth about the Mormons.** London: Rider; 1920. [$45.00]

Jones, Daniel Webster. **Forty Years among the Indians.** Salt Lake City: Juvenile Instructor Office; 1890. [$150.00]

Jones, David. **A Journal of Two Visits Made to Some Nations of Indians on the West Side of the River Ohio, in the Years 1772 and 1773.** NY: Sabin; 1865. [rebound, $65.00]

Jones, Electa F. **Stockbridge, Past and Present.** Springfield, MA: Bowles; 1854. [$175.00]

Jones, Evan Rowland. **The Emigrant's Friend.** rev. ed. London: Tyne; 1881. [$75.00] [$125.00]

Jones, Evan Rowland. **Four Years in the Army of the Potomac.** London: Tyne; 1881. [$150.00]

Jones, Evan Rowland. **Lincoln, Stanton and Grant.** London; NY: Warne; Scribner, Welford and Armstrong; 1875. [$65.00]

Jones, Fayette Alexander. **Old Mining Camps of New Mexico, 1854-1904.** Santa Fe: Stagecoach; 1964. [$45.00]

Jones, George Roberts. **Joseph Russell Jones.** Chicago: [s.n.]: 1964. [$15.00]

Jones, Howard Mumford. **America and French Culture, 1750-1848.** Chapel Hill; London: U. of North Carolina; Oxford UP; 1927. [$35.00]

Jones, Howard Mumford. **Life of Moses Coit Tyler.** Ann Arbor, MI: U. of Michigan; 1933. [$15.00]

Jones, Idwal. **High Bonnet.** NY: Prentice Hall; 1945. [inscribed, $40.00]

Jones, Idwal. **Vines in the Sun.** NY: Morrow; 1949. [$20.00]

Jones, J. B. **A Rebel War Clerk's Diary at the Confederate States Capital.** Philadelphia: Lippincott; 1866. 2 v. [bindings rubbed, $250.00]

Jones, James Sawyer. **Life of Andrew Johnson.** Greeneville, TN: East Tennessee; 1901. [title page loose, cover spotted, $22.50]

Jones, Jenkin Lloyd. **An Artilleryman's Diary.** Madison: Wisconsin Hist. Comm.; 1914. [$75.00]

Jones, John Paul. **John Paul Jones in Russia.** Garden City: Doubleday, Page; 1927. [$35.00]

Jones, John Paul. **Life and Correspondence of.** NY: Fanshaw; 1830. [$125.00]

Jones, John Price. **America Entangled: The Secret Plotting of German Spies in the United States.** NY: Laut; 1917. [$17.50]

Jones, John William. **Army of Northern Virginia Memorial Volume.** Richmond: Randolph & English; 1880. [$125.00]

Jones, John William. **Christ in the Camp.** Richmond: Johnson; 1887. [$37.50]

Jones, Joseph Seawell. **Defence of the Revolutionary History of the State of North Carolina.** Boston: Bowen; 1834. [very worn, water and mildew stained, $35.00]

Jones, Justin. **The Nun of St. Ursula.** 1st ed. Boston: Gleason; 1845. [$135.00]

Jones, Katharine M. **Heroines of Dixie.** lst ed. Indianapolis: Bobbs-Merrill; 1955. [$10.00] [signed, $20.00]

Jones, Katharine M. **The Plantation South.** 1st ed. Indianapolis: Bobbs-Merrill; 1957. [$22.50]

Jones, Katharine M. **When Sherman Came.** Indianapolis: Bobbs-Merrill; 1964. [$47.50]

Jones, Lance George Edward. **The Jeanes Teacher in the United States, 1908-1933.** Chapel Hill: U. of North Carolina; 1937. [mildew, $25.00]

Jones, LeRoi. see, Baraka, Imamu Amiri.

Jones, Louis Thomas. **Aboriginal American Oratory.** Los Angeles: Southwest Museum; 1965. [$25.00]

Jones, Louis Thomas. **Quakers of Iowa.** Iowa City: State Hist. Soc.; 1914. [$37.50]

Jones, Nelson Edwards. **Squirrel Hunters of Ohio.** Cincinnati: Clarke; 1898. [$85.00]

Jones, Pomroy. **Annals and Recollections of Oneida County.** Rome, NY: The Author; 1851. [$125.00]

Jones, Robert Huhn. **The Civil War in the Northwest.** 1st ed. Norman: U. of Oklahoma; 1960. [$20.00] [$25.00]

Jones, Rufus Matthew. **The Quakers in the American Colonies.** London: Macmillan; 1923, c1911. [$50.00]

Jones, Samuel. **The Siege of Charleston.** NY: Neale; 1911. [$175.00]

Jones, Uriah James. **History of the Early Settlement of the Juniata Valley.** Harrisburg, PA: Harrisburg Pub. Co.; 1889. [$45.00]

Jones, Uriah James. **Simon Girty.** Harrisburgh, PA: Aurand; 1931. [$45.00]

Jones, Virgil Carrington. **The Hatfields and McCoys.** 1st ed. Chapel Hill: U. of North Carolina; 1948; [$32.50]

Jones, Virgil Carrington. **Ranger Mosby.** Chapel Hill: U. of North Carolina; 1944. [1st printing, $45.00] [later printings?, $22.50; $25.00]

Jones, Walter Burgwyn. **Confederate War Poems.** Montgomery, AL: [s.n.]; 1959. [$13.50]

Jones, William Frank. **Experiences of a Deputy U. S. Marshall of the Indian Territory.** Tulsa: [s.n.]; 1937. [mended, $45.00]

Jones, Winfield. **Knights of the Ku Klux Klan.** NY: Tocsin; 1941. [$75.00]

Jones, Winfield. **Story of the Ku Klux Klan.** Washington: American Newspaper Syndicate; 1921. [$60.00]

Jordan, David Starr. **Blood of the Nation.** 1st ed. Boston: American Unitarian Assn.; 1902. [$90.00]

Jordan, David Starr. **The Days of a Man.** Yonkers-on-Hudson, NY: World; 1922. 2 v. [$100.00]

Jordan, George Racey. **From Major Jordan's Diaries.** 1st ed. NY: Harcourt, Brace; 1952. [$12.50]

Jordan, John. **Serious Actual Dangers of Foreigners and Foreign Commerce, in the Mexican States.** Philadelphia: Lafourcade; 1826. [$275.00]

Jordan, John Woolf. **Genealogical and Personal History of Beaver County, Pennsylvania.** NY: Lewis; 1914. 2 v. [rebound, $125.00]

Jordan, John Woolf. **Genealogical and Personal History of Fayette County, Pennsylvania.** NY: Lewis; 1912. 3 v. [vol. 1 lacks flyleaf, $175.00] [rebound, $125.00]

Jordan, William George. **Feodor Vladimir Larrovitch; an Appreciation of His Life and Works.** NY: Authors Club; 1918. [labels silverfished, $45.00]

Jordon, Thomas. **Campaigns of Lieut. Gen. N. B. Forrest, and of Forrest's Cavalry.** New Orleans, NY: Blelock; 1868. [rebound in grey cloth, $200.00]

Joseph, Alice. **The Desert People.** Chicago: U. of Chicago; 1949. [$30.00]

Josephson, Hannah. **Golden Threads.** NY: Duell, Sloan and Pearce; 1949. [frayed dj, $20.00]

Josephy, Alvin M. **The Patriot Chiefs.** NY: Viking; 1961. [4th printing, $15.00]

Josephy, Alvin M. **Red Power.** NY: American Heritage Press; 1971. [$17.50]

Josselyn, John. **Account of Two Voyages to New-England.** London: Widdows; 1674. [$5000.00]

Joughin, Louis. **The Legacy of Sacco and Vanzetti.** NY: Harcourt, Brace; 1948. [$17.50]

Joyce, John Alexander. **A Checkered Life.** Chicago: Rounds; 1883. [x-lib., $25.00]

Judd, Laura Fish. **Honolulu.** Honolulu: Star-Bulletin; 1928. [corners bumped, $100.00]

Judson, Katharine Berry. **Early Days in Old Oregon.** Chicago: McClurg; 1916. [$25.00]

Judson, Katharine Berry. **Myths and Legends of the Mississippi Valley and the Great Lakes.** Chicago: McClurg; 1914. [$22.50]

Juergens, George. **Joseph Pulitzer and the New York World.** Princeton: Princeton UP; 1966. [$15.00]

Junius. **Annexation of Texas.** see, Colton, Calvin.

Justement, Louis. **New Cities for Old.** NY, London: McGraw-Hill; 1946. [dj chipped, $30.00]

Kahn, Ely Jacques. **The Big Drink.** NY: Random; 1960. [repaired dj, $35.00]

Kahn, Ely Jacques. **Ely Jacques Kahn.** 1st ed. NY; London: Whittlesey; McGraw-Hill; 193l. [$29.50]

Kahn, Ely Jacques. **The Voice.** 1st ed. NY, London: Harper; 1947. [$35.00]

Kahn, Roger. **The Battle for Morningside Heights.** NY: Morrow; 1970. [$20.00]

Kalkhorst, Anton. **House of Berendsen.** San Francisco: Nash; 1919. [top of spine missing, $75.00]

Kalm, Pehr. **Peter Kalm's Travels in North America.** NY: Wilson-Erickson; 1937. 2 v. [$100.00] [$125.00]

Kane, Harnett Thomas. **Bride of Fortune.** 1st ed. Garden City: Doubleday; 1948. [$12.50]

Kane, Harnett Thomas. **Deep Delta Country.** 1st ed. NY: Duell, Sloan & Pearce; 1944. [signed, 2nd printing, $10.00]

Kane, Harnett Thomas. **Louisiana Hayride.** NY: Morrow; 1941. [x-lib., later printing, $7.50]

Kane, Harnett Thomas. **Queen New Orleans.** NY: Morrow; 1949. [$10.00]

Kane, Harnett Thomas. **Spies for the Blue and Gray.** 1st ed. Garden City: Hanover; 1954. [$18.50]

Kane, Paul. **Wanderings of an Artist among the Indians of North America.** Toronto: Radison Society; 1925. [$75.00]

Kane, Thomas P. **Romance and Tragedy of Banking.** NY: Bankers Pub.; 1922. [one vol. issue, inscribed, $35.00]

Kaplan, Justin. **Mr. Clemens and Mark Twain.** NY: Simon and Schuster; 1966. [$12.50]

Karsner, David. **Andrew Jackson.** NY: Brentano's; 1929. [$17.50]

Karsner, David. **Silver Dollar.** NY: Covici, Friede; 1932. [bumped, $20.00] [1951 Crown reprint, $12.00]

Kauffman, Henry. **Early American Copper, Tin, and Brass.** NY: McBride; 1950. [$40.00]

Kawakami, Kiyoshi Karl. **The Real Japanese Question.** NY: Macmillan; 1921. [$40.00]

Kean, Robert Garlick Hill. **Inside the Confederate Government.** NY: Oxford UP; 1957. [$25.00]

Kearney, Belle. **A Slaveholder's Daughter.** NY: Abbey; 1900. [$35.00]

Kearney Business and Professional Women's Club. **Where the Buffalo Roamed.** Shenandoah, IA: World; 1967. [$25.00]

Keating, Paul W. **Lamps for a Brighter America.** NY: McGraw-Hill; 1954. [$15.00]

Keating, William Hypolitus. **Narrative of an Expedition to the Sources of St. Peter's River, Lake Winnepeek, Lake of the Woods . . . Performed in the Year 1823.** Philadelphia: Carey & Lea; 1824. 2 v. [some foxing, $1500.00] [rebound, $1000.00] [1825 London ed., $1000.00]

Keeler, William Frederick. **Aboard the USS Monitor: 1862.** Annapolis: U.S. Naval Institute; 1964. [$17.50]

Keep, Rosalind Amelia. **Fourscore and Ten Years: A History of Mills College.** Oakland, CA: Mills College; 1946. [signed, $17.50]

Kegley, Frederick Bittle. **Kegley's Virginia Frontier.** Roanoke: Southwest Virginia Historical Society; 1938. [$150.00]

Keighton Printing House, Phildelphia. **Delaware's Industries.** Philadelphia: Keighton; 1891. [$75.00]

Keim, De B. Randolph. **Sheridan's Troopers on the Borders.** Philadelphia: Claxton Remsen & Haffelfinger; 1870. [$150.00] [rebound, $75.00] [1891 McKay imprint, $60.00]

Keith, Charles Penrose. **Provincial Councillors of Pennsylvania.** Philadelphia: [s.n.]; 1883. [$75.00] [$100.00]

Keithley, Ralph. **Buckey O'Neill.** Caldwell, ID: Caxton; 1949. [covers faded, $40.00]

Keleher, William Aloysius. **The Fabulous Frontier.** Santa Fe: Rydal; 1945. [dj repaired and chipped, $100.00] [signed, $130.00]

Keleher, William Aloysius. **Maxwell Land Grant.** Santa Fe: Rydal; 1942. [$185.00] [1964 Argosy ed., $25.00]

Keleher, William Aloysius. **Memoirs, 1892-1969.** Santa Fe: Rydal; 1969. [$28.00]

Keleher, William Aloysius. **Violence in Lincoln County, 1869-1881.** Albuquerque: U. of New Mexico; 1957. [presentation, $65.00] [$75.00] [$45.00] [$90.00]

Kelemen, Pal. **Baroque and Rococo in Latin America.** NY: Macmillan; 1951. [$60.00]

Keller, Julius. **Inns and Outs.** NY: Putnam; 1939. [$15.00]

Kelley, Hall J. **Narrative of Events and Difficulties in the Colonization of Oregon, and the Settlement of California.** Boston: Thurston, Torry & Emerson; 1852. [3/4 blue morocco, $3000.00]

Kelley, William D. **Farmers, Mechanics, and Laborers Need Protection-Capital Can Take Care of Itself.** Washington: Rives & Bailey; 1870. [$20.00]

Kelley, William D. **Old South and the New.** NY: Putnam; 1888, c1887. [$125.00]

Kellock, Harold. **Parson Weems of the Cherry-Tree.** NY, London: Century; 1928. [$15.00]

Kellogg, John Harvey. **Plain Facts about Sexual Life.** 1st ed. Battle Creek, MI: Health Reformer; 1877. [$60.00]

Kellogg, Louise Phelps. **The British Regime in Wisconsin and the Northwest.** Madison: State Hist. Soc.; 1935. [$35.00] [presentation, $47.00] [$30.00]

Kellogg, Louise Phelps. **Frontier Advance on the Upper Ohio, 1778-1779.** Madison: State Historical Society; 1916. [$45.00]

Kellogg, Louise Phelps. **Frontier Retreat on the Upper Ohio, 1779-1781.** Madison: State Hist. Soc.; 1917. [$45.00]

Kellogg, Robert H. **Life and Death in Rebel Prisons.** Hartford, CT: Stebbins; 1865. [binding worn, $20.00] [$30.00] [$25.00]

Kelly, Alfred Hinsey. **The American Constitution.** NY: Norton; 1948. [$25.00]

Kelly, Arthur Randolph. **Physical Anthropology of a Mexican Population in Texas.** New Orleans: Middle American Research Institute, Tulane; 1947. [$45.00]

Kelly, Charles. **Holy Murder.** NY: Minton, Balch; 1934. [$90.00]

Kelly, Charles. **Miles Goodyear.** limited ed. Salt Lake City: Western; 1937. [$150.00]

Kelly, Charles. **Old Greenwood.** limited ed. Salt Lake City: Western; 1936. [$125.00] [$175.00]

Kelly, Charles. **Outlaw Trail.** Salt Lake City: The Author; 1938. [$275.00] [1959 Bonanza reprint, $30.00]

Kelly, Charles. **Salt Desert Trails.** Salt Lake City: Western; 1930. [$75.00] [$100.00]

Kelly, Fanny. **Narrative of My Captivity among the Sioux Indians.** Hartford, CT: Mutual; 1871. [shaken, $40.00]

Kelly, John Frederick. **Early Connecticut Meetinghouses.** NY: Columbia UP; 1948. 2 v. [$100.00]

Kelly, Luther Sage. **Yellowstone Kelly.** New Haven: Yale UP; 1926. [$60.00]

Kelly, Samuel. **Samuel Kelly, an Eighteenth Century Seaman.** London: Cape; 1925. [$35.00, Canadian]

Kelly, William. **Excursion to California over the Prairie, Rocky Mountains, and Great Sierra Nevada.** London: Chapman and Hall; 1851. 2 v. in 1. [$350.00]

Kelly, William. **Stroll through the Diggings of California.** Oakland: Biobooks; 1950. [$25.00]

Kelsey, D. M. **Our Pioneer Heroes and Their Daring Deeds.** Philadelphia: Scammell; 1883, c1882. [$50.00] [1893 Buckland ed., $50.00]

Kelsey, Henry. **The Kelsey Papers.** Ottawa: Acland; 1929. [$60.00] [$75.00]

Kelsey, Vera. **Red River Runs North!** 1st ed. NY: Harper; 1951. [signed, $25.00]

Kelso, Isaac. **The Stars & Bars.** Boston: Williams; 1863. [$135.00] [worn, $20.00]

Kemble, Fanny. **Journal of a Residence on a Georgian Plantation in 1838-1839.** NY: Harper; 1863. [$150.00] [1961 Knopf ed., $15.00]

Kemler, Edgar. **The Irreverent Mr. Mencken.** 1st ed. Boston: Little, Brown; 1950. [$15.00]

Kemmerer, Donald Lorenzo. **Path to Freedom.** Princeton; London: Princeton UP; Oxford UP; 1940. [$60.00]

Kemp, Ben W. **Cow Dust and Saddle Leather.** 1st ed. Norman: U. of Oklahoma; 1968. [$30.00]

Kendall, George Wilkins. **Narrative of the Texan Sante Fe Expedition.** NY: Harper; 1844. 2 v. [$650.00] [$600.00] [$875.00] [$700.00] [1845 London ed., $425.00]

Kenderdine, Thaddeus S. **A California Tramp and Later Footprints.** Newtown, PA: Globe; 1888. [$125.00] [$150.00]

Kendrick, Benjamin Burks. **The South Looks at Its Past.** Chapel Hill: U. of North Carolina; 1935. [$15.00]

Kenly, John Reese. **Memoirs of a Maryland Volunteer.** Philadelphia: Lippincott; 1873. [$125.00]

Kennan, George. **The Salton Sea.** NY: Macmillan; 1917. [$25.00]

Kennaway, John Henry. **On Sherman's Track.** London: Seeley, Jackson, and Halliday; 1867. [spine repaired, $100.00] [$125.00]

Kennedy, Captain. **Life and History of Francisco Villa.** see, title.

Kennedy, Charles E. **Fifty Years of Cleveland.** Cleveland: Weidenthal; 1925. [signed, $25.00]

Kennedy, Elijah Robinson. **The Contest for California in 1861.** Boston, NY: Houghton Mifflin; 1912. [$20.00]

Kennedy, Howard Angus. **The Book of the West.** Toronto: Ryerson; 1925. [$20.00, Canadian]

Kennedy, Jean de Chantal. **Biography of a Colonial Town, Hamilton, Bermuda, 1790-1897.** Hamilton: Bermuda Book Stores; [1961?]. [$25.00]

Kennedy, John F. **Profiles in Courage.** 1st ed. NY: Harper; 1956. [dj chipped, $65.00] [$100.00]

Kennedy, Marguerite. **My Home on the Range.** 1st ed. Boston: Little, Brown; 1951. [frayed dj, $22.50]

Kennedy, Stetson. **Palmetto Country.** 1st ed. NY: Duell, Sloan; 1942. [$10.00]

Kennedy, William Sloane. **Plan of Union.** Hudson, OH: Pentagon; 1856. [$85.00]

Kenner, Scipio A. **Utah As It Is.** Salt Lake City: Deseret News; 1904. [$85.00]

Kennerly, William Clark. **Persimmon Hill.** 1st ed. Norman: U. of Oklahoma; 1948. [chipped dj, $27.50] [$40.00]

Kenny, Daniel J. **Illustrated Cincinnati.** Cincinnati: Stevens; 1875. [$30.00]

Kenny, Michael. **Catholic Culture in Alabama.** NY: America; 1931. [$20.00]

Kent, Frank Richardson. **Story of Alexander Brown & Sons.** Baltimore: [s.n.]; 1925. [$25.00] [1950, 2nd? ed., $35.00]

Kent, Henry Brainard. **Graphic Sketches of the West.** Chicago: Donnelley; 1890. [$175.00]

Kent, Rockwell. **A Northern Christmas.** NY: American Artists Group; 1941. [$35.00]

Kenton, Edna. **Simon Kenton.** 1st ed. Garden City: Doubleday, Doran; 1930. [$30.00]

Kephart, Horace. **Our Southern Highlanders.** NY: Macmillan; 1921, c1913. [$12.50]

Ker, Henry. **Travels through the Western Interior of the United States.** Elizabethtown, NJ: The Author; 1816. [$950.00]

Kercheval, Samuel. **History of the Valley of Virginia.** 3rd ed. Woodstock, VA: Grabill; 1902. [$125.00] [1925 4th ed., $45.00]

Kerr, Hugh. **A Poetical Description of Texas.** Houston: Jones; 1936. [$45.00]

Kersey, Ralph T. **Buffalo Jones.** Garden City, KS: Elliott; 1958. [$35.00]

Kesey, Ken. **One Flew over the Cuckoo's Nest.** 1st British ed. London: Methuen; 1962. [$75.00] [$90.00]

Kesey, Ken. **Sometimes a Great Notion.** 1st ed. NY: Viking; 1964. [very good in dj, $65.00] [chipped dj, $50.00] [$60.00]

Kettell, Russell Hawes. **Pine Furniture of Early New England.** Garden City: Doubleday; 1929. [defective slipcase, $50.00]

Kettell, Samuel. **Specimens of American Poetry.** Boston: Goodrich; 1829. 3 v. [$250.00]

Keyes, Erasmus Darwin. **Fifty Years' Observations of Men and Events.** NY: Scribner; 1884. [$75.00]

Keyes, Erasmus Darwin. **From West Point to California.** Oakland: Biobooks; 1950. [$15.00]

Kibbe, Pauline R. **Latin Americans in Texas.** Albuquerque: U. of New Mexico; 1946. [presentation, $30.00]

Kibler, Lillian Adele. **Benjamin F. Perry.** Durham, NC: Duke UP; 1946. [$20.00]

Kidder, Daniel P. **Brazil and the Brazilians Portrayed in Historical and Descriptive Sketches.** Philadelphia; NY: Childs & Peterson; Sheldon, Blakeman; 1857. [rebound, $150.00] [1868 Boston 8th ed., $45.00]

Kidder, Daniel P. **Mormonism and the Mormons.** NY: Lane & Sandford; 1842. [front hinge cracked, $90.00]

Kidder, Daniel P. **Sketches of Residence and Travels in Brazil.** Philadelphia; London: Sorin & Ball; Wiley & Putnam; 1845. 2 v. [$175.00]

Kidder, Frederic. **History of the Boston Massacre, March 5, 1770.** Albany, NY: Munsell; 1870. [$65.00]

Kidder, Frederic. **History of the First New Hampshire Regiment in the War of the Revolution.** Albany, NY: Munsell; 1868. [$100.00]

Kidwell, J. H. **Silver Fleece.** NY: Avondale; 1927. [$25.00]

Kieffer, Henry Martin. **Recollections of a Drummer-Boy.** Boston; NY: Houghton Mifflin; 1888. [covers worn, $30.00]

Killikelly, Sarah H. **The History of Pittsburgh.** Pittsburgh, PA: Montgomery; 1906. [$40.00] [$65.00]

Kimball, Fiske. **Domestic Architecture of the American Colonies and of the Early Republic.** NY: Scribner; 1922. [$85.00]

Kimball, Gertrude Selwyn. **Providence in Colonial Times.** Boston, NY: Houghton Mifflin; 1912. [$37.50]

Kimball, Marie Goebel. **Jefferson: The Scene of Europe, 1784 to 1789.** NY: Coward-McCann; 1950. [$15.00]

Kimball, Marie Goebel. **Jefferson, War and Peace, 1776 to 1784.** NY: Coward-McCann; 1947. [$15.00]

Kimmel, Stanley Preston. **The Mad Booths of Maryland.** 1st ed. Indianapolis: Bobbs-Merrill; 1940. [x-lib., rear hinge weak, $12.50] [$30.00]

Kincaid, Robert Lee. **The Wilderness Road.** 1st ed. Indianapolis, NY: Bobbs-Merrill; 1947. [$25.00]

Kinchen, Oscar Arvle. **Daredevils of the Confederate Army.** Boston: Christopher; 1959. [$30.00]

Kinchion, L. Brackett. **Life and Works of Arthur Smith Jackson.** Nashville: A. M. E. Sunday School Union; 1944. [$125.00]

Kindelan, Joseph. **Trackman's Helper.** Mitchell, Dakota: Mitchell Printing; 1888. [$35.00]

King, B. A. **Faces of the Great Lakes.** San Francisco: Sierra Club; 1977. [$25.00]

King, Charles. **Campaigning with Crook.** Milwaukee: Sentinel; 1880. [$300.00]

King, Charles. **Daughter of the Sioux.** NY: Hobart; 1902. [$25.00] [1903 printing, $35.00]

King, Charles. **Laramie.** Philadelphia: Lippincott; 1889. [loose, $25.00]

King, Charles. **The True Ulysses S. Grant.** Philadelphia, London: Lippincott; 1914. [$16.00]

King, Clarence. **Mountaineering in the Sierra Nevada.** NY: Norton; 1935. [torn dj, $30.00]

King, Edward. **The Great South.** Hartford, CT: American Pub. Co.; 1875. [$150.00] [$125.00]

King, Frank Marion. **Mavericks.** 1st ed. Pasadena, CA: Trail's End; 1947. [$45.00]

King, Frank Marion. **Wranglin' the Past.** 1st rev. ed. Pasadena, CA: Trail's End; 1946. [presentation, $100.00] [$50.00]

King, Grace Elizabeth. **Creole Families of New Orleans.** NY: Macmillan; 1921. [$12.50]

King, Grace Elizabeth. **Memories of a Southern Woman of Letters.** NY: Macmillan; 1932. [$65.00]

King, Henry Melville. **Summer Visit of Three Rhode Islanders to the Massachusetts Bay in 1651.** Providence: Preston and Rounds; 1896. [$35.00]

King, James T. **War Eagle.** Lincoln: U. of Nebraska; 1963. [$30.00]

King, John Anthony. **Twenty-Four Years in the Argentine Republic.** NY, Philadelphia: Appleton; 1846. [$150.00]

King, John Henry. **Three Hundred Days in a Yankee Prison.** Atlanta: Daves; 1904. [wraps chipped, tape repairs, $137.50]

King, Martin Luther. **Stride toward Freedom.** 1st ed. NY: Harper; 1958. [dj sunned and soiled, $75.00]

King, Moses. **King's Handbook of the U.S.** see, Sweetser, M. F.

King, Moses. **Philadelphia and Notable Philadelphians.** NY: King; 1902. [rebound, $100.00]

King, Moses. **Poets' Tributes to Garfield.** Cambridge, MA: King; 1882. [$45.00]

King, Pauline. **American Mural Painting.** Boston: Noyes, Platt; 1902. [$50.00]

King, Sidney A. **Story of the Sesqui-Centennial Celebration of Pittsburgh.** Pittsburgh: Johnston Studios; 1910. [$40.00]

King, T. Butler. **California, the Wonder of the Age.** NY: Gowans; 1850. [$75.00]

King, Thomas Starr. **The White Hills.** Boston: Crosby, Nichols, Lee; 1860, c1859. [$50.00] [1864 printing, $35.00]

King, William C. **Camp-Fire Sketches and Battlefield Echoes.** Springfield, MA: King, Richardson; 1888. [2nd issue, waterstained, $17.50]

King, Willis Percival. **Stories of a Country Doctor.** rev. ed. Kansas City: Burton; 1906. [$50.00]

King's Book of Quebec. Ottawa: Mortimer; 1911. 2 v. [$50.00]

Kingsbury, Alice. **Ho! for Elf-Land!** San Francisco: Bancroft; 1878. [$50.00]

Kingsbury, Henry D. **Illustrated History of Kennebec County, Maine; 1625-1799-1892.** NY: Blake; 1892. 2 v. [rebound, $175.00]

Kingsley, Charles. **At Last; a Christmas in the West Indies.** NY: Harper; 1871. [$30.00]

Kingsley, Zephaniah. **Treatise on the Patriarchal, or Co-Operative, System of Society.** Tallahassee: [s.n.]; 1829. [2nd issue, $225.00]

Kinney, Bruce. **Mormonism; the Islam of America.** NY, Chicago: Revell; 1912. [spine darkened, $20.00]

Kinney, Jay P. **A Continent Lost--a Civilization Won; Indian Land Tenure in America.** Baltimore: Hopkins; 1937. [$27.50]

Kino, Eusebio Francisco. **Kino's Historical Memoir of Pimeria Alta.** Berkeley, CA: U. of California; 1948. 2 v. in 1. [$75.00]

Kinsley, Earle S. **Calvin Coolidge, Vermonter.** Plymouth, VT: Home Town Coolidge Club; [1924?]. [$20.00]

Kinzie, Juliette Augusta (Magill). **Wau-Bun, the "Early Day" in the North-West.** NY; Cincinnati: Derby & Jackson; Derby; 1856. [$280.00] [1932 Lakeside ed., binding scratched, $15.00]

Kip, Leonard. **California Sketches.** Albany, NY: Pease; 1850. [$1000.00]

Kip, William Ingraham. **The Early Days of My Episcopate.** NY: Whittaker; 1892. [$30.00]

Kip, William Ingraham. **The Early Jesuit Missions in North America.** London: Wiley and Putnam; 1847, c1846. 2 v. [$150.00]

Kipnis, Ira. **American Socialist Movement, 1897-1912.** NY: Columbia UP; 1952. [$30.00]

Kirk, Charles H. **History of the Fifteenth Pennsylvania Volunteer Cavalry.** Philadelphia: [s.n.]; 1906. [with pocket map, rebound, $100.00]

Kirk, H. L. **Pablo Casals.** 1st ed. NY: Holt, Rinehart and Winston; 1974. [$15.00]

Kirk, Russell. **Academic Freedom.** Chicago: Regnery; 1955. [$17.50]

Kirk, Russell. **Randolph of Roanoke.** Chicago: U. of Chicago; 1951. [scuffed, $10.00]

Kirkbride, Thomas Story. **On the Construction, Organization and General Arrangements of Hospitals for the Insane.** Philadelphia: [s.n.]; 1854. ["crisp," $375.00]

Kirker, Harold. **Bulfinch's Boston, 1787-1817.** NY: Oxford UP; 1964. [$17.50]

Kirkland, Frazor. **Reminiscenses of the Blue and Gray.** see, Devens, Richard Miller.

Kirkpatrick, Add Y. **The Early Settlers Life in Texas and the Organization of Hill County.** Hillsboro, TX: [s.n.; 1909?]. [$45.00]

Kirkpatrick, Frederick Alexander. **The Spanish Conquistadores.** London: Black; 1934. [$35.00]

Kirkpatrick, J. M. **Heroes of Battle Rock, or the Miners' Reward.** [s.l.: s.n.]; 1904. [$25.00]

Kirkpatrick, John Ervin. **Timothy Flint.** Cleveland: Clark; 1911. [$50.00] [$75.00]

Kirlin, Joseph Louis J. **Catholicity in Philadelphia.** Philadelphia: McVey; 1909. [$55.00]

Kirsten, A. **Skizzen aus den Vereinigten Staaten von Nordamerika.** 2nd ed. Leipzig: Brockhaus; 1851. [rebacked, $200.00]

Kittredge, George Lyman. **The Old Farmer and His Almanack.** Cambridge: Harvard UP; 1920, c1904. [$30.00]

Kittredge, Henry Crocker. **Mooncussers of Cape Cod.** Boston, NY: Houghton Mifflin; 1937. [covers faded, $17.50]

Kittredge, Henry Crocker. **Shipmasters of Cape Cod.** Boston, NY: Houghton Mifflin; 1935. [$35.00]

Klah, Hasteen. **Tleji or Yehbechai Myth.** Santa Fe: House of Navajo Religion; 1938. [$25.00]

Klah, Hasteen. **Wind Chant.** Santa Fe: Museuem of Navajo Ceremonial Art; 1946. [$25.00]

Klamkin, Marian. **American Patriotic and Political China.** NY: Scribner; 1973. [x-lib., $25.00]

Klauder, Charles Zeller. **College Architecture in America and Its Part in the Development of the Campus.** NY, London: Scribner; 1929. [$45.00]

Klees, Fredric. **The Pennsylvania Dutch.** NY: Macmillan; 1950. [$24.50]

Klein, Harry Martin John. **History and Customs of the Amish People.** York, PA: Maple; 1946. [$25.00]

Klein, Harry Martin John. **Lancaster County, Pennsylvania, a History.** NY, Chicago: Lewis; 1924. 4 v. [$150.00]

Klement, Frank L. **The Copperheads in the Middle West.** Chicago: U. of Chicago; 1960. [$20.00] [$16.50]

Kletke, H. **Skildringar fran Amerika.** Stockholm: Berg; 1860-61. 2 v. [$175.00]

Klinckowstrom, Axel Leonhard. **Bref om de Forenta Staterna Forfattade under en Resa till Amerika.** Stockholm: Ecksteinska; 1824. 2 v. in 1. [lacks plates, $75.00]

Kline, John Jacob. **History of the Lutheran Church in New Hanover.** New Hanover, PA: The Congregation; 1910. [$85.00]

Klingberg, Frank Joseph. **An Appraisal of the Negro in Colonial South Carolina.** Washington: Associated Pub.; 1941. [waterstained, some ink underlines, $15.00]

Kluckhohn, Clyde. **Navaho Witchcraft.** Boston: Beacon; 1944. [$20.00]

Kluckhohn, Clyde. **To the Foot of the Rainbow.** NY, London: Century; 1927. [$50.00] [$25.00]

Kmen, Henry A. **Music in New Orleans: The Formative Years, 1791-1841.** Baton Rouge: Louisiana State UP; 1966. [$17.50]

Knapp, Frances. **The Thlinkets of Southeastern Alaska.** Chicago: Stone and Kimball; 1896. [x-lib., $50.00]

Knapp, Horace S. **History of the Maumee Valley.** Toledo: Blade; 1872. [$100.00]

Knapp, Samuel Lorenzo. **Life of Aaron Burr.** NY: Wiley & Long; 1835. [frayed and stained, $60.00] [x-lib., faded and foxed, $35.00]

Knauff, Ellen Raphael. **Ellen Knauff Story.** 1st ed. NY: Norton; 1952. [frayed dj, $20.00]

Knauss, James Owen. **Social Conditions among the Pennsylvania Germans in the Eighteenth Century.** Lancaster: Pennsylvania German Soc.; 1922. [$40.00]

Knickerbocker, Hubert Renfro. **Is Tomorrow Hitler's?** NY: Reynal & Hitchcock; 1941. [$15.00]

Knight, Edgar Wallace. **Documentary History of Education in the South before 1860.** Chapel Hill: U. of North Carolina; 1949-53. 5 v. [$60.00]

Knight, James. **Founding of Churchill.** Toronto: Dent; 1932. [$70.00, Canadian]

Knight, John. **Indian Atrocities.** see, Brackenridge, Hugh Henry.

Knight, Oliver. **Following the Indian Wars.** 1st ed. Norman: U. of Oklahoma; 1960. [$30.00] [$32.50]

Knight, Oliver. **Fort Worth.** 1st ed. Norman: U. of Oklahoma; 1953. [signed, $45.00]

Knittle, Rhea Mansfield. **Early Ohio Taverns.** Ashland, OH: Priv. Print.; 1937. [$25.00]

Knower, Daniel. **Adventures of a Forty-Niner.** Albany: Weed-Parsons; 1894. [$75.00]

Knowles, Ruth Sheldon. **The Greatest Gamblers.** 1st ed. NY: McGraw-Hill; 1959. [$15.00]

Knox, Charles E. **Origin and Annals of the "Old Church on the Green."** Bloomfield, NJ: Hulin; 1901. [$20.00]

Knox, Dudley W. **The Naval Genius of George Washington.** Boston: Houghton Mifflin; 1932. [$15.00]

Knox, John. **Historical Journal of the Campaigns in North-America for the Years 1757, 1758, 1759, and 1760.** London: The Author; 1769. 2 v. [$2750.00]

Knox, John P. **Historical Account of St. Thomas, W.I.** NY: Scribner; 1852. [inscribed, $275.00]

Knox, Katharine. **The Sharples.** New Haven; London: Yale UP; Oxford UP; 1930. [$50.00]

Knox, Thomas Wallace. **Camp-Fire and Cotton-Field.** Philadelphia, Cincinnati: Jones; 1865. [$85.00]

Knox, Thomas Wallace. **Life and Work of Henry Ward Beecher.** Chicago: Haines; 1887. [x-lib., rebound, $12.50]

Kocher, Alfred Lawrence. **Shadows in Silver.** NY: Scribner; 1954. [$30.00]

Koebel, William Henry. **In Jesuit Land.** London: Paul; [1912?]. [x-lib., $35.00]

Koerner, Gustave Philipp. **Memoirs of.** Cedar Rapids, IA: Torch; 1909. 2 v. [$175.00]

Koerner, James D. **Parsons College Bubble.** NY: Basic Books; 1970. [$20.00]

Koford, Henning. **Dr. Samuel Merritt.** Oakland, CA: Kennedy; 1938. [inscribed, $20.00]

Kohl, Johann George. **History of the Discovery of the East Coast of North America, Particularly the Coast of Maine.** Portland: Maine Hist. Soc.; 1869. [$85.00]

Kohl, Johann Georg. **Reisen in Canada und durch die Staaten von New York und Pennsylvanien.** Stuttgart, Augsburg: Cotta; 1856. [$300.00]

Koiner, George W. see, Virginia. Dept. of Agriculture and Immigration.

Kolb, Ellsworth Leonardson. **Through the Grand Canyon from Wyoming to Mexico.** NY: Macmillan; 1914. [inscribed, $50.00] [1952 reissue, $12.00]

Konkle, Burton Alva. **John Motley Morehead and the Development of North Carolina.** Philadelphia: Campbell; 1922. [$45.00]

Konkle, Burton Alva. **Joseph Hopkinson.** Philadelphia; London: U. of Pennsylvania; Oxford UP; 1931. [$20.00] [$30.00]

Konkle, Burton Alva. **Life and Times of Thomas Smith, 1745-1809.** Philadelphia: Campion; 1904. [$40.00]

Konkle, Burton Alva. **Thomas Willing and the First American Financial System.** Philadelphia; London: U. of Pennsylvania; Oxford UP; 1937. [$40.00]

Koontz, Louis Knott. **Robert Dinwiddie.** Glendale, CA: Clark; 1941. [$60.00]

Korn, Bertram Wallace. **American Jewry and the Civil War.** Philadelphia: Jewish Publication Soc. of America; 1951. [$30.00]

Korson, George Gershon. **Black Rock.** 1st ed. Baltimore: Hopkins; 1960. [$17.50] [$22.00]

Korson, George Gershon. **Pennsylvania Songs and Legends.** Philadelphia: U. of Pennsylvania; 1949. [$22.50] [$20.00] [$26.00]

Koster, Henry. **Travels in Brazil.** Philadelphia: Carey; 1817. 2 v. [few marginal ink notes, foxing, $500.00]

Kouwenhoven, John Atlee. **Columbia Historical Portrait of New York.** 1st ed. Garden City: Doubleday; 1953. [$35.00]

Krafft, Michael August. **The American Distiller.** Philadelphia: Dobson; 1804. [spine crudely repaired, $375.00]

Krakel, Dean Fenton. **The Saga of Tom Horn.** 1st ed. Laramie, WY: Powder River; 1954. [1st state, $125.00]

Kraus, Michael. **History of American History.** NY: Farrar & Rinehart; 1937. [$25.00] [$15.00]

Krause, Hans. **Geschichte der Ersten Evangelisch-Lutherischen Synode von Texas.** Chicago: Im Selbst-Verlag der Synode; 1926. [$75.00]

Krehbiel, Henry Edward. **Afro-American Folksongs.** NY: Schirmer; 1914. [5th issue, x-lib., spine frayed, $20.00]

Kreidberg, Marvin A. **History of Military Mobilization in the United States Army.** Washington: Dept. of the Army; 1955. [some browning and loosening, $22.50]

Kriebel, Howard Wiegner. **Schwenkfelders in Pennsylvania.** Lancaster: Pennsylvania German Society; 1904. [$50.00]

Kroeber, Alfred Louis. **Handbook of the Indians of California.** Washington: USGPO; 1925. [$100.00] [x-lib., $65.00] [1967 Berkeley ed., $100.00]

Krotee, Walter. **Shipwrecks off the New Jersey Coast.** Philadelphia: [s.n.]; 1966. [$50.00]

Krug, Merton E. **DuBay.** 1st ed. Appleton, WI: Nelson; 1946. [signed, $15.00]

Kruger, Franz Jacob. **First Discovery of America, and Its Early Civilization.** NY: Sheldon; 1863. [$20.00]

Krutch, Joseph Wood. **Baja California and the Geography of Hope.** San Francisco: Sierra Club; 1967. [$65.00]

Kuhlman, Charles. **Gen. George A. Custer; A Lost Trail and the Gall Saga.** limited signed ed. Billings: Kuhlman; 1940; [$185.00]

Kuhlman, Charles. **Legend into History: The Custer Mystery.** 1st ed. Harrisburg: Stackpole; 1951. [with map, $125.00] [lacks map, $75.00] [1952 printing, $30.00]

Kuhns, Levi Oscar. **German and Swiss Settlements of Colonial Pennsylvania.** new ed. NY: Eaton & Mains; 1914. [$22.00] [1945 Aurand ed., $20.00]

Kulp, George Brubaker. **Families of the Wyoming Valley.** Wilkes-Barre, PA: Yordy; 1885-90. 3 v. [$275.00]

Kumlien, Ludwig. **Birds of Wisconsin.** Madison: Wisconsin Society for Ornithology; 1951. [$10.00]

Kunstler, William Moses. **The Minister and the Choir Singer.** NY: Morrow; 1964. [$12.50]

Kurtz, Benjamin Putnam. **Charles Mills Gayley.** Berkeley: U. of California; 1943. [$17.50]

Kurz, Rudolph Friedrich. **Journal of.** Washington: USGPO; 1937. [$150.00]

Kuykendall, Ivan Lee. **Ghost Riders of the Mogollon.** San Antonio: Naylor; 1954. [$450.00]

Kuykendall, Ralph S. **The Hawaiian Kingdom.** Honolulu: U. of Hawaii; 1938-67. 3 v. [vol. 1 only, $50.00]

Kyne, Peter Bernard. **Never the Twain Shall Meet.** NY: Cosmopolitan; 1923. [$17.50]

Kyne, Peter Bernard. **The Three Godfathers.** NY: Doran; 1913. [$75.00]

Kyne, Peter Bernard. **Tide of Empire.** NY: Cosmopolitan; 1928. [$40.00]

La Bree, Benjamin. **The Confederate Soldier in the Civil War, 1861-1865.** Louisville, KY: Courier-Journal; 1895. [$150.00]

La Dame, Mary. **The Filene Store.** NY: Sage; 1930. [x-lib., $15.00]

La Farge, Oliver. **The Changing Indian.** Norman: U. of Oklahoma; 1942. [$20.00] [$75.00]

La Farge, Oliver. **A Pause in the Desert.** Boston: Houghton Mifflin; 1957. [dj frayed, $20.00]

La Farge, Oliver. **Pictorial History of the American Indian.** NY: Crown; 1957, c1956. [$15.00]

La Farge, Oliver. **Santa Eulalia.** Chicago: U. of Chicago; 1947. [$45.00]

La Farge, Oliver. **Santa Fe.** Norman: U. of Oklahoma; 1959. [$20.00]

La Follette, Robert Hoath. **Eight Notches.** Albuquerque: Valliant; 1950. [$15.00]

Lackey, Vinson. **The Chouteaus and the Founding of Salina.** Tulsa, OK: Tulsa Print. Co.; 1961. [$4.00]

Lafora, Nicolas de. **Frontiers of New Spain.** Berkeley: Quivira; 1958. [x-lib., $75.00]

Lahontan, Louis Armand de Lom d'Arce baron de. **New Voyages to North-America Containing an Account of the Several Nations of That Vast Continent.** London: Bonwicke; 1703. 2 v. [rebound, $3500.00] [1735 2nd ed., $1700.00] [1905 McClurg ed., $100.00]

Lair, John. **Songs Lincoln Loved.** 1st ed. NY: Duell, Sloan, and Pearce; 1954. [$10.00]

Lake, Stuart N. **Wyatt Earp.** Boston, NY: Houghton Mifflin; 1931. [cover worn, hinges cracked, $45.00] [dj worn, $125.00] [1955 reprint, $18.00]

Lamar, Clarinda. **Life of Joseph Rucker Lamar.** NY: Putnam; 1926. [$37.50]

Lamar, Howard Roberts. **The Far Southwest, 1846-1912.** New Haven: Yale UP; 1966. [$40.00]

Lamb, Dean Ivan. **The Incurable Filibuster.** NY: Farrar & Rinehart; 1934. [$17.50]

Lamb, Roger. **Original and Authentic Journal of Occurrences during the Late American War.** Dublin: Wilkinson & Courtney; 1809. [$375.00]

Lambert, George. see, Fernandez, Nicholas.

Lambert, George Cannon. **Precious Memories.** Salt Lake City: [s.n.]; 1914. [$45.00]

Lambert, George Cannon. **Treasures in Heaven.** Salt Lake City: [s.n.]; 1914. [$35.00]

Lambert, John. **Travels through Canada, and the United States of North America.** London; Edinburgh: Cradock and Joy; Doig and Stirling; 1813. [$1100.00] [1814 2nd ed., in 2 vols., $1250.00]

Lambert, Joseph R. **Objections to the Book of Mormon and the Book of Doctrine and Covenants Answered and Refuted.** Lamoni, IA: Herald; 1894. [$35.00]

Lambert, Marcus Bachman. **Dictionary of the Non-English Words of the Pennsylvania-German Dialect.** Lancaster, PA: Pennsylvania German Society; 1924. [$36.00]

Lambourne, Alfred. **Scenic Utah.** NY: Dewing; 1891. [$250.00]

Lamon, Ward Hill. **Life of Abraham Lincoln.** Boston: Osgood; 1872. [$75.00]

Lamon, Ward Hill. **Recollections of Abraham Lincoln, 1847-1865.** 2nd ed. Washington: The Editor; 1911. [$150.00]

Lampman, Clinton Parks. **Great Western Trail.** NY: Putnam; 1939. [worn dj, $45.00]

Lamson, David Rich. **Two Years' Experience among the Shakers.** West Boylston: The Author; 1848. [x-lib., $170.00]

Lamson, Joseph. **Round Cape Horn.** Bangor: Knowles; 1878. [binding worn, x-lib., $49.50]

Lancaster, Robert Alexander. **Historic Virginia Homes and Churches.** Philadelphia: Lippincott; 1915. [$100.00] [shaken, $100.00]

Lanctot, Gustave. **Canada & the American Revolution, 1774-1783.** Cambridge: Harvard UP; 1967. [$25.00]

Landers, H. L. **The Virginia Campaign and the Blockade and Siege of Yorktown, 1781.** Washington: USGPO; 1931. [$55.00]

Landes, Ruth. **The Prairie Potawatomi.** Madison: U. of Wisconsin; 1970. [$25.00]

Landry, Stuart Omer. **Cult of Equality.** New Orleans: Pelican; 1945. [$15.00]

Lane, Allen Stanley. **Emperor Norton.** Caldwell, ID: Caxton; 1939. [$50.00]

Lane, Frederic Chapin. **Ships for Victory.** Baltimore: Hopkins; 1951. [$17.50]

Lane, John J. **History of the University of Texas.** 1st ed. Austin: Hutchings; 1891. [$45.00]

Lane, Samuel. **Journal for the Years 1739-1803.** Concord: New Hampshire Historical Society; 1937. [$30.00]

Lane, Walter Paye. **Adventures and Recollections of.** Marshall, TX: News Messenger; 1928. [$90.00]

Lane, Wheaton Joshua. **From Indian Trail to Iron Horse.** 1st ed. Princeton: Princeton UP; 1939. [$50.00]

Lang, Theodore F. **Loyal West Virginia from 1861 to 1865.** Baltimore: Deutsch; 1895. [$165.00]

Langford, Nathaniel Pitt. **Vigilante Days and Ways.** 2nd ed. NY: Merrill; 1893. 2 v. [inscribed, $150.00] [1912 Burt reprint, $20.00]

Lanier, Henry Wysham. **A Century of Banking in New York, 1822-1922.** NY: Doran; 1922. [$25.00]

Lanier, Sidney. **Letters of.** NY: Scribner; 1911. [$25.00]

Lanks, Herbert Charles. **Highway to Alaska.** NY, London: Appleton-Century; 1944. [$10.00]

Lanman, Charles. **Adventures in the Wilds of the United States and British American Provinces.** Philadelphia: Moore; 1856. 2 v. [$275.00] [$400.00]

Lanman, Charles. **Letters from the Alleghany Mountains.** NY: Putnam; 1849. [$175.00]

Lanman, Charles. **Private Life of Daniel Webster.** NY: Harper; 1852. [spine chipped, $38.00]

Lanman, James Henry. **History of Michigan.** NY: Harper; 1843. [text foxed, binding mended, $50.00]

Lanning, John Tate. **The Diplomatic History of Georgia.** Chapel Hill: U. of North Carolina; 1936. [$40.00]

Lanning, John Tate. **Spanish Missions of Georgia.** Chapel Hill: U. of North Carolina; 1935. [$85.00]

Lansdowne, J. Fenwick. **Birds of the Northern Forest.** Toronto: McClelland and Stewart; 1966. [signed, $95.00, Canadian]

Lansford, William Douglas. **Pancho Villa.** Los Angeles: Sherbourne; 1965. [$20.00]

Lapham, William Berry. **History of Rumford, Oxford County, Maine.** Augusta: Maine Farmer; 1890. [$100.00]

Lardner, Ring Wilmer. **Round Up.** NY: Scribner; 1929. [$35.00]

Lardner, Ring Wilmer. **Story of a Wonder Man.** NY: Scribner; 1927. [$15.00]

Larkin, Thomas Oliver. **Chapters in the Early Life of.** San Francisco: California Historical Society; 1939. [$30.00]

Larpenteur, August Louis. **Reminiscences and Recollections of St. Paul and Its People.** St. Paul: [s.n.]; 1898. [$45.00]

Larpenteur, Charles. **Forty Years a Fur Trader on the Upper Missouri.** NY: Harper; 1898. 2 v. [$275.00] [$250.00] [1933 Lakeside ed., $15.00]

Larrison, Earl. **Owyhee.** Caldwell, ID: Caxton; 1957. [$25.00]

Larsen, Ellouise Baker. **American Historical Views on Staffordshire China.** 1st ed. NY: Doubleday, Doran; 1939. [$95.00]

Larson, Gustive Olof. **Prelude to the Kingdom.** Francestown, NH: Jones; 1947. [$25.00]

Larson, Laurence Marcellus. **The Log Book of a Young Immigrant.** Northfield, MN: Norwegian-American Historical Association; 1939. [$20.00]

Lasky, Victor. **J. F. K.: The Man and the Myth.** NY: Macmillan; 1963. [chipped dj, $30.00]

Latham, Henry. **Black and White.** London: Macmillan; 1867. [x-lib., $60.00]

Lathrop, Amy. **Tales of Western Kansas.** Kansas City: La Rue; 1948. [$45.00]

Lathrop, Cornelia. **Black Rock.** New Haven: Tuttle, Morehouse & Taylor; 1930. [$45.00]

Lathrop, Elise L. **Early American Inns and Taverns.** NY: Tudor; 1935. [$25.00]

Lathrop, George. **Some Pioneer Recollections.** Philadelphia: Jacobs; 1927. [cover worn and fraying, $32.50]

Lathrop, John. **Discourse before the Society for "Propagating the Gospel among the Indians, and Others, in North-America."** Boston: Manning & Loring; 1804. [$125.00]

Lathrop, William Gilbert. **Brass Industry in the United States.** rev. ed. Mount Carmel, CT: Lathrop; 1926. [$25.00] [$35.00]

Latour, Arsene Lacarriere. **Historical Memoir of the War in West Florida and Louisiana in 1814-15 .** Philadelphia: Conrad; 1816. [with atlas vol., $2750.00]

Latrobe, Benjamin Henry. **Impressions Respecting New Orleans.** NY: Columbia UP; 1951. [$50.00]

Latrobe, Benjamin Henry. **Journal of.** NY: Appleton; 1905. [$90.00]

Latrobe, John H. B. **The First Steamboat Voyage on the Western Waters.** Baltimore: Murphy; 1871. [$45.00]

Latta, Estelle. **Controversial Mark Hopkins.** NY: Greenberg; 1953. [$12.50]

Laubin, Reginald. **The Indian Tipi.** Norman: U. of Oklahoma; 1957. [1st printing, $25.00]

Laude, G. A. **Kansas Shorthorns.** Iola, KS: Laude; 1920. [$30.00]

Laughlin, J. Laurence. **History of Bimetallism in the United States.** NY: Appleton; 1896. [$65.00] [$60.00]

Laughlin, Ledlie Irwin. **Pewter in America.** Boston: Houghton Mifflin; 1940. 2 v. [$225.00]

Laughlin, Ruth. **Caballeros.** NY, London: Appleton; 1931. [$30.00]

Laumer, Frank. **Massacre!** Gainesville: U. of Florida; 1968. [$25.00]

Laurens, J. Wayne. **The Crisis.** Philadelphia: Miller; 1855. [$50.00]

Laut, Agnes Christiana. **Pathfinders of the West.** NY, London: Macmillan; 1904. [$50.00]

Laut, Agnes Christiana. **Pilgrims of the Santa Fe.** NY: Stokes; 1931. [$25.00]

Lavender, David Sievert. **Bent's Fort.** Garden City: Doubleday; 1954. [frayed dj, $20.00] [$35.00] [$30.00]

Lavender, David Sievert. **One Man's West.** 1st ed. Garden City: Doubleday, Doran; 1943. [$27.50]

Law, John. **Colonial History of Vincennes.** Vincennes, IN: Harvey, Mason; 1858. [rebound, $125.00]

Lawes, Lewis Edward. **Twenty Thousand Years in Sing Sing.** NY: Long & Smith; 1932. [$22.50]

Lawrence, Alexander A. **James Moore Wayne, Southern Unionist.** Chapel Hill: U. of North Carolina; 1943. [signed, $25.00] [dj silverfished, $17.50]

Lawrence, D. H. **Mornings in Mexico.** London: Secker; 1927. [$60.00] [$75.00]

Lawrence, Joseph. **Caves Beyond.** NY: Funk & Wagnalls; 1955. [$15.00]

Lawrence, Robert Carbelle. **Here in Carolina.** Lumberton, NC: [s.n.]; 1939. [bumped, spotted & sunned, $20.00]

Lawrence, Robert Means. **New England Colonial Life.** Cambridge: Cosmos; 1927. [rebound, $25.00]

Lawson, J. Murray. **Yarmouth Past and Present.** Yarmouth, NS: Herald; 1902. [$85.00]

Lawson, John. **History of Carolina.** Raleigh: Perry; 1860. [rebound, $100.00]

Lawson, William Pinkney. **Log of a Timber Cruiser.** NY: Duffield; 1926. [$30.00]

Lawton, Mary. **A Lifetime with Mark Twain.** NY: Harcourt, Brace; 1925. [$30.00]

Lawyer, James Patterson. **History of Ohio from the Glacial Period to the Present Time.** Guernsey, OH: Lawyer; 1912. [$30.00]

Lay, Bennett. **Lives of Ellis P. Bean.** Austin: U. of Texas; 1960. [$15.00]

Le Conte, Joseph. **'Ware Sherman.** Berkeley: U. of California; 1937. [$45.00] [1938 2nd ed., $25.00]

Le Fors, Joe. **Wyoming Peace Officer.** Laramie, WY: Laramie Print.; 1953. [2nd printing, $75.00]

Le Grange, H. M. see, Cameron, Rebecca.

Le Moine, James MacPherson. **L'album du touriste.** 2nd ed. Quebec: Cote; 1872. [spine faded, $85.00]

Le Page du Pratz, Antoine. **Histoire de la Louisiane.** Paris: De Bure; 1758. 3 v. [$1500.00]

Le Sueur, Meridel. **North Star Country.** NY: Duell, Sloan & Pearce; 1945. [signed, $17.50]

Lea, J. Henry. **The Ancestry of Abraham Lincoln.** Boston, NY: Houghton Mifflin; 1909. [$135.00]

Lea, Tom. **The Brave Bulls.** 1st ed. Boston: Little, Brown; 1949. [$17.50]

Lea, Tom. **Hands of Cantu.** 1st ed. Boston: Little, Brown; 1964. [$45.00]

Lea, Tom. **The King Ranch.** Boston: Little, Brown; 1957. 2 v. [$125.00] [$125.00] [1st state, $185.00] [lacks box, $75.00]

Lea, Tom. **Wonderful Country.** Boston: Little, Brown; 1952. [$40.00]

Leach, A. J. **Early Day Stories.** Norfolk, NE: Huse; 1916. [$100.00]

Leach, A. J. **History of Antelope County, Nebraska.** Chicago: Donnelley; 1909. [$250.00]

Leacock, Stephen Butler. **Canada, the Foundation of Its Future.** 1st ed. Montreal: Priv. Print.; 1941. [slipcase frayed, $65.00]

Leakey, John. **The West That Was.** Dallas: Southern Methodist UP; 1958. [$35.00]

Leary, John Joseph. **Talks with T.R.** Boston, NY: Houghton Mifflin; 1920. [$30.00]

Leary, Peter J. **Newark, N.J. Illustrated.** Newark: Baker; 1891. [$125.00]

Lechford, Thomas. **Plain Dealing; or, News from New England.** Boston: Wiggin & Lunt; 1867. [$125.00]

Leckie, William H. **The Military Conquest of the Southern,Plains.** 1st ed. Norman: U. of Oklahoma; 1963. [$28.50]

LeConte, Emma. **When the World Ended.** NY: Oxford UP; 1957. [$22.50]

Lecouvreur, Frank. **From East Prussia to the Golden Gate.** NY, Los Angeles: Angelitia; 1906. [$50.00]

Leder, Lawrence H. **Robert Livingston, 1654-1728.** Chapel Hill: U. of North Carolina; 1961. [$22.50]

Lederer, John. **Discoveries of.** Rochester: Humphrey; 1902. [$85.00]

Lee, Alfred McClung. **Race Riot.** NY: Dryden; 1943. [$25.00]

Lee, Daniel. **Ten Years in Oregon.** NY: Collard; 1844. [$200.00]

Lee, Francis Bazley. **History of Trenton, New Jersey.** Trenton: Murphy; 1895. [$75.00]

Lee, Guy Carleton. **True History of the Civil War.** Philadelphia, London: Lippincott; 1903. [$17.50]

Lee, Hannah Farnham Sawyer. **Memoir of Pierre Toussaint.** 2nd ed. Boston: Crosby, Nichols; 1854. [$125.00]

Lee, Henry. **Memoirs of the War in the Southern Department of the United States.** new ed. London: Low & Marston; 1869. [scuffed and worn, hinges cracked, $40.00] [1870 NY ed., $27.00]

Lee, James. **Operation Lifeline: History and Development of the Naval Air Transport Service.** Chicago, NY: Ziff-Davis; 1947. [$35.00]

Lee, John Doyle. **Journals of.** Salt Lake City: Western Printing; 1938. [covers dampstained, $75.00]

Lee, Nelson. **Three Years among the Comanches.** Norman: U. of Oklahoma; 1967, c1957. [second printing, $45.00]

Lee, Richard Henry. **Letters of.** NY: Macmillan; 1911-14. 2 v. [$75.00]

Lee, Richard Henry. **Life of Arthur Lee.** Boston: Wells and Lilly; 1829. 2 v. [$225.00]

Lee, Robert Edward. **Recollections and Letters of.** Garden City: Doubleday, Page; 1924. [$40.00] [Garden City reprint, $12.50]

Lee, Robert Edward. **Wartime Papers of.** Boston: Little, Brown; 1961. [2nd printing, $20.00]

Lee, William. **A Yankee Jeffersonian.** Cambridge: Harvard UP; 1958. [$20.00]

Leech, Harper. **Armour and His Times.** NY, London: Appleton-Century; 1938. [$35.00]

Leech, Margaret. **Reveille in Washington, 1860-1865.** 1st ed. NY, London: Harper; 1941. [$15.00]

Leeper, Wesley Thurman. **Rebels Valiant.** Little Rock: Pioneer Press; 1964. [$37.50]

Lefler, Hugh Talmage. **Orange County, 1752-1952.** Chapel Hill, NC: [s.n.]; 1953. [$30.00]

Leforge, Thomas H. **Memoirs of a White Crow Indian.** NY, London: Century; 1928. [$75.00]

Left Handed. **Son of Old Man Hat.** NY: Harcourt, Brace; 1938. [$100.00] [$65.00]

Leftwich, Bill J. **Tracks along the Pecos.** [s.l.: s.n.]; 1957. [$35.00]

Leftwich, Nina. **Two Hundred Years at Muscle Shoals.** Tuscumbia, AL: [s.n.]; 1935. [presentation, $45.00]

Legard, Allayne Beaumont. **Colorado.** London: Chapman and Hall; 1872. [$325.00]

Lehmann, Herman. **Nine Years among the Indians, 1870-1879.** Austin: Von Boeckmann-Jones; 1927. [$125.00]

Lehmann, Karl. **Thomas Jefferson.** NY: Macmillan; 1947. [$7.50]

Lehmann-Haupt, Hellmut. **Bookbinding in America.** Portland, ME: Southworth-Anthoensen; 1941. [$50.00]

Leiding, Harriette Kershaw. **Charleston.** Philadelphia: Lippincott; 1931. [$15.00]

Leiding, Harriette Kershaw. **Historic Houses of South Carolina.** Philadelphia, London: Lippincott; 1921. [$85.00]

Leigh, Frances. **Ten Years on a Georgia Plantation since the War.** London: Bentley; 1883. [$85.00]

Leigh, Randolph. **American Enterprise in Europe.** Paris: Bellenard; 1945. [$12.50]

Leighton, Clare. **Sometime--Never.** NY: Macmillan; 1939. [dj silverfished and soiled, $25.00]

Leighton, Clare. **Southern Harvest.** NY: Macmillan; 1942. [signed, dj very chipped, $60.00] [dj badly chipped, $52.50, Canadian]

Leland, Charles Godfrey. **Hans Breitmann's Ballads.** Philadelphia: McKay; 1897. [$20.00]

Lemke, Walter John. **The Battle of Prairie Grove, December 7, 1862.** Fayetteville, AK: Washington County Hist. Soc.; 1952. [$25.00]

Lemmon, Ed. **Boss Cowman.** Lincoln: U. of Nebraska; 1969. [$40.00]

Leng, John. **America in 1876.** Dundee: Advertiser; 1877. [lacks half title, $125.00]

Leonard, Thomas Henry. **From Indian Trail to Electric Rail.** Atlantic Highlands, NJ: Journal; 1923. [$75.00]

Leonard, William Norris. **Railroad Consolidation under the Transportation Act of 1920.** NY: Columbia UP; 1946. [$30.00]

Leonard, Zenas. **Adventures of.** Norman: U. of Oklahoma Press; 1959. [$20.00]

Leonard, Zenas. **Narrative of the Adventures of Zenas Leonard.** Chicago: Lakeside Press; 1934. [$25.00]

Lequear, John W. **Traditions of Hunterdon.** Flemington, NJ: Moreau; 1957. [$30.00]

Lerski, Jerzy Jan. **A Polish Chapter in Jacksonian America.** Madison: U. of Wisconsin; 1958. [$12.50]

Lesesne, Thomas Petigru. **Landmarks of Charleston.** Richmond: Garrett & Massie; 1932. [$20.00]

Lesley, Susan Inches Lyman. **Memoir of the Life of Mrs. Anne Jean Lyman.** Cambridge, MA: Wilson; 1876. [$35.00]

Leslie, Anita. **The Remarkable Mr. Jerome.** NY: Holt; 1954. [$12.50]

Leslie, Charles. **New History of Jamaica.** 2nd ed. London: Hodges; 1740. [$250.00]

Leslie, Frank. **Frank Leslie's Illustrated History of the Civil War.** NY: Leslie; 1895. [$50.00]

Lester, Charles Edwards. **Life and Public Services of Charles Sumner.** NY: United States Publishing; 1874. [$35.00]

Lester, Charles Edwards. **Life and Voyages of Americus Vespucius.** NY: Baker & Scribner; 1846. [$50.00] [1858 New Haven imprint, rebound, $40.00]

Lester, Charles Edwards. **Life of Sam Houston.** NY; Boston: Derby; Phillips, Sampson; 1855. [$135.00] [2nd printing, $200.00]

Lester, Charles Edwards. **Sam Houston and His Republic.** NY: Burgess, Stringer; 1846. [inscribed, $1750.00]

Lester, John Ashby. **A Century of Philadelphia Cricket.** Philadelphia: U. of Pennsylvania; 1951. [$20.00]

Lester, John C. **Ku Klux Klan: Its Origin, Growth and Disbandment.** Nashville: Wheeler, Osborn & Duckworth; 1884. [$250.00]

Lester, Paul. **The Great Galveston Disaster.** Chicago: Kuhlman; 1900. [$15.00]

Lesure, Thomas B. **Adventures in Arizona.** San Antonio: Naylor; 1956. [$20.00]

Letts, John M. **California Illustrated.** NY: Holdredge; 1852. [$600.00]

Letts, John M. **Pictorial View of California.** NY: Bill; 1853. [with 48 plates, $500.00] [lacks some plates?, $200.00]

Leuchs, Frederick Adolph Herman. **Early German Theatre in New York, 1840-1872.** NY: Columbia UP; 1928. [$50.00]

Leupp, Francis Ellington. **The Indian and His Problem.** NY: Scribner; 1910. [x-lib., $15.00]

Levasseur, Auguste. **Lafayette in America in 1824 and 1825.** NY: White, Gallaher & White; 1829. 2 v. [$75.00]

Levens, Henry C. **History of Cooper County, Missouri.** St. Louis: Perrin & Smith; 1876. [$125.00]

Levering, Julia. **Historic Indiana.** NY, London: Putnam; 1909. [$40.00]

Levermore, Charles H. **Forerunners and Competitors of the Pilgrims and Puritans.** Brooklyn: New England Society; 1912. 2 v. [$85.00]

Levermore, Charles H. **Republic of New Haven.** Baltimore: Hopkins; 1886. [$35.00]

Levi, Carolissa. **Chippewa Indians of Yesterday and Today.** 1st ed. NY: Pageant; 1956. [$25.00]

Levine, Samuel Walter. **The Business of Pawnbroking.** NY: Halpern; 1913. [$35.00]

Levy, Babette May. **Preaching in the First Half Century of New England History.** Hartford, CT: American Society of Church History; 1945. [$25.00]

Levy, Lester S. **Grace Notes in American History.** 1st ed. Norman: U. of Oklahoma; 1967. [$45.00]

Lewis, Alfred Henry. **The Throwback.** NY: Outing; 1906. [$20.00]

Lewis, Alfred Henry. **Wolfville.** NY: Stokes; 1897. [first issue, $125.00]

Lewis, Alfred Henry. **Wolfville Days.** NY: Stokes; 1902. [$25.00]

Lewis, Anthony. **Gideon's Trumpet.** NY: Random; 1964. [2nd printing, $15.00]

Lewis, Charles Lee. **David Glasgow Farragut.** Annapolis, MD: United States Naval Institute; 1943. [$35.00]

Lewis, Claudia Louise. **Children of the Cumberland.** NY: Columbia UP; 1946. [$25.00]

Lewis, Elisha Jarrett. **The American Sportsman.** Philadelphia: Lippincott; 1857. [$150.00] [1885 ed., rubbed, rear endpapers lacking, $47.00]

Lewis, Elisha Jarrett. **Hints to Sportsmen.** Philadelphia: Lea and Blanchard; 1851. [$125.00]

Lewis, George W. **Campaigns of the 124th Regiment Ohio Volunteer Infantry.** Akron: Werner; 1894. [rebound, $150.00]

Lewis, John W. **Life, Labors, and Travels of Elder Charles Bowles.** Watertown, NY: Ingalls & Stowell's; 1852. [fine, $250.00] [$150.00]

Lewis, Lloyd. **Captain Sam Grant.** 1st ed. Boston: Little, Brown; 1950. [worn and chipped dj, $18.50] [$25.00]

Lewis, Lloyd. **Chicago, the History of Its Reputation.** NY: Harcourt, Brace; 1929. [2nd printing, $15.00]

Lewis, Lloyd. **John S. Wright.** Chicago: Prairie Farmer; 1941. [$15.00]

Lewis, Lloyd. **Sherman, Fighting Prophet.** NY: Harcourt, Brace; 1932. [$35.00]

Lewis, Matthew Gregory. **Journal of a West-India Proprietor.** London: Murray; 1834. [$285.00]

Lewis, McMillan. **Woodrow Wilson of Princeton.** Narberth, PA: Livingston; 1952. [$20.00]

Lewis, Meriwether. **History of the Expedition under the Command of Captains Lewis and Clark.** Philadelphia: Bradford and Inskeep; 1814. 2 v. [$9500.00] [1893 Harper "large paper" ed., in 4 vols., $450.00]

Lewis, Meriwether. **The Journals of Lewis and Clark.** Boston: Houghton Mifflin; 1953. [$20.00] [$25.00]

Lewis, Meriwether. **Journals of the Expedition under the Command of Capts. Lewis and Clark.** NY: Heritage; 1962. 2 v. [$47.50]

Lewis, Meriwether. **Travels of Capts. Lewis and Clark . . .** see, title.

Lewis, Meriwether. **Travels to the Source of the Missouri River and across the American Continent to the Pacific Ocean.** London: Longman, etc.; 1814. [$3500.00]

Lewis, Oscar. **Autobiography of the West.** 1st ed. NY: Holt; 1958. [signed, $25.00]

Lewis, Oscar. **The Big Four.** NY: Knopf; 1938. [$20.00] [1941 printing, $20.00]

Lewis, Oscar. **Bonanza Inn.** NY, London: Knopf; 1939. [$10.00]

Lewis, Oscar. **Here Lived the Californians.** NY: Rinehart; 1957. [signed, $35.00]

Lewis, Oscar. **High Sierra Country.** 1st ed. NY: Duell, Sloan and Pearce; 1955. [$35.00]

Lewis, Oscar. **On the Edge of the Black Waxy.** Saint Louis: Washington U.; 1948. [$15.00]

Lewis, Oscar. **The Town That Died Laughing.** 1st ed. Boston: Little, Brown; 1955. [$15.00] [signed, $25.00]

Lewis, Sinclair. **Babbitt.** 1st ed. NY: Harcourt, Brace; 1922. [1st state, spine chipped, $20.00]

Lewis, Sinclair. **Dodsworth.** 1st ed. NY: Harcourt, Brace; 1929. [$12.50] [$20.00]

Lewis, Sinclair. **The Man Who Knew Coolidge.** NY: Harcourt, Brace; 1928. [$30.00]

Lewis, Sinclair. **The Prodigal Parents.** Garden City,: Doubleday, Doran; 1938. [$15.00]

Lewis, Sinclair. **Work of Art.** 1st ed. Garden City: Doubleday, Doran; 1934. [dj repaired, $35.00]

Lewis, Tracy Hammond. **Along the Rio Grande.** NY: Lewis; 1916. [$60.00] [$45.00]

Lewis, Virgil Anson. **Story of the Louisiana Purchase.** St. Louis: Woodward & Tiernan; 1903. [$45.00]

Lewis, William. **Biographical Sketch of the Life of Sam Houston.** Dallas: Herald; 1882. [$485.00]

Lewis, Willie Newbury. **Between Sun and Sod.** Clarendon, TX: Clarendon; 1938. [2nd issue, $100.00]

Leyda, Jay. **Melville Log.** 1st ed. NY: Harcourt, Brace; 1951. 2 v. [$65.00]

Libby, Orin Grant. **The Arikara Narrative of the Campaign against the Hostile Dakotas, June, 1876.** Bismarck, ND: State Historical Society; 1920. [$125.00]

Library of Congress. Manuscript Division. **Naval Records of the American Revolution 1775-1788.** Washington: USGPO; 1906. [$150.00]

Lichtenstein, Gaston. **Thomas Jefferson as War Governor.** Richmond: Byrd; 1925. [$75.00]

Lick, David E. **Plant Names and Plant Lore among the Pennsylvania Germans.** Lancaster: Pennsylvania German Society; 1923. [$45.00]

Liddell Hart, Basil Henry. **Sherman: Soldier, Realist, American.** NY: Dodd, Mead; 1929. [x-lib., $25.00]

Lieb, Frederick George. **Baltimore Orioles.** NY: Putnam; 1955. [$15.00]

Lieber, Francis. **Letters to a Gentleman in Germany.** Philadelphia: Carey, Lea & Blanchard; 1834. [foxed, $125.00]

Lieber, Francis. **Stranger in America.** London: Bentley; 1835. 2 v. [$75.00]

Liebling, A. J. **Chicago, the Second City.** 1st ed. NY: Knopf; 1952. [$35.00]

Liebling, A. J. **The Earl of Louisiana.** NY: Simon and Schuster; 1961. [$15.00]

Lieuwen, Edwin. **Petroleum in Venezuela.** Berkeley: U. of California; 1954. [$20.00]

Life and History of Francisco Villa. Baltimore: Ottenheimer; 1916. [$55.00]

Life and Public Services of Gen. Z. Taylor. NY: Long; 1846. [$55.00]

Life and Reminiscences of Jefferson Davis. Baltimore: Woodward; 1890. [$45.00] [$25.00]

Life at Vassar. Poughkeepsie: Vassar Cooperative Bookshop; 1940. [$20.00]

Life in the West. Philadelphia, NY: American Sunday-School Union; 1851. [$35.00]

Life of General Lewis Cass. Philadelphia: Zieber; 1848. [$75.00]

Life of Major-General the Marquis de Lafayette. Easton, PA: Maroon Club of Lafayette College; 1943. [$25.00]

Lillard, Richard Gordon. **Desert Challenge.** 1st ed. NY: Knopf; 1942. [$40.00]

Lincklaen, John. **Travels in the Years 1791 and 1792 in Pennsylvania, New York and Vermont.** NY, London: Putnam; 1897. [$125.00]

The Lincoln Catechism wherein the Eccentricities & Beauties of Despotism Are Fully Set Forth. NY: Feeks; 1864. [wraps chipped, $135.00]

Lincoln, Abraham. **Abraham Lincoln: His Speeches and Writings.** Cleveland, NY: World; 1946. [$35.00]

Lincoln, Abraham. **Autobiography of.** Indianapolis: Bobbs-Merrill; 1926. [$15.00]

Lincoln, Abraham. **Conversations with Lincoln.** NY: Putnam; 1961. [$50.00]

Lincoln, Abraham. **Created Equal?** Chicago: U. of Chicago; 1958. [signed by editor, $32.00]

Lincoln, Abraham. **A House Divided against Itself Cannot Stand.** Chicago, NY: Black Cat; 1936. [one of 140 copies, $75.00]

Lincoln, Abraham. **Lincoln Letters, Hitherto Unpublished.** Providence, RI: Brown University Library; 1927. [$30.00]

Lincoln, Abraham. **Political Debates between Hon. Abraham Lincoln and Hon.Stephen A. Douglas.** Columbus: Follett, Foster; 1860. [$100.00] [1912 Putnam ed., $25.00]

Lincoln, Charles Henry. **Narratives of the Indian Wars, 1675-1699.** NY: Scribner; 1913. [$40.00]

Lincoln, Jonathan Thayer. **City of the Dinner-Pail.** Boston: Houghton Mifflin; 1909. [$30.00]

Lincoln, William. **History of Worcester.** Worcester, MA: Hersey; 1862. 2 v. in 1. [$40.00]

Lincoln, William Sever. **Life with the Thirty-Fourth Mass. Infantry in the War of the Rebellion.** Worcester: Noyes, Snow; 1879. [x-lib., $100.00]

Lindbergh, Charles A. **We.** NY, London: Putnam; 1927. [$25.00]

Linder, Usher F. **Reminiscences of the Early Bench and Bar of Illinois.** 2nd ed. Chicago: Chicago Legal News; 1879. [binding worn, $60.00]

Linderman, Frank Bird. **Lige Mounts.** NY: Scribner; 1922. [$75.00]

Lindestrom, Peter Martensson. **Geographia Americae; with an Account of the Delaware Indians.** Philadelphia: Swedish Colonial Society; 1925. [$95.00]

Lindley, Walter. **California of the South.** NY: Appleton; 1888. [spine worn, $50.00]

Lindquist, Emory Kempton. **Smoky Valley People.** Lindsborg, KS: Bethany College; 1953. [signed, $30.00]

Lindquist, Gustavus Elmer Emanuel. **Bland Nordamerikas Indianer.** Uppsala: Lindblad; 1926. [$12.50]

Lindsay, Julian Ira. **Tradition Looks Forward: The University of Vermont.** Burlington: U. of Vermont; 1954. [$25.00]

Lindsay, Vachel. **General William Booth Enters into Heaven.** 1st ed. NY: Kennerley; 1913. [fine in dj, $200.00]

Linford, Velma. **Wyoming, Frontier State.** Denver: Old West; 1947. [$35.00]

Linforth, James. **Route from Liverpool to Great Salt Lake Valley.** Los Angeles: Westernlore; [1959?]. [$85.00]

Linn, Elizabeth A. **Life and Public Services of Dr. Lewis F. Linn.** NY: Appleton; 1857. [$125.00]

Linn, John Blair. **Pennsylvania in the War of the Revolution.** Harrisburg: Hart; 1880. 2 v. [spines repaired, $90.00] [$65.00]

Linn, John Joseph. **Reminiscences of Fifty Years in Texas.** NY: Sadlier; 1883. [$400.00]

Linn, William Alexander. **Story of the Mormons.** NY: Macmillan; 1923. [$22.50]

Lipman, Jean. **American Folk Art in Wood, Metal and Stone.** NY: Pantheon; 1948. [$50.00]

Lipman, Jean. **American Folk Decoration.** NY: Oxford UP; 1951. [$40.00]

Lippard, George. **Legends of the American Revolution.** Philadelphia: Leary, Stuart; 1876. [$17.50]

Lippincott, Horace Mather. **Early Philadelphia.** Philadelphia, London: Lippincott; 1917. [$75.00]

Lippincott, Mary Shoemaker. **Life and Letters of.** Philadelphia: Pile's; 1893. [$30.00]

Lipsky, George Arthur. **John Quincy Adams, His Theory and Ideas.** NY: Crowell; 1950. [$15.00]

Littell, John. **Family Records, or, Genealogies of the First Settlers of Passaic Valley.** Feltville, NJ: Stationers' Hall; 1851. [$150.00]

Little, Arthur West. **From Harlem to the Rhine.** NY: Covici, Friede; 1936. [inscribed, $125.00; $95.00]

Little, James A. **From Kirtland to Salt Lake City.** Salt Lake City: Little; 1890. [$275.00]

Little, John Peyton. **History of Richmond.** Richmond: Dietz; 1933. [$40.00]

Littlefield, George Emery. **Early Schools and School-Books of New England.** Boston: Club of Odd Volumes; 1904. [$60.00]

Littlejohn, Elbridge Gerry. **Texas History Stories.** Richmond: Johnson; 1901. [$75.00]

Litton, Gaston. **History of Oklahoma.** NY: Lewis; 1957. 4 v. [x-lib., $70.00]

Lively, Robert. **Fiction Fights the Civil War.** Chapel Hill: U. of North Carolina; 1957. [$20.00]

Livermore, Abiel Abbot. **War with Mexico Reviewed.** Boston: American Peace Society; 1850. [x-lib., $50.00] [$40.00]

Livermore, George. **An Historical Research Respecting the Opinions of the Founders of the Republic on Negroes as Slaves, as Citizens, and as Soldiers.** 3rd ed. Boston: Williams; 1863. [wraps soiled and chipped, $25.00]

Livermore, Mary Ashton Rice. **My Story of the War.** Hartford: Worthington; 1888. [binding spotted, some foxing, $25.00] [1890 issue, $27.50]

Livermore, Mary Ashton Rice. **Story of My Life.** Hartford: Worthington; 1898. [$20.00]

Livermore, S. T. **Condensed History of Cooperstown.** Albany: Munsell; 1862. [$45.00]

Livermore, S. T. **History of Block Island.** Hartford, CT: Case, Lockwood & Brainard; 1877. [$60.00]

Livingston, Luther Samuel. **Franklin and His Press at Passy.** NY: Grolier; 1914. [$175.00]

Livingston, Walter Ross. **Responsible Government in Nova Scotia.** Iowa City: U. of Iowa; 1930. [spine faded, $30.00]

Lloyd, Everett. **Law West of the Pecos: The Story of Roy Bean.** San Antonio: Naylor; 1935. [$35.00]

Lloyd, Herbert. **Vaudeville Trails thru the West.** Chicago: [s. n.]; 1919. [$50.00]

Locke, David Ross. **Ekkoes from Kentucky.** Boston: Lee and Shepard; 1868. [$150.00]

Locke, David Ross. **Inflation at the Cross Roads.** NY: American News; 1875. [wrinkled, $95.00]

Locke, David Ross. **Swingin round the Cirkle.** Boston: Lee and Shepard; 1867. [x-lib., $15.00]

Locke, E. W. **Three Years in Camp and Hospital.** Boston: Russell; 1870. [$30.00] [$25.00]

Lockhart, John Washington. **Sixty Years on the Brazos.** limited, signed ed. Los Angeles: Dunn; 1930. [$1000.00]

Lockman, John. **Travels of the Jesuits, into Various Parts of the World.** 2nd ed. London: Piety; 1762. 2 v. [spines chipped, boards loose, $400.00]

Lockwood, Charles A. **Through Hell and Deep Water.** NY: Greenberg; 1956. [$17.50]

Lockwood, Francis Cummins. **The Apache Indians.** 1st ed. NY: Macmillan; 1938. [$85.00] [dj chipped, $65.00]

Lockwood, Francis Cummins. **Arizona Characters.** Los Angeles: Times-Mirror; 1928. [loose, $125.00]

Lockwood, Francis Cummins. **Life in Old Tucson, 1854-1864.** Tucson: Civic Committee; 1943. [$35.00]

Lockwood, Francis Cummins. **Life of Edward E. Ayer.** Chicago: McClurg; 1929. [$35.00]

Lockwood, Francis Cummins. **Pioneer Days in Arizona.** NY: Macmillian; 1932. [inscribed, $110.00]

Lockwood, Francis Cummins. **With Padre Kino on the Trail.** Tucson: U. of Arizona; 1934. [$25.00]

Lockwood, George Browning. **The New Harmony Communities.** Marion, IN: Chronicle; 1902. [x-lib., $65.00]

Lockwood, George Browning. **The New Harmony Movement.** NY: Appleton; 1905. [$27.50]

Lodge, Henry Cabot. **The Democracy of the Constitution.** NY: Scribner; 1915. [$45.00]

Lodge, Henry Cabot. **The Pilgrims of Plymouth.** Washington: USGPO; 1921. [$20.00]

Loederer, Richard A. **Voodoo Fire in Haiti.** NY: Doubleday, Doran; 1935. [$15.00]

Loehr, Rodney C. **Minnesota Farmers' Diaries.** St. Paul: MN Hist. Soc.; 1939. [$15.00]

Logan, Deborah Norris. **Memoir of Dr. George Logan of Stenton.** Philadelphia: Historical Society of Pennsylvania; 1899. [$45.00]

Logan, Herschel C. **Buckskin and Satin.** 1st ed. Harrisburg, PA: Stackpole; 1954. [$35.00]

Logan, John Alexander. **Great Conspiracy.** NY: Hart; 1886. [$20.00] [$22.00] [$35.00]

Logan, John Alexander. **Principles of the Democratic Party.** Washington: Union Republican Congressional Committee; 1868. [$25.00]

Logan, John Alexander. **The Volunteer Soldier of America.** Chicago, NY: Peale; 1887. [rebound, $30.00] [$40.00]

Logan, Mary Simmerson. **Reminiscences of a Soldier's Wife.** NY: Scribner; 1913. [$35.00] [$37.50]

Logan, Rayford Whittingham. **What the Negro Wants.** Chapel Hill: U. of North Carolina; 1944. [dj chipped and sunned, $20.00]

Lomask, Milton. **Andrew Johnson: President on Trial.** NY: Farrar, Straus; 1960. [$20.00]

Lomax, Elizabeth. **Leaves from an Old Washington Diary, 1854-1863.** 1st ed. NY: Books, Inc.; 1943. [$27.50]

Lomax, John Avery. **Adventures of a Ballad Hunter.** NY: Macmillan; 1947. [presentation, lst printing, $75.00]

Lomax, John Avery. **Songs of the Cattle Trail and Cow Camp.** 1st ed. NY: Macmillan; 1920, c1919. [$65.00]

Lomen, Carl J. **Fifty Years in Alaska.** NY: McKay; 1954. [$7.50]

London, Charmian. **Jack London.** London: Mills and Boon; 1921. 2 v. [$125.00]

London, Charmian. **Our Hawaii.** NY: Macmillan; 1917. [$90.00]

London, Jack. **The Abysmal Brute.** 1st Canadian ed. Toronto: Bell & Cockburn; 1913. [$150.00, Canadian]

London, Jack. **The Call of the Wild.** 1st ed. NY, London: Macmillan; 1903. [$250.00]

London, Jack. **The Game.** London: Heinemann; 1905. [$100.00]

London, Jack. **Jerry of the Islands.** 1st ed. NY: Macmillan; 1917. [$75.00] [$70.00]

London, Jack. **John Barleycorn.** 1st ed. NY: Century; 1913. [$65.00] [$80.00]

London, Jack. **The Little Lady of the Big House.** 1st ed. NY: Macmillan; 1916. [$65.00] [$70.00]

London, Jack. **Michael, Brother of Jerry.** 1st ed. NY: Macmillan; 1917. [$65.00]

London, Jack. **White Fang.** 1st ed. NY, London: Macmillan; 1906. [$75.00] [$80.00]

Long, Armistead Lindsay. **Memoirs of Robert E. Lee.** NY, Philadelphia: Stoddart; 1886. [$75.00]

Long, Edwin McKean. **The Union Tabernacle, or, Movable Tent-Church.** Philadelphia: Perry & McMillan; 1859. [$65.00]

Long, Harry W. **Gettysburg as the Battle Was Fought.** Gettysburg, PA: Long; 1927. [$10.00]

Long, Huey Pierce. **Every Man a King.** New Orleans: National Book Co.; 1933. [$35.00]

Long, Huey Pierce. **My First Days in the White House.** Harrisburg, PA: Telegraph; 1935. [$50.00]

Long, John. **Voyages and Travels of an Indian Interpreter and Trader.** London: The Author; 1791. [rebacked, $1500.00] [$1600.00]

Long, John Cuthbert. **Lord Jeffery Amherst.** NY: Macmillan; 1933. [$22.50] [$30.00]

Long, John Cuthbert. **Motor Camping.** NY: Dodd, Mead; 1923. [dj chipped, $50.00]

Longfellow, Henry Wadsworth. **Belfry of Burges and Other Poems.** 1st ed. Cambridge: Owen; 1846. [rebound, $150.00]

Longfellow, Henry Wadsworth. **Courtship of Miles Standish.** 1st ed. Boston: Ticknor and Fields; 1858. [1st printing, $200.00]

Longfellow, Henry Wadsworth. **The Divine Tragedy.** 1st ed. Boston: Osgood; 1871. [$10.00] [large paper issue, rear hinge cracked, $75.00]

Longfellow, Henry Wadsworth. **The Golden Legend.** Boston: Ticknor, Reed, and Fields; 1851. [1st printing, $165.00]

Longfellow, Henry Wadsworth. **Hanging of the Crane.** 1st ed. Boston: Osgood; 1875. [$35.00]

Longfellow, Henry Wadsworth. **The Seaside and the Fireside.** 1st ed. Boston: Ticknor, Reed and Fields; 1850. [special red publisher's binding, $175.00] [$150.00] [top of spine missing, $12.50]

Longfellow, Henry Wadsworth. **Skeleton in Armor.** Boston: Osgood; 1877. [$35.00]

Longfellow, Henry Wadsworth. **Song of Hiawatha.** 1st ed. Boston: Ticknor and Fields; 1855. [1st printing, spine frayed, $250.00] [2nd printing, $75.00]

Longfellow, Henry Wadsworth. **Ultima Thule.** 1st ed. Boston: Houghton Mifflin; 1880. [lacks front endpaper, $55.00]

Longfellow, Henry Wadsworth. **Voices of the Night.** Boston: Redding; 1845. [covers frayed, $85.00]

Longstreet, Augustus Baldwin. **Georgia Scenes.** 2nd ed. NY: Harper; 1845. [$85.00] [1894 Quitman, GA, imprint, $45.00]

Longstreet, James. **From Manassas to Appomattox.** Philadelphia: Lippincott; 1896. [rebound, $135.00] [1960 Indiana UP ed., $40.00]

Longstreet, Stephen. **Sportin' House.** 1st ed. Los Angeles: Sherbourne; 1965. [$20.00]

Longstreth, Thomas Morris. **The Adirondacks.** NY: Century; 1917. [$20.00]

Longstreth, Thomas Morris. **The Catskills.** NY: Century; 1918. [$15.00]

Lonn, Ella. **Reconstruction in Louisiana after 1868.** NY: Putnam; 1918. [538 page issue, $85.00]

Looker, Earle. **Colonel Roosevelt, Private Citizen.** NY, London: Revell; 1932. [$25.00]

Loomis, Noel M. **Pedro Vial and the Roads to Santa Fe.** 1st ed. Norman: U. of Oklahoma; 1967. [$35.00]

Loomis, Noel M. **The Texan-Santa Fe Pioneers.** 1st ed. Norman: U. of Oklahoma; 1958. [$35.00]

Looney, Louisa Preston. **Tennessee Sketches.** Chicago: McClurg; 1901. [$12.50]

Loos, Anita. **But Gentlemen Marry Brunettes.** NY: Boni & Liveright; 1928. [x-lib., $15.00]

Lorant, Stefan. **Lincoln: His Life in Photographs.** 1st ed. NY: Duell, Sloan and Pearce; 1941. [$55.00]

Lorant, Stefan. **The New World.** NY: Duell, Sloan & Pearce; 1946. [$25.00]

Lord, Eliot. **Comstock Mining and Miners.** Berkeley, CA: Howell-North; 1959. [$25.00]

Lord, John. **Frontier Dust.** Hartford, CT: Mitchell; 1926. [spine rubbed, $40.00]

Lord, John King. **History of Dartmouth College, 1815-1909.** Concord, NH: Rumford; 1913. [$35.00]

Lord, Priscilla Sawyer. **Folk Arts and Crafts of New England.** Radnor, PA: Chilton; 1975. [$20.00]

Lord, Walter. **A Time to Stand.** 1st ed. NY: Harper; 1961. [$25.00]

Lorz, Robert Michael. **Shadow of a Man.** [Batavia?, IL: s.n.]; 1964. [$15.00]

Loskiel, George Henry. **Extempore on a Wagon.** Lancaster, PA: Zahm; 1887. [$60.00]

Loskiel, George Henry. **Geschichte der Mission der Evangelischen Bruder unter den Indianern in Nordamerika.** Leipzig: Kummer; 1789. [$400.00]

Loskiel, George Henry. **History of the Mission of the United Brethren among the Indians in North America.** London: Brethren's Society for the Furtherance of the Gospel; 1794. [$300.00] [$375.00]

Lossing, Benson John. **The American Centenary.** Philadelphia: Porter; 1876. [$120.00]

Lossing, Benson John. **Biographical Sketches of the Signers of the Declaration of American Independence.** NY: Derby & Jackson; 1859, c1848. [$25.00]

Lossing, Benson John. **The Empire State.** Hartford, CT: American Pub. Co.; 1888. [$55.00]

Lossing, Benson John. **History of New York City.** NY: Perine; 1884. 2 v. [$150.00]

Lossing, Benson John. **History of the Civil War.** NY: War Memorial Association; 1912. [one hinge broken, $50.00] [$55.00]

Lossing, Benson John. **The Home of Washington.** Hartford, CT; Chicago: Hale; Rogers; 1870. [$20.00] [$75.00]

Lossing, Benson John. **The Hudson from the Wilderness to the Sea.** Troy, NY: Nims; 1866. [$150.00] [$100.00] [1866 Virtue & Yorston imprint, $85.00]

Lossing, Benson John. **The Pictorial Field-Book of the Revolution.** NY: Harper; 1850. 2 v. [spine faded, $175.00] [2nd printing?, in 3/4 morocco, $150.00] [1859 printing, $150.00] [1869 one vol. ed., $75.00]

Lossing, Benson John. **Vassar College and Its Founder.** NY: Alvord; 1867. [$85.00]

Lossing, Benson John. **Washington and the American Republic.** NY: Virtue & Yorston; 1870. 3 v. [$100.00]

Loughborough, John Norton. **The Great Second Advent Movement.** Nashville: Southern Publishing Assn.; 1905. [$22.50]

Louisiana Commissioner of Military Records. **Records of Louisiana Confederate Soldiers and Louisiana Confederate Commands.** New Orleans: [s.n.]; 1920. 3 v. in 4. [$240.00]

Louisiana Constitutional Convention. **Journal Officiel des Travaux de la Convention Reunie four [sic] Reviser et Amender la Constitution de l' Etat de la Louisiane.** Nouvelle Orleans: Fish; 1864. [$125.00]

Louisiana Native American Association. **Address of the Louisiana Native American Association to the Citizens of Louisiana and the Inhabitants of the United States.** New Orleans: Felt; 1839. [$85.00]

Lounsberry, Clement Augustus. **Early History of North Dakota.** Washington: Liberty; 1919. [$125.00]

Love, Paul Emilius. **Rube Burrow, the Outlaw.** Baltimore: Ottenheimer; 1908. [cover and spine torn, $65.00]

Love, Robertus. **Rise and Fall of Jesse James.** NY, London: Putnam; 1926. [$75.00]

Love, William De Loss. **Colonial History of Hartford.** limited ed. Hartford, CT: The Author; 1914. [$40.00]

Lovejoy, Joseph Cammet. **Memoir of the Rev. Elijah P. Lovejoy.** NY: Taylor; 1838. [lightly foxed, $225.00] [x-lib., $100.00]

Lovelace, Leland. **Lost Mines and Hidden Treasure.** San Antonio: Naylor; 1956. [$8.00]

Lovell, James. **Oration Delivered April 2d, 1771 at the Request of the Inhabitants of the Town of Boston.** Boston: Edes and Gill; 1771. [worn morocco, restored, $350.00]

Lowe, Percival Green. **Five Years a Dragoon.** Kansas City, MO: Hudson; 1906. [disbound, uncut, and unopened, $75.00] [$150.00] [rebound, $60.00] [1965 Oklahoma ed., $35.00]

Lowell, Edward Jackson. **The Hessians and the Other German Auxiliaries of Great Britain in the Revolutionary War.** NY: Harper; 1884. [$37.50]

Lowell, James Russell. **The Anti-Slavery Papers.** Boston: Houghton Mifflin; 1902. 2 v. [$170.00]

Lowell, James Russell. **The Cathedral.** 1st ed. Boston: Fields, Osgood; 1870. [spine sunned and chipped, $85.00]

Lowell, James Russell. **Heartsease and Rue.** 1st ed. London: Macmillan; 1888. [1st printing, $160.00]

Lowell, James Russell. **Poems.** Boston: Ticknor, Reed, and Fields; 1849. 2 v. [covers stained, $95.00]

Lowell, James Russell. **Poems (second series).** 1st ed. Cambridge; Boston: Nichols; Mussey; 1848. [endpapers missing, $30.00] [2nd state, rebacked, $125.00]

Lowell, James Russell. **Reader! Walk Up at Once.** 2nd ed. Boston: Ticknor and Fields; 1859. [x-lib., $125.00]

Lowell, James Russell. **Under the Willows, and Other Poems.** 1st ed. Boston: Fields, Osgood; 1869. [spine chewed, $15.00]

Lowell, James Russell. **Works.** standard library ed. Boston: Houghton-Mifflin; 1899-1902. 13 v. [$450.00]

Lowell, James Russell. **A Year's Life.** 1st ed. Boston: Little and Brown; 1841. [fine, $500.00]

Lowell, John. **The New-England Patriot.** Boston: Russell and Cutler; 1810. [$60.00]

Lower, Arthur Reginald Marsden. **Settlement and the Forest Frontier in Eastern Canada.** Toronto: Macmillan; 1936. [x-lib., $15.00]

Lowery, Woodbury. **Spanish Settlements within the Present Limits of the United States.** NY, London: Putnam; 1901. [$45.00]

Lowie, Robert Harry. **Indians of the Plains.** NY: McGraw-Hill; 1954. [$35.00]

Lowndes, Marie Adelaide. **Lizzie Borden.** 1st ed. NY, Toronto: Longmans, Green; 1939. [$35.00]

Lowry, Thomas. **Personal Reminiscences of Abraham Lincoln.** London: Chiswick; 1910. [signed by Beatrice Lowry, $200.00]

Loyal, C. see, Burton, Maria Amparo.

Lubbock, Alfred Basil. **The Down Easters.** Glasgow: Brown & Ferguson; 1930. [$35.00]

Lubbock, Alfred Basil. **The Nitrate Clippers.** Glascow: Brown & Ferguson; 1932. [$50.00]

Lubbock, Francis Richard. **Six Decades in Texas.** Austin: Jones; 1900. [$475.00]

Lucas, Daniel Bedinger. **Maid of Northumberland.** NY: Putnam; 1879. [$45.00]

Lucas, Netley. **Autobiography of a Crook.** NY: Dial; 1925. [$25.00]

Lucia, Ellis. **Klondike Kate.** NY: Hastings; 1962. [torn dj, $23.00]

Lucia, Ellis. **Saga of Ben Holladay.** NY: Hastings; 1959. [$20.00] [$30.00]

Luckey, John. **Life in Sing Sing State Prison.** NY: Tibbals; 1860. [missing endpapers, $40.00]

Ludlow, Noah Miller. **Dramatic Life As I Found It.** St. Louis: Jones; 1880. [$100.00]

Ludlow, William. **Report of a Reconnaissance from Carroll, Montana Territory, on the Upper Missouri, to the Yellowstone National Park.** Washington: USGPO; 1876. [$175.00]

Ludlow, William. **Report of a Reconnaissance of the Black Hills.** see, United States. Army. Corp of Engineers.

Ludlum, David McWilliams. **Social Ferment in Vermont, 1791-1850.** NY: Columbia UP; 1939. [$30.00]

Ludwig, Ella A. **History of the Harbor District of Los Angeles.** California: Historic Record Company; [1927?]. [$65.00] [$150.00]

Lueders, August. **Sixty Years in Chicago.** Chicago: Klein; 1929. [$35.00]

Luff, Joseph. **The Old Jerusalem Gospel.** Independence, MO: Luff; 1903. [$25.00]

Luhan, Mabel Dodge. **Edge of Taos Desert.** 1st ed. NY: Harcourt, Brace; 1937. [$100.00]

Luhan, Mabel Dodge. **Taos and Its Artists.** NY: Duell, Sloan and Pearce; 1947. [$175.00]

Lui, Garding. **Inside Los Angeles Chinatown.** [Los Angeles?: s.n.]; 1948. [$15.00]

Luke, L. D. **A Journey from the Atlantic to the Pacific Coast by Way of Salt Lake City.** Utica: Roberts; 1884. [$250.00]

Lumholtz, Carl. **New Trails in Mexico.** NY: Scribner; 1912. [spine chipped, $75.00]

Lumholtz, Carl. **Unknown Mexico.** NY: Scribner; 1902. 2 v. [$175.00]

Lummis, Charles Fletcher. **King of the Broncos.** NY: Scribner; 1897. [$60.00]

Lummis, Charles Fletcher. **The Land of Poco Tiempo.** NY: Scribner; 1925. [$15.00]

Lummis, Charles Fletcher. **Some Strange Corners of Our Country.** NY: Century; 1892. [$50.00] [$60.00]

Lummis, Charles Fletcher. **The Spanish Pioneers.** Chicago: McClurg; 1893. [$25.00]

Lummis, Charles Fletcher. **A Tramp across the Continent.** NY: Scribner; 1892. [$125.00]

Lumsden, James. **The Skipper Parson on the Bays & Barrens of Newfoundland.** NY: Eaton; 1905. [$12.50]

Lundin, Leonard. **Cockpit of the Revolution.** Princeton; London: Princeton UP; Oxford UP; 1940. [$65.00]

Lundy, Benjamin. **Life, Travels, and Opinions of.** Philadelphia: Parrish; 1847. [rebound, $475.00] [$1000.00]

Lundy, Benjamin. **The War in Texas.** Philadelphia: The Author; 1836. [$650.00]

Lunettes, Henry. **The American Gentleman's Guide to Politeness and Fashion.** NY: Darby & Jackson; 1863. [spine sunned, some stains, $30.00]

Lunt, Dolly Sumner. see, Burge, Dolly Sumner.

Lurie, Edward. **Louis Agassiz.** Chicago: U. of Chicago; 1960. [$25.00]

Luzerne, Frank. **The Lost City!** NY; Chicago: Wells; Parker; 1872. [$90.00]

Lydens, Z. Z. **Story of Grand Rapids.** Grand Rapids: Kregel; 1966. [$25.00]

Lyell, Charles. **Travels in North America, in the Years 1841-2.** 1st American ed. NY: Wiley and Putnam; 1845. 2 v. [$350.00]

Lyell, Charles. **Zweite Reise nach den Vereinigten Staaten von Nordamerika.** Braunschweig: Wieweg; 1851. 2 v. [$185.00]

Lyman, Chester Smith. **Around the Horn to the Sandwich Islands and California, 1845-1850.** New Haven: Yale UP; 1924. [$77.50]

Lyman, George D. **John Marsh, Pioneer.** NY: Scribner; 1930. [$30.00] [1931 Chautauqua ed., $15.00]

Lyman, George D. **The Saga of the Comstock Lode.** NY, London: Scribner; 1934. [$25.00] [$30.00]

Lynch, Anne C. **The Rhode-Island Book.** Providence; Boston: Fuller; Weeks, Jordan; 1841. [$95.00]

Lynch, Charles H. **Civil War Diary, 1862-1865.** Hartford, CT: Case, Lockwood & Brainard; 1915. [lacks front endpaper, $45.00]

Lynch, Denis Tilden. **"Boss" Tweed.** NY: Boni and Liveright; 1927. [$12.50]

Lynch, Denis Tilden. **An Epoch and a Man.** NY: Liveright; 1929. [$65.00]

Lynch, James Daniel. **The Bench and Bar of Texas.** St. Louis: Nixon-Jones; 1885. [rebound, $225.00]

Lynch, Jeremiah. **A Senator of the Fifties.** San Francisco: Robertson; 1911. [$25.00]

Lynn, Ernest. **The Blazing Horizon.** Chicago: White House; 1929. [$20.00]

Lynn, Stuart M. **New Orleans.** NY: Hastings; 1949. [$20.00]

Lyon, Elijah Wilson. **Louisiana in French Diplomacy, 1759-1804.** Norman: U. of Oklahoma; 1934. [$37.50]

Lyon, George Francis. **Brief Narrative of an Unsuccessful Attempt to Reach Repulse Bay.** London: Murray; 1825. [$400.00]

Lyon, George Francis. **Journal of a Residence and Tour in the Republic of Mexico in the Year 1826.** London: Murray; 1828. 2 v. [$285.00]

Lyon, Irving Whitall. **Colonial Furniture of New England.** limited ed. Boston, NY: Houghton Mifflin; 1924. [$125.00]

Lyon, Peter. **Eisenhower: Portrait of the Hero.** 1st ed. Boston: Little, Brown; 1974. [$25.00]

Lyons, Eugene. **Herbert Hoover.** 1st ed. Garden City: Doubleday; 1964. [$20.00]

Lyons, Eugene. **Life and Death of Sacco and Vanzetti.** NY: International; 1927. [$25.00]

Lysaght, Averil M. **Joseph Banks in Newfoundland and Labrador, 1766.** Berkeley: U. of California Press; 1971. [$35.00]

Lytle, Andrew Nelson. **Bedford Forrest and His Critter Company.** NY: Putnam; 1931. [$40.00] [4th printing, $25.00]

Maass, John. **The Gingerbread Age.** NY: Rinehart; 1957. [$25.00]

Mabie, Janet. **Neither Wealth nor Poverty.** Montpelier: Vermont Historical Society; 1944. [$20.00]

Macbride, Thomas Huston. **In Cabins and Sod-Houses.** Iowa City: State Historical Society; 1928. [worn, $12.50]

MacCurdy, George Grant. **Study of Chiriquian Antiquities.** New Haven: Yale UP; 1911. [$225.00]

Macdermott, Hugh Fairon. **Poems, Epic, Comic, and Satiric.** San Francisco: The Author; 1857. [$100.00]

Macdonald, Donald. **Diaries of.** Indianapolis: Indiana Historical Society; 1942. [$30.00]

Macdonald, Dwight. **The Ford Foundation.** NY: Reynal; 1956. [$15.00]

Macdougall, Hamilton Crawford. **Early New England Psalmody.** Brattleboro: Daye; 1940. [$35.00]

MacFadden, Harry Alexander. **Rambles in the Far West.** Hollidaysburg, PA: Standard; 1906. [$50.00]

Macfarlan, Allan A. **American Indian Legends.** Los Angeles: Limited Editions Club; 1968. [$75.00]

MacGregor, John. **British America.** Edinburgh; London: Blackwood; Cadell; 1832. 2 v. [$350.00]

MacGregor, John. **Progress of America.** London: Whittaker; 1847. 2 v. [x-lib., $250.00]

MacIntyre, William Irwin. **Colored Soldiers.** Macon, GA: Burke; 1923. [$20.00]

Mack, Effie Mona. **Mark Twain in Nevada.** 1st ed. NY, London: Scribner; 1947. [dj frayed $20.00]

Mack, Gerstle. **The Land Divided.** 1st ed. NY: Knopf; 1944. [$20.00]

Mackenzie, Alexander. **Voyages from Montreal, on the River St. Laurence, through the Continent of North America, to the Frozen and Pacific Oceans; in the Years 1789 and 1793.** London: Cadell; 1801. [some repair, $1750.00] [1922 Allerton ed., $35.00] [1927 Radison ed., $40.00]

Mackenzie, Alexander Slidell. **Life of Stephen Decatur.** Boston: Little and Brown; 1848. [$45.00]

Mackenzie, William Lyon. **Life and Times of Martin Van Buren.** Boston: Cooke; 1846. [lacks rear wrap, pages creased, $30.00]

Mackey, Albert Gallatin. **Lexicon and History of Freemasonry.** Philadelphia: McClure; 1910. [$50.00]

Mackey, Margaret Gilbert. **Early California Costumes.** Stanford; London: Stanford UP; Oxford UP; 1932. [$30.00]

Mackintosh, J. see, McIntosh, John.

Mackintosh, William Archibald. **Economic Problems of the Prairie Provinces.** Toronto: Macmillan; 1935. [x-lib., $20.00]

MacLaren, Gay. **Morally We Roll Along.** 1st ed. Boston: Little, Brown; 1938. [x-lib., $7.50]

MacLaren, Malcolm. **Rise of the Electrical Industry during the Nineteenth Century.** Princeton: Princeton UP; 1943. [$45.00]

Maclay, Edgar Stanton. **A History of American Privateers.** London: Sampson, Low, Marston; 1900. [$85.00]

Maclay, William. **Sketches of Debate in the First Senate of the United States.** Harrisburg: Hart; 1880. [$65.00]

Maclean, John. **History of the College of New Jersey.** Philadelphia: Lippincott; 1877. 2 v. [$50.00]

MacLeish, Archibald. **The American Cause.** NY: Duell, Sloan and Pearce; 1941. [$10.00]

MacLeish, Archibald. **Poems, 1924-1933.** Boston, NY: Houghton Mifflin; 1933. [$10.00]

MacLeod, Alexander Samuel. **Spirit of Hawaii.** NY, London: Harper; 1943. [$15.00]

MacMinn, Edwin. **On the Frontier with Colonel Antes.** Camden, NJ: Chew; 1900. [x-lib., $45.00]

Macomber, Benjamin. **Jewel City.** San Francisco, Tacoma: Williams; 1915. [$35.00]

Macon, Thomas Joseph. **Life Gleanings.** Richmond: Adams; 1913. [$75.00]

Macon, Thomas Joseph. **Reminiscences of the First Company of Richmond Howitzers.** Richmond: Whittey & Shepperson; [1909?]. [$125.00]

Macoun, John. **Manitoba and the Great Northwest.** London: Jack; 1883. [x-lib., $150.00]

Macpherson, James Pennington. **Life of the Right Hon. Sir John A. Macdonald.** St. John, NB: Earle; 1891. 2 v. [binding worn and chipped, $35.00]

Macy, Obed. **History of Nantucket.** Boston: Halliard, Gray; 1835. [$225.00]

Madariaga, Salvador de. **Rise of the Spanish American Empire.** NY: Macmillan; 1947. [$10.00]

Maddox, John Lee. **The Medicine Man.** NY: Macmillan; 1923. [$65.00]

Madison, Dolley (Payne) Todd. **Memoirs and Letters of.** Boston: Houghton Mifflin; 1887, c1886. [$45.00]

Madsen, Brigham D. **The Bannock of Idaho.** Caldwell, ID: Caxton; 1958. [$35.00]

Magee, James D. **Bordentown, 1682-1932.** Bordentown, NJ: Register; 1932. [$50.00]

Magoffin, Susan. **Down the Santa Fe Trail and into Mexico.** New Haven; London: Yale UP; Oxford UP; 1926. [binding worn and soiled, $37.50]

Magoun, F. Alexander. **The Frigate Constitution and Other Historic Ships.** Salem, MA: Marine Research Society; 1928. [dj chipped, $200.00]

Maguire, John Francis. **The Irish in America.** 4th ed. NY, Montreal: Sadlier; 1873. [$65.00]

Mahan, A. T. **The Interest of America in Sea Power.** Boston: Little, Brown; 1897. [$30.00]

Mahan, A. T. **Sea Power in Its Relations to the War of 1812.** London: Low, Marston; 1905. 2 v. [$125.00]

Mahan, Bruce Ellis. **Old Fort Crawford and the Frontier.** Iowa City: State Hist. Soc.; 1926. [$35.00]

Mahony, D. A. **The Prisoner of State.** NY: Carleton; 1863. [$75.00]

Mailer, Norman. **Advertisements for Myself.** NY: Putnam; 1959. [fine, $35.00]

Mailer, Norman. **Barbary Shore.** 1st ed. NY: Rinehart; 1951. [very good in dj, $125.00]

Mails, Thomas E. **Dog Soldiers, Bear Men, and Buffalo Women.** Englewood Cliffs, NJ: Prentice-Hall; 1973. [$65.00]

Maine, Floyd Shuster. **Lone Eagle, the White Sioux.** Albuquerque: U. of New Mexico; 1956. [$35.00]

Maine (District) Constitutional Convention, 1819. **Petition of a Convention of the People of the District of Maine: Praying to be Admitted into the Union.** Washington: Gales & Seaton; 1819. [$150.00]

Maine Federation of Women's Clubs. **Trail of the Maine Pioneer.** Lewiston, ME: Journal; 1916. [$35.00]

Mair, Charles. **Tecumseh, a Drama, and Canadian Poems.** Toronto: Radisson Society; 1926. [$35.00]

Mair, Charles. **Through the Mackenzie Basen.** Toronto: Briggs; 1908. [$100.00]

Maissin, Eugene. **The French in Mexico and Texas, 1838-1839.** Salado, TX: Jones; 1961. [$125.00]

Major, Howard. **Domestic Architecture of the Early American Republic, the Greek Revival.** Philadelphia, London: Lippincott; 1926. [$75.00]

Major, Mabel. **Southwest Heritage.** rev. ed. Albuquerque: U. of New Mexico; 1948. [$25.00]

Malcom, Malcolm Vartan. **The Armenians in America.** Boston, Chicago: Pilgrim; 1919. [$30.00]

Mallet, Thierry. **Glimpses of the Barren Lands.** NY: Revillon; 1930. [$17.00]

Mallison, Sam Thomas. **The Great Wildcatter.** Charleston: Education Foundation of West Virginia; 1953. [$25.00] [$15.00]

Malone, Dumas. **The Story of the Declaration of Independence.** NY: Oxford UP; 1954. [$15.00]

Maltby, William J. **Captain Jeff; or, Frontier Life in Texas with the Texas Rangers.** 2nd ed. Colorado, TX: Whipkey; 1906. [$175.00] [spine chipped, $175.00]

Manchester, Herbert. **The Diamond Match Company.** NY, Chicago: [s.n.]; 1935. [x-lib., $12.50]

Manchester, William Raymond. **A Rockefeller Family Portrait.** 1st ed. Boston: Little, Brown; 1959. [$15.00]

Mangan, John. **History of the Steam Fitters' Protective Association of Chicago.** Chicago: Steam Fitters' Protective Association; 1930. [$35.00]

Mange, Juan Mateo. **Unknown Arizona and Sonora, 1693-1721.** 1st ed. Tucson: Arizona Silhouettes; 1954. [$30.00]

Manly, William Lewis. **Death Valley in '49.** San Jose, CA: Pacific Tree and Vine; 1894. [$150.00] [1927 Lakeside reprint, $25.00] [1929 Hebberd ed., $35.00]

Manly, William Lewis. **Jayhawkers' Oath.** Los Angeles: Lewis; 1949. [$15.00]

Mann, Albert William. **Walks & Talks about Historic Boston.** Boston: Mann; 1917. [$60.00]

Mann, Arthur. **La Guardia.** Philadelphia: Lippincott; 1959. [$15.00]

Mann, Henry. **Our Police.** Providence, RI: [s.n.]; 1889. [$65.00]

Mann, Horace. **Lecture on the Best Mode of Preparing and Using Spelling.** 1st ed. Boston: Ticknor; 1841. [x-lib., shaken, $42.50]

Mann, William B. see, Probst, Anton.

Manross, William Wilson. **History of the American Episcopal Church.** NY, Milwaukee: Morehouse; 1935. [$25.00]

Mansfield, Edward Deering. **Life of General Winfield Scott.** NY: Barnes; 1846. [$45.00]

Mansfield, Edward Deering. **The Mexican War.** NY; Cincinnati: Barnes; Derby; 1848. [$90.00] [10th ed., 1851, covers worn, $50.00]

Mansfield, Edward Deering. **Personal Memories.** Cincinnati: Clarke; 1879. [$60.00] [$75.00]

Mansfield, Joseph King Fenno. **Mansfield on the Condition of the Western Forts, 1853-54.** 1st ed. Norman: U. of Oklahoma; 1963. [$75.00]

Manship, Andrew. **National Jewels.** Philadelphia: Manship; 1865. [$45.00]

Manter, Ethel H. **Rocket of the Comstocks.** Caldwell, ID: Caxton; 1950. [$35.00]

Manvill, P. D.(Mrs.). **Lucinda.** Johnstown: Child; 1807. [$1250.00]

Manypenny, George Washington. **Our Indian Wards.** Cincinnati: Clarke; 1880. [$150.00]

Mapp, Alf Johnson. **Frock Coats and Epaulets.** NY: Yoseloff; 1963. [$27.50]

Marable, Mary Hays. **Handbook of Oklahoma Writers.** 1st ed. Norman: U. of Oklahoma; 1939. [$55.00]

Marberry, M. Marion. **Splendid Poseur.** NY: Crowell; 1953. [$17.50]

Marcosson, Isaac Frederick. **Metal Magic.** NY: Farrar, Straus; 1949. [$15.00]

Marcus, Jacob Rader. **Early American Jewry.** Philadelphia: Jewish Publication Society of America; 1951- 53. 2 v. [$50.00]

Marcy, Randolph Barnes. **Border Reminiscences.** NY: Harper; 1872. [$125.00]

Marcy, Randolph Barnes. **Exploration of the Red River.** see, United States. War Department.

Marcy, Randolph Barnes. **The Prairie Traveler.** Denver: Mumey; 1959. [$35.00]

Marcy, Randolph Barnes. **Thirty Years of Army Life on the Border.** NY: Harper; 1866. [$165.00] [$250.00] [x-lib., $100.00]

Maritime Canal Company of Nicaragua. **Nicaragua, the Gateway to the Pacific.** NY: Bien; 1889. [loose, x-lib., $35.00]

Markham, Clements Robert. **Early Spanish Voyages to the Strait of Magellan.** London: Hakluyt Society; 1911. [$40.00]

Markham, Clements Robert. **War between Peru and Chile, 1879-1882.** London: Low, Marston, etc.; 1882. [good only, $35.00]

Markham, Edwin. **The Man with the Hoe.** NY: Doubleday, Page; 1899. [$20.00] [1899 San Francisco imprint, in elaborate slipcase, $100.00]

Marks, David. **Memoirs of the Life of.** Dover, NH: Free-Will Baptist; 1846. [$150.00]

Marmontel, Jean Francois. **Les Incas.** Leide: Murray; 1783. 2 v. [disbound, $100.00]

Marquis, Don. **The Almost Perfect State.** 1st ed. Garden City: Doubleday, Page; 1927. [x-lib., $15.00]

Marquis, Don. **Chapters for the Orthodox.** 1st ed. Garden City: Doubleday, Doran; 1934. [x-lib., $15.00]

Marquis, Don. **Hermione and Her Little Group of Serious Thinkers.** NY: Appleton; 1916. [x-lib., $15.00]

Marquis, Don. **Lives and Times of Archy and Mehitable.** NY: Doubleday, Doran; 1933. [1936 issue, x-lib., $15.00]

Marquis, Don. **Master of the Revels.** 1st ed. Garden City: Doubleday, Doran; 1934. [x-lib., $15.00]

Marquis, Don. **Off the Arm.** 1st ed. Garden City: Doubleday, Doran; 1930. [x-lib., $15.00]

Marquis, Don. **Prefaces.** NY: Appleton; 1919. [covers rubbed, bumped, dull, $12.50]

Marquis, Don. **Sonnets to a Red-Haired Lady.** 1st ed. Garden City: Doubleday, Page; 1922. [$22.50] [1925 issue, $15.00]

Marr, Harriet Webster. **Old New England Academies Founded before 1826.** NY: Comet; 1959. [$20.00]

Marriott, Alice Lee. **Greener Fields.** NY: Crowell; 1953. [$15.00]

Marriott, Alice Lee. **Indians on Horseback.** NY: Crowell; 1948. [$35.00]

Marriott, Alice Lee. **Maria, the Potter of San Ildefonso.** 1st ed. Norman: U. of Oklahoma; 1948. [$50.00]

Marriott, Alice Lee. **These Are the People.** Santa Fe, NM: Laboratory of Anthropology; 1949. [$17.00]

Marriott, Alice Lee. **Winter-Telling Stories.** NY: Sloane; 1947. [$35.00]

Marryat, Francis Samuel. **Mountains and Molehills.** NY: Harper; 1855. [$325.00]

Marryat, Frederick. **Diary in America.** NY: Appleton; 1839. [$75.00]

Marryat, Frederick. **Second Series of a Diary in America.** Philadelphia: Collins; 1840. [$45.00]

Marsh, Edith L. **A History of the County of Grey.** Owen Sound, Ontario: Fleming; 1931. [$50.00, Canadian]

Marsh, Edith L. **Where the Buffalo Roamed.** Toronto: Briggs; 1908. [$155.00, Canadian]

Marsh, George Perkins. **The Camel.** Boston; NY: Gould and Lincoln; Sheldon, Blakeman; 1856. [x-lib., worn, $47.50]

Marsh, J. B. T. **Story of the Jubilee Singers.** new ed. Cleveland: Cleveland Print. & Pub. Co.; 1892. [bumped, sunned, $15.00]

Marsh, John. **Temperance Hymn Book and Minstrel.** NY: American Temperance Union; 1841. [$25.00]

Marshall, Carrington T. **History of the Courts and Lawyers of Ohio.** NY: American Historical Society; 1934. 4 v. [$125.00]

Marshall, Christopher. **Extracts from the Diary Kept in Philadelphia and Lancaster.** Albany, NY: Munsell; 1877. [x-lib., $75.00]

Marshall, David Trumbull. **Recollections of Boyhood Days in Old Metuchen.** Flushing, NY: Case; 1930. [$25.00]

Marshall, James Leslie. **Santa Fe.** limited, signed ed. NY: Random; 1945. [$55.00]

Marshall, James Leslie. **Swinging Doors.** Seattle: McCaffrey; 1949. [$45.00]

Marshall, John. **Autobiographical Sketch.** Ann Arbor: U. of Michigan; 1937. [$85.00]

Marshall, John. **History of the Colonies Planted by the English on the Continent of North America.** Philadelphia: Small; 1824. [$65.00]

Marshall, John. **Life of George Washington.** Philadelphia: Wayne; 1804-1807. 5 v. [atlas from later edition, rebound, $150.00]

Marshall, John. **Writings of John Marshall . . . upon the Federal Constitution.** Boston: Munroe; 1839. [$100.00]

Marshall, Robert. **Arctic Wilderness.** Berkeley: U. of California; 1956. [$16.00]

Marshall, Theodora Britton. **They Found It in Natchez.** New Orleans: Pelican; 1940, c1939. [$12.50]

Marshall, Thomas Riley. **Recollections of.** Indianapolis: Bobbs-Merrill; 1925. [$12.50]

Marshall, William Isaac. **Acquisition of Oregon.** Seattle: Lowman & Hanford; 1911. 2 v. [$100.00]

Marshall, William Isaac. **History vs. the Whitman Saved Oregon Story.** Chicago: Blakely; 1904. [$50.00]

Martin, Alexander Campbell. **American Wildlife & Plants.** NY: McGraw-Hill; 1951. [$20.00]

Martin, Charles Lee. **Sketch of Sam Bass.** new ed. Norman: U. of Oklahoma; 1956. [first printing, $45.00] [$30.00]

Martin, Douglas. **The Earps of Tombstone.** 1st ed. Tombstone, AZ: Epitaph; 1959. [$30.00]

Martin, Douglas. **Tombstone's Epitaph.** Albuquerque: U. of New Mexico; 1951. [$20.00]

Martin, Edwin Thomas. **Thomas Jefferson.** NY: Schuman; 1952. [$20.00]

Martin, George Washington. **First Two Years of Kansas.** Topeka: State Print. Office; 1907. [$85.00]

Martin, Jack. **Border Boss.** San Antonio: Naylor; 1942. [x-lib., $50.00]

Martin, James Lee. **It Happened Here--in West Texas.** Dallas: Mathis, Van Nort; 1945. [$35.00]

Martin, John Bartlow. **Call It North Country: The Story of Upper Michigan.** NY: Knopf; 1944. [$10.00]

Martin, Michael. **Captain Lightfoot, the Last of the New England Highwaymen.** Topsfield, MA: Wayside; 1926. [$30.00]

Martin, Percy Falcke. **Maximilian in Mexico.** London: Constable; 1914. [$40.00]

Martin, Roscoe Coleman. **The People's Party in Texas.** Austin: The University; 1933. [$150.00]

Martin, Thomas H. **Atlanta and Its Builders.** Atlanta: Century Memorial; 1902. 2 v. [rebound, $125.00]

Martindale, Thomas. **With Gun and Guide.** Philadelphia: Jacobs; 1910. [$25.00]

Martineau, Harriet. **Retrospect of Western Travel.** NY: Lohman; 1838. 2 v. [v. 1 spine repaired, $75.00] [1942 Harper facs. ed., $35.00]

Martineau, Harriet. **Society in America.** 2nd ed. London: Saunders and Otley; 1839. 3 v. [$85.00]

Martinez Caro, Ramon. **Verdadera Idea de la Primera Xampana de Tejas.** Mexico: Santiago Perez; 1837. [$2500.00]

Martyn, Benjamin. **An Impartial Enquiry into the State and Utility of the Province of Georgia.** London: Meadows; 1741. [rebound, $675.00]

Martyn, Charles. **Life of Artemas Ward.** NY: Ward; 1921. [with box, $45.00]

Marvin, Henry. **Complete History of Lake George.** NY: Sibells and Maigne; 1853. [$65.00]

Marx, Groucho. **Beds.** NY: Farrar & Rinehart; 1930. [$50.00]

Marzolf, Marion. **Up from the Footnote.** NY: Hastings; 1977. [$15.00]

Mason, Alpheus Thomas. **Harlan Fiske Stone.** NY: Viking; 1956. [$20.00] [$27.00]

Mason, Emily Virginia. **Popular Life of Gen. Robert Edward Lee.** 2nd ed. Baltimore: Murphy; 1872. [$25.00]

Mason, George Champlin. **Life and Works of Gilbert Stuart.** NY: Scribner; 1879. [$75.00]

Mason, George Champlin. **Re-Union of the Sons and Daughters of Newport, R.I.** Newport, RI: Pratt; 1859. [hinge worn, $35.00]

Mason, Gregory. **Columbus Came Late.** NY, London: Century; 1931. [$15.00]

Mason, Richard. **The Gentleman's New Pocket Farrier.** Richmond: Cottom; 1835. [$2750.00]

Mason, Robert Lindsay. **Lure of the Great Smokies.** Boston: Houghton Mifflin; 1927. [water stained, bumped, sunned, $20.00]

Massachusetts Constitutional Convention. **Address of the Convention, for Framing a New Constitution of Government for the State of Massachusetts-Bay, to Their Constituents.** Boston: White and Adams; 1780. [half morocco, $185.00]

Massachusetts Infantry. 19th Regt., 1861-1865. **History of.** Salem, MA: Salem Press; 1906. [$55.00]

Massett, Stephen C. **Drifting About.** NY: Carleton; 1863. [covers worn, foxing, $25.00]

Massey, Beatrice. **It Might Have Been Worse.** San Francisco: Wagner; 1920. [$40.00]

Massey, Ernest de. **A Frenchman in the Gold Rush.** San Francisco: California Historical Society; 1927. [$35.00]

Massie, J. W. **America: The Origin of Her Present Conflict.** London: Snow; 1864. [$45.00]

Massie, Susanne Williams. **Homes and Gardens in Old Virginia.** Richmond: Garrett & Massie; 1931. [$20.00]

Masson, L. R. **Les Bourgeois de la Compagnie du Nord-Ouest.** NY: Antiquarian Press; 1960. 2 v. [$125.00]

Masters, Edgar Lee. **A Book of Verses.** 1st ed. Chicago: Way & Williams; 1898. [inscribed, $ 600.00]

Masters, Edgar Lee. **The Golden Fleece of California.** limited, signed ed. Weston, VT: Countryman; 1936. [$60.00]

Masters, Edgar Lee. **Vachel Lindsay.** NY, London: Scribner; 1935. [$25.00] [$20.00]

Masterson, V. V. **The Katy Railroad and the Last Frontier.** Norman: U. of Oklahoma Press; 1952. [$40.00]

Masterson, William H. **William Blount.** Baton Rouge: Louisiana State UP; 1954. [$20.00]

Mather, Cotton. **Diary of.** NY: Ungar; [1957?]. 2 v. [$45.00]

Mather, Cotton. **Life of Sir William Phips.** NY: Covici-Friede; 1929. [$30.00]

Mather, Cotton. **Magnalia Christi Americana; or, The Ecclesiastical History of New England.** London: Parkhurst; 1702. [$2750.00]

Mather, Cotton. **Triumphs of the Reformed Religion, in America.** Boston: Brunning; 1691. [$6500.00]

Mather, Cotton. **Wonders of the Invisible World.** London: Smith; 1862. [$49.50] [$35.00]

Mather, Samuel. **Abridgment of the Life of the Late Reverend and Learned Dr. Cotton Mather.** London: Oswald and Brackstone; 1744. [$300.00]

Mather, Samuel. **Life of the Very Reverend and Learned Cotton Mather.** Boston: Gerrish; 1729. [$300.00]

Mathers, James H. **From Gun to Gavel.** NY: Morrow; 1954. [$20.00] [dj worn, $25.00]

Mathes, Charles Hodge. **Tall Tales from Old Smoky.** Kingsport, TN: Southern; 1952. [worn dj, $13.00] [$15.00]

Mathew, Catharine Van Cortlandt. **Andrew Ellicott, His Life and Letters.** NY: Grafton; 1908. [$75.00]

Mathews, Alfred Edward. **Pencil Sketches of Colorado.** signed limited ed. Denver: Mumey; 1961. [$125.00]

Mathews, Donald G. **Slavery and Methodism.** Princeton: Princeton UP; 1965. [$25.00]

Mathews, John Joseph. **Life and Death of an Oilman.** 1st ed. Norman: U. of Oklahoma; 1951. [$20.00]

Mathews, John Joseph. **The Osages.** 1st ed. Norman: U. of Oklahoma; 1961. [dj chipped, $60.00]

Mathews, John Joseph. **Wah'kon-Tah: The Osage and the White Man's Road.** Norman: U. of Oklahoma; 1932. [$25.00] [$10.00]

Mathews, Mary McNair. **Ten Years in Nevada.** Buffalo: Baker, Jones; 1880. [$325.00]

Mathews, Thomas. **Puerto Rican Politics and the New Deal.** Gainesville: U. of Florida; 1960. [$25.00]

Mathis, Harry R. **Along the Border.** Oxford, NC: Coble; 1964. [mildew stained, $30.00]

Mathison, Richard R. **Three Cars in Every Garage.** Garden City: Doubleday; 1968. [$12.00]

Matschat, Cecile Hulse. **Suwannee River.** NY: Literary Guild; 1938. [$9.00]

Matson, Nehemiah. **Memories of Shaubena.** Chicago: Cooke; 1878. [$125.00]

Matson, Nehemiah. **Pioneers of Illinois.** Chicago: Knight & Leonard; 1882. [inscribed, $150.00]

Mattes, Merrill J. **Indians, Infants and Infantry.** Denver: Old West; 1960. [inscribed, $40.00]

Matthews, Sallie Reynolds. **Interwoven.** El Paso: Hertzog; 1958. [$350.00]

Matthiessen, F. O. **Achievement of T. S. Eliot.** 2nd ed. NY: Oxford UP; 1947. [$15.00]

Mattson, Hans. **Reminiscences.** St.Paul: Merrill; 1891. [$30.00]

Maude, John. **Visit to the Falls of Niagara in 1800.** London: Longman, Rees, Orme, Brown & Green; 1826. [spine repaired, $500.00]

Mauldin, Bill. **Back Home.** NY: Sloan; 1947. [$15.00]

Mauldin, Bill. **What's Got Your Back Up?** NY: Harper; 1961. [$15.00]

Maule, Harry. **Fall Roundup.** see, Western Writers of America.

Maurey, Edward B. **Where the West Began.** Coraopolis, PA: Record; 1930. [damp stained, $35.00]

Maurice, Frederick Barton. **Robert E. Lee, the Soldier.** Boston, NY: Houghton Mifflin; 1925. [$17.50]

Maurice, Frederick Barton. **Statesmen and Soldiers of the Civil War.** Boston: Little, Brown; 1926. [$20.00]

Maurois, Andre. **Eisenhower the Liberator.** NY: Didier; 1945. [$25.00]

Maury, Dabney Herndon. **Recollections of a Virginian in the Mexican, Indian, and Civil Wars.** NY: Scribner; 1894. [presentation, $55.00]

Maverick, Augustus. **Henry J. Raymond and the New York Press for Thirty Years.** Hartford: Hale; 1870. [$75.00]

Maverick, Mary Ann. **Memoirs of.** San Antonio: Alamo; 1921. [first state, $50.00]

Maxwell, Archibald Montgomery. **A Run through the United States, during the Autumn of 1840.** London: Colburn; 1841. 2 v. [spines worn, $125.00]

Maxwell, Hu. **History of Tucker County, West Virginia.** Kingwood, WV: Preston; 1884. [$200.00] [1898 Acme ed., $135.00]

Maxwell, Will J. **Greek Letter Men of Pittsburg.** NY: College Book Co.; 1901. [$8.50]

Maxwell, William Audley. **Crossing the Plains.** San Francisco: Sunset; 1915. [water stained, $20.00]

Maxwell, William Quentin. **Lincoln's Fifth Wheel.** 1st ed. NY: Longmans, Green; 1956. [signed, $27.50]

May, Caroline. **The American Female Poets.** Philadelphia: Lindsay & Blakiston; 1854. [cloth repaired spine, $65.00]

May, Earl Chapin. **The Canning Clan.** NY: Macmillan; 1937. [$15.00]

May, Earl Chapin. **Century of Silver.** NY: McBride; 1947. [$12.50]

May, John Bichard. **Hawks of North America.** NY: National Association of Audubon Societies; 1935. [$60.00]

May, Samuel Joseph. **Some Recollections of Our Antislavery Conflict.** Boston: Fields, Osgood; 1869. [$55.00] [x-lib., $20.00]

Mayer, Brantz. **Mexico As It Was and As It Is.** NY: Winchester; 1844. [$60.00]

Mayer, Frank H. **Buffalo Harvest.** Denver: Sage; 1958. [x-lib., $12.50]

Mayes, Edward. **Lucius Q. C. Lamar.** Nashville: M. E. Church, South; 1896. [$55.00] [$45.00]

Mayhall, Mildred P. **The Kiowas.** 1st ed. Norman: U. of Oklahoma; 1962. [x-lib., $15.00] [$45.00] [$30.00]

Mayhew, Henry. **The Mormons; or, Latter-Day Saints.** London: National Illustrated Library; 1851. [$100.00]

Maynard, Henrietta Sturdevant. **Was Abraham Lincoln a Spiritualist?** Chicago: Progressive Thinker; 1917. [$60.00]

Maynard, Olga. **The American Ballet.** Philadelphia: Macrae Smith; 1959. [$17.50]

Mayo, Amory Dwight. **Industrial Education in the South.** Washington: USGPO; 1888. [$15.00]

Mayo, Amory Dwight. **Symbols of the Capital; or, Civilization in New York.** NY: Thatcher & Hutchinson; 1859. [$60.00]

Mazo, Earl. **Richard Nixon.** 1st ed. NY: Harper; 1959. [$20.00]

Mazzanovich, Anton. **Trailing Geronimo.** Los Angeles: Gem; 1926. [$95.00]

Mazzuchelli, Samuel. **Memoirs, Historical and Edifying of a Missionary Apostolic.** Chicago: Hall; 1915. [rear hinge cracked, $45.00]

McAllester, David Park. **Peyote Music.** NY: Viking Fund; 1949. [$45.00]

McAllister, Joseph Thompson. **Virginia Militia in the Revolutionary War.** Hot Springs, VA: McAllister; 1913. [x-lib., $35.00]

McAllister, Ward. **Society As I Have Found It.** NY: Cassell; 1890. [$30.00]

M'Callum, Pierre Franc. **Travels in Trinidad.** Liverpool: Jones; 1805. [$375.00]

McBeth, Kate Christine. **The Nez Perces Since Lewis and Clark.** NY, Chicago: Revell; 1908. [$30.00]

McCabe, Gillie Cary. **The Story of an Old Town, Hampton, Virginia.** Richmond: Old Dominion; 1929. [bumped, sunned, rubbed, $20.00]

McCabe, James Dabney. **Illustrated History of the Centennial Exhibition.** Philadelphia: National; 1876. [$120.00]

McCabe, James Dabney. **Secrets of the Great City.** Philadelphia: National; 1868. [spine sunned, front hinge weak, $45.00]

McCain, Charles W. **History of the SS. "Beaver."** Vancouver: Evans & Hastings; 1894. [$195.00, Canadian]

McCall, George Archibald. **New Mexico in 1850.** Norman: U. of Oklahoma; 1968. [$15.00]

McCalla, William Latta. **Adventures in Texas.** 1st ed. Philadelphia: The Author; 1841. [spine worn, $1100.00] [$1800.00]

McCalla, William Latta. **The Unitarian Baptist of the Robinson School Exposed.** Philadelphia: Young; 1826. [rebound, $65.00]

McCallum, Henry D. **The Wire That Fenced the West.** Norman: U. of Oklahoma; 1965. [$18.00]

McCallum, James. **A Brief Sketch of the Settlement and Early History of Giles County, Tennessee.** Pulaski, TN: Citizen; 1928. [$75.00]

McCann, Irving Goff. **With the National Guard on the Border.** St. Louis: Mosby; 1917. [$125.00]

McCarthy, Carlton. **Detailed Minutiae of Soldier Life in the Army of Northern Virginia, 1861-1865.** Richmond: McCarthy; 1882. [$100.00]

McCarthy, Charles Hallan. **Lincoln's Plan of Reconstruction.** NY: McClure, Phillips; 1901. [$125.00]

McCarty, John Lawton. **Adobe Walls Bride.** San Antonio: Naylor; 1955. [$35.00]

McCarty, John Lawton. **Maverick Town.** Norman: U. of Oklahoma; 1968. [$15.00]

McCauley, James Emmit. **Stove-Up Cowboy's Story.** limited ed. Austin: Texas Folklore Soc.; 1943. [$325.00]

McClellan, Carswell. **Notes on the Personal Memoirs of P. H. Sheridan.** St. Paul: Banning; 1889. [$75.00]

McClellan, Elisabeth. **Historic Dress in America, 1800-1870.** Philadelphia: Jacobs; 1910. [$75.00]

McClellan, Elisabeth. **History of American Costume, 1607-1870.** NY: Tudor; 1937. [$35.00]

McClellan, George Brinton. **McClellan's Own Story: The War for the Union.** NY: Webster; 1887. [$60.00] [$45.00]

McClellan, George Brinton. **Report on the Organization and Campaigns of the Army of the Potomac.** NY: Sheldon; 1864. [$85.00]

McClellan, Henry Brainerd. **I Rode with Jeb Stuart.** Bloomington: Indiana UP; 1958. [worn dj, $35.00]

McClellan, William Smith. **Smuggling in the American Colonies at the Outbreak of the Revolution.** NY: Moffat, Yard; 1912. [x-lib., $15.00]

McClernand, Edward J. **With the Indian and the Buffalo in Montana.** Glendale, CA: Clark; 1969. [$110.00]

McClintock, James H. **Mormon Settlement in Arizona.** Phoenix: Manufacturing Stationers; 1921. [$69.50]

McClintock, Walter. **Old Indian Trails.** Boston, NY: Houghton Mifflin; 1923. [$75.00]

McClintock, Walter. **The Old North Trail.** London: Macmillan; 1910. [hinges cracked, $100.00]

McCloskey, Joseph J. **Christmas in the Gold Fields, 1849.** San Francisco: California Historical Society; 1959. [$17.50]

McClung, John Alexander. **Sketches of Western Adventure.** Maysville, KY: Collin's; 1832. [$850.00]

McClure, Alexander Kelly. **Authentic Life of William McKinley.** [Philadelphia?]: Scull; 1901. [$25.00]

McClure, Alexander Kelly. **Colonel Alexander K. McClure's Recollections.** Salem, MA: Salem Press; 1902. [$35.00]

McCollom, Albert O. **War-Time Letters.** Fayetteville, AR: Washington County Historical Society; 1961. [$12.00]

McCombs, Vernon Monroe. **From over the Border.** NY: Council of Women for Home Missions and Missionary Education Movement; 1925. [presentation, $12.50] [$20.00]

McConkey, Harriet E. Bishop. **Dakota War Whoop.** rev. ed. St. Paul: Moses; 1864. [$90.00]

McConnell, Burt M. **Mexico at the Bar of Public Opinion.** NY: Mail and Express; 1939. ["reading copy," $15.00]

McConnell, H. H. **Five Years a Cavalryman.** Jacksboro, TX: Rogers; 1889, c1888. [$250.00]

McCordock, Robert Stanley. **The Yankee Cheese Box.** Philadelphia: Dorrance; 1938. [$75.00]

McCorkle, John. **Three Years with Quantrell.** Armstrong, MO: Herald; 1914. [rebound, $300.00]

McCormick, Cyrus. **Century of the Reaper.** Boston; NY: Houghton Mifflin; 1931. [$15.00]

McCormick, Leander Hamilton. **Characterology.** Chicago, NY: Rand McNally; 1920. [x-lib., $10.00]

McCormick, Richard Patrick. **History of Voting in New Jersey.** New Brunswick: Rutgers UP; 1953. [$15.00]

McCoy, Joseph G. **Historic Sketches of the Cattle Trade of the West and Southwest.** Kansas City, MO: Ramsey, Millett & Hudson; 1874. [$1500.00] [1940 Clark ed., $85.00] [1951 Long's reprint, $27.50]

McCracken, Harold. **The Charles M. Russell Book.** Garden City: Doubleday; 1957. [chipped dj, $55.00] [fine, $60.00]

McCracken, Harold. **Frederic Remington.** 1st ed. Philadelphia: Lippincott; 1947. [worn dj, $55.00]

McCracken, Harold. **George Catlin and the Old Frontier.** NY: Dial; 1959. [$40.00] [$30.00]

McCracken, Harold. **Portrait of the Old West.** 1st ed. NY: McGraw-Hill; 1952. [$45.00] [$25.00]

McCreight, Major Israel. **Chief Flying Hawk's Tales.** NY: Alliance; 1936. [$35.00]

McCullers, Carson. **Member of the Wedding.** 1st ed. Boston: Houghton Mifflin; 1946. [$60.00]

McCulloh, James Haines. **Researches, Philosophical and Antiquarian, Concerning the Aboriginal History of America.** Baltimore: Lucas; 1829. [rebound in buckram, "3rd edition," $400.00]

McDaniel, Ruel. **Vinegarroon.** Kingsport, TN: Southern; 1936. [$9.00] [$15.00]

McDanield, H. F. **The Coming Empire.** NY: Barnes; 1877. [$200.00]

McDermott, John Francis. **George Caleb Bingham.** Norman: U. of Oklahoma; 1959. [$55.00]

McDermott, John Francis. **Lost Panoramas of the Mississippi.** Chicago: U. of Chicago; 1958. [$12.00]

McDonald, Cornelia Peake. **A Diary with Reminiscences of the War and Refugee Life in the Shenandoah Valley, 1860-1865.** Nashville: Cullom & Ghertner; 1935. [$100.00]

McDonald, James Joseph. **Life in Old Virginia.** Norfolk: Old Virginia; 1907. [some mildew, $30.00]

McDougall, John. **Saddle, Sled and Snowshoe.** Cincinnati; NY: Curts and Jennings; Eaton and Mains; 1896. [$45.00, Canadian] [$60.00]

McElroy, John. **The Struggle for Missouri.** Washington: National Tribune; 1913, c1909. [$20.00]

McElroy, Robert McNutt. **Grover Cleveland, the Man and the Statesman.** 1st ed. NY, London: Harper; 1923. 2 v. [$45.00]

McElroy, Robert McNutt. **Kentucky in the Nation's History.** NY: Moffat, Yard; 1909. [$75.00]

McElroy, Robert McNutt. **The Winning of the Far West.** NY, London: Putnam; 1914. [$60.00]

McFarland, John Horace. **Eagles Mere and the Sullivan Highlands.** Harrisburg, PA: McFarland; 1944. [$40.00]

McFarling, Lloyd. **Exploring the Northern Plains, 1804-1876.** Caldwell, ID: Caxton; 1955. [$35.00]

McGavin, Elmer Cecil. **The Mormon Pioneers.** Salt Lake City: Stevens & Wallis; 1947. [$45.00]

McGee, Thomas D'Arcy. **Catholic History of North America.** Boston: Donahoe; 1855. [x-lib., hinges cracked, worn, $20.00]

McGill, William Mahone. **Caverns of Virginia.** University, VA: State Commission on Conservation and Development; 1933. [$22.00]

McGillycuddy, Julia E. **McGillycuddy, Agent.** Stanford; London: Stanford UP; Oxford UP; 1941. [$65.00]

McGlashan, Charles Fayette. **History of the Donner Party.** 2nd ed. San Francisco: Bancroft; 1880. [$300.00] [9th ed., 1907, Crocker, $50.00]

McGrane, Reginald Charles. **William Allen.** Columbus: Ohio State Archaeological and Historical Society; 1925. [$35.00]

McGrath, Paul of the Cross, Sister. **Political Nativism in Texas.** Washington: Catholic University; 1930. [$45.00]

McGregor, James Herman. **The Wounded Knee Massacre from the Viewpoint of the Sioux.** Baltimore: Wirth; 1940. [$110.00]

McGuire, Hunter Holmes. **The Confederate Cause and Conduct in the War between the States.** Richmond: Jenkins; 1907. [$45.00]

McGuire, Hunter Holmes. **Memory of "Stonewall" Jackson.** NY: Kellogg; [1898?]. [lacks rear wrap, $100.00]

McHenry, George. **The Cotton Trade.** London: Saunders, Otley; 1863. [bumped, stained, and worn, $50.00]

McHenry, James. **The Wilderness; or, Braddock's Times.** Pittsburgh: Morse; 1848. 2 v. in 1. [$35.00]

McIlhany, Edward Washington. **Recollections of a '49er.** Kansas City: Hailman; 1908. [$95.00]

McIlvaine, Mabel. **Reminiscences of Chicago during the Civil War.** Chicago: Lakeside; 1914. [cover wear and minor stains, $28.00]

McIlwaine, Richard. **Memories of Three Score Years and Ten.** NY, Washington: Neale; 1908. [$90.00]

McIlwaine, Shields. **Memphis Down in Dixie.** 1st ed. NY: Dutton; 1948. [$20.00]

McIntosh, John. **The Discovery of America by Christopher Columbus; and the Origin of the North American Indians.** Toronto: Coates; 1836. [$150.00]

McIntosh, Maria Jane. **Two Pictures.** NY, London: Appleton; 1863. [$45.00]

McKay, Claude. **Home to Harlem.** NY, London: Harper; 1928. [$15.00]

McKay, Richard Cornelius. **South Street, a Maritime History of New York.** NY: Putnam; 1934. [$35.00]

McKay, Seth Shepard. **W. Lee O'Daniel and Texas Politics, 1938-1942.** Lubbock: Texas Research Funds; 1944. [$85.00]

McKelvey, Blake. **Rochester, the Flower City 1855-1890.** Cambridge: Harvard UP; 1949. [$25.00]

McKelvey, Susan Delano. **Botanical Exploration of the Trans-Mississippi West, 1790-1850.** Jamaica Plain, MA: Arnold Arboretum; 1955. [$110.00]

McKenna, James A. **Black Range Tales.** NY: Wilson-Erickson; 1936. [$75.00] [$40.00]

McKenney, Thomas Loraine. **Memoirs, Official and Personal.** NY: Paine and Burgess; 1846. 2 v. in 1. [$275.00] [$350.00]

McKenzie, Thomas. **My Life as a Soldier.** St. John, NB: McMillan; 1898. [$45.00, Canadian]

McKeown, Martha. **Alaska Silver.** NY: Macmillan; 1951. [presentation, $12.50]

McKeown, Martha. **Trail Led North.** NY: Macmillan; 1948. [$15.00] [presentation, $18.50]

McKinley, Carlyle. **An Appeal to Pharaoh: The Negro Problem, and Its Radical Solution.** 3rd ed. Columbia, SC: State; 1907. [silverfished and spotted, $20.00]

McKinley, Silas Bent. **Old Rough and Ready.** NY: Vanguard; 1946. [$30.00]

McKittrick, Myrtle Mason. **Vallejo, Son of California.** 1st ed. Portland, OR: Binfords & Mort; 1944. [$30.00]

McLain, John Scudder. **Alaska and the Klondike.** NY: McClure, Phillips; 1907. [$35.00]

McLane, Hiram H. **Irene Viesca: A Tale of the Magee Expedition in the Gauchipin War in Texas.** San Antonio: San Antonio Print. Co.; 1886. [$375.00]

McLane, Lucy Neely. **A Piney Paradise by Monterey Bay, Pacific Grove.** San Francisco: Kennedy; 1952. [$25.00] [$39.50]

McLaughlin, James. **My Friend the Indian.** Baltimore: Proof Press; 1936. [$45.00]

McLendon, Samuel Guyton. **History of the Public Domain of Georgia.** Atlanta: Foote & Davies; 1924. [slightly bumped and silverfished, $17.50] [$25.00]

McLennan, John Stewart. **Louisbourg, from Its Foundation to Its Fall, 1713-1758.** London: Macmillan; 1918. [$150.00]

McLeod, Alexander. **Pigtails and Gold Dust.** Caldwell, ID: Caxton; 1948, c1947. [2nd printing, $20.00]

McLeod, Robert Randall. **Markland or Nova Scotia.** Berwick, NS: Markland Publishing; 1903. [$125.00]

M'Clintock, Francis Leopold. **The Voyage of the "Fox" in the Arctic Seas.** Boston: Ticknor and Fields; 1860. [$100.00]

McLoughlin, James Joseph. **The Jack Lafaience Book.** New Orleans: American; 1922. [$25.00]

McMahon, William H. **South Jersey Towns, History and Legend.** New Brunswick: Rutgers U.P.; 1973. [$20.00]

McManus, Thomas J. Luke. **The Boy and the Outlaw.** NY: Grafton; 1904. [$15.00]

McMaster, John Bach. **Daniel Webster.** NY: Century; 1902. [$12.50]

McMaster, S. W. **60 Years on the Upper Mississippi.** Rock Island, IL: [s.n.]; 1893 [i.e.1895]. [$90.00]

McMechen, Edgar Carlisle. **Moffat Tunnel of Colorado.** Denver: Wahlgreen; 1927. 2 v. [x-lib., $75.00] [$150.00]

McMeekin, Clark. **Old Kentucky Country.** 1st ed. NY: Duell, Sloan and Pearce; 1957. [$20.00]

McMurray, William Josiah. **History of the Twentieth Tennessee Regiment Volunteer Infantry, C.S.A.** Nashville: Publication Committee; 1904. [spine faded, $250.00]

McMurry, Donald Le Crone. **The Great Burlington Strike of 1888.** Cambridge: Harvard UP; 1956. [$35.00]

McNall, Neil Adams. **Agricultural History of the Genesee Valley, 1790-1860.** Philadelphia: U. of Pennsylvania; 1952. [$30.00]

McNeal, Thomas Allen. **When Kansas Was Young.** NY: Macmillan; 1922. [x-lib., front hinge weak, $15.00]

McNeal, Violet. **Four White Horses and a Brass Band.** 1st ed. Garden City: Doubleday; 1947. [$10.00]

McNeill, John Charles. **Lyrics from Cotton Land.** Charlotte, NC: Stone; 1922. [rebacked, $85.00]

McNitt, Frank. **The Indian Traders.** 1st ed. Norman: U. of Oklahoma; 1962. [$30.00]

McPhail, Alexander James. **Diary of.** Toronto: U. of Toronto; 1940. [$80.00 Canadian]

Mcpherson, Aimee Semple. **Give Me My Own God.** NY: Kinsey; 1936. [$25.00]

McPherson, Aimee Semple. **This Is That.** Los Angeles: Echo Park Evangelistic Assn.; 1923. [$75.00]

McPherson, Alexander. **The History of Faulkner County, Arkansas.** Conway: Times; 1927. [$15.00] [$25.00]

McQuade, James. **The Cruise of the Montauk to Bermuda, the West Indies and Florida.** NY: Knox; 1885. [$25.00]

McReynolds, Edwin C. **Oklahoma: The Story of Its Past and Present.** Norman: U. of Oklahoma; 1967. [$13.00]

McSherry, Richard. **El Puchero.** Philadelphia: Lippincott, Grambo; 1850. [$150.00]

McTyeire, Holland Nimmons. **Duties of Christian Masters.** Nashville: Southern Methodist Publishing; 1859. [x-lib., $45.00]

McVaugh, Rogers. **Edward Palmer: Plant Explorer of the American West.** Norman: U. of Oklahoma; 1956. [$25.00]

McWatters, George S. **Knots Untied: or Ways and By-Ways in the Hidden Life of American Detectives.** Hartford: Burr and Hyde; 1871. [$50.00]

McWilliams, Carey. **Southern California Country.** NY: Duell, Sloan & Pearce; 1946. [$12.50]

M'Dowall, John R. **Memoir and Select Remains of.** NY: Leavitt, Lord; 1838. [$40.00]

Meacham, Albert Gallatin. **Compendious History of the Rise and Progress of the Methodist Church, both in Europe and America.** Hallowell, UC: Wilson; 1832. [foxed, endpapers missing, $225.00, Canadian]

Mead, Edward C. **Historic Homes of the South-West Mountains, Virginia.** Philadelphia: Lippincott; 1899. [$125.00]

Mead, Margaret. **Changing Culture of an Indian Tribe.** NY: Columbia UP; 1932. [$65.00]

Mead, Peter B. **An Elementary Treatise on American Grape Culture and Wine Making.** NY: Harper; 1867. [slight water damage, $125.00]

Meade, Robert Douthat. **Judah P. Benjamin.** NY, London: Oxford UP; 1943. [$25.00] [$35.00]

Meade, Robert Douthat. **Patrick Henry, Patriot in the Making.** 1st ed. Philadelphia: Lippincott; 1957. [$15.00]

Meade, William. **Old Churches, Ministers and Families of Virginia.** Philadelphia: Lippincott; 1857. 2 v. [$125.00] [1861 issue, $75.00] [1894 reissue, $65.00]

Meader, J. W. **The Merrimack River.** Boston: Russell; 1869. [$75.00]

Means, Gaston Bullock. **The Strange Death of President Harding.** NY: Gold Label; 1930. [$35.00]

Means, Philip Ainsworth. **Fall of the Inca Empire and the Spanish Rule in Peru; 1530-1780.** NY, London: Scribner; 1932. [$25.00]

Means, Philip Ainsworth. **Newport Tower.** NY: Holt; 1942. [fine in dj, $25.00]

Meares, John. **Voyages Made in the Years 1788 and 1789, from China to the North West Coast of America.** London: Logographic; 1790. [rebacked, $3250.00]

Mearns, David Chambers. **Lincoln Papers.** Garden City: Doubleday; 1948. 2 v. [box worn, djs chipped, $60.00]

Mears, Anne de Benneville. **Old York Road.** Philadelphia: Harper; 1870. [$38.00]

Mease, James. **Picture of Philadelphia.** Philadelphia: Kite; 1811. [spine and map repaired, $200.00]

Mecklenburg, George. **Last of the Old West.** Washington: Capital; 1927. [signed, $35.00]

Mecklin, John Moffatt. **The Ku Klux Klan.** NY: Harcourt, Brace; 1924. [$27.50] [x-lib., 1963 Russell imprint, $6.00]

Meeker, Nathan Cook. **Life in the West.** NY: Wells; 1868. [$125.00]

Meggers, Betty Jane. **Aboriginal Cultural Development in Latin America.** Washington: Smithsonian; 1963. [$15.00]

Meginness, John Franklin. **Biography of Frances Slocum.** Williamsport, PA: Heller; 1891. [x-lib., $60.00] [$150.00]

Mehling, Harold. **The Most of Everything.** 1st ed. NY: Harcourt, Brace; 1960. [$6.00]

Meigs, William Montgomery. **Life of Charles Jared Ingersoll.** Philadelphia: Lippincott; 1897. [$25.00]

Meine, Franklin Julius. **Tall Tales of the Southwest.** NY: Knopf; 1930. [spine stained, $17.50]

Melish, John. **A Geographical Description of the United States: With the Contiguous British and Spanish Possessions, Intended as an Accompaniment to Melish's Map of These Countries.** Philadelphia: Melish; 1816. [lacks general map, $50.00]

Melish, John. **Necessity of Protecting and Encouraging the Manufactures of the United States.** Philadelphia: Melish; 1818. [foxed, $75.00]

Mellen, Kathleen. **Magnificent Matriarch: Kaahumanu, Queen of Hawaii.** NY: Hastings; 1952. [$12.50]

Mellick, Andrew D. **The Story of an Old Farm.** Somerville, NJ: Unionist-Gazette; 1889. [flyleaf missing, hinges glued, $100.00]

Mellon, Matthew Taylor. **Early American Views on Negro Slavery.** Boston: Meador; 1934. [$20.00]

Mellquist, Jerome. **Emergence of an American Art.** NY: Scribner; 1942. [worn dj, $25.00]

Melone, Harry R. **History of Central New York.** Indianapolis: Historical; 1932. [$100.00]

Meltzer, Gilbert. **Beginnings of Elmira College, 1851-1868.** Elmira, NY: Commercial; 1941. [$25.00]

Melville, George W. **In the Lena Delta.** Boston: Houghton Mifflin; 1885. [$50.00]

Melville, Herman. **Battle-Pieces.** NY: Harper; 1866. [cover stained, $350.00]

Melville, Herman. **Benito Cereno.** London: Nonesuch; 1926. [$100.00]

Melville, Herman. **Billy Budd.** London: Lehmann; 1947. [dj chipped, $45.00]

Melville, Herman. **Clarel.** London: Constable; 1924. 2 v. [2nd printing, chipped dj, $75.00]

Melville, Herman. **The Confidence-Man.** 1st ed. NY: Dix, Edwards; 1857. [$750.00]

Melville, Herman. **John Marr.** Princeton: Princeton UP; 1922. [near fine, $75.00] [$45.00]

Melville, Herman. **Mardi.** NY: Harper; 1849. 2 v. [spine ends chipped, $950.00] [$850.00]

Melville, Herman. **Moby-Dick.** NY: Harper; 1851. [rebound in full calf, $3600.00] [little wear and light foxing, $5000.00]

Melville, Herman. **Piazza Tales.** NY: Dix & Edwards; 1856. [rear hinge cracked, spine chipped, $1000.00]

Melville, Herman. **Redburn.** 1st ed. NY: Harper; 1849. [1st printing, $750.00] [2nd state, $650.00]

Melville, Herman. **Typee.** rev. ed. NY; London: Harper; Murray; 1849. [$225.00]

Melville, Herman. **White-Jacket.** NY; London: Harper; Bentley; 1850. [$700.00]

Memoir of Frank Russell Firth. Boston: Lee & Shepard; 1873. [$100.00]

Memory of Washington. Newport, RI: Farnsworth; 1800. [$75.00]

Mencken, H. L. **The American Language.** 4th ed. NY: Knopf; 1960, c1936-1946. 3 v. [$50.00]

Mencken, H. L. **Americana 1925.** NY: Knopf; 1925. [presentation, $185.00] [$80.00]

Mencken, H. L. **Christmas Story.** NY: Knopf; 1946. [very good in dj, $40.00]

Mencken, H. L. **Days of.** NY: Knopf; 1947. [$22.50]

Mencken, H. L. **George Bernard Shaw; His Plays.** Boston, London: Luce; 1905. [$225.00]

Mencken, H. L. **Heathen Days, 1890-1936.** 1st ed. NY: Knopf; 1943. [$50.00] [$30.00]

Mencken, H. L. **Heliogabalus.** NY: Knopf; 1920. [$65.00] [$85.00]

Mencken, H. L. **In Defense of Women.** NY: Knopf; 1922. [$12.50]

Mencken, H. L. **A Little Book in C Major.** NY: Lane; 1916. [as new, $120.00]

Mencken, H. L. **Notes on Democracy.** limited signed ed. NY: Knopf; 1926. [very good in slipcase, $325.00]

Mencken, H. L. **The Philosophy of Friedrich Nietzsche.** Boston: Luce; 1908. [$125.00]

Menefee, C. A. **Historical and Descriptive Sketch Book of Napa, Sonoma, Lake, and Mendocino.** Napa City, CA: Reporter; 1873. [$150.00]

Mera, H. P. **Navajo Textile Arts.** Santa Fe: Laboratory of Anthropology; 1947. [$50.00]

Mercer, Asa Shinn. **The Banditti of the Plains.** new ed. Norman: U. of Oklahoma; 1954. [$18.00]

Mercer, Asa Shinn. **Powder River Invasion.** Los Angeles: [s.n.]; 1923. [binding soiled, $75.00]

Mercer, Henry Chapman. **The Bible in Iron.** 2nd ed. Doylestown, PA: Bucks County Historical Society; 1941. [$50.00]

Mercier, Henry James. **Life in a Man-of-War.** Boston, NY: Houghton Mifflin; 1927. [$75.00]

Meredith, Roy. **The Face of Robert E. Lee in Life and Legend.** NY: Scribner; 1947. [$20.00]

Meredith, Roy. **Mr. Lincoln's Camera Man.** NY: Scribner; 1946. [$30.00]

Meredith, Roy. **Storm over Sumter.** NY: Simon and Schuster; 1957. [$14.50]

Mereness, Newton Dennison. **Maryland as a Proprietary Province.** NY, London: Macmillan; 1901. [$60.00]

Meriwether, Elizabeth Avery. **Facts and Falsehoods Concerning the War on the South.** Memphis: Taylor; 1904. [rebound, $65.00]

Merkley, Christopher. **Biography of.** Salt Lake City: Parry; 1887. [$100.00]

Merriam, C. Hart. **Dawn of the World.** Cleveland: Clark; 1910. [$75.00]

Merrifield, Edward. **Story of the Captivity and Rescue from the Indians of Luke Swetland.** Scranton, PA: [s.n.]; 1915. [$60.00]

Mersfelder, Louis Calhoun. **Cowboy--Fisherman--Hunter: True Stories of the Great Southwest.** Kansas City, MO: Brown-White-Lowell; 1951. [signed, $35.00]

Mershon, Stephen Lyon. **Power of the Crown in the Valley of the Hudson.** Brattleboro: Vermont Printing; 1925. [$35.00]

Meserve, Frederick Hill. **The Photographs of Abraham Lincoln.** NY: Harcourt, Brace; 1944. [$50.00]

Messiter, Charles Alston. **Sport and Adventures among the North-American Indians.** London: Porter; 1890. [$125.00]

Meyer, Annie. **Barnard Beginnings.** Boston, NY: Houghton Mifflin; 1935. [$17.50]

Meyer, Carl of Basel. **Nach dem Sacramento.** Aarau: Sauerlander; 1855. [wraps chipped and worn, $100.00]

Meyer, Isadore S. **Early History of Zionism in America.** see, American Jewish Historical Society.

Meyer, Leland Winfield. **Life and Times of Colonel Richard M. Johnson of Kentucky.** NY; London: Columbia UP; King; 1932. [$40.00]

Meyer, Roy Willard. **History of the Santee Sioux.** Lincoln: U. of Nebraska; 1967. [$25.00]

Meyers, William H. **Journal of a Cruise to California and the Sandwich Islands.** San Francisco: Book Club of California; 1955. [$150.00]

Michaux, Francois Andre. **Travels to the Westward of the Allegany [sic.] Mountains.** London: Phillips; 1805. [rebound, $300.00]

Michelson, Truman. **Observations on the Thunder Dance of the Bear Gens of the Fox Indians.** Washington: USGPO; 1929. [$25.00]

Michener, Ezra. **Retrospect of Early Quakerism.** Philadelphia: Zell; 1860. [$35.00]

Michie, Allan Andrew. **Dixie Demagogues.** NY: Vanguard; 1939. [$15.00]

Michigan Commissioner of Immigration. **Michigan and Its Resources.** 3rd ed. Lansing: George; 1883. [$35.00]

Middlebrook, Louis Frank. **History of Maritime Connecticut during the American Revolution.** Salem, MA: Essex Institute; 1925. 2 v. [$50.00]

Middleton, Philip Harvey. **Half Century of Teamwork.** Chicago: Railway Progress Institute; 1958. [$15.00]

Middleton, Thomas C. **Historical Sketch of the Augustinian Monastery, College and Mission of St. Thomas of Villanova.** Philadelphia: Villanova College; 1893. [$22.00]

Miers, Earl Schenck. **The General Who Marched to Hell.** 1st ed. NY: Knopf; 1951. [$25.00]

Miers, Earl Schenck. **The Web of Victory.** NY: Knopf; 1955. [$18.00]

Mighels, Ella Sterling. **The Story of the Files.** San Francisco: Cooperative Print.; 1893. [cover rubbed, $125.00]

Milbank, Jeremiah. **The First Century of Flight in America.** Princeton: Princeton UP; 1943. [$35.00]

Milburn, William Henry. **The Pioneers, Preachers and People of the Mississippi Valley.** 1st ed. NY: Derby & Jackson; 1860. [binding faded, $45.00]

Milburn, William Henry. **The Rifle, Axe, and Saddle-Bags.** NY; Cincinnati: Derby & Jackson; Derby; 1857. [$65.00]

Milburn, William Henry. **Ten Years of Preacher-Life.** NY: Derby & Jackson; 1859. [$60.00]

Miles, Nelson Appleton. **Personal Recollections and Observations of.** Chicago, NY: Werner; 1896. [spine repaired, hinges starting, $100.00] [$175.00] [$125.00] [2nd issue, $100.00] [1897 printing, $150.00]

Miles, Nelson Appleton. **Serving the Republic.** NY: Harper; 1911. [$75.00]

Milfort, Louis. **Memoirs.** Kennesaw, GA: Continental; 1959. [$20.00]

Milham, Charles G. **Gallant Pelham.** Washington: Public Affairs; 1959. [$50.00]

Milhollen, Hirst Dillon. **Divided We Fought.** NY: Macmillan; 1956. [$25.00]

Military Historical Society of Massachusetts. **Civil War and Miscellaneous Papers.** Boston: The Society; 1918. [$45.00]

Millais, John Guille. **Newfoundland and Its Untrodden Ways.** London, NY: Longmans, Green; 1907. [$75.00] [1967 Arno reprint, $30.00]]

Miller, A. P. **Tom's Experience in Dakota.** Minneapolis: Miller, Hale; 1883. [$225.00]

Miller, Alexander Quintella. **Jayhawk Editor.** 1st ed. Los Angeles: Sterling; 1955. [chipped dj, $10.00]

Miller, Alfred Jacob. **The West of Alfred Jacob Miller (1837).** 1st ed. Norman: U. of Oklahoma; 1951. [$60.00]

Miller, Alice Duer. **Barnard College.** NY: Columbia UP; 1939. [$25.00]

Miller, Amy. **The Pioneer Doctor in the Ozarks White River Country.** Kansas City, MO: Burton; 1949. [$16.00]

Miller, Daniel. **Early History of the Reformed Church in Pennsylvania.** Reading: Miller; 1906. [$25.00]

Miller, David E. **Hole-in-the-Rock.** 2nd ed. Salt Lake City: U. of Utah; 1966. [$30.00]

Miller, David Humphreys. **Custer's Fall.** 1st ed. NY: Duell, Sloan and Pearce; 1957. [1st printing, $45.00]

Miller, Delavan S. **Drum Taps in Dixie.** Watertown, NY: Hungerford-Holbrook; 1905. [$45.00]

Miller, Floyd. **Bill Tilghman.** 1st ed. Garden City: Doubleday; 1968. [$17.50]

Miller, Francis Trevelyan. **Photographic History of the Civil War.** NY: Review of Reviews; 1911. 10 v. [fine, $350.00] [$250.00]

Miller, Henry. **Colossus of Maroussi.** San Francisco: Colt; 1941. [chipped dj, $90.00]

Miller, Henry. **Remember to Remember.** NY: New Directions; 1947. [front hinge loose, taped dj, $50.00]

Miller, Henry. **Sunday after the War.** Norfolk, CT: New Directions; 1944. [$50.00]

Miller, Henry. **Wisdom of the Heart.** Norfolk, CT: New Directions; 1941. [back flap of dj missing, $50.00]

Miller, James McDonald. **Genesis of Western Culture.** Columbus: Ohio State Archaeological and Hist. Soc.; 1938. [$22.50]

Miller, Joaquin. **Overland in a Covered Wagon.** NY, London: Appleton; 1930. [$40.00] [$35.00]

Miller, Joaquin. **Songs of the Sierras.** Roberts; 1871. [cover worn and bumped, $40.00]

Miller, Joaquin. **True Bear Stories.** Chicago: Rand, McNally; 1900. [2nd printing, $40.00]

Miller, Joaquin. **Unwritten History: Life amongst the Modocs.** Hartford: American Pub. Co.; 1874. [$175.00]

Miller, John. **Description of the Province and City of New York.** new ed. NY: Gowans; 1862. [$50.00]

Miller, John Chester. **Origins of the American Revolution.** Boston: Little, Brown; 1943. [$15.00]

Miller, Joseph. **The Arizona Story.** NY: Hastings; 1952. [$22.50]

Miller, Joseph. **Arizona: The Last Frontier.** NY: Hastings; 1956. [chipped dj, $17.50]

Miller, Joseph. **Monument Valley and the Navajo Country.** NY: Hastings; 1951. [$30.00]

Miller, Lee Graham. **An Ernie Pyle Album.** NY: Sloane; 1946. [$15.00]

Miller, Marion Mills. **Great Debates in American History.** national ed. NY: Current Literature; 1913. [$150.00]

Miller, Max. **The Great Trek.** Garden City: Doubleday, Doran; 1935. [$18.00]

Miller, Perry. **Life of the Mind in America, from the Revolution to the Civil War.** 1st ed. NY: Harcourt, Brace & World; 1965. [$20.00]

Miller, Perry. **New England Mind: From Colony to Province.** Cambridge: Harvard UP; 1953. [$20.00]

Miller, Perry. **The New England Mind: The Seventeenth Century.** NY: Macmillan; 1939. [spine faded, $20.00] [1954 Harvard ed., $20.00]

Miller, Perry. **The Transcendentalists.** Cambridge: Harvard UP; 1950. [$20.00]

Miller, Robert Ryal. **For Science and National Glory.** Norman: U. of Oklahoma; 1968. [$16.00]

Miller, Samuel. **Life of Samuel Miller.** Philadelphia: Claxton, Remsen and Haffelfinger; 1869. 2 v. [$40.00]

Miller, Sidney Lincoln. **Tomorrow in West Texas.** Lubbock: Texas Tech; 1956. [dj chipped, $30.00]

Miller, William. **Evidence from Scripture and History of the Second Coming of Christ about the Year 1843.** Troy, NY: Kemble & Hooper; 1836. [$350.00]

Miller, William. **Views of the Prophecies and Prophetic Chronology.** Boston: Dow; 1841. [$125.00]

Miller, William D. **Memphis during the Progressive Era, 1900-1917.** Memphis: Memphis State UP; 1957. [$20.00]

Millis, Walter. **The Martial Spirit.** Cambridge: Riverside Press; 1931. [$15.00]

Mills, Anson. **My Story.** Washington: The Author; 1918. [$100.00]

Mills, Bill. **25 Years behind Prison Bars.** Emory, TX: Mills; [1939?]. [$75.00]

Mills, Enos Abijah. **Spell of the Rockies.** Boston, NY: Houghton Mifflin; 1911. [$25.00]

Mills, George S. **Little Man with the Long Shadow.** Des Moines: Hubbell Estate; 1955. [$17.50]

Mills, Randall Vause. **Stern-Wheelers up Columbia.** Palo Alto, CA: Pacific; 1947. [$35.00]

Mills, Samuel John. **Report of a Missionary Tour through That Part of the United States Which Lies West of the Allegany [sic.] Mountains.** Andover, MA: Flagg and Gould; 1815. [$225.00]

Milner, Joe E. **California Joe.** Caldwell, ID: Caxton; 1935. [$75.00] [$85.00]

Milton, George Fort. **Age of Hate; Andrew Johnson and the Radicals.** NY: Coward-McCann; 1930. [$25.00] [$40.00]

Milton, George Fort. **The Eve of Conflict.** Boston, NY: Houghton Mifflin; 1934. [$20.00]

M'Ilvaine, William. **Sketches of Scenery and Notes of Personal Adventure in California and Mexico.** Philadelphia: Smith & Peters; 1850. [$3000.00]

Mindlin, Henrique E. **Modern Architecture in Brazil.** Rio de Janeiro: Colibris; 1956. [inscribed, $30.00]

Miner, Charles. **History of Wyoming.** Philiadelphia: Crissy; 1845. [$75.00]

Miner, H. Craig. **The St. Louis-San Francisco Transcontinental Railroad.** Lawrence: UP of Kansas; 1972. [$15.00]

Minnesota. Bureau of Statistics. **Minnesota: Its Resources and Progress.** St. Paul: Press Print.; 1870. [$100.00]

Minnesota. State Board of Immigration. **State of Minnesota.** St. Paul: The Board; 1885. [$35.00]

Minnigh, Luther William. **Gettysburg: "What They Did Here."** [s.l.:s.n.]; 1892. [$25.00] [some underlining, $10.00]

Minter, John Easter. **The Chagres.** NY: Rinehart; 1948. [near fine in dj, $22.00]

Mirabeau, Gabriel-Honore de Riqueti comte de. **Discours du Comte de Mirabeau, dans la Seance du 11 Juin, sur la Mort de Benjamin Francklin.** Paris: Baudouin; 1790. [$145.00]

Miranda, Francisco de. **Diary of.** NY: Hispanic Society of America; 1928. [$45.00]

Miranda, Francisco de. **The New Democracy in America.** 1st ed. Norman: U. of Oklahoma; 1963. [$20.00]

Mississippi State Geologist. **Report on the Agriculture and Geology of Mississippi.** Jackson: Barksdale; 1854. [$75.00]

Mitchel, Frederic Augustus. **Chattanooga.** 1st ed. NY: American News; 1891. [$35.00]

Mitchell, Broadus. **William Gregg.** Chapel Hill: U. of North Carolina; 1928. [silverfished, bumped, and rubbed, $30.00]

Mitchell, David W. **Ten Years in the United States.** London: Smith, Elder; 1862. [$100.00]

Mitchell, Frances Letcher. **Georgia: Land and People.** Atlanta: Franklin; 1900. [silverfished, hinges repaired, $40.00]

Mitchell, John. **Reminiscences of Scenes and Characters in College.** New Haven: Maltby; 1847. [$25.00]

Mitchell, John Donald. **Lost Mines & Buried Treasures along the Old Frontier.** Palm Desert, CA: Desert Magazine; 1953. [$35.00]

Mitchell, Joseph Brady. **Decisive Battles of the American Revolution.** NY: Putnam; 1962. [x-lib., $12.50]

Mitchell, Joseph Brady. **Decisive Battles of the Civil War.** NY: Putnam; 1955. [$30.00]

Mitchell, Lige. **Daring Exploits of Jesse James.** Baltimore: Ottenheimer; 1912. [$35.00]

Mitchell, S. Augustus. **Texas, Oregon, and California.** Oakland, CA: Biobooks; 1948. [$45.00]

Mitchell, S. Weir. **The Red City.** NY: Century; 1908. [$20.00]

Mitgang, Herbert. **The Man Who Rode the Tiger.** 1st ed. Philadelphia: Lippincott; 1963. [$18.50]

Mizener, Arthur. **The Far Side of Paradise.** Boston: Houghton Mifflin; 1951. [fine in dj, $25.00]

Mizner, Addison. **Florida Architecture of.** NY: Helburn; 1928. [$150.00]

M'Lean, James. **Seventeen Years' History of the Life and Sufferings of.** 1st ed. Hartford: Russell; 1814. [$500.00]

M'Leod, Donald. **A Brief Review of the Settlement of Upper Canada by the U. E. Loyalists and Scotch Highlanders.** Cleveland: The Author; 1841. [crudely rebacked, $395.00]

Moat, Louis Shepheard. **Frank Leslie's Illustrated Famous Leaders and Battle Scenes of the Civil War.** NY: Leslie; 1896. [$200.00]

Mockridge, Norton. **The Big Fix.** 1st ed. NY: Holt; 1954. [$12.50]

Moffett, Thomas Clinton. **The American Indian on the New Trail.** NY: Missionary Education Movement; 1914. [$35.00]

Moger, Allen Wesley. **Virginia: Bourbonism to Byrd.** Charlottesville: U. of Virginia; 1968. [$25.00]

Mohler, J. L. **Description of Weyer's Cave in Augusta County, Virginia.** [s.l.: s.n.]; 1852. [$150.00]

Mohr, Robert Landis. **Thomas Henry Burrowes.** Philadelphia; London: U. of Pennsylvania; Oxford UP; 1946. [$12.50]

Molina, Giovanni Ignacio. **The Geographical, Natural and Civil History of Chili.** Middletown, CT: Riley; 1808. 2 v. [covers worn, map repaired, $200.00] [front cover of vol. 2 detached, $125.00] [$150.00]

Molyneaux, Peter. **The Romantic Story of Texas.** NY, Dallas: Cordova; 1936. [$28.00] [$40.00]

Momaday, N. Scott. **House Made of Dawn.** 1st ed. NY: Harper & Row; 1968. [$50.00]

Mombert, Jacob Isidor. **Authentic History of Lancaster County in the State of Pennsylvania.** Lancaster: Barr; 1869. [rebound, $120.00]

Monaghan, Frank. **John Jay, Defender of Liberty.** 1st ed. NY, Indianapolis: Bobbs-Merrill; 1935. [$25.00]

Monaghan, Jay. **The Book of the American West.** NY: Messner; 1963. [$30.00]

Monaghan, Jay. **Civil War on the Western Border.** 1st ed. Boston: Little, Brown; 1955. [$35.00]

Monaghan, Jay. **Diplomat in Carpet Slippers.** 1st ed. Indianapolis, NY: Bobbs-Merrill; 1945. [$25.00]

Monaghan, Jay. **The Great Rascal.** 1st ed. Boston: Little, Brown; 1952, c1951. [$10.00] [$15.00]

Monaghan, Jay. **Last of the Bad Men.** 1st ed. Indianapolis: Bobbs-Merrill; 1946. [$35.00] [later printing, $15.00]

Monaghan, Jay. **The Overland Trail.** 1st ed. Indianapolis: Bobbs-Merrill; 1947. [$25.00]

Monardes, Nicolas. **Joyfull Newes out of the Newe Founde Worlde.** London; NY: Constable; Knopf; 1925. 2 v. [$125.00]

Moncrieff, Ascott Robert Hope. **The Men of the Backwoods.** London; NY: Griffith and Farran; Dutton; 1880. [x-lib., hinge cracked, $15.00]

Monette, John Wesley. **History of the Discovery and Settlement of the Valley of the Mississippi by the Three Great European Powers.** NY: Harper; 1846. 2 v. [$350.00]

Monk, Maria. **Awful Disclosures of the Hotel Dieu Nunnery of Montreal.** NY: De Witt & Davenport; 1855. [$75.00]

Monro, Alexander. **The United States and the Dominion of Canada: Their Future.** Saint John, NB: Barnes; 1879. [pencil annotations, $40.00, Canadian]

Monroe, Harriet. **Valeria and Other Poems.** Chicago: McClurg; 1892. [$60.00]

Monroe, James. **Narrative of a Tour of Observation Made during the Summer of 1817.** Philadelphia: Mitchell & Ames; 1818. [needs rebinding, $75.00]

Montague, Gilbert Holland. **Rise and Progress of the Standard Oil Company.** NY, London: Harper; 1904. [$30.00] [$50.00]

Montana. Dept. of Agriculture and Publicity. **The Resources and Opportunities of Montana.** Helena: Independent; 1915. [x-lib., $30.00]

Monteiro, Aristides. **War Reminiscences.** Richmond: Waddey; 1890. [$135.00]

Montenegro, Roberto. **Pintura Mexicana.** Mexico: 1933. [crudely rebacked, $75.00]

Montgomery, Cora. see, Cazneau, Jane Maria.

Montgomery, Henry. **Life of Major General Zachary Taylor.** 20th ed. Auburn, NY: Derby, Miller; 1850. [$150.00]

Montgomery, Henry. **Life of Major-General William H. Harrison.** alta ed. Philadelphia: Porter & Coates; 1852. [$25.00]

Montgomery, Thomas Harrison. **History of the University of Pennsylvania.** Philadelphia: Jacobs; 1900. [$27.50]

Montoya, Juan de. **New Mexico in 1602.** Albuquerque: Quivira Society; 1938. [$185.00]

Montross, Lynn. **Rag, Tag, and Bobtail.** NY: Harper; 1952. [$10.00]

Montule, Edouard de. **Travels in America, 1816-1817.** Bloomington: Indiana UP; 1951, c1950. [$35.00]

Montule, Edouard de. **A Voyage to North America and the West Indies in 1817.** London: Phillips; 1821. [$300.00] [$250.00]

Moodie, Susannah. **Roughing It in the Bush.** Toronto: McClelland; 1923. [$15.00]

Moody, Dan W. **Life of a Rover.** Chicago: Moody; 1926. [$26.00] [rebound, $10.00]

Moody, Helen. **The Unquiet Sex.** NY: Scribner; 1898. [$47.50]

Moody, Loring. **Facts for the People.** Boston: Anti-Slavery Office; 1847. [title page stained, $125.00]

Moody, Loring. **History of the Mexican War.** 2nd ed. Boston: Marsh; 1848. [$250.00]

Moody, Ralph. **Little Britches.** 1st ed. NY: Norton; 1950. [$12.50]

Moody, Ralph. **The Old Trails West.** NY: Crowell; 1963. [$30.00]

Moody, Ralph. **Stagecoach West.** NY: Promontory; 1967. [$12.00]

Moody, William Vaughn. **Masque of Judgment.** Boston: Small, Maynard; 1900. [$25.00]

Mooney, Booth. **Lyndon Johnson Story.** NY: Farrar, Straus and Cudahy; 1956. [$20.00]

Moore, Albert Burton. **Conscription and Conflict in the Confederacy.** NY: Macmillan; 1924. [$45.00]

Moore, Clarence Bloomfield. **Antiquities of the St. Francis, White, and Black Rivers, Arkansas.** Philadelphia: Stockhausen; 1910. [$65.00]

Moore, Clarence Bloomfield. **Certain Mounds of Arkansas and of Mississippi.** Philadelphia: Stockhausen; 1908. [$65.00]

Moore, Edward Alexander. **Story of a Cannoneer under Stonewall Jackson.** NY, Washington: Neale; 1907. [$150.00] [1910 Bell ed., $110.00; dj chipped, $200.00]

Moore, Francis Jr. **Map and Description of Texas.** Philadelphia; NY: Tanner; Tanner & Disturnell; 1840. [lacks map and plates, $1500.00]

Moore, Frank. **The Civil War in Song and Story.** NY: Collier; 1882. [$25.00]

Moore, Frank. **Diary of the American Revolution.** NY: Scribner; 1860. 2 v. [$110.00]

Moore, Frank. **Women of the War.** Hartford; Chicago: Scranton; Treat; 1866. [foxed, hinges cracked, worn, $15.00] [$50.00] [1867 ed., $40.00]

Moore, George Henry. **Notes on the History of Slavery in Massachusetts.** NY: Appleton; 1866. [$50.00] [$85.00]

Moore, George Henry. **Treason of Charles Lee.** 1st ed. NY: Scribner; 1860. [binding dampstained and wrinkled, $50.00] [$65.00] [x-lib., inscribed, $75.00]

Moore, Glover. **The Missouri Controversy, 1819-1821.** Lexington: U. of Kentucky; 1953. [$30.00]

Moore, H. Judge. **Scott's Campaign in Mexico.** Charleston: Nixon; 1849. [$165.00]

Moore, Hugh. **Memoir of Col. Ethan Allen.** Plattsburg, NY: Cook; 1834. [$100.00]

Moore, James. **Kilpatrick and Our Cavalry.** NY: Widdleton; 1865. [badly worn and foxed, $20.00]

Moore, Lucia Wilkins. **Story of Eugene.** NY: Stratford; 1949. [$25.00]

Moore, Martin. **Boston Revival, 1842.** Boston: Putnam; 1842. [$40.00]

Moore, Merrill. **The Fugitive.** Boston: [s.n.]; 1939. [$25.00]

Moore, Nathaniel Fish. **Historical Sketch of Columbia College.** NY: The College; 1876. [$25.00]

Moore, Powell A. **The Calumet Region.** Indianapolis: Indiana Historical Bureau; 1959. [x-lib., $15.00]

Moore, Terris. **Mt. McKinley: The Pioneer Climbs.** College: U. of Alaska; 1967. [signed, $27.50]

Moore, William V. **Indian Wars of the United States from the Discovery to the Present Time.** Philadelphia: Smith; 1841. [$25.00] [1852 Pomeroy imprint, $25.00]

Moorehead, Warren King. **American Indian in the United States, Period 1850-1914.** Andover, MA: Andover Press; 1914. [$85.00]

Moorhead, Max L. **The Apache Frontier.** 1st ed. Norman: U. of Oklahoma; 1968. [$30.00] [$20.00]

Moorhead, Max L. **New Mexico's Royal Road.** 1st ed. Norman: U. of Oklahoma; 1958. [x-lib., $15.00]

Moorhouse, Lee. **Souvenir Album of Noted Indian Photographs.** 2nd ed. Pendleton, OR: Moorhouse; 1906. [$50.00]

Moors, J. F. **History of the Fifty-Second Regiment, Massachusetts Volunteers.** Boston: Ellis; 1893. [$55.00]

Mora, Joseph Jacinto. **Californios.** 1st ed. Garden City: Doubleday; 1949. [very good in dj, $35.00]

Mordecai, Samuel. **Richmond in By-Gone Days.** Richmond: West; 1856. [$60.00]

More, Charles Albert. **A French Volunteer of the War of Independence.** 2nd ed. Paris: Carrington; 1898. [$45.00] [1898 Appleton imprint, $25.00]

Moreau de Saint-Mery, M. L. E. **Moreau de St. Mery's American Journey (1793-1798).** 1st ed. Garden City: Doubleday; 1947. [$15.00] [$10.00]

Morfi, Juan Agustin. **History of Texas, 1673-1779.** Albuquerque: Quivira Society; 1935. 2 v. [$485.00]

Morgan, A. T. **Yazoo.** Washington: Morgan; 1884. [$75.00] [$150.00]

Morgan, Arthur Ernest. **Nowhere Was Somewhere.** Chapel Hill: U. of North Carolina; 1946. [$20.00]

Morgan, Dale Lowell. **Jedediah Smith and His Maps of the American West.** San Francisco: California Historical Soc.; 1954. [$500.00]

Morgan, Edward E. P. **God's Loaded Dice: Alaska, 1897-1930.** Caldwell, ID: Caxton; 1948. [$20.00] [$15.00]

Morgan, George. **Life of James Monroe.** Boston: Small, Maynard; 1921. [$45.00]

Morgan, James. **Theodore Roosevelt.** NY: Macmillan; 1907. [$12.50]

Morgan, James Morris. **Recollections of a Rebel Reefer.** Boston, NY: Houghton Mifflin; 1917. [$60.00] [$100.00] [$55.00]

Morgan, John Hill. **Life Portraits of Washington and Their Replicas.** Philadelphia: Lancaster; 1931. [$250.00]

Morgan, Lewis Henry. **Indian Journals, 1859-62.** Ann Arbor: U. of Michigan; 1959. [fine, $50.00] [$45.00]

Morgan, Lewis Henry. **League of the Ho-De-No-Sau-Nee or Iroquois.** new ed. NY: Dodd, Mead; 1901. 2 v. [$175.00] [1904 one vol. issue, $120.00]

Morgan, Murray Cromwell. **Last Wilderness.** NY: Viking; 1955. [$12.00]

Morgan, Murray Cromwell. **Skid Road.** rev. ed. NY: Viking; 1960. [$25.00]

Morgan, Thomas. **My Story of the Last Indian War in the Northwest.** [Forest Grove?, OR: s.n.]; 1954. [signed, $35.00]

Morgan, William. **Human-Wolves among the Navaho.** New Haven; London: Yale UP; Oxford UP; 1936. [$25.00]

Morgan, William. **Memoirs of the Life of the Rev. Richard Price.** London: Hunter; 1815. [inscribed, $25.00]

Morgenstern, George Edward. **Pearl Harbor.** NY: Devin-Adair; 1947. [$12.50]

Morison, John Lyle. **British Supremacy and Canadian Self-Government.** Glasgow: MacLehose; 1919. [$20.00, Canadian]

Morison, Samuel Eliot. **Builders of the Bay Colony.** Boston: Houghton Mifflin; 1930. [$35.00]

Morison, Samuel Eliot. **Development of Harvard University since the Inauguration of President Eliot, 1869-1929.** Cambridge: Harvard UP; 1930. [$30.00] [$35.00]

Morison, Samuel Eliot. **Harvard College in the Seventeenth Century.** Cambridge: Harvard UP; 1936. [$55.00]

Morison, Samuel Eliot. **Life and Letters of Harrison Gray Otis.** Boston, NY: Houghton Mifflin; 1913. 2 v. [$125.00]

Morison, Samuel Eliot. **Maritime History of Massachusetts, 1783-1860.** Boston: Houghton Mifflin; 1941. [$20.00]

Morison, Samuel Eliot. **The Puritan Pronaos.** 1st ed. NY; London: New York UP; Oxford UP; 1936. [$35.00] [$40.00]

Morison, Samuel Eliot. **Three Centuries of Harvard.** Cambridge: Harvard UP; 1936. [$15.00] [$25.00]

Morleigh. **A Merry Briton in Pioneer Wisconsin.** Madison: State Hist. Soc.; 1950. [$10.00]

Morley, Margaret Warner. **The Carolina Mountains.** Boston, NY: Houghton Mifflin; 1913. [$22.00]

Morley, Sylvanus Griswold. **Ancient Maya.** 2nd ed. Stanford: Stanford UP; 1947. [$45.00]

Morley, Sylvanus Griswold. **Covered Bridges of California.** Berkeley: U. of California; 1938. [$45.00] [$40.00]

Morphis, James M. **History of Texas from Its Discovery and Settlement.** NY: United States Pub. Co.; 1874. [map repaired, $350.00]

Morrel, Martha McBride. **Young Hickory.** 1st ed. NY: Dutton; 1949. [$45.00]

Morrell, Zenos N. **Flowers and Fruits in the Wilderness.** 3rd ed. St. Louis: Commercial; 1882, c1872. [$485.00]

Morris, Benjamin Franklin. **Historical Sketch of Rising Sun, Indiana, and the Presbyterian Church.** Cincinnati: Moore, Wilstach, Keys; 1858. [$100.00]

Morris, Charles. **Autobiography of.** Boston: Williams; 1880. [$75.00]

Morris, Edward Parmelee. **The Fore-and-Aft Rig in America: A Sketch.** New Haven; London: Yale UP; Oxford UP; 1927. [$100.00]

Morris, Gouverneur. **Diary and Letters of.** NY: Scribner; 1888. 2 v. [$75.00]

Morris, Henry Curtis. **Desert Gold and Total Prospecting.** Washington: [s.n.];1955. [$45.00]

Morris, Lerona Rosamond. **Oklahoma, Land of Opportunity.** Guthrie: Co-Operative; 1934. [$50.00]

Morris, Lerona Rosamond. **Oklahoma, Yesterday--Today--Tomorrow.** Guthrie: Co-Operative; 1930. [$45.00]

Morris, Lloyd R. **The Rebellious Puritan.** NY: Harcourt, Brace; 1927. [$17.50]

Morris, Robert C. **The Carnegie Public Library, Cheyenne, Wyoming.** Cheyenne: Daily Leader; 1902. [signed, $25.00]

Morrison, Hugh. **Early American Architecture from the First Colonial Settlements to the National Period.** NY: Oxford UP; 1952. [$20.00]

Morrison, Okey J. **The Slaughter of the Pfost-Greene Family of Jackson County West Virginia.** Cincinnati: Gibson and Sorin; 1898. [$50.00]

Morse, Anson Ely. **Federalist Party in Massachusetts to the Year 1800.** Princeton: University Library; 1909. [$45.00]

Morse, Jedidiah. **Annals of the American Revolution.** Hartford: [s.n.]; 1824. [rubbed, worn, foxed, $40.00] [$100.00]

Morse, John Frederick. **Illustrated Historical Sketches of California.** Sacramento: Democratic State Journal; 1854. [$1250.00]

Morse, John Torrey. **Life of Alexander Hamilton.** 1st ed. Boston: Little, Brown; 1876. 2 v. [$40.00]

Morse, Samuel Finley Breese. **Foreign Conspiracy against the Liberties of the United States.** 6th ed. NY: American Protestant Soc.; 1844. [foxed, $40.00]

Morse, Samuel Finley Breese. **Samuel F. B. Morse; His Letters and Journals.** Boston, NY: Houghton Mifflin; 1914. 2 v. [$35.00]

Mortimer, William Golden. **Peru. History of Coca, "The Divine Plant" of the Incas.** NY: Vail; 1901. [$200.00]

Morton, Arthur Silver. **History of the Canadian West to 1870-71.** London, NY: Nelson; 1939. [$200.00, Canadian]

Morton, John S. **History of the Origin of the Appellation Keystone State.** Philadelphia: Claxton, Remsen & Haffelfinger; 1874. [$20.00]

Morton, Joseph W. **Sparks from the Camp Fire.** new ed. Philadelphia: Keystone; 1890. [rear hinge cracked, $20.00]

Morton, Nathaniel. **New England's Memorial.** 6th ed. Boston: Congregational Board of Publication; 1855. [spine chipped, $65.00]

Morton, Sarah Wentworth. **Beacon Hill.** Boston: Manning & Loring; 1797. [book one all published, edges frayed, $150.00]

Mosby, John Singleton. **Memoirs of.** Boston: Little, Brown; 1917. [some underlining, $125.00]

Mosby, John Singleton. **Stuart's Cavalry in the Gettysburg Campaign.** NY: Moffat, Yard; 1908. [rebound, $60.00]

Moseley, Mary. **Bahamas Handbook.** Nassau: Guardian; 1926. [$30.00]

Moser, Brian. **The Cocaine Eaters.** London: Longmans; 1965. [minor cover stains, $17.50]

Moses, Frederick Taft. **Firemen of Industry.** Providence: Fireman's Mutual Insurance; 1954. [$10.00]

Mosgrove, George Dallas. **Kentucky Cavaliers in Dixie.** Jackson, TN: McCowart-Mercer; 1957. [$45.00] [$50.00]

Motley, John Lothrop. **The Causes of the American Civil War.** NY: Gregory; 1861. [$30.00]

Motley, John Lothrop. **Merry-Mount.** Boston, Cambridge: Munroe; 1849, c1848. 2 v. in 1. [x-lib., $85.00]

Mott, Edward Harold. **Between the Ocean and the Lakes.** NY: Collins; 1901. [x-lib., $100.00] [1908 Ticker imprint, $75.00]

Mott, Emma. **Legends and Lore of the Long Ago.** Los Angeles: Wetzel; 1929. [$20.00]

Mott, George Scudder. **History of the Presbyterian Church in Flemington, New Jersey.** NY: Ketcham; 1894. [$25.00]

Motte, Jacob Rhett. **Journey into Wilderness.** Gainesville: U. of Florida; 1953. [$65.00]

Mountain Minstrelsy of Pennsylvania. Philadelphia: McGirr; 1931. [$32.00]

Mowery, William Byron. **Tales of the Ozarks.** NY: Bouregy & Curl; 1954. [$7.50]

Mowry, William Augustus. **Recollections of a New England Educator.** NY, Boston: Silver, Burdett; 1908. [$17.50]

Moyle, Seth. **My Friend, O. Henry.** NY: Fly; 1914. [$30.00]

M'Robert, Patrick. **Tour through Part of the Northern Provinces of America.** Philadelphia: Pennsylvania Magazine of History and Biography; 1935. [$35.00]

Muir, John. **Cruise of the Corwin.** Boston, NY: Houghton Mifflin; 1917. [$85.00] [$150.00]

Muir, John. **John of the Mountains.** Boston: Houghton Mifflin; 1938. [$55.00]

Muir, John. **The Mountains of California.** NY: Century; 1894. [$275.00]

Muir, John. **My First Summer in the Sierra.** Boston: Houghton Mifflin; 1916. [$185.00]

Muir, John. **Our National Parks.** Boston, NY: Houghton Mifflin; 1901. [$100.00]

Muir, John. **Steep Trails.** Boston: Houghton Mifflin; 1918. [$100.00]

Muir, John. **Stickeen.** Boston, NY: Houghton Mifflin; 1909. [$35.00]

Muir, John. **A Thousand-Mile Walk to the Gulf.** 1st ed. Boston: Houghton Mifflin; 1916. [$175.00]

Muir, John. **The Yosemite.** NY: Century; 1912. [$200.00]

Muir, John. **Yosemite and the Sierra Nevada.** Boston: Houghton Mifflin; 1948. [chipped dj, $125.00]

Muir, Ross L. **Over the Long Term.** NY: Seligman; 1964. [$15.00]

Muirhead, James Fullarton. **Land of Contrasts.** Boston, NY: Lamson, Wolffe; 1898. [$55.00]

Mulder, William. **Homeward to Zion.** Minneapolis: U. of Minnesota; 1957. [$15.00]

Mulford, Prentice. **Life by Land and Sea.** NY: Needham; 1889. [$100.00]

Mulford, Prentice. **Prentice Mulford's Story.** Oakland: Biobooks; 1953. [$15.00] [$20.00]

Mulhern, Donald S. **Donald Stephenson's Reminiscences.** Pittsburgh: Johnston; 1891. [$60.00]

Mullaney, Thomas W. **Four-Score Years: A Contribution to the History of the Catholic Germans in Rochester.** Rochester: Monroe Printing; 1916. [$35.00]

Mullendore, William Clinton. **History of the United States Food Administration, 1917-1919.** Stanford; London: Stanford UP; Oxford UP; 1941. [worn dj, $30.00]

Muller, Dan. **Chico of the + Up Ranch.** 1st ed. Chicago: Reilly & Lee; 1938. [$15.00]

Muller, Dan. **My Life with Buffalo Bill.** Chicago: Reilly & Lee; 1948. [$20.00]

Muller, Johann Wilhelm von. **Reisen in den Vereinigten Staaten, Canada und Mexico.** Leipzig: Brockhaus; 1864-65. 3 v. [spines worn, $200.00]

Mullins (W. H.) Company. **Statues in Stamped Copper and Bronze.** Salem, OH: The Company; 1913. [$25.00]

Mulvihill, William F. **You Tell 'Em; Why Roosevelt and His "Brainstormers" Should Be Defeated . . . and How!** Chicago: Cook County Republican Party; 1936. [$25.00]

Mumey, Nolie. **Calamity Jane, 1852-1903.** limited ed. Denver: Range; 1950. [signed, $250.00]

Mumey, Nolie. **Early Mining Laws of Buckskin Joe--1859.** limited ed. Boulder, CO: Johnson; 1961. [signed, $50.00]

Mumey, Nolie. **History and Laws of Nevadaville.** limited ed. Boulder, CO: Johnson; 1962. [signed, $45.00]

Mumey, Nolie. **History of Tin Cup, Colorado (Virginia City).** signed limited ed. Boulder, CO: Johnson; 1963. [lacks the cup, $85.00]

Mumey, Nolie. **James Pierson Beckwourth, 1856-1866.** limited signed ed. Denver: Old West; 1957. [$135.00] [$165.00]

Mumey, Nolie. **John Williams Gunnison, 1812-1853.** signed limited ed. Denver: Artcraft; 1955. [$150.00]

Mumey, Nolie. **Nathan Addison Baker, 1843-1934.** Denver: Old West; 1965. [$35.00]

Mumey, Nolie. **Old Forts and Trading Posts of the West: Bent's Old Fort and Bent's New Fort on the Arkansas River.** signed limited ed. Denver: Artcraft; 1956. [$150.00]

Mumey, Nolie. **Pioneer Denver.** signed limited ed. Denver: Artcraft; 1948. [$150.00]

Mumey, Nolie. **Poker Alice.** signed limited ed. Denver: Artcraft; 1951. [$50.00]

Mumey, Nolie. **Wigwam.** Boulder, CO: Johnson; 1969. [numbered and signed, fine, $50.00]

Mumford, Lewis. **Roots of Contemporary American Architecture.** NY: Reinhold; 1952. [1956 printing?, $15.00]

Munford, Beverley Bland. **Virginia's Attitude toward Slavery and Secession.** new ed. NY: Longmans, Green; 1910. [$22.50]

Munk, Joseph Amasa. **Activities of a Lifetime.** Los Angeles: Times-Mirror; 1924. [$45.00] [$25.00]

Munk, Joseph Amasa. **Arizona Sketches.** NY: Grafton; 1905. [inscribed, $85.00]

Munk, Joseph Amasa. **Southwest Sketches.** NY, London: Putnam; 1920. [$65.00]

Munro, George Campbell. **Birds of Hawaii.** Honolulu: Tongg; 1944. [$25.00]

Munro, Wilfred Harold. **History of Bristol, R. I.** Providence: Reid; 1880. [$75.00]

Munro, Wilfred Harold. **Tales of an Old Sea Port.** Princeton: Princeton UP; 1917. [$25.00]

Munroe, John A. **Federalist Delaware, 1775-1815.** New Brunswick, NJ: Rutgers UP; 1954. [$15.00]

Munsell, Marion Ebenezer. **Flying Sparks.** Kansas City: Tiernan-Dart; 1914. [wraps worn, $100.00] [$100.00]

Murbarger, Nell. **Sovereigns of the Sage.** 1st ed. Palm Desert, CA: Desert Magazine; 1958. [$45.00]

Murdoch, Angus. **Boom Copper.** NY: Macmillan; 1943. [$15.00]

Murdock, Harold. **The Nineteenth of April, 1775.** Boston: Houghton Mifflin; 1925, c1923. [$35.00]

Murdock, Kenneth Ballard. **Increase Mather, the Foremost American Puritan.** Cambridge: Harvard UP; 1925. [$37.50]

Murfin, James V. **Gleam of Bayonets.** NY: Yoseloff; 1965. [$32.50]

Murie, Adolph. **Naturalist in Alaska.** NY: Devin-Adair; 1961. [$14.00]

Murphy, Celeste G. **The People of the Pueblo.** Sonoma, CA: Murphy; 1935. [lacks front endpaper, $35.00]

Murphy, DuBose. **Short History of the Protestant Episcopal Church in Texas.** Dallas: Turner; 1935. [$55.00]

Murphy, Elmer A. **The Thirtieth Division in the World War.** Lepanto, AR: Old Hickory; 1936. [$45.00]

Murphy, John Mortimer. **Sporting Adventures in the Far West.** London: Low, Marston, Searle, & Rivington; 1879. [worn, rebacked, $75.00]

Murphy, Larry. **Out in God's Country.** 1st ed. Springer, NM: Springer Pub. Co.; 1969. [$17.50]

Murphy, Thomas Dowler. **On Sunset Highways.** Boston: Page; 1915. [$55.00]

Murphy, Thomas Dowler. **Three Wonderlands of the American West.** Boston: Page; 1912. [$75.00]

Murphy, Thomas F. **Hearts of the West.** Boston: Christopher; 1928. [$75.00]

Murray, Amelia Matilda. **Letters from the United States, Cuba and Canada.** NY: Putnam; 1856. [sunned and silverfished, $30.00] [$60.00]

Murray, Charles Augustus. **The Prairie-Bird.** London: Bentley; 1844. 3 v. [$100.00]

Murray, Charles Augustus. **Travels in North America during the Years 1834, 1835 & 1836.** London: Bentley; 1839. 2 v. [$585.00]

Murray, Elizabeth Dunbar. **Early Romances of Historic Natchez.** Natchez, MS: Natchez Printing & Stationery; 1938. [signed, $20.00]

Murray, Elizabeth Dunbar. **My Mother Used to Say.** see, Dunbar, Mary Conway.

Murray, Henry Anthony. **Lands of the Slave and the Free.** London: Parker; 1855. 2 v. [$325.00] [1857 one vol. Routledge ed., lacks map, $75.00]

Murray, Hugh. **Historical Account of Discoveries and Travels in North America.** London: Longman, etc.; 1829. 2 v. [rebound, $325.00]

Murray, Lois Lovina Abbott. **Incidents of Frontier Life in Two Parts.** Goshen, IN: Mennonite; 1880. [$175.00]

Murray, Louise Welles. **History of Old Tioga Point and Early Athens, Pennsylvania.** Athens, PA: [s.n.]; 1908, c1907. [somewhat shaken, $60.00]

Murray, Philip Alcemus. **Fishing in the Carolinas.** Chapel Hill: U. of North Carolina; 1941. [$25.00]

Murray, Robert Keith. **Red Scare.** Minneapolis: U. of Minnesota; 1955. [fine in dj, $30.00]

Murray, William Henry Harrison. **Adventures in the Wilderness.** Boston: Fields, Osgood; 1869. [$85.00]

Murray, William Henry Harrison. **Cones for the Camp Fire.** Boston: De Wolfe, Fiske; 1891. [$40.00]

Murrell, William. **History of American Graphic Humor, 1865-1938.** NY: Macmillan; 1938. [$25.00]

Murrett, John C. **Tar Heel Apostle.** NY: Longmans, Green; 1944. [bumped stained, $15.00]

Musmanno, Michael Angelo. **After Twelve Years.** NY, London: Knopf; 1939. [$20.00]

Musmanno, Michael Angelo. **Verdict!** Garden City: Doubleday; 1958. [$15.00]

Musser, Amos Milton. **The Fruits of "Mormonism."** Salt Lake City: Deseret News; 1878. [$40.00]

Muzzey, David Saville. **James G. Blaine.** NY: Dodd-Mead; 1934. [$45.00]

Myers, Albert Cook. **Narratives of Early Pennsylvania, West New Jersey and Delaware, 1630-1707.** NY: Scribner; 1912. [$25.00]

Myers, Frank M. **The Comanches.** Baltimore: Kelly, Piet; 1871. [rubbed, sunned, frayed, $1250.00] [1956 Continental reprint, $55.00]

Myers, Gustavus. **History of Bigotry in the United States.** NY: Random; 1943. [$25.00]

Myers, John Myers. **The Alamo.** 1st ed. NY: Dutton; 1948. [$35.00] [$20.00]

Myers, John Myers. **Deaths of the Bravos.** 1st ed. Boston: Little, Brown; 1962. [$18.00]

Myers, John Myers. **Doc Holliday.** 1st ed. Boston: Little, Brown; 1955. [cover worn, hinge loose, $27.50] [$25.00]

Myers, John Myers. **I, Jack Swilling.** NY: Hastings; 1961. [$20.00]

Myers, John Myers. **The Last Chance; Tombstone's Early Years.** 1st ed. NY: Dutton; 1950. [dj chipped, $30.00]

Myers, John Myers. **San Francisco's Reign of Terror.** 1st ed. Garden City: Doubleday; 1966. [$10.00]

Myers, William Starr. **Fifty Years of the Prudential.** Newark, NJ: The Company; 1927. [$20.00]

Myers, William Starr. **Self-Reconstruction of Maryland, 1864-1867.** Baltimore: Hopkins; 1909. [$65.00]

Myrick, Herbert. **Cache la Poude.** NY, Chicago: Orange Judd; 1905. [$75.00]

Myrthe, A. T. see, Ganilh, Anthony.

Nabuco, Joaquim. **Guerra del Paraguay.** Paris: Garnier; 1901. [$45.00]

Nahm, Milton Charles. **Las Vegas and Uncle Joe.** 1st ed. Norman: U. of Oklahoma; 1964. [$35.00] [$30.00]

Napoleao, Aluizio. **Santos-Dumont and the Conquest of the Air.** Rio de Janeiro: National Print. Off.; 1945. 2 v. [x-lib., $195.00]

Nasatir, Abraham Phineas. **French Activities in California.** Stanford; London: Stanford UP; Oxford UP; 1945. [fine in dj, $40.00]

Nasby, Petroleum V. see, Locke, David Ross.

Nash, George H. **The Conservative Intellectual Movement in America, since 1945.** NY: Basic; 1976. [$20.00]

Nash, Wallis. **Two Years in Oregon.** NY: Appleton; 1882. [$35.00] [$65.00]

Nason, Elias. **A Monogram on Our National Song.** Albany: Munsell; 1869. [$35.00]

Nason, Elias. **Sir Charles Henry Frankland, Baronet.** Albany: Munsell; 1865. [$65.00]

Nathan, George Jean. **American Credo.** NY: Knopf; 1920. [$65.00]

Nathan, Maud. **Once upon a Time and Today.** NY, London: Putnam; 1933. [$35.00]

Nathan, Paul D. **San Saba Papers.** San Francisco: Howell; 1959. [with map in pocket, $30.00]

National Press Club (U.S.). **Harding in Canada.** Vancouver, BC: Sun; 1924. [$125.00]

National Society of the Colonial Dames of America. Connecticut. **Old Inns of Connecticut.** Hartford: Prospect; 1937. [$75.00]

National Speleological Society. **The Caves of Texas.** Washington: The Society; 1948. [$85.00]

National Woman Suffrage and Educational Committee. **Appeal to the Women of the United States.** Hartford: Case, Lockwood & Brainard; 1871. [$85.00]

Naughton, W. W. **Kings of the Queensberry Realm.** Chicago: Continental; 1902. [rear hinge weak, $37.50]

Nead, Daniel Wunderlich. **The Pennsylvania-German in the Settlement of Maryland.** Lancaster: Pennsylvania German Society; 1914. [$30.00]

Neal, Daniel. **History of New England.** London: Clark, Ford, and Cruttenden; 1720. 2 v. [hinges repaired, $475.00] [$500.00]

Nebraska Question. NY: Redfield; 1854. [$45.00]

Neely, Frank Tennyson. **Greater America.** NY, London: Neely; 1898. [$20.00]

Neff, Andrew Love. **History of Utah, 1847-1869.** 1st ed. Salt Lake City: Deseret News; 1940. [$30.00]

Neff, Jacob K. **The Army and Navy of America.** Philadelphia: Pearsol; 1845. [$80.00]

Neide, Charles A. **The Canoe Aurora.** NY: Forest & Stream; 1885. [$47.00]

Neihardt, John Gneisenau. **The River and I.** new ed. NY: Macmillan; 1927. [dj chipped, $25.00] [$35.00]

Neihardt, John Gneisenau. **Song of Jed Smith.** NY: Macmillan; 1941. [$25.00]

Neihardt, John Gneisenau. **Splendid Wayfaring.** NY: Macmillan; 1920. [$65.00]

Neill, Edward D. **English Colonization of America during the Seventeenth Century.** London: Strahan; 1871. [$85.00]

Neill, Edward D. **History of Minnesota.** Philadelphia: Lippincott; 1858. [$100.00]

Neilson, Charles. **An Original, Compiled, and Corrected Account of Burgoyne's Campaign.** Albany: Munsell; 1844. [$150.00]

Nelligan, John Emmett. **Life of a Lumberman.** [s.l.: s.n.]; 1929. [$25.00]

Nelson, Alanson Henery. **Battles of Chancellorsville and Gettysburg.** Minneapolis: [s.n.]; 1899. [$75.00]

Nelson, Bruce Opie. **Land of the Dacotahs.** Minneapolis; London: U. of Minnesota; Oxford UP; 1946. [$25.00]

Nelson, Lowry. **The Mormon Village.** Salt Lake City: U. of Utah; 1952. [$35.00] [$25.00]

Nelson, Oliver. **Cowman's Southwest.** Glendale, CA: Clark; 1953. [$150.00]

Nelson, William Hamilton. **Alluring Arizona.** San Francisco: Nelson; 1927. [$35.00]

Nelson Valley Railway and Transportation Company, Montreal. **A New Route from Europe to the Interior of North America.** Montreal: Lovell; 1881. [wraps chipped, $150.00, Canadian]

Nemerov, Howard. **The Image and the Law.** NY: Holt; 1947. [$50.00]

Neuhaus, Eugen. **William Keith.** Berkeley: U. of California; 1938. [cover rubbed, $85.00]

Neuner, Edward J. **The Natural Gas Industry.** 1st ed. Norman: U. of Oklahoma; 1960. [$20.00]

Neutra, Richard Joseph. **Survival through Design.** NY: Oxford UP; 1954. [$15.00]

Nevins, Allan. **American Social History as Recorded by British Travellers.** NY: Holt; 1923. [$25.00]

Nevins, Allan. **The Emergence of Lincoln.** NY: Scribner; 1950. 2 v. [$30.00]

Nevins, Allan. **Fremont, the West's Greatest Adventurer.** NY, London: Harper; 1928. 2 v. [$75.00]

Nevins, Allan. **The Greater City: New York, 1898-1948.** NY: Columbia UP; 1948. [$25.00]

Nevins, Allan. **Grover Cleveland.** NY: Dodd, Mead; 1933. [$15.00]

Nevins, Allan. **Hamilton Fish.** NY: Dodd, Mead; 1936. [dj chipped, $60.00]

Nevins, Allan. **Ordeal of the Union.** NY: Scribner; 1947. 2 v. [$30.00]

New England Journalist. **The Ramrod Broken.** Boston: Colby; 1859. [$50.00]

New York (City) Mercantile Library Association. **New York City during the American Revolution.** NY: The Association; 1861. [x-lib., $40.00]

Newbery, George Harkness. **Pampa Grass.** Buenos Aires: Guarania; 1953. [$40.00]

Newbrough, John Ballou. **Oahspe.** 1st ed. London: Oahspe; 1882. [worming, $350.00]

Newcomb, Bobby. **Tambo.** NY: Wehman; 1882. [x-lib., $30.00]

Newcomb, Pearson. **The Alamo City.** San Antonio: Newcomb; 1926. [$20.00]

Newcomb, Rexford. **Architecture of the Old Northwest Territory.** Chicago: U. of Chicago; 1950. [$135.00]

Newcomb, Richard. **Our Lost Explorers.** see, Bliss, Richard W.

Newell, Chester. **History of the Revolution in Texas.** NY: Wiley & Putnam; 1838. [with map, $650.00]

Newhall, John B. **Sketches of Iowa, or, The Emigrant's Guide.** NY: Colton; 1841. [lacks map, spine repaired, $100.00]

Newhouse, S. **The Trapper's Guide.** 2nd ed. Wallingford, CT: Oneida Community; 1867. [$320.00]

Newlin, Claude Milton. **Life and Writings of Hugh Henry Brackenridge.** Princeton: Princeton UP; 1932. [x-lib., $30.00]

Newman, Henry Stanley. **Memories of Stanley Pumphrey.** NY: Friends' Book and Tract Committee; 1883. [$20.00]

Newman, James A. **Autobiography of an Old Fashioned Boy.** Oklahoma City: Harlow; 1923. [$85.00]

Newmark, Harris. **Sixty Years in Southern California.** 3rd ed. Boston, NY: Houghton Mifflin; 1930. [$30.00]

Newsome, J. A. **Life and Practice of the Wild and Modern Indian.** Oklahoma City: Harlow; 1923. [$100.00]

Newson, Thomas McLean. **Pen Pictures of St. Paul, Minnesota.** Saint Paul: The Author; 1886. [vol. 1 all published, $125.00]

Newson, Thomas McLean. **Thrilling Scenes among the Indians.** Chicago, NY: Belford, Clarke; 1884. [$100.00]

Newton, Arthur Percival. **Colonising Activities of the English Puritans.** New Haven: Yale UP; 1914. [$35.00]

Newton, Earle W. **Vermont Story.** Montpelier: Vermont Hist. Soc.; 1949. [$15.00]

Newton, John. **Authentic Narrative of Some Remarkable and Interesting Particulars in the Life of Mr. Newton.** Philadelphia: Young; 1795. [$48.00]

Newton, Joseph Fort. **Lincoln and Herndon.** Cedar Rapids, IA: Torch; 1910. [$40.00]

Nicholl, Edith M. **Observations of a Ranchwoman in New Mexico.** London, NY: Macmillan; 1898. [$125.00]

Nichols, Alice. **Bleeding Kansas.** NY: Oxford UP; 1954. [dj frayed, $18.00] [$35.00]

Nichols, Edward Jay. **Zach Taylor's Little Army.** 1st ed. Garden City: Doubleday; 1963. [$15.00]

Nichols, George Ward. **Story of the Great March.** NY: Harper; 1865. [$75.00] [$60.00] [$65.00] [24th ed., 1866, $25.00]

Nichols, James Wilson. **Now You Hear My Horn.** Austin: U. of Texas; 1967. [1st printing, $35.00]

Nichols, Roy Franklin. **The Democratic Machine, 1850-1854.** NY: Columbia UP; 1923. [$45.00]

Nichols, Roy Franklin. **Franklin Pierce.** Philadelphia; London: U. of Pennsylvania; Oxford UP; 1931. [$30.00] [$50.00]

Nichols, Thomas Low. **Forty Years of American Life.** NY: Stackpole; 1937. [fine, $50.00]

Nicholson, Henry Whalley. **From Sword to Share; or, A Fortune in Five Years at Hawaii.** London: Allen; 1881. [$425.00]

Nickerson, Hoffman. **Turning Point of the Revolution; or, Burgoyne in America.** Boston, NY: Houghton Mifflin; 1928. [$40.00] [bumped, rubbed, $20.00]

Nicol, John. **Life & Adventures of.** NY, Toronto: Farrar & Rinehart; 1936. [$35.00]

Nicolay, Charles Grenfell. **The Oregon Territory.** London: Knight; 1846. [binding waterstained, $125.00]

Nicolay, John G. **Outbreak of Rebellion.** NY: Scribner; 1881. [$35.00]

Niles, Grace Greylock. **The Hoosac Valley.** NY: Putnam; 1912. [$37.50]

Niles, Hezekiah. **Principles and Acts of the Revolution in America.** Baltimore: Niles; 1822. [$75.00] [1876 Barnes ed., $45.00]

Niles, John Milton. **History of South America and Mexico.** Hartford: Huntington; 1838. 2 v. in 1. [$135.00]

Niles, John Milton. **Life of Oliver Hazard Perry.** 2nd ed. Hartford: Cooke; 1821. [spine chipped, $150.00]

Niles, John Milton. **View of South-America and Mexico.** NY: Huntington; 1825. 2 v. in 1. [spine worn, with frontis, $125.00] [$95.00] [1826 issue, $90.00]

Nin, Anaïs. **Children of the Albatross.** NY: Dutton; 1947. [inscribed, very good in fine dj, $125.00]

Nin, Anaïs. **Ladders to Fire.** NY: Dutton; 1946. [inscribed, fine with fine dj, $125.00]

Nin, Anaïs. **The Novel of the Future.** NY: Macmillan; 1968. [first printing, inscribed, as new in fine dj, $95.00]

Nin, Anaïs. **Seduction of the Minotaur.** Denver: Swallow; 1961. [inscribed, book fine, dj soiled, $110.00]

Nin, Anaïs. **Under a Glass Bell.** 1st ed. NY: Dutton; 1948. [worn dj, $30.00]

Nix, Evett Dumas. **Oklahombres.** St. Louis: [s.n.]; 1929. [$75.00]

Nixon, H. C. **Forty Acres and Steel Mules.** Chapel Hill: U. of North Carolina; 1938. [x-lib., $15.00]

Noall, Claire Augusta. **Intimate Disciple.** Salt Lake City: U. of Utah; 1957. [$20.00]

Noble, Louis Legrend. **After Icebergs with a Painter.** NY: Appleton; 1861. [$375.00]

Noel, Baptist Wriothesley. **Freedom and Slavery in the United States of America.** London: Nisbet; 1863. [$150.00]

Noel, Theophilus. **Autobiography and Reminiscences of.** Chicago: Noel; 1904. [$200.00] [x-lib., $125.00]

Nogales Mendez, Rafael de. **The Looting of Nicaragua.** London: Wright & Brown; [1928?]. [$75.00]

Noice, Harold H. **Back of Beyond.** NY: Putnam; 1939. [$13.00]

Nolan, Alan T. **The Iron Brigade.** NY: Macmillan; 1961. [$40.00]

Nolan, James Bennett. **The Schuylkill.** New Brunswick: Rutgers UP; 1951. [$30.00]

Noll, Arthur Howard. **History of the Church in the Diocese of Tennessee.** NY: Pott; 1900. [$45.00]

Nolte, Vincent Otto. **Fifty Years in Both Hemispheres.** NY: Redfield; 1854. [rebound, $50.00] [$100.00]

Norcross, Frank W. **History of the New York Swamp.** NY: Chiswick; 1901. [$45.00]

Nordhoff, Charles. **California: For Health, Pleasure, and Residence.** NY: Harper; 1873. [$100.00] [$75.00]

Nordhoff, Charles. **Communistic Societies of the United States.** NY: Harper; 1875. [worn and spotted, $125.00] [$115.00]

Nordhoff, Charles. **Northern California, Oregon, and the Sandwich Islands.** NY: Harper; 1874. [$100.00]

Nordskog, Andrae B. **Spiking the Gold.** Los Angeles: Gridiron; 1932. [worn and soiled, $25.00]

Nordyke, Lewis. **Great Roundup.** special ed. NY: Morrow; 1955. [$30.00]

Nordyke, Lewis. **John Wesley Hardin, Texas Gunman.** NY: Morrow; 1957. [$30.00]

Norfleet, J. Frank. **Norfleet.** Fort Worth, TX: White; 1924. [presentation, $30.00]

Norlie, Olaf Morgan. **History of the Norwegian People in America.** Minneapolis: Augsburg; 1925. [x-lib., $30.00]

Norman, Benjamin Moore. **Rambles by Land and Water.** NY; New Orleans: Paine & Burgess; Norman; 1845. [spine torn, $60.00]

Norman, Benjamin Moore. **Rambles in Yucatan.** 2nd ed. NY; Philadelphia: Langley; Thomas, Cowperthwait; 1843, c1842. [$150.00]

Norman, William M. **A Portion of My Life.** Winston-Salem, NC: Blair; 1959. [$15.00]

Norris, Charles Gilman. **Seed.** Garden City: Doubleday, Doran; 1930. [$35.00]

Norris, Edwin Mark. **Story of Princeton.** Boston: Little, Brown; 1917. [$20.00]

Norris, Frank. **The Complete Edition of.** Garden City: Doubleday, Doran; 1928. 10 v. [some djs chipped, $200.00]

Norris, Frank. **A Deal in Wheat and Other Stories of the New and Old West.** NY: Wessels; 1903. [$75.00]

Norris, Frank. **The Pit.** special presentation ed. NY: Doubleday, Page; 1903. [$80.00] [$100.00]

Norris, Frank. **Works.** Argonaut Manuscript Limited ed. Garden City: Doubleday, Doran; 1928. 10 v. [$750.00, Canadian]

Norris, Thaddeus. **American Angler's Book.** Philadelphia: Butler; 1864. [needs rebinding, $60.00]

North, Luther Hedden. **Man of the Plains.** Lincoln: U. of Nebraska; 1961. [$23.50]

North, Simon Newton Dexter. **Simeon North.** Concord, NH: Rumford; 1913. [inscribed, $20.00]

North, Thomas. **Five Years in Texas.** Cincinnati: Elm Street; 1871. [$375.00]

Northend, Mary Harrod. **We Visit Old Inns.** Boston: Small, Maynard; 1925. [$25.00]

Northrop, Henry Davenport. **Life and Deeds of General Sherman.** Philadelphia: Moore; 1891. [$22.50]

Northrop, John Worreil. **Chronicles from the Diary of a War Prisoner.** Wichita, KS: The Author; 1904. [presentation, $300.00]

Northup, Solomon. **Twelve Years a Slave.** London; Auburn, NY: Low; Derby & Miller; 1853. [$65.00]

Norton, A. Tiffany. **History of Sullivan's Campaign against the Iroquois.** Lima, NY: Norton; 1879. [$65.00]

Norton, Charles Eliot. **Letters of.** Boston: Houghton Mifflin; 1913. 2 v. [$35.00]

Norton, Francis L. **Cuba.** NY: [s.n.]; 1873. [1st printing, $75.00]

Norton, Frank Henry. **Life and Public Services of Winfield Scott Hancock.** NY: Appleton; 1880. [$25.00]

Norton, Lewis Adelbert. **Life and Adventures of.** Oakland: Pacific; 1887. [$80.00]

Norton, Oliver Willcox. **The Attack and Defense of Little Round Top, Gettysburg.** NY: Neale; 1913. [$95.00]

Norvell, Saunders. **Forty Years of Hardware.** 1st ed. NY: Hardware Age; 1924. [presentation, $35.00]

Noun, Louise R. **Strong-Minded Women.** 1st ed. Ames: Iowa State UP; 1969. [$25.00]

Nowlin, William. **The Bark Covered House.** Chicago: Lakeside; 1937. [$17.50]

Noyes, Alva Josiah. **In the Land of Chinook.** Helena, MT: State; 1917. [$150.00]

Noyes, George Wallingford. **Religious Experience of John Humphrey Noyes.** NY: Macmillan; 1923. [foxed, $25.00]

Noyes, John Humphrey. **The Berean.** Putney, VT: Spiritual Magazine; 1847. [worn and soiled, $75.00]

Noyes, John Humphrey. **History of American Socialisms.** NY: Hillary; 1961. [$17.50] [$25.00]

Nuckolls, Benjamin Floyd. **Pioneer Settlers of Grayson County, Virginia.** Bristol, TN: King; 1914. [$75.00]

Nuermberger, Ruth Anna. **Charles Osborn in the Anti-Slavery Movement.** Columbus: Ohio State Archaeological and Historical Soc.; 1937. [inscribed, $25.00]

Nunan, Thomas. **Diary of an Old Bohemian.** San Francisco: Wagner; 1927. [$35.00]

Nunez Cabeza de Vaca, Alvar. **Relation et Naufrages d'Alvar Nunez Cabecà de Vaca.** Paris: Bertrand; 1837. [$850.00]

Nunez Cabeza de Vaca, Alvar. **Relation That Alvar Nunez Cabeca de Vaca Gave of What Befel.** San Francisco: Grabhorn; 1929. [$475.00]

Nute, Grace Lee. **Caesars of the Wilderness.** NY, London: Appleton-Century; 1943. [$20.00]

Nuttall, Thomas. **The Genera of North American Plants.** Philadelphia: The Author; 1818. 2 v. [$225.00]

Nuttall, Thomas. **Journal of Travels into the Arkansas Territory during the Year 1819.** Philadelphia: Palmer; 1821. [foxed, $850.00]

Nutting, Wallace. **Maine Beautiful.** Framingham, MA: Old America; 1924. [$35.00]

Nye, Bill. **Bill Nye and Boomerang.** Chicago: Belford, Clarke; 1881. [covers worn, last leaf torn, $12.50]

Nye, Bill. **Guest at the Ludlow and Other Stories.** Indianapolis, Kansas City: Bowen-Merrill; 1897. [x-lib., $15.00]

Nye, Bill. **Nye and Riley's Railway Guide.** Chicago; NY: Dearborn; 1888. [first printing, inscribed by Riley, $400.00]

Nye, Russel Blaine. **George Bancroft.** NY: Knopf; 1944. [$15.00]

Nye, Wilbur Sturtevant. **Carbine & Lance.** 1st ed. Norman: U. of Oklahoma; 1943. [$19.50] [$20.00] [$35.00]

Nye, Wilbur Sturtevant. **Plains Indian Raiders.** 1st ed. Norman: U. of Oklahoma; 1968. [$30.00]

Oaks, Lewis Weston. **Medical Aspects of the Latter-Day Saint Word of Wisdom.** Provo: Brigham Young; 1929. [$30.00]

Oates, Joyce Carol. **By the North Gate.** 1st ed. NY: Vanguard; 1963. [rubbed dj, worn spine, $100.00]

Oates, Joyce Carol. **Them.** 1st ed. NY: Vanguard; 1966. [slightly worn dj, $40.00]

Oates, Joyce Carol. **Upon the Sweeping Flood.** 1st ed. NY: Vanguard; 1966. [inscribed, slightly worn dj, $100.00]

Oates, Joyce Carol. **With Shuddering Fall.** NY: Vanguard; 1964. [inscribed, slightly worn dj, $100.00]

O'Beirne, Harry F. **Leaders and Leading Men of the Indian Territory.** Chicago: American Publishers; 1891. [$200.00]

Ober, Frederick Albion. **Guide to the West Indies, Bermuda and Panama.** NY: Dodd, Mead; 1913, c1908. [$40.00]

Ober, Frederick Albion. **Our West Indian Neighbors.** NY: Pott; 1904. [$35.00]

Ober, Frederick Albion. **Travels in Mexico and Life among the Mexicans.** San Francisco: Dewing; 1884, c1883. [binding loosened, $70.00] [1884 Boston imprint, $40.00]

Oberholser, Harry C. **Bird Life of Louisiana.** New Orleans: Louisiana Dept. of Conservation; 1938. [$20.00]

Oberholtzer, Ellis Paxson. **Jay Cooke, Financier of the Civil War.** Philadelphia: Jacobs; 1907. 2 v. [$75.00]

Obermann, Karl. **Joseph Weydemeyer.** NY: International; 1947. [$15.00]

O'Brien, Michael Joseph. **Hercules Mulligan, Confidential Correspondent of General Washington.** NY: Kenedy; 1937. [signed, $15.00]

O'Brien, Michael Joseph. **A Hidden Phase of American History.** NY: Dodd, Mead; 1920, c1919. [$45.00]

O'Byrne, John. **Pikes Peak or Bust.** 2nd ed. Colorado Springs: [s.n.]; 1923, c1922. [$40.00]

O'Callaghan, Edmund B. **Documentary History of the State of New York.** see, title.

Och, Joseph. **Missionary in Sonora.** San Francisco: California Hist. Soc.; 1965. [$20.00]

O'Connell, Daniel. **Lyrics.** San Francisco: Bancroft; 1881. [$40.00]

O'Connor, Paul. **Eskimo Parish.** Milwaukee: Bruce; 1947. [$7.50]

O'Connor, Richard. **Bat Masterson.** 1st ed. Garden City: Doubleday; 1957. [$15.00] [$14.00]

O'Connor, Richard. **High Jinks on the Klondike.** 1st ed. Indianapolis: Bobbs-Merrill; 1954. [$12.50]

O'Connor, Richard. **Hood, Cavalier General.** 1st ed. NY: Prentice-Hall; 1949. [$35.00] [$45.00]

O'Connor, Richard. **Thomas, Rock of Chickamauga.** 1st ed. NY: Prentice-Hall; 1948. [$45.00]

O'Connor, Richard. **Wild Bill Hickok.** 1st ed. Garden City: Doubleday; 1959. [$35.00]

O'Daniel, Victor Francis. **Dominicans in Early Florida.** NY: U. S. Catholic Historical Soc.; 1930. [$27.50]

Oden, Bill Arp. **Early Days on the Texas-New Mexico Plains.** Canyon, TX: Palo Duro; 1965. [$55.00]

O'Donovan, Jeremiah. **Brief Account of the Author's Interviews with His Countrymen.** Pittsburgh: The Author; 1864. [$300.00]

Odum, Howard Washington. **Southern Regions of the United States.** Chapel Hill: U. of North Carolina; 1936. [$45.00] [$65.00]

Oehser, Paul Henry. **Sons of Science.** NY: Schuman; 1949. [$18.00]

O'Ferrall, Charles Triplett. **Forty Years of Active Service.** NY, Washington: Neale; 1904. [$125.00]

O'Flaherty, Daniel. **General Jo Shelby.** Chapel Hill: U. of North Carolina; 1954. [dj worn, $38.00]

Ogden, John Cosens. **Excursion into Bethlehem & Nazareth, in Pennsylvania.** Philadelphia: Cist; 1800. [$350.00]

Ogden, Uzal. **Antidote to Deism.** Newark: Woods; 1795. 2 v. [$125.00]

Ogg, Frederic Austin. **Opening of the Mississippi.** NY, London: Macmillan; 1904. [$55.00]

Oglesby, Richard Edward. **Manuel Lisa and the Opening of the Missouri Fur Trade.** 1st ed. Norman: U. of Oklahoma; 1963. [x-lib., $15.00]

O'Hanlon, John. **Irish-American History of the United States.** NY: Murphy; 1907. 2 v. [$100.00]

O'Hara, Barratt. **From Figg to Johnson.** Chicago: Blossom; 1909. [$50.00]

O'Kane, Walter Collins. **The Hopis.** 1st ed. Norman: U. of Oklahoma; 1953. [some underlining, $35.00]

O'Kane, Walter Collins. **Sun in the Sky.** 1st ed. Norman: U. of Oklahoma; 1950. [$27.50]

O'Kieffe, Charley. **Western Story.** Lincoln: U. of Nebraska; 1960. [$25.00]

Olcott, Charles Sumner. **Life of William McKinley.** Boston, NY: Houghton Mifflin; 1916. 2 v. [$75.00] [$65.00]

Old South Church (Boston, Mass.). **Catalogue of the Loan Collection of Revolutionary Relics.** 5th ed. Boston: Ellis; 1876. [wraps frayed, $12.50]

Older, Fremont (Mrs.). **San Francisco; Magic City.** 1st ed. NY: Longmans, Green; 1961. [$7.50]

Olin, Oscar Eugene. **Akron and Environs.** Chicago: Lewis; 1917. [$95.00]

Oliphant, J. Orin. **On the Cattle Ranges of the Oregon Country.** Seattle: U. of Washington; 1968. [$35.00] [$50.00]

Oliphant, Laurence. **Minnesota and the Far West.** Edinburgh, London: Blackwood; 1855. [map repaired, binding worn, $60.00] [$275.00]

Oliver, Isabella. see, Sharp, Isabella.

Oliver, John William. **History of American Technology.** NY: Ronald; 1956. [$25.00]

Oliver, Smith Hempstone. **The First Quarter-Century of Steam Locomotives in North America.** Washington: Smithsonian; 1956. [$10.00]

Olmsted, Frederick Law. **The Cotton Kingdom.** NY: Knopf; 1953. [$20.00]

Olmsted, Frederick Law. **Frederick Law Olmsted, Landscape Architect, 1822-1903.** NY, London: Putnam; 1922-1928. 2 v. [vol. 2 only, $100.00]

Olmsted, Frederick Law. **Journey through Texas.** NY; London: Dix, Edwards; Low; 1857. [$275.00]

Olmsted, Frederick Law. **Walks and Talks of an American Farmer in England.** London: Bogue; 1852. [$100.00]

Olsson, Jan Olof. **Welcome to Tombstone.** London: Elek; 1956. [$25.00] [$30.00]

Olsson, Karl A. **By One Spirit.** Chicago: Covenant; 1962. [$20.00]

Olsson, Nils William. **Swedish Passenger Arrivals in New York, 1820-1850.** Chicago: Swedish Pioneer Historical Society; 1967. [$25.00]

O'Meara, James. **Broderick and Gwin.** San Francisco: Bacon; 1881. [cover worn and stained, hinges weak, $30.00]

O'Meara, James. **The Vigilance Committee of 1856.** San Francisco: Barry; 1887. [2nd printing, $90.00]

Omwake, John. **Conestoga Six-Horse Bell Teams of Eastern Pennsylvania.** Cincinnati: Ebbert & Richardson; 1930. [$70.00]

Onderdonk, Henry. **Documents and Letters Intended to Illustrate the Revolutionary Incidents of Queens County.** NY: Leavitt, Trow; 1846. [inscribed, $85.00]

Onderdonk, Henry. **Revolutionary Incidents of Suffolk and Kings Counties.** NY: Leavitt; 1849. [$100.00]

Oneal, James. **Workers in American History.** 3rd ed. St. Louis: National Rip-Saw; 1912. [$27.50]

O'Neall, John Belton. **The Negro Law of South Carolina.** Columbia: Bowman; 1848. [$135.00]

O'Neil, James Bradas. **They Die But Once.** NY: Knight; 1935. [dj very worn, $55.00] [$35.00]

O'Neill, Charles Kendall. **Wild Train.** NY: Random; 1956. [$20.00]

O'Neill, Eugene. **All God's Chillun Got Wings, and Welded.** 1st ed. NY: Boni and Liveright; 1924. [near fine, dj repaired, $130.00] [lacks dj, $50.00]

O'Neill, Eugene. **The Iceman Cometh.** NY: Random; 1946. [$165.00]

O'Neill, Eugene. **Long Day's Journey into Night.** New Haven: Yale UP; 1956. [front cover spotted, $10.00]

O'Neill, Eugene. **A Touch of the Poet.** New Haven: Yale UP; 1957. [$12.50]

Opotowsky, Stan. **The Longs of Louisiana.** 1st ed. NY: Dutton; 1960. [$9.50]

Orcutt, Ada M. **Tillamook.** Portland, OR: Binfords & Mort; 1951. [signed, $20.00]

Orcutt, Samuel. **Indians of the Housatonic and Naugatuck Valleys.** Hartford, CT: Case, Lockwood & Brainard; 1882. [$85.00]

Orgain, Kate Alma. **Southern Authors in Poetry and Prose.** NY: Neale; 1908. [$30.00]

Ormerod, Leonard. **The Curving Shore; the Gulf Coast from Brownsville to Key West.** NY: Harper; 1957. [$20.00]

Ormsbee, Thomas H. **Early American Furniture Makers.** NY: Tudor; 1936. [$17.50]

Orpen, Adela Elizabeth Richards. **Memories of the Old Emigrant Days in Kansas.** NY: Harper; 1928. [$45.00]

Orton, James. **Underground Treasures: How and Where to Find Them.** new ed. Philadelphia: Baird; 1881. [$100.00]

Osborn, Campbell. **Let Freedom Ring.** Tokyo: Inter-Nation; 1954. [lacks front flyleaf, $16.00] [$30.00]

Osborn, Hartwell. **Trials and Triumphs.** Chicago: McClurg; 1904. [inscribed, $195.00]

Osborn, Henry Fairfield. **Evolution and Religion in Education.** NY: Scribner; 1926. [$20.00]

Osborne, Joseph Alexander. **Williamsburg in Colonial Times.** Richmond: Dietz; 1935. [$15.00]

Osborne, Lilly de Jongh. **Indian Crafts of Guatemala and El Salvador.** 1st ed. Norman: U. of Oklahoma; 1965. [$35.00]

Osborne, Thomas. **True and Particular Relation of the Dreadful Earthquake Which Happen'd at Lima.** 2nd ed. London: Osborne; 1748. [$300.00]

Osgood, Cornelius. **Archeological Survey of Venezuela.** New Haven; London: Yale UP; Oxford UP; 1943. [$65.00]

Osgood, Herbert Levi. **The American Colonies in the Seventeenth Century.** NY, London: Macmillan; 1904-07. 3 v. [$100.00] [1924-25 Columbia 4 vol. ed., $150.00]

Osgood, Samuel. **New York in the Nineteenth Century.** NY: New York Hist. Soc.; 1867. [$20.00]

O'Shaughnessy, Edith. **Diplomat's Wife in Mexico.** NY: Harper; 1916. [$27.50] [$30.00]

Oskison, John Milton. **Tecumseh and His Times.** NY: Putnam; 1938. [$30.00]

Osler, William. **An Alabama Student.** NY: Oxford UP; 1908. [$40.00]

Osler, William. **Principles and Practice of Medicine.** NY: Appleton; 1892. [covers scuffed and stained, $200.00]

Ossoli, Sarah Margaret. **Woman in the Nineteenth Century.** 1st ed. NY: Greeley & McElrath; 1845. [very good in wraps, $300.00]

Ostenso, Martha. **Wild Geese.** NY: Dodd, Mead; 1925. [$17.50]

Ostrander, Alson Bowles. **An Army Boy of the Sixties.** Yonkers-on-Hudson: World; 1924. [$20.00]

Oswald, John Clyde. **Benjamin Franklin, Printer.** Garden City: Doubleday, Page; 1917. [x-lib., $30.00]

Oswald, John Clyde. **Printing in the Americas.** NY, Chicago: Gregg; 1937. [$75.00]

Oswalt, Wendell H. **The Ethnoarcheology of Crow Village, Alaska.** Washington: USGPO; 1967. [$17.50]

Otero, Miguel Antonio. **My Life on the Frontier.** NY: Press of the Pioneers; 1935-39. 2 v. [v. 2 published by U. of New Mexico, $150.00]

Otero, Miguel Antonio. **My Nine Years as Governor of the Territory of New Mexico, 1897-1906.** 1st trade ed. Albuquerque: U. of New Mexico; 1940. [tattered dj, $65.00]

Otero, Miguel Antonio. **The Real Billy the Kid.** NY: Wilson; 1936. [$100.00]

Otis, Fessenden N. **Isthmus of Panama.** NY: Harper; 1867. [$125.00]

Otis, Philo Adams. **The Chicago Symphony Orchestra.** Chicago: Summy; 1924. [$27.50]

Ottley, Roi. **New World A-Coming.** Boston: Houghton Mifflin; 1943. [spine creased, dj soiled and chipped, $15.00]

Outlines of the Life of General Lafayette. Tappan, NY: Broadwell; 1830. [$75.00]

Overton, Richard Cleghorn. **Burlington West.** Cambridge: Harvard UP; 1941. [$30.00]

Overton, Richard Cleghorn. **Gulf to Rockies.** 1st ed. Austin: U. of Texas; 1953. [$35.00]

Owen, Henry Wilson. **Edward Clarence Plummer History of Bath, Maine.** Bath, ME: Times; 1936. [$60.00]

Owen, Mary Alicia. **Folk-Lore of the Musquakie Indians of North America.** London: Nutt; 1904. [$100.00]

Owen, Richard. **Second Report . . .** see, Arkansas. State Geologist.

Owen, Robert Dale. **Future of the North-West.** Philadelphia: Crissy & Markley; 1863. [wraps chipped, $60.00]

Owen, William Miller. **In Camp and Battle with the Washington Artillery of New Orleans.** Boston: Ticknor; 1885. [$250.00]

Owens, James. **Recollections of a Runaway Boy.** Pittsburg: Keystone Label; 1903. [$20.00]

Paddock, A. G. (Mrs.). **Fate of Madame La Tour.** NY: Fords, Howard, & Hulbert; 1881. [$50.00]

Paddock, B. B. **History of Central and Western Texas.** Chicago: Lewis; 1911. 2 v. [$550.00]

Paddock, Zachariah. **Memoir of Rev. Benjamin G. Paddock.** NY; Cincinnati: Nelson and Phillips; Hitchcock and Walden; 1875. [binding mottled, $25.00]

Paden, Irene Dakin. **The Big Oak Flat Road.** San Francisco: Schlichtmann; 1955. [$75.00]

Paden, Irene Dakin. **The Wake of the Prairie Schooner.** 1st ed. NY: Macmillan; 1943. [$35.00] [$20.00]

Padover, Saul Kussiel. **A Jefferson Profile.** see, Jefferson, Thomas.

Page, Elizabeth. **Wild Horses and Gold.** NY: Farrar & Rinehart; 1932. [$35.00]

Page, James Madison. **The True Story of Andersonville Prison.** NY, Washington: Neale; 1908. [$95.00]

Page, Rosewell. **Iliads of the South.** Richmond: Garrett and Massie; 1932. [signed, $35.00]

Page, Thomas Nelson. **The Old South.** 1st ed. NY: Scribner; 1892. [$45.00]

Page, Thomas Nelson. **Social Life in Old Virginia before the War.** NY: Scribner; 1897. [$30.00]

Paine, Albert Bigelow. **Captain Bill McDonald, Texas Ranger.** NY: Little & Ives; 1909. [$125.00]

Paine, Albert Bigelow. **In One Man's Life.** NY, London: Harper; 1921. [$20.00]

Paine, Albert Bigelow. **Thomas Nast.** NY: Macmillan; 1904. [$85.00]

Paine, George Taylor. **Denial of the Charges of Forgery in Connection with the Sachems' Deed to Roger Williams.** Providence: Standard; 1896. [$50.00]

Paine, Lauran. **Tom Horn; Man of the West.** 1st American ed. Barre, MS: Barre Pub.; 1963. [$20.00]

Paine, Ralph Delahaye. **Joshua Barney.** NY, London: Century; 1924. [$23.50]

Paine, Ralph Delahaye. **Ships and Sailors of Old Salem.** new ed. Chicago: McClurg; 1912. [$75.00]

Paine, Thomas. **Agrarian Justice.** Philadelphia: Bache; [1797?]. [$375.00]

Paine, Thomas. **Common Sense.** London: Symonds; 1792. [$325.00]

Paine, Thomas. **Dissertation on First-Principles of Government.** Paris: English Press; 1795. [$650.00] [$300.00]

Paine, Thomas. **Letter Addressed to the Abbe Raynal.** London: Ridgway; 1792. [$100.00] [$125.00]

Paine, Thomas. **Letter Addressed to the Addressers on the Late Proclamation.** London: Symonds and Rickman; 1792. [$400.00] [$250.00]

Paine, Thomas. **Life and Works of.** patriots' ed. New Rochelle, NY: Thomas Paine National Historical Assn.; 1925. 10 v. [$150.00]

Paine, Thomas. **Rights of Man.** London: Symonds; 1792. [$150.00]

Paine, Thomas. **Writings of.** Albany, NY: Webster; [1792?]. [$200.00]

Painter, James Henry. **The Iowa Pulpit of the Church of Christ.** St. Louis: Christian; 1886. [front hinge weak, $30.00]

Paley, William. **Principles of Moral and Political Philosophy.** 7th ed. Philadelphia: Dobson; 1788. [spine cracked, $60.00]

Palfrey, Francis Winthrop. **The Antietam and Fredericksburg.** NY: Scribner; 1882. [$35.00]

Palfrey, John Gorham. **History of New England.** Boston: Little, Brown; 1882-90. 5 v. [$185.00]

Palgrave, William Gifford. **Dutch Guiana.** London: Macmillan; 1876. [$50.00]

Palladino, Lawrence Benedict. **Indian and White in the Northwest.** Baltimore: Murphy; 1894. [$150.00]

Palliser, John. **The Solitary Hunter.** London, NY: Routledge; 1856. [rebacked, $150.00]

Palmer, George Herbert. **Life of Alice Freeman Palmer.** 1st ed. Boston, NY: Houghton Mifflin; 1908. [$25.00]

Palmer, Howard. **Edward W. D. Holway.** Minneapolis: U. of Minnesota; 1931. [$22.50]

Palmer, John Williamson. **The New and the Old.** NY: Rudd & Carleton; 1859. [cover worn, $50.00]

Palmer, Sarah A. **Story of Aunt Becky's Army-Life.** NY: Trow; 1867. [2nd printing?, hinges weak, $90.00]

Palou, Francisco. **The Founding of the First California Missions.** San Francisco: Nueva California; 1934. [$80.00]

Pancoast, Charles Edward. **A Quaker Forty-Niner.** Philadelphia; London: U. of Pennsylvania; Oxford UP; 1930. [$20.00]

Pancoast, Henry Spackman. **Impressions of the Sioux Tribes in 1882.** Philadephia: Franklin; 1883. [$85.00]

Pannell, Walter. **Civil War on the Range.** Los Angeles: Welcome News; 1943. [$40.00]

Park, Willard Zerbe. **Shamanism in Western North America.** Evanston and Chicago: Northwestern UP; 1938. [$35.00]

Parke, John E. **Recollections of Seventy Years.** Boston: Rand, Avery; 1886. [$22.50]

Parker, Amos Andrew. **Trip to the West and Texas.** Concord, NH: White & Fisher; 1835. [$1500.00] [1826 issue, $1500.00]

Parker, Arthur Caswell. **Analytical History of the Seneca Indians.** Rochester, NY: Morgan Chapter, State Archeological Assn.; 1926. [$40.00]

Parker, Augustus G. **Parker in America.** Buffalo: Niagara Frontier; 1911. [spine chipped, hinges cracked, worn, $25.00]

Parker, David Bigelow. **A Chautauqua Boy in '61 and Afterward.** Boston: Small, Maynard; 1912. [$50.00]

Parker, Dorothy. **Collected Stories of.** NY: Modern Library; 1942. [presentation, $30.00]

Parker, Dorothy. **Here Lies.** London, NY: Longmans, Green; 1939. [$12.50]

Parker, Edward Griffin. **Reminiscences of Rufus Choate.** NY: Mason; 1860. [$37.50]

Parker, Emma. **Fugitives.** Dallas: Ranger; 1934. [dj split, $85.00]

Parker, George Frederick. **Recollections of Grover Cleveland.** NY: Century; 1909. [$12.50]

Parker, Granville. **The Formation of the State of West Virginia.** Wellsburg, WV: Glass; 1875. [x-lib., $25.00]

Parker, James. **The Old Army.** Philadelphia: Dorrance; 1929. [$125.00]

Parker, James. **Rear-Admirals Schley, Sampson and Cervera.** NY, Washington: Neale; 1910. [$65.00]

Parker, Margaret Terrell. **Lowell.** NY: Macmillan; 1940. [$27.50]

Parker, Nathan Howe. **Iowa As It Is in 1856.** Chicago: Keen and Lee; 1856. [$80.00]

Parker, Nathan Howe. **Minnesota Handbook for 1856-7.** Boston; NY: Jewett; Sheldon, Blakeman; 1857. [lacks map, rebacked, $125.00]

Parker, Robert Allerton. **A Yankee Saint.** NY: Putnam; 1935. [$15.00]

Parker, Samuel. **Journal of an Exploring Tour beyond the Rocky Mountains.** Ithaca, NY: The Author; 1838. [foxed, $300.00] [$500.00]

Parker, Solomon. **Parker's American Citizen's Sure Guide.** Sag-Harbor: Spooner; 1808. [$65.00]

Parker, Theodore. **Letter to the People of the United States Touching the Matter of Slavery.** Boston: Munroe; 1848. [$75.00]

Parker, William B. **Notes Taken during the Expedition Commanded by Capt. R. B. Marcy.** Philadelphia: Hayes & Zell; 1856. [$650.00] [$750.00]

Parker, William Thornton. **Personal Experiences among our North American Indians from 1867 to 1885.** Northampton, MA: [s.n.]; 1913. [$100.00]

Parkhill, Forbes. **The Blazed Trail of Antoine Leroux.** Los Angeles: Westernlore; 1965. [$35.00]

Parkhill, Forbes. **The Wildest of the West.** 1st ed. NY: Holt; 1951. [signed, $30.00]

Parkin, George Robert. **The Rhodes Scholarships.** Boston, NY: Houghton Mifflin; 1912. [$15.00, Canadian]

Parkinson, Edward S. **Wonderland; or, Twelve Weeks in and out of the United States.** Trenton: MacCrellish & Quigley; 1894. [inscribed, $35.00]

Parkinson, Richard. **A Tour in America in 1798, 1799, and 1800.** London: Harding; 1805. 2 v. [$500.00]

Parkman, Ebenezer. **Diary of.** Westborough, MA: Westborough Hist. Soc.; 1899. [$37.50]

Parkman, Francis. **Battle for North America.** 1st ed. Garden City: Doubleday; 1948. [$25.00]

Parkman, Francis. **The California and Oregon Trail.** NY: Putnam; 1849. [lacks covers, $1000.00] [$1500.00] [3rd printing, $600.00]

Parkman, Francis. **History of the Conspiracy of Pontiac.** Boston; London: Little and Brown; Bentley; 1851. [$175.00] [spine chipped, $37.50]

Parkman, Francis. **Journals of.** 1st ed. NY: Harper; 1947. 2 v. [$40.00] [$35.00] [$45.00]

Parkman, Francis. **La Salle and the Discovery of the Great West.** 12th ed. Boston: Little, Brown; 1891, c1879. [$45.00]

Parkman, Francis. **Letters of.** 1st ed. Norman: U. of Oklahoma; 1960. 2 v. [$50.00]

Parkman, Francis. **The Oregon Trail.** Boston: Little, Brown; 1894. [spine sunned, $40.00]

Parkman, Francis. **Pioneers of France in the New World.** 1st ed. Boston: Little, Brown; 1865. [$45.00]

Parris, John. **Mountain Bred.** Asheville, NC: Citizen-Times; 1967. [signed, $27.50]

Parris, John. **My Mountains, My People.** Asheville, NC: Citizen-Times; 1957. [signed, mildew, dj badly chipped, $20.00]

Parrish, John. **Remarks on the Slavery of the Black People.** Philadelphia: The Author; 1806. [$200.00]

Parrish, Randall. **The Great Plains.** Chicago: McClurg; 1907. [$27.00]

Parry, Albert. **Garrets and Pretenders.** NY: Covici, Friede; 1933. [$30.00]

Parry, Albert. **Tattoo.** NY: Simon and Schuster; 1933. [$35.00]

Parry, William Edward. **Journal of a Third Voyage for the Discovery of a Northwest Passage.** Philadelphia: Carey and Lee; 1826. [$175.00]

Parsons, Elsie Worthington Clews. **American Indian Life.** NY: Huebsch; 1922. [$65.00]

Parsons, George Frederic. **Life and Adventures of James W. Marshall.** Sacramento: Marshall and Burke; 1870. [rebound, $125.00]

Parsons, Horatio Adams. **The Book of Niagara Falls.** 3rd ed. Buffalo: Steele; 1836. [$85.00] [1847 11th ed., $55.00]

Parsons, Horatio Adams. **Guide to Travelers Visiting the Falls of Niagara.** 2nd ed. Buffalo: Steele; 1835. [$85.00]

Parsons, William Barclay. **Robert Fulton and the Submarine.** NY: Columbia UP; 1922. [$37.50]

Parton, James. **General Butler in New Orleans.** 8th ed. NY; Boston: Mason; Mason & Hamlin; 1864. [shabby, reading copy, $15.00] [$30.00]

Parton, James. **General Jackson.** large paper ed. NY: Appleton; 1892. [$27.50]

Parton, James. **Life and Times of Aaron Burr.** 10th ed. NY: Mason; 1858. [$50.00] [$45.00]

Parton, James. **Life and Times of Benjamin Franklin.** NY: Mason; 1864. 2 v. [$225.00]

Parton, James. **Life of Andrew Jackson.** NY: Mason; 1860. 3 v. [1861 issue, $75.00] [1864 printing, $75.00]

Parton, James. **Life of Horace Greeley.** NY: Mason; 1855. [front hinge broken, $25.00]

Partridge, Bellamy. **Sir Billy Howe.** London, NY: Longmans, Green; 1932. [$35.00]

Patri, Giacomo. **White Collar.** San Francisco: Pisani; [1940?]. [signed, $65.00]

Patrick, Rembert Wallace. **Florida Fiasco.** Athens: U. of Georgia; 1954. [$28.50]

Patrick, Rembert Wallace. **Florida under Five Flags.** Gainesville: U. of Florida; 1945. [signed, $15.00]

Patrick, Rembert Wallace. **Jefferson Davis and His Cabinet.** Baton Rouge: Louisiana State UP; 1944. [$22.50]

Patrick, Wiley Jones. **History of Salt River Association, Missouri.** Columbia, MO: Stephens; 1909. [rebound, $30.00]

Pattee, William S. **History of Old Braintree and Quincy.** Quincy, MA: Green & Prescott; 1878. [$85.00]

Patten, Matthew. **Diary of.** Concord, NH: Rumford; 1903. [$100.00]

Patterson, C. L. **Sensational Texas Manhunt.** San Antonio: Murray; 1939. [$30.00]

Patterson, Samuel. **Narrative of the Adventures and Sufferings of.** Palmer, MA: Press in Palmer; 1817. [lacks pages 87-94, $50.00] [$350.00]

Pattie, James O. **Personal Narrative of.** Cincinnati: Flint; 1833. [rebound, $2500.00]

Paul, Rodman Wilson. **Mining Frontiers of the Far West, 1848-1880.** NY: Holt, Rinehart and Winston; 1963. [$30.00]

Paulding, James Kirke. **John Bull in America.** 2nd ed. NY: Wiley; 1825. [$100.00]

Paulding, James Kirke. **Life of Washington.** NY: Harper; 1835. 2 v. [$65.00]

Paullin, Charles Oscar. **Commodore John Rodgers.** Cleveland: Clark; 1910. [$40.00]

Pausch, Georg. **Journal of.** Albany, NY: Munsell; 1886. [$90.00]

Paxson, Frederic L. **History of the American Frontier, 1763-1893.** Boston, NY: Houghton Mifflin; 1924. [$45.00] [$20.00] [$30.00]

Paxton, Philip. see, Hammett, Samuel A.

Payne, Buckner H. **The Negro: What Is His Ethnological Status?** 2nd ed. Cincinnati: The Proprietor; 1867. [$75.00]

Payne, Doris Palmer. **Captain Jack.** 1st ed. Portland, OR: Binfords & Mort; 1938. [$30.00]

Payne, Edwin Chancellor. **The Hillsville Tragedy.** Chicago: Donohue; 1913. [$45.00]

Payne, Leonidas Warren. **When the Woods Were Burnt.** Austin: Texas Folklore Society; 1946. [$45.00]

Payne, Stephen. **Where the Rockies Ride Herd.** Denver: Sage; 1965. [$25.00]

Payson, Seth. **Proofs of the Real Existence, and Dangerous Tendency, of Illuminism.** Charlestown, MA: Etheridge; 1802. [disbound, $75.00]

Paytiamo, James. **Flaming Arrow's People.** NY: Duffield and Green; 1932. [$125.00]

Pazos Kanki, Vicente. **Letters on the United Provinces of South America.** NY; London: Seymour; Miller; 1819. [$150.00]

Peabody, Francis Greenwood. **Education for Life.** Garden City: Doubleday, Page; 1918. [$20.00] [$27.50]

Peabody, George Augustus. **South American Journals.** Salem, MA: Peabody Museum; 1937. [$30.00] [$50.00]

Peabody, Robert Ephraim. **Log of the Grand Turks.** Boston, NY: Houghton Mifflin; 1926. [$35.00]

Peabody, Robert Ephraim. **Merchant Venturers of Old Salem.** Boston, NY: Houghton Mifflin; 1912. [$25.00]

Peak, Howard Wallace. **A Ranger of Commerce.** 1st ed. San Antonio: Naylor; 1929. [signed, $45.00]

Peake, Ora Brooks. **History of the United States Indian Factory System, 1795-1822.** Denver: Sage; 1954. [$50.00]

Pearce, Hamilton. **Kidnapping of Billy Whitla.** Cleveland: Hamilton; 1909. [$75.00]

Pearce, Roy Harvey. **Continuity of American Poetry.** Princeton: Princeton UP; 1961. [$20.00]

Pearse, Eleanor Howard. **Florida's Vanishing Era.** rev. ed. [s.l.: s.n.]; 1954. [$12.50]

Pearse, James. **Narrative of the Life of.** Rutland, VT: Fay; 1825. [$350.00]

Pearson, Drew. **The Nine Old Men.** Garden City: Doubleday, Doran; 1937. [$20.00]

Pearson, Edmund Lester. **Dime Novels.** Boston: Little, Brown; 1929. [$25.00]

Pearson, Edmund Lester. **The Old Librarian's Almanack.** Woodstock, VT: Elm Tree; 1909. [$40.00]

Pearson, Henry Greenleaf. **An American Railroad Builder, John Murray Forbes.** Boston, NY: Houghton Mifflin; 1911. [$25.00]

Pearson, Jim Berry. **The Maxwell Land Grant.** 1st ed. Norman: U. of Oklahoma; 1961. [$60.00]

Peary, Josephine. **My Arctic Journal.** NY, Philadelphia: Contemporary; 1893. [$65.00]

Peary, Robert E. **Nearest the Pole.** London: Hutchinson; 1907. [$150.00] [1907 Doubleday imprint, $125.00]

Peary, Robert E. **The North Pole.** NY: Stokes; 1910. [$125.00] [$100.00]

Pease, Theodore Calvin. **George Rogers Clark and the Revolution in Illinois.** Springfield: Illinois State Historical Library; 1929. [$15.00]

Peat, Frank Edwin. **Legion Airs.** NY: Feist; 1932. [shaken, $15.00]

Peattie, Donald Culross. **Road of a Naturalist.** Boston: Houghton Mifflin; 1941. [$35.00]

Peattie, Roderick. **The Black Hills.** NY: Vanguard; 1952. [$20.00] [dj chipped, $35.00]

Peattie, Roderick. **Friendly Mountains.** NY: Vanguard; 1942. [$25.00]

Peattie, Roderick. **Pacific Coast Ranges.** NY: Vanguard; 1946. [$10.00]

Peck, Cassius R. **A Vermont Tenderfoot in Oklahoma Territory.** La Jolla, CA: The Author; 1956. [presentation, $45.00]

Peck, Charles Henry. **The Jacksonian Epoch.** NY, London: Harper; 1899. [$85.00] [$55.00]

Peck, George. **Early Methodism within the Bounds of the Old Genesee Conference from 1788 to 1828.** NY: Carlton & Porter; 1860. [$45.00]

Peck, George Bacheler. **A Recruit before Petersburg.** Providence: Williams; 1880. [$45.00]

Peck, George W. **Peck's Bad Boy and His Pa.** complete ed. Chicago: Thompson; 1900. [$35.00]

Peck, Taylor. **Round-Shot to Rockets.** Annapolis: U.S. Naval Institute; 1949. [dj rubbed, $20.00]

Peckham, Howard Henry. **Captured by Indians.** New Brunswick: Rutgers UP; 1954. [$25.00]

Peckham, Howard Henry. **Pontiac and the Indian Uprising.** Princeton: Princeton UP; 1947. [$30.00]

Pedley, Charles. **The History of Newfoundland from the Earliest Times to the Year 1860.** London: Longman; 1863. [has map, one gathering loose, $175.00]

Peel, Alfreda Marion. **Witch in the Mill.** Richmond: Dietz; 1947. [$20.00]

Peirce, Ebenezer Weaver. **Indian History, Biography and Genealogy.** North Abington, MA: Mitchell; 1878. [$40.00]

Peixotto, Ernest Clifford. **Our Hispanic Southwest.** NY: Scribner; 1916. [$40.00]

Peixotto, Ernest Clifford. **A Revolutionary Pilgrimage.** NY: Scribner; 1917. [$10.00]

Pelzer, Louis. **The Cattlemen's Frontier.** Glendale, CA: Clark; 1936. [$165.00] [$125.00]

Pelzer, Louis. **Marches of the Dragoons in the Mississippi Valley.** Iowa City, IA: State Historical Society; 1917. [$100.00]

Pember, Phoebe Yates. **A Southern Woman's Story.** Jackson, TN: McCowat-Mercer; 1959. [$65.00]

Pemberton, John Clifford. **Pemberton, Defender of Vicksburg.** Chapel Hill: U. of North Carolina; 1942. [inscribed, $50.00]

Penhallow, Samuel. **History of the Wars of New-England with the Eastern Indians.** reprint ed. Cincinnati: Harpel; 1859. [$200.00] [map repaired, $165.00]

Penn, Thomas Jefferson. **My Black Mammy.** [Reidsville?, NC: s.n.]; 1942. [$25.00]

Penn, William. **Primitive Christianity Revived.** Philadelphia: Crukshank; 1783. [$75.00] [$50.00]

Penn, William. **Select Works of.** London: 1771. [needs rebinding, $150.00]

Penn, William. **Three Treatises.** Philadelphia: Crukshank; 1770. [$150.00]

Pennsylvania Ornithologist. **Report on the Birds of Pennsylvania.** 2nd ed. Harrisburg: Meyers; 1890. [$85.00]

Pennypacker, Samuel W. **Annals of Phoenixville and Its Vicinity.** Philadelphia: Bavis & Pennypacker; 1872. [$85.00] [$100.00]

Penrose, Charles William. **"Mormon" Doctrine, Plain and Simple or Leaves from the Tree of Life.** Salt Lake City: Juvenile Instructor Office; 1888. [binding worn, $110.00]

Pepper, William. **The Medical Side of Benjamin Franklin.** Philadelphia: Campbell; 1911. [rebound, $125.00]

Pepper, William. **System of Practical Medicine.** Philadelphia: Lea; 1885-86. 5 v. [$160.00]

Perelman, Sidney Joseph. **Acres and Pains.** NY: Reynal & Hitchcock; 1947. [x-lib., $15.00]

Perelman, Sidney Joseph. **Best of.** NY: Modern Library; 1947. [x-lib., $15.00]

Perelman, Sidney Joseph. **Keep It Crisp.** 1st ed. NY: Random; 1946. [chipped dj, $25.00]

Perelman, Sidney Joseph. **Listen to the Mocking Bird.** NY: Simon and Schuster; 1949. [worn, x-lib., $15.00]

Perelman, Sidney Joseph. **One Touch of Venus.** 1st ed. Boston: Little, Brown; 1944. [$15.00]

Perez de Luxan, Diego. **Expedition into New Mexico Made by Antonio de Espejo, 1582-1583.** Los Angeles: Quivira Society; 1929. [new spine, $185.00]

Perkins, Charles Elliott. **The Pinto Horse.** 1st ed. Santa Barbara: Hebberd; 1927. [$135.00]

Perkins, Dexter. **The Monroe Doctrine, 1823-1926.** Cambridge; London: Harvard UP; Oxford UP; 1927. [$30.00]

Perkins, Dexter. **The Monroe Doctrine, 1867-1907.** Baltimore: Hopkins; 1937. [$25.00]

Perkins, Dexter. **The United States and the Caribbean.** Cambridge: Harvard UP; 1947. [$25.00]

Perkins, Edward T. **Na Motu; or, Reef-Rovings in the South Seas.** NY: Pudney & Russell; 1854. [$275.00]

Perkins, Elisha Douglass. **Gold Rush Diary.** Lexington: U. of Kentucky; 1967. [x-lib., $15.00]

Perkins, Frances. **The Roosevelt I Knew.** NY: Viking; 1946. [$25.00]

Perkins, Frederic Beecher. **President Greeley, President Hoffman and the Resurrection of the Ring.** Budlongton [i.e. Boston]: Printed for the Purchasers; 1876 [i.e. 1872]. [resewn, $42.50]

Perkins, J. R. **Trails, Rails and War.** 1st ed. Indianapolis: Bobbs-Merrill; 1929. [$32.50] [$30.00]

Perkins, James H. **Annals of the West.** Pittsburgh: Haven; 1857. [rebound, $85.00] [$60.00]

Perkins, Simeon. **Diary of.** Toronto: Champlain Society; 1948-1978. 5 v. [missing vol. 3, $400.00]

Pernety, Antoine-Joseph. **History of a Voyage to the Malouine (or Falkland) Islands.** London: Jefferys; 1771. [rebound, x-lib., $975.00]

Perrin, William Henry. **History of Stark County with an Outline Sketch of Ohio.** Chicago: Baskin & Battey; 1881. [$75.00]

Perrin du Lac, Francois Marie. **Travels through the Two Louisianas.** London: Phillips; 1807. [x-lib., $300.00]

Perrin du Lac, Francois Marie. **Voyage dans les Deux Louisianes.** Paris: Capelle et Renand; 1805. [half morocco binding, $2000.00]

Perry, Bliss. **And Gladly Teach.** Boston, NY: Houghton Mifflin; 1935. [$17.50]

Perry, Charles Milton. **Henry Philip Tappan.** Ann Arbor: U. of Michigan; 1933. [x-lib., $15.00]

Perry, Clair Willard. **Underground New England.** Brattleboro: Daye; 1939. [$20.00]

Perry, George Sessions. **Hold Autumn in Your Hand.** NY: Viking; 1941. [third printing, inscribed, $35.00]

Perry, George Sessions. **Roundup Time.** NY; London: Whittlesey; McGraw-Hill; 1943. [signed, $35.00]

Perry, George Sessions. **Story of Texas A and M.** NY: McGraw-Hill; 1951. [$20.00]

Perry, Lynn. **A Branch of the Peery Family Tree.** Strasburg, VA: Shenandoah; 1931. [shaken and soiled, $25.00]

Perry, Matthew Calbraith. **Narrative of the Expedition of an American Squadron to the China Seas and Japan.** Washington: Nicholson; 1856. 3 v. [$1100.00]

Perry, Milton F. **Patton and His Pistols.** Harrisburg: Stackpole; 1957. [$45.00]

Pershing, John J. **My Experiences in the World War.** 1st ed. NY: Stokes; 1931. 2 v. [$35.00] [$25.00]

Persons, Stow. **Evolutionary Thought in America.** NY: Braziller; 1956. [$15.00]

Peter, Grace Dunlop. **Portrait of Old George Town.** Richmond: Garrett & Massie; 1933. [bumped, rubbed, sunned, $35.00]

Peters, Charles. **Autobiography of.** Sacramento: La Grave; 1915. [$40.00]

Peters, De Witt Clinton. **Kit Carson's Life and Adventures.** Hartford; Cincinnati: Dustin, Gilman; Queen City; 1874. [x-lib., $35.00] [$55.00]

Peters, De Witt Clinton. **Life and Adventures of Kit Carson, the Nestor of the Rocky Mountains.** NY: Clark; 1858. [$250.00]

Peters, Harry Twyford. **America on Stone; the Other Printmakers to the American People.** Garden City: Doubleday, Doran; 1931. [$500.00]

Peters, Harry Twyford. **Currier & Ives.** Garden City: Doubleday, Doran; 1942. [$12.00]

Peters, Samuel. **General History of Connecticut.** New Haven: Clark; 1829. [$85.00] [1877 Appleton ed., $50.00]

Petersen, Frederick A. **Military Review of the Campaign in Virginia & Maryland.** NY: Tousey, Dexter; 1862-63. 2 pt. in 1 v. [$100.00]

Petersen, William John. **Steamboating on the Upper Mississippi.** Iowa City: State Historical Society of Iowa; 1937. [some water stains, $85.00] [$75.00]

Peterson, Charles Jacobs. **The Cabin and Parlor.** Philadelphia: Peterson; 1852. [$34.00]

Peterson, J. W. **Joseph Smith Defended and His Divine Mission Vindicated.** Lamoni, IA: Herald; 1904. [rebound, $25.00]

Peterson, Purl Dewey. **Through the Black Hills and Bad Lands of South Dakota.** Pierre: Olander; 1929. [$45.00] [$65.00]

Peto, Samuel Morton. **Resources and Prospects of America.** London, NY: Strahan; 1866. [$90.00]

Petrie, George. **Church and State in Early Maryland.** Baltimore: Hopkins; 1892. [$35.00]

Petrullo, Vincenzo. **The Diabolic Root.** Philadelphia: U. of Pennsylvania; 1934. [rebound, x-lib., $30.00]

Pettengill, Ray Waldron. **Letters from America, 1776-1779.** Boston, NY: Houghton Mifflin; 1924. [$65.00]

Peyton, Green. see, Wertenbaker, Green Peyton.

Pflueger, Donald H. **Glendora.** lst ed. Claremont, CA: Saunders; 1951. [presentation, $49.50]

Phares, Ross. **Bible in Pocket, Gun in Hand.** Lincoln: U. of Nebraska; 1964. [dj worn, $25.00]

Phares, Ross. **Texas Tradition.** 1st ed. NY: Holt; 1954. [$25.00]

Phelan, James. **History of Tennessee.** Boston, NY: Houghton Mifflin; 1889. [x-lib., binding torn, $15.00]

Phelps, Albert. **Louisiana; a Record of Expansion.** Boston, NY: Houghton Mifflin; 1905. [$40.00]

Phelps, H. **Phelps' Strangers and Citizens' Guide to New York City.** NY: Watson; 1857. [map repaired, $100.00]

Phelps, Martha Bennett. **Frances Slocum, the Lost Sister of Wyoming.** NY: Knickerbocker; 1905. [$35.00]

Phelps, William Dane. **Fore and Aft.** Boston: Nichols & Hall; 1871. [rebound, $100.00]

Philips, Shine. **Big Spring.** NY: Prentice-Hall; 1942. [presentation, $12.00]

Phillips, Catherine Coffin. **Jessie Benton Fremont.** San Francisco: Nash; 1935. [inscribed, $75.00] [$65.00]

Phillips, Ephraim. **Lost in the Adirondacks!** Schenectady, NY: Burrows; 1890. [$75.00]

Phillips, Mary Elizabeth. **Reminiscences of William Wetmore.** Chicago, NY: Rand McNally; 1897. [inscribed, $75.00]

Phillips, Ulrich Bonnell. **American Negro Slavery.** NY: Appleton; 1929, c1918. [$30.00]

Phillips, Walter Shelley. **The Old-Timer's Tale.** Chicago: Canterbury; 1929. [$35.00] [$45.00] $50.00]

Phillips, Wilbur H. **Oberlin Colony.** limited ed. Oberlin: Oberlin Print.; 1933. [$50.00]

Phillips, Willard. **Propositions Concerning Protection and Free Trade.** Boston: Little and Brown; 1850. [$65.00]

Phillips, William Addison. **Conquest of Kansas by Missouri and Her Allies.** Boston: Phillips, Sampson; 1856. [$85.00] [$70.00]

Phinney, Elias. **History of the Battle of Lexington.** Boston: Phelps and Farnham; 1825. [$75.00]

Pickard, Madge E. **The Midwest Pioneer.** 1st ed. Crawfordsville, IN: Banta; 1945. [$50.00]

Pickard, Samuel. **Autobiography of a Pioneer.** Chicago: Church & Goodman; 1866. [$135.00]

Pickering, John. **Vocabulary; or Collection of Words and Phrases.** Boston; Cambridge: Cummings and Hilliard; Hilliard and Metcalf; 1816. [spine chipped, $175.00]

Pickett, George Edward. **Soldier of the South.** Boston, NY: Houghton Mifflin; 1928. [$35.00]

Pickford, Mary. **Sunshine and Shadow.** 1st ed. Garden City: Doubleday; 1955. [$12.50]

Pickrell, Annie Doom. **Pioneer Women in Texas.** 1st ed. Austin: Steck; 1929. [$75.00]

Pictet, Charles. **Tableau de la Situation Actuelle des Etats-'Unis d'Ameriques d'apres J. Morse et les Meilleurs Auteurs Americains.** Paris: Du Pont; 1795. 2 v. [$275.00]

Pidgeon, William. **Traditions of De-Coo-Dah.** NY: Thayer, Bridgman & Fanning; 1853. [lacks map, $60.00] [spine repaired, $50.00]

Pidgin, Charles Felton. **Quincy Adams Sawyer and Mason's Corner Folks.** Boston: Clark; 1900. [$35.00]

Pierce, Arthur D. **Iron in the Pines.** New Brunswick: Rutgers UP; 1957. [$12.50]

Pierce, Arthur D. **Smugglers' Woods.** New Brunswick: Rutgers UP; 1960. [$12.50]

Pierce, Calvin P. **Ryal Side from Early Days of Salem County.** Cambridge: Beverly Hist. Soc.; 1931. [$45.00]

Pierce, Gerald S. **Texas under Arms.** Austin: Encino; 1969. [$25.00]

Pierce, Josiah. **Letters to Laura.** Boston: Godine; 1974. [$12.50]

Pierpont, John. **The Portrait.** Boston: Bradford and Read; 1812. [$35.00]

Piers, Harry. **Robert Field.** NY: Sherman; 1927. [$200.00]

Pierson, Emily Catherine. **Jamie Parker, the Fugitive.** Hartford: Brockett, Fuller; 1851. [spine chipped, $150.00]

Pierson, George Wilson. **Tocqueville and Beaumont in America.** NY: Oxford UP; 1938. [$45.00]

Pierson, Hamilton Wilcox. **In the Brush.** NY: Appleton; 1881. [$25.00]

Pigman, Walter Griffith. **Journal of.** Mexico, MO: Staley; 1942. [$75.00]

Pike, Albert. **Prose Sketches and Poems Written in the Western Country.** Boston: Light & Horton; 1834. [$2250.00]

Pike, James. **The Scout and Ranger.** Cincinnati, NY: Hawley; 1865. [first issue, $850.00] [1932 Princeton UP ed., $65.00]

Pike, James Shepherd. **The Prostrate South.** NY: Appleton; 1874. [$100.00]

Pike, Warburton Mayer. **The Barren Ground of Northern Canada.** London, NY: Macmillan; 1892. [$135.00]

Pike, Zebulon Montgomery. **The Expeditions of Zebulon Montgomery Pike to Headwaters of the Mississippi River.** new ed. NY: Harper; 1895. 3 v. [rebound, $150.00]

Pike, Zebulon Montgomery. **Journals of.** 1st ed. Norman: U. of Oklahoma; 1966. 2 v. [$75.00]

Pilcher, Elijah Holmes. **Protestantism in Michigan.** Detroit: Tyler; 1878. [rebacked, $65.00]

Pillsbury, Dorothy L. **Adobe Doorways.** Albuquerque: U. of New Mexico; 1952. [$15.00] [$17.50]

Pillsbury, Parker. **Acts of the Anti-Slavery Apostles.** Concord, NH: Clague, Wegman, Schlicht; 1883. [$40.00]

Pinchon, Edgcumb. **Dan Sickles.** 1st ed. Garden City: Doubleday, Doran; 1945. [$15.00] [$16.50]

Pinchot, Gifford. **Breaking New Ground.** 1st ed. NY: Harcourt, Brace; 1947. [covers stained, $15.00]

Pinckney, Charles. **Three Letters.** Philadelphia: Aurora; 1799. [disbound, $150.00]

Pine, George W. **Beyond the West.** Utica: Griffiths; 1870. [$250.00] [second ed., 1871, $75.00]

Pinkerton, Allan. **Mississippi Outlaws and the Detectives.** NY: Carleton; 1879. [x-lib., $15.00]

Pinkerton, Allan. **Professional Thieves and the Detective.** Chicago: Nettleton; 1881. [$125.00]

Pinkerton, Allan. **Thirty Years a Detective.** NY: Carlton; 1884. [1886 issue, $45.00]

Pinkerton, Robert Eugene. **Hudson's Bay Company.** NY: Holt; 1931. [x-lib., rebound, $15.00] [$45.00]

Pino, Pedro Bautista. **Three New Mexico Chronicles.** Albuquerque: Quivira; 1942. [$150.00]

Pioneer and General History of Geauga County. Burton, OH: Historical Society of Geauga County; 1880. [$50.00]

Pitezel, John H. **Lights and Shades of Missionary Life.** Cincinnati: Western Book Concern; 1860. [$65.00]

Pitkin, Timothy. **A Political and Civil History of the United States of America.** 1st ed. New Haven: Howe, Durrie & Peck; 1828. 2 v. [$95.00] [foxed, $150.00]

Pitman, Benn. **The Assassination of President Lincoln and the Trial of the Conspirators.** Cincinnati: Moore, Wilstach & Baldwin; 1865. [$125.00]

Pitt, William. **Correspondence of.** NY, London: Macmillan; 1906. 2 v. [$85.00]

Pittenger, William. **Daring and Suffering.** Philadelphia: Daughaday; 1864. [$45.00]

Pittenger, William. **The Great Locomotive Chase.** 9th ed. Philadelphia: Penn; 1929. [$25.00]

Platt, Charles Davis. **Ballads of New Jersey in the Revolution.** Morristown: Jerseyman; 1896. [$35.00]

Platt, Rutherford Hayes. **The Great American Forest.** Englewood Cliffs: Prentice-Hall; 1965. [$15.00]

Platt, Thomas Collier. **Autobiography of.** NY: Dodge; 1910. [$35.00]

Plaut, W. Gunther. **The Jews in Minnesota.** NY: American Jewish Hist. Soc.; 1959. [signed, $10.00]

Player, Cyril Arthur. **Barons of the Virginia Rivers.** Detroit: News; 1930. [$20.00]

Playter, George Frederick. **History of Methodism in Canada.** Toronto: Green; 1862. [second vol. never published, x-lib., $75.00]

Plenn, Jaime Harrysson. **Saddle in the Sky.** 1st ed. Indianapolis, NY: Bobbs-Merrill; 1940. [dj very worn, $35.00]

Plowden, David. **Floor of the Sky.** San Francisco: Sierra Club; 1972. [$25.00]

Plummer, Albert. **History of the Forty-Eighth Regiment, M.V.M. during the Civil War.** Boston: New England Druggist; 1907. [x-lib., $50.00]

Plyler, Alva Washington. **Iron Duke of the Methodist Itinerancy.** Nashville: Cokesbury; 1925. [mildewed, $20.00]

Poague, William Thomas. **Gunner with Stonewall.** Jackson, TN: McCowat-Mercer; 1957. [signed, $30.00]

Poe, Clarence Hamilton. **True Tales of the South at War.** Chapel Hill: U. of North Carolina; 1961. [$22.50]

Poe, Edgar Allan. **Complete Works of.** Arnheim ed. NY: Putnam; 1902. 10 v. [$650.00, Canadian]

Poe, Edgar Allan. **Edgar Allan Poe Letters.** Philadelphia, London: Lippincott; 1925. [$125.00]

Poe, Edgar Allan. **Eureka.** 1st ed. NY: Putnam; 1848. [$1250.00]

Poe, Edgar Allan. **Mesmerism "In Articulo Mortis."** London: Short; 1846. [$1750.00]

Poe, Edgar Allan. **Narrative of Arthur Gordon Pym.** London: Wiley and Putnam; 1838. [$950.00]

Poe, Edgar Allan. **The Raven, and Other Poems.** NY: Wiley and Putnam; 1845. [in blue morocco, $4200.00] [1942 Facs. Text Soc. imprint, $75.00]

Poe, Edgar Allan. **Tales.** NY: Wiley and Putnam; 1845. [$1850.00]

Poe, Edgar Allan. **Works of.** Edinburgh: Black; 1874-75. 4 v. [$785.00]

Poe, Edgar Allan. **Works of the Late.** NY: Redfield; 1850. 2 v. [2nd printing, signatures somewhat loose, $800.00]

Poe, John William. **Death of Billy the Kid.** Boston, NY: Houghton Mifflin; 1933. [$35.00] [corners bumped, $50.00] [$45.00]

Poe, Sophie. **Buckboard Days.** Caldwell, ID: Caxton; 1936. [$60.00] [dj worn, $85.00]

Poindexter, Miles. **The Ayar-Incas.** NY: Liveright; 1930. 2 v. [$85.00]

Point, Nicolas. **Wilderness Kingdom, Indian Life in the Rocky Mountains: 1840-1847.** 1st ed. NY: Holt, Rinehart and Winston; 1967. [$35.00] [$30.00]

Polk, James K. **The Diary of.** Chicago: McClurg; 1910. 4 v. [$550.00]

Polk, James K. **Polk; the Diary of a President, 1845-1849.** London, NY: Longmans, Green; 1952. [$45.00] [$22.50]

Polk, William Mecklenburg. **Leonidas Polk.** new ed. NY: Longmans, Green; 1915. 2 v. [$125.00]

Pollack, Norman. **Populist Mind.** Indianapolis: Bobbs-Merrill; 1967. [$15.00]

Pollard, Edward Alfred. **First Year of the War.** NY: Richardson; 1866. [$45.00]

Pollard, Edward Alfred. **Lee and His Lieutenants.** NY; Baltimore: Treat; Morrow; 1867. [rebound, $125.00]

Pollard, Edward Alfred. **The Lost Cause.** NY: Treat; 1866. [rebound, $40.00]

Pollard, Edward Alfred. **The Lost Cause Regained.** NY: Carleton; 1868. [$60.00]

Pollard, Edward Alfred. **Observations in the North.** Richmond: Ayres; 1865. [inscribed, $450.00]

Pollard, Edward Alfred. **Southern History of the War.** NY: Richardson; 1866. 2 v. [spine of v. 2 split, $65.00]

Pollard, Henry Robinson. **Memoirs and Sketches of the Life of.** Richmond: Lewis; 1923. [$35.00]

Polley, Joseph Benjamin. **Hood's Texas Brigade.** NY, Washington: Neale; 1910. [$950.00] [$875.00]

Polley, Joseph Benjamin. **A Soldier's Letters to Charming Nellie.** NY, Washington: Neale; 1908. [$375.00]

Pollock, Edwin Taylor. **The Hatchet of the United States Ship "George Washington."** NY: Little & Ives; 1919. [$35.00]

Pomeroy, Earl Spencer. **In Search of the Golden West.** 1st ed. NY: Knopf; 1957. [$15.00]

Pomfret, John Edwin. **California Gold Rush Voyages, 1848-1849.** San Marino: Huntington; 1954. [$25.00]

Pond, Edgar Le Roy. **The Tories of Chippeny Hill, Connecticut.** NY: Grafton; 1909. [$25.00]

Pond, Frederick Eugene. **Life and Adventures of "Ned Buntline."** NY: Cadmus; 1919. [$100.00]

Pons, Francois Raymond Joseph de. **Voyage to the Eastern Part of Terra Firma.** NY: Riley; 1806. 3 v. [$350.00]

Ponting, Tom Candy. **Life of.** Evanston, IL: Branding Iron; 1952. [$65.00]

Pool, Bettie Freshwater. **The Eyrie and Other Southern Stories.** NY: Broadway; 1905. [$20.00]

Poole, D. C. **Among the Sioux of Dakota.** NY: Van Nostrand; 1881. [$45.00]

Poole, Ernest. **Nurses on Horseback.** NY: Macmillan; 1932. [$25.00]

Poolman, Kenneth. **Guns off Cape Ann.** London: Evans; 1961. [$17.50]

Poor, Alfred Easton. **Colonial Architecture of Cape Cod, Nantucket and Martha's Vineyard.** NY: Helburn; 1932. [$60.00]

Poor, Meredith Clarence. **Denver, South Park & Pacific.** Denver: Rocky Mountain Railroad Club; 1949. [signed edition, $200.00]

Poore, Benjamin Perley. **Perley's Reminiscences.** Philadelphia; NY: Hubbard; Houghton; 1886. 2 v. [$125.00]

Pope, Charles Henry. **Pioneers of Massachusetts.** Boston: Pope; 1900. [rebound. $35.00]

Pope, Joseph. **Jacques Cartier.** Ottawa: Woodburn; 1890. [x-lib., $30.00, Canadian]

Pope, Katherine. **Hawaii, the Rainbow Land.** NY: Crowell; 1924. [$15.00]

Pope, Liston. **Millhands & Preachers.** New Haven; London: Yale UP; Oxford UP; 1942. [x-lib., $12.50]

Pope, W. C. **Leisure Moments.** Raleigh: Edwards & Broughton; 1919. [$25.00]

Porter, Anthony Toomer. **History of a Work of Faith and Love in Charleston, South Carolina.** 4th ed. NY: Appleton; 1882. [binding stained, $27.50]

Porter, Burton B. **One of the People.** Colton, CA: The Author; 1907. [x-lib., $55.00]

Porter, Burton P. **Old Canal Days.** premiere ed. Columbus, OH: Heer; 1942. [signed, $42.50]

Porter, Charles T. **Review of the Mexican War.** Auburn, NY: Alden & Parsons; 1849. [pages stained and foxed, $75.00]

Porter, David Dixon. **Incidents and Anecdotes of the Civil War.** NY: Appleton; 1885. [$85.00]

Porter, David Dixon. **Naval History of the Civil War.** NY: Sherman; 1886. [$100.00] [rebound, $90.00]

Porter, Eliot. **The Place No One Knew.** San Francisco: Sierra Club; 1963. [$55.00]

Porter, Eliphalet. **A Discourse before the Society for Propagating the Gospel among the Indians and Others in North America.** Boston: Munroe, Francis, & Parker; 1808. [disbound, $85.00]

Porter, Henry M. **Pencilings of an Early Western Pioneer.** Denver: World; 1929. [$85.00]

Porter, Katherine Anne. **Hacienda.** NY: Harrison of Paris; 1934. [$75.00]

Porter, Mae Reed. **Scotsman in Buckskin.** NY: Hastings; 1963. [$25.00]

Porter, Nannie Francisco. **Romantic Record of Peter Francisco.** Staunton, VA: McClure; 1929. [silverfished, bumped, $20.00]

Porter, Rufus. **Aerial Navigation.** San Francisco: Kennedy; 1935. [$100.00]

Porter, Valentine Mott. **History of Battery "A" of St. Louis.** St. Louis: Missouri Hist. Soc.; 1905. [$75.00]

Porter, William Dennison. **State Sovereingty and the Doctrine of Coercion.** Charleston: Evans and Cogswell; 1860. [$65.00] [$80.00]

Porter, William Trotter. **Colonel Thorpe's Scenes in Arkansaw.** Philadelphia: Peterson; 1858. [$75.00]

Portlock, Nathaniel. **A Voyage round the World.** London: Stockdale and Goulding; 1789. [$975.00] [x-lib., $1200.00]

Posey, Alexander Lawrence. **Poems of.** Topeka, KS: Crane; 1910. [$45.00]

Posey, Walter Brownlow. **The Presbyterian Church in the Old Southwest, 1778-1838.** Richmond: Knox; 1952. [$30.00]

Post, Charles Asa. **Those Were the Days When Hearts Were Kind and Sports Were Simple.** Cleveland: Caxton; 1935. [$15.00]

Post, Charles Clement. **Ten Years a Cowboy.** Chcigao [sic]: Rhodes & McClure; 1895. [$20.00]

Post, Charles Johnson. **Across the Andes.** NY: Outing; 1912. [$25.00]

Post, Emily. **By Motor to the Golden Gate.** NY, London: Appleton; 1916. [$40.00]

Post, Lydia. **Grace Barclay's Diary.** 2nd ed. NY: Randolph; 1866. [$40.00]

Poston, Charles Debrille. **Apache-Land.** San Francisco: Bancroft; 1878. [$450.00]

Potter, Chandler Eastman. **History of Manchester, Formerly Derryfield in New Hampshire.** Manchester: Potter; 1856. [$75.00]

Potter, Elisha Reynolds. **Memoir Concerning the French Settlements and French Settlers in the Colony of Rhode Island.** Providence: Rider; 1879. [$40.00]

Potter, Helen. **Impersonations.** NY: Werner; 1891. [$95.00]

Potter, Jack Myers. **Cattle Trails of the Old West.** Clayton, NM: Krehbiel; 1939. [$75.00]

Potter, Woodburne. **The War in Florida.** Baltimore: Lewis and Coleman; 1836. [x-lib., waterstained, $175.00] [$650.00] [$500.00]

Pottle, Frederick Albert. **Stretchers.** New Haven; London: Yale UP; Oxford UP; 1929. [$15.00]

Pound, Arthur. **Johnson of the Mohawks.** NY: Macmillan; 1930. [$40.00] [$35.00] [$30.00]

Pound, Arthur. **Lake Ontario.** Indianapolis: Bobbs-Merrill; 1945. [$14.00]

Pound, Ezra. **The Cantos of.** NY: New Directions; 1948. [2nd printing?, $12.50]

Pound, Ezra. **Eleven New Cantos, XXXI-XLI.** NY: Farrar and Rinehart; 1934. [dj intact, back cover dented, $50.00]

Pound, Ezra. **Seventy Cantos.** London: Faber & Faber; 1950. [$30.00]

Pound, Merritt Bloodworth. **Benjamin Hawkins, Indian Agent.** Athens: U. of Georgia; 1951. [$15.00]

Poussin, Guillaume Tell. **The United States; Its Power and Progress.** 1st American ed. Philadelphia: Lippincott, Grambo; 1851. [$75.00]

Powderly, Terence Vincent. **The Path I Trod.** NY: Columbia UP; 1940. [$27.50]

Powell, Addison M. **Trailing and Camping in Alaska.** NY: Wessels; 1909. [$50.00] [London, 1910, $42.00]

Powell, Donald M. **The Peralta Grant.** 1st ed. Norman: U. of Oklahoma; 1960. [$25.00]

Powell, E. Alexander. **Brothers in Arms.** Boston, NY: Houghton Mifflin; 1917. [$15.00]

Powell, J. H. **Bring Out Your Dead.** Philadelphia: U. of Pennsylvania; 1949. [$25.00]

Powell, John J. **The Golden State and Its Resources.** San Francisco: Bacon; 1874. [x-lib., $50.00]

Powell, John Wesley. **Exploration of the Colorado River.** Chicago: U. of Chicago; 1957. [$11.00]

Powell, John Wesley. **Outlines of the Philosophy of the North American Indians.** NY: Taylor; 1877. [$75.00]

Powell, Lyman Pierson. **Historic Towns of New England.** NY, London: Putnam; 1898. [$35.00]

Powell, Peter J. **Sweet Medicine.** 1st ed. Norman: U. of Oklahoma; 1969. 2 v. [with worn box, $75.00]

Powell, Samuel. **Notes on "Southern Wealth and Northern Profits."** Philadelphia: Sherman; 1861. [$35.00]

Power, John Carroll. **History of an Attempt to Steal the Body of Abraham Lincoln.** Springfield, IL: Rokker; 1890, c1887. [x-lib., $200.00]

Powers, Alfred. **Poems of the Covered Wagons.** 1st ed. Portland, OR: Pacific; 1947. [$20.00]

Powers, Alfred. **Redwood Country.** 1st ed. NY: Duell, Sloan & Pearce; 1949. [$15.00]

Powers, Caleb. **Great Speech of.** [s.l.: s.n.; 1903?]. [$45.00]

Powers, Edwin. **Crime and Punishment in Early Massachusetts.** Boston: Beacon; 1966. [$20.00]

Powers, Laura Bride. **The Missions of California.** San Francisco: Doxey; 1897. [$20.00]

Powers, Stephen. **Afoot and Alone.** Hartford: Columbian; 1872. [spine rubbed, corners bumped, soiled, $125.00]

Pratt, Josiah. **Life of David Brainerd.** London: Seeley, Jackson, and Halliday; 1856. [$150.00]

Pratt, Julius Howard. **Reminiscences, Personal and Otherwise.** [s.l.]: Priv. Print.; 1910. [$125.00]

Pratt, Orson. **Absurdities of Immaterialism.** Liverpool: [s.n.]; 1849. [$75.00]

Pratt, Parley P. **A Voice of Warning and Instruction to All People.** 2nd ed. Plano, IL: Reorganized Church of Jesus Christ of Latter Day Saints; 1867. [boards rubbed, $250.00]

Preble, George Henry. **Origin and History of the American Flag.** new ed. Philadelphia: Brown; 1917. 2 v. [$100.00]

Preece, Harold. **The Dalton Gang.** NY: Hastings; 1963. [$25.00]

Preece, Harold. **Living Pioneers.** 1st ed. Cleveland: World; 1952. [dj soiled, $30.00]

Preece, Harold. **Lone Star Man: Ira Aten.** NY: Hastings; 1960. [$35.00] [$30.00]

Preedy, George. **Life of Rear-Admiral John Paul Jones.** London: Jenkins; 1940. [$45.00]

Prendergast, Thomas F. **Forgotten Pioneers.** San Francisco: Trade Pressroom; 1942. [$49.50]

Prentiss, A. **History of the Utah Volunteers in the Spanish-American War and in the Philippine Islands.** Salt Lake City: Ford; 1900. [hinges cracked, $39.50]

Prentiss, Charles. **Life of the Late Gen. William Eaton.** Brookfield: Merriam; 1813. [$135.00]

Presbyterian Church in the U.S.A. Presbyteries. Geneva-Lyons. **Narrative of the Late Revivals of Religion.** Geneva, NY: Merrell; 1832. [$150.00]

Prescott, William Hickling. **Histoire de la Conquete du Mexique.** nouv. ed. Paris: Didot; 1863-1864. [$125.00]

Prescott, William Hickling. **History of the Conquest of Peru.** NY: Harper; 1848, c1847. 2 v. [$150.00] [$175.00] [1864 Lippincott ed., $75.00]

Preston, Richard Arthur. **Royal Fort Frontenac.** Toronto: Champlain Soc.; 1958. [$25.00]

Preston, Walter Creigh. **Lee, West Point and Lexington.** Yellow Springs, OH: Antioch; 1934. [x-lib., $30.00]

Prettyman, William S. **Indian Territory.** 1st ed. Norman: U. of Oklahoma; 1957. [$25.00]

Price, Alfred. **Rail Life.** Toronto: Allen; 1925. [$35.00, Canadian]

Price, Doughbelly. **Short Stirrups.** Los Angeles: Westernlore; 1960. [$20.00]

Price, Joseph Cooper. **Wild Oats.** Toledo: Barkdull; 1879. [$350.00]

Price, Richard. **Observations on the Importance of the American Revolution.** Amherst, NH: Cushing; 1805. [$75.00]

Price, Richard. **Observations on the Nature of Civil Liberty, the Principles of Government, and the Justice and Policy of the War with America.** 7th ed. London: Cadell; 1776. [$150.00]

Price, Rose Lambart. **The Two Americas.** Philadelphia: Lippincott; 1877. [$55.00]

Price, Samuel Goodale. **Ghosts of Golconda.** Deadwood, SD: Western Publishers; 1952. [$40.00] [$25.00]

Prichard, Hesketh Vernon Hesketh. **Through the Heart of Patagonia.** NY: Appleton; 1902. [$100.00]

Pride, Woodbury Freeman. **History of Fort Riley.** Fort Riley, KS: Cavalry School, Book Dept.; 1926. [$50.00] [$40.00]

Priest, Josiah. **American Antiquities, and Discoveries in the West.** 3rd ed. Albany, NY: Hoffman & White; 1833. [worn, $60.00] [lacks map and 2nd plate, $65.00] [5th ed., 1835, $85.00]

Priest, William. **Travels in the United States of America.** London: Johnson; 1802. [waterstained, spotted, $200.00]

Priestley, Joseph. **Letters to the Inhabitants of Northumberland and Its Neighbourhood.** 2nd ed. Philadelphia: Bioren; 1801. [disbound, $250.00]

Prieto, Guillermo. **San Francisco in the Seventies.** San Francisco: Nash; 1938. [$70.00]

Prime, Alfred Coxe. **Arts & Crafts in Philadelphia, Maryland and South Carolina.** Topsfield, MA: Walpole Soc.; 1929-33. 2 v. [$150.00]

Prime, Nathaniel S. **History of Long Island.** NY: Carter; 1845. [rebacked, $75.00]

Prince, Le Baron Bradford. **Historical Sketches of New Mexico, from the Earliest Records to the American Occupation.** NY; Kansas City: Leggat; Ramsey, Millett & Hudson; 1883. [signature tipped in, $125.00]

Prince, Thomas. **Chronological History of New-England.** new ed. Boston: Cummings, Hilliard; 1826. [x-lib., rebound, hinges cracked, $40.00]

Prince, William Meade. **The Southern Part of Heaven.** NY: Rinehart; 1950. [signed, bumped, $20.00]

Pringle, George Charles Fraser. **Tillicums of the Trail.** Toronto: McClelland & Stewart; 1922. [$30.00, Canadian]

Pringle, Henry Fowles. **Life and Times of William Howard Taft.** NY, Toronto: Farrar & Rinehart; 1939. 2 v. [$65.00]

Pritchard, James A. **The Overland Diary of.** 1st ed. Denver: Rosenstock; 1959. [unopened, $100.00]

Pritchett, John Perry. **The Red River Valley.** New Haven; Toronto: Yale UP; Ryerson; 1942. [$45.00]

Probst, Anton. **Trial, Life and Execution of.** Philadelphia: Peterson; 1866. [$35.00]

Procter, Ben H. **Not without Honor.** Austin: U. of Texas; 1962. [$25.00]

Procter, Gil. **Tucson, Tubac, Tumacacori, Tohell.** 1st limited ed. Tucson: Arizona Silhouettes; 1956. [$35.00]

Proctor, Alexander Phimister. **Alexander Phimister Proctor.** 1st ed. Norman: U. of Oklahoma; 1971. [$20.00]

Proper, Ida Sedgwick. **Monhegan, the Cradle of New England.** Portland, ME: Southworth; 1930. [$15.00]

Prosch, Thomas Wickham. **McCarver and Tacoma.** Seattle: Lowman & Hanford; 1906. [inscribed, $225.00]

Prowell, George Reeser. **History of the Eighty-Seventh Regiment, Pennsylvania Volunteers.** York: Daily; 1901. [$75.00]

Prucha, Francis Paul. **Broadax and Bayonet.** Madison: State Hist. Soc. of Wisconsin; 1953. [$35.00]

Prudden, Theophil Mitchell. **On the Great American Plateau.** NY, London: Putnam; 1906. [$55.00] [1907 printing, $25.00]

Pruiett, Moman. **Moman Pruiett, Criminal Lawyer.** Oklahoma City: Harlow; 1944. [$75.00] [3rd printing, 1945, $35.00]

Pryor, Sara Agnes. **Birth of the Nation; Jamestown, 1607.** NY, London: Macmillan; 1907. [presentation, $17.50]

Pryor, Sara Agnes. **Reminiscences of Peace and War.** NY, London: Macmillan; 1904. [$45.00]

Puddefoot, William George. **Minute Man on the Frontier.** NY: Crowell; 1895. [$35.00] [$50.00]

Pullen, John J. **The Twentieth Maine.** Philadelphia: Lippincott; 1957. [$35.00]

Pulsifer, David. **Sights in Boston and Suburbs.** Boston: Munroe; 1857. [with two folding maps, $75.00]

Pumpelly, Raphael. **Across America and Asia.** 4th ed. NY: Leopoldt & Holt; 1870. [$110.00]

Purviance, Robert. **Narrative of Events Which Occurred in Baltimore Town during the Revolutionary War.** Baltimore: Robinson; 1849. [presentation, $85.00]

Pusey, Merlo John. **Charles Evans Hughes.** NY: Macmillan; 1952, c1951. 2 v. [$35.00]

Putnam, George Granville. **Salem Vessels and Their Voyages.** Salem, MA: Essex Institute; 1924-30. 4 v. [$125.00]

Putnam, George Haven. **Memories of My Youth, 1844-1865.** NY, London: Putnam; 1914. [covers scuffed, $35.00]

Putnam, George Haven. **Prisoner of War in Virginia, 1864-5.** NY, London: Putnam; 1912. [$15.00] [$25.00]

Putnam, George Haven. **Some Memories of the Civil War.** NY, London: Putnam; 1924. [$35.00] [$25.00]

Putnam, George Palmer. **Death Valley and Its Country.** NY: Duell, Sloan and Pearce; 1946. [$7.50]

Putnam, Israel. **General Orders Issued by Major-General Israel Putnam.** Brooklyn: Historical Printing Club; 1893. [$45.00]

Putnam, Israel. **The Two Putnams, Israel and Rufus.** Hartford: Connecticut Hist. Soc.; 1931. [$45.00]

Putnam, Royal Porter. **Journal of.** Porterville, CA: Farm Tribune; 1961. [$25.00]

Putnam, Sallie A. **In Richmond during the Confederacy.** NY: McBride; 1961. [$35.00]

Put's Golden Songster. see, Stone, John A.

Puxley, W. Lavallin. **Magic Land of the Maya.** London: Allen and Unwin; 1928. [$35.00]

Pyle, Ernie. **Last Chapter.** NY: Holt; 1946. [$10.00]

Quad, M. **Brother Gardner's Lime-Kiln Club.** Chicago: Belford, Clark; 1882. [$150.00]

Quaife, Milo Milton. **Attainment of Statehood.** Madison: State Historical Society of Wisconsin; 1928. [$50.00]

Quaife, Milo Milton. **Chicago's Highways, Old and New.** Chicago: Keller; 1923. [$50.00]

Quaife, Milo Milton. **Convention of 1846.** Madison: Wisconsin State Historical Society; 1919. [$65.00]

Quaife, Milo Milton. **Pictures of Gold Rush California.** Chicago: Lakeside; 1949. [$17.50]

Quarles, Benjamin. **The Negro in the Civil War.** 1st ed. Boston: Little, Brown; 1953. [$35.00] [$20.00]

Queeny, Edgar M. **Cheechako.** NY: Scribner; 1941. [$75.00]

Quick, Arthur Craig. **Wild Flowers of the Northern States and Canada.** Chicago: Donahue; 1939. [$12.50]

Quick, Herbert. **Mississippi Steamboatin'.** NY: Holt; 1926. [$37.50] [$25.00]

Quincy, Josiah. **Memoir of the Life of John Quincy Adams.** Boston: Phillips, Sampson; 1858. [$50.00] [$45.00]

Quinn, Arthur Hobson. **Edgar Allan Poe.** NY, London: Appleton-Century; 1941. [worn dj, $35.00]

Quinn, John Philip. **Fools of Fortune; or, Gambling and Gamblers.** Chicago: Anti-Gambling Assn.; 1892. [browning, $65.00]

Quint, Wilder Dwight. **Story of Dartmouth.** Boston: Little, Brown; 1914. [$45.00]

Quisenberry, Anderson Chenault. **Lopez's Expeditions to Cuba, 1850 and 1851.** Louisville: Morton; 1906. [$85.00]

R***, J. see, Romanet, Joseph.

Rademaker, John Adrian. **These Are Americans.** Palo Alto, CA: Pacific Books; 1951. [signed, $100.00]

Radin, Paul. **Indians of South America.** 1st ed. Garden City: Doubleday, Doran; 1942. [$38.00] [$29.00]

Radoff, Morris Leon. **Buildings of the State of Maryland at Annapolis.** Annapolis: Hall of Records Commission; 1954. [$45.00]

Rae, W. Fraser. **Westward by Rail.** London: Longmans, Green; 1870. [rebound, $65.00]

Raht, Carlysle Graham. **Romance of Davis Mountains and Big Bend Country.** El Paso: Raht; 1919. [$100.00]

Railroad Communication with the Pacific with an Account of the Central Pacific Railroad of California. NY: Brown; 1867. [$145.00]

Raine, James Watt. **Land of Saddle-Bags.** NY: Council of Women for Home Missions and Missionary Education Movement of the U.S. and Canada; 1924. [$23.00]

Raine, William MacLeod. **Cattle.** 1st ed. NY: Doubleday, Doran; 1930. [$50.00] [Grosset & Dunlap reprint, $17.50]

Raine, William MacLeod. **Famous Sheriffs & Western Outlaws.** 1st ed. Garden City: Doubleday, Doran; 1929. [loose at spine, $40.00] [1944 New Home Lib. ed., $18.00]

Raine, William MacLeod. **Guns of the Frontier.** Boston: Houghton Mifflin; 1940. [$30.00] [dj sunned, $40.00]

Raine, William MacLeod. **The Yukon Trail.** Boston, NY: Houghton Mifflin; 1917. [$12.50]

Rainey, George. **The Cherokee Strip.** Guthrie, OK: Co-Operative Pub. Co.; 1933. [$50.00]

Rainey, Luretta Gilbert. **In Memory.** Enid, OK: Rainey; 1949. [$20.00]

Rainsford, Marcus. **An Historical Account of the Black Empire of Hayti.** London: Cundee; 1805. [plates browning, $250.00] [$600.00]

Rak, Mary Kidder. **A Cowman's Wife.** Boston: Houghton Mifflin; 1934. [$45.00]

Ralph, Julian. **Dixie; or, Southern Scenes and Sketches.** NY: Harper; 1896. [bumped, sunned, $20.00]

Ralph, Julian. **On Canada's Frontier.** NY: Harper; 1892. [$35.00]

Ralph, Julian. **Our Great West.** NY: Harper; 1893. [$50.00]

Ramon, Jose Domingo. **Captain Don Domingo Ramon's Diary of His Expedition into Texas in 1716.** Austin: St. Edward's; 1933. [$35.00]

Ramsay, David. **History of South-Carolina.** Charleston: Longworth; 1809. 2 v. [lacks map, covers hanging, spines split, $75.00]

Ramsay, David. **History of the American Revolution.** Philadelphia: Aitken; 1789. 2 v. [covers worn, rebacked, $300.00]

Ramsay, David. **Vie de Georges Washington.** Paris: Parsons, Galignani; 1809. [$75.00]

Ramsdell, Charles William. **Reconstruction in Texas.** NY: Columbia UP; 1910. [$100.00]

Ramsey, Carolyn. **Cajuns on the Bayous.** NY: Hastings; 1957. [$15.00] [$12.50]

Ramsey, James Gettys McGready. **Annals of Tennessee to the End of the Eighteenth Century.** Kingsport: Kingsport Press; 1926. [ink notes, water damage, $40.00]

Ramsey, Robert Wayne. **Carolina Cradle.** Chapel Hill: U. of North Carolina; 1964. [scattered ink marks, dj chipped and torn, $25.00]

Rand, Ayn. **Atlas Shrugged.** NY: 1st ed. Random; 1957. [dj chipped, $45.00]

Randall, Clarence Belden. **Over My Shoulder.** 1st ed. Boston: Little, Brown; 1956. [$12.50]

Randall, E. O. **Masterpieces of the Ohio Mound Builders.** Columbus: Ohio State Archaeological and Historical Society; 1916. [$35.00]

Randall, E. O. **The Serpent Mound.** 2nd ed. Columbus: Ohio State Archaelogical and Historical Society; 1907. [$30.00]

Randall, Henry Stephens. **Life of Thomas Jefferson.** Philadelphia: Lippincott; 1871. 3 v. [x-lib., $125.00]

Randall, John Herman. **The Landscape and the Looking Glass.** Boston: Houghton Mifflin; 1960. [$20.00]

Randall, Ruth. **I, Varina.** 1st ed. Boston: Little, Brown; 1962. [$14.50]

Randall, Thomas E. **History of the Chippewa Valley.** Eau Claire, WI: Free Press; 1875. [covers worn and spotted, some worming, $85.00]

Randell, Jack. **I'm Alone.** Indianapolis: Bobbs-Merrill; 1930. [spine faded, $25.00, Canadian]

Randolph, Edmund. **Hell among the Yearlings.** 1st ed. NY: Norton; 1955. [signed, $30.00]

Randolph, Edmund. **A Vindication of Mr. Randolph's Resignation.** Philadelphia: Smith; 1795. [$150.00]

Randolph, John. **Letters of John Randolph, to a Young Relative.** Philadelphia: Carey, Lea & Blanchard; 1834. [$49.00]

Randolph, Vance. **Gun-Fighters of the Old West.** Giraud, KS: Haldeman-Julius; 1943. [$25.00]

Randolph, Vance. **Kate Bender, the Kansas Murderess.** Girard, KS: Haldeman-Julius; 1944. [$30.00]

Randolph, Vance. **The Texas Rangers.** Girard, KS: Haldeman-Julius; 1944. [$45.00]

Rankin, Henry Bascom. **Intimate Character Sketches of Abraham Lincoln.** Philadelphia, London: Lippincott; 1924. [spine faded, $15.00]

Rankin, Melinda. **Twenty Years among the Mexicans.** 2nd ed. Cincinnati: Chase & Hall; 1875. [$100.00]

Ranney, David James. **Dave Ranney; or, Thirty Years on the Bowery.** NY: American Tract Soc.; 1910. [$20.00]

Ransom, Frank Leslie. **The Sunshine State; a History of South Dakota.** Mitchell, SD: Educator School Supply; 1917. [$35.00]

Ransom, John L. **John Ransom's Diary.** NY: Eriksson; 1963. [$20.00]

Raper, Charles Lee. **North Carolina: A Study in English Colonial Government.** NY, London: Macmillan; 1904. [spine frayed, $17.50]

Rascoe, Burton. **Belle Starr, "The Bandit Queen."** NY: Random; 1941. [worn dj, $25.00] [$30.00]

Rath, Ida Ellen. **The Rath Trail.** Wichita: McCormick-Armstrong; 1961. [$35.00]

Rather, Ethel Zivley. **Recognition of the Republic of Texas by the United States.** Austin: U. of Texas; 1911. [$125.00]

Ratigan, William. **Great Lakes Shipwrecks & Survivals.** Grand Rapids: Eerdmans; 1960. [$15.00]

Raumer, Friedrich Ludwig Georg von. **America and the American People.** NY: Langley; 1846. [$95.00] [rebacked, $35.00]

Rawley, James A. **Turning Points of the Civil War.** Lincoln: U. of Nebraska; 1966. [$20.00]

Rawlings, Marjorie Kinnan. **Cross Creek Cookery.** NY: Scribner; 1942. [dj chipped, $35.00]

Rawson, Marion. **New Hampshire Borns a Town.** 1st ed. NY: Dutton; 1942. [$10.00]

Ray, Clarence Everly. **The Border Outlaws, Frank and Jesse James.** Chicago: Regan; [192-?]. [$20.00]

Ray, Clarence Everly. **Harry Tracy.** Chicago: Regan; [1915?]. [$15.00]

Ray, Clarence Everly. **Life of Bob and Cole Younger with Quantrell.** Chicago: Regan; [1916?]. [$15.00]

Ray, Clarence Everly. **Rube Burrow.** Chicago: Regan; [19--?]. [$10.00]

Ray, Clarence Everly. **Tracy, the Bandit.** Chicago: Regan; [19--?]. [$20.00]

Ray, Patrick H. see, International Polar Expedition, 1882-1883.

Ray, Perley Orman. **Repeal of the Missouri Compromise.** Cleveland: Clark; 1909. [publisher's inscription, $50.00]

Ray, Worth Stickley. **Austin Colony Pioneers.** Austin: Pemberton; 1970, c1949. [$17.50]

Raymond, Dora. **Captain Lee Hall of Texas.** 1st ed. Norman: U. of Oklahoma; 1940. [$75.00]

Raymond, Henry Jarvis. **History of the Administration of President Lincoln.** NY: Derby & Miller; 1864. [$100.00]

Raymond, Henry Jarvis. **Life and Public Services of Abraham Lincoln.** NY: Derby and Miller; 1865. [$85.00]

Raymond, Walter. **Grand Tour through the Sunny South, Mexico and California.** Boston: [s.n.]; 1887. [$45.00]

Raynal, abbe. **Revolution de l'Amerique.** Londres: Davis; 1781. [backstrip missing, $150.00]

Raynal, abbe. **The Revolution of America.** London: Lockyer, Davis, Holborn; 1781. [$80.00]

Rayne, Martha Louise. **What Can a Woman Do.** Petersburgh, NY: Eagle; 1893. [$35.00]

Read, Thomas Buchanan. **Wagoner of the Alleghanies.** Philadelphia: Lippincott; 1862. [$30.00]

Read, William Alexander. **Florida Place Names of Indian Origin and Seminole Personal Names.** Baton Rouge: Louisiana State UP; 1934. [$30.00]

Read, William Alexander. **Louisiana-French.** Baton Rouge: Louisiana State UP; 1931. [$45.00]

Reagan, Albert B. **Don Diego; or, The Pueblo Indian Uprising of 1680.** NY: Harriman; 1914. [$45.00]

Reagan, John Henninger. **Memoirs.** NY, Washington: Neale; 1906. [$225.00] [$150.00]

Reavis, L. U. **A Change of National Empire.** St. Louis: Torrey; 1869. [x-lib., $55.00]

Red, William Stuart. **The Texas Colonists and Religion, 1821-1836.** Austin: Shettles; 1924. [$65.00]

Redpath, James. **Public Life of Capt. John Brown.** Boston: Thayer and Eldridge; 1860. [$25.00]

Reed, Hugh T. **Cadet Life at West Point.** Chicago: The Author; 1896. [$125.00]

Reed, Nelson. **The Caste War of Yucatan.** Stanford: Stanford UP; 1964. [$10.00]

Reed, Rebecca Theresa. **Six Months in a Convent.** Boston; NY: Russell, Odiorne & Metcalf; Hall; 1835. [$90.00] [$50.00] [$40.00]

Reed, Sampson. **Observations on the Growth of the Mind.** Boston: Cummings, Hilliard; 1826. [removed, $100.00]

Reed, Verner Zevola. **Lo-To-Kah.** NY, London: Continental; 1897. [$100.00]

Reeves, Marian Calhoun Legare. **Randolph Honor.** NY: Richardson; 1868. [$75.00]

Reichard, Gladys Amanda. **Social Life of the Navajo Indians.** NY: Columbia UP; 1928. [$65.00]

Reichard, Harry Hess. **Pennsylvania-German Dialect Writings and Their Writers.** Lancaster: New Era; 1918. [$32.00]

Reichel, Levin T. **Moravians in North Carolina.** Salem, NC: Keehln; 1857. [$200.00]

Reid, Arthur. **Reminiscences of the Revolution.** Utica: Roberts; 1859. [$50.00] [$75.00]

Reid, Edith Gittings. **The Great Physician.** NY, London: Oxford UP; 1931. [$25.00]

Reid, Hugo. **Indians of Los Angeles County.** Los Angeles: Priv. Print.; 1926. [$100.00]

Reid, John Coleman. **Reid's Tramp.** Selma, AL: Hardy; 1858. [fine, $12,500.00] [1935 Steck ed., $75.00]

Reid, Samuel Chester. **The Scouting Expeditions of McCulloch's Texas Rangers.** Philadelphia: Bradley; 1859. [foxed, $250.00] [1890 Keystone ed., spine loose, $65.00] [1859 Potter imprint, $65.00]

Reid, William. Maxwell. **Lake George and Lake Champlain.** NY: Putnam; 1910. [$75.00]

Reid, William. Maxwell. **Mohawk Valley.** NY: Putnam; 1901. [later printing?, $27.50]

Reid, William. Maxwell. **Story of Old Fort Johnson.** NY, London: Putnam; 1906. [$35.00]

Reifsnyder, Henry G. **A Second Class Private in the Great World War.** Philadelphia: [s.n.]; 1923. [presentation, $50.00]

Reigart, John Franklin. **Life of Robert Fulton.** Philadelphia: Henderson; 1856. [$150.00]

Reign of Terror in Kanzas. Boston: Briggs; 1856. [$1250.00]

Reimann, Lewis Charles. **Hurley--Still No Angel.** Ann Arbor: Northwoods; 1954. [signed, $20.00]

Reimann, Lewis Charles. **When Pine Was King.** Ann Arbor, MI: Northwoods; 1952. [$17.50]

Reisner, Robert George. **Bird.** NY: Citadel; 1962. [$20.00]

Remington, Frederic. **Crooked Trails.** NY, London: Harper; 1898. [in slipcase and dj, $350.00] [slight wear and foxing, $165.00] [$125.00]

Remington, Frederic. **Done in the Open.** NY: Collier; 1903. [$225.00]

Remington, Frederic. **Drawings.** limited signed ed. NY; London: Russell; Lawrence & Bullen; 1897. [text signed by Owen Wister, $1500.00]

Remington, Frederic. **Men with the Bark On.** 1st ed. NY, London: Harper; 1900. [2nd issue, $100.00]

Remington, Frederic. **Pony Tracks.** NY: Harper; 1895. [$40.00] [$275.00] [1961 Oklahoma ed., $45.00]

Remington, Frederic. **Remington's Frontier Sketches.** Chicago, NY: Werner; 1898. [$500.00] [$300.00]

Remington, Frederic. **Way of an Indian.** NY: Fox, Duffield; 1906. [$300.00]

Remlap, L. T. **Life of General U.S. Grant.** Chicago: Fairbanks & Palmer; 1887. [$17.50]

Remy, Jules. **Journey to Great-Salt-Lake City.** London: Jeffs; 1861. 2 v. [$550.00] [$400.00]

Renick, L. W. **Che-Le-Co-The, Glimpses of Yesterday.** Chillicothe, OH: Knickerbocker; 1896. [$65.00]

Rennolds, Edwin Hansford. **History of the Henry County Commands Which Served in the Confederate States Army.** Jacksonville, FL: Sun; 1904. [$120.00] [1961 Continental ed., $35.00]

Reno, Marcus A. **Abstract of the Official Record of Proceedings of the Reno Court of Inquiry.** Harrisburg, PA: Stackpole; 1954. [$60.00] [dj taped, $45.00]

Replogle, Charles. **Among the Indians of Alaska.** London: Headley; 1904. [$85.00]

Repton, Humphry. **Art of Landscape Gardening.** Boston, NY: Houghton Mifflin; 1907. [$150.00]

Reutter, Winifred. **Early Dakota Days.** [White River?, SD: s.n.]; 1962. [$25.00]

Revere, Joseph Warren. **Keel and Saddle.** Boston: Osgood; 1872. [$90.00]

Revere, Joseph Warren. **Tour of Duty in California.** NY, Boston: Francis; 1849. [rebound, $175.00] [$300.00] [faded and worn, corners bumped, $200.00]

Revoil, Benedict Henry. **Chasses dans l'Amerique du Nord.** nouvelle ed. Tours: Mame; 1884. [$65.00]

Reynolds, Florence. **The Rawhide Tree.** 1st ed. Clarendon, TX: Clarendon Press; 1957. [dj defective, $25.00]

Reynolds, John. **Pioneer History of Illinois.** Belleville: Randall; 1852. [rebound, scattered foxing, $375.00]

Reynolds, John Earle. **In French Creek Valley.** Meadville, PA: Crawford County Hist. Soc.; 1938. [$35.00]

Reynolds, John Hugh. **History of the University of Arkansas.** Fayetteville: U. of Arkansas; 1910. [$40.00]

Reynolds, John N. **The Twin Hells.** Chicago: Thompson & Thomas; 1890. [$25.00]

Reynolds, R. E. **Illustrated Southern Kansas.** 1st ed. Kingman: Daily and Weekly News; 1887. [x-lib., $200.00]

Rhees, William Jones. **Manual of Public Libraries.** Philadelphia: Lippincott; 1859. [spine badly chipped, $75.00]

Rhodes, Eugene Manlove. **A Bar Cross Man.** 1st ed. Norman: U. of Oklahoma; 1956. [$45.00]

Rhodes, Eugene Manlove. **Best Novels and Stories of.** Boston: Houghton Mifflin; 1949. [$25.00]

Rhodes, Eugene Manlove. **Beyond the Desert.** Boston: Houghton Mifflin; 1934. [$35.00]

Rhodes, Eugene Manlove. **Bransford in Arcadia.** NY: Holt; 1914. [$30.00]

Rhodes, Eugene Manlove. **Once in the Saddle and Paso por Aqui.** Boston, NY: Houghton Mifflin; 1927. [$25.00]

Rhodes, Eugene Manlove. **The Rhodes Reader.** 1st ed. Norman: U. of Oklahoma; 1957. [$25.00]

Rhodes, James A. **Trial of Mary Todd Lincoln.** 1st ed. Indianapolis: Bobbs-Merrill; 1959. [presentation, in dj, $27.50]

Rhodes, James Ford. **History of the United States: From the Compromise of 1850 to the Final Restoration of Home Rule at the South in 1877.** NY, London: Macmillan; 1913-1919. 8 v. [spines sun faded, $500.00]

Rhodes, May Davison. **The Hired Man on Horseback.** Boston: Houghton Mifflin; 1938. [x-lib., $25.00]

Rice, Craig. **Los Angeles Murders.** NY: Duell, Sloan, and Pearce; 1947. [$15.00]

Rice, Harvey. **Letters from the Pacific Slope.** NY: Appleton; 1870. [covers soiled and worn, $60.00]

Rice, Wallace de Groot Cecil. **The Chicago Stock Exchange.** Committee on Library of the Chicago Stock Exchange; 1923. [$25.00]

Rice, William Henry. **David Zeisberger and His Brown Brethren.** 2nd ed. Bethlehem, PA: Moravian; 1902. [$26.00]

Rich, Ben E. **Mr. Durant of Salt Lake City.** Salt Lake City: Cannon; 1893. [$45.00]

Rich, E. E. **The Fur Trade and the Northwest to 1857.** Toronto: McClelland and Stewart; 1967. [$25.00, Canadian]

Rich, Louise Dickinson. **We Took to the Woods.** Philadelphia, NY: Lippincott; 1942. [$7.00] [$12.50]

Richards, Henry Melchior Muhlenberg. **The Pennsylvania-German in the Revolutionary War.** Lancaster: Pennsylvania German Society; 1908. [$36.00]

Richards, John Thomas. **Abraham Lincoln, the Lawyer-Statesman.** Boston, NY: Houghton Mifflin; 1916. [$25.00]

Richards, Laura Elizabeth Howe. **Julia Ward Howe, 1819-1910.** Boston, NY: Houghton Mifflin; 1915. 2 v. ["large paper edition," $125.00] [$35.00]

Richards, Lysander Salmon. **History of Marshfield.** Plymouth, MA: Memorial; 1901-1905. 2 v. [$100.00]

Richards, Thomas Cole. **Samuel J. Mills.** Boston, NY: Pilgrim; 1906. [$17.50]

Richardson, Albert Deane. **Beyond the Mississippi.** Hartford; NY: American Pub. Co.; Bliss; 1867. [$100.00] [rebound, $20.00]

Richardson, Albert Deane. **Personal History of Ulysses S. Grant.** Hartford: Winter & Hatch; 1885. [$14.50]

Richardson, Albert Deane. **The Secret Service, the Field, the Dungeon, and the Escape.** Hartford; Philadelphia: American Pub. Co.; Jones; 1865. [x-lib.,$35.00]

Richardson, E. **History of Woonsocket.** Woonsocket: Foss; 1876. [inscribed, $45.00]

Richardson, Ethel. **American Mountain Songs.** NY: Greenberg; 1927. [$25.00]

Richardson, Eudora Ramsay. **Little Aleck.** 1st ed. Indianapolis: Bobbs-Merrill; 1932. [$45.00]

Richardson, James. **Wonders of the Yellowstone.** NY: Scribner, Armstrong; 1873. [$55.00] [$45.00]

Richardson, John. **Hardscrabble.** NY: Pollard and Moss; 1888. [$40.00]

Richardson, John Anderson. **Richardson's Defense of the South.** Atlanta: Caldwell; 1914. [x-lib., $15.00]

Richardson, Leon Burr. **An Indian Preacher in England.** Hanover, NH: Dartmouth College; 1933. [$30.00]

Richardson, Richard. **Memoir of Josiah White.** Philadelphia: Lippincott; 1873. [$60.00]

Richardson, Rupert Norval. **Frontier of Northwest Texas, 1846 to 1876.** Glendale, CA: Clark; 1963. [$85.00]

Richardson, Rupert Norval. **The Greater Southwest.** Glendale, CA: Clark; 1934. [$85.00]

Richardson, Rupert Norval. **Texas, the Lone Star State.** NY: Prentice-Hall; 1943. [$75.00]

Richardson, W. R. **Brief Sketch of the History of the Protestant Episcopal Church in the Missionary District of Western Texas.** San Antonio: Sigmund; 1902. [$125.00]

Richardson, William H. **Journal of.** 3rd ed. NY: Richardson; 1849. [last page in facsimilie, $550.00]

Richley, John William. **Obstacles No Barrier.** [York?, PA: s.n.]; 1951. [presentation, $40.00]

Richman, Irving Berdine. **California under Spain and Mexico, 1535-1847.** Boston, NY: Houghton Mifflin; 1911. [$40.00]

Richman, Irving Berdine. **Ioway to Iowa.** Iowa City: State Hist. Soc.; 1931. [$17.50]

Richmond, A. B. **What I Saw at Cassadaga Lake.** 2nd ed. Boston· Colby & Rich; 1888. [$25.00]

Richmond, C. W. **History of the County of Du Page, Illinois.** Chicago: Scripps, Bross & Spears; 1857. [foxed, $50.00]

Richmond, James Cook. **Mid-Summer's Day-Dream.** Boston; NY: Jordan & Wiley; Burgess, Stringer; 1847. [$75.00]

Richter, Conrad. **Sea of Grass.** 1st ed. NY: Knopf; 1937. [$35.00]

Rickaby, Franz Lee. **Ballads and Songs of the Shanty-Boy.** Cambridge: Harvard UP; 1926. [$30.00]

Rickard, Maxine Elliott. **Everything Happened to Him.** NY: Stokes; 1936. [$15.00]

Rickard, T. A. **Journeys of Observation.** San Francisco: Dewey;. 1907. [presentation, $100.00]

Rickards, Colin. **Buckskin Frank Leslie.** El Paso: Texas Western; 1964. [$60.00]

Rickey, Don. **Forty Miles a Day on Beans and Hay.** 1st ed. Norman: U. of Oklahoma; 1963. [$35.00]

Rickman, John. **Authentic Narrative of a Voyage Performed by Captain Cook and Captain Clerke . . . During the Years 1776, 1777, 1778, 1779, and 1780.** London: Robinson, Sewell and Debrett; 1783. 2 v. [$1850.00]

Rickman, Thomas Clio. **Life of Thomas Paine.** London: Rickman; 1819. [$50.00]

Riddell, William Renwick. **The Slave in Canada.** Washington: Association for the Study of Negro Life and History; 1920. [$40.00]

Riddle, A. G. **Ansel's Cave.** Cleveland: Burrows; 1893. [publisher's presentation, $47.50] [$30.00]

Riddle, A. G. **Bart Ridgeley.** Boston: Nichols and Hall; 1873. [front flyleaf missing, shaken, $35.00]

Riddle, A. G. **The Tory's Daughter.** NY, London: Putnam; 1888. [inscribed, $45.00]

Riddle, Donald Wayne. **Congressman Abraham Lincoln.** Urbana: U. of Illinois; 1957. [$25.00]

Riddle, William. **Nicholas Comenius.** Lancaster, PA: Wickersham; 1897. [$12.00]

Riddle, William. **One Hundred and Fifty Years of School History in Lancaster, Pennsylvania.** Lancaster: The Author; 1905. [$35.00]

Rideal, Charles Frederick. **History of the E. I. Du Pont de Nemours Powder Company.** NY: Business America; 1912. [$35.00]

Rideout, Jacob Barzilla. **Camping Out in California.** San Francisco: Patterson; 1889. [stained, hinges weak, $35.00]

Ridge, John Rollin. **Crimes and Career of Tiburcio Vasquez.** Hollister, CA: Evening Free Lance; 1927. [$35.00]

Ridge, John Rollin. **Life and Adventures of Joaquin Murieta.** Norman: U. of Oklahoma; 1955. [$12.50] [$20.00]

Ridgely, David. **Annals of Annapolis.** Baltimore: Cushing; 1841. [$125.00]

Ridgely, Mabel Lloyd. **What Them Befell.** Portland, ME: Anthoensen; 1949. [$60.00]

Ridings, Sam P. **The Chisholm Trail.** Guthrie, OK: Co-operative; 1936. [fine, $175.00]

Riedesel, Friederike Charlotte Luise. **Letters and Memoirs Relating to the War of American Independence.** NY: Carvill; 1827. [disbound, $44.00]

Riegel, Oscar Wetherhold. **Crown of Glory.** New Haven: Yale UP; 1935. [cover dampstained, $25.00]

Riegel, Robert Edgar. **Story of the Western Railroads.** NY: Macmillan; 1926. [$35.00]

Riel, Louis. **Poesies Religieuses et Politiques.** Montreal: L'Etendard; 1886. [$20.00]

Riesenberg, Felix. **Cape Horn.** NY: Dodd, Mead; 1939. [$40.00] [presentation, $45.00]

Riggs, Stephen Return. **Mary and I.** Chicago: Holmes; 1880. [$75.00] [$40.00]

Rights, Douglas Le Tell. **The American Indian in North Carolina.** Durham: Duke UP; 1947. [mildewed and rubbed, $45.00]

Riis, Jacob A. **Making of an American.** NY: Macmillan; 1924. [$15.00]

Riley, Henry Hiram. **The Puddleford Papers.** NY; Cincinnati: Derby & Jackson; Derby; 1857. [$45.00]

Riley, James Whitcomb. **Armazindy.** Indianapolis: Bobbs-Merrill; 1894. [$10.00]

Riley, James Whitcomb. **Out to Old Aunt Mary's.** Indianapolis: Bobbs-Merrill; 1904. [$15.00]

Riley, James Whitcomb. **The Raggedy Man.** Indianapolis: Bobbs-Merrill; 1907. [chipped dj, $75.00]

Riley, James Whitcomb. **When She Was about Sixteen.** Indianapolis: Bobbs-Merrill; 1911. [$40.00]

Rimmer, William. **Elements of Design. Book First.** Boston: Wilson; 1864. [$175.00]

Rindge, Frederick Hastings. **Happy Days in Southern California.** Cambridge, Los Angeles: Riverside; 1898. [$125.00]

Ringwalt, J. Luther. **Development of Transportation Systems in the United States.** Philadelphia: The Author, Railway World Office; 1888. [$125.00]

Rios, Eduardo Enrique. **Life of Fray Antonio Margil, O. F. M.** Washington: Academy of American Franciscan History; 1959. [$30.00]

Ripley, Eliza Moore. **Social Life in Old New Orleans.** NY, London: Appleton; 1912. [$15.00]

Ripley, Roswell Sabine. **War with Mexico.** NY: Harper; 1849. 2 v. [rebound, $185.00]

Ripley, Thomas. **They Died with Their Boots On.** 1st ed. Garden City: Doubleday, Doran; 1935. [binding worn, $45.00]

Rippy, James Fred. **United States and Mexico.** NY: Knopf; 1926. [$60.00]

Rister, Carl Coke. **Border Command.** 1st ed. Norman: U. of Oklahoma; 1944. [$45.00] [slightly worn dj, $25.00]

Rister, Carl Coke. **Fort Griffin on the Texas Frontier.** 1st ed. Norman: U. of Oklahoma; 1956. [x-lib., $14.00]

Rister, Carl Coke. **Oil! Titan of the Southwest.** 1st ed. Norman: U. of Oklahoma; 1949. [$60.00]

Rister, Carl Coke. **The Southwestern Frontier.** Cleveland: Clark; 1928. [$175.00]

Ritch, William Gillet. **Illustrated New Mexico.** 3rd ed. Santa Fe: New Mexican Print. & Pub. Co; 1883. [$285.00]

Ritchie, James S. **Wisconsin and Its Resources.** 3rd ed. Philadelphia: Desilver; 1860. [$125.00] [x-lib., $95.00]

Ritter, Abraham. **History of the Moravian Church in Philadelphia.** Philadelphia: Hayes & Zell; 1857. [spine repaired, $38.00]

Ritter, Mary Bennett. **More Than Gold in California, 1849-1933.** Berkeley: [s.n.]; 1933. [inscribed, $115.00]

Roa Barcena, Jose Maria. **Recuerdos de la Invasion Norte-Americana, 1846-1848.** Mexico: Buxo; 1883. [hinges cracked, internal repairs, $275.00]

Roark, Garland. **Star in the Rigging.** 1st ed. Garden City: Doubleday; 1954. [inscribed, $55.00]

Robbins, Charles Henry. **The Gam.** New Bedford: Hutchinson; 1899. [$24.00]

Roberts, B. H. **The Missouri Persecutions.** Salt Lake City: Cannon; 1900. [$30.00]

Roberts, Bruce. **Springs from the Parched Ground.** Uvalde, TX: Hornby; 1950. [$35.00]

Roberts, Daniel Webster. **Rangers and Sovereignty.** San Antonio, TX: Wood; 1914. [$100.00]

Roberts, Edwards. **Shoshone and Other Western Wonders.** NY: Harper; 1888. [$65.00] [$35.00]

Roberts, Ellwood. **Biographical Annals of Montgomery County, Pennsylvania.** NY: Benham; 1904. 2 v. [spined taped, $120.00]

Roberts, Howard. **Story of Pro Football.** Chicago: Rand McNally; 1953. [$12.50]

Roberts, Job. **The Pennsylvania Farmer.** Philadelphia: Johnson; 1804. [$450.00]

Roberts, Kenneth Lewis. **The Battle of Cowpens.** 1st trade ed. Garden City: Doubleday; 1958, c1957. [$30.00] [$32.50]

Roberts, Kenneth Lewis. **March to Quebec.** Garden City: Doubleday; 1953, c1940. [$17.50]

Roberts, Kenneth Lewis. **Northwest Passage.** 1st trade ed. Garden City: Doubleday, Doran; 1937. [$45.00]

Roberts, Kenneth Lewis. **Trending into Maine.** Boston: Little, Brown; 1938. [$65.00] ["Arundel Edition" inscribed, $500.00]

Roberts, Leonard W. **South from Hell-fer-Sartin.** Lexington: U. of Kentucky; 1955. [$30.00] [$20.00]

Roberts, Oran Milo. **Description of Texas.** St. Louis: Gilbert; 1881. [$650.00]

Roberts, Robert Ellis. **Sketches of the City of Detroit.** Detroit: [s.n.]; 1855. [$125.00]

Roberts, Thomas S. **Birds of Minnesota.** Minneapolis; London: U. of Minnesota; Oxford UP; 1932. 2 v. [$150.00]

Roberts, Walter Adolphe. **Lake Pontchartrain.** Indianapolis: Bobbs-Merrill; 1946. [$12.00]

Roberts, Walter Adolphe. **Semmes of the Alabama.** 1st ed. Indianapolis, NY: Bobbs-Merrill; 1938. [$40.00]

Robertson, Archibald Thomas. **Slow Train to Yesterday.** Boston: Houghton Mifflin; 1945. [$40.00]

Robertson, Charles Franklin. **Attempts Made to Separate the West from the American Union.** St. Louis: Missouri Hist. Soc.; 1885. [$75.00]

Robertson, David. **Reports of the Trials.** see, Burr, Aaron.

Robertson, Elizabeth Wells. **American Quilts.** NY: Studio; 1948. [inscribed, $25.00]

Robertson, Frank C. **Soapy Smith.** NY: Hastings; 1961. [dj chipped, $35.00]

Robertson, James Alexander. **Louisiana under the Rule of Spain, France, and the United States.** Cleveland: Clark; 1911. 2 v. [$175.00]

Robertson, William. **History of America.** 7th ed. London: Strahan and Cadell; 1796. 3 v. [spines chipped, $75.00] [9th ed., 1880 in 4 vols., $250.00]

Robeson, Eslanda Goode. **Paul Robeson, Negro.** NY, London: Harper; 1930. [covers worn, spine sunned, $22.50]

Robinson, Alfred. **Life in California.** Oakland: Biobooks; 1947. [$35.00]

Robinson, Conway. **Account of Discoveries in the West until 1519.** Richmond: Shepherd and Colin; 1848. [spine split, $150.00]

Robinson, Doane. **History of South Dakota.** [Logansport?, IN]: Bowen; 1904. 2 v. [binding repaired, $225.00]

Robinson, Edwin Arlington. **Children of the Night.** 1st ed. Boston: Badger; 1897. [$375.00]

Robinson, Fayette. **Account of the Organization of the Army of the United States.** Philadelphia: Butler; 1848. 2 v. [rebound, $40.00]

Robinson, Fayette. **Mexico and Her Military Chieftains.** Philadelphia: Butler; 1847. [$125.00]

Robinson, Frank Torrey. **Living New England Artists.** Boston: Cassino; 1888. [some silverfishing, $45.00]

Robinson, George F. **History of Greene County, Ohio.** Chicago: Clarke; 1902. [$125.00]

Robinson, Leigh. **The South before and at the Battle of the Wilderness.** Richmond: Goode; 1878. [$150.00]

Robinson, Luther Emerson. **Abraham Lincoln as a Man of Letters.** NY, London: Putnam; 1923. [front hinge weak, $15.00]

Robinson, Morgan Poitiaux. **Concerning the Boyson Essay and Its Defence.** Richmond: [s.n.]; 1909. [$22.50]

Robinson, Philip Stewart. **Sinner and Saints.** Boston: Roberts; 1883. [$30.00]

Robinson, Rowland Evans. **Vermont: A Study of Independence.** Boston, NY: Houghton Mifflin; 1897. [$20.00]

Robinson, Sara Tappan Doolittle. **Kansas; Its Interior and Exterior Life.** [6th ed.?] Boston: Crosby, Nichols; 1856. [$65.00]

Robinson, W. W. **Land in California.** Berkeley: U. of California; 1948. [$12.50]

Robinson, William Davis. **Memoirs of the Mexican Revolution.** London: Lackington, Huges, Harding, Mavor & Lepard; 1821. [rebacked, portrait missing, $350.00]

Robinson, William Henry. **Under Turquoise Skies.** NY: Macmillan; 1928. [$45.00]

Robinson, William Morrison. **The Confederate Privateers.** New Haven; London: Yale UP; Oxford UP; 1928. [$75.00]

Robinson, William Stevens. **"Warrington" Pen-Portraits.** Boston: Robinson; 1877. [$45.00]

Robison, Daniel Merritt. **Bob Taylor and the Agrarian Revolt in Tennessee.** Chapel Hill: U. of North Carolina; 1935. [presentation, $25.00]

Robley, Thomas F. **History of Bourbon County, Kansas.** Fort Scott, KS: Monitor; 1894. [$55.00]

Robotti, Frances Diane. **Whaling and Old Salem.** 1st ed. Salem: Newcomb & Gauss; 1950. [$100.00]

Roca, Paul M. **Paths of the Padres through Sonora.** Tucson: Arizona Pioneers Historical Society; 1967. [$85.00]

Rockefeller, John D. **The Colorado Industrial Plan.** NY: The Author; 1916. [$40.00]

Rockfellow, John Alexander. **Log of an Arizona Trail Blazer.** Tucson: Acme; 1933. [$65.00]

Rockwell, Paul Ayres. **American Fighters in the Foreign Legion, 1914-1918.** Boston, NY: Houghton Mifflin; 1930. [binding soiled, $25.00]

Rockwell, Wilson. **No Way Back.** Denver: Bradford-Robinson; 1950. [$25.00]

Rockwell, Wilson. **Sunset Slope.** Denver: Big Mountain; 1956. [presentation, $25.00]

Rockwood, Caroline Washburn. **In Biscayne Bay.** NY: Dodd, Mead; 1891. [$35.00]

Roddis, Louis H. **Indian Wars of Minnesota.** Cedar Rapids, IA: Torch; 1956. [$50.00]

Rodney, George Brydges. **As a Cavalryman Remembers.** Caldwell, ID: Caxton; 1944. [$50.00]

Roe, Frances Marie Antoinette. **Army Letters from an Officer's Wife.** NY: Appleton; 1909. [$75.00]

Roeder, Ralph. **Juarez and His Mexico.** NY: Viking; 1947. 2 v. [$60.00]

Roemer, Ferdinand. **Texas.** San Antonio: Standard; 1935. [$185.00]

Rogers, Cameron. **The Magnificent Idler.** Toronto; Garden City: Gundy; Doubleday, Page; 1926. [$10.00]

Rogers, Donald I. **Since You Went Away.** New Rochelle, NY: Arlington; 1973. [$12.50]

Rogers, Ernest Elias. **Connecticut's Naval Office at New London during the War of the American Revolution.** New London, CT: [s. n.]; 1933. [$50.00]

Rogers, John Godfrey. **Sport in Vancouver and Newfoundland.** London: Chapman and Hall; 1912. [$35.00]

Rogers, Mary Cochrane. **Rogers' Rock, Lake George, March 13, 1758.** Derry, NH: The Author; 1917. [$65.00]

Rogers, Samuel. **Autobiography of.** 3rd ed. Cincinnati: Standard; 1881, c1880. [$15.00]

Rogers, Will. **Autobiography of.** Boston: Houghton Mifflin; 1949. [$8.00]

Rogers, Will. **Will Rogers Wit and Wisdom.** pictorial ed. NY: Stokes; 1936. [x-lib., $12.50]

Rohan, Jack. **Yankee Arms Maker.** rev. ed. NY: Harper; 1948. [$17.50] [$35.00]

Roland, Charles Pierce. **The Confederacy.** Chicago: U. of Chicago; 1960. [$20.00]

Rolfe, Abial. **Reminiscences of Concord.** Penacook, NH: [s.n.]; 1901. [$35.00]

Rollins, Philip Ashton. **The Cowboy.** NY: Scribner; 1922. [pencil notes in text, $50.00] [frontis loose, $20.00] [$75.00]

Rollinson, John K. **Hoofprints of a Cowboy and U. S. Ranger.** Caldwell, ID: Caxton; 1941. [$40.00]

Rollinson, John K. **Wyoming Cattle Trails.** Caldwell, ID: Caxton; 1948. [$60.00]

Rolvaag, O. E. **Giants in the Earth.** lst ed. NY: Harper; 1927. [dj worn, $25.00]

Romanet, Joseph. **Voyage 'a la Martinique.** Paris: Pelletier; 1804. [$525.00]

Romer, Frank. **Makers of History.** Hartford, CT: Colt's Patent Fire Arms Manufacturing Co.; 1926. [$30.00]

Rood, Hosea W. **Story of the Service of Company E: And the Twelfth Wisconsin Regiment.** Milwaukee: Swain & Tate; 1893. [spine worn, hinges cracked, $125.00]

Roosevelt, Eleanor. **It's Up to the Women.** NY: Stokes; 1933. [$50.00]

Roosevelt, Franklin D. **The Happy Warrior.** Boston, NY: Houghton Mifflin; 1928. [$17.50]

Roosevelt, Franklin D. **Wit and Wisdom of.** Boston: Beacon; 1950. [$12.50]

Roosevelt, Robert Barnwell. **Game Birds of the Coasts and Lakes of the Northern States of America.** NY: Carleton; 1866. [$45.00]

Roosevelt, Theodore. **African Game Trails.** NY: Scribner; 1920, c1910. 2 v. [x-lib., $12.50]

Roosevelt, Theodore. **Autobiography.** 1st ed. NY: Macmillan; 1913. [$50.00]

Roosevelt, Theodore. **Book-Lover's Holidays in the Open.** NY: Scribner; 1916. [$45.00]

Roosevelt, Theodore. **Hunting Trips of a Ranchman.** NY, London: Putnam; 1886. [$200.00]

Roosevelt, Theodore. **Realizable Ideals.** San Francisco: Whittaker & Ray-Wiggin; 1912. [spine faded, $30.00]

Roosevelt, Theodore. **Roosevelt in the Kansas City Star.** Boston, NY: Houghton Mifflin; 1921. [large paper limited ed., $25.00]

Roosevelt, Theodore. **The Rough Riders.** NY: Scribner; 1920. [x-lib., $10.00]

Roosevelt, Theodore. **Theodore Roosevelt's Letters to His Children;.** NY: Scribner; 1919. [$20.00]

Roosevelt, Theodore. **Theodore Roosevelt, an Autobiography.** NY: Scribner; 1923, c1913. [$19.00]

Roosevelt, Theodore. **Thomas Hart Benton.** 1st ed. Boston, NY: Houghton Mifflin; 1886. [$55.00]

Roosevelt, Theodore. **Through the Brazilian Wilderness.** NY: Scribner; 1926. [cover soiled, edges dampstained, $20.00]

Roosevelt, Theodore. **Winning of the West.** NY: Putnam; 1889-1896. 6 v. in 3. [$40.00]

Root, Edward Wales. **Philip Hooker.** NY: Scribner; 1929. [$175.00]

Root, Henry. **Personal History and Reminiscences.** San Francisco: 1921. [$30.00]

Rooth, Signe Alice. **Seeress of the Northland.** 1st ed. Philadelphia: American Swedish Historical Foundation; 1955. [$15.00]

Rosa, Joseph G. **The Gunfighter.** 1st ed. Norman: U. of Oklahoma; 1969. [$20.00]

Rosa, Joseph G. **They Called Him Wild Bill.** 1st ed. Norman: U. of Oklahoma; 1964. [$30.00]

Rosch, John. **Historic White Plains.** White Plains, NY: Balletto-Sweetman; 1939. [$20.00]

Roscoe, Theodore. **The Web of Conspiracy.** Englewood Cliffs, NJ: Prentice-Hall; 1959. [$35.00] [1960 issue, $25.00]

Rose, Barbara. **American Art since 1900.** NY: Praeger; 1967. [$20.00]

Rose, George B. **Art Work of the State of Arkansas.** Racine, WI: Harney; 1905. [nine parts bound separately, $450.00]

Rose, Theodore F. **Historical and Biographical Atlas of the New Jersey Coast.** Philadelphia: Woolman & Rose; 1878. [$900.00]

Rose, Victor M. **Ross' Texas Brigade.** Kennesaw, GA: Continental; 1960. [$40.00]

Rose, Victor M. **Texas Vendetta.** Houston: Frontier; 1956. [$35.00]

Roseboom, Eugene Holloway. **History of Ohio.** NY: Prentice Hall; 1934. [$40.00]

Rosebush, Waldo Emerson. **American Firearms and the Changing Frontier.** Spokane: Eastern Washington State Historical Society; 1962. [$10.00]

Roske, Ralph Joseph. **Lincoln's Commando.** 1st ed. NY: Harper; 1957. [$15.00] [$20.00]

Ross, Alexander. **Fur Hunters of the Far West.** Norman: U. of Oklahoma; 1956. [fine in dj, $45.00] [1961 issue, $20.00]

Ross, Fitzgerald. **Cities and Camps of the Confederate States.** Urbana: U. of Illinois; 1958. [$25.00]

Ross, Frederick Augustus. **Slavery Ordained of God.** Philadelphia: Lippincott; 1857. [$85.00]

Ross, Ishbel. **Proud Kate.** 1st ed. NY: Harper; 1953. [$22.50]

Ross, Ishbel. **Rebel Rose.** 1st ed. NY: Harper; 1954. [$17.50]

Ross, Joel H. **What I Saw in New York.** 2nd ed. Auburn, NY: Derby & Miller; 1852, c1851. [$42.00]

Ross, William Potter. **Life and Times of.** Fort Smith, AR: Weldon & Williams; 1893. [$200.00]

Roth, Philip. **The Great American Novel.** 1st ed. NY: Holt, Rinehart and Winston; 1973. [$20.00]

Rothermel, Abraham Heckman. **The Dumb Dutch, by One of Them.** Myerstown, PA: Church Center; 1948. [$24.00]

Rothrock, Mary Utopia. **French Broad-Holston Country.** see, East Tennessee Historical Society.

Rounds, Glen. **Rodeo: Bulls, Broncs & Buckaroos.** NY: Holiday; 1949. [$20.00]

Rourke, Constance. **Audubon.** NY: Harcourt, Brace; 1936. [$8.00]

Rowland, Dunbar. **History of Mississippi.** Chicago, Jackson: Clarke; 1925. 2 v. [$125.00]

Rowland, Dunbar. **Symposium on the Place of Discovery of the Mississippi River by Hernando de Soto.** Jackson, MS: Mississippi Historical Society; 1927. [$35.00]

Rowland, Eron Opha Moore. **Andrew Jackson's Campaign against the British.** NY: Macmillan; 1926. [$55.00] [$25.00]

Rowlands, John J. **Cache Lake Country.** NY: Norton; 1959. [$9.00]

Rowlandson, Mary. **Narrative of the Captivity and Restoration of.** Lancaster ed. Boston: Houghton Mifflin; 1930. [$25.00]

Rowlandson, Thomas. **The Sheep Breeder's Guide.** San Francisco: Warren; 1861. [waterstained, $68.50]

Roxborough, Henry Hall. **Canada at the Olympics.** Toronto: Ryerson; 1963. [$15.00, Canadian]

Royce, Josiah. **The Feud of Oakfield Creek.** 1st ed. Boston, NY: Houghton Mifflin; 1887. [$50.00]

Royce, Sarah Bayliss. **A Frontier Lady.** New Haven; London: Yale UP; Oxford UP; 1932. [$45.00]

Roys, Ralph Loveland. **Indian Background of Colonial Yucatan.** Washington: Carnegie Institute; 1943. [$35.00]

Ruby, James S. **Blue and Gray.** see, Georgetown University, Washington, D. C. Alumni Association.

Ruby, Robert H. **Half-Sun on the Columbia.** 1st ed. Norman: U. of Oklahoma; 1965. [$33.00]

Ruffner, William Henry. **Report on Washington Territory.** NY, Seattle: Lake Shore and Eastern Railway; 1889. [$125.00] [$100.00]

Ruggles, Eleanor. **The West-Going Heart.** 1st ed. NY: Norton; 1959. [signed, $20.00]

Ruiz, Hipolito. **Florae Peruviane et Chilensis Prodromus.** Madrid: De Sancha; 1794. [wormed, $250.00]

Rulofson, William Herman. **Dance of Death.** 3rd ed. San Francisco: Keller; 1877. [$50.00]

Rumple, Jethro. **History of Rowan County, North Carolina.** Salisbury, NC: Bruner; 1881. [silverfished, covers and spine frayed, preface defective, $135.00]

Rupp, Israel Daniel. **History of Northampton, Lehigh, Monroe, Carbon, and Schuylkill Counties.** Lancaster, PA: Hills; 1845. [rebacked, $125.00]

Rupp, Israel Daniel. **He Pasa Ekklesia.** Philadelphia: Humphreys; 1844. [$75.00]

Rush, Benjamin. **Account of the Manners of the German Inhabitants of Pennsylvania.** Lancaster: Pennsylvania German Society; 1910. [$22.00]

Rush, Benjamin. **Enquiry into the Effects of Public Punishments upon Criminals, and upon Society.** Philadelphia: James; 1787. [disbound, $1700.00]

Rush, Benjamin. **Letter on the Rebellion.** Philadelphia: Campbell; 1862. [$45.00]

Rush, Richard. **Memoranda of a Residence at the Court of London.** Philadelphia: Carey, Lea & Blanchard; 1833. [$250.00]

Rush, Richard. **Occasional Productions.** Philadelphia: Lippincott; 1860. [$40.00]

Rusk, Ralph Leslie. **Life of Ralph Waldo Emerson.** NY: Scribner; 1949. [$15.00]

Rusling, James Fowler. **Across America.** NY: Sheldon; 1874. [x-lib., $60.00]

Russel, Robert Royal. **Improvement of Communication with the Pacific Coast as an Issue in American Politics, 1783-1864.** Cedar Rapids, IA: Torch; 1948. [$37.50]

Russell, Carl Parcher. **Firearms, Traps, & Tools of the Mountain Men.** 1st ed. NY: Knopf; 1967. [$45.00]

Russell, Carl Parcher. **Guns on the Early Frontiers.** Berkeley: U. of California; 1957. [$40.00]

Russell, Charles Edward. **A-Rafting on the Mississip'.** NY: Century; 1928. [$20.00]

Russell, Charles Edward. **Bare Hands and Stone Walls.** NY: Scribner; 1933. [$12.50]

Russell, Charles Edward. **The Greatest Trust in the World.** NY: Ridgway-Thayer; 1905. [worn, $30.00]

Russell, Charles Edward. **Haym Salomon and the Revolution.** 1st ed. NY: Cosmopolitan; 1930. [$35.00]

Russell, Charles M. **Back-Trailing on the Old Frontiers.** Great Falls, MT: Cheely-Raban; 1922. [$500.00]

Russell, Charles M. **Good Medicine.** Garden City: Doubleday, Doran; 1930. [with dj, $200.00]

Russell, Charles M. **Rawhide Rawlins Stories.** Great Falls, MT: Montana Newspaper Assn.; 1921. [4th printing, $175.00]

Russell, Charles M. **Trails Plowed Under.** Garden City: Doubleday, Page; 1927. [spine and front cover chewed, $40.00]

Russell, Charles Russell. **Diary of a Visit to the United States of America in the Year 1883.** NY: U. S. Catholic Hist. Soc.; 1910. [$90.00] [$40.00]

Russell, Francis. **Tragedy in Dedham.** NY: McGraw-Hill; 1962. [$20.00]

Russell, Virgil Yates. **Indian Artifacts.** rev. ed. Boulder, CO: Johnson; 1962, c1951. [fine, $25.00]

Russell, William Howard. **My Diary North and South.** NY: Harper; 1863. [hinges cracking, $35.00] [binding worn, $65.00] [1954 Harper reprint, $20.00]

Russell, William Shaw. **Guide to Plymouth and Recollections of the Pilgrims.** Boston: Coolidge; 1846. [rebound, $60.00]

Russell, Willis. **Quebec As It Was, and As It Is.** Quebec: Lamoureaux; 1857. [$20.00]

Rutgers, Lispenard. **On and Off the Saddle.** NY, London: Putnam; 1894. [presentation, $85.00]

Ruth, John A. **Decorum; a Practical Treatise on Etiquette and Dress of the Best American Society.** Chicago: Ruth; 1877. [$30.00]

Ruth, Kent. **Great Day in the West.** 1st ed. Norman: U. of Oklahoma; 1963. [$27.00] [$30.00]

Rutherford, Mary Louise. **Influence of the American Bar Association on Public Opinion and Legislation.** Philadelphia: U. of Pennsylvania; 1937. [$15.00]

Rutland, Robert Allen. **Birth of the Bill of Rights.** Chapel Hill: U. of North Carolina; 1955. [$24.50]

Ruxton, George Federick Augustus. **Adventures in Mexico and the Rocky Mountains.** NY: Harper; 1848. [rebacked, $250.00]

Ruxton, George Frederick Augustus. **Life in the Far West.** Edinburgh: Blackwood; 1849. [$300.00] [1951 Oklahoma ed., $45.00]

Ruxton, George Frederick Augustus. **Ruxton of the Rockies.** 1st ed. Norman: U. of Oklahoma; 1950. [$45.00]

Ryan, J. Clyde. **A Skeptic Dude in Arizona.** San Antonio: Naylor; 1952. [$35.00]

Ryan, William Morris. **Shamrock and Cactus.** San Antonio, Houston: Southern Literary Institute; 1936. [$65.00]

Ryan, William Redmond. **Personal Adventures in Upper and Lower California, in 1848-9.** London: Shoberl; 1850. 2 v. [lacks frontis., $175.00] [rebound, $475.00]

Ryder, David Warren. **Memories of the Mendocino Coast.** San Francisco: Priv. Print.; 1948. [$25.00]

Rynning, Thomas Harbo. **Gun Notches.** NY: Stokes; 1931. [$40.00]

Ryus, William Henry. **The Second William Penn.** Kansas City, MO: Riley; 1913. [$40.00]

Rywell, Martin. **Samuel Colt.** Harriman, TN: Pioneer; 1952. [$45.00]

Saarinen, Aline. **The Proud Possessors.** NY: Random; 1958. [$15.00]

Saber, Clifford. **Desert Rat Sketch Book.** 1st ed. NY: Sketchbook; 1959. [$100.00]

Sabin, Edwin Legrand. **Kit Carson Days, 1809-1868.** rev. ed. NY: Press of the Pioneers; 1935. 2 v. [$135.00]

Sabine, Lorenzo. **Biographical Sketches of Loyalists of the American Revolution with an Historical Essay.** Boston: Little, Brown; 1864. 2 v. [rebound, $150.00]

Sachse, Julius Friedrich. **Diary of a Voyage from Rotterdam to Philadelphia in 1728.** Lancaster, PA: Pennsylvania German Society; 1909. [$20.00]

Sachse, Julius Friedrich. **German Pietists of Provincial Pennsylvania.** Philadelphia: The Author; 1895. [$200.00]

Sachse, Julius Friedrich. **German Sectarians of Pennsylvania.** Philadelphia: The Author; 1899-1900. 2 v. [$300.00]

Sachse, Julius Friedrich. **Justus Falckner.** Philadelphia: The Author; 1903. [$75.00]

Sack, John. **The Butcher; the Ascent of Yerupaja.** NY: Rinehart; 1952. [$15.00]

Sackett, Frances Robertson. **Dick Dowling.** Houston: Gulf; 1937. [$85.00]

Safford, Susan Darling. **Quaint Epitaphs.** 3rd ed. Boston: Ochs; 1900, c1898. [$15.00]

Safford, William Harrison. **Life of Harman Blennerhassett.** Chillicothe, OH: Ely, Allen & Looker; 1850. [$135.00] [$50.00]

Sage, Lee. **The Last Rustler.** Boston: Little, Brown; 1930. [soiled, $32.50] [$20.00] [$35.00] [$50.00]

Sage, Rufus B. **Rocky Mountain Life.** Cincinnati: Rulison; 1857. [$50.00]

Saint Amant, Pierre Charles Fournier de. **Des Colonies.** Paris: Barroi-Delaunay; 1822. [$350.00]

Saint-Germain, C. de. see, Valcourt-Vermont, Edgar de.

Salinger, Jerome David. **Raise High the Roof Beam, Carpenters: and Seymour--an Introduction.** 1st ed. Boston: Little, Brown; 1959. [2nd state, fine in dj, $47.50]

Salisbury, Albert P. **Two Captains West.** 1st ed. Seattle: Superior; 1950. [$25.00]

Salmons, C. H. **The Burlington Strike.** Aurora, IL: Bunnell and Ward; 1889. [$50.00]

Salomon, Julian Harris. **Book of Indian Crafts & Indian Lore.** NY, London: Harper; 1928. [$25.00]

Salpointe, John Baptist. **Soldiers of the Cross.** Banning, CA: St. Boniface's Industrial School; 1898. [x-lib., rebound, $100.00] [$175.00]

Salter, William. **Memoirs of Joseph W. Pickett.** Burlington, IA: Love; 1880. [$85.00]

Sampson, York. **South Dakota; Fifty Years of Progress.** Sioux Falls: SD Golden Anniversary Book Co.; 1939. [spine torn, wraps creased and soiled, $15.00]

Sanborn, F. B. **Life and Letters of John Brown.** 2nd ed. Boston: Roberts; 1891, c1885. [$27.50]

Sanborn, Helen Josephine. **A Winter in Central America and Mexico.** Boston, NY: Lee and Shepard; 1886. [$75.00]

Sanchez, Nellie Van de Grift. **Spanish and Indian Place Names of California.** San Francisco: Robertson; 1922. [$22.50]

Sandburg, Carl. **Abraham Lincoln, the Prairie Years.** NY: Harcourt, Brace; 1926. 2 v. [inscribed, $60.00]

Sandburg, Carl. **Abraham Lincoln: The War Years.** trade ed. NY: Harcourt, Brace; 1939. 4 v. [$80.00]

Sandburg, Carl. **Chicago Poems.** 1st ed. NY: Holt; 1916. [$100.00] [1st state, as new, $145.00]

Sandburg, Carl. **Cornhuskers.** NY: Holt; 1918. [$85.00]

Sandburg, Carl. **Correspondence.** 1st ed. NY: Harcourt, Brace & World; 1968. [$17.50]

Sandburg, Carl. **Good Morning, America.** 1st ed. NY: Harcourt, Brace; 1928. [fine, $65.00]

Sandburg, Carl. **Mary Lincoln.** trade ed. NY: Harcourt, Brace; 1932. [$25.00]

Sandburg, Carl. **Poems of the Midwest.** Cleveland, NY: World; 1946. [lacks publisher's slipcase, $80.00]

Sandburg, Carl. **Rootabaga Country.** NY: Harcourt, Brace; 1929. [signed, $75.00]

Sanders, Alvin Howard. **At the Sign of the Stock Yard Inn.** Chicago: Breeder's Gazette; 1915. [$65.00]

Sanders, Alvin Howard. **Red, White, and Roan.** Chicago: American Shorthorn Breeders' Assn.; 1936. [$50.00]

Sanders, Alvin Howard. **Story of the Herefords.** Chicago: Breeder's Gazette; 1914. [$40.00]

Sanders, Helen Fitzgerald. **History of Montana.** Chicago: Lewis; 1913. 3 v. [vol. 1-2 only, rebacked, $150.00]

Sandoz, Mari. **Battle of the Little Bighorn.** 1st ed. Philadelphia: Lippincott; 1966. [in frayed dj, $18.00] [$30.00] [$35.00]

Sandoz, Mari. **The Buffalo Hunters.** NY: Hastings; 1954. [$45.00]

Sandoz, Mari. **Capital City.** Boston: Little, Brown; 1939. [chipped dj, $25.00]

Sandoz, Mari. **Crazy Horse.** 1st ed. NY: Knopf; 1942. [$100.00] [worn dj, $75.00] [Hastings reprint, $30.00]

Sandoz, Mari. **Love Song to the Plains.** 1st ed. NY: Harper; 1961. [$20.00]

Sandoz, Mari. **Old Jules.** Boston: Little, Brown; 1935. [1st issue, $17.50] [dj reinforced, $30.00]

Sandoz, Mari. **Son of the Gamblin' Man.** 1st ed. NY: Potter; 1960. [signed, dj stained, $25.00] [$20.00]

Sandoz, Mari. **The Story Catcher.** Philadelphia: Westminster; 1963. [$15.00]

Sandoz, Mari. **These Were the Sioux.** NY: Hastings; 1961. [$30.00] [$20.00]

Sanger, Donald Bridgman. **James Longstreet.** Baton Rouge: Louisiana State UP; 1952. [$50.00]

Sanger, Samuel F. **The Olive Branch of Peace and Good Will to Men.** Elgin, IL: Brethren; 1907. [covers worn, $20.00]

Santee, Ross. **Hardrock and Silver Sage.** NY: Scribner; 1951. [$35.00]

Santee, Ross. **The Rummy Kid Goes Home.** NY: Hastings; 1965. [$17.50]

Santleben, August. **A Texas Pioneer.** NY, Washington: Neale; 1910. [$375.00]

Sappington, Joe. **Joe Sap's Tales.** Belton, TX: [s.n.]; 1908. [$125.00]

Sardi, Vincent. **Sardi's.** 1st ed. NY: Holt; 1953. [$15.00]

Sarett, Lew R. **Collected Poems of.** NY: Holt; 1944, c1941. [$25.00]

Sargent, Martin P. **Pioneer Sketches.** Erie, PA: Herald; 1891. [some wear, $175.00]

Sargent, Winthrop. **History of an Expedition against Fort Du Quesne, in 1755.** Philadelphia: Historical Soc. of PA; 1856. [rebound, water stained, $45.00]

Sargent, Winthrop. **Life and Career of Major John Andre.** Boston: Ticknor and Fields; 1861. [$35.00]

Saroyan, William. **Adventures of Wesley Jackson.** 1st ed. NY: Harcourt, Brace; 1946. [$20.00]

Saroyan, William. **The Assyrian.** 1st ed. NY: Harcourt, Brace; 1950. [$25.00] [$20.00]

Saroyan, William. **Dear Baby.** 1st ed. NY: Harcourt, Brace; 1944. [$20.00]

Saroyan, William. **The Human Comedy.** 1st ed. NY: Harcourt, Brace; 1943. [$25.00] [$35.00]

Saroyan, William. **My Heart's in the Highlands.** NY: Harcourt, Brace; 1939. [$35.00]

Saroyan, William. **Selections.** 1st ed. NY: Braziller; 1958. [$30.00]

Saroyan, William. **Three Plays.** 1st ed. NY: Harcourt, Brace; 1941. [dj frayed, $30.00]

Saroyan, William. **The Time of Your Life.** 1st ed. NY: Harcourt, Brace; 1939. [$25.00]

Sartain, John. **Reminiscences of a Very Old Man.** NY: Appleton; 1899. [$70.00]

Sasnett, William J. **Discussions in Literature and Religion.** Nashville: Southern Methodist Pub. House; 1859. [front endpaper missing, $25.00]

Sasse, Fred A. **Rookie Days of a Soldier.** St. Paul: Greene; 1924. [$25.00]

Saunders, Charles Francis. **Finding the Worth While in the Southwest.** rev. ed. NY: McBride; 1928, c1918. [$45.00]

Saunders, Charles Francis. **Indians of the Terraced Houses.** NY: Putnam; 1912. [$60.00]

Saunders, Charles Francis. **The Southern Sierras of California.** Boston, NY: Houghton Mifflin; 1923. [$25.00]

Saunders, Charles Francis. **Under the Sky in California.** NY: McBride, Nast; 1913. [$20.00]

Saunders, Keith. **Independent Man.** Washington: Saunders; 1962. [dj torn, $20.00]

Saunders, William Oscar. **A Concept of Life and Other Editorial Cocktails.** rev. ed. Elizabeth City, NC: Independent; 1932. [$12.50]

Saunderson, Mont H. **Western Land and Water Use.** 1st ed. Norman: U. of Oklahoma; 1950. [$12.50]

Savage, Henry Lyttleton. **Nassau Hall, 1756-1956.** Princeton: Nassau Hall Bicentennial Committee; 1956. [$15.00]

Savage, John. **Life and Public Services of Andrew Johnson.** NY: Derby & Miller; 1866. [x-lib., $50.00]

Savelle, Max. **Diplomatic History of the Canadian Boundary.** New Haven; Toronto: Yale UP; Ryerson; 1940. [x-lib., $30.00, Canadian]

Savitt, Sam. **Rodeo.** Garden City: Doubleday; 1963. [$9.00]

Sawtelle, Ithamar B. **History of the Town of Townsend, Middlesex County, Massachusetts.** Fitchburg, MA: The Author; 1878. [$75.00]

Sawyer, Charles Winthrop. **Firearms in American History, 1600 to 1800.** Boston: The Author; 1910. [$45.00]

Saxon, Lyle. **Fabulous New Orleans.** NY: Appleton-Century; 1943, c1928. [$14.50] [1947 New Orleans imprint, $10.00]

Saxon, Lyle. **Father Mississippi.** NY, London: Century; 1927. [$22.00]

Say, Jean Baptiste. **Catechism of Political Economy.** Philadelphia: Carey; 1817. [$475.00]

Sayles, E. B. **Fantasies of Gold.** Tucson: U. of Arizona; 1968. [$10.00]

Scarborough, Dorothy. **From a Southern Porch.** NY, London: Putnam; 1919. [$40.00]

Scarborough, Dorothy. **In the Land of Cotton.** NY: Macmillan; 1923. [$40.00]

Scarborough, Katherine. **Homes of the Cavaliers.** NY: Macmillan; 1930. [$15.00]

Schachner, Nathan. **Aaron Burr.** NY: Stokes; 1937. [$12.50]

Schacht, Alexander. **Clowning through Baseball.** NY: Barnes; 1941. [$15.00]

Schaefer, Jack. **The Plainsmen.** Boston: Houghton Mifflin; 1963. [$25.00]

Schaff, David Schley. **Life of Philip Schaff.** NY: Scribner; 1897. [x-lib., $17.50]

Schain, Josephine. **Women and the Franchise.** Chicago: McClurg; 1918. [front hinge glued, $20.00]

Schaller, Waldemar Theodore. **Crystal Cavities of the New Jersey Zeolite Region.** Washington: USGPO; 1932. [$15.00]

Schantz, Franklin Jakob Fogel. **Domestic Life & Characteristics of the Pennsylvania-German Pioneer.** Lancaster: Pennsylvania German Society; 1900. [$22.00]

Scharf, J. Thomas. **Chronicles of Baltimore.** Baltimore: Turnbull; 1874. [$85.00]

Scharf, J. Thomas. **History of Baltimore City and County.** Philadelphia: Everts; 1881. [rebacked, $125.00]

Scharf, J. Thomas. **History of Delaware.** Philadelphia: Richards; 1888. 2 v. [titlepage of vol. 1 in facs., rebound, $550.00]

Scharf, J. Thomas. **History of Philadelphia, 1609-1884.** Philadelphia: Everts; 1884. 3 v. [$175.00]

Scharf, J. Thomas. **History of the Confederate States Navy.** NY; San Francisco: Rogers & Sherwood; Bancroft; 1887. [rebound in grey cloth, $175.00]

Schenck, Martin. **Up Came Hill.** Harrisburg, PA: Stackpole; 1958. [$65.00]

Scherer, James Augustin Brown. **The First Forty-Niner and the Story of the Golden Tea-Caddy.** NY: Minton, Balch; 1925. [$25.00]

Scherzer, Karl. **Travels in the Free States of Central America.** London: Longman, etc.; 1857. 2 v. [bound in one vol., $275.00]

Schiel, Jacob Heinrich Wilhelm. **Journey through the Rocky Mountains and the Humboldt Mountains to the Pacific Ocean.** Norman: U. of Oklahoma; 1959. [$25.00]

Schiff, Jacob H. **Jacob H. Schiff; His Life and Letters.** Garden City: Doubleday, Doran; 1928. 2 v. [$25.00]

Schindler, Harold. **Orrin Porter Rockwell.** Salt Lake City: U. of Utah; 1966. [$35.00]

Schlesinger, Arthur Meier. **Age of Jackson.** 1st ed. Boston: Little, Brown; 1945. [2nd printing, $15.00]

Schlesinger, Arthur Meier. **Colonial Merchants and the American Revolution.** NY: Columbia UP; 1918. [$125.00] [1957 Ungar ed., x-lib., $15.00]

Schlesinger, Arthur Meier. **A Thousand Days.** Boston: Houghton Mifflin; 1965. [$20.00]

Schlesinger, Julia. **Workers in the Vineyard.** San Francisco: [s.n.]; 1896. [v. 1 only--no more published?, $75.00]

Schley, Winfield Scott. **Rescue of Greely.** NY: Scribner; 1885. [$55.00]

Schmeckebier, Laurence Eli. **John Steuart Curry's Pageant of America.** NY: American Artists Group; 1943. [$35.00]

Schmitt, Jo Ann. **Fighting Editors.** San Antonio: Naylor; 1958. [$30.00] [without dj, $20.00]

Schmitt, Martin Ferdinand. **Fighting Indians of the West.** NY: Scribner; 1948. [$40.00]

Schmitt, Martin Ferdinand. **The Settlers' West.** NY: Scribner; 1955. [$25.00]

Schmitz, Joseph William. **Thus They Lived.** San Antonio: Naylor; 1935. [$125.00]

Scholte, Leonora R. **A Stranger in a Strange Land.** Grand Rapids, MI: Eerdmans; 1942. [$12.50]

Schomburgk, Robert Hermann. **Twelve Views in the Interior of Guiana.** 1st ed. London: Ackerman; 1841. [boards detached, x-lib., $1250.00]

Schoolcraft, Henry Rowe. **Archives of Aboriginal Knowledge.** Philadelphia: Lippincott; 1860. 6 v. [x-lib., $1500.00]

Schoolcraft, Henry Rowe. **Historical and Statistical Information Respecting the History, Condition, and Prospects of the Indian Tribes of the United States.** Philadelphia: Lippincott, Grambo; 1851-57. 6 v. [$4500.00]

Schoolcraft, Henry Rowe. **Incentives to the Study of the Ancient Period of American History.** NY: NY Historical Society; 1847. [$35.00]

Schoolcraft, Henry Rowe. **Journal of a Tour into the Interior of Missouri and Arkansaw.** London: Phillips; 1821. [$245.00]

Schoolcraft, Henry Rowe. **The Myth of Hiawatha and Other Oral Legends.** Philadelphia: Lippincott; 1856. [$175.00] [$225.00]

Schoolcraft, Henry Rowe. **Narrative of an Expedition through the Upper Mississippi to Itasca Lake.** NY: Harper; 1833. [$225.00]

Schoolcraft, Henry Rowe. **Personal Memoirs of a Residence of Thirty Years with the Indian Tribes on the American Frontiers.** Philadelphia: Lippincott, Grambo; 1851. [$200.00]

Schoolcraft, Henry Rowe. **Schoolcraft in the Ozarks.** Van Buren, AR: Press-Argus; 1955. [$35.00]

Schoolcraft, Henry Rowe. **Summary Narrative of an Exploratory Expedition to the Sources of the Mississippi River.** Philadelphia: Lippincott, Grambo; 1855. [$150.00]

Schoolman, Regina. see, Slatkin, Regina Schoolman.

Schoonover, Thomas J. **Life and Times of Gen'l John A. Sutter.** Sacramento: Johnston; 1895. [$75.00]

Schreyvogel, Charles. **My Bunkie, and Others.** NY: Moffat, Yard; 1909. [$850.00]

Schull, Joseph. **100 Years of Banking in Canada.** Vancouver: Copp Clark; 1958. [$15.00]

Schultz, Christian. **Travels on an Inland Voyage.** NY: Riley; 1810. 2 v. in 1. [$1000.00]

Schultz, Edward T. **History of Freemasonry in Maryland.** Baltimore: Medairy; 1884-1887. 3 v. [$105.00]

Schultz, Gerard. **Early History of the Northern Ozarks.** Jefferson City, MO: Midland; 1937. [$25.00]

Schultz, James Willard. **My Life as an Indian.** Boston, NY: Houghton Mifflin; 1907. [inscribed, $75.00] [$65.00] [1914 printing, $30.00]

Schultz, James Willard. **With the Indians in the Rockies.** Boston, NY: Houghton Mifflin; 1912. [$50.00]

Schurz, Carl. **The New South.** NY: American News; 1885. [$40.00]

Schwartz, Delmore. **The World Is a Wedding.** 1st ed. Norfolk, CT: New Directions; 1948. [very good in dj, $55.00]

Schwarze, Edmund. **History of the Moravian Missions among Southern Indian Tribes of the United States.** Bethlehem, PA: Times; 1923. [$60.00]

Schwatka, Frederick. **Along Alaska's Great River.** Chicago: Henry; 1898. [$75.00]

Schwatka, Frederick. **A Summer in Alaska.** St. Louis: Henry; 1894. [$50.00]

Scobee, Barry. **Old Fort Davis.** San Antonio: Naylor; 1947. [$45.00]

Scopes, John Thomas. see, Waller, William

Scott, Carroll De Wilton. **Here's Don Coyote.** Los Angeles: Westernlore; 1956. [$20.00]

Scott, Eben Greenough. **Reconstruction during the Civil War in the United States of America.** Boston, NY: Houghton Mifflin; 1895. [x-lib., $35.00] [$75.00]

Scott, Hugh Lenox. **Some Memories of a Soldier.** NY: Century; 1928. [$125.00]

Scott, Job. **Journal of the Life, Travels and Gospel Labours of That Faithful Servant and Minister of Christ.** NY: Collins; 1797. [$350.00] [worn, $125.00]

Scott, John F. **Brudder Bones' Book of Stump Speeches, and Burlesque Orations.** NY: Dick & Fitzgerald; 1868. [$45.00]

Scott, Nancy N. **Memoir of Hugh Lawson White.** Philadelphia: Lippincott; 1856. [$100.00]

Scott, Natalie Vivian. **Old Plantation Houses in Louisiana.** see, Spratling, William Philip.

Scott, Reva Lucile. **Samuel Brannan and the Golden Fleece.** NY: Macmillan; 1944. [caps bumped, $30.00]

Scott, William Anderson. **A Discourse for the Times.** San Francisco: [s.n.]; 1856. [covers missing, $50.00]

Scott, William Anderson. **The Wedge of Gold.** San Francisco: Whitton, Towne; 1855. [$100.00]

Scott, William J. **Historic Eras and Paragraphic Pencilings.** Atlanta: Constitution; 1892. [$22.50]

Scott, Winfield. **Infantry Tactics.** new ed. NY: Harper; 1860. 3 v. [hinges weak, $135.00]

Scott, Winfield. **Memoirs of Lieut.-General Scott, LL.D.** NY: Sheldon; 1864. 2 v. [$60.00]

Scowcroft, Richard. **Children of the Covenant.** Boston: Houghton Mifflin; 1945. [dj repaired, $20.00] [$25.00]

Scribner, Benjamin Franklin. **How Soldiers Were Made.** New Albany, IN: Donohue & Henneberry; 1887. [hinges weak, $125.00]

Scrymser, James Alexander. **Personal Reminiscences of.** Easton, PA: Eschenbach; 1915. [$40.00]

Seager, Robert. **Alfred Thayer Mahan.** Annapolis: Naval Institute; 1977. [$25.00]

Seager, Robert. **And Tyler Too.** 1st ed. NY: McGraw-Hill; 1963. [$45.00]

Seale, William. **Sam Houston's Wife.** Norman: U. of Oklahoma; 1970. [$25.00]

Sealsfield, Charles. **Frontier Life.** Buffalo: Derby, Orton & Mulligan; 1853. [$45.00]

Sealsfield, Charles. **Life in the New World.** NY: Winchester; 1842. [$250.00] [$225.00]

Searight, Thomas B. **The Old Pike.** Uniontown, PA: The Author; 1894. [$75.00]

Seaver, James Everett. **Narrative of the Life of Mrs. Mary Jemison.** Howden, Eng.: Parkin; 1826. [$300.00] [1877, 5th ed., NY, $75.00] [1932 NY ed., $20.00]

Sedgwick, Catharine Maria. **Hope Leslie.** NY: White, Gallaher & White; 1827. 2 v. [$85.00]

Sedgwick, Sarah Cabot. **Stockbridge, 1739-1939.** bicentennial limited ed. Great Barrington, MA: Berkshire Courier; 1939. [$30.00]

Sedgwick, Theodore. **Memoir of the Life of William Livingston.** NY: Harper; 1833. [$12.50]

Sedgwick, Theodore. **Thoughts on the Proposed Annexation of Texas to the United States.** NY: Fanshaw; 1844. [first issue, $135.00]

Seeger, Eugen. **Chicago: Entwickelung, Zerstorung und Wiederaufbau der Wunderstadt.** Chicago: Stern; 1872. [$300.00]

Seelye, Laurenus Clark. **Early History of Smith College, 1871-1910.** Boston, NY: Houghton Mifflin; 1923. [$17.50] [$15.00]

Seeman, Elizabeth. **In the Arms of the Mountain.** NY: Crown; 1961. [dj chipped, $15.00]

Segale, Blandina. **At the End of the Santa Fe Trail.** Columbus, OH: Columbian; 1932. [$45.00]

Seger, John. **Narrative of the Life and Ministry of.** NY: Holman; 1863. [worn, $45.00]

Seitz, Don Carlos. **From Kaw Teepee to Capitol.** NY: Stokes; 1928. [$25.00]

Seitz, Don Carlos. **Lincoln the Politician.** NY: Coward-McCann; 1931. [$15.00]

Sell, Henry Blackman. **Buffalo Bill and the Wild West.** NY: Oxford UP; 1955. [$30.00]

Selle, Ralph Abraham. **Big Bend.** Houston: Carroll; [1938?]. [limited signed, $75.00]

Sellers, Charles Coleman. **Benedict Arnold.** NY: Minton, Balch; 1930. [$15.00]

Sellstedt, Lars Gustaf. **From Forecastle to Academy.** Buffalo: Matthews-Northrup; 1904. [$60.00]

Selous, Frederick Courteney. **Recent Hunting Trips in British North America.** London: Witherby; 1907. [$160.00]

Selvig, Conrad George. **A Tale of Two Valleys.** Los Angeles: Jones; 1951. [$20.00]

Semmens, John. **The Field and the Work.** Toronto: Methodist Mission Rooms; 1884. [$95.00, Canadian]

Semmes, Raphael. **Campaign of General Scott, in the Valley of Mexico.** Cincinnati: Moore & Anderson; 1852. [$150.00]

Semmes, Raphael. **Crime and Punishment in Early Maryland.** Baltimore: Hopkins; 1938. [$45.00]

Semmes, Raphael. **Service Afloat.** Baltimore: Baltimore Pub. Co.; 1887. [rebound, $80.00]

Senan, Jose Francisco de Paula. **Letters of.** San Francisco: Ventura County Historical Society; 1962. [$40.00]

Senour, Faunt Le Roy. **Morgan and His Captors.** Cincinnati, Chicago: Vent; 1865. [$55.00]

Senter, E. G. **Bailey Case Boiled Down.** Dallas: Flag; 1908. [$35.00]

Separk, Joseph H. **Gastonia and Gaston County, North Carolina, 1846-1949.** Gastonia: [s.n.; 1949?]. [$17.50]

Service, Robert W. **Ballads of a Cheechako.** NY: Barse & Hopkins; 1909. [$20.00, Canadian]

Service, Robert W. **More Collected Verse.** NY: Dodd, Mead; 1959. [$7.00]

Service, Robert W. **Rhymes of a Rolling Stone.** 1st ed. Toronto: Briggs; 1912. [$50.00] [$75.00] [1925 Dodd, Mead ed., $7.00]

Service, Robert W. **Songs of a Sourdough.** Toronto: Briggs; 1908. [later printing, $13.00]

Service, Robert W. **Spell of the Yukon.** 1st ed. Philadelphia: Stern; 1907. [covers soiled, $50.00]

Seton, Ernest Thompson. **America.** NY: Devin-Adair; 1954. [$11.00]

Seton, Ernest Thompson. **Arctic Prairies.** NY: Scribner; 1911. [$125.00]

Seton, Ernest Thompson. **Book of Woodcraft and Indian Lore.** Garden City: Doubleday, Page; 1925, c1921. [$13.00]

Seton, Ernest Thompson. **The Preacher of Cedar Mountain.** Garden City: Doubleday, Page; 1917. [$35.00]

Seton, William. **Pride of Lexington.** 1st ed. NY: O'Shea; 1874. [hinge broken, $47.50]

Settle, Raymond W. **Empire on Wheels.** Stanford: Stanford UP; 1949. [$15.00]

Settle, Raymond W. **Saddles and Spurs.** Harrisburg, PA: Stackpole; 1955. [$40.00]

Settle, William A. **Jesse James Was His Name.** Columbia: U. of Missouri; 1966. [$35.00]

Sevareid, Arnold E. **Canoeing with the Cree.** NY: Macmillan; 1935. [$40.00]

Severance, Frank Hayward. **Old Trails on the Niagara Frontier.** 2nd ed. Cleveland: Burrows; 1903. [$35.00, Canadian]

Sevier, Cora Bales. **Sevier Family History.** Washington: [s.n.]; 1961. [bumped, mildewed, $60.00]

Seward, Frederick William. **Reminiscences of a War-Time Statesman and Diplomat.** NY, London: Putnam; 1916. [$30.00] [$21.50]

Seward, William Henry. **Elements of Empire in America.** NY: Shepard; 1844. [$55.00]

Seward, William Henry. **Life and Public Services of John Quincy Adams.** Auburn, NY: Derby, Miller; 1849. [$75.00]

Seward, William Henry. **William H. Seward.** new ed. NY: Derby and Miller; 1891. 3 v. [$45.00]

Sewel, William. **History of the Rise, Increase, and Progress, of the Christian People Called Quakers.** 3rd ed. Burlington, NJ: Collins; 1774. [worn binding, $275.00]

Sexton, Grover F. **The Arizona Sheriff.** [s.l.]: Studebaker; 1925. [$100.00]

Sexton, Randolph Williams. **Spanish Influence on American Architecture and Decoration.** NY: Brentano's; 1927. [$35.00]

Seymour, Charles. **American Diplomacy during the World War.** Baltimore: Hopkins; 1934. [$20.00]

Seymour, Flora Warren. **Indian Agents of the Old Frontier.** NY, London: Appleton-Century; 1941. [$55.00]

Seymour, Flora Warren. **Lords of the Valley.** 1st ed. London: Longmans, Green; 1930. [$35.00] [$30.00]

Seymour, George Dudley. **Captain Nathan Hale, 1755-1776: Yale College 1773; Major John Palsgrave Wyllys, 1754-1790: Yale College 1773.** New-Haven: The Author; 1933. [rubbed, scuffed, soiled, sunned, $25.00] [$32.50]

Seymour, Silas. **Incidents of a Trip through the Great Platte Valley, to the Rocky Mountains and Laramie Plains, in the Fall of 1866.** NY: Van Nostrand; 1867. [portrait lacking, $50.00] [$350.00]

Shackleford, William Yancey. **Belle Starr, the Bandit Queen.** Girard, KS: Haldeman-Julius; 1943. [$30.00]

Shackleton, Robert. **The Book of Boston.** Philadelphia: Penn; 1920. [box broken, $25.00]

Shafer, Hugh B. **A Stockman's Poems.** San Antonio: San Antonio Print.; 1903. [$45.00]

Shaker Heights. Ohio. Board of Education. **Shaker Heights, Then and Now.** Cleveland: Copifyer Lithograph; 1938. [$100.00]

Shakers. **A Summary View of the Millennial Church.** Albany: Packard & Van Benthuysen; 1823. [$225.00] [$150.00] [1848 ed., $75.00]

Shaler, Nathaniel Southgate. **Kentucky, a Pioneer Commonwealth.** Boston, NY: Houghton Mifflin; 1885. [$11.00] [1912 Houghton reissue, $30.00]

Shallenberger, Eliza Jane. **Stark County and Its Pioneers.** Cambridge, IL: Seaton; 1876. [spine eroded, $175.00]

Shambaugh, Benjamin Franklin. **Iowa City.** Iowa City: State Hist. Soc.; 1893. [$40.00]

Shambaugh, Bertha Maud. **Amana That Was and Amana That Is.** Iowa City: State Hist. Soc.; 1932. [x-lib., $17.50] [$30.00]

Shambaugh, Bertha Maud. **Amana, the Community of True Believers.** Iowa City: State Hist. Soc.; 1908. [$40.00] [$50.00]

Shankle, George Earlie. **American Nicknames.** 2nd ed. NY: Wilson; 1955. [x-lib., $17.50]

Shanks, Henry Thomas. **The Secession Movement in Virginia, 1847-1861.** Richmond: Garrett and Massie; 1934. [inscribed, $45.00]

Shannon, James P. **Catholic Colonization on the Western Frontier.** New Haven: Yale UP; 1957. [$15.00]

Sharp, Abigale Gardner. **History of the Spirit Lake Massacre and Captivity of.** Des Moines: Iowa Print. Co.; 1885. [inner hinge worn, $65.00]

Sharp, Isabella. **Poems.** 1st ed. Carlisle, PA: London; 1805. [$100.00]

Sharpe, Bill. **Tar on My Heels.** Winston-Salem, NC: Tar Heels; 1946. [dj chipped and soiled, $15.00]

Sharpe, William Carvasso. **Records of the Sharpe Family in England and America, from 1580 to 1870.** Seymour, CT: Sharpe; 1874. [spine worn, $35.00]

Shaw, Albert. **Abraham Lincoln.** NY: Review of Reviews; 1929. 2 v. [$45.00]

Shaw, Anna Howard. **Story of a Pioneer.** NY, London: Harper; 1915. [$40.00]

Shaw, Charles. **Topographical and Historical Description of Boston.** Boston: Spear; 1817. [rebacked, $50.00]

Shaw, Edward Richard. **Legends of Fire Island Beach and the South Side.** NY: Lovell, Coryell; 1895. [presentation, $60.00]

Shaw, James. **Our Last Campaign and Subsequent Service in Texas.** Providence: Rhode Island Soldiers & Sailors Hist. Soc.; 1905. [$35.00]

Shaw, James Clay. **North from Texas.** Evanston, IL: Branding Iron; 1952. [$55.00]

Shaw, Lloyd. **Cowboy Dances.** Caldwell, ID: Caxton; 1939. [signed, $50.00]

Shaw, Reuben Cole. **Across the Plains in Forty-Nine.** Chicago: Lakeside; 1948. [$17.50]

Shaw, William. **Golden Dreams and Waking Realities.** London: Smith, Elder; 1851. [minor repair to binding, $150.00]

Shaw, William H. **History of Essex and Hudson Counties, New Jersey.** Philadelphia: Everts & Peck; 1884. 2 v. [rebound, $150.00]

Shay, Felix. **Elbert Hubbard of East Aurora.** NY: Wise; 1926. [worn dj, $15.00]

Shay, Frank. **Iron Men & Wooden Ships.** Garden City: Doubleday, Page; 1924. [$60.00]

Shea, John Dawson Gilmary. **Discovery and Exploration of the Mississippi Valley.** NY: Redfield; 1852. [$250.00]

Shea, John Dawson Gilmary. **Fallen Brave.** NY: Richardson; 1861. [spine replaced, $75.00]

Shea, John Dawson Gilmary. **History of the Catholic Church in the United States.** NY: McBride; 1886-92. 4 v. [spines of vols. 1 & 2 worn and torn, $60.00]

Sheahan, James Washington. **The Great Conflagration: Chicago.** Chicago: Union; 1872. [$60.00]

Sheeran, James B. **Confederate Chaplain.** Milwaukee: Bruce; 1960. [$20.00]

Sheffield, John Holroyd. **Observations on the Commerce of the American States.** new ed. London: Debrett; 1784. [$300.00]

Sheffy, Lester Fields. **The Francklyn Land & Cattle Company.** Austin: U. of Texas; 1963. [$45.00]

Sheldon, Charles. **The Wilderness of Denali.** NY: Scribner; 1960, c1958. [near fine in frayed dj, $45.00] [$22.50]

Sheldon, Electa M. **Early History of Michigan from the First Settlement to 1815.** NY; Detroit: Barnes; Morley; 1856. [$125.00]

Sheldon, W. **Mormonism Examined.** Brodhead, WI: Sheldon; [1876?]. [some underlining, $75.00]

Sheller, Roscoe. **Bandit to Lawman.** Yakima, WA: Franklin; 1966. [signed, $15.00]

Sheller, Roscoe. **Ben Snipes: Northwest Cattle King.** 1st ed. Portland, OR: Binfords & Mort; 1957. [signed, $35.00]

Sheller, Roscoe. **Courage and Water, a Story of Yakima Valley's Sunnyside.** Portland, OR: Binfords & Mort; 1952. [$10.00]

Shelley, Henry Charles. **John Harvard and His Times.** Boston: Little, Brown; 1907. [$15.00]

Shepherd, William. **Prairie Experiences in Handling Cattle and Sheep.** London: Chapman and Hall; 1884. [$195.00] [1885 Judd ed., $135.00]

Sheppard, Eric William. **The American Civil War, 1864-1865.** Aldershot: Gale & Polden; 1938. [x-lib., $65.00]

Sheppard, Muriel. **Cloud by Day.** Chapel Hill: U. of North Carolina; 1947. [$20.00]

Shepperson, Archibald Bolling. **John Paradise and Lucy Ludwell.** Richmond: Dietz; 1942. [$15.00]

Sherburne, Andrew. **Memoirs of.** Utica: Williams; 1828. [$75.00] [1831 2nd ed., Brown, $75.00]

Sheridan, Martin. **Comics and Their Creators.** 1st ed. Boston: Hale; 1942. [fine in dj, $30.00]

Sheridan, Philip Henry. **Personal Memoirs of.** NY: Webster; 1888. 2 v. [$75.00] [scuffed, boards hanging, spines chipped, $30.00]

Sherlock, Chesla Clella. **Homes of Famous Americans.** Des Moines: Meredith; 1926. 2 v. [$40.00]

Sherman, Andrew Magoun. **Life of Captain Jeremiah O'Brien.** Morristown, NJ: Sherman; 1902. [$20.00]

Sherman, Edwin Allen. **Life of the Late Rear Admiral John Drake Sloat.** monumental ed. Oakland: Carruth & Carruth; 1902. [$175.00]

Sherman, Frederic Fairchild. **American Painters of Yesterday and Today.** NY: Priv. Print.; 1919. [$75.00]

Sherman, Frederic Fairchild. **John Ramage.** NY: Priv. Print.; 1929. [$100.00]

Sherman, John. **John Sherman's Recollections of Forty Years in the House, Senate and Cabinet.** Chicago, NY: Werner; 1895. [$25.00]

Sherman, John H. **General Account of Miranda's Expedition.** NY: McFarlane and Long; 1808. [$150.00]

Sherman, William T. **General W. T. Sherman as College President.** Cleveland: Clark; 1912. [$85.00]

Sherman, William T. **Memoirs of.** NY: Appleton; 1875. 2 v. [$85.00] [1876 1 vol. issue, $75.00]

Sherrill, William Lander. **Annals of Lincoln County, North Carolina.** Charlotte: Observer; 1937. [inscribed, rubbed, soiled, sunned, $50.00]

Sherwin, W. T. **Memoirs of the Life of Thomas Paine.** London: Carlile; 1819. [$585.00]

Shields, George O. **Cruisings in the Cascades.** Chicago, NY: Rand, McNally; 1889. [$30.00] [$45.00]

Shiflet, Kenneth E. **The Convenient Coward.** 1st ed. Harrisburg, PA: Stackpole; 1961. [$30.00]

Shimeall, Richard Cunningham. **Age of the World . . . Historic and Prophetic; and the "Sign of the Time."** 1st ed. NY: Swords, Standford; 1842. [chipped, shaken, $47.50]

Shinkle, James D. **Reminiscences of Roswell Pioneers.** Roswell, NM: Hall-Poorbaugh; 1966. [$35.00]

Shinn, Charles Howard. **Mining Camps.** NY: Knopf; 1948. [dj chipped and torn, $15.00]

Shipherd, Jacob R. **History of the Oberlin-Wellington Rescue.** Boston: Jewett; 1859. [rebound, $125.00]

Shipman, Alice Jack. **Taming the Big Bend.** Austin: Von Boeckmann-Jones; 1926. [$325.00]

Shipp, Albert Micajah. **History of Methodism in South Carolina.** Nashville: Southern Methodist; 1883. [bumped, silverfished, $45.00]

Shipp, Barnard. **History of Hernando de Soto and Florida.** Philadelphia: Collins; 1881. [$250.00] [1881 Lindsay imprint, presentation, $275.00]

Shipp, Barnard. **The Indian and Antiquities of America.** Philadelphia: Sherman; 1897. [x-lib., $25.00]

Shirk, David Lawson. **Cattle Drives of.** Portland, OR: Champoeg; 1956. [$60.00] [$50.00]

Shirley, Glenn. **Buckskin and Spurs.** NY: Hastings; 1958. [$25.00]

Shirley, Glenn. **Heck Thomas.** 1st ed. Philadelphia: Chilton; 1962. [$35.00]

Shirley, Glenn. **Henry Starr.** NY: McKay; 1965. [$18.00] [$25.00]

Shirley, Glenn. **Law West of Fort Smith.** 1st ed. NY: Holt; 1957. [$25.00] [dj repaired and chipped, $35.00]

Shirley, Glenn. **Pawnee Bill.** 1st ed. Albuquerque: U. of New Mexico; 1958. [$28.50] [$20.00] [$30.00]

Shirley, Glenn. **Six-Gun and Silver Star.** Albuquerque: U. of New Mexico; 1955. [$35.00]

Shirley, Glenn. **Toughest of Them All.** Albuquerque: U. of New Mexico; 1953. [$19.50] [$35.00]

Shirley, William. **Correspondence of.** NY: Macmillan; 1912. 2 v. [$60.00]

Shoemaker, Henry Wharton. **Juniata Memories.** Philadelphia: McVey; 1916. [x-lib., $30.00]

Shoemaker, Henry Wharton. **North Pennsylvania Minstrelsy.** 2nd ed. Altoona: Times Tribune; 1923. [$32.50]

Shores, Cyrus Wells. **Memoirs of a Lawman.** Denver: Sage; 1962. [$35.00]

Short, Wayne. **The Cheechakoes.** NY: Random; 1964. [$10.00]

Shostak, Arthur B. **Blue-Collar World.** Englewood Cliffs: Prentice-Hall; 1964. [x-lib., $15.00]

Shoup, Paul. **Side Tracks from the Main Line.** San Francisco: Priv. Print.; 1924. [inscribed, $50.00]

Shreve, Royal Ornan. **Finished Scoundrel.** Indianapolis: Bobbs-Merrill; 1933. [$30.00]

Shriver, Joseph Alexis. **Lafayette in Harford County, 1781.** signed, limited ed. Bel Air, MD: Waverly; 1931. [rebound, $45.00]

Shugg, Roger W. **Origins of Class Struggle in Louisiana.** University: Louisiana State UP; 1939. [x-lib., $10.00] [$45.00]

Shulman, Harry Manuel. **Slums of New York.** NY: Boni; 1938. [$30.00]

Shulman, Max. **Barefoot Boy with Cheek.** 1st ed. Garden City: Doubleday, Doran; 1943. [x-lib., $15.00]

Shulman, Max. **The Feather Merchants.** Garden City: Sun Dial; 1945, c1944. [x-lib., $12.50]

Shulman, Max. **Sleep till Noon.** 1st ed. Garden City: Doubleday; 1950. [$15.00]

Shulman, Max. **The Zebra Derby.** 1st ed. Garden City: Doubleday; 1946. [x-lib., $15.00]

Shurtleff, Harold Robert. **The Log Cabin Myth.** Cambridge: Harvard UP; 1939. [$25.00] [rebound. $20.00]

Shutes, Milton H. **Lincoln and California.** Stanford: Stanford UP; 1943. [$35.00]

Sibbald, George. **Notes and Observations, on the Pine Lands of Georgia.** Augusta: Bruce; 1801. [$1250.00]

Sidney, Margaret. **Old Concord.** Boston: Lothrop; 1888. [$45.00]

Siedel, Frank. **Out of the Midwest.** 1st ed. Cleveland: World; 1953. [$6.50]

Sievers, Harry Joseph. **Benjamin Harrison, Hoosier Statesman; from the Civil War to the White House, 1865-1888.** NY: University Publishers; 1959. [$25.00]

Sievers, Harry Joseph. **Benjamin Harrison: Hoosier Warrior, 1833-1865.** Chicago: Regnery; 1952. [$30.00]

Sigaud, Louis Adrien. **Belle Boyd, Confederate Spy.** 2nd ed. Richmond: Dietz; 1945. [$20.00]

Sigourney, L. H. **Select Poems.** 3rd ed. Philadelphia: Greenough; 1838. [$20.00]

Sigsbee, Charles Dwight. **The "Maine."** NY: Century; 1899. [$17.50]

Sigsby, William. **Life and Adventures of Timothy Murphy.** Middleburgh, NY: Gazette; 1912. [$85.00]

Siguenza y Gongora, Carlos de. **The Mercurio Volante of.** Los Angeles: Quivira Society; 1932. [$150.00]

Simkins, Francis Butler. **South Carolina during Reconstruction.** Chapel Hill: U. of North Carolina; 1932. [$75.00] [x-lib., $15.00]

Simkins, Francis Butler. **The Tillman Movement in South Carolina.** Durham: Duke UP; 1926. [$45.00]

Simkins, Francis Butler. **Women of the Confederacy.** Richmond: Garrett and Massie; 1936. [frayed dj, $37.50] [$50.00] [$47.50]

Simmons, Edward. **From Seven to Seventy.** NY: Harper; 1922. [spine faded, $30.00]

Simmons, John Collinsworth. **History of Southern Methodism on the Pacific Coast.** Nashville: Southern Methodist Pub. House; 1886. [$75.00]

Simmons, William E. **The Nicaragua Canal.** NY, London: Harper; 1900. [$25.00]

Simms, Jeptha Root. **Frontiersmen of New York.** Albany: Riggs; 1882-83. 2 v. [$175.00]

Simms, Jeptha Root. **Trappers of New York.** Albany: Munsell; 1850. [front cover detached, rear cover loose, $50.00]

Simms, William Gilmore. **History of South Carolina.** new ed. NY: Redfield; 1860. [x-lib., $25.00]

Simms, William Gilmore. **Life of Francis Marion.** NY: Langley; 1844. [$42.00] [11th ed., 1854, $15.00]

Simms, William Gilmore. **Martin Faber.** NY: Harper; 1837. 2 v. [$275.00]

Simpson, Charles H. **Life in the Mines.** 1st ed. Chicago: Rhodes & McClure; 1898. [$15.00]

Simpson, George. **An Overland Journey round the World, during the Years 1841 and 1842.** Philadelphia: Lea and Blanchard; 1947. [$150.00]

Simpson, James Hervey. **Journal of a Military Reconnaissance from Santa Fe, New Mexico, to the Navajo Country.** Philadelphia: Lippincott, Grambo; 1852. [$800.00]

Simpson, James Hervey. **Navaho Expedition.** 1st ed. Norman: U. of Oklahoma; 1964. [$30.00] [$35.00]

Simpson, James Hervey. **Report of Explorations across the Great Basin of the Territory of Utah.** see, United States. Army. Corps of Engineers.

Simpson, Samuel Leonidas. **The Gold-Gated West.** Philadelphia, London: Lippincott; 1910. [$15.00] [$25.00]

Simpson, William R. **Hockshop.** NY: Random; 1954. [$25.00]

Sims, Carlton C. **A History of Rutherford County.** [Murfreesboro?, TN: s.n.]; 1947. [bumped, silverfished, ink marks, $45.00]

Sims, J. Marion. **Story of My Life.** NY: Appleton; 1884. [spine badly torn, $25.00]

Sims, Orland L. **Gun-Toters I Have Known.** 1st limited ed. Austin: Encino; 1967. [signed, $85.00]

Sinclair, Upton. **Autobiography.** 1st ed. NY: Harcourt, Brace & World; 1962. [$15.00]

Sinclair, Upton. **Between Two Worlds.** NY: Viking; 1941. [$12.50]

Sinclair, Upton. **Book of Life, Mind and Body.** Girard: Haldeman-Julius; 1922. [$12.50]

Sinclair, Upton. **Brass Check.** Pasadena: The Author; [1920?]. [$10.00]

Sinclair, Upton. **Cry for Justice.** Pasadena: Sinclair; 1921. [$15.00]

Sinclair, Upton. **Damaged Goods.** Pasadena: Sinclair; 1913. [$20.00]

Sinclair, Upton. **The Goslings.** 1st ed. Pasadena: Sinclair; 1924. [$30.00] [$40.00]

Sinclair, Upton. **The Industrial Republic.** NY: Doubleday; 1907. [$65.00]

Sinclair, Upton. **The Jungle.** 1st ed. NY: Doubleday, Page; 1906. [$100.00] [1st issue, $125.00]

Sinclair, Upton. **Mammonart.** Pasadena: The Author; 1925. [$15.00]

Sinclair, Upton. **O Shepherd, Speak!** NY: Viking; 1949. [$10.00]

Sinclair, Upton. **The Profits of Religion.** Pasadena: The Author; 1918. [$25.00]

Sinclair, Upton. **Roman Holiday.** special presentation ed. NY: Farrar & Rinehart; 1931. [$40.00]

Singer, Kurt D. **Danny Kaye Story.** NY: Nelson; 1958. [$12.50]

Sipe, C. Hale. **Fort Ligonier and Its Times.** Harrisburg, PA: Telegraph; 1932. [$50.00]

Sipe, C. Hale. **The Indian Wars of Pennsylvania.** Harrisburg, PA: Telegraph; 1929. [signed, $115.00]

Siringo, Charles A. **Cowboy Detective.** Chicago: Conkey; 1912. [$250.00]

Siringo, Charles A. **History of "Billy the Kid."** Austin: Steck-Vaughn; 1967. [$20.00]

Siringo, Charles A. **Riata and Spurs.** Boston, NY: Houghton Miffin; 1927. [1st issue, $185.00; $175.00] [rev. ed., $125.00]

Siringo, Charles A. **A Texas Cow Boy.** Chicago: Siringo & Dobson; 1886. [$200.00] [$350.00] [1886 Rand McNally imprint, $200.00] [1950 Sloane ed., $55.00]

Siringo, Charles A. **Two Evilisms.** Austin: Steck-Vaughn; 1968, c1967. [$40.00]

Sissons, Charles Bruce. **History of Victoria University.** Toronto: U. of Toronto; 1952. [$15.00, Canadian]

Sitterson, Joseph Carlyle. **Sugar Country.** Lexington: U. of Kentucky; 1953. [$65.00]

Siviter, Anna. **Recollections of War and Peace, 1861-1868.** NY: Putnam; 1938. [$20.00]

Six Missions of Texas. 1st ed. Waco: Texian Press; 1965. [$30.00]

Skaggs, William Henry. **The Southern Oligarchy.** NY: Devin-Adair; 1924. [$35.00]

Skarsten, M. O. **George Drouillard.** 1st ed. Glendale, CA: Clark; 1964. [$65.00]

Skelton, R. A. **The Vinland Map and the Tartar Relation.** New Haven: Yale UP; 1965. [$25.00]

Skeyhill, Thomas John. **Sergeant York: Last of the Long Hunters.** Philadelphia, Chicago: Winston; 1930. [$20.00]

Skiff, Frederick Woodward. **Adventures in Americana.** Portland, OR: Metropolitan; 1935. [x-lib., $40.00]

Skinner, Constance Lindsay. **Beaver, Kings and Cabins.** NY: Macmillan; 1933. [$25.00, Canadian] [$15.00]

Slafter, Edmund F. **John Checkley.** Boston: Prince Society; 1897. 2 v. [$175.00]

Slatkin, Regina Shoolman. **Enjoyment of Art in America.** 1st ed. Philadelphia: Lippincott; 1942. [$30.00]

Slattery, Charles Lewis. **Felix Reville Brunot.** NY: Longmans, Green; 1901. [$30.00]

Slaughter, Philip. **History of St. Mark's Parish, Culpeper County, Virginia.** Baltimore: Innes; 1877. [spine torn, bumped, and worn, $60.00]

Slick, Jonathan. see, Stephens, Ann Sophia.

Slocum, Charles Elihu. **Ohio Country between the Years 1783 and 1815.** NY: Putnam; 1910. [$40.00]

Small, Henry Beaumont. **The Canadian Handbook and Tourist's Guide.** Montreal: Longmoore; 1867. [$250.00]

Smalley, George Herbert. **My Adventures in Arizona.** Tucson: Arizona Pioneers' Hist. Soc.; 1966. [$25.00]

Smedes, Susan Dabney. **Memorials of a Southern Planter.** Baltimore: Cushings & Bailey; 1887. [$60.00]

Smedley, Robert Clemens. **History of the Underground Railroad in Chester and the Neighboring Counties of Pennsylvania.** Lancaster: Journal; 1883 [$135.00]

Smet, Pierre-Jean de. **Letters and Sketches.** Philadelphia: Fithian; 1843. [with folded plate, $1500.00] [$1750.00]

Smet, Pierre-Jean de. **Life, Letters and Travels.** NY: Harper; 1905. 4 v. [$650.00]

Smith, Aaron. **Atrocities of the Pirates.** London: Whittaker; 1824. [$250.00]

Smith, Abbot Emerson. **Colonists in Bondage.** Chapel Hill: U. of North Carolina; 1947. [$40.00]

Smith, Alice Ravenel Huger. **Charles Fraser.** NY: Sherman; 1924. [$100.00]

Smith, Alice Ravenel Huger. **Dwelling Houses of Charleston, South Carolina.** Philadelphia, London: Lippincott; 1917. [$75.00]

Smith, Alson Jesse. **Men against the Mountains.** NY: Day; 1965. [$17.50]

Smith, Amanda Berry. **Autobiography.** Chicago: Meyer; 1893. [$45.00]

Smith, Arthur Douglas Howden. **Old Fuss and Feathers.** 1st ed. NY: Greystone; 1937. [signed, $17.50]

Smith, Baxter Perry. **History of Dartmouth College.** Boston: Houghton Osgood; 1878. [$17.50]

Smith, Bradford. **Bradford of Plymouth.** 1st ed. Philadelphia: Lippincott; 1951. [$7.50]

Smith, C. Alphonso. **O. Henry Biography.** Garden City: Doubleday, Page; 1916. [$45.00] [1916 London ed., $17.50]

Smith, Chard Powers. **Yankees and God.** 1st ed. NY: Hermitage; 1954. [$12.50]

Smith, Charles W. **Journal of a Trip to California across the Continent.** NY: Cadmus; 1920. [$35.00] [$25.00]

Smith, Charles William. **Old Charleston.** Richmond: Dale; 1933. [rubbed, hinges weak, $75.00] [x-lib., hinges weak, signed, $75.00]

Smith, Cornelius Cole. **William Sanders Oury.** Tucson: U. of Arizona; 1967. [$20.00]

Smith, De Cost. **Martyrs of the Oblong and Little Nine.** Caldwell, ID: Caxton; 1948. [$20.00]

Smith, Edmund Ware. **The One-Eyed Poacher and the Maine Woods.** NY: Fell; 1955. [$15.00]

Smith, Edmund Ware. **Upriver and Down.** NY: Holt, Rinehart and Winston; 1965. [$18.00]

Smith, Ephraim Kirby. **To Mexico with Scott.** Cambridge: Harvard UP; 1917. [x-lib., $60.00] [$65.00]

Smith, Erwin Evans. **Life on the Texas Range.** 1st ed. Austin: U. of Texas; 1952. [in slipcase, $135.00] [$75.00]

Smith, Ethan. **Dissertation on the Prophecies Relative to Antichrist and the Last Times.** 2nd ed. Boston: Armstrong; 1814. [crude homemade binding, $100.00]

Smith, Ethel Sabin. **A Furrow Deep and True.** NY: Norton; 1964. [$10.00] [$12.50]

Smith, Frederick Dumont. **Summit of the World.** 4th ed. Chicago: Rand McNally; 1909. [$25.00]

Smith, George Albert. **The Rise, Progress, and Travels of the Church of Jesus Christ of Latter-Day Saints.** 2nd ed. Salt Lake City: Deseret News; 1872. [$150.00]

Smith, George Gilman. **Story of Georgia and the Georgia People, 1732 to 1860.** Macon: The Author; 1900. [$100.00]

Smith, George Washington. **When Lincoln Came to Egypt.** limited ed. Herrin, IL: Trovillion; 1940. [signed, $75.00]

Smith, Gustavus Woodson. **Confederate War Papers.** NY: Atlantic; 1884. [$65.00]

Smith, H. P. **History of the City of Buffalo and Erie County.** Syracuse: Mason; 1884. 2 v. [very worn, one cover detached, $65.00]

Smith, H. P. **Modern Babes in the Wood.** Hartford; Syracuse: Columbian Book; Gill; 1872. [$75.00]

Smith, Harry. **Fifty Years of Slavery in the United States of America.** Grand Rapids, MI: West Michigan Print.; 1891. [wraps soiled and chipped, $35.00]

Smith, Harry Worcester. **A Sporting Family of the Old South.** Albany: Lyon; 1936. [$60.00]

Smith, Helena Huntington. **War on Powder River.** NY: McGraw-Hill; 1966. [$35.00]

Smith, Henry Nash. **Virgin Land.** Cambridge: Harvard UP; 1950. [$25.00]

Smith, Herbert Huntington. **Brazil, the Amazons and the Coast.** NY: Scribner; 1879. [hinges cracked, $45.00]

Smith, Horace Wemyss. **Nuts for Future Historians to Crack.** Philadelphia: Smith; 1856. [$37.50] [$20.00]

Smith, Isaac M. **The Book of Mormon Vindicated.** 2nd ed. Independence, MO: Ensign; 1900. [$75.00]

Smith, John. **Advertisements for the Unexperienced Planters of New England.** Boston: Veazie; 1865. [$75.00]

Smith, John. **The Generall Historie of Virginia, New-England, and the Summer Isles.** London: World; 1966. [$75.00]

Smith, John. **True Travels, Adventures and Observations of.** Richmond: Franklin; 1819. 2 v. [joints starting, rebound, $255.00] [bound in 1 vol., $250.00]

Smith, John Jay. **American Historical and Literary Curiosities.** 5th ed. NY: Putnam; 1852. [$45.00]

Smith, John Thomas. **History of the Thirty-First Regiment of Indiana Volunteer Infantry in the War of the Rebellion.** Cincinnati: Western Methodist; 1900. [$85.00]

Smith, Joseph. **Book of Mormon.** 1st ed. Palmyra: Grandin; 1830. [rebacked, pages darkened, $6000.00]

Smith, Joseph. **Old Redstone, or, Historical Sketches of Western Presbyterianism.** Philadelphia: Lippincott, Grambo; 1854. [$65.00]

Smith, Joseph. **Visions of Joseph Smith the Seer.** Plano, IL: Reorganized Church of Jesus Christ of Latter Day Saints; 1879. [$35.00]

Smith, Joseph Aubin. **Reminiscences of Saratoga.** NY: Knickerbocker; 1897. [$40.00]

Smith, Joseph Frazer. **White Pillars.** NY: Helburn; 1941. [$30.00]

Smith, Joseph P. **History of the Republican Party in Ohio and Memoirs of Its Representative Supporters.** Chicago: Lewis; 1898. 2 v. [$40.00]

Smith, Joshua Hett. **An Authentic Narrative of the Causes Which Led to the Death of Major Andre.** London: Mathews and Leigh; 1808. [$200.00]

Smith, Julia. **Aaron Copland.** 1st ed. NY: Dutton; 1955. [$15.00]

Smith, Justin Harvey. **Annexation of Texas.** corrected ed. NY: Barnes & Noble; 1941. [$165.00]

Smith, Justin Harvey. **Our Struggle for the Fourteenth Colony.** NY, London: Putnam; 1907. 2 v. [$75.00, Canadian] [$85.00]

Smith, Justin Harvey. **The War with Mexico.** NY: Macmillan; 1919. 2 v. [$125.00]

Smith, Lawrence Breese. **Dude Ranches and Ponies.** NY: Coward-McCann; 1936. [$45.00]

Smith, Lawrence Breese. **The Sunlight Kid.** 1st ed. NY: Dutton; 1935. [ratty dj, $25.00]

Smith, Matthew Hale. **Bulls and Bears of New York with the Crisis of 1873.** Hartford: Burr; 1873. [$85.00]

Smith, Matthew Hale. **Sunshine and Shadow in New York.** Hartford: Burr; 1868. [$45.00]

Smith, Mortimer Brewster. **Life of Ole Bull.** Princeton: Princeton UP; 1947. [$12.50]

Smith, Page. **John Adams.** Garden City: Doubleday; 1962. 2 v. [$20.00]

Smith, Peter. **The Indian Doctor's Dispensatory.** Cincinnati: Browne and Looker; 1813. [$3500.00]

Smith, Ralph Dunning. **The History of Guilford, Connecticut from Its First Settlement in 1639.** Albany, NY: Munsell; 1877. [$75.00]

Smith, Randolph Wellford. **Benighted Mexico.** NY, London: Lane; 1916. [$20.00]

Smith, Rixey. **Carter Glass.** 1st ed. NY, Toronto: Longmans, Green; 1939. [$20.00]

Smith, S. Compton. **Chile Con Carne.** NY; Milwaukee: Miller & Curtis; Ford & Fairbanks; 1857. [$285.00]

Smith, Samuel. **History of the Colony of Nova-Caesaria, or New Jersey.** Burlington, NJ; Philadelphia: Parker; Hall; 1765. [$1000.00]

Smith, Theodore Clarke. **Life and Letters of James Abram Garfield.** New Haven: Yale UP; 1925. 2 v. [covers spotted, $40.00]

Smith, Thomas. **Journals of the Rev. Thomas Smith, and the Rev. Samuel Deane.** 2nd ed. Portland: Bailey; 1849. [$65.00]

Smith, Thomas Edward Vermilye. **The City of New York in the Year of Washington's Inauguration, 1789.** NY: Randolph; 1889. [$15.00]

Smith, William. **History of the Province of New York, from the First Discovery to the Year M.DCC.XXXII.** London: Wilcox; 1757. [$850.00] [1776 Almon ed., front hinge weak, $325.00] [1814 Albany, NY, ed., $165.00]

Smith, William L. G. **Life at the South, or, "Uncle Tom's Cabin" As It Is.** Buffalo: Derby; 1852. [$45.00]

Smith, William Robert Lee. **Story of the Cherokees.** Cleveland, TN: Church of God; 1928. [$45.00] [$35.00]

Smith, William Rudolph. **Incidents of a Journey from Pennsylvania to Wisconsin Territory.** limited ed. Chicago: Howes; 1927. [$135.00]

Smithsonian Institution. **Exploration of the Colorado River of the West and Its Tributaries.** Washington: USGPO; 1875. [lacks maps, $135.00]

Smithwick, Noah. **Evolution of a State.** Austin, TX: Gammel; 1900. [$225.00]

Smucker, Samuel M. **Arctic Explorations and Discoveries during the Nineteenth Century.** NY: Miller, Orton; 1857. [binding worn, $25.00]

Smucker, Samuel M. **Life and Times of Thomas Jefferson.** Philadelphia: Potter; 1857. [$35.00]

Smyth, Augustine T. **The Carolina Low-Country.** see, Society for the Preservation of Spirituals.

Smythe, William Ellsworth. **Conquest of Arid America.** NY, London: Harper; 1900. [$150.00]

Snively, William Daniel. **Satan's Ferryman.** NY: Ungar; 1968. [$25.00]

Snodgrass, Charles Albert. **History of Freemasonry in Tennessee, 1789-1943.** Nashville: Ambrose; 1944. [$25.00]

Snow, Edward Rowe. **Great Storms and Shipwrecks of New England.** 1st ed. Boston: Yankee; 1943. [$25.00]

Snow, Lorenzo. **The Italian Mission.** London: Aubrey; 1851. [$95.00]

Snow, William Parker. **Lee and His Generals.** NY: Richardson; 1867. [internal dampstaining, $50.00]

Snowden, James Henry. **The Truth about Mormonism.** NY: Doran; 1926. [lacks front endpaper, $20.00]

Snowden, Richard. **History of North and South America.** Philadelphia: Warner; 1819. 2 v. in 1. [$145.00]

Snowden, William H. **Some Old Historic Landmarks of Virginia and Maryland.** [4th-7th? ed.] Alexandria: Ramey; 1904. [wraps worn, $35.00]

Snyder, Ann E. **The Civil War from a Southern Standpoint.** Nashville: M. E. Church, South; 1890. [$40.00]

Snyder, John Francis. **Adam W. Snyder and His Period in Illinois History, 1817-1842.** 2nd ed. Virginia, IL: Needham; 1906. [inscribed, $17.50]

Snyder, Margaret Irene. **The Chosen Valley.** 1st ed. NY: Norton; 1948. [$17.50]

Sobel, Robert. **The Big Board.** NY: Free Press; 1965. [$15.00]

Social Anthropology of North American Tribes. Chicago: U. of Chicago; 1937. [$25.00]

Society for the Preservation of Spirituals. **The Carolina Low-Country.** NY: Macmillan; 1931. [bumped and soiled, spine torn, $25.00]

Society of Colonial Wars. New Jersey. **Historic Roadsides in New Jersey.** Plainfield: The Society; 1928. [$10.00]

Society of Friends. Philadelphia. **View of the Present State of the African Slave Trade.** Philadelphia: Brown; 1824. [$85.00]

Somerville, George B. **Lure of Long Beach.** Long Beach, NJ: Board of Trade; 1914. [$30.00]

Sommer, Charles Henry. **Quanah Parker.** St. Louis: [s.n.]; 1945. [$60.00]

Sommerville, Charles William. **History of Hopewell Presbyterian Church.** [Charlotte?, NC]: Hopewell Presbyterian Church; 1939. [bumped, stained, some ink notes, $35.00]

Sonne, Conway Ballantyne. **World of Wakara.** San Antonio: Naylor; 1962. [$15.00] [$23.50]

Sonnichsen, C. L. **Alias Billy the Kid.** Albuquerque: U. of New Mexico; 1955. [$30.50] [$25.00] [$35.00]

Sonnichsen, C. L. **Billy King's Tombstone.** 1st ed. Caldwell, ID: Caxton; 1942. [$50.00]

Sonnichsen, C. L. **Cowboys and Cattle Kings.** 1st ed. Norman: U. of Oklahoma; 1950. [$20.00] [inscribed, $55.00] [$30.00]

Sonnichsen, C. L. **The El Paso Salt War, 1877.** 1st ed. El Paso: Hertzog; 1961. [$37.50]

Sonnichsen, C. L. **I'll Die Before I'll Run.** NY: Harper; 1951. [$45.00]

Sonnichsen, C. L. **The Mescalero Apaches.** 1st ed. Norman: U. of Oklahoma; 1958. [$50.00] [x-lib., $22.50]

Sonnichsen, C. L. **Pass of the North.** 1st ed. El Paso: Texas Western; 1968. [fine, $45.00]

Sonnichsen, C. L. **Roy Bean.** NY: Macmillan; 1943. [$45.00]

Sonnichsen, C. L. **Ten Texas Feuds.** 1st ed. Albuquerque: U. of New Mexico; 1957. [dj chipped, $55.00]

Sonnichsen, C. L. **Tularosa.** NY: Devin-Adair; 1960. [$25.00]

Sorensen, Theodore C. **Kennedy.** NY: Harper & Row; 1965. [inscribed, limited edition, $100.00]

Sorin, Scota. **Blackbird: A Story of Mackinac Island.** Detroit: Citator; 1907. [$50.00]

Sorrel, Gilbert Moxley. **Recollections of a Confederate Staff Officer.** 2nd ed. NY: Neale; 1917. [$85.00]

Sosey, Frank Hanley. **Robert Devoy: A Tale of the Palmyra Massacre.** Palmyra, MO: Sosey; 1903. [$60.00]

Southern Pacific Company. **Autographs of Prominent Men of the Southern Confederacy.** Houston: Cumming; [190-?]. [$35.00]

Southern Sociological Congress 2d, Atlanta, 1913. **The South Mobilizing for Social Service.** Nashville: Southern Sociological Congress; 1913. [$45.00]

Southern, Terry. **Flash and Filigree.** NY: Coward-McCann; 1958. [chipped dj, $25.00]

Southwood, Marion. **"Beauty and Booty," the Watchword of New Orleans.** NY: Doolady; 1867. [bumped, rubbed, stained, $20.00]

Southworth, Alvan S. **Four Thousand Miles of African Travel.** NY; London: Baker, Pratt; Sampson, Low; 1875. [$85.00]

Sowell, Andrew Jackson. **Early Settlers and Indian Fighters of Southwest Texas.** Austin: Jones; 1900. [first issue, original binding, $850.00]

Sowell, Andrew Jackson. **Rangers and Pioneers of Texas.** San Antonio: Shepard; 1884. [$1000.00]

Spahr, Charles Barzillai. **America's Working People.** 1st ed. NY, London: Longmans, Green; 1900. [$25.00]

Spalding, Henry Harmon. **Diaries and Letters of Henry H. Spalding and Asa Bowen Smith Relating to the Nez Perce Mission, 1838-1842.** Glendale, CA: Clark; 1958. [signed by Drury, $40.00]

Spalding, John A. **From New England to the Pacific.** Hartford, CT: Case, Lockwood & Brainard; 1884. [worn, $65.00]

Spanish Explorers in the Southern United States, 1528-1543. NY: Scribner; 1907. [$150.00]

Sparks, Jared. **Correspondence of the American Revolution.** Boston: Little, Brown; 1853. 4 v. [$100.00]

Sparks, Jared. **Life of George Washington.** Boston: Andrews; 1839. [text water stained, spine cracked, $45.00] [1856 NY imprint, $25.00]

Sparks, Jared. **Life of Gouverneur Morris.** Boston: Gray & Bowen; 1832. 3 v. [re-spined, $75.00]

Sparks, Jared. **Life of John Ledyard.** Cambridge; NY: Hilliard and Brown; Carvill; 1828. [$385.00]

Sparks, William. **The Apache Kid, a Bear Fight, and Other True Stories of the Old West.** Los Angeles: Skelton; 1926. [$40.00]

Speare, Eva Augusta. **Colonial Meeting-Houses of New Hampshire.** Littleton: Courier; 1938. [$40.00]

Spears, John Randolph. **American Slave Trade.** NY: Scribner's; 1901, c1900. [$50.00]

Spears, John Randolph. **Illustrated Sketches of Death Valley and Other Borax Deserts of the Pacific Coast.** Chicago, NY: McNally; 1892. [$225.00]

Spears, Raymond S. **A Trip on the Great Lakes.** Columbus, OH: Harding; 1913. [covers stained, $40.00]

Speck, Frank Gouldsmith. **Cherokee Dance and Drama.** Berkeley: U. of California; 1951. [$25.00]

Speck, Frank Gouldsmith. **Naskapi, the Savage Hunters of the Labrador Peninsula.** 1st ed. Norman: U. of Oklahoma; 1935. [$150.00] [rebound, $30.00]

Speck, Frank Gouldsmith. **Study of the Delaware Indian Big House Ceremony.** Harrisburg: Pennsylvania Historical Commission; 1931. [$22.50]

Speck, Gordon. **Northwest Explorations.** Portland, OR: Binfords & Mort; 1954. [$25.00]

Speer, Marion Artemus. **Western Trails.** Huntington Beach, CA: News; 1931. [$50.00]

Speer, William. **The Oldest and the Newest Empire.** Hartford, CT: Scranton; 1870. [some wear, $65.00]

Speer, William S. **Encyclopedia of the New West.** see, title.

Spell, Lota May. **Music in Texas.** Austin: [s.n.]; 1936. [$125.00] [$95.00]

Spence, Clark C. **British Investments and the American Mining Frontier, 1860-1901.** Ithaca: Cornell UP; 1958. [$30.00]

Spence, James Mudie. **The Land of Bolivar.** London: Low, Marston, Searle & Rivington; 1878. 2 v. [$60.00]

Spence, Lewis. **Mexico of the Mexicans.** London, NY: Pitman; 1918. [spine darkened, $20.00]

Spence, Thomas. **Manitoba, and the North-West of the Dominion.** Toronto: Hunter, Rose; 1871. [$175.00]

Spencer, Ambrose. **Narrative of Andersonville.** NY: Harper; 1866. [$50.00]

Spencer, Bella Zilfa. **Tried and True.** Springfield, MA: Holland; 1873. [$35.00]

Spencer, Betty Goodwin. **The Big Blowup.** Caldwell, ID: Caxton; 1956. [$7.50]

Spencer, Clarissa Young. **One Who Was Valiant.** Caldwell, ID: Caxton; 1940. [chipped dj, $45.00]

Spencer, Cornelia. **The Last Ninety Days of the War in North Carolina.** NY: Watchman; 1866. [silverfished and stained, $100.00]

Spencer, Elma Dill. **Gold Country, 1828-1858.** San Antonio: Naylor; 1958. [$25.00]

Spencer, Elma Dill. **Green Russell and Gold.** Austin: U. of Texas; 1966. [$18.00]

Spencer, Ichabod Smith. **Fugitive Slave Law.** NY: Dodd; 1850. [$135.00]

Spicer, Edward Holland. **Pascua.** Chicago: U. of Chicago; 1940. [$65.00]

Spier, Leslie. **Yuman Tribes of the Gila River.** Chicago: U. of Chicago; 1933. [$65.00]

Spiller, Robert Ernest. **The Oblique Light.** NY: Macmillan; 1968. [$12.50]

Spinka, Matthew. **History of Illinois Congregational and Christian Churches.** Chicago: Congregational and Christian Conference of Illinois; 1944. [$20.00]

Spiro, Edward. **Baron of Arizona.** NY: Day; 1967. [$12.50]

Splawn, Andrew Jackson. **Ka-Mi-Akin, Last Hero of the Yakimas.** Yakima, WA: [s.n.]; 1958, c1944. [$25.00]

Splitstone, Fred John. **Orcas.** Sedro-Woolley, WA: Courier-Times; 1946. [$15.00]

Spokesfield, Walter Earnest. **History of Wells County, North Dakota, and Its Pioneers.** Valley City, ND: [s.n.]; 1929. [$175.00]

Spooner, Ruth Hopkins. **Lasell's First Century.** Boston: Abbey; 1951. [$12.50]

Spooner, Walter Whipple. **The Back-Woodsman.** Cincinnati: Dibble; 1883. [covers soiled, $65.00]

Spotsylvania Co., VA. **Spotsylvania County Records, 1721-1800.** Baltimore: Southern; 1955. [bumped, sunned, some underlining, $25.00]

Sprague, John Titcomb. **The Treachery in Texas.** NY: NY Hist. Soc.; 1862. [$125.00]

Sprague, Marshall. **A Gallery of Dudes.** 1st ed. Boston: Little, Brown; 1967, c1966. [$30.00]

Sprague, Marshall. **The Great Gates.** 1st ed. Boston: Little, Brown; 1964. [x-lib., $12.50]

Sprague, Marshall. **Massacre.** 1st ed. Boston: Little, Brown; 1957. [$33.00] [dj worn and chipped, $28.00]

Sprague, Marshall. **Money Mountain.** Boston: Little, Brown; 1954, c1953. [$15.00]

Spratling, William Philip. **Old Plantation Houses in Louisiana.** NY; New Orleans: Helburn; Pelican; 1927. [bumped, worn, stained, silverfished, $20.00]

Sprengel, Matthias Christian. **Geschichte der Revolution von Nord-Amerika.** Frankentahl: Gegelische; 1788. [$40.00]

Spring, Agnes Wright. **Bloomer Girl on Pike's Peak, 1858.** limited ed. Denver: Public Library; 1949. [$25.00]

Spring, Agnes Wright. **Caspar Collins.** NY: Columbia UP; 1927. [$50.00] [$80.00]

Spring, Agnes Wright. **William Chapin Deming of Wyoming.** limited ed. Glendale, CA: Clark; 1944. [$50.00] [$60.00]

Spring, Lindley. **The Negro at Home.** NY: The Author; 1868. [$50.00]

Sprunt, James. **Derelicts.** Wilmington, NC: [s.n.]; 1920. [x-lib., $100.00]

Spurr, Howard W. **Paul Revere Album.** 6th ed. Boston: Spurr Coffee; 1904. [$17.50]

Spurzheim, J. G. **Phrenology in Connection with the Study of Physiognomy.** 1st American ed. Boston: Marsh, Capen & Lyon; 1833. [x-lib., $95.00]

Squier, Ephraim George. **Honduras.** London: Trubner; 1870. [$65.00]

Squier, Ephraim George. **Nicaragua.** NY: Appleton; 1852. 2 v. [$300.00]

Squier, Ephraim George. **Peru.** NY: Harper; 1877. [$175.00]

Squier, Ephraim G. **Waikna.** London: Low; 1855. [$100.00]

Squier, Louise Smith. **Sketches of Southern Scenes.** NY: Pratt; 1885. [bumped, rubbed, and worn, $45.00]

Squire, Belle. **Woman Movement in America.** Chicago: McClurg; 1911. [$47.50]

Squires, William Henry Tappey. **Days of Yester-Year in Colony and Commonwealth.** limited, signed ed. Portsmouth, VA: Printcraft; 1928. [$45.00] [$50.00]

Squires, William Henry Tappey. **Through Centuries Three.** limited, signed ed. Portsmouth, VA: Printcraft; 1929. [$45.00]

Squires, William Henry Tappey. **Unleashed at Long Last.** 1st ed. Portsmouth, VA: Printcraft; 1939. [$30.00]

St. John de Crevecoeur, J. Hector. **Letters from an American Farmer.** London: Davies; 1782. [$750.00]

St. John de Crevecoeur, J. Hector. **Lettres d'un Cultivateur Americain.** Paris: Cuchet; 1784. 2 v. [$775.00]

St. John de Crevecoeur, J. Hector. **Sketches of Eighteenth Century America.** New Haven: Yale UP; 1925. [$45.00]

St. John de Crevecoeur, J. Hector. **Voyage dans la Haute Pensylvanie et dans l' Etat de New-York.** Paris: Maradan; 1801. 3 v. [$750.00]

Stacey, May Humphreys. **Uncle Sam's Camels.** Cambridge: Harvard UP; 1929. [$100.00] [$80.00] [$75.00]

Stackpole, Edouard A. **Sea-Hunters.** 1st ed. Philadelphia: Lippincott; 1953. [$30.00]

Stackpole, Edward J. **Chancellorsville; Lee's Greatest Battle.** 1st ed. Harrisburg, PA: Stackpole; 1958. [$20.00]

Stackpole, Edward J. **Sheridan in the Shenandoah.** 1st ed. Harrisburg, PA: Stackpole; 1961. [$35.00]

Stackpole, Everett Schermerhorn. **Old Kittery and Her Families.** Lewiston, ME: Journal; 1903. [$90.00]

Stafford, Jean. **A Mother in History.** NY: Farrar, Straus and Giroux; 1966. [$25.00]

Staley, Eugene. **History of the Illinois State Federation of Labor.** Chicago: U. of Chicago; 1930. [$25.00]

Stallings, Laurence. **The Doughboys.** 1st ed. NY: Harper & Row; 1963. [$8.50]

Stallman, R. W. **Stephen Crane.** NY: Braziller; 1968. [$15.00]

Stanard, Mary Mann. **Colonial Virginia.** Philadelphia, London: Lippincott; 1917. [$60.00]

Stanard, Mary Mann. **Story of Bacon's Rebellion.** NY: Neale; 1907. [$30.00]

Stanard, Mary Mann. **Story of Virginia's First Century.** Philadelphia, London: Lippincott; 1928. [$45.00]

Standing Bear, Luther. **Land of the Spotted Eagle.** Boston, NY: Houghton Mifflin; 1933. [$30.00]

Standing Bear, Luther. **My People the Sioux.** Boston: Houghton Mifflin; 1928. [1st printing, $45.00]

Stanger, Frank Merriman. **South from San Francisco.** San Mateo: County Hist. Assn.; 1963. [signed, $25.00]

Stanley, Clark. **Life and Adventures of the American Cow-Boy.** Providence: Stanley; 1897. [very stained, $275.00]

Stanley, Edwin James. **Life of Rev. L. B. Stateler.** Nashville: M.E. Church, South; 1907. [$250.00] [1916 rev. ed., $50.00]

Stanley, Edwin James. **Rambles in Wonderland.** NY: Appleton; 1878. [$100.00]

Stanley, F. **Apaches of New Mexico, 1540-1940.** Pampa, TX: Pampa Print Shop; 1962. [signed, $75.00] [presentation, $45.00]

Stanley, F. **Civil War in New Mexico.** Denver: World; 1960. [presentation, $65.00]

Stanley, F. **Clay Allison.** Denver: World; 1956. [$95.00]

Stanley, F. **Dave Rudabaugh.** Denver: World; 1961. [signed, $37.50] [$45.00]

Stanley, F. **Desperadoes of New Mexico.** Denver: World; 1953. [presentation, $65.00] [$75.00]

Stanley, F. **Fort Union.** Denver: World; 1953. [dj badly chipped, $65.00]

Stanley, F. **Ike Stockton.** limited, signed ed. Denver: World; 1959. [$37.50]

Stanley, F. **Jim Courtright.** limited, signed ed. Denver: World; 1957. [$45.00] [$75.00]

Stanley, F. **The Las Vegas Story (New Mexico).** Denver: World; 1951. [presentation, $150.00]

Stanley, F. **No Tears for Black Jack Ketchum.** Rotan, TX: Stanley; 1958. [signed, $35.00] [1958 Denver ed., limited and signed, $75.00]

Stanley, F. **Socorro, the Oasis.** Denver: World; 1950. [presentation, $150.00]

Stanley, Reva. **Biography of Parley P. Pratt.** Caldwell, ID: Caxton; 1937. [$40.00]

Stansbery, Lon R. **The Passing of 3-D Ranch.** Tulsa: Henry; [1928?]. [$250.00]

Stansbury, Charles Frederick. **Lake of the Great Dismal.** NY: Boni; 1925. [$50.00]

Stansbury, Howard. **Exploration and Survey of the Valley of the Great Salt Lake.** see, United States. Army. Corps of Topographical Engineers.

Stanton, Daniel. **Journal of the Life, Travels, and Gospel Labours, of a Faithful Minister of Jesus Christ.** Philadelphia: Crukshank; 1772. [x-lib., $225.00]

Stanton, Gerrit Smith. **When the Wildwood Was in Flower.** NY: Ogilvie; 1909. [$85.00]

Stanwell-Fletcher, Theodora Morris. **The Tundra World.** 1st ed. Boston: Little, Brown; 1952. [$8.00]

Staples, Thomas Starling. **Reconstruction in Arkansas.** NY: Longmans; 1923. [$50.00]

Staples, William Read. **Rhode Island in the Continental Congress.** Providence: Providence Press; 1870. [$45.00] [$75.00]

Stapleton, Ammon. **Memorials of the Huguenots in America.** Carlisle, PA: Huguenot; 1901. [$75.00]

Stapleton, Isaac. **Moonshiners in Arkansas.** 1st ed. Independence, MO: Lackey; 1948. [$100.00]

Stapp, William Preston. **Prisoners of Perote.** Philadelphia: Zieber; 1845. [$1200.00]

Starbuck, Alexander. **History of the American Whale Fishery.** NY: Argosy; 1964. 2 v. [$60.00]

Stark, James Henry. **Loyalists of Massachusetts and the Other Side of the American Revolution.** Boston: Stark; 1910. [$95.00] [$75.00]

Starkey, Marion Lena. **The Cherokee Nation.** 1st ed. NY: Knopf; 1946. [$35.00] [$25.00]

Starkey, Marion Lena. **The Devil in Massachusetts.** 1st ed. NY: Knopf; 1950. [$10.00]

Starr, Emmet. **History of the Cherokee Indians and Their Legends and Folk Lore.** Oklahoma City: Warden; 1921. [$225.00]

Starrett, Agnes Lynch. **Through One Hundred and Fifty Years.** Pittsburgh: U. of Pittsburgh; 1937. [$17.50]

State University of New York at Albany. **Historical Sketch of the State Normal College at Albany.** Albany: Brandow; [1894?]. [$25.00]

Stead, W. T. **If Christ Came to Chicago.** Chicago: Laird & Lee; 1894. [wraps worn, $75.00]

Stearns, Amanda Akin. **The Lady Nurse of Ward E.** NY: Baker & Taylor; 1909. [hinges weak, $70.00]

Steckmesser, Kent Ladd. **The Western Hero in History and Legend.** 1st ed. Norman: U. of Oklahoma; 1965. [$35.00] [2nd printing, $25.00]

Stedman, Ebenezer Hiram. **Bluegrass Craftsman.** Lexington: U. of Kentucky; 1959. [$17.50]

Stedman, John Gabriel. **Narrative of a Five Years' Expedition against the Revolted Negroes of Surinam.** Barre, MA: Imprint Society; 1971. 2 v. [$75.00]

Stedman, John W. **Norwich Jubilee.** Norwich, CT: Stedman; 1859. [$30.00]

Steele, David McConnell. **Going Abroad Overland.** NY, London: Putnam; 1917. [$35.00]

Steele, David McConnell. **Vacation Journeys East and West.** NY, London: Putnam; 1918. [$30.00]

Steele, James. **Old California Days.** Chicago: Belford-Clarke; 1889. [soiled, $40.00]

Steele, James William. **Frontier Army Sketches.** Chicago: Jansen, McClurg; 1883. [$125.00]

Steele, John Washington. **Coal Oil Johnny.** Franklin, PA: [s.n.]; 1902. [shabby, $30.00]

Steele, Mathew Forney. **American Campaigns.** Washington: U. S. Infantry Assn.; 1922. 2 v. [$47.00] [$55.00]

Steele, Oliver Gray. **Book of Niagara Falls.** see, Parsons, Horatio Adams.

Steele, Zadock. **Indian Captive.** Woodstock, VT: Elm Tree; 1934. [$45.00]

Steell, Willis. **Benjamin Franklin of Paris, 1776-1785.** NY: Minton, Balch; 1928. [$30.00]

Stefansson, Evelyn. **Here Is Alaska.** statehood ed. NY: Scribner; 1959. [$10.00]

Stefansson, Vilhjalmur. **My Life with the Eskimos.** abridged ed. NY: Macmillan; 1927. [$18.00]

Stefansson, Vilhjalmur. **Northward Course of Empire.** NY: Harcourt, Brace; 1922. [presentation, $35.00]

Stefansson, Vilhjalmur. **Northwest to Fortune.** 1st ed. NY: Duell, Sloan and Pearce; 1958. [$25.00]

Stegner, Wallace Earle. **The Big Rock Candy Mountain.** 1st ed. NY: Duell, Sloan and Pearce; 1943. [$25.00]

Stegner, Wallace Earle. **The Gathering of Zion.** 1st ed. NY: McGraw-Hill; 1964. [$30.00]

Stegner, Wallace Earle. **The Potter's House.** limited ed. Muscatine, IA: Prairie Press; 1938. [$300.00]

Stegner, Wallace Earle. **The Preacher and the Slave.** Boston: Houghton Mifflin; 1950. [$17.50]

Stegner, Wallace Earle. **Wolf Willow.** NY: Viking; 1962. [$30.00] [$35.00]

Steichen, Edward. **The Blue Ghost.** 1st ed. NY: Harcourt, Brace; 1947. [$125.00]

Stein, Gertrude. **Everybody's Autobiography.** NY: Random; 1937. [dj "fair," $165.00]

Stein, Gertrude. **Four Saints in Three Acts.** NY: Random; 1934. [$200.00]

Stein, Gertrude. **How to Write.** 1st ed. Paris: Plain Edition; 1931. [$165.00]

Stein, Leon. **The Triangle Fire.** 1st ed. Philadelphia: Lippincott; 1962. [$20.00]

Steinbeck, John. **Bombs Away.** 1st ed. NY: Viking; 1942. [$50.00]

Steinbeck, John. **Cup of Gold.** 1st ed. NY: McBride; 1929. [covers soiled, tape marks on endpapers, $900.00]

Steinbeck, John. **East of Eden.** 1st ed. NY: Viking; 1952. [dj repaired, $75.00]

Steinbeck, John. **Grapes of Wrath.** NY: Viking Press; 1939. [1st issue, dj chipped, $350.00]

Steinbeck, John. **The Log from the Sea of Cortez.** NY: Viking; 1951. [$100.00]

Steinbeck, John. **Of Mice and Men.** NY: Covici-Friede; 1937. [chipped dj, 1st state, $150.00]

Steinbeck, John. **The Moon Is Down.** 1st ed. NY: Viking; 1942. [frayed dj, $37.50]

Steinbeck, John. **The Red Pony.** signed limited ed. NY: Covici-Friede; 1937. [almost fine, $500.00]

Steinbeck, John. **Sea of Cortez.** NY: Viking; 1941. [dj worn, $225.00]

Steiner, Bernard Christian. **Beginnings of Maryland, 1631-1639.** Baltimore: Hopkins; 1903. [x-lib., $45.00]

Steiner, Paul E. **Disease in the Civil War.** Springfield, IL: Thomas; 1968. [$50.00]

Steinmetz, Rollin C. **Vanishing Crafts and Their Craftsmen.** New Brunswick, NJ: Rutgers UP; 1959. [$55.00]

Stelle, James Parish. **The Gunsmith's Manual.** NY: Excelsior; 1883. [$165.00]

Stellman, Louis John. **Sam Brannan.** 1st ed. NY: Exposition; 1953. [$15.00]

Stenhouse, Fanny. **Expose of Polygamy in Utah.** 2nd ed. NY: American News; 1872. [rebound, $25.00]

Stenhouse, Fanny. **Tell It All.** Hartford, CT: Worthington; 1874. [hinges cracked, backstrip chipped, $39.50]

Stenhouse, Thomas B. H. **The Rocky Mountain Saints.** Salt Lake City: Shepard; 1904. [$69.50]

Stephens, Alexander Hamilton. **Recollections of.** NY: Doubleday, Page; 1910. [$35.00] [$45.00]

Stephens, Ann Sophia. **High Life in New York.** London: How; 1844. 2 v. [$40.00]

Stephens, Henry. **South American Travels.** NY: Knickerbocker; 1915. [$20.00]

Stephens, John Lloyd. **Incidents of Travel in Central America, Chiapas, and Yucatan.** NY: Harper; 1841. 2 v. [elegantly rebound, $650.00] [$325.00] [$450.00] [1843 issue, $750.00]

Stephens, John Vant. **Causes Leading to the Organization of the Cumberland Presbyterian Church.** Nashville: Cumberland Presbyterian; 1898. [x-lib., pencil underlining, $20.00]

Stephens, Robert W. **Walter Durbin.** Clarendon, TX: Clarendon Press; 1970. [$45.00]

Stephenson, Nathaniel Wright. **Texas and the Mexican War.** New Haven: Yale UP; 1921. [$45.00] [$25.00]

Stephenson, Orlando Worth. **Ann Arbor, the First Hundred Years.** Ann Arbor, MI: Chamber of Commerce; 1927. [$37.50]

Stephenson, Terry E. **Caminos Viejos.** Santa Ana, CA: Santa Ana High School and Junior College; 1930. [$200.00]

Sterling, George. **Yosemite.** San Francisco: Robertson; 1916. [$65.00]

Stern, Philip Van Doren. **The Man Who Killed Lincoln.** NY: Random; 1939. [$14.50] [$15.00]

Stern, Philip Van Doren. **Prologue to Sumter.** Bloomington: Indiana UP; 1961. [$20.00]

Stern, Philip Van Doren. **Secret Missions of the Civil War.** NY: Bonanza; c1959. [$12.00]

Stern, Philip Van Doren. **Tin Lizzie.** NY: Simon and Schuster; 1955. [$15.00]

Stern, Susan. **With the Weathermen.** 1st ed. NY: Doubleday; 1975. [$15.00]

Stevens, Charles McClellan. **Lucky Ten Bar of Paradise Valley.** Chicago: Rhodes and McClure; 1900. [$100.00]

Stevens, George E. **City of Cincinnati.** Cincinnati: Blanchard; 1869. [sunned, $250.00]

Stevens, James Wilson. **An Historical and Geographical Account of Algiers.** Philadelphia: Hogan & M'Elroy; 1797. [$650.00]

Stevens, John H. **Personal Recollections of Minnesota and Its People.** Minneapolis: Tribune; 1890. [$75.00]

Stevens, Lewis Townsend. **History of Cape May County, New Jersey.** Cape May City: Stevens; 1897. [$135.00]

Stevens, Wallace. **The Man with the Blue Guitar, Including Ideas of Order.** 1st combined ed. NY: Knopf; 1952. [frayed dj, $200.00]

Stevens, William Bacon. **History of Georgia.** NY: Appleton; 1847-1859. 2 v. [$350.00] [x-lib., spine missing, front covers hanging, offered "as is," $125.00]

Stevens, William Burnham. **History of the Fiftieth Regiment of Infantry, Massachusetts Volunteer Militia.** Boston: Griffith-Stillings; 1907. [$70.00]

Stevens, William Oliver. **Pistols at Ten Paces.** Boston: Houghton Mifflin; 1940. [$28.50]

Stevenson, Charles S. **We Met at Camelback!** 1st ed. Scottsdale: Arizona Desert; 1968. [$15.00]

Stevenson, R. Randolph. **The Southern Side; or, Andersonville Prison.** Baltimore: Turnbull; 1876. [$130.00]

Stevenson, William Bennet. **Historical and Descriptive Narrative of Twenty Years' Residence in South America.** London: Hurst, Robinson; 1825. 3 v. [rebound, $250.00]

Stevenson, William G. **Thirteen Months in the Rebel Army.** NY: Barnes & Burr; 1862. [$75.00] [1959 Barnes ed., $35.00]

Steward, Austin. **Twenty-Two Years a Slave, and Forty Years a Freeman.** 2nd ed. Rochester, NY: Allings & Cory; 1859. [loose, worn, bumped, spine chipped, $15.00]

Stewart, Charles West. **John Paul Jones Commemoration at Annapolis, April 24, 1906.** Washington: USGPO; 1907. [$30.00] [$8.00]

Stewart, Donald M. **Frontier Port.** Los Angeles: Ritchie; 1965. [$10.00]

Stewart, Edgar Irving. **Custer's Luck.** 1st ed. Norman: U. of Oklahoma; 1955. [$50.00]

Stewart, Edgar Irving. **Penny-an-Acre Empire in the West.** 1st ed. Norman: U. of Oklahoma; 1968. [$25.00]

Stewart, Elinore. **Letters of a Woman Homesteader.** Boston, NY: Houghton Mifflin; 1914. [$17.50]

Stewart, Frank H. **Indians of Southern New Jersey.** Woodbury, NJ: Gloucester County Hist. Soc.; 1932. [$20.00]

Stewart, George. **Canada under the Administration of the Earl of Dufferin.** Toronto: Rose-Belford; 1878. [$20.00, Canadian]

Stewart, George Rippey. **The California Trail.** 1st ed. NY: McGraw-Hill; 1962. [$18.00] [$25.00]

Stewart, George Rippey. **Doctor's Oral.** NY: Random; 1939. [$30.00]

Stewart, George Rippey. **East of the Giants.** NY: Holt; 1938. [$17.50] [$30.00]

Stewart, George Rippey. **Ordeal by Hunger.** NY: Holt; 1936. [$30.00]

Stewart, George Rippey. **Pickett's Charge.** Boston: Houghton Mifflin; 1959. [$35.00] [$45.00]

Stewart, George Rippey. **The Year of the Oath.** 1st ed. Garden City: Doubleday; 1950. [$20.00]

Stewart, Philemon. **Holy, Sacred, and Divine Roll and Book.** Canterbury, NH: United Society; 1843. [front hinge cracked, $225.00]

Stewart, Randall. **Nathaniel Hawthorne.** New Haven: Yale UP; 1948. [$15.00]

Stewart, Robert. **The American Farmer's Horse Book.** Cincinnati: Vent; 1867. [worn, front joint repaired, $50.00]

Stewart, William George Drummond. **Altowan.** NY: Harper; 1846. 2 v. [spines restored, $1750.00]

Stewart, William Henry. **Spirit of the South.** NY, Washington: Neale; 1908. [$75.00]

Stewart, William M. **Reminiscences of.** NY: Neale; 1908. [x-lib., $85.00] [$125.00]

Stick, David. **Fabulous Dare.** Kitty Hawk, NC: Dare Press; 1949. [signed, $30.00]

Stiefel, H. C. **Slices from a Long Loaf: Logbook of an Eventful Voyage.** Pittsburg, PA: Bissell; 1905. [$12.50]

Stiehl, Henry. **Life of a Frontier Builder.** 1st ed. Salt Lake City: Utah Print.; 1941. [$30.00]

Stiff, Edward. **The Texan Emigrant.** Cincinnati: Conclin; 1840. [rebound, lacks maps and plates, $850.00]

Stiles, Edward Holcomb. **Recollections and Sketches of Notable Lawyers and Public Men of Early Iowa.** Des Moines: Homestead; 1916. [$30.00]

Stiles, Ezra. **History of Three of the Judges of King Charles I.** Hartford: Babcock; 1794. [frontis missing, binding worn and torn, $50.00] [fine, $325.00]

Stiles, Henry Reed. **Bundling; Its Origin, Progress and Decline in America.** Albany, NY: Munsell; 1869. [$60.00] [1934 Book Collector's ed., $30.00]

Stiles, Robert. **Four Years under Marse Robert.** 3rd ed. NY: Neale; 1904. [silverfished, sunned, $25.00]

Still, William. **The Underground Rail Road.** Philadelphia: Porter & Coates; 1872. [$225.00] [rebound, $100.00]

Stillman, Jacob Davis Babcock. **The Horse in Motion as Shown by Instantaneous Photography.** Boston: Osgood; 1882. [$750.00]

Stillman, Jacob Davis Babcock. **Seeking the Golden Fleece.** San Francisco, NY: Roman; 1877. [$325.00]

Stillwell, Leander. **The Story of a Common Soldier.** 2nd ed. [Erie?, KS]: Hudson; 1920. [$75.00]

Stillwell, Lucille. **Born to Be a Statesman: John Cabell Breckinridge.** Caldwell, ID: Caxton; 1936. [$20.00]

Stilwell, Hart. **Border City.** 1st ed. Garden City: Doubleday, Doran; 1945. [$17.50]

Stilwell, Joseph Warren. **Stilwell Papers.** NY: Sloane; 1948. [$9.50]

Stimson, Henry Lewis. **On Active Service in Peace and War.** 1st ed. NY: Harper; 1948. [signed, $75.00]

Stimson, Hiram K. **From the Stage Coach to the Pulpit.** Saint Louis: Campbell; 1874. [spine worn, $15.00]

Stine, James Henry. **History of the Army of the Potomac.** Philadelphia: Rodgers; 1892. [$85.00]

Stine, Thomas Ostenson. **Scandinavians on the Pacific, Puget Sound.** [Seattle?: s.n.]; 1900. [$65.00]

Stock, Ralph. **Confessions of a Tenderfoot.** NY: Holt; 1914. [$50.00]

Stockbridge, Frank Parker. **Florida in the Making.** NY: De Bower; 1926. [$35.00]

Stockbridge, Frank Parker. **So This Is Florida.** Jacksonville, FL: Perry; 1938. [$25.00] [$12.50]

Stockwell, Elisha. **Private Elisha Stockwell, Jr., Sees the Civil War.** 1st ed. Norman: U. of Oklahoma; 1958. [$30.00]

Stoddard, Amos. **Sketches, Historical and Descriptive, of Louisiana.** Philadelphia: Carey; 1812. [$375.00]

Stoddard, Henry Luther. **Presidential Sweepstakes.** NY: Putnam; 1948. [$7.50]

Stoddard, Seneca Ray. **The Adirondacks.** 22nd ed. Glens Falls, NY: Stoddard; 1892. [x-lib., $15.00]

Stoke, Will E. **Episodes of Early Days in Central and Western Kansas.** Great Bend, KS: [s.n.]; 1926. [vol. 1 all published, $35.00]

Stokes, George W. **Deadwood Gold.** Yonkers-on-Hudson: World; 1926. [2nd printing, $15.00]

Stokes, Olivia Egleston Phelps. **Letters and Memories of Susan and Anna Bartlett Warner.** NY, London: Putnam; 1925. [dj worn, $20.00]

Stone, Edwin Winchester. **Rhode Island in the Rebellion.** Providence: Whitney; 1864. [presentation, $65.00]

Stone, Irving. **Clarence Darrow for the Defense.** 1st ed. Garden City: Doubleday, Doran; 1941. [$20.00]

Stone, Irving. **Men to Match My Mountains.** 1st ed. Garden City: Doubleday; 1956. [$14.00]

Stone, John A. **Put's Golden Songster.** San Francisco: Appleton; 1858. [$125.00]

Stone, Kate. **Brokenburn.** Baton Rouge: Louisiana State UP; 1955. [worn dj, $37.50]

Stone, William Alexis. **Tale of a Plain Man.** 2nd ed. Philadelphia: Winston; 1918. [$45.00]

Stone, William Leete. **Ballads and Poems Relating to the Burgoyne Campaign.** Albany: Munsell; 1893. [$75.00]

Stone, William Leete. **Life and Times of Red-Jacket, or Sa-Go-Ye-Wat-Ha.** NY, London: Wiley and Putnam; 1841. [$175.00] [dampstained, $40.00] [$275.00]

Stone, William Leete. **Life of Joseph Brant (Thayendenegea).** Buffalo, NY: Phinney; 1840, c1838. 2 v. [4th printing of 1st ed, corners bumped, $125.00]

Stone, William Leete. **Matthias and His Impostures.** 3rd ed. NY: Harper; 1835. [$175.00]

Stone, William Leete. **The Poetry and History of Wyoming.** 3rd ed. Albany: Munsell; 1864. [$38.00]

Stone, William Leete. **Uncas and Miantonomoh.** NY: Dayton & Newman; 1842. [$50.00]

Stone, William Leete. **Campaign of Lieut. Gen. John Burgoyne and the Expedition of Lieut. Col. Barry St. Leger.** Albany, NY: Munsell; 1877. [$60.00]

Stookey, Walter M. **Fatal Decision.** Salt Lake City: Deseret Book Co.; 1950. [$65.00]

Storey, Samuel. **To the Golden Land.** London: Scott; 1889. [$125.00]

Stork, William. **An Account of East-Florida.** London: Woodfall; 1766. [$3000.00]

Storm, Barry. **Thunder Gods Gold.** Tortilla Flat, AZ: Southwest; 1945. [presentation, $17.00]

Storrick, William C. **Battle of Gettysburg.** 8th ed. Harrisburg, PA: McFarland; 1947. [$9.00]

Storrick, William C. **Gettysburg; the Place, the Battles, the Outcome.** Harrisburg, PA: McFarland; 1932. [$30.00]

Storrs, Charles. **Storrs Family.** NY: Priv. Print.; 1886. [binding detached, worn, $35.00]

Story of Champ d'Asile as Told by Two of the Colonists. Dallas: Book Club of Texas; 1937. [$300.00]

Story Without an End. 1st ed. Boston: Francis; 1836. [shaken, $250.00]

Story, Thomas. **Journal of the Life of.** Newcastle upon Tyne: Thompson; 1747. [binding worn, $100.00]

Stout, Tom. **Montana, Its Story and Biography.** Chicago: American Historical Society; 1921. 2 v. [$150.00]

Stover, Elizabeth Matchett. **Son-of-a-Gun Stew.** Dallas: Southern Methodist UP; 1945. [$85.00]

Stover, John F. **Railroads of the South, 1865-1900.** Chapel Hill: U. of North Carolina; 1955. [x-lib., $12.00]

Stowe, Harriet Beecher. **Agnes of Sorrento.** 1st ed. Boston: Ticknor & Fields; 1862. [$40.00]

Stowe, Harriet Beecher. **Dred.** 1st ed. Boston: Sampson; 1856. 2 v. [$85.00] [$60.00]

Stowe, Harriet Beecher. **Key to Uncle Tom's Cabin.** London: Bosworth; 1853. [$75.00]

Stowe, Harriet Beecher. **Little Pussy Willow.** Boston: Houghton Mifflin; 1881. [bumped, spine worn, $45.00]

Stowe, Harriet Beecher. **Sunny Memories of Foreign Lands.** Boston; NY: Phillips, Sampson; Derby; 1854. 2 v. [$75.00]

Stowe, Harriet Beecher. **Uncle Tom's Cabin.** 1st ed. Boston: Jewett; 1852. 2 v. ["gift binding," spine chipped, corners bumped, $1500.00] [later issue, $125.00] [1852 London ed., $125.00]

Stowe, Harriet Beecher. **We and Our Neighbors.** NY: Ford; 1875. [near fine, $20.00]

Stowell, Fred W. **Ragtime Philosophy.** San Francisco: News; 1902. [$75.00]

Stowell, Myron R. **"Fort Frick," or the Siege of Homestead.** Pittsburg: Pittsburg Printing; 1893. [binding worn, shaken, soiled, $85.00] [$50.00]

Strahorn, Carrie Adell. **Fifteen Thousand Miles by Stage.** NY: Putnam; 1911. [$375.00]

Strahorn, Robert Edmund. **Resources and Attractions of Idaho Territory.** Boise City: Idaho Legislature; 1881. [$200.00]

Strahorn, Robert Edmund. **To the Rockies and Beyond.** Omaha: Omaha Republican; 1878. [x-lib., lacks map, $225.00]

Straight, Michael Whitney. **Carrington.** 1st ed. NY: Knopf; 1960. [$18.00]

Straley, W. **Pioneer Sketches, Nebraska and Texas.** Hico, TX: Hico Printing; 1915. [$35.00]

Strand, Paul. **Time in New England.** NY: Oxford UP; 1950. [$75.00]

Stranger's Guide in Philadelphia. Philadelphia: Lindsay & Blakiston; 1863. [$40.00]

Stratton, Chester R. **Thrilling Adventures in the Wilds of Africa.** 1st ed. [s.l.: s.n.; 19??]. [$25.00]

Stratton, Florence. **When the Storm God Rides.** NY: Scribner; 1936. [$25.00]

Stratton, Royal B. **Captivity of the Oatman Girls.** NY: Carlton & Porter; 1858. [$350.00]

Straube, Carl Frederick. **Rise and Fall of Harmony Society.** Pittsburgh: National Printing; 1911. [$17.00]

Strauss, Wallace Patrick. **Americans in Polynesia, 1783-1842.** East Lansing: Michigan State UP; 1963. [$16.00]

Street, George G. **Che! Wah! Wah! or, the Modern Montezumas in Mexico.** Rochester, NY: Andrews; 1883. [rebound, $400.00] [$900.00]

Street, Julian Leonard. **Abroad at Home.** NY: Century; 1914. [$20.00]

Street, Julian Leonard. **The Most Interesting American.** NY: Century; 1915. [$20.00]

Streeter, Floyd Benjamin. **Ben Thompson.** NY: Fell; 1957. [$18.00]

Streeter, Floyd Benjamin. **Prairie Trails & Cow Towns.** NY: Devin Adair; 1963. [$28.00]

Streeter, Sebastian Ferris. **Papers Relating to the Early History of Maryland.** Baltimore: Murphy; 1876. [x-lib., $10.00]

Stribling, Robert Mackey. **Gettysburg Campaign and Campaigns of 1864-1865 in Virginia.** Petersburg, VA: Franklin; 1905. [$75.00]

Strickland, Reba Carolyn. **Religion and the State in Georgia in the Eighteenth Century.** NY: Columbia UP; 1939. [$30.00]

Strickler, Theodore D. **When and Where We Met Each Other on Shore and Afloat.** Washington: National Tribune; 1899. [$55.00]

Strobel, P. A. **The Salzburgers and Their Descendants.** Baltimore: Kurtz; 1855. [$30.00] [1953 U. of Georgia ed., $45.00]

Strode, Hudson. **Jefferson Davis.** 1st ed. NY: Harcourt, Brace; 1955-64. 3 v. [$60.00]

Strong, George Templeton. **Diary of.** NY: Macmillan; 1952. 4 v. [$75.00]

Strong, Henry W. **My Frontier Days & Indian Fights on the Plains of Texas.** [s.l.: s.n.; 1926?]. [$55.00]

Strong, Moses McCure. **History of the Territory of Wisconsin, from 1836 to 1848.** Madison: Democrat; 1885. [$75.00]

Strong, Nathaniel T. **Appeal to the Christian Community.** NY: Clayton; 1841. [$175.00]

Strong, Robert Hale. **A Yankee Private's Civil War.** Chicago: Regnery; 1961. [$16.50]

Strong, William Emerson. **Canadian River Hunt.** 1st ed. Norman: U. of Oklahoma; 1960. [$45.00]

Strother, David Hunter. **Virginia Illustrated.** NY: Harper; 1857. [$175.00]

Strother, David Hunter. **Virginia Yankee in the Civil War.** Chapel Hill: U. of North Carolina; 1961. [$30.00] [$25.00]

Stroyer, Jacob. **My Life in the South.** Salem, MA: Observer; 1891. [$90.00]

Strubberg, Friedrich Armand. **The Backwoodsman.** see, Wraxall, Frederick Charles.

Stryker, Lloyd Paul. **Andrew Johnson.** NY: Macmillan; 1929. [$45.00] [later issue, $25.00]

Stryker, William Scudder. **Affair at Egg Harbor, New Jersey, October 15, 1778.** Trenton: Naar, Day & Naar; 1894. [$35.00]

Stryker, William Scudder. **Battle of Monmouth.** Princeton: Princeton UP; 1927. [$75.00]

Stryker, William Scudder. **Battles of Trenton and Princeton.** Boston: Houghton Mifflin; 1898. [$85.00]

Stuart, Addison A. **Iowa Colonels and Regiments.** Des Moines: Mills; 1865. [$150.00]

Stuart, Granville. **Forty Years on the Frontier.** 1st ed. Cleveland: Clark; 1925. 2 v. [$250.00]

Stuart, James. **Three Years in North America.** NY: Harper; 1833. 2 v. [rebound in one vol., $100.00]

Stuart, Merah Steven. **An Economic Detour.** 1st ed. NY: Malliet; 1940. [bumped, rubbed, sunned, hinges weak, $40.00]

Stuart, Robert. **Discovery of the Oregon Trail.** NY, London: Scribner; 1935. [$85.00]

Stuart, Ruth. **The River's Children.** NY: Century; 1904. [$12.50]

Stuart, Villiers. **Adventures amidst the Equatorial Forests and Rivers of South America.** London: Murray; 1891. [one plate missing, $125.00]

Stuart-Wortley, Emmeline. **Travels in the United States, etc.: During 1849 and 1850.** NY: Harper; 1851. [$200.00] [rebound, $50.00]

Stubbs, William Carter. **Hand-Book of Louisiana.** New Orleans: Picayune; 1895. [rebound, $75.00]

Sturge, Joseph. **A Visit to the United States in 1841.** London: Hamilton, Adams; 1842. [$125.00]

Sturge, Joseph. **The West Indies in 1837.** 2nd ed. London: Hamilton, Adams; 1838. [inscribed by Thomas Harvey, $285.00]

Sturgis, William. **The Oregon Question.** Boston: Jordan, Swift & Wiley; 1845. [$60.00]

Styles, John. **Life of David Brainerd.** 1st American ed. Boston: Armstrong; 1812. [$25.00]

Styron, Arthur. **Last of the Cocked Hats.** 1st ed. Norman: U. of Oklahoma; 1945. [binding soiled, $60.00]

Styron, William. **Lie Down in Darkness.** 1st ed. Indianapolis: Bobbs-Merrill; 1951. [dj sunned and worn, $95.00]

Styron, William. **Set This House on Fire.** NY: Random; 1960. [bumped, rubbed, dj torn, $25.00]

Sugranes, Eugene Joseph. **The Old San Gabriel Mission.** San Gabriel, CA: [s.n.]; 1909. [$25.00]

Sullins, David. **Recollections of an Old Man.** Bristol, TN: King; 1910. [shelf-cocked, $85.00]

Sullivan, Aloysius Michael. **Ballad of John Castner.** NY: Fine Editions; 1943. [$12.50]

Sullivan, Dulcie. **The LS Brand.** Austin: U. of Texas; 1968. [$50.00]

Sullivan, Edward Dean. **Benedict Arnold, Military Racketeer.** NY: Vanguard; 1932. [$20.00]

Sullivan, Edward Robert. **Rambles and Scrambles in North and South America.** London: Bentley; 1852. [$185.00]

Sullivan, John. **Letters and Papers of.** Concord: New Hampshire Hist. Soc.; 1930-39. 3 v. [$175.00]

Sullivan, Mark. **The Education of an American.** 1st ed. NY: Doubleday, Doran; 1938. [$10.00]

Sullivan, William. **The Public Men of the Revolution.** Philadelphia: Carey and Hart; 1847. [$50.00]

Summerfield, Charles. see, Arrington, Alfred W.

Summerhayes, Martha. **Vanished Arizona.** 2nd ed. Salem, MA: Salem Press; 1911. [$45.00]

Sumner, Charles. **The Barbarism of Slavery.** Washington: Buell & Blanchard; 1860. [$20.00]

Sumner, Charles. **Demands of Freedom.** Washington: Buell & Blanchard; 1855. [$25.00]

Sumner, Charles. **Last Three Speeches on Kansas and Freedom.** Boston: Higgins and Bradley; 1856. [$100.00]

Sumner, Charles. **Promises of the Declaration of Independence.** Boston: Ticknor & Fields; 1865. [$45.00]

Sumner, Charles. **Prophetic Voices Concerning America.** Boston; NY: Lee and Shepard; Lee, Shepard, and Dillingham; 1874. [$40.00]

Sumner, Charles. **Security and Reconciliation for the Future.** Boston: Rand & Avery; 1865. [$25.00]

Sumner, Charles. **War System of the Commonwealth of Nations.** Boston: American Peace Soc.; 1854. [$45.00]

Sunday, Billy. **Face to Face with Satan.** Knoxville: Prudential; 1923. [$10.00]

Sunder, John E. **Bill Sublette.** 1st ed. Norman: U. of Oklahoma; 1959. [$45.00]

Sunder, John E. **Fur Trade on the Upper Missouri, 1840-1865.** 1st ed. Norman: U. of Oklahoma; 1965. [$45.00]

Sunder, John E. **Joshua Pilcher.** 1st ed. Norman: U. of Oklahoma; 1968. [$20.00]

Sunderland, La Roy. **Anti Slavery Manual.** 2nd ed. NY: Piercy & Reed; 1837. [$65.00]

Surby, Richard W. **Grierson Raids, and Hatch's Sixty-Four Days March.** Chicago: Rounds and James; 1865. [$500.00]

Surrey, Nancy Maria. **Commerce of Louisiana during the French Regime, 1699-1763.** NY: Columbia UP; 1916. [$65.00]

Survivor of Two Wars: Biographical Sketch of Gen. Joseph A. Cooper. Knoxville: Bean; 1895. [$75.00]

Sutherland, William Alexander. **Out Where the West Be-Grins.** Las Cruces, NM: Southwest; 1942. [$27.00] [$30.00]

Sutley, Zachary Taylor. **The Last Frontier.** NY: Macmillan; 1930. [binding worn, $17.50] [$35.00]

Sutton, Ernest Venable. **A Life Worth Living.** 1st ed. Pasadena, CA: Trail's End; 1948. [$30.00]

Sutton, Fred Ellsworth. **Hands Up!** Indianapolis: Bobbs-Merrill; 1927. [$35.00]

Svedelius, Jacob Michael. **De Effectu Detect Americ in Europam.** Upsaliae: Edman; 1800-02. 2 v. [$50.00]

Svinin, Pavel Petrovich. **Picturesque United States of America, 1811, 1812, 1813.** NY: Rudge; 1930. [$50.00]

Swan, Howard. **Music in the Southwest, 1825-1950.** San Marino, CA: Huntington; 1952. [$25.00]

Swanberg, W. A. **First Blood.** NY: Scribner; 1957. [$10.00]

Swanberg, W. A. **Sickles the Incredible.** NY: Scribner; 1956. [$25.00]

Swanson, Neil Harmon. **The First Rebel.** NY: Farrar & Rinehart; 1937. [limited signed, $40.00]

Swartwout, Annie Fern. **Missie.** Blanchester, OH: Brown; 1947. [presentation, $37.50]

Swartzlow, Ruby Johnson. **Peter Lassen.** San Francisco: California Hist. Soc.; 1940. [$15.00]

Sweet, Alexander Edwin. **Humoristische Reise durch Texas von Galveston bis zum Rio Grande.** Jena: Costenoble; 1884. [rebound, $55.00]

Sweet, Alexander Edwin. **On a Mexican Mustang, through Texas.** Hartford, CT: Scranton; 1883. [$85.00]

Sweet, Alexander Edwin. **Sketches from "Texas Siftings."** NY: Texas Siftings; 1882. [$100.00]

Sweetman, Luke Decatur. **Back Trailing on Open Range.** Caldwell, ID: Caxton; 1951. [$45.00]

Sweetser, M. F. **King's Handbook of the United States.** Buffalo: King; 1891. [$50.00]

Swett, Charles. **Trip to British Honduras, and to San Pedro, Republic of Honduras.** New Orleans: Price Current; 1868. [$125.00]

Swift, Louis Franklin. **The Yankee of the Yards.** Chicago, NY, London: Shaw; 1927. [$45.00]

Swiggett, Howard. **Forgotten Leaders of the Revolution.** 1st ed. Garden City: Doubleday; 1955. [$17.50]

Swihart, Altman K. **Since Mrs. Eddy.** NY: Holt; 1931. [$17.50]

Swinton, William. **Campaigns of the Army of the Potomac.** NY: Richardson; 1866. [$75.00]

Swisher, Carl Brent. **Stephen J. Field.** Washington: Brookings; 1930. [$47.50]

Swisher, Jacob Armstrong. **The American Legion in Iowa, 1919-1929.** Iowa City: State Historical Society of Iowa; 1929. [x-lib., $20.00]

Swisher, James. **How I Know.** Cincinnati: The Author; 1880. [spine torn, $100.00]

Swisshelm, Jane Grey Cannon. **Crusader and Feminist.** Saint Paul: Minnesota Hist. Soc.; 1934. [spine faded, $15.00]

Sydnor, Charles S. **A Gentleman of the Old Natchez Region, Benjamin L.C. Wailes.** Durham: Duke UP; 1938. [$35.00]

Sylvester, Nathaniel Bartlett. **Historical Sketches of Northern New York and the Adirondack Wilderness.** Troy, NY: Young; 1877. [$90.00] [$35.00]

Symes, Lillian. **Rebel America.** NY, London: Harper; 1934. [$15.00]

Symonds, John. **Remarks upon an Essay, Intituled, the History of the Colonization of the Free States of Antiquity.** London: Nichols; 1778. [$400.00]

Symons, Thomas William. see, United States. Army. Corps of Engineers.

Syrett, Harold Coffin. **Interview in Weehawken.** 1st ed. Middletown, CT: Wesleyan UP; 1960. [$25.00]

Taft, Helen Herron. **Recollections of Full Years.** NY: Dodd, Mead; 1914. [$30.00]

Taft, Robert. **Artists and Illustrators of the Old West.** NY: Scribner; 1953. [$50.00]

Taft, William H. **Representative Government in the United States.** NY: New York UP; 1921. [$25.00]

Tait, Archibald Campbell. **Death of President Garfield.** London: Stevens; 1881. [spine chipped, covers soiled, $30.00]

Tait, Samuel W. **The Wildcatters.** Princeton: Princeton UP; 1946. [2nd printing, $35.00]

Talbert, Thomas B. **My Sixty Years in California.** Huntington Beach, CA: News; 1952. [$50.00]

Talbot, Edith Armstrong. **Samuel Chapman Armstrong.** NY: Doubleday, Page; 1904. [$22.50]

Talbot, Edward Allen. **Five Years' Residence in the Canadas.** London: Longman, Hurst, etc.; 1824. 2 v. [$325.00]

Taliaferro, Hardin E. **Carolina Humor.** Richmond: Dietz; 1938. [mildewed, dj chipped, $12.00]

Tallant, Robert. **Romantic New Orleanians.** 1st ed. NY: Dutton; 1950. [$17.50]

Talleyrand-Perigord, Charles Maurice de. **Memoir Concerning the Commercial Relations of the United States with England.** London: Longman, Hurst, etc.; 1806. [$150.00]

Tallmadge, Benjamin. **Memoir of.** NY: Holman; 1858. [$125.00] [1904 Gilliss imprint, $100.00]

Tallmadge, Frank. **Horseback Riding in and around Columbus, 1774-1924.** Columbus, OH: Riding Club; 1925. [$25.00]

Talmage, James Edward. **"The Book of Mormon"; an Account of Its Origin.** Salt Lake City: Deseret News; 1899. [$125.00]

Tannenbaum, Frank. **Slave and Citizen.** NY: Knopf; 1947, c1946. [$45.00]

Tanner, George C. **Fifty Years of Church Work in the Diocese of Minnesota, 1857-1907.** St. Paul: Pope; 1909. [$65.00]

Tanner, John. **Narrative of the Captivity and Adventures of.** NY: Carvill; 1830. [$850.00]

Tappan, Lewis. **Side-Light on Anglo-American Relations, 1839-1858.** Lancaster, PA: Assn. for the Study of Negro Life and History; 1927. [$40.00]

Taraval, Sigismundo. **The Indian Uprising in Lower California, 1734-1737.** Los Angeles: Quivira Society; 1931. [$125.00] [$150.00]

Tarbell, Ida M. **In the Footsteps of the Lincolns.** NY, London: Harper; 1924. [$50.00]

Tarbell, Ida M. **Life of Elbert H. Gary.** NY: Appleton; 1925. [$12.50] [$18.50]

Tarbox, Increase N. **Life of Israel Putnam.** Boston: Lockwood, Brooks; 1876. [$35.00]

Tardy, William Thomas. **Trials and Triumphs.** Marshall, TX: Tardy; 1919. [$45.00]

Targ, William. **The American West.** Cleveland, NY: World; 1946. [$25.00]

Tate, Allen. **Jefferson Davis: His Rise and Fall.** NY: Minton, Balch; 1929. [chipped dj, $45.00]

Tate, Allen. **Stonewall Jackson, the Good Soldier.** NY: Minton, Balch; 1928. [1st printing, $175.00] [2nd printing, $20.00]

Tatum, George B. **Penn's Great Town.** Philadelphia: U. of Pennsylvania; 1961. [$45.00]

Tatum, Lawrie. **Our Red Brothers and the Peace Policy of President Ulysses S. Grant.** Philadelphia: Winston; 1899. [some dampstaining, $85.00]

Taverner, Percy Algernon. **Birds of Western Canada.** Ottawa: Acland; 1926. [$50.00]

Tayler, Charles Benjamin. **Mark Wilton, the Merchant's Clerk.** NY: Stanford and Swords; 1848. [$45.00]

Taylor, Bayard. **At Home and Abroad (2nd series).** NY: Putnam; 1883, c1862. [spine worn, $35.00]

Taylor, Bayard. **Colorado: A Summer Trip.** NY: Putnam; 1867. [$65.00]

Taylor, Bayard. **Eldorado; or, Adventures in the Path of Empire.** NY; London: Putnam; Bentley; 1850. 2 v. [$385.00] [$450.00] [4th ed. 1854, $50.00] [1850 Bohn ed. in one vol., $125.00]

Taylor, Bayard. **Ximena.** 1st ed. Philadelphia: Hooker; 1844. [$200.00]

Taylor, Benjamin Cook. **Annals of the Classis of Bergen.** 3rd ed. NY: Reformed Protestant Dutch Church; 1857. [$125.00]

Taylor, Benjamin Franklin. **Between the Gates.** 8th ed. Chicago: Griggs; 1880, c1878. [$12.50] [$15.00]

Taylor, Benjamin Franklin. **Pictures of Life in Camp and Field.** Chicago: Griggs; 1875. [$40.00]

Taylor, Benjamin Franklin. **Summary-Savory.** Chicago: Griggs; 1879. [$40.00]

Taylor, C. B. **Universal History of the United States of America.** NY: Strong; 1834. [$25.00]

Taylor, Edward Livingston. **Ohio Indians and Other Writings.** Columbus, OH: Heer; 1909. [$45.00]

Taylor, Fitch Waterman. **The Broad Pennant.** 1st ed. NY: Leavitt, Trow; 1848. [covers rubbed, $75.00]

Taylor, James W. **History of the State of Ohio.** Cincinnati, Sandusky: Derby; 1854. [all published, $95.00]

Taylor, Joseph Henry. **Sketches of Frontier and Indian Life on the Upper Missouri and Great Plains.** Pottstown, PA: The Author; 1889. [$1000.00]

Taylor, Landon. **The Battlefield Reviewed.** Chicago: The Author; 1881. [$65.00]

Taylor, Mary Geraldine Guinness. **Peru; Its Story, People and Religion.** London: Morgan & Scott; 1909. [$17.50]

Taylor, Richard. **Destruction and Reconstruction.** NY: Appleton; 1879. [binding worn and soiled, $65.00] [1955 Appleton ed., $40.00]

Taylor, T. U. **Bill Longley and His Wild Career.** Bandera, TX: Frontier Times; [192-?]. [$85.00]

Taylor, Walter Herron. **Four Years with General Lee.** NY: Appleton; 1877. [rebacked, worn, $35.00] [$125.00]

Taylor, William. **California Life Illustrated.** NY: Carlton & Porter; 1858. [lacking Sacramento plate, $40.00] [1861 reissue, $47.50]

Teague, Charles Collins. **Fifty Years a Rancher.** 2nd ed. [s.l.]: California Fruit Growers Association; 1944. [$20.00]

Teeters, Negley King. **They Were in Prison.** Philadelphia, Chicago: Winston; 1937. [x-lib., $45.00]

Teetor, Henry B. **Past and Present of Mill Creek Valley.** Cincinnati: Cohen; 1882. [$65.00]

Temple, Edmond. **Travels in Various Parts of Peru Including a Year's Residence in Potosi.** London: Colburn and Bentley; 1830. 2 v. [$275.00]

Temple, Oliver Perry. **Notable Men of Tennessee from 1833 to 1875.** NY: Cosmopolitan; 1912. [x-lib., $65.00]

Tennessee Constitutional Convention. **Journal of the Proceedings.** Nashville: Jones, Purvis; 1870. [$65.00]

Tennessee Historical Quarterly. **Landmarks of Tennessee History.** Nashville: Tennessee Hist. Soc.; 1965. [$25.00]

Tenney, Horace Addison. **Memorial Record of the Fathers of Wisconsin.** Madison: Atwood; 1880. [$50.00]

Terral, Rufus. **The Missouri Valley.** New Haven: Yale UP; 1947. [$10.00]

Terrell, Charles Vernon. **The Terrells.** Austin: [Texas Heritage Foundation?]; 1948. [$90.00] [inscribed, worn dj, $80.00]

Terrell, John Upton. **Black Robe.** 1st ed. Garden City: Doubleday; 1964. [$18.00] [$12.50]

Terrell, John Upton. **Estevanico the Black.** Los Angeles: Westernlore; 1968. [$25.00]

Terrell, John Upton. **Faint the Trumpet Sounds.** 1st ed. NY: McKay; 1966. [$40.00] [$30.00]

Terrell, John Upton. **Furs by Astor.** NY: Morrow; 1963. [$12.50]

Terrell, John Upton. **Journey into Darkness.** NY: Morrow; 1962. [$20.00]

Terrell, John Upton. **Pueblo of the Hearts.** Palm Desert, CA: Best-West; 1966. [$10.00]

Terrell, John Upton. **Traders of the Western Morning.** Los Angeles: Southwest Museum; 1967. [$20.00]

Terrell, John Upton. **War for the Colorado River.** Glendale, CA: Clark; 1965. 2 v. [$50.00]

Terrell, John Upton. **Zebulon Pike.** NY: Weybright and Talley; 1968. [$15.00] [$25.00]

Terry, Marian Dickinson. **Old Inns of Connecticut.** see, National Society of the Colonial Dames of America.

Tevis, James Henry. **Arizona in the '50's.** Albuquerque: U. of New Mexico; 1954. [$30.00]

Texas Convention, 1861. **Journal of the Secession Convention of Texas, 1861.** Austin: Austin Printing; 1912. [$85.00]

Texas in 1840. NY: Allen; 1840. [$325.00]

Thacher, James. **Military Journal of the American Revolution.** Hartford, CT: Hurlbut, Williams; 1861. [hinges weak, $60.00]

Thackrah, Charles Turner. **Effects of the Principal Arts, Trades, and Professions.** Philadelphia: Porter; 1831. [2nd printing?, $225.00]

Tharp, Louise Hall. **Adventurous Alliance.** 1st ed. Boston: Little, Brown; 1959. [$12.50]

Thayer, Eli. **History of the Kansas Crusade.** NY: Harper; 1889. [x-lib., $35.00]

Thayer, Eli. **The New England Emigrant Aid Company.** Worcester, MA: Rice; 1887. [wraps chipped, $65.00]

Thayer, Emma. **Wild Flowers of the Rocky Mountains.** NY: Cassell; 1887. [$150.00]

Thayer, William Makepeace. **Marvels of the New West.** Norwich, CT: Bill; 1887. [edge wear, $75.00]

Thayer, William Makepeace. **The Printer Boy.** London: Hogg; 1861. [$15.00]

Thayer, William Roscoe. **Life and Letters of John Hay.** Boston, NY: Houghton Mifflin; 1915. 2 v. [$45.00]

Thayer, William Roscoe. **Theodore Roosevelt.** Boston, NY: Houghton Mifflin; 1919. [$30.00]

Thayer, William Sydney. **Osler and Other Papers.** Baltimore; London: Hopkins; Oxford UP; 1931. [$25.00]

Thenault, Georges. **Story of the Lafayette Escadrille.** Boston: Small, Maynard; 1921. [$85.00]

Thicknesse, Philip. **Memoirs and Anecdotes of.** Dublin: Jones; 1790. [$400.00]

Thoburn, Joseph Bradfield. **History of Oklahoma.** San Francisco: Doub; 1908. [$45.00]

Thomas, Addison Charles. **Roosevelt among the People.** Chicago: Walter; 1910. [$85.00]

Thomas, Alfred Barnaby. **After Coronado.** 1st ed. Norman: U. of Oklahoma; 1935. [dj repaired, $45.00]

Thomas, Alfred Barnaby. **Forgotten Frontiers.** Norman: U. of Oklahoma; 1932. [spine faded, $40.00] [1969 reissue, $15.00]

Thomas, Benjamin Platt. **Portrait for Posterity.** New Brunswick: Rutgers UP; 1947. [$35.00]

Thomas, Benjamin Platt. **Stanton.** 1st ed. NY: Knopf; 1962. [$16.00]

Thomas, Charles Marion. **Thomas Riley Marshall, Hoosier Statesman.** Oxford, OH: Mississippi Valley; 1939. [$45.00]

Thomas, David Yancey. **Arkansas in War and Reconstruction.** Little Rock: United Daughters of the Confederacy; 1926. [x-lib., $45.00] [binding worn and stained, $48.00]

Thomas, Dorothy Swaine. **Japanese American Evacuation and Resettlement: The Spoilage.** Berkeley: U. of California; 1946. [$35.00]

Thomas, Ebenezer Smith. **Reminiscences of the Last Sixty-Five Years.** Hartford: The Author; 1840. 2 v. [$95.00]

Thomas, Elbert Duncan. **Thomas Jefferson.** NY: Modern Age; 1942. [$12.50]

Thomas, Evangeline. **Footprints on the Frontier.** Westminster, MD: Newman; 1948. [$15.00]

Thomas, Jeannette Bell. **The Singin' Gatherin'.** complete ed. NY, Boston: Silver, Burdett; 1939. [covers soiled, $22.50]

Thomas, Jeannette Bell. **The Sun Shines Bright.** NY: Prentice-Hall; 1940. [$40.00]

Thomas, John J. **Fifty Years on the Rail.** NY: Knickerbocker; 1912. [hinges repaired, ink notes inside front cover, $20.00]

Thomas, Lately. **A Debonair Scoundrel.** 1st ed. NY: Holt, Rinehart and Winston; 1962. [$25.00]

Thomas, Lowell. **Old Gimlet Eye.** NY: Farrar & Rinehart; 1933. [$32.50]

Thomas, William Isaac. **The Polish Peasant in Europe and America.** 2nd ed. NY: Knopf; 1927. 2 v. [$65.00]

Thomas, William S. **Trails and Tramps in Alaska and Newfoundland.** NY, London: Putnam; 1913. [$75.00]

Thomason, John W. **Jeb Stuart.** NY, London: Scribner; 1930. [binding faded, $32.50] [$35.00] [$30.00]

Thome, James Armstrong. **Emancipation in the West Indies.** NY: American Anti-Slavery Soc.; 1838. [489 page issue, $125.00]

Thomlinson, Matthew H. **The Garrison of Fort Bliss, 1849-1916.** El Paso: Hertzog & Resler; 1945. [$65.00]

Thompson, Albert W. **They Were Open Range Days.** Denver: World; 1946. [$75.00]

Thompson, Charles Nebeker. **Sons of the Wilderness.** Indianiapolis: Indiana Hist. Soc.; 1937. [$20.00]

Thompson, Daniel Pierce. **Gaut Gurley.** 1st ed. Boston: Jewett; 1857. [$35.00]

Thompson, Daniel Pierce. **Green Mountain Boys.** rev. ed. Boston: Sanborn, Carter, Bazin; 1857. 2 v. in 1. [shaken, $32.00]

Thompson, Daniel Pierce. **May Martin.** 1st ed. Montpelier, VT: Walton; 1835. [lacks binding, $175.00]

Thompson, Daniel Pierce. **The Rangers; or, The Tory's Daughter.** 4th ed. Boston: Bazin and Ellsworth; 1851. 2 v. in 1. [$28.00]

Thompson, Edwin Porter. **History of the First Kentucky Brigade.** Cincinnati: Caxton; 1868. [$350.00]

Thompson, Fred D. **At That Point in Time.** NY: Quadrangle; 1975 [$20.00]

Thompson, George. **Prison Life and Reflections.** Hartford: Work; 1847. [rebacked, stained, $40.00] [rebound, $50.00] [1847 Oberlin ed., bumped, spine chipped, $200.00]

Thompson, George Alexander. **Narrative of an Official Visit to Guatemala from Mexico.** London: Murray; 1829. [lacks front endpaper, $550.00]

Thompson, George Greene. **Bat Masterson: The Dodge City Years.** Topeka: Kansas State Printing; 1943. [$35.00]

Thompson, Hunter S. **Fear and Loathing: On the Campaign Trail '72.** San Francisco: Straight Arrow; 1973. [$35.00]

Thompson, John Eric Sidney. **Mexico before Cortez.** NY, London: Scribner; 1933. [$15.00]

Thompson, Josiah. **Six Seconds in Dallas.** NY: Geis; 1968, c1967. [$35.00]

Thompson, Robert A. **Conquest of California, Capture of Sonoma by Bear Flag Men.** Santa Rosa: Sonoma Democrat; 1896. [$85.00]

Thompson, Robert A. **The Russian Settlement in California.** Oakland: Biobooks; 1951. [unopened, $20.00]

Thompson, Robert Luther. **Wiring a Continent.** Princeton: Princeton UP; 1947. [$35.00] [$45.00]

Thompson, Samuel Hunter. **Highlanders of the South.** NY: Eaton & Mains; 1910. [bumped and rubbed, $35.00]

Thompson, Slason. **Short History of American Railways.** Chicago: Bureau of Railway News and Statistics; 1925. [$30.00]

Thompson, Stith. **Round the Levee.** Austin: Texas Folklore Society; 1935, c1916. [$55.00]

Thompson, Vance. **Life of Ethelbert Nevin.** Boston: Boston Music; 1913. [$25.00]

Thompson, Waddy. **Recollections of Mexico.** NY, London: Wiley and Putnam; 1846. [$140.00] [$225.00]

Thompson, William. **Reminiscences of a Pioneer.** San Francisco: [s.n.]; 1912. [cover worn, $35.00] [$75.00]

Thomson, Matt. **Early History of Wabaunsee County, Kansas.** Alma, KS: [s.n.]; 1901. [paper browning, cover stains, $25.00]

Thord-Gray, I. **Gringo Rebel.** 1st ed. Coral Gables: Miami UP; 1960.

Thoreau, Henry David. **Anti-Slavery and Reform Papers.** London: Sonnenschein; 1890. [$175.00]

Thoreau, Henry David. **Cape Cod.** 1st ed. Boston: Ticknor and Fields; 1865. [bright copy, $250.00] [1896 Houghton ed. in 2 vols., $75.00]

Thoreau, Henry David. **Walden.** 1st ed. Boston: Ticknor and Fields; 1854. [$1800.00] [$2200.00]

Thoreau, Henry David. **A Week on the Concord and Merrimack Rivers.** rev. ed. Boston: Ticknor and Fields; 1868. [$75.00]

Thoreau, Henry David. **Yankee in Canada.** Boston: Houghton Osgood; 1879, c1866. [$30.00, Canadian]

Thornton, Dave. **America's First Big Parade.** Little Rock: Cooley; 1932. [$15.00]

Thornton, Jessy Quinn. **The California Tragedy.** Oakland: Biobooks; 1945. [$25.00]

Thornton, Jessy Quinn. **Oregon and California in 1848.** NY: Harper; 1849. 2 v. [slight foxing, $400.00]

Thornton, Randolph J. see, Peterson, Charles Jacobs.

Thornton, Thomas C. **Inquiry into the History of Slavery.** Washington: Morrison; 1841. [$250.00]

Thornton, Willis. **Nine Lives of Citizen Train.** NY: Greenberg; 1948. [$15.00]

Thorp, Joseph. **Early Days in the West.** Liberty, MO: Gilmer; 1924. [$100.00]

Thorp, N. Howard. **Pardner of the Wind.** Caldwell, ID: Caxton; 1945. [$45.00] [2nd printing, $25.00]

Thorp, N. Howard. **Songs of the Cowboys.** Boston, NY: Houghton Mifflin; 1921. [$45.00]

Thorp, N. Howard. **Tales of the Chuck Wagon.** 1st ed. Santa Fe: Thorp; 1926. [$65.00]

Thorp, Raymond W. **Bowie Knife.** Albuquerque: U. of New Mexico; 1948. [$55.00] [$50.00]

Thorp, Raymond W. **Crow Killer.** Bloomington: Indiana UP; 1958. [$35.00]

Thorp, Raymond W. **Spirit Gun of the West.** Glendale, CA: Clark; 1957. [$50.00]

Thorpe, Thomas Bangs. **Our Army on the Rio Grande.** Philadelphia: Carey and Hart; 1846. [$875.00]

Thouar, Arthur. **Explorations dans l'Amerique du Sud.** Paris: Hachette; 1891. [x-lib., $70.00]

Thrall, Homer S. **Pictorial History of Texas.** 3rd ed. St. Louis: Thompson; 1883, c1878. [rebound, $90.00]

Thrapp, Dan L. **Al Sieber, Chief of Scouts.** 1st ed. Norman: U. of Oklahoma; 1964. [$40.00] [$45.00]

Thrasher, Frederic Milton. **The Gang.** Chicago: U. of Chicago; 1929, c1927. [spine scratched, $20.00]

Throop, Benjamin H. **A Half Century in Scranton.** Scranton, PA: Republican; 1895. [$60.00]

Thurber, James. **Alarms and Diversions.** 1st ed. NY: Harper; 1957. [$15.00]

Thurber, James. **Fables for Our Time and Famous Poems Illustrated.** 1st ed. NY: Harper; 1940. [$20.00]

Thurber, James. **Let Your Mind Alone!** London: Hamilton; 1937. [dj rubbed, $125.00]

Thurber, James. **A Thurber Garland.** London: Hamilton; 1955. [$90.00]

Thurber, James. **The Wonderful O.** London: Hamilton; 1957. [very good in dj, $150.00]

Thurston, George H. **Allegheny County's Hundred Years.** Pittsburgh: Anderson; 1888. [$50.00]

Thurston, Lorrin Andrews. **Hand-Book on the Annexation of Hawaii.** St. Joseph, MI: Morse; 1897. [$125.00]

Thwaites, Reuben Gold. **Daniel Boone.** NY: Appleton; 1928, c1902. [x-lib., $12.50]

Thwaites, Reuben Gold. **Father Marquette.** NY: Appleton; 1902. [$35.00]

Thwaites, Reuben Gold. **How George Rogers Clark Won the Northwest.** 6th ed. Chicago: McClurg; 1931. [$19.00]

Thwaites, Reuben Gold. **On the Storied Ohio.** Chicago: McClurg; 1903. [$30.00]

Tibbles, Thomas Henry. **Buckskin and Blanket Days.** 1st ed. Garden City: Doubleday; 1957. [$25.00]

Tibbles, Thomas Henry. **The Ponca Chiefs.** Boston: Lockwood, Brooks; 1880. [x-lib., $85.00]

Tice, John H. **Over the Plains and on the Mountains.** St. Louis: Book and News; [1872?]. [$165.00]

Ticknor, Caroline. **May Alcott.** Boston: Little, Brown; 1928. [2nd printing?, $37.50]

Ticknor, Caroline. **New England Aviators 1914-1918.** Boston, NY: Houghton Mifflin; 1919-20. 2 v. [$250.00]

Tilden, Samuel J. **The New York City "Ring."** NY: Polhemus; 1873. [$45.00]

Tilghman, Oswald. **History of Talbot County, Maryland, 1661-1861.** Baltimore: Williams & Wilkins; 1915. 2 v. [$75.00]

Tilghman, Zoe Agnes. **Marshal of the Last Frontier.** Glendale, CA: Clark; 1949. [$100.00] [$75.00] [1964 ed., $60.00]

Tilghman, Zoe Agnes. **Outlaw Days.** Oklahoma City: Harlow; 1926. [$50.00]

Tilghman, Zoe Agnes. **Quanah.** Oklahoma City: Harlow; 1938. [inscribed, $160.00]

Tilghman, Zoe Agnes. **Spotlight.** San Antonio: Naylor; 1960. [$35.00]

Tiling, Moritz Philipp Georg. **History of the German Element in Texas from 1820-1850.** 1st ed. Houston: The Author; 1913. [$195.00]

Tillotson, F. H. **How to Be a Detective.** [s.l.: s.n.]; 1909. [$75.00]

Timberlake, Henry. **Lieut. Henry Timberlake's Memoires: 1756-1765.** Marietta, GA: Continental; 1948. [$30.00]

Tinkcom, Harry Marlin. **John White Geary.** Philadelphia: U. of Pennsylvania; 1940. [$15.00]

Tinker, Edward Larocque. **Horsemen of the Americas and the Literature They Inspired.** NY: Hastings; 1953. [$35.00]

Tinkle, Lon. **Cowboy Reader.** 1st ed. NY: Longmans, Green; 1959. [$35.00]

Titus, Frances W. see, Gilbert, Olive.

Tobie, Harvey Elmer. **No Man like Joe.** Portland, OR: Binfords & Mort; 1949. [$30.00]

Tocqueville, Alexis de. **De la Democratie en Amerique.** 13th ed. Paris: Pagnerre; 1850. 2 v. [$85.00]

Tocqueville, Alexis de. **Democracy in America.** 2nd American ed. NY: Adlard; 1838. [bumped and rubbed, $75.00]

Todd, Frank Morton. **Story of the Exposition.** NY, London: Putnam; 1921. 5 v. [$150.00]

Todd, Glenn Haywood. **The Immortal Nick Arrington.** Chicago: Adams; 1965. [$35.00]

Todd, John. **The Sunset Land.** Boston: Lee and Shepard; 1870. [rubbed, $85.00] [$75.00]

Tomes, Robert. **Battles of America by Sea and Land.** NY: Virtue; 1878. 3 v. [$325.00]

Tomes, Robert. **The War with the South.** NY: Virtue; 1862. 30 pts. bound in 3 v. [$350.00]

Tomkins, Calvin. **The Lewis and Clark Trail.** 1st ed. NY: Harper & Row; 1965. [inscribed, $14.00]

Tomlin, Charles. **Cape May Spray.** Philadelphia: Bradley; 1913. [$35.00]

Tompkins, Frank. **Chasing Villa.** Harrisburg, PA: Military Service; 1934. [$75.00]

Tompkins, Stuart Ramsay. **Alaska, Promyshlennik and Sourdough.** 1st ed. Norman: U. of Oklahoma; 1945. [dj worn, $25.00]

Tooker, Elva. **Nathan Trotter.** Cambridge: Harvard UP; 1955. [$25.00]

Tooker, William Wallace. **The Bocootawanaukes.** NY: Harper; 1901. [$20.00]

Tooker, William Wallace. **Significance of John Eliot's Natick and the Name Merrimac.** NY: Harper; 1901. [$20.00]

Toombs, Robert Augustus. **Correspondence of Robert Toombs, Alexander H. Stephens, and Howell Cobb.** Washington: AHA; 1913. [$100.00] [x-lib., $75.00]

Toombs, Samuel. **New Jersey Troops in the Gettysburg Campaign.** Orange, NJ: Evening Mail; 1887. [$50.00] [$40.00]

Topographical Description of the State of Ohio. see, Culter, Jervis.

Topp, Mildred. **Smile Please.** Boston: Houghton Mifflin; 1948. [$15.00]

Topping, Eugene Sayre. **Chronicles of the Yellowstone.** St. Paul: Pioneer Press; 1888. [covers worn, $100.00] [$225.00]

Tornel Y Mendivil, Jose Maria. **Tejas y los Estados-Unidos de America en Sus Relaciones con la Republica Mexicana.** Mexico: Cumplido; 1837. [hinge cracked, later leather binding, $2000.00]

Torrey, Bradford. **Field-Days in California.** Boston, NY: Houghton Mifflin; 1913. [$25.00]

Torrey, Bradford. **Florida Sketch-Book.** Boston, NY: Houghton Mifflin; 1894. [x-lib., $30.00]

Torrey, Edwin C. **Early Days in Dakota.** Minneapolis: Farnham; 1925. [$95.00]

Totten, George Oakley. **Maya Architecture.** Washington: Maya; 1926. [$150.00]

Toulmin, Harry Aubrey. **With Pershing in Mexico.** 1st ed. Harrisburg, PA: Military Service; 1935. [$75.00]

Toussaint, Manuel. **Arte Colonial en Mexico.** Mexico: Universidad Nacional Autonoma de Mexico, Instituto de Investigaciones Estesticas; 1948. [$200.00]

Tower, Philo. **Slavery Unmasked.** Rochester: Darrow; 1856. [spine frayed, shaken, $65.00]

Towle, Margaret Ashley. **The Ethnobotany of Pre-Columbian Peru.** Chicago: Aldine; 1961. [$30.00]

Towle, Nancy. **Vicisitudes Illustrated.** 2nd ed. Portmouth, NH: Caldwell; 1833. [spine badly worn, foxed, $225.00]

Towle, Virginia Rowe. **Vigilante Women.** South Brunswick: Barnes; 1966. [$10.00]

Towne, Arthur Elisha. **Old Prairie Days.** Otsego, MI: Otsego Union; 1941. [presentation, $45.00]

Towne, Charles Wayland. **Cattle & Men.** 1st ed. Norman: U. of Oklahoma; 1955. [$25.00] [$30.00]

Townsend, George Alfred. **Campaigns of a Non-Combatant.** NY: Blelock; 1866. [$45.00]

Townsend, George Alfred. **Rustics in Rebellion.** Chapel Hill: U. of North Carolina; 1950. [worn dj, $20.00] [$10.00]

Townsend, John Kirk. **Narrative of a Journey across the Rocky Mountains, to the Columbia River, and a Visit to the Sandwich Islands.** Philadelphia; Boston: Perkins; Perkins & Marvin; 1839. [$500.00]

Townsend, William Henry. **Lincoln and the Bluegrass.** Lexington: U. of Kentucky; 1955. [signed, $35.00]

Townshend, Richard Baxter. **A Tenderfoot in Colorado.** 1st ed. London: Lane; 1923. [$60.00]

Townshend, Richard Baxter. **The Tenderfoot in New Mexico.** London: Lane; 1923. [$60.00] [$80.00] [$75.00]

Tracy, Joseph. **History of American Missions to the Heathen.** Worcester: Spooner & Howland; 1840. [rebound, $35.00]

Traill, Catherine Parr Strickland. **Backwoods of Canada.** London: Knight; 1836. [x-lib., $275.00]

Traill, Catherine Parr Strickland. **Canada and the Oregon.** London: Nattali; 1846. [$325.00]

Travels of Capts. Lewis and Clarke from St. Louis, by way of the Missouri and Columbia Rivers, to the Pacific Ocean. London: Longman, etc.; 1809. [$600.00]

Traylor, Samuel White. **Out of the Southwest.** Allentown, PA: Schlicher; 1936. [signed, $50.00]

Treadwell, Edward F. **Cattle King.** NY: Macmillan; 1931. [$45.00] [inscribed, $60.00]

Tremain, Henry Edwin. **Last Hours of Sheridan's Cavalry.** NY: Bonnell, Silver & Bowers; 1904. [$35.00] [binding worn, $45.00]

Tremenheere, Hugh Seymour. **Notes on Public Subjects, Made during a Tour in the United States and in Canada.** London: Murray; 1852. [$150.00]

Trenholm, Virginia Cole. **Footprints on the Frontier.** signed limited ed. Douglas, WY: Enterprise; 1945. [$150.00]

Trenholm, Virginia Cole. **The Shoshonis.** 1st ed. Norman: U. of Oklahoma; 1964. [$35.00]

Treves, Frederick. **The Cradle of the Deep.** London: Smith, Elder; 1908. [foxed, $20.00]

Trinka, Zena Irma. **North Dakota of Today.** 3rd ed. Saint Paul: Dow; 1920, c1919. [$35.00]

Trinka, Zena Irma. **Out Where the West Begins.** St. Paul: Pioneer; 1920. [hinges cracked, shaken, $25.00]

Triplett, Frank. **Conquering the Wilderness.** NY: Thompson; 1883. [spine loose, $95.00]

Trissal, Francis Marion. **Public Men of Indiana.** Hammond, IN: Conkey; 1922-23. 2 v. [$40.00]

Trobriand, Regis de. **Army Life in Dakota.** Chicago: Lakeside; 1941. [$17.50]

Trobriand, Regis de. **Military Life in Dakota.** St. Paul: Alvord Memorial; 1951. [$35.00]

Trollope, Anthony. **West Indies and the Spanish Main.** NY: Harper; 1860. [spine wormed, $30.00]

Trollope, Frances Milton. **Domestic Manners of the Americans.** 4th ed. London; NY: Whittaker, Treacher; The Booksellers; 1832. [bumped, rubbed, worn, spine detached, $35.00]

Trow, Harrison. **Charles W. Quantrell.** Vega, TX: Burch; 1923. [$25.00] [$16.50]

Trow, James. **Manitoba and North West Territories.** Ottawa: Dept. of Agriculture; 1878. [x-lib., $175.00]

Trowbridge, J. T. **The South.** Hartford, CT: Stebbins; 1866. [$85.00]

Troxell, William S. **Aus Pennsylfawnia.** Philadelphia: U. of Pennsylvania; 1938. [$20.00]

True and Particular Relation of the Dreadful Earthquake Which Happen'd at Lima. 2nd ed. London: Osborne; 1748. [one plate missing, $150.00]

Trueheart, James L. **Perote Prisoners.** San Antonio: Naylor; 1934. [$250.00]

Truman, Benjamin Cummings. **Occidental Sketches.** San Francisco: News; 1881. [presentation, $150.00]

Truman, Benjamin Cummings. **Semi-Tropical California.** San Francisco: Bancroft; 1874. [$100.00]

Trumbull, Gurdon. **Names and Portraits of Birds Which Interest Gunners.** NY: Harper; 1888. [$35.00]

Trumbull, Henry. **History of the Discovery of America.** Norwich: Springer; 1812. [lacking plates, $165.00] [$125.00] [1833 Clark ed., $125.00]

Trumbull, Henry. **History of the Indian Wars.** new ed. Philadelphia: Bill; 1851. [$140.00]

Tryon, Rolla Milton. **Household Manufactures in the United States, 1640-1860.** Chicago: U. of Chicago; 1917. [x-lib., $45.00]

Tschudi, Johann Jakob von. **Travels in Peru during the Years 1838-1842.** NY: Putnam; 1849. [$80.00]

Tucker, Arthur Holmes. **Hope Atherton and His Times.** [Deerfield?, MA: Pocumtuck Valley Mem. Assn.; 1926?]. [$25.00]

Tucker, George Fox. **The Monroe Doctrine.** Boston: Reed; 1885. [$45.00]

Tucker, Glenn. **Dawn like Thunder.** Indianapolis: Bobbs-Merrill; 1963. [$22.50] [$17.50]

Tucker, Glenn. **Hancock the Superb.** 1st ed. Indianapolis: Bobbs-Merrill; 1960. [$45.00]

Tucker, Glenn. **High Tide at Gettysburg.** 1st ed. Indianapolis: Bobbs-Merrill; 1958. [x-lib., $17.50]

Tucker, Glenn. **Poltroons and Patriots.** 1st ed. Indianapolis: Bobbs-Merrill; 1954. 2 v. [$20.00] [$35.00]

Tucker, Glenn. **Tecumseh; Vision of Glory.** 1st ed. Indianapolis: Bobbs-Merrill; 1956. [$32.50] [$20.00]

Tucker, Sophie. **Some of These Days.** 1st ed. Garden City: Doubleday, Doran; 1945. [x-lib., $20.00]

Tucker, William Franklin. **Historical Sketch of the Town of Charlestown in Rhode Island.** Westerly, RI: Utter; 1877. [x-lib., $35.00]

Tuckerman, Bayard. **Life of General Lafayette.** London: Low, Marston, Searle, & Rivington; 1889. 2 v. [$30.00]

Tuckerman, Bayard. **Life of General Philip Schuyler.** NY: Dodd, Mead; 1903. [$20.00]

Tudor, William. **Life of James Otis.** Boston: Wells and Lilly; 1823. [x-lib., $75.00]

Tufts, James. **Tract Descriptive of Montana Territory.** NY: Craighead; 1865. [$500.00]

Tugwell, Rexford G. **The Democratic Roosevelt.** 1st ed. Garden City: Doubleday; 1957. [$25.00]

Tully, Samuel. **Life of.** Boston: Watson & Bangs; 1812. [$175.00]

Tumblety, Francis. **A Few Passages in the Life of.** Cincinnati: The Author; 1866. [$30.00]

Tunnard, William H. **A Southern Record: The History of the Third Regiment Louisiana Infantry.** Baton Rouge: The Author; 1866. [signed, $795.00]

Tunnels and Water System of Chicago. Chicago: Wing; 1874. [$175.00]

Tunstall, John Henry. **Life and Death of.** 1st ed. Carson City, NV: State Museum; 1965. [$25.00] [$35.00]

Turchin, John Basil. **Chickamauga.** Chicago: Fergus; 1888. [darkened covers, $65.00]

Turnbull, George Stanley. **History of Oregon Newspapers.** Portland: Binfords & Mort; 1939. [$65.00]

Turner, Frederick Jackson. **Frontier in American History.** NY: Holt; 1920. [some underlining, $25.00]

Turner, Frederick Jackson. **Reuben Gold Thwaites.** Madison: State Historical Society of Wisconsin; 1914. [$10.00]

Turner, Frederick Jackson. **Significance of the Frontier in American History.** Washington: USGPO; 1894. [$125.00]

Turner, George Edgar. **Victory Rode the Rails.** 1st ed. Indianiapolis: Bobbs-Merrill; 1953. [$35.00]

Turner, John Peter. **North-West Mounted Police.** Ottawa: Cloutier; 1950. 2 v. [$80.00, Canadian]

Turner, Jonathan Baldwin. **Mormonism in All Ages.** NY: Platt & Peters; 1842. [$235.00]

Turner, Katharine C. **Red Men Calling on the Great White Father.** 1st ed. Norman: U. of Oklahoma; 1951. [$45.00]

Turney, Ida Virginia. **Paul Bunyan Comes West.** Eugene: University Press; [19-?]. [presentation, $30.00] [1928 Houghton ed., $12.50]

Turton, M. Conway. **Cassiar.** London: Macmillan; 1934. [$45.00, Canadian]

Tuttle, Charles R. **Our North Land.** Toronto: Robinson; 1885. [lacks frontis map, rear hinge broken, $75.00, Canadian]

Tuttle, Daniel Sylvester. **Reminiscences of a Missionary Bishop.** NY: Whittaker; 1906. [2nd printing, $75.00]

Tuttle, James Harvey. **Field and the Fruit.** Boston: Universalist; 1891. [$45.00]

Twain, Mark. **Adventures of Huckleberry Finn.** 1st ed. London: Chatto & Windus; 1884. [2nd issue, $1000.00] [1st issue, $1350.00] [1885 Webster ed., $900.00]

Twain, Mark. **Adventures of Thomas Jefferson Snodgrass.** Chicago: Covici; 1928. [$75.00]

Twain, Mark. **The American Claimant.** 1st ed. NY: Webster; 1892. [$120.00] [$85.00] [1892 Chatto & Windus ed., $150.00]

Twain, Mark. **Connecticut Yankee in King Arthur's Court.** 1st ed. NY: Webster; 1889. [$350.00] [second state, $165.00]

Twain, Mark. **The Curious Republic of Gondour, and Other Whimsical Sketches.** NY: Boni and Liveright; 1919. [$125.00] [near fine in dj, $175.00]

Twain, Mark. **Editorial Wild Oats.** NY: Harper; 1905. [$20.00]

Twain, Mark. **English As She Is Taught.** Boston: Mutual; 1900. [$150.00]

Twain, Mark. **Eve's Diary.** 1st ed. London: Harper; 1906. [$75.00]

Twain, Mark. **Extracts from Adam's Diary.** NY, London: Harper; 1904. [$60.00]

Twain, Mark. **Following the Equator.** Hartford, CT: American Pub. Co.; 1897. [inner hinge ragged, worn, $22.50] [1st issue, near fine, $165.00]

Twain, Mark. **A Horse's Tale.** NY: Harper; 1907. [$100.00]

Twain, Mark. **Is Shakespeare Dead?** NY, London: Harper; 1909. [$60.00]

Twain, Mark. **The Jumping Frog in English, Then in French, Then Clawed Back into a Civilized Language Once More by Patient, Unremunerated Toil.** NY, London: Harper; 1903. [$45.00]

Twain, Mark. **Letters of Quintus Curtius Snodgrass.** Dallas: Southern Methodist UP; 1946. [$50.00] [dj chipped, $40.00]

Twain, Mark. **Life on the Mississippi.** 1st ed. Boston: Osgood; 1883. [spine frayed, a few gatherings loose, $200.00] [$185.00][latter issue, 125.00]

Twain, Mark. **Lotos Leaves.** see, Brougham, John.

Twain, Mark. **Love Letters of.** 1st ed. NY: Harper; 1949. [worn dj, $30.00]

Twain, Mark. **Mark Twain, Business Man.** Boston: Little, Brown; 1946. [$15.00]

Twain, Mark. **Mark Twain's Autobiography.** NY, London: Harper; 1924. 2 v. [$55.00] [1925 Collier reprint, $75.00]

Twain, Mark. **Mark Twain's (Burlesque) Autobiography and First Romance.** NY: Sheldon; 1871. [$165.00] [2nd state, $65.00]

Twain, Mark. **Mark Twain's San Francisco.** 1st ed. NY: McGraw-Hill; 1963. [$17.50]

Twain, Mark. **Mark Twain's Sketches, New and Old.** Hartford, Chicago: American Pub. Co.; 1875. [2nd state, $85.00] [2nd printing, $65.00]

Twain, Mark. **Mark Twain's Travels with Mr. Brown.** NY: Knopf; 1940. [fine in dj, $65.00]

Twain, Mark. **Merry Tales.** NY: Webster; 1892. [1st issue, $150.00]

Twain, Mark. **Old Times on the Mississippi.** Toronto: Belford; 1876. [$250.00]

Twain, Mark. **The One Million Pound Bank-Note.** NY: Webster; 1893. [$85.00] [binding spotted, $125.00]

Twain, Mark. **The Prince and the Pauper.** 1st ed. London: Chatto & Windus; 1881. [$300.00] [1st American ed., 1st printing, $650.00]

Twain, Mark. **Pudd'nhead Wilson.** London: Chatto & Windus; 1894. [1st issue, $250.00] [March 1895 ads, $225.00]

Twain, Mark. **Roughing It.** 1st ed. Hartford: American Pub. Co.; 1872. [front joint cracked, front endpaper detached, $120.00] [pencil underlining, rebound, $50.00] [2nd issue, rebacked, $75.00]

Twain, Mark. **Sketches.** [Toronto?]: Belford; 1880. [$30.00]

Twain, Mark. **Stolen White Elephant.** 1st ed. Boston: Osgood; 1882. [$95.00] [$85.00]

Twain, Mark. **Tom Sawyer Abroad.** 1st English ed. London: Chatto & Windus; 1894. [near fine, $95.00]

Twain, Mark. **Tragedy of Pudd'nhead Wilson.** 1st ed. Hartford: American Pub. Co.; 1894. [1st printing, $200.00]

Twain, Mark. **A Tramp Abroad.** Hartford; London: American Publishing; Chatto & Windus; 1880. [$185.00] [1880 Toronto ed., wraps worn and loose, $125.00]

Twain, Mark. **The Washoe Giant in San Francisco.** San Francisco: Fields; 1938. [signed by editor, fine in good dj, $105.00] [$65.00]

Tweedsmuir, John Norman Stuart Buchan baron. **Hudson's Bay Trader.** NY: Norton; 1951. [$13.00]

Twiss, Travers. **The Oregon Question Examined.** London: Longman, Brown, etc.; 1846. [with 2 folding maps, $450.00] [$300.00]

Twitchell, Ralph Emerson. **History of the Military Occupation of the Territory of New Mexico from 1846 to 1851.** Denver: Smith-Brooks; 1909. [$100.00]

Twitchell, Ralph Emerson. **Leading Facts of New Mexican History.** Cedar Rapids, IA: Torch; 1911-1917. 5 v. [$1350.00]

Tyler, Hamilton A. **Pueblo Gods and Myths.** 1st ed. Norman: U. of Oklahoma; 1964. [$50.00] [$25.00]

Tyler, Lyon Gardiner. **Cradle of the Republic.** 2nd ed. Richmond: Hermitage; 1906. [$20.00]

Tyler, Lyon Gardiner. **Letters and Times of the Tylers.** Richmond: Whittet & Shepperson; 1884-96. 3 v. [rebound, lacks third vol., $325.00]

Tyler, Lyon Gardiner. **Narratives of Early Virginia, 1606-1625.** NY: Scribner; 1907. [$45.00]

Tyler, Mason Whiting. **Recollections of the Civil War.** NY, London: Putnam; 1912. [$25.00] [$40.00]

Tyler, Moses Coit. **Literary History of the American Revolution, 1763-1783.** 2nd ed. NY: Putnam; 1898, c1897. 2 v. [$35.00]

Tyler, Sydney. **San Francisco's Great Disaster.** Philadelphia: Ziegler; 1906. [$30.00]

Tylor, Edward Burnett. **Anahuac.** London: Longman, etc.; 1861. [$150.00]

Tyrner-Tyrnauer, A. R. **Lincoln and the Emperors.** 1st ed. NY: Harcourt, Brace & World; 1962. [$25.00]

Udall, David King. **Arizona Pioneer Mormon.** Tucson: Arizona Silhouettes; 1959. [$25.00]

Udell, John. **Incidents of Travel to California, across the Great Plains.** Jefferson, OH: Sentinel; 1856. [signed, $850.00]

Ueland, Andreas. **Recollections of an Immigrant.** NY: Minton, Balch; 1929. [$20.00]

Uhden, Hermann Ferdinand. **New England Theocracy.** Boston; NY: Gould and Lincoln; Sheldon, Blakeman; 1859. [$50.00]

Underhill, Ann Leah. **The Missing Link in Modern Spiritualism.** NY: Knox; 1885. [presentation, $50.00]

Underhill, Ruth Murray. **First Penthouse Dwellers of America.** 1st ed. NY: Augustin; 1938. [$25.00] [2nd ed., 1946, $27.50]

Underhill, Ruth Murray. **The Navajos.** Norman: U. of Oklahoma; 1956. [$30.00] [$25.00]

Underhill, Ruth Murray. **Pueblo Crafts.** Phoenix: Indian School; 1945. [spine chipped, $10.00]

Underhill, Ruth Murray. **Red Man's America.** Chicago: U. of Chicago; 1953. [$15.00]

Underhill, Ruth Murray. **Workaday Life of the Pueblos.** Washington: U.S. Office of Indian Affairs; 1946. [$30.00]

Underwood, John Jasper. **Alaska, an Empire in the Making.** NY: Dodd, Mead; 1913. [$50.00]

Underwood, John Levi. **Women of the Confederacy.** NY, Washington: Neale; 1906. [x-lib., $75.00]

United Confederate Veterans. **Flags of the Confederate States of America.** Baltimore: Hoen; 1907. [$8.00]

United States. Army. 693d Field Artillery Battalion. **On the Way.** [Salzburg?: s.n.]; 1945. [$65.00]

United States. Army. Corps of Engineers. **Report of a Reconnaissance of the Black Hills of Dakota.** Washington: USGPO; 1875. [covers rubbed, $150.00]

United States. Army. Corps of Engineers. **Report of an Examination of the Upper Columbia River.** Washington: USGPO; 1882. [$75.00]

United States. Army. Corps of Engineers. **Report of Explorations across the Great Basin of the Territory of Utah.** Washington: USGPO; 1876. [$425.00]

United States. Army. Corps of Engineers. **Report upon the Colorado River of the West Explored in 1857 and 1858 by Joseph C. Ives.** Washington: USGPO; 1861. [$600.00] [front hinge split, $450.00]

United States. Army. Corps of Topographical Engineers. **Expedition to the Valley of the Great Salt Lake of Utah.** Philadelphia: Lippincott, Grambo; 1855. 2 v. [$275.00]

United States. Army. Corps of Topographical Engineers. **Exploration and Survey of the Valley of the Great Salt Lake of Utah.** Philadelphia: Lippincott, Grambo; 1852. [$400.00]

United States. Army. Corps of Topographical Engineers. **Message from the President of the United States, Communicating the Report of Lieutenant Webster of a Survey of the Gulf Coast at the Mouth of the Rio Grande.** Washington: [s.n.]; 1850. [$125.00]

United States. Army. Corps of Topographical Engineers. **Message from the President of the United States, in Compliance with a Resolution of the Senate,**

Communicating a Report of an Expedition Led by Lieutenant Abert, on the Upper Arkansas and through the Country of the Camanche Indians, in the Fall of the Year 1845. Washington: [s.n.];1846. [$375.00]

United States. Army. Corps of Topographical Engineers. **Notes of Military Reconnoissance from Fort Leavenworth, in Missouri, to San Diego, in California.** Washington: Wendell and Van Benthuysen; 1848. [with folding map, $250.00] [$400.00]

United States. Army. Corps of Topographical Engineers. **Report of the Secretary of War, Communicating, in Answer to a Resolution of the Senate, a Report and Map of the Examination of New Mexico.** Washington: [s.n.]; 1848. [$1500.00]

United States. Bureau of Education. **Education in Alaska, 1889-90.** Washington: USGPO; 1893. [$45.00]

United States. Census Office. 7th Census, 1850. **Statistical View of the United States.** Washington: Nicholson; 1854. [$75.00]

United States. Census Office. 11th Census, 1890. **Indians Taxed and Indians Not Taxed in the United States (except Alaska).** Washington: USGPO; 1894. [19 color plates, $750.00]

United States. Congress. Committee Appointed to Enquire into the Spirit and Manner in Which the War Has Been Waged by the Enemy. **Barbarities of the Enemy Exposed.** Worcester: Sturtevant; 1814. [$150.00]

United States. Congress. House. **Labor Troubles in the Anthracite Regions of Pennsylvania 1887-1888.** Washington: USGPO; 1889. [$85.00]

United States. Congress. House. Committe on Naval Affairs. **Report of the Naval Committee to the House of Representatives, August, 1850, in Favor of the Establishment of a Line of Mail Steamships to the Western Coast of Africa and Thence via the Mediterranean to London.** Washington: Gideon; 1850. [$135.00]

United States. Congress. Senate Committee on Privileges and Elections. **Testimony on the Alleged Election Outrages in Texas.** Washington: USGPO; 1889. [$225.00]

United States. Constitutional Convention (1787). **Secret Proceedings and Debates.** Albany, NY: Websters and Skinners; 1821. [unbound, $325.00]

United States. Continental Army. **Revolutionary Orders of General Washington Issued during the Years 1778, '80, '81, & '82.** NY: Wiley and Putnam; 1844. [$75.00]

United States. Dept. of State. **Assassination of Abraham Lincoln.** Washington: USGPO; 1867. [$50.00]

United States. Dept. of State. **Instructions to the Envoys Extraordinary and Ministers Plenipotentiary from the United States of America to the French Republic.** Philadelphia: Ross; 1798. [$135.00]

United States. Dept. of State. **Mexico and Texas.** Washington: Blair & Rives; 1837. [$150.00]

United States. Dept. of State. **Report of the Secretary of State, Communicating the Report of the Rev. R. R. Gurley.** Washington: [s.n.]; 1850. [$45.00]

United States. Dept. of State. **Revolutionary Diplomatic Correspondence of the U. S.** Washington: USGPO; 1889. 6 v. [$300.00]

United States. Dept. of the Interior. **Report on the United States and Mexican Boundary Survey.** Washington: Wendell; 1857-59. 2 v. in 3. [$2250.00]

United States. National Park Service. **Soldier and Brave.** 1st ed. NY: Harper & Row; 1963. [$30.00]

United States. Navy Dept. **Narrative of the North Polar Expedition U.S. Ship Polaris.** Washington: USGPO; 1876. [$95.00]

United States. Office of Education. **Report on Education in Alaska.** Washington: USGPO; 1886. [$50.00]

United States. President (1801-1809: Jefferson). **Message from the President of the United States: Communicating Discoveries Made in Exploring the Missouri, Red River and Washita.** Washington: Way; 1806. [folding map in facs., $2500.00]

United States. President (1801-1809: Jefferson). **Message from the President of the United States, to Both Houses of Congress at the Commencement of the Second Session of the Tenth Congress.** Washington: Way; 1808. [$185.00]

United States. President (1857-1861: Buchanan). **Message from the President of the United States Relative to the Seizure of General William Walker and His Followers in Nicaragua.** Washington: [s.n.]; 1858. [$35.00]

United States. Sanitary Commission. **Narrative of Privations and Sufferings of United States Officers and Soldiers While Prisoners of War in the Hands of the Rebel Authorities.** Philadelphia: King and Baird; 1864. [$85.00]

United States. Supreme Court. **Report of the Decision of the Supreme Court of the United States and the Opinions of the Judges Thereof, in the Case of Dred Scott Versus John F. A. Sandford. December Term, 1856.** Washington: Wendell; 1857. [lacks back wrapper, $185.00] [1857 Appleton issue, $350.00]

United States. Treasury Dept. **Rules and Regulations Concerning Commerical Intercourse with and in States and Parts of States Declared in Insurrection.** Washington: [s.n.]; 1864. [$45.00]

United States. War Dept. **Adventure on Red River.** Norman: U. of Oklahoma; 1937. [$60.00]

United States. War Dept. **Defence of Western Frontier.** Washington: [s.n.]; 1840. [$85.00]

United States. War Dept. **Exploration of the Red River of Louisiana in the Year 1852:.** Washington: Armstrong; 1853. [$200.00] [1854 Tucker imprint, hinges weak, $95.00]

United States. War Dept. **Letter from the Secretary of War in Answer to a Resolution of the House of the 4th Ultimo, Transmitting Copies of General Terry's Report on Georgia.** Washington: USGPO; 1870. [$55.00]

United States. War Dept. **Message of the President of the United States Communicating in Compliance with a Resolution of the Senate of February 26, Calling for a Copy of the Report and Maps of Captain Marcy of His Explorations of the Big Wichita and Head Waters of the Brazos Rivers.** Washington: [s.n.]; 1856. [$385.00]

United States. War Dept. **Report of Lieutenant Gustavus C. Doane, upon the So-Called Yellowstone Expedition of 1870.** Washington: USGPO; 1871. [$125.00]

United States Cartridge Company. **Where to Hunt American Game.** Lowell, MA: United States Cartridge Company; 1898. [$100.00]

Unknown Author. **America's First Big Parade.** see, Thornton, Dave.

Unonius, Gustaf Elias Marius. **Minnen fran en Sauttonarig Vistelse i Nordvestra Amerika.** 2nd ed. Upsala: Schultz; 1862. 2 v. [$175.00]

Updike, John. **Of the Farm.** lst ed. NY: Knopf; 1965. [inscribed, $35.00]

Upham, Charles Wentworth. **Life, Explorations and Public Services of John Charles Fremont.** Boston: Ticknor & Fields; 1856. [$45.00] [$40.00]

Upham, Samuel Curtis. **Notes of a Voyage to California via Cape Horn.** Philadelphia: The Author; 1878. [$225.00]

Upham, Thomas Cogswell. **American Cottage Life.** 2nd ed. Brunswick, ME: Griffin; 1850-51. [$50.00]

Upshur, George Lyttleton. **As I Recall Them.** NY: Wilson-Erickson; 1936. [2nd printing, $60.00]

Upson Family Association of America. **The Upson Family in America.** New Haven: Tuttle, Morehouse & Taylor; 1940. [bumped, hinges weak, some ink notes, $20.00]

Upton, Harriet Taylor. **History of the Western Reserve.** Chicago, NY: Lewis; 1910. 3 v. [$135.00]

Utley, Robert Marshall. **Frontiersmen in Blue.** NY: Macmillan; 1967. [$30.00]

Vail, Eugene A. **Notice sur les Indiens de l'Amerique du Nord.** Paris: Bertrand; 1840. [rebound, $600.00]

Vail, Stephen Montford. **The Bible against Slavery.** Concord: Fogg, Hadley; 1864. [$65.00]

Vaillant, George Clapp. **Aztecs of Mexico.** Garden City: Doubleday; 1944. [$25.00]

Valcourt-Vermont, Edgar de. **The Dalton Brothers and Their Astounding Career of Crime.** NY: Fell; 1954. [$18.00] [$15.00]

Valentine, Alan Chester. **Vigilante Justice.** NY: Reynal; 1956. [$10.00]

Valentine, Benjamin Batchelder. **Ole Marster.** Richmond: Whittet & Shepperson; 1921. [$10.00]

Van Cleve, Charlotte Ouisconsin. **Three Score Years and Ten.** Minneapolis: Harrison & Smith; 1888. [bumped, spine frayed, hinges cracked, 1st issue, $75.00] [$80.00]

Van Court, Catharine. **In Old Natchez.** 1st ed. Garden City: Doubleday, Doran; 1937. [soiled, sunned, and signed, $15.00]

Van de Water, Frederic Franklyn. **The Captain Called It Mutiny.** NY: Washburn; 1954. [$10.00]

Van de Water, Frederic Franklyn. **Glory-Hunter.** Indianapolis, NY: Bobbs-Merrill; 1934. [$50.00] [1963 Argosy reprint, $30.00]

Van de Water, Frederic Franklyn. **Lake Champlain and Lake George.** Indianapolis, NY: Bobbs-Merrill; 1946. [$14.00]

Van de Water, John. **Street of Forgotten Men.** Grand Rapids: Eerdmans; [n.d.]. [$30.00]

Van Deusen, John George. **The Black Man in White America.** Washington: Associated Publishers; 1938. [bumped, front hinge cracked, $25.00]

Van Doren, Carl. **Mutiny in January.** NY: Viking; 1943. [$15.00]

Van Doren, Carl. **Secret History of the American Revolution.** 1st ed. NY: Viking; 1941. [signed limited, $50.00] [trade ed., $12.50]

Van Dyke, John Charles. **The Desert.** NY: Scribner; 1901. [$20.00]

Van Dyke, John Charles. **The Grand Canyon of the Colorado.** NY: Scribner; 1920. [$40.00]

Van Dyke, Theodore S. Millionaires of a Day. NY: Fords, Howard & Hulbert; 1890. [$50.00]

Van Every, Dale. Men of the Western Waters. Boston: Houghton Mifflin; 1956. [$15.00] [$25.00]

Van Evrie, John H. Negroes and Negro "Slavery." NY: Van Evrie, Horton; 1861. [$35.00]

Van Evrie, John H. White Supremacy and Negro Subordination. NY: Van Evrie, Horton; 1868. [$75.00]

Van Horne, Thomas Budd. History of the Army of the Cumberland. Cincinnati: Clarke; 1875. 3 v. [$350.00]

Van Meter, Anna Hunter. Relics of ye Olden Days in Salem County, New Jersey. Salem: Gwynne; 1892. [rebacked, x-lib., $75.00]

Van Meter, Benjamin Franklin. Genealogies and Sketches of Some Old Families Who Have Taken Prominent Part in the Development of Virginia and Kentucky Especially. Louisville: Morton; 1901. [bumped, worn, endpapers and half title lacking, $75.00]

Van Metre, Isaiah. History of Black Hawk County, Iowa. Chicago: Biographical; 1904. [rebacked, $150.00]

Van Ness, William Peter. Speeches at Full Length of Mr. Van Ness, Mr. Caines, the Attorney-General [Ambrose Spencer], Mr. Harrison, and General Hamilton, in the Great Cause of the People, against Harry Croswell. NY: Waite; 1804. [$175.00]

Van Orman, Richard A. Room for the Night. Bloomington: Indiana UP; 1966. [$20.00]

Van Roosbroeck, Gustave Leopold. Reincarnation of H. L. Mencken. [s.l.: s.n.]; 1925. [inscribed, $35.00]

Van Santvoord, George. Sketches of the Lives and Judicial Services of the Chief-Justices of the Supreme Court of the United States. NY: Scribner; 1854. [$185.00]

Van Schaack, Henry Cruger. Life of Peter Van Schaack. NY: Appleton; 1842. [spine frayed, corners bumped, $175.00] [$25.00]

Van Tramp, John C. Prairie and Rocky Mountain Adventures. Columbus: Segner & Condit; 1867. [$100.00]

Van Tyne, Claude Halstead. Loyalists in the American Revolution. 1st ed. NY: Macmillan; 1902. [hinges weak, $35.00]

Van Vorst, Bessie. The Woman Who Toils. NY: Doubleday, Page; 1903. [$35.00]

Vance, James Scott. **Proof of Rome's Political Meddling in America.** Washington: Fellowship Forum; 1927. [$12.50]

Vance, Robert H. **A Camera in the Gold Rush.** San Francisco: Book Club of California; 1946. [$150.00]

Vanderbilt, Gertrude Lefferts. **Social History of Flatbush.** NY: Appleton; 1881. [$85.00]

Vanderpoel, Emily. **More Chronicles of a Pioneer School.** NY: Cadmus; 1927. [$27.50]

Vanderslice, John Mitchell. **Gettysburg, Then and Now.** NY: Dillingham; 1899. [inscribed, $75.00]

Vandiveer, Clarence A. **Fur-Trade and Early Western Exploration.** Cleveland: Clark; 1929. [$45.00, Canadian] [$75.00]

Vandiver, Frank Everson. **Rebel Brass.** Baton Rouge: Louisiana State UP; 1956. [$17.50] [signed, $32.50]

Vandiver, Louise Ayer. **Traditions and History of Anderson County.** Atlanta: Ruralist; 1928. [frayed rubbed, spotted, $45.00]

Vanzetti, Bartolomeo. **Background of the Plymouth Trial.** Boston: Road to Freedom; [1926?]. [$50.00]

Varick, Richard. **The Varick Court of Inquiry.** Boston: Bibliophile Society; 1907. [x-lib., $50.00]

Vaughn, Jesse Wendell. **Indian Fights.** 1st ed. Norman: U. of Oklahoma; 1966. [$35.00]

Vaughn, Jesse Wendell. **The Reynolds Campaign on Powder River.** Norman: U. of Oklahoma; 1961. [chipped dj, $37.50]

Vaughn, Robert. **Then and Now; or, Thirty-Six Years in the Rockies.** Minneapolis: Tribune; 1900. [rubbed, $175.00] [$150.00]

Veblen, Thorstein. **The Higher Learning in America.** NY: Huebsch; 1918. [$20.00]

Veech, James. **Monongahela of Old.** Pittsburgh: [s.n.]; 1858-92. [$65.00]

Vega, Garcilaso de la. **La Florida del Inca.** Madrid: Franco; 1723. [contemporary vellum binding, x-lib., $1000.00]

Vega, Garcilaso de la. **Florida of the Inca.** Austin: U. of Texas; 1962. [$25.00]

Velasco, Jose Francisco. **Sonora.** San Francisco: Bancroft; 1861. [cloth rippled, few leaves stained, $260.00]

Velazquez, Loreta Janeta. **Story of the Civil War.** NY: Worthington; 1890. [rubbed, hinges weak, $85.00]

Velez de Escalante, Silvestre. **Pageant in the Wilderness.** Salt Lake City: Utah State Hist. Soc.; 1950. [$50.00]

Venegas, Miguel. **Natural and Civil History of California.** London: Rivington and Fletcher; 1759. 2 v. [1st English ed., $1250.00]

Vennor, Henry George. **Our Birds of Prey.** Montreal: Dawson; 1876. [binding scuffed, spine replaced, $875.00]

Vercheres de Boucherville, Rene Thomas. **War on the Detroit.** Chicago: Lakeside; 1940. [endpapers foxed, $35.00]

Very, Lydia Louisa Anna. **Poems.** 1st ed. Andover, MA: Draper; 1856. [spine spoiled, $75.00]

Vestal, Stanley. **'Dobe Walls.** Boston, NY: Houghton Mifflin; 1929. [$35.00]

Vestal, Stanley. **Jim Bridger.** NY: Morrow; 1946. [worn dj, $35.00] [$50.00]

Vestal, Stanley. **Joe Meek.** Caldwell, ID: Caxton; 1952. [$40.00]

Vestal, Stanley. **Kit Carson.** Boston, NY: Houghton Mifflin; 1928. [worn dj, $35.00]

Vestal, Stanley. **The Missouri.** NY, Toronto: Farrar & Rinehart; 1945. [$25.00]

Vestal, Stanley. **New Sources of Indian History, 1850-1891.** Norman: U. of Oklahoma; 1934. [$85.00]

Vestal, Stanley. **Queen of Cowtowns: Dodge City.** 1st ed. NY: Harper; 1952. [$22.50] [$35.00] [1st printing, $25.00]

Vestal, Stanley. **Revolt on the Border.** Bostòn: Houghton Mifflin; 1938. [$40.00]

Vestal, Stanley. **Short Grass Country.** 1st ed. NY: Duell, Sloan & Pearce; 1941. [$45.00] [covers very worn, $25.00]

Vestal, Stanley. **Sitting Bull.** Boston, NY: Houghton Mifflin; 1932. [$50.00] [1957 Oklahoma ed., $30.00]

Vestal, Stanley. **Warpath and Council Fire.** NY: Random; 1948. [$45.00] [$55.00]

Vetromile, Eugene. **The Abnakis and Their History.** NY: Kirker; 1866. [$125.00]

Vickers, George Edward. **Philadelphia.** Philadelphia: Dunlap; 1893. [x-lib., $35.00]

Victor, Frances Fuller. **River of the West.** Hartford; San Francisco: Columbian; Trumbill; 1870. [$150.00]

Vidal, Gore. **The Best Man.** 1st ed. Boston: Little, Brown; 1960. [torn, frayed dj, $15.00]

Viele, Teresa. **Following the Drum.** NY: Rudd & Carleton; 1858. [$300.00]

Vigneron, Lucien. **De Montreal 'a Washington (Amerique du Nord).** nouv. ed. Paris: Delhomme et Briguet; 1895. [$40.00]

Villagra, Gaspar Perez de. **History of New Mexico.** Los Angeles: Quivira Society; 1933. [$195.00]

Villard, Henry. **Memoirs of.** Boston, NY: Houghton Mifflin; 1904. 2 v. [x-lib., $35.00]

Villard, Henry. **The Past and Present of the Pike's Peak Gold Regions.** Princeton: Princeton UP; 1932. [$40.00] [$50.00]

Villard, Oswald Garrison. **John Brown.** Boston, NY: Houghton Mifflin; 1910. [$35.00]

Vinton, Stallo. **John Colter.** limited ed. NY: Eberstadt; 1926. [$50.00]

Virgines, George E. **Saga of the Colt Six-Shooter.** NY: Fell; 1969. [dj chipped, $40.00]

Virginia. Dept. of Agriculture and Immigration. **Hand Book of Virginia Information for the Homeseeker and Investor.** Lynchburg: Bell; 1906. [x-lib., $35.00]

Vischer, Edward. **Sketches of the Washoe Mining Regions.** San Francisco: Valentine; 1862. [lacking the sketches, $85.00]

Visit to Texas: Being the Journal of a Traveller Through Those Parts Most interesting to American Settlers. NY: Goodrich & Wiley; 1834. [map in facs., $750.00]

Visscher, William L. **A Thrilling and Truthful History of the Pony Express.** Chicago: Rand, McNally; 1908. [$35.00] [$45.00]

Vivian, Thomas Jondrie. **Fall of Santiago.** NY: Fenno; 1898. [$65.00]

Vizetelly, Henry. **Four Months among the Gold-Finders in California.** NY, Philadelphia: Appleton; 1849. [$250.00]

Vlekke, Bernard Hubertus Maria. **Hollanders Who Helped Build America.** NY: American Biographical Co.; 1942. [$40.00]

Voegelin, Charles Frederick. **Tubatulabal Grammar.** Berkeley: U. of California; 1935. [$7.50]

Voegelin, Charles Frederick. **Tubatulabal Texts.** Berkeley: U. of California; 1935. [$6.50]

Vollmer, Carl Gottfried Wilhelm. **Kalifornien och Guldfebern.** Stockholm: Fahlstedt; 1862. [bound in 2 vols., $300.00]

Volney, C. F. **View of the Soil and Climate of the United States of America.** Philadelphia, Baltimore: Conrad; 1804. [$300.00]

Volunteer Nurse! 1st ed. Philadelphia: Old Franklin; 1878. [loose binding, $75.00]

Volwiler, Albert T. **George Croghan and the Westward Movement.** Cleveland: Clark; 1926. [$125.00]

Von Hagen, Victor Wolfgang. **The Ancient Sun Kingdoms of the Americas.** 1st ed. Cleveland: World; 1961. [$25.00]

Von Hagen, Victor Wolfgang. **Aztec and Maya Papermakers.** NY: Augustin; 1944. [$100.00]

Von Hagen, Victor Wolfgang. **Highway of the Sun.** 1st ed. NY: Duell, Sloan and Pearce; 1955. [$12.50]

Von Hagen, Victor Wolfgang. **Maya Explorer.** 1st ed. Norman: U. of Oklahoma; 1947. [$18.00]

Voorhis, Robert. **Life and Adventures of.** Providence, RI: Trumbull; 1829. [$75.00]

Voyage of H. M. S. Blonde to the Sandwich Island, in the Years 1824-1825. London: Murray; 1826. [x-lib., $1600.00]

Wack, Henry Wellington. **Newark Anniversary Poems.** NY: Gomme; 1917. [spine darkened, corners worn, $200.00]

Waddell, Alfred Moore. **Some Memories of My Life.** Raleigh: Edwards & Broughton; 1908. [bumped, stained, $35.00]

Wade, John Donald. **Augustus Baldwin Longstreet.** Athens: U. of Georgia; 1969. [$20.00]

Wafer, Lionel. **A New Voyage and Description of the Isthmus of America.** Cleveland: Burrows; 1903. [$85.00] [1934 Hakluyt ed., $60.00]

Waggoner, Madeline Sadler. **The Long Haul West.** NY: Putnam; 1958. [$15.00]

Wagner, Charles Abraham. **Harvard; Four Centuries and Freedoms.** 1st ed. NY: Dutton; 1950. [$20.00]

Wagner, Glendolin Damon. **Old Neutriment.** Boston: Hill; 1934. [$100.00]

Wagner, Henry Raup. **Discovery of Yucatan.** Berkeley, CA: Cortes Soc.; 1942. [$100.00]

Wagner, Henry Raup. **Peter Pond.** limited ed. New Haven: Yale Univ. Library; 1955. [in slipcase with 3 maps, $50.00]

Wagner, Henry Raup. **Spanish Voyages to the Northwest Coast of America in the Sixteenth Century.** San Francisco: California Hist. Soc.; 1929. [inscribed, $250.00]

Wait, Benjamin. **Letters from Van Dieman's Land.** Buffalo: Wilgus; 1843. [front cover detached, $250.00]

Waite, Catherine. **The Mormon Prophet and His Harem.** 5th ed. Cambridge, MA: Riverside; 1867. [$75.00]

Waite, Otis Frederick Reed. **New Hampshire in the Great Rebellion.** Claremont: Tracy, Chase; 1870. [$60.00]

Waitt, Ernest Linden. **History of the Nineteenth Regiment.** see, Massachusetts. Infantry 19th Regt., 1861-1865.

Waldo, Edna. **Dakota.** Bismarck: Capital; 1932. [$50.00] [1936 Caxton ed., signed, $60.00]

Waldo, Edna. **From Travois to Iron Trail.** NY: Ackerman; 1944. [$15.00]

Waldo, Samuel Putnam. **Memoirs of Andrew Jackson.** 1st ed. Hartford: Russell; 1818. [spine badly chipped, prelims missing, boards warped, $75.00]

Waldo, Samuel Putnam. **Tour of James Monroe.** Hartford: Bolles; 1818. [$125.00] [$90.00] [1820 2nd ed. Andrus, $35.00]

Waldron, Holman D. **With Pen and Camera on the Field of Gettysburg in War and Peace.** Portland, ME: Chisholm; 1898. [$10.00]

Waldron, Holman D. **With Pen and Camera thro' the "Land of the Sky."** 10th ed. Portland, ME: Chisholm; 1911. [$35.00]

Walker, Adam. **Journal of Two Campaigns of the Fourth Regiment of U. S. Infantry in the Michigan and Indiana Territories.** Keene, NH: Sentinel; 1816. [$1350.00]

Walker, Aldace F. **The Vermont Brigade in the Shenandoah Valley.** Burlington: Free Press; 1869. [$55.00]

Walker, Alexander. **Jackson and New Orleans.** NY, Cincinnati: Derby; 1856. [$125.00]

Walker, Alexander. **Life of Andrew Jackson.** Philadelphia: Potter; 1867. [$85.00]

Walker, Anne Kendrick. **Russell County in Retrospect.** Richmond: Dietz; 1950. [$50.00]

Walker, Charles Rumford. **Steeltown.** 1st ed. NY: Harper; 1950. [$20.00]

Walker, Franklin Dickerson. **Literary History of Southern California.** Berkeley: U. of California; 1950. [$25.00] [$30.00]

Walker, Franklin Dickerson. **San Francisco's Literary Frontier.** NY: Knopf; 1939. [$35.00]

Walker, Henry J. **Jesse James, the Outlaw.** 1st ed. [Des Moines?]: Walker; 1961. [vol. 1 all published, $35.00]

Walker, Henry P. **The Wagonmasters.** 1st ed. Norman: U. of Oklahoma; 1966. [$30.00]

Walker, Hovenden. **A Journal: Or Full Account of the Late Expedition to Canada.** London: Browne; 1720. [hinges worn, $785.00]

Walker, James Herbert. **Rafting Days in Pennsylvania.** Altoona: Times-Tribune; 1922. [very x-lib., $40.00]

Walker, Robert Sparks. **Torchlights to the Cherokees; the Brainerd Mission.** NY: Macmillan; 1931. [$75.00]

Walker, Tacetta B. **Stories of Early Days in Wyoming.** Casper: Prairie; 1936. [$200.00]

Walker, William. **Injun Summer.** Caldwell, ID: Caxton; 1952. [$30.00]

Walker, William. **The Longest Rope.** Caldwell, ID: Caxton; 1940. [x-lib., $10.00]

Walker, William. **War in Nicaragua.** Mobile, NY: Goetzel; 1860. [rebacked, folding map in facs., $175.00]

Wall, Caleb Arnold. **The Historic Boston Tea Party of December 16, 1773.** Worcester, MA: Blanchard; 1896. [$45.00]

Wallace, Alfred Russel. **A Narrative of Travels on the Amazon and Rio Negro.** 2nd ed. London, NY: Lock; 1889. [hinge taped, spine chipped, $50.00]

Wallace, Alfred Russel. **Travels on the Amazon.** London: Ward, Lock; 1911. [$20.00]

Wallace, Allie B. **Frontier Life in Oklahoma.** Washington: Public Affairs; 1964. [inscribed, $55.00]

Wallace, Charles. **Confession of the Awful and Bloody Transactions in the Life of.** 1st ed. New Orleans: Barclay; 1851. [rear wrap loose, $1250.00]

Wallace, Edward Seccomb. **Destiny and Glory.** NY: Coward-McCann; 1957. [$18.50]

Wallace, Edward Seccomb. **General William Jenkins Worth.** Dallas: Southern Methodist UP; 1953. [$40.00]

Wallace, Edward Seccomb. **The Great Reconnaissance.** 1st ed. Boston: Little, Brown; 1955. [$16.00]

Wallace, Elizabeth. **Mark Twain and the Happy Island.** Chicago: McClurg; 1913. [$135.00]

Wallace, Ernest. **The Comanches.** 1st ed. Norman: U. of Oklahoma; 1952. [$48.00] [$55.00]

Wallace, Ernest. **Texas in Turmoil, 1849-1875.** Austin: Steck-Vaughn; 1965. [$30.00]

Wallace, Joseph. **History of Illinois and Louisiana under the French Rule.** Cincinnati: Clarke; 1893. [$85.00]

Wallace, Susan Arnold. **Land of the Pueblos.** NY: Alden; 1888. [$40.00] [1889 2nd ed., $20.00]

Wallace, Willard Mosher. **Traitorous Hero.** 1st ed. NY: Harper; 1954. [$25.00]

Wallace, William H. **Speeches and Writings of.** Kansas City, MO: Western Baptist; 1914. [$25.00]

Waller, Brown. **Last of the Great Western Train Robbers.** South Brunswick, NJ: Barnes; 1968. [$35.00]

Waller, William. **In the Supreme Court of Tennessee at Nashville by Transfer from Knoxville, John Thomas Scopes, Plaintiff-in Error, vs. State of Tennessee, Defendant-in Error.** Nashville: Baird-Ward; [1926?]. [$325.00]

Wallihan, Allen Grant. **Hoofs, Claws and Antlers of the Rocky Mountains.** Denver: Thayer; 1894. [$300.00]

Wallington, Nellie. **Historic Churches of America.** NY: Duffield; 1907. [$22.50]

Walter, Richard. **A Voyage round the World in the Years MDCCXL, I, II, III, IV.** London: Knapton; 1748. [$150.00]

Walters, Lorenzo D. **Tombstone's Yesterday.** Tucson: Acme; 1928. [signed, $100.00]

Walters, Ray. **Albert Gallatin: Jeffersonian Financier and Diplomat.** NY: Macmillan; 1957. [$25.00]

Walton, Frank Ledyard. **Tomahawks to Textiles.** NY: Appleton Century Crofts; 1953. [$15.00]

Walton, Joseph Solomon. **Conrad Weiser and the Indian Policy of Colonial Pennsylvania.** Philadelphia: Jacobs; 1900. [very x-lib., $50.00]

Walton, William. **Narrative of the Captivity and Sufferings of Benjamin Gilbert and His Family.** Philadelphia: Phillips; 1790. [$125.00]

Walton, William M. **Life and Adventures of Ben Thompson.** Austin: The Author; 1884. [$3500.00] [1954 Frontier Press ed., $20.00] [1926 Frontier Times ed., $125.00] [1956 Steck reprint, $35.00]

Wandell, Samuel Henry. **Aaron Burr.** NY, London: Putnam; 1925. 2 v. [$45.00]

War Reports of General of the Army George C. Marshall, Chief of Staff, General of the Army H. H. Arnold, Commanding General, Army Air Forces [and] Fleet Admiral Ernest J. King. 1st ed. Philadelphia: Lippincott; 1947. [$25.00]

War Songs of the Blue and the Gray. NY: Hurst; 1905. [$15.00]

Warburg, Paul Moritz. **Federal Reserve System.** NY: Macmillan; 1930. 2 v. [$37.50]

Ward, Artemus. **Artemus Ward: His Works, Complete.** NY: Carleton; 1877. [$25.00]

Ward, Artemus. **Complete Works of.** rev. ed. NY: Dillingham; 1898. [shaken, $20.00]

Ward, Christopher. **War of the Revolution.** NY: Macmillan; 1952. [$35.00]

Ward, Don. **Bits of Silver.** NY: Hastings; 1961. [$20.00]

Ward, Henry George. **Mexico in 1827.** London: Colburn; 1828. 2 v. [$950.00]

Ward, Hortense. **Cattle Brands and Cow Hides.** Dallas: Story Book; 1953. [$45.00]

Ward, J. O. **My Grandpa Went West.** Caldwell, ID: Caxton; 1956. [$12.50]

Ward, John. **Overland Route to California, and Other Poems.** NY: Tompkins; 1874. [$35.00]

Ward, John William. **Andrew Jackson, Symbol for an Age.** NY: Oxford UP; 1955. [$20.00]

Ward, Lester Frank. **Young Ward's Diary.** 2nd ed. NY: Putnam; 1935. [$30.00]

Ward, Maria. **Female Life among the Mormons.** 1st ed. NY: Derby; 1855. [$35.00] [1855 London ed., $40.00]

Ward, Samuel. **Sam Ward in the Gold Rush.** Stanford: Stanford UP; 1949. [$20.00]

Ward, Theodora. **The Capsule of the Mind.** Cambridge, MA: Belknap; 1961. [$17.50]

Ward, William. **Harry Tracy.** Cleveland: Westbrook; 1908. [$50.00]

Wardell, Morris L. **Political History of the Cherokee Nation, 1838-1907.** 1st ed. Norman: U. of Oklahoma; 1938. [presentation, x-lib., $35.00] [$85.00]

Warden, D. B. **Chorographical and Statistical Description of the District of Columbia.** Paris: Smith; 1816. [$325.00]

Wardner, James F. **Jim Wardner, of Wardner, Idaho.** NY: Anglo-American; 1900. [$150.00]

Ware, Eugene Fitch. **Indian War of 1864.** NY: St. Martin; 1960. [$17.50] [$18.00]

Ware, Norman Joseph. **Labor Movement in the United States, 1860-1895.** NY: Vintage; 1929. [$10.00]

Waring, George Edwin. **Whip and Spur.** Boston: Osgood; 1875. [inscribed, $50.00]

Waring, Guy. **My Pioneer Past.** Boston: Humphries; 1936. [$45.00]

Warman, Cy. **The Prospector.** Denver: Great Divide; 1894. [presentation, $50.00]

Warmoth, Henry Clay. **War, Politics, and Reconstruction.** NY: Macmillan; 1930. [$25.00]

Warne, Frank Julian. **The Immigrant Invasion.** NY: Dodd, Mead; 1913. [$27.50]

Warner, Charles Dudley. **On Horseback.** Boston, NY: Houghton Mifflin; 1888. [$35.00] [2nd issue, $30.00]

Warner, Louis Henry. **Archbishop Lamy.** Santa Fe: New Mexican; 1936. [x-lib., $15.00] [$30.00]

Warren, Charles. **Odd Byways in American History.** Cambridge: Harvard UP; 1942. [bumped, $10.00]

Warren, John. **Eulogy on the Honourable Thomas Russell.** Boston: Sweetser; 1796. [disbound, $40.00]

Warren, John Esaias. **Para.** NY: Putnam; 1851. [foxed and waterstained, $120.00]

Warren, John Quincy Adams. **California Ranchos and Farms.** Madison: State Historical Society of Wisconsin; 1967. [$12.50]

Warren, Robert Penn. **Brother to Dragons.** NY: Random; 1953. [dj chipped, $22.50]

Warren, Robert Penn. **How Texas Won Her Freedom.** San Jacinto Monument, TX: Museum of History; 1959, c1958. [$25.00]

Warren, Robert Penn. **John Brown; the Making of a Martyr.** 1st ed. NY: Payson & Clarke; 1929. [in slipcase, $350.00]

Warren, Robert Penn. **You, Emperors, and Others.** NY: Random; 1960. [$20.00]

Warren, Thomas Robinson. **Dust and Foam.** NY: Scribner; 1859. [$125.00]

Warren, William Whipple. **History of the Ojibway.** St. Paul: MN Hist. Soc.; 1885. [x-lib., $45.00]

Washburn, Charles G. **Theodore Roosevelt.** London: Heinemann; 1916. [$20.00]

Washburn, Stanley. **Trails, Trappers, and Tender-Feet in the New Empire of Western Canada.** NY: Holt; 1912. [binding torn, $40.00]

Washburn, Wilcomb E. **The Governor and the Rebel.** Chapel Hill: U. of North Carolina; 1957. [water damaged, $20.00]

Washburne, Elihu Benjamin. **Sketch of Edward Coles.** Chicago: Jansen, McClurg; 1882. [$45.00]

Washington, Booker T. **Future of the American Negro.** 2nd ed. Boston: Small, Maynard; 1900. [$25.00]

Washington, Booker T. **My Larger Education.** 1st ed. Garden City: Doubleday, Page; 1911. [rubbed, $20.00]

Washington, George. **Diaries of George Washington, 1748-1799.** regents' ed. Boston, NY: Houghton Mifflin; 1925. 4 v. [$90.00]

Washington, George. **George Washington, Colonial Traveller, 1732-1775.** Indianapolis: Bobbs-Merrill; 1927. [$40.00]

Washington, George. **Journal of Major George Washington.** limited ed. NY: Sabin; 1865. [$45.00]

Washington, George. **Letters and Recollections of.** London: Constable; 1906. [$55.00]

Washington, George. **Letters from General Washington to Several of His Friends, in June and July, 1776.** Philadelphia: Federal; 1795. [lacks half title, $100.00]

Washington, George. **Letters from His Excellency George Washington, to Arthur Young, Esq., F. R. S., and Sir John Sinclair, Bart., M. P.** Alexandria, VA: Cottom and Stewart; 1803. [$125.00]

Washington, George. **Monuments of Washington's Patriotism.** 4th ed. Washington: Knight; 1844. [$45.00]

Washington, George. **Revolutionary Orders.** see, United States. Continental Army.

Washington, George. **Selections from the Correspondence of General Washington and James Anderson.** London: Cumming; 1800. [$125.00]

Washington, George. **Washington and the West.** NY: Century; 1905. [spine silverfished, $35.00]

Washington, George. **Washington's Political Legacies.** NY: Forman; 1800. [x-lib., $75.00]

Watchem, Timothy. **War-Horseiana.** [Philadelphia?: s.n.]; 1851. [$85.00]

Waterhouse, Benjamin. **Journal, of a Young Man of Massachusetts.** Boston: Rowe and Hooper; 1816. [rebacked, frontis partly missing, $75.00]

Waterhouse, Sylvester. **Resources of Missouri.** St. Louis: Wiebusch; 1867. [$75.00]

Waterman, Thomas Tileston. **Mansions of Virginia, 1706-1776.** Chapel Hill: U. of North Carolina; 1946. [$37.50]

Waters, Frank. **The Colorado.** NY, Toronto: Rinehart; 1946. [$30.00] [signed, $75.00]

Waters, Frank. **The Dust within the Rock.** NY: Liveright; 1940. [$45.00]

Waters, Frank. **The Earp Brothers of Tombstone.** 1st ed. NY: Potter; 1960. [dj chipped, $40.00]

Waters, Frank. **Masked Gods.** 1st ed. Albuquerque: U. of New Mexico; 1950. [dj worn, $75.00]

Waters, Frank. **Midas of the Rockies.** Denver: U. of Denver; 1949. [$20.00]

Waters, William. **Gallery of Western Badmen.** Covington, KY: Americana; 1954. [$12.00] [$35.00]

Waterston, Elizabeth. **Churches in Delaware during the Revolution.** Wilmington: Historical Soc. of Delaware; 1925. [$25.00]

Waterton, Charles. **Wanderings in South America.** new ed. London: Macmillan; 1879. [corners bumped, $75.00]

Watkins, T. H. **The Grand Colorado.** Palo Alto, CA: American West; 1969. [$15.00]

Watson, Douglas Sloane. **West Wind.** Los Angeles: Priv. Print.; 1934. [limited ed., $450.00]

Watson, Elkanah. **Men and Times of the Revolution.** NY: Dana; 1856. [$165.00]

Watson, Elmo Scott. **The Professor Goes West.** Bloomington: Illinois Wesleyan UP; 1954. [$15.00]

Watson, Frederick. **A Century of Gunmen.** London: Nicholson & Watson; 1931. [dj worn, $40.00]

Watson, Margaret G. **Silver Theatre.** Glendale, CA: Clark; 1964. [$25.00]

Watson, Paul Barron. **The Tragic Career of Commodore James Barron.** NY: Coward-McCann; 1942. [$10.00]

Watson, Robert. **Lower Fort Garry.** 1st ed. Winnipeg: Hudson's Bay Co.; 1928. [$15.00]

Watson, Thomas E. **Life and Times of Andrew Jackson.** Thomson, GA: Jeffersonian; 1912. [$45.00]

Watson, Winslow C. **Military and Civil History of the County of Essex, New York.** Albany, NY: Munsell; 1869. [binding worn and stained, $95.00] [$85.00]

Watt, Roberta Frye. **Four Wagons West.** Portland, OR: Binfords & Mort; 1931. [$11.00]

Watters, Leon Laizer. **Pioneer Jews of Utah.** NY: American Jewish Hist. Soc.; 1952. [$25.00]

Watterson, Henry. **History of the Spanish-American War.** Hartford, CT: American Pub. Co.; 1898. [$85.00] [1898 Richmond ed., $25.00]

Watts, Isaac. **Miscellaneous Thoughts.** 1st American ed. Elizabeth-Town: Shepard Kollock; 1796. [$75.00]

Waugh, Lorenzo. **Autobiography of.** Oakland, CA: Pacific; 1883. [$100.00]

Waugh, William Templeton. **James Wolfe.** Montreal, NY: Carrier; 1928. [$85.00]

Way, Frederick. **The Allegheny.** NY, Toronto: Farrar & Rinehart; 1942. [signed, $30.00]

Way, Frederick. **Directory of Western Rivers' Steam Towboats Corrected to June, 1953.** limited ed. Sewickley, PA: [s.n.]; 1954. [mimeographed, $75.00]

Way, Frederick. **She Takes the Horns.** [Cincinnati: Picture Marine]; 1953. [with chart, $22.50]

Wayland, Francis. **Affairs of Rhode Island.** Boston: Ticknor; 1842. [$45.00]

Wayland, John Walter. **Battle of New Market.** New Market, VA: Henkel; 1926. [$35.00]

Wayne, Anthony. **Anthony Wayne, a Name in Arms.** Pittsburgh: U. of Pittsburgh; 1959, c1960. [$32.50]

Weadock, Jack. **Dust of the Desert.** Tucson: Arizona Silhouettes; 1963. [$12.00]

Weare, W. K. **Songs of the Western Shore.** San Francisco: Bacon; 1879. [covers worn, $35.00]

Weatherford, Willis Duke. **James Dunwoody Brownson De Bow.** Charlottesville, VA: Historical Pub. Co.; 1935. [$45.00]

Weatherford, Willis Duke. **Life and Religion in Southern Appalachia.** NY: Friendship; 1964, c1962. [2nd printing, $7.50]

Weatherwax, Paul. **Story of the Maize Plant.** Chicago: U. of Chicago; 1923. [$35.00]

Weaver, Ethan Allen. **The Forks of the Delaware Illustrated.** Easton, PA: Escheubach; 1900. [$175.00]

Weaver, James Baird. **A Call to Action.** Des Moines: Iowa Printing; 1892. [$45.00]

Weaver, Warren A. **Lithographs of N. Currier and Currier & Ives.** NY: Holport; 1925. [$25.00]

Webb, J. Watson. **Altowan.** see, Stewart, William George Drummond.

Webb, James Josiah. **Adventures in the Santa Fé Trade, 1844-1847.** Glendale, CA: Clark; 1931. [$65.00]

Webb, Laura S. **Custer's Immortality.** NY: Evening Post; [1876?]. [$125.00]

Webb, Nancy. **Hawaiian Islands from Monarchy to Democracy.** NY: Viking; 1956. [$35.00]

Webb, Samuel Blachley. **Correspondence and Journals of.** letterpress ed. Lancaster, PA: Wickersham; 1893. 3 v. [$200.00]

Webb, Walter Prescott. **Divided We Stand.** NY, Toronto: Farrar & Rinehart; 1937. [$65.00]

Webb, Walter Prescott. **The Great Frontier.** Boston: Houghton Mifflin; 1952. [$20.00]

Webb, Walter Prescott. **The Great Plains.** Boston: Ginn; 1931. [1st ed., 2nd state, $40.00] [$25.00] [$27.50]

Webb, Walter Prescott. **Handbook of Texas.** Austin: Texas State Hist. Assn.; 1952-76. 3 v. [vols. 1-2 only, worn djs, $75.00]

Webb, Walter Prescott. **The Texas Rangers.** Boston: Houghton Mifflin; 1935. [dj worn, $75.00]

Webb, William Edward. **Buffalo Land.** Cincinnati, Chicago: Hannaford; 1872. [$90.00] [$100.00]

Webb, William Larkin. **Centennial History of Independence, Mo.** [s.l.]: Webb; 1927. [$50.00]

Webber, Charles Wilkins. **Old Hicks.** NY: Harper; 1848. [soiled, loose in binding, $180.00] [$250.00]

Webber, Charles Wilkins. **Prairie Scout.** NY: Dewitt & Davenport; 1852. [$37.50]

Webster, Daniel. **The Private Correspondence.** Boston: Little, Brown; 1857. 2 v. [$200.00]

Webster, Daniel. **Works of.** Boston: Little and Brown; 1851. 6 v. [spines faded, $145.00]

Webster, Noah. **Compendious Dictionary of the English Language.** 1st ed. Hartford; New Haven: Hudson & Goodwin; Cooke; 1806. [front hinge cracked, $325.00]

Webster, Noah. **The Prompter.** 4th ed. NY: Bunce; 1793. [binding very worn, endpapers lacking, $175.00]

Webster, Thomas. **Free Military School for Applicants for Commands of Colored Troops.** Philadelphia: King & Baird; 1863. [$475.00]

Webster, William Henry Bayley. **Narrative of a Voyage to the Southern Atlantic Ocean in the Years 1828, 29, 30.** London: Bentley; 1834. 2 v. [$585.00]

Wechsler, James Arthur. **Age of Suspicion.** NY: Random; 1953. [$7.50]

Wecter, Dixon. **Age of the Great Depression.** NY: Macmillan; 1948. [$12.50]

Wecter, Dixon. **Sam Clemens of Hannibal.** Boston: Houghton Mifflin; 1952. [$12.50]

Wedel, Peter J. **Story of Bethel College.** North Newton, KS: Bethel; 1954. [$17.50]

Wedel, Waldo Rudolph. **Introduction to Pawnee Archeology.** Washington: USGPO; 1936. [some insect damage, $35.00]

Weeks, Alvin Gardner. **Massasoit of the Wampanoags.** Fall River, MA: Plimpton; 1919. [$15.00]

Weeks, Joseph Dame. **History of the Knights of Pythias.** Cincinnati: Powers and Weeks; 1871. [$35.00]

Weems, Mason Locke. **Das Leben des Georg Washington.** Baltimore: Schaffer und Maund; 1817. [$75.00]

Weems, Mason Locke. **Life of General Francis Marion.** Philadelphia: Allen; 1829, c1824. [taped spine, hinges cracked, $45.00]

Weems, Mason Locke. **Life of George Washington.** 27th ed. Philadelphia: Allen; 1834. [rebacked, $22.50]

Weems, Mason Locke. **Life of William Penn.** Philadelphia: Carey & Lea; 1822. [rebound, foxed, $60.00] [1829 Hunt ed., stained, front cover loose, $20.00]

Wehlitz, Lou Rogers. **Tar Heel Women.** Raleigh: Warren; 1949. [$20.00]

Weise, Arthur James. **History of the City of Albany, New York.** Albany: Bender; 1884. [$40.00] [$75.00]

Weisel, George Ferdinand. **Men and Trade on the Northwest Frontier.** Missoula: Montana State UP; 1955. [$35.00]

Weiss, Harry B. **Thomas Say.** Springfield, Baltimore: Thomas; 1931. [$35.00]

Welch, Andrew. **Narrative of the Early Days and Remembrances of Oceola Nikkanochee.** London: Hatchard; 1841. [$750.00]

Welch, Robert Henry Winborne. **Life of John Birch.** 1st ed. Chicago: Regnery; 1954. [presentation, dj stained, $15.00]

Weld, Isaac. **Travels through the States of North America and the Provinces of Upper and Lower Canada.** London: Stockdale; 1799. [$850.00] [1800 issue, $400.00]

Welde, Thomas. see, Winthrop, John.

Weldon, Martin. **Babe Ruth.** NY: Crowell; 1948. [$40.00]

Welles, C. M. **Three Years' Wanderings of a Connecticut Yankee, in South America, Africa, Australia, and California.** NY: American Subscription; 1859. [$75.00]

Welles, Gideon. **Diary of.** Boston, NY: Houghton Mifflin; 1911. 3 v. [$55.00] [$45.00] [1960 Norton ed., $50.00]

Wellman, Manly Wade. **Fastest on the River.** 1st ed. NY: Holt; 1957. [$16.00]

Wellman, Manly Wade. **Rebel Boast: First at Bethel--Last at Appomattox.** 1st ed. NY: Holt; 1956. [$25.00] [$30.00]

Wellman, Manly Wade. **They Took Their Stand.** NY: Putnam; 1959. [$25.00]

Wellman, Paul Iselin. **Death in the Desert.** NY: Macmillan; 1935. [$45.00]

Wellman, Paul Iselin. **A Dynasty of Western Outlaws.** 1st ed. Garden City: Doubleday; 1961. [$35.00]

Wellman, Paul Iselin. **Glory, God, and Gold.** 1st ed. Garden City: Doubleday; 1954. [$30.00] [$25.00]

Wellman, Paul Iselin. **Trampling Herd.** NY: Carrick & Evans; 1939. [$40.00] [$35.00]

Wells, Charles Knox Polk. **Life and Adventures of.** Halls, MO: Warnica; 1907. [$120.00]

Wells, Edward Laight. **Hampton and His Cavalry in '64.** Richmond: Johnson; 1899. [$135.00]

Wells, James Monroe. **The Chisolm Massacre.** 2nd ed. Washington: Chisolm Monument Assn.; 1878. [$45.00]

Wells, Tom Henderson. **Commodore Moore and the Texas Navy.** Austin: U. of Texas; 1960. [$35.00]

Wells, William Vincent. **Walker's Expedition to Nicargua.** NY: Stringer and Townsend; 1856. [spine torn, $100.00]

Welsh, Herbert. **Civilization among the Sioux Indians.** Philadelphia: Indian Rights Assn.; 1893. [$35.00]

Welsh, Willard. **Hutchinson, a Prairie City in Kansas.** Wichita, KS: McCormick-Armstrong; 1946. [$25.00]

Welty, Eudora. **The Ponder Heart.** 1st ed. NY: Harcourt, Brace; 1954. [soiled dj, $75.00]

Wendell, George Blunt. **George Blunt Wendell.** Mystic, CT: Marine Hist. Assn.;1949. [$15.00]

Wenner, Fred L. **Story of Oklahoma and the Eighty-Niners.** Guthrie: Co-Operative Pub.; 1939. [$35.00]

Wentworth, Frank L. **Aspen on the Roaring Fork.** Lakewood, CO: [s.n.]; 1950. [$85.00]

Wentworth, John. **Congressional Reminiscences.** Chicago: Fergus; 1882. [$45.00]

Wentworth, John. **Early Chicago.** Chicago: Fergus; 1876. [wraps chipped, $45.00]

Wentz, Abdel Ross. **Beginnings of the German Element in York County, Pennsylvania.** Lancaster: New Era; 1916. [$45.00]

Wentz, Abdel Ross. **Lutheran Church in American History.** 2nd ed. Philadelphia: United Lutheran; 1933. [$15.00]

Werner, Morris Robert. **Brigham Young.** 1st ed. Harcourt, Brace; 1925. [$40.00]

Werner, Morris Robert. **Tammany Hall.** Garden City: Doubleday, Doran; 1928. [$15.00]

Werner, Morris Robert. **Teapot Dome.** NY: Viking; 1959. [$15.00]

Wertenbaker, Green Peyton. **For God and Texas; the Life of P. B. Hill.** NY; London: Whittlesey; McGraw-Hill; 1947. [$20.00]

Wertenbaker, Thomas Jefferson. **Father Knickerbocker Rebels.** NY: Scribner; 1948. [$12.50] [$10.00]

Wertenbaker, Thomas Jefferson. **Founding of American Civilization; the Middle Colonies.** NY, London: Scribner; 1938. [$15.00]

West, D. Porter. **Early History of Pope County.** Little Rock: Foreman-Payne; 1968. [$10.00]

West, Edward. **Homesteading.** London: Unwin; 1918. [$85.00, Canadian]

West, Nathanael. **Complete Work.** NY: Farrar, Straus and Cudahy; 1957. [$12.50]

West, Nathaniel. **Ancestry, Life, and Times of Hon. Henry Hastings Sibley.** Saint Paul: Pioneer; 1889. [$30.00]

West, Ray Benedict. **Rocky Mountain Reader.** 1st ed. NY: Dutton; 1946. [$17.50]

West, Richard Sedgewick. **Gideon Welles, Lincoln's Navy Department.** Indianapolis, NY: Bobbs-Merrill; 1943. [$35.00]

West, Richard Sedgewick. **Lincoln's Scapegoat General.** Boston: Houghton Mifflin; 1965. [$35.00]

West, Richard Sedgewick. **Mr. Lincoln's Navy.** 1st ed. NY: Longmans, Green; 1957. [$25.00]

Westcott, Edward Noyes. **David Harum.** 1st ed. NY: Appleton; 1889. [$50.00]

Westcott, Thompson. **Centennial Portfolio: A Souvenir of the International Exhibition at Philadelphia.** Philadelphia: Hunter; 1876. [$400.00]

Western Writers of America. **The Fall Roundup.** NY: Random; 1955. [$12.00]

Weston, George Melville. **Progress of Slavery in the United States.** Washington: The Author; 1857. [$75.00]

Wethey, Harold E. **Colonial Architecture and Sculpture in Peru.** Cambridge: Harvard UP; 1949. [$60.00]

Wetmore, Helen Cody. **Last of the Great Scouts.** Duluth, MN: Duluth Press; 1899. [$175.00] [1899 Chicago imprint, $75.00]

Weygandt, Cornelius. **The Blue Hills.** NY: Holt; 1936. [signed, $12.50]

Weygandt, Cornelius. **The Red Hills.** Philadelphia: U. of Pennsylvania; 1929. [signed, $40.00] [2nd printing, $15.00]

Weygandt, Cornelius. **Wissahickon Hills.** Philadelphia: U. of Pennsylvania; 1930. [$20.00]

Wharton, Anne Hollingsworth. **Social Life in the Early Republic.** 2nd ed. Philadelphia: Lippincott; 1903, c1902. [signed, $17.50]

Wharton, Clarence Ray. **Gail Borden, Pioneer.** San Antonio: Naylor; 1941. [$55.00]

Wharton, Clarence Ray. **El Presidente.** Austin: Gammel's; 1926. [$85.00]

Wharton, Clarence Ray. **Satanta.** Dallas: Banks Upshaw; 1935. [$95.00]

Wharton, Henry Marvin. **War Songs and Poems of the Southern Confederacy.** Philadelphia: [s.n.]; 1904. [$25.00]

Wheatley, Phillis. **Poems of.** Philadelphia: Wright; 1909. [$25.00]

Wheatley, Phillis. **Poems on Various Subjects, Religious and Moral.** 1st ed. London: Bell; 1773. [elegantly rebound, $1950.00]

Wheeler, A. O. **Eye-Witness; or, Life Scenes in the Old North State.** Boston; Chicago: Russell; Boyden; 1865. [$75.00]

Wheeler, Alfred. **Land Titles in San Francisco.** San Francisco: Alta California Steam Print.; 1852. [map extensively repaired, $950.00]

Wheeler, Andrew Carpenter. **Chronicles of Milwaukee.** Milwaukee: Jermain & Brightman; 1861. [x-lib., $45.00]

Wheeler, George Augustus. **Castine, Past and Present.** Boston: Rockwell; 1896. [rebound, $40.00]

Wheeler, Gervase. **Rural Homes.** Detroit: Kerr & Doughty; 1854, c1851. [inner hinge cracked, $125.00]

Wheeler, Homer Webster. **Buffalo Days.** Indianapolis: Bobbs-Merrill; 1925. [in dj, $30.00]

Wheeler, Homer Webster. **The Frontier Trail.** Los Angeles: Times-Mirror; 1923. [$60.00]

Wheeler, Mary. **Steamboatin' Days.** Baton Rouge: Louisiana State UP; 1944. [bumped, stained, $15.00]

Wheeler, Olin Dunbar. **Wonderland 1906.** St. Paul: Northern Pacific Railway; 1906. [$30.00]

Wheeler, Osgood Church. **Chinese in America.** Oakland, CA: Times; 1880. [$200.00]

Wheelwright, Mary C. **Myth of Sontso.** Santa Fe: Museum of Navajo Ceremonial Art; 1940. [$25.00]

Wheildon, William Willder. **New History of the Battle of Bunker Hill.** 2nd ed. Boston: Lee & Shepard; 1875. [$25.00]

Whipple, Amiel Weeks. **Pathfinder in the Southwest.** Norman: U. of Oklahoma; 1941. [$50.00]

Whipple, Amiel Weeks. **The Whipple Report.** Los Angeles: Westernlore; 1961. [$45.00]

Whipple, Henry Benjamin. **Lights and Shadows of a Long Episcopate.** NY, London: Macmillan; 1902. [third printing, $40.00]

Whitaker, Epher. **Whitaker's Southold.** Princeton: Princeton UP; 1931. ["covers quite scratched," $15.00]

Whitaker, Fess. **History of Corporal Fess Whitaker.** Louisville, KY: Standard; 1918. [$55.00]

Whitaker, Richard H. **Whitaker's Reminiscences.** Raleigh: Edwards & Broughton; 1905. [$65.00]

White Horse Eagle. **We Indians.** 1st ed. NY: Dutton; 1931. [$30.00]

White, Andrew. **Declaration of the Lord Baltemore's Plantation in Maryland.** Baltimore: Lord Baltimore Press; 1929. [$40.00]

White, Charley C. **No Quittin' Sense.** Austin: U. of Texas; 1969. [$40.00]

White, Edward P. **Ballads of Tombstone's Yesterdays.** Bisbee, AZ: McKinney; 1929. [dampstained, $15.00]

White, Elijah. **Testimonials and Records Together with Arguments in Favor of Special Action for Our Indian Tribes.** Washington: Waters; 1861. [morocco slipcase, repaired, $750.00]

White, Eugene E. **Service on the Indian Reservations.** Little Rock: Diploma; 1893. [$850.00]

White, George. **Historical Collections of Georgia.** 3rd ed. NY: Pudney & Russell; 1855. [x-lib., $25.00]

White, George. **Statistics of the State of Georgia.** Savannah: Williams; 1849. [x-lib., $25.00] [$175.00]

White, George Savage. **Memoir of Samuel Slater.** Philadelphia: White; 1836. [$185.00]

White, Henry. **Indian Battles.** NY: Evans; 1859. [$45.00]

White, John E. **My Old Confederate.** Atlanta: Atlanta Camp No. 159; 1908. [$35.00]

White, Leonard Dupee. **The Jacksonians.** NY: Macmillan; 1954. [$30.00]

White, Owen Payne. **Autobiography of a Durable Sinner.** NY: Putnam; 1942. [first issue, $150.00]

White, Owen Payne. **Lead and Likker.** NY: Minton, Balch; 1932. [$50.00]

White, Owen Payne. **My Texas 'Tis of Thee.** NY: Putnam; 1936. [$35.00]

White, Owen Payne. **Texas.** NY: Putnam; 1945. [$25.00]

White, Owen Payne. **Them Was the Days.** NY: Minton, Balch; 1925. [presentation, dj, $150.00] [$50.00]

White, Owen Payne. **Trigger Fingers.** NY, London: Putnam; 1926. [$95.00]

White, Richard Grant. **The New Gospel of Peace, according to St. Benjamin.** NY: Tousey; 1863-66. 4 v. [bound together, $75.00]

White, Stewart Edward. **Arizona Nights.** 1st ed. NY: McClure; 1907. [$55.00]

White, Stewart Edward. **The Cabin.** 1st ed. Garden City: Doubleday, Page; 1911. [$30.00]

White, Stewart Edward. **Folded Hills.** 1st ed. Garden City: Doubleday Doran; 1934. [$40.00]

White, Stewart Edward. **Gold.** 1st ed. Garden City: Doubleday, Page; 1913. [dj chipped, $50.00]

White, Stewart Edward. **The Gray Dawn.** 1st ed. Garden City: Doubleday, Page; 1915. [$20.00]

White, Stewart Edward. **The Mountains.** 1st ed. NY: McClure, Phillips; 1904. [$65.00]

White, Stewart Edward. **Old California in Picture and Story.** 1st ed. Garden City: Doubleday, Doran; 1937. [dj chipped & rubbed, $40.00]

White, Stewart Edward. **On Tiptoe.** 1st ed. NY: Doran; 1922. [$20.00]

White, Stewart Edward. **Ranchero.** 1st ed. Garden City: Doubleday, Doran; 1933. [$20.00]

White, Stewart Edward. **The Rules of the Game.** 1st ed. NY: Doubleday, Page; 1910. [$20.00]

White, Stewart Edward. **The Westerners.** 1st ed. NY: McClure, Phillips; 1901. [$20.00]

White, William Allen. **Emporia and New York.** Emporia, KS: Gazette; 1908, c1906. [$85.00]

White, William Allen. **Puritan in Babylon.** NY: Macmillan; 1938. [$25.00]

White, William Francis. **Picture of Pioneer Times in California.** San Francisco: Hinton; 1881. [cloth faded, $75.00]

Whitefield, George. **Journals.** London: Banner of Truth Trust; 1960. [$25.00]

Whitehead, L. **The New House That Jack Built.** NY: Beadle; 1865. [lacks wraps, $50.00]

Whitehead, William A. **Contributions to the Early History of Perth Amboy and Adjoining Country.** NY: Appleton; 1856. [$185.00] [x-lib., $30.00]

Whitehill, Walter Muir. **East India Marine Society and the Peabody Museum of Salem.** Salem, MA: Peabody Museum; 1949. [$40.00]

Whitehouse, Arthur George Joseph. **Legion of the Lafayette.** 1st ed. Garden City: Doubleday; 1962. [$15.00]

Whitelaw, William Menzies. **Maritimes and Canada before Confederation.** Toronto: Oxford UP; 1934. [$17.50]

Whitely, Issac H. **Rural Life in Texas.** Atlanta: Harrison; 1891. [$300.00]

Whitener, Daniel Jay. **History of Watauga County.** Boone, NC: [s.n.]; 1949. [$17.50]

Whiteshot, Charles Austin. **The Oil-Well Driller.** 2nd ed. Mannington, WV: Whiteshot; 1905. [$100.00]

Whitfield, Henry. **Strength out of Weakness.** NY: Sabin; 1865. [$45.00]

Whitford, William Clarke. **Colorado Volunteers in the Civil War.** Denver: State Historical and Natural History Society; 1906. [$125.00]

Whitley, Edythe Johns. **Sam Davis.** [Nashville?: s.n.]; 1947. [$50.00]

Whitlock, Ernest Clyde. **Music and Dance in Texas, Oklahoma, and the Southwest.** Hollywood, CA: Bureau of Musical Research; 1950. [$9.00]

Whitlock, Vivian H. **Cowboy Life on the Llano Estacado.** 1st ed. Norman: U. of Oklahoma; 1970. [$25.00]

Whitman, Walt. **After All, Not to Create Only.** Boston: Roberts; 1871. [$125.00]

Whitman, Walt. **Poems.** London: Hotten; 1868. [second binding, shaken, spine darkened, $125.00]

Whitman, Willson. **Bread and Circuses.** NY: Oxford UP; 1937. [$15.00]

Whitman, Willson. **God's Valley.** NY: Viking; 1939. [$15.00]

Whitman, Zacheriah Gardner. **Historical Sketch of the Ancient and Honourable Artillery Company.** Boston: House; 1820. [spine chipped, $75.00]

Whitmore, William Henry. **Cavalier Dismounted.** Salem, MA: Whipple & Smith; 1864. [lacks wraps, $15.00]

Whitney, Harry. **Hunting with the Eskimos.** NY: Century; 1911. [$50.00]

Whitney, Henry Clay. **Life on the Circuit with Lincoln.** Caldwell, ID: Caxton; 1940. [$40.00]

Whitney, James Parker. **Silver Mining Regions of Colorado.** NY: Van Nostrand; 1865. [$1250.00]

Whitney, Janet Payne. **John Woolman.** Boston: Little, Brown; 1942. [$20.00]

Whitney, Luna M. **History of Madison County.** Syracuse: Truair, Smith; 1872. [rebound, $75.00]

Whitney, Orson Ferguson. **Popular History of Utah.** Salt Lake City: Deseret News; 1916. [$35.00]

Whitney, Peter. **History of the County of Worcester.** Worcester, MA: Thomas; 1793. [$1200.00]

Whitsitt, William Heth. **Life and Times of Judge Caleb Wallace.** Louisville: Morton; 1888. [$65.00]

Whittaker, Frederick. **Complete Life of Gen. George A. Custer.** NY; Chicago: Sheldon; Nettleton; 1876. [$45.00] [$100.00]

Whittaker, Frederick. **Popular Life of Gen. George A. Custer.** NY; Chicago: Sheldon; Nettleton; c1876. [$125.00]

Whittier, John Greenleaf. **At Sundown.** 1st ed. Cambridge: Priv. Print.; 1890. [$225.00]

Whittier, John Greenleaf. **Ballads of New England.** 1st ed. Boston: Fields, Osgood; 1870. [$75.00]

Whittier, John Greenleaf. **Chapel of the Hermits.** Boston: Ticknor, Reed and Fields; 1853. [$45.00]

Whittier, John Greenleaf. **Hazel-Blossoms.** 1st ed. Boston: Osgood; 1875. [$10.00]

Whittier, John Greenleaf. **In War Time, and Other Poems.** 1st ed. Boston: Ticknor and Fields; 1863. [$28.00] [$25.00]

Whittier, John Greenleaf. **Literary Recreations and Miscellanies.** Boston: Ticknor and Fields; 1854. [$45.00]

Whittier, John Greenleaf. **Mabel Martin.** Boston: Osgood; 1876, c1875. [$10.00]

Whittier, John Greenleaf. **The Pennsylvania Pilgrim.** Boston: Osgood; 1872. [$10.00]

Whittier, John Greenleaf. **Pictures and Stories from Uncle Tom's Cabin.** Boston: Jewett; 1853. [$100.00]

Whittier, John Greenleaf. **Poems.** Boston: Mussey; 1854, c1848. [$25.00]

Whittier, John Greenleaf. **Poetical Works of.** Boston, NY: Houghton Mifflin; 1892. [$45.00]

Whittier, John Greenleaf. **Proceedings of a Convention of Delegates.** see, Boston Convention of Delegates on Proposed Annexation of Texas, 1845.

Whittier, John Greenleaf. **Songs of Labor, and Other Poems.** Boston: Ticknor, Reed, and Fields; 1851. [second printing, $40.00]

Whittlesey, Charles. **Early History of Cleveland, Ohio.** large paper ed. Cleveland: Fairbanks, Benedict; 1867. [$75.00]

Wibberley, Leonard. **The Coming of the Green.** 1st ed. NY: Holt; 1958. [$7.50]

Wick, Barthinius Larson. **The Amish Mennonites.** Iowa City: State Hist. Soc.; 1894. [$75.00]

Wickersham, James. **Old Yukon: Tales--Trails--and Trials.** Washington: Washington Law Book; 1938. [$45.00] [$35.00]

Wieder, Arnold A. **Early Jewish Community of Boston's North End.** Waltham, MA: Brandeis U.; 1962. [$20.00]

Wiggin, Kate Douglas Smith. **A Summer in a Canon.** Boston, NY: Houghton Mifflin; 1891, c1889. [cover worn and bumped, $15.00]

Wightman, William May. **Life of William Capers.** Nashville: Southern Methodist; 1858. [$100.00]

Wilbarger, J. W. **Indian Depredations in Texas.** Austin: Hutchings; 1890. [$450.00]

Wilber, C. D. **The Great Valleys and Prairies of Nebraska and the Northwest.** 3rd ed. Omaha: Daily Republican; 1881. [worn, $30.00]

Wilber, Edwin L. **Silver Wings.** NY: Appleton-Century; 1948. [$47.50]

Wilbur, Henry Watson. **Life and Labors of Elias Hicks.** Philadelphia: Friends' General Conference Advancement Committee; 1910. [$25.00]

Wilbur, Marguerite Knowlton. **John Sutter, Rascal and Adventurer.** NY: Liveright; 1949. [$20.00]

Wilbur, Ray Lyman. **The Hoover Policies.** NY: Scribner; 1937. [$12.50]

Wilcox, Alanson. **History of the Disciples of Christ in Ohio.** Cincinnati: Standard; 1918. [$20.00]

Wilcox, Ella Wheeler. **Custer, and Other Poems.** Chicago: Conkey; 1896. [loose, $15.00]

Wilcox, Walter Dwight. **Camping in the Canadian Rockies.** 2nd ed. NY: Putnam; 1897. [rebound, $85.00]

Wildavsky, Aaron B. **Leadership in a Small Town.** Totowa, NJ: Bedminster; 1964. [$15.00]

Wilde, Richard Henry. **Speech of Mr. Wilde, of Georgia, on the Bill for Removing the Indians from the East to the West Side of the Mississippi.** Washington: Gales & Seaton; 1830. [$65.00]

Wilder, Daniel Webster. **Annals of Kansas.** Topeka: Martin; 1875. [$65.00]

Wilder, Thornton. **The Bridge of San Luis Rey.** 1st ed. NY: Boni; 1927. [dj chipped, $15.00]

Wiles, Robert. **Cuban Cane Sugar.** 1st ed. Indianapolis: Bobbs-Merrill; 1916. [$12.50]

Wiley, Bell Irvin. **The Common Soldier in the Civil War.** Indianapolis: Bobbs-Merrill; 1943-1951. 2 v. [$70.00]

Wiley, Bell Irvin. **The Plain People of the Confederacy.** Baton Rouge: Louisiana State UP; 1943. [$50.00]

Wiley, Bell Irvin. **The Road to Appomattox.** Memphis: Memphis State College; 1956. [$25.00]

Wiley, Bell Irvin. **They Who Fought Here.** 1st ed. NY: Macmillan; 1959. [$30.00]

Wilhelm, Lewis Webb. **Sir George Calvert, Baron of Baltimore.** Baltimore: Murphy; 1884. [rebound, $25.00]

Wilkes, Charles. **Columbia River to the Sacramento.** Oakland: Bio-Books; 1958. [$35.00]

Wilkie, Franc B. **Davenport, Past and Present.** Davenport: Luce, Lane; 1858. [$175.00]

Wilkie, Franc B. **Walks about Chicago, 1871-1881.** Chicago: Kenney and Sumner; 1869. [$185.00]

Wilkins, Benjamin Harrison. **War Boy.** Tullahoma, TN: Wilson; 1938. [signed, $75.00]

Wilkins, Isaac. **My Services and Losses.** Brooklyn: Historical Printing Club; 1890. [x-lib., $120.00]

Wilkins, Robert P. **God Giveth the Increase.** Fargo: North Dakota Institute for Regional Studies; 1959. [$20.00]

Wilkins, Thurman. **Thomas Moran, Artist of the Mountains.** 1st ed. Norman: U. of Oklahoma; 1966. [$65.00]

Wilkinson, Cecil J. **The University Club of Washington.** Washington: The Club; 1954. [$12.50]

Wilkinson, Douglas. **Land of the Long Day.** London: Harrap; 1956. [$11.00]

Wilkinson, Herbert Arnold. **The American Doctrine of State Succession.** Baltimore: Hopkins; 1934. [$45.00]

Wilkinson, James. **Memoirs of My Own Times.** Philadelphia: Small; 1816. 3 v. [3 vols. and folio atlas, $1850.00]

Wilkinson, William. **Memorials of the Minnesota Forest Fires in the Year 1894.** Minneapolis: Wilkinson; 1895. [spine faded, $50.00]

Willard, Charles Dwight. **The Herald's History of Los Angeles City.** Los Angeles: Kingsley-Barnes & Neuner; 1901. [$60.00]

Willard, Frances Elizabeth. **A Wheel within a Wheel.** 1st ed. NY, Chicago: Revell; 1895. [$75.00]

Willard, Joseph A. **Half a Century with Judges and Lawyers.** Boston: Houghton Mifflin; 1895. [$50.00]

Willard, Theodore Arthur. **City of the Sacred Well.** NY, London: Century; 1926. [hinges cracked, $25.00]

Willey, Austin. **History of the Antislavery Cause in State and Nation.** Portland, ME: Thruston; 1886. [$40.00]

Willey, Worcester. **Tale of Home and War.** Portland, ME: Brown, Thurston; 1888. [$350.00]

Williams, Aaron. **Harmony Society, at Economy, Penn'a.** Pittsburgh: Haven; 1866. [$275.00]

Williams, Catherine Read. **Biography of Revolutionary Heroes.** Providence; NY: The Author; Wiley & Putnam; 1839. [$65.00] [$35.00]

Williams, Charles Richard. **Life of Rutherford Birchard Hayes.** Columbus: Ohio State Arch. and Hist. Soc.; 1928. 2 v. [$65.00]

Williams, Chauncy Pratt. **Lone Elk.** 1st ed. Denver: Van Male; 1935-36. 2 v. [$150.00]

Williams, Gaar. **Among the Folks in History.** Winnetka, IL: Book and Print Guild; 1935. [$12.00]

Williams, Henry T. **The Pacific Tourist.** NY: Williams; 1876. [lacks map and timetable, $75.00] [1877 issue, some pages torn, $50.00]

Williams, James. **Rise and Fall of "The Model Republic."** London: Bentley; 1863. [$175.00]

Williams, James. **Seventy-Five Years on the Border.** Kansas City: Standard; 1912. [inscribed, $80.00] [$60.00]

Williams, Jay P. **Alaskan Adventure.** Harrisburg, PA: Stackpole; 1952. [$22.00]

Williams, Jesse Wallace. **Big Ranch Country.** Wichita Falls, TX: Terry; 1954. [in good dj, $45.00]

Williams, John Edward. **Butcher's Crossing.** NY: Macmillan; 1960. [$30.00]

Williams, John Jay. **Isthmus of Tehuantepec.** NY: Appleton; 1852. [x-lib., rebacked, $250.00]

Williams, John S. **History of the Invasion and Capture of Washington.** NY: Harper; 1857. [$60.00]

Williams, Mary Floyd. **History of the San Francisco Committee of Vigilance of 1851.** Berkeley: U. of California; 1921. [$75.00]

Williams, Samuel Cole. **Beginnings of West Tennessee in the Land of the Chickasaws.** Johnson City: Watauga; 1930. [mildewed, spotted, $65.00]

Williams, Stanley Thomas. **Life of Washington Irving.** 1st ed. NY, London: Oxford UP; 1935. 2 v. [$30.00]

Williams, Stephen West. **Biographical Memoir of the Rev. John Williams.** Greenfield, MA: Ingersoll; 1837. [$180.00]

Williams, T. Harry. **Huey Long.** London: Thames & Hudson; 1970. [$15.00]

Williams, T. Harry. **Lincoln and His Generals.** 1st ed. NY: Knopf; 1952. [covers dampstained, $14.50]

Williams, T. Harry. **P. G. T. Beauregard; Napoleon in Gray.** Baton Rouge: Louisiana State UP; 1954. [$40.00]

Williams, Tennessee. **One Arm.** NY: New Directions; 1954. [bumped, $20.00]

Williams, Walter. **History of Northwest Missouri.** Chicago: Lewis; 1915. 3 v. [v.1-2 only, $125.00]

Williams, Whiting. **What's on the Worker's Mind.** NY: Scribner; 1920. [$20.00]

Williams, William. **Journal of the Life, Travels, and Gospel Labours of.** Cincinnati: Lodge, L'Hommedieu, and Hammond; 1828. [$175.00]

Williams, William Carlos. **Collected Earlier Poems.** NY: New Directions; 1951. [$20.00]

Williamson, Harold Francis. **Winchester: The Gun That Won the West.** 1st ed. Washington: Combat Forces Press; 1952. [$45.00] [lacks front endpaper, $20.00]

Williamson, Hugh. **History of North Carolina.** Philadelphia: Dobson; 1812. 2 v. [spines badly chipped, hinges crudely repaired, worn, $450.00]

Williamson, James Joseph. **Prison Life in the Old Capitol.** West Orange, NJ: [s.n.]; 1911. [$75.00]

Williamson, Peter. **Travels of.** Edinburgh: [s.n.]; 1768. [$2785.00]

Willis, Bailey. **Yanqui in Patagonia.** Stanford: Stanford UP; 1947. [x-lib., $25.00]

Willis, Henry Augustus. **Fifty-Third Regiment Massachusetts Volunteers.** Fitchburg: Blanchard & Brown; 1889. [$60.00]

Willis, Nathaniel Parker. **American Scenery.** London: Virtue; 1840. 2 v. [lacks plate #39, $850.00]

Willis, Nathaniel Parker. **Out-Doors at Idlewild.** NY: Scribner; 1855. [$225.00]

Willison, George Findlay. **Here They Dug the Gold.** NY: Brentano's; 1931. [$30.00]

Wills, Charles Wright. **Army Life of an Illinois Soldier.** Washington: Globe; 1906. [x-lib., $75.00]

Willson, Minnie (Moore). **Seminoles of Florida.** rev. ed. NY: Moffat, Yard; 1914. [$45.00]

Willson, Roscoe G. **No Place for Angels.** Phoenix: Arizona Republic; 1958. [$30.00] [$17.50]

Wilson, Adelaide. **Historic and Picturesque Savannah.** Boston: Photogravure; 1889. [$60.00]

Wilson, Augusta Jane Evans. **Inez.** NY: Harper; 1855. [bumped, rubbed, stained, worn, hinges weak, $125.00]

Wilson, Bird. **Memoir of the Life of the Right Reverend William White.** Philadelphia, Pittsburgh: Kay; 1839. [x-lib., $20.00]

Wilson, Carol Green. **California Yankee.** Claremont: Saunders; 1946. [dj chipped, $15.00]

Wilson, Charles Morrow. **Meriwether Lewis of Lewis and Clark.** NY: Crowell; 1934. [$35.00]

Wilson, Edmund. **The American Earthquake.** 1st ed. Garden City: Doubleday; 1958. [dj chafed, $40.00]

Wilson, Edmund. **Boys in the Back Room.** 1st ed. San Francisco: Colt; 1941. [$50.00]

Wilson, Ella Grant. **Famous Old Euclid Avenue of Cleveland.** Cleveland: Wilson; 1932-37. 2 v. [signed, $100.00]

Wilson, Frank John. **Special Agent.** NY: Holt, Rinehart and Winston; 1965. [$12.50]

Wilson, Henry. **History of the Antislavery Measures of the Thirty-Seventh and Thirty-Eighth United States Congresses, 1861-64.** Boston: Walker, Wise; 1864. [$45.00]

Wilson, James Andrew. **James Andrew Wilson.** Austin: Gammel's; 1927. [$35.00]

Wilson, James Grant. **Biographical Sketches of Illinois Officers Engaged in the War against the Rebellion of 1861.** Chicago: Barnet; 1862. [$325.00]

Wilson, John Laird. **Story of the War.** Philadelphia: National; 1881. [$75.00]

Wilson, Neill Compton. **Silver Stampede.** NY: Macmillan; 1937. [$20.00]

Wilson, Neill Compton. **Treasure Express.** NY: Macmillan; 1936. [dj very worn, $35.00]

Wilson, Robert. **Half Forgotten By-Ways of the Old South.** Columbia, SC: State; 1928. [$50.00]

Wilson, Robert Anderson. **Mexico and Its Religion.** NY: Harper; 1855. [spine faded, $75.00]

Wilson, Rufus Rockwell. **Lincoln in Caricature.** NY: Horizon; 1953. [$25.00]

Wilson, Rufus Rockwell. **Out of the West.** NY: Press of the Pioneers; 1933. [$50.00] [1936 Wilson-Erickson imprint, $25.00]

Wilson, Samuel Paynter. **Chicago by Gaslight.** Chicago: [s.n.]; 1910. [soiled, dampstained, $85.00]

Wilson, Thomas L. **Sufferings Endured for a Free Government.** Washington: The Author; 1864. [$200.00]

Wilson, Thomas William. **The Island of Cuba in 1850.** New Orleans: La Patria; 1850. [$85.00]

Wilson, William Bender. **History of the Pennsylvania Railroad Company.** autograph ed. Philadelphia: Coates; 1899. 2 v. [$250.00]

Wilson, Woodrow. **Divison and Reunion, 1829-1889.** 1st ed. NY: Longmans, Green; 1893. [$65.00]

Wilson, Woodrow. **In Our First Year of War.** NY, London: Harper; 1918. [$25.00]

Wilson, Woodrow. **Mere Literature, and Other Essays.** Boston, NY: Houghton Mifflin; 1896. [$25.00] [$65.00]

Wilson, Woodrow. **On Being Human.** NY: Harper; 1916. [$25.00]

Wilson, Woodrow. **The State.** Boston: Heath; 1889. [$50.00]

Wilson, Woodrow. **Why We Are at War.** NY: Harper; 1917. [$25.00]

Wilson, Woodrow. **Wit and Wisdom of Woodrow Wilson.** Garden City: Doubleday, Page; 1916. [$25.00]

Wilstach, Frank Jenners. **Wild Bill Hickock.** Garden City: Doubleday, Doran; 1928, c1926. [corners bumped, $22.50]

Wilstach, Paul. **Tidewater Maryland.** 1st ed. Indianapolis: Bobbs-Merrill; 1931. [$15.00]

Wiltsee, Ernest Abram. **Pioneer Miner and Pack Mule Express.** San Francisco: California Hist. Soc.; 1931. [$55.00] [$60.00]

Wiltsey, Norman B. **Brave Warriors.** Caldwell, ID: Caxton; 1964, c1963. [$25.00]

Winch, Frank. **Thrilling Lives of Buffalo Bill . . . and Pawnee Bill.** 3rd ed. NY: Parsons; 1911. [$15.00]

Windolph, Charles A. **I Fought with Custer.** NY, London: Scribner; 1947. [$35.00] [1950 issue, $20.00]

Wing, Joseph Elwyn. **Sheep Farming in America.** new ed. Chicago: Breeder's Gazette; 1912. [$17.50]

Wingate, George Wood. **History of the Twenty-Second Regiment of the National Guard of the State of New York.** NY: Dayton; 1896. [$125.00]

Winget, De Witt Harris. **Anecdotes of Buffalo Bill.** Clinton, IA: [s.n.]; 1912. [cover stained, text browned, $20.00]

Winkler, John Kennedy. **Morgan the Magnificent.** NY: Garden City; 1930. [$10.00]

Winship, George Parker. **The Coronado Expedition, 1540-1542.** Washington: USGPO; 1896. [$275.00]

Winslow, Edith. **In Those Days.** San Antonio: Naylor; 1950. [worn dj, $15.00]

Winslow, Ola Elizabeth. **American Broadside Verse.** New Haven; London: Yale UP; Oxford UP; 1930. [edition of 500 copies, $75.00]

Winslow, Ola Elizabeth. **John Eliot, Apostle to the Indians.** 1st ed. Boston: Houghton Mifflin; 1968. [$10.00]

Winslow, Ola Elizabeth. **Jonathan Edwards, 1703-1758.** NY: Macmillan; 1940. [$45.00]

Winslow, William Henry. **Cruising and Blockading.** Pittsburgh: Weldin; 1885. [$65.00]

Winsor, Justin. **Christopher Columbus and How He Received and Imparted the Spirit of Discovery.** Boston, NY: Houghton Mifflin; 1892. [$50.00]

Winsor, Justin. **History of the Town of Duxbury, Massachusetts.** Boston: Crosby & Nichols; 1849. [$75.00]

Winsor, Justin. **Memorial History of Boston Including Suffolk County, Massachusetts.** Boston: Ticknor; 1880-81. 4 v. [$85.00] [$125.00]

Winsor, Justin. **Narrative and Critical History of America.** Boston, NY: Houghton Mifflin; 1889. 8 v. [x-lib., $100.00] [$325.00]

Winsor, Justin. **The Westward Movement.** Boston, NY: Houghton Mifflin; 1897. [$65.00]

Winston, Robert Watson. **High Stakes and Hair Trigger.** NY: Holt; 1930. [$20.00]

Winter, Nevin Otto. **Brazil and Her People of To-Day.** Boston: Page; 1910. [book and dj fine, box worn, $40.00]

Winter, Nevin Otto. **Texas, the Marvellous.** Texas Centennial ed. Garden City: Garden City Publishing; 1936. [$13.00]

Winter, William. **Life of David Belasco.** NY: Moffat, Yard; 1918. 2 v. [x-lib., lacks front endpaper, $25.00]

Winterbotham, William Wrigley. **Recollections.** Pittsburgh: Priv. Print.; 1950. [$50.00]

Winters, John D. **The Civil War in Louisiana.** Baton Rouge: Louisiana State UP; 1963. [$40.00]

Winther, Oscar Osburn. **The Great Northwest.** 1st ed. NY: Knopf; 1947. [$20.00]

Winther, Oscar Osburn. **The Old Oregon Country.** Stanford: Stanford UP; 1950. [x-lib., $17.50]

Winthrop, John. **Short Story of the Rise, Reign, and Ruine of the Antinomians.** London: Smith; 1644. [$975.00]

Winthrop, Robert C. **Life and Letters of John Winthrop.** Boston: Ticknor and Fields; 1864-67. 2 v. [v. 1 only, $45.00]

Winthrop, Theodore. **The Canoe and the Saddle.** Boston: Ticknor & Fields; 1863, c1862. [$50.00]

Winzerling, Oscar William. **Acadian Odyssey.** Baton Rouge: Louisiana State UP; 1955. [$10.00]

Wirkus, Faustin. **The White King of La Gonave.** Garden City: Doubleday, Doran; 1931. [$20.00]

Wirt, William. **Letters of the British Spy.** 5th ed. Baltimore: Lucas; 1813. [scuffed, $45.00] [1832 Harper ed., $45.00]

Wirt, William. **Sketches of the Life and Character of Patrick Henry.** Philadelphia: Webster; 1817. [$60.00] [1832, 15th ed., $20.00]

Wise, Jennings Cropper. **The Red Man in the New World Drama.** Washington: Roberts; 1931. [worn dj, $35.00]

Wise, John. **Vindication of the Government of New England Churches.** Boston: Boyles; 1772. [$175.00]

Wise, John S. **End of an Era.** Boston, NY: Houghton Mifflin; 1899. [shaken, $15.00]

Wisehart, Marion Karl. **Sam Houston, American Giant.** Washington: Luce; 1962. [$35.00]

Wissler, Clark. **Societies and Dance Associations of the Blackfoot Indians.** NY: American Musuem of Natural History; 1913. [$30.00]

Wistar, Isaac Jones. **Autobiography of.** Philadelphia: Wistar Institute; 1914. 2 v. [$250.00] [1937 1 vol. reprint, $40.00; $90.00]

Wister, Owen. **The Jimmyjohn Boss.** NY, London: Harper; 1900. [$50.00]

Wister, Owen. **A Journey in Search of Christmas.** Toronto: Musson; 1904. [$60.00]

Wister, Owen. **Owen Wister Out West.** Chicago: U. of Chicago; 1958. [$15.00] [$25.00]

Wister, Owen. **Roosevelt, the Story of a Friendship, 1880-1919.** NY: Macmillan; 1930. [$20.00] [$30.00]

Wister, Owen. **When West Was West.** NY: Macmillan; 1928. [$20.00]

Withers, Alexander Scott. **Chronicles of Border Warfare.** Clarksburg, VA: Israel; 1831. [$250.00]

Wittke, Carl Frederick. **History of the State of Ohio.** Columbus: Ohio State Arch. and Hist. Soc.; 1941-1944. 6 v. [$125.00]

Wittke, Carl Frederick. **Refugees of Revolution; the German Forty-Eighters in America.** Philadelphia: U. of Pennsylvania; 1952. [$20.00]

Woldman, Albert A. **Lincoln and the Russians.** 1st ed. Cleveland: World; 1952. [$15.00]

Wolf, Eric Robert. **Sons of the Shaking Earth.** Chicago: U. of Chicago; 1959. [$15.00]

Wolf, Hazel Catherine. **On Freedom's Altar.** Madison: U. of Wisconsin; 1952. [$10.00]

Wolf, Simon. **The American Jew as Patriot, Soldier and Citizen.** Philadelphia: Levytype; 1895. [$35.00]

Wolf, Simon. **Presidents I Have Known from 1860-1918.** Washington: Adams; 1918. [$40.00]

Wolfe, Samuel M. **Helper's Impending Crisis Dissected.** Philadelphia: Lloyd; 1860. [$65.00]

Wolfe, Thomas. **The Hills Beyond.** 1st ed. NY, London: Harper; 1941. [ragged dj, $35.00]

Wolfe, Thomas. **Of Time and the River.** 1st ed. NY: Scribner; 1935. [mildew, dj chipped and worn, $85.00]

Wolfe, Thomas. **Thomas Wolfe's Letters to His Mother.** NY: Scribner; 1943. [dj chipped and creased, $35.00]

Wolfe, William G. **Stories of Guernsey County, Ohio.** Cambridge, OH: The Author; 1943. [$60.00]

Wolfenstine, Manfred R. **Manual of Brands and Marks.** 1st ed. Norman: U. of Oklahoma; 1970. [$20.00]

Wolle, Muriel Vincent Sibell. **Bonanza Trail.** Bloomington: Indiana UP; 1953. [$25.00]

Wolle, Muriel Vincent Sibell. **Stampede to Timberline.** Boulder: Wolle; 1949. [$35.00]

Wolseley, Garnet Joseph. **Story of a Soldier's Life.** NY: Scribner; 1903. 2 v. [x-lib., $125.00]

Woman's Centennial Executive Committee, Wisconsin. **Centennial Records of the Women of Wisconsin.** Madison: Atwood and Culver; 1876. [$125.00]

Wood, John. **Correct Statement of the Various Sources from Which the History of the Administration of John Adams Was Compiled and the Motives for Its Suppression by Col. Burr.** 2nd ed. NY: Waite; 1802. [$85.00]

Wood, John. **Suppressed History of the Administration of John Adams.** Philadelphia: The Editor; 1846, c1845. [$40.00]

Wood, Norman Barton. **White Side of a Black Subject.** Chicago: American Pub. House; 1897. [rear cover waterstained, $22.50]

Wood, Ralph Charles. **Pennsylvania Germans.** Princeton: Princeton UP; 1943. [$18.00]

Wood, Richard Coke. **Murphys, Queen of the Sierra.** Angels Camp, CA: Calaveras Californian; 1948. [$30.00]

Wood, Richard George. **Stephen Harriman Long.** Glendale, CA: Clark; 1966. [$30.00] [$35.00]

Wood, Stanley. **Over the Range to the Golden Gate.** Chicago: Donnelley; 1889. [$75.00]

Wood, Violet. **So Sure of Life.** NY: Friendship; 1950. [$17.50]

Wood, William Charles. **Fight for Canada.** Boston: Little, Brown; 1906. [$45.00]

Woodcock, Eldred Nathaniel. **Fifty Years a Hunter and Trapper.** Columbus, OH: Harding; 1913. [$45.00]

Woodley, Thomas Frederick. **Thaddeus Stevens.** Harrisburgh, PA: Telegraph; 1934. [$22.50] [$27.50]

Woodman, Abby Johnson. **Picturesque Alaska.** 3rd ed. Boston, NY: Houghton Mifflin; 1890, c1889. [$22.50] [$30.00]

Woodroffe, Joseph Froude. **The Upper Reaches of the Amazon.** London: Methuen; 1914. [spine sunned, $35.00]

Woodruff, William Edward. **With the Light Guns in '61-'65.** Little Rock: Central; 1903. [rebacked, $350.00] [$325.00]

Woods, Alva. **Intellectual and Moral Culture.** Lexington, KY: Norwood; 1828. [$125.00]

Woods, Daniel B. **Sixteen Months at the Gold Diggings.** NY: Harper; 1851. [$150.00]

Woods, Edgar. **Albemarle County in Virginia.** Charlottesville: Michie; 1901. [stained, $50.00]

Woods, John. **Two Years' Residence in the Settlement on the English Prairie, in the Illinois Country.** London: Longman, etc.; 1822. [$950.00]

Woodsworth, James. **Thirty Years in the Canadian North-West.** Toronto: McClelland, Goodchild & Stewart; 1917. [$45.00, Canadian]

Woodward, Arthur. **Brief History of Navajo Silversmithing.** 2nd ed. Flagstaff: Northern Arizona Society of Science and Art; 1946, c1938. [$10.00]

Woodward, Arthur. **Feud on the Colorado.** Los Angeles: Westernlore; 1955. [$40.00]

Woodward, Ashbel. **Review of Uncle Tom's Cabin.** Cincinnati: Applegate; 1853. [bumped, foxed, rubbed, stained, $75.00]

Woodward, C. Vann. **Origins of the New South, 1877-1913.** Baton Rouge: Louisiana State UP; 1951. [$20.00]

Woodward, E. M. **Our Campaigns.** Philadelphia: Potter; 1865. [$37.50]

Woodward, Grace Steele. **Pocahontas.** 1st ed. Norman: U. of Oklahoma; 1969. [$15.00]

Woodward, Sara Day. **Early New Haven.** New Haven, CT: Judd; 1929. [$25.00]

Woodward, William E. **Lafayette.** NY, Toronto: Farrar & Rinehart; 1938. [$25.00]

Woodward, William E. **Meet General Grant.** NY: Liveright; 1928. [binding worn, $25.00]

Woody, Thomas. **Quaker Education in the Colony and State of New Jersey.** Philadelphia: The Author; 1923. [$20.00]

Woollen, William Watson. **Inside Passage to Alaska, 1792-1920.** Cleveland: Clark; 1924. 2 v. [$200.00]

Woolman, John. **Journal of the Life, Gospel Labours, and Christian Experiences, of.** Philadelphia: Chapman; 1837. [$50.00]

Woolman, John. **Works of.** 1st ed. Philadelphia: Crukshank; 1774. [$350.00]

Woolworth, Laura. **Littleton Fowler, 1803-1846.** Shreveport, LA: [s.n.]; 1936. [$125.00]

Worcester, Dean C. **The Philippines Past and Present.** 2nd ed. NY: Macmillan; 1914. 2 v. [$50.00]

Workingman's Guide and the Laborer's Friend and Advocate. San Francisco: Bacon; 1886. [$150.00]

Wormington, Hannah Marie. **Prehistoric Indians of the Southwest.** Denver: Museum of Natural History; 1961. [$12.50]

Wormser, Richard Edward. **The Yellowlegs.** 1st ed. Garden City: Doubleday; 1966. [$37.50]

Worner, William Frederic. **Old Lancaster Tales and Traditions.** Lancaster, PA: The Author; 1927. [$35.00]

Wortham, Louis J. **History of Texas from Wilderness to Commonwealth.** Fort Worth: Wortham-Molyneaux; 1924. 5 v. [$175.00]

Wraxall, Frederick Charles. **The Backwoodsman.** London: Maxwell; 1864. [$385.00]

Wray, Angelina W. **Tales and Poems.** New Brunswick, NJ: Heidingsfeld; 1890. [$20.00]

Wright, A. F. **G. W. Wright and the Early Settlers.** NY: Carlton; 1963. [$20.00]

Wright, Carroll Davidson. **Some Ethical Phases of the Labor Question.** Boston: American Unitarian Assn.; 1903. [$17.50]

Wright, Charles Will. **The Mammoth Cave of Kentucky.** Louisville: [s.n.]; 1859. [soiled, $40.00]

Wright, Frances. **Views of Society and Manners in America.** 2nd ed. NY: Bliss and White; 1821. [x-lib., hinges split, $125.00]

Wright, Frank Lloyd. **An American Architecture.** NY: Horizon; 1955. [$150.00]

Wright, Frank Lloyd. **The Natural House.** NY: Bramhall; 1954. [$45.00]

Wright, Frank Lloyd. **When Democracy Builds.** Chicago: U. of Chicago; 1945. [$65.00]

Wright, Harold Bell. **The Mine with the Iron Door.** NY: Appleton; 1923. [signed, $40.00]

Wright, Henry H. **History of the Sixth Iowa Infantry.** Iowa City: State Hist. Soc.; 1923. [$45.00] [$50.00]

Wright, James Frederick Church. **Saskatchewan.** Toronto: McClelland and Stewart; 1955. [$16.00]

Wright, Louise Wigfall. **A Southern Girl in '61.** NY: Doubleday, Page; 1905. [$35.00] [some wear, $50.00]

Wright, Marcus Joseph. **Official History of the Spanish American War.** Washington: [s.n.]; 1900. [$125.00]

Wright, Muriel Hazel. **Guide to the Indian Tribes of Oklahoma.** 1st ed. Norman: U. of Oklahoma; 1951. [$65.00]

Wright, Richard. **Native Son.** 1st ed. NY, London: Harper; 1940. [2nd issue, chipped dj, $50.00]

Wright, Richardson Little. **Grandfather Was Queer.** 1st ed. Philadelphia, NY: Lippincott; 1939. [$15.00]

Wright, Robert Marr. **Dodge City.** Witchita, KS: Eagle; 1913. [$175.00]

Wright, William. **The Big Bonanza.** NY: Knopf; 1947. [$15.00]

Wright, William. **History of the Big Bonanza.** Hartford; San Francisco: American Pub. Co.;Bancroft; 1877. [rebound, $80.00]

Wright, William Henry. **The Grizzly Bear.** NY: Scribner; 1909. [$35.00] [$40.00]

Wriston, Jennie Amelia. **A Pioneer's Odyssey.** Menasha, WI: Priv. Print.; 1943. [$45.00]

Writers' Program. see also, Federal Writers' Project.

Writers' Program. Arizona. **Arizona.** NY: Hastings; 1940. [$45.00]

Writers' Program. Georgia. **Atlanta, Capital of the South.** NY: Durrell; 1949. [$25.00]

Writers' Program. Kentucky. **In the Land of Breathitt.** Northport, NY: Bacon, Percy & Daggett; 1941. [x-lib., $28.50]

Writers' Program. Nevada. **Nevada.** Portland, OR: Binfords & Mort; 1940. [$45.00]

Writers' Program. New Hampshire. **New Hampshire.** Boston: Houghton; 1938. [$30.00]

Writers' Program. Ohio. **Ohio Guide.** NY: Oxford UP; 1940. [$30.00]

Writers' Program. Oregon. **Oregon, End of the Trail.** Portland, OR: Binfords & Mort; 1940. [$35.00]

Writers' Program. Pennsylvania. **Pennsylvania Cavalcade.** Philadelphia: U. of Pennsylvania; 1942. [$35.00]

Writers' Program. Tennessee. **God Bless the Devil! Liars' Bench Tales.** Chapel Hill: U. of North Carolina; 1940. [$17.50] [worn dj, $30.00]

Writers' Program. Virginia. **Dinwiddie County.** Richmond: Whittet & Shepperson; 1942. [stained and mildewed, $35.00]

Wrong, George McKinnon. **The Canadians.** NY: Macmillan; 1942, c1938. [$7.50]

Wuorinen, John H. **The Finns on the Delaware, 1638-1655.** NY: Columbia UP; 1938. [$25.00]

Wyatt, Frank S. **Brief History of Oklahoma.** Oklahoma City: Webb; 1919. [$25.00]

Wyeth, John A. **That Devil Forrest.** NY: Harper; 1959. [$40.00]

Wyeth, Walter Newton. **Isaac McCoy; Early Indian Missions.** Philadelphia: Wyeth; 1895. [$35.00]

Wylder, Meldrum Keplinger. **Rio Grande Medicine Man.** Sante Fe: Rydal; 1958. [$20.00]

Wyllys, Rufus Kay. **Arizona.** 1st ed. Phoenix: Hobson & Herr; 1950. [$30.00]

Wyman, Lillie Buffum. **American Chivalry.** Boston: Clarke; 1913. [$45.00]

Wyman, Walker Demarquis. **California Emigrant Letters.** NY: Bookman Associates; 1952. [$10.00]

Wynn, Marcia Rittenhouse. **Desert Bonanza.** rev. ed. Glendale, CA: Clark; 1963. [$45.00] [$40.00]

Xantus, Janos. **Utazas Kalifornia deli Reszeiben.** Pesten: Lauffer; 1860. [$200.00]

Ximenes, Ben Cuellar. **Gallant Outcasts.** San Antonio: Naylor; 1963. [$25.00]

A Yankee. **The Southwest.** see, Ingraham, Joseph Holt.

Yardley, Herbert O. **The American Black Chamber.** 1st ed. Indianapolis: Bobbs-Merrill; 1931. [$10.00]

Yates, Emma Hayden. **70 Miles from a Lemon.** Boston: Houghton Mifflin; 1947. [$15.00]

Yen, Chin-Yung. **Rights of Citizens and Persons under the Fourteenth Amendment.** NY: New Era; 1905. [$15.00]

Yoakum, Henderson K. **History of Texas from Its First Settlement in 1685 to Its Annexation to the United States in 1846.** NY: Redfield; 1856. 2 v. [$950.00]

Yorke, Dane. **Able Men of Boston.** Boston: Manufacturers Mutual Fire Insurance; 1950. [$15.00]

Yost, Edna. **Frank and Lillian Gilbreth.** New Brunswick: Rutgers UP; 1949. [$20.00]

Young, Alexander. **Chronicles of the First Planters of the Colony of Massachusetts Bay.** Boston: Little and Brown; 1846. [$75.00]

Young, Alexander. **Chronicles of the Pilgrim Fathers of the Colony of Plymouth.** 2nd ed. Boston: Little and Brown; 1844. [$45.00]

Young, Alfred Fabian. **The Democratic Republicans of New York.** Chapel Hill: U. of North Carolina; 1967. [$20.00]

Young, Andrew W. **History of Chautauqua County, New York.** Buffalo, NY: Matthews & Warren; 1875. [$65.00]

Young, Bennett Henderson. **Confederate Wizards of the Saddle.** Kennesaw, GA: Continental; 1958. [$65.00]

Young, Charles E. **Dangers of the Trail in 1865.** Geneva, NY: Humphrey; 1912. [$85.00]

Young, Donald Ramsay. **American Minority Peoples.** 1st ed. NY, London: Harper; 1932. [$15.00]

Young, Egerton Ryerson. **By Canoe and Dog-Train among the Cree and Salteaux Indians.** NY: Hunt & Eaton; 1891. [$25.00] [1892 London ed., $50.00]

Young, Egerton Ryerson. **Stories from Indian Wigwams and Northern Camp-Fires.** London: Kelly; 1893. [$48.50]

Young, George. **Manitoba Memories.** Toronto: Briggs; 1897. [$85.00]

Young, Harry. **Hard Knocks: A Life Story of the Vanishing West.** Portland, OR: Wells; 1915. [covers spotted, $65.00] [1916 Chicago reprint, worn binding, $50.00]

Young, John Philip. **Journalism in California.** San Francisco: Chronicle; 1915. [$35.00]

Young, John Philip. **San Francisco, a History of the Pacific Coast Metropolis.** Chicago: Clarke; 1912. 2 v. [$175.00]

Young, Klyde H. **Heirs Apparent.** 1st ed. NY: Prentice-Hall; 1948. [$10.00]

Young, Levi Edgar. **First Hundred Years.** Salt Lake City: Tribune; 1930. [lacks wraps, $35.00]

Young, Lucien. **The Real Hawaii.** NY: Doubleday & McClure; 1899. [$20.00]

Young, Mary Elizabeth. **Redskins, Ruffleshirts and Rednecks.** Norman: U. of Oklahoma; 1961. [$20.00]

Young, Otis E. **First Military Escort on the Santa Fe Trail, 1829.** Glendale, CA: Clark; 1952. [$65.00] [$50.00]

Young, Otis E. **The West of Philip St. George Cooke.** 1st ed. Glendale, CA: Clark; 1955. [$65.00]

Young, Samuel Hall. **Alaska Days with John Muir.** NY, Chicago: Revell; 1915. [$16.00] [$25.00]

Yount, George Calvert. **George C. Yount and His Chronicles of the West.** Denver: Old West; 1966. [$50.00]

Yukon Bill. **Derby Day in the Yukon.** NY: Doran; 1910. [$17.50]

Zahm, John Augustine. **Along the Andes and down the Amazon.** NY, London: Appleton; 1911. [$35.00]

Zarate, Agustin de. **Histoire de la Decouverte et de la Conquete du Perou.** Amsterdam: Louis de Lorme; 1700. [$175.00]

Zehnpfennig, Gladys. **Nathaniel Leverone.** Minneapolis: Denison; 1963. [$17.50]

Zeigler, Wilbur Gleason. **Heart of the Alleghanies; or, Western North Carolina.** Raleigh, Cleveland: Williams; 1883. [$275.00]

Zeisberger, David. **Diary of.** Cincinnati: Clarke; 1885. 2 v. [$250.00]

Zeisberger, David. **History of Northern American Indians.** Columbus: Ohio State Arch. and Hist. Soc.; 1910. [$85.00]

Ziegler, Jesse A. **Wave of the Gulf.** 1st ed. San Antonio: Naylor; 1938. [$50.00]

Zierold, Norman J. **Little Charley Ross.** 1st ed. Boston: Little, Brown; 1967. [$15.00]

Zigler, David H. **History of the Brethren in Virginia.** rev. ed. Elgin, IL: Brethren; 1914. [rear endpaper missing, $35.00]

Zimmerman, Arthur Franklin. **Francisco de Toledo.** Caldwell, ID: Caxton; 1938. [binding waterstained, $12.50]

Zimmerman, W. F. A. see, Vollmer, Carl Gottfried Wilhelm.

Zink, Harold. **City Bosses in the United States.** Durham: Duke UP; 1930. [$30.00]

Zinman, David. **The Day Huey Long Was Shot.** NY: Obolensky; 1963. [$12.50]

Zolotow, Maurice. **Marilyn Monroe.** 1st ed. NY: Harcourt, Brace; 1960. [$30.00]

Zornow, William Frank. **Kansas.** 1st ed. Norman: U. of Oklahoma; 1957. [$45.00]

Zornow, William Frank. **Lincoln & the Party Divided.** 1st ed. Norman: U. of Oklahoma; 1954. [$25.00] [fine in dj, $40.00]

Zwierlein, Frederick James. **Religion in New Netherland, 1623-1664.** Rochester, NY: Smith; 1910. [$50.00]

Zylyff. see, Tibbles, Thomas Henry.